The
ENCYCLOPEDIA
—of—
RELIGIOUS
QUOTATIONS

The
ENCYCLOPEDIA
—of—
RELIGIOUS
QUOTATIONS

Edited and Compiled by
Frank S. Mead

Fleming H. Revell Company
Old Tappan, New Jersey

0-8007-1410-5

Mead, Frank Spencer *ed.*
    The encyclopedia of religious quotations. Edited and
compiled by Frank S. Mead. Westwood, N. J., Revell
[1965]
    534 p. 26 cm.

    1. Quotations. 2. Religious literature (Selections: ex-
tracts, etc.) ɪ. Title.
PN6084.R3M4   808.882   65–23623

Contents

Preface

Ecclesiastes has it that "Of making many books there is no end; and much study is a weariness of the flesh," and Martin Luther said once that "The multitude of books is a great evil." We agree with both. The labor involved in the making of this book has seemed endless, and it produced a great weariness; behind it there are years of searching, separating, typing, cataloguing, analyzing, checking and re-checking, and now that it is done we know that more than one will ask, "Why *another* book of quotations?"

It has been compiled in the knowledge that such a work is in demand, and long overdue; so far as we are able to determine, there is no other comprehensive anthology of strictly religious quotations available. We have proceeded from that premise as a first rule—that every quote must be of a religious nature, or at least bear religious connotation.

Ancient, medieval and modern quotations have been arranged topically, from Adversity to Zeal; from dim B.C. to yesterday's newspaper and best-seller. Both Christian and non-Christian material has been included; we hear from the Koran, the gentle Buddha, Zoroaster and Confucius, the Hindu Vedas and the seers and prophets of other world faiths living or dead. Nothing has been selected because of special appeal or interest to this or that group or sect: Montaigne, Voltaire, Paine and H. G. Wells are included because they had something of importance to say on or against religion and said it well—because they are profitable in stirring the mind to further, deeper thought. As Christopher Morley said in his preface to *Bartlett's*, a book of quotations is "not just a work of reference, but a work of conference; a nest-egg of the mind."

Wherever possible, the names and dates of authors are included, together with the titles of volumes from which their words are taken. That created mountainous problems at every turn. Often we found the same quotation, in varying form, claimed by a dozen different authors; any statement or story suffers change in transition. One might be credited to Henry James Jones, another to H. J. Jones, still another to H. James Jones, or simply Jones! Were they one and the same? And when did they live and speak? Many were dead, many said a fine thing or two and then were kidnapped by oblivion—with their words still in copyright! Publishers published and then went out of business. Some would ask exorbitant fees; some wrote, "I do not remember having said that." Permission would be secured from an American publisher, only to have permission denied by a publisher abroad (where copyrights often hold for fifty years after an author's death). Better than ten percent of our original manuscript went into the waste-basket. Often we were rescued by that ever-present help in time of trouble, the beloved benefactor known only as "Anonymous."

Every effort has been made to credit the original author, to secure every necessary permission, and to make full and just acknowledgment of source; if we have failed in any case, and if your favorite quote in any department does not appear, we ask for mercy and understanding and offer correction in another and enlarged edition.

We find ourselves hopelessly in debt to a ten-foot shelf of previous works, to most helpful and patient staffs in many libraries, to a host of book, magazine and newspaper publishers, to a great company of long-suffering and gracious "permissions people" in who knows how many publishers' offices, and especially to the three associates without whom the book could never have been completed: Joan Hampson, who typed it; Judy Mead, who catalogued it; and Ethel Elsea, who fought her way through a card file of fifteen thousand cards and quotes, and gave the printer his manuscript.

Books are the food of the spirit; we offer this one in the hope that it may supply a delectable morsel or two for those who know that "he who never quotes is never quoted."

Frank S. Mead

A

ADVERSITY

Prosperity is the blessing of the Old Testament; adversity of the New, which carrieth the greater benediction and the clearer revelation of God's favor. Prosperity is not without many fears and distastes; adversity not without many comforts and hopes.

Sir Francis Bacon: *Of Adversity*

Rightly conceived, time is the friend of all who are in any way in adversity, for its mazy road winds in and out of the shadows sooner or later into sunshine, and when one is at its darkest point one can be certain that presently it will grow brighter.

Arthur Bryant: *Illustrated London News*

The brightest crowns that are worn in heaven have been tried, and smelted, and polished, and glorified through the furnace of tribulation.

Edwin Hubbell Chapin

He that can heroically endure adversity will bear prosperity with equal greatness of soul; for the mind that cannot be dejected by the former is not likely to be transported with the latter.

Henry Fielding

Adversities do not make the man either weak or strong, but they reveal what he is.

Faith Forsyte: *Tit-Bits*

And these vicissitudes come best in youth;
    For when they happen at a riper age,
People are apt to blame the Fates, forsooth,
    And wonder Providence is not more sage.
Adversity is the first path to truth.

George Gordon, Lord Byron: *Don Juan,* Canto XII, st. 50

Adversity is the diamond dust Heaven polishes its jewels with.

Robert Leighton

The long, dull, monotonous years of middle-aged prosperity or middle-aged adversity are excellent campaigning weather (for the Devil).

C. S. Lewis: *The Screwtape Letters,* XXVIII

Adversity reminds men of religion.

Livy: *Annales,* V, 51

Different people must contend with different trials, but adversities in some shape or other come to everyone. Life is a procession of people bearing crosses and when one carries his awkwardly he interferes with his fellow-marchers.

R. C. McCarthy: *Safeguarding Mental Health*

A friend loveth at all times, and a brother is born for adversity.

Old Testament: *Proverbs 17: 17*

If thou faint in the day of adversity, thy strength is small.

Old Testament: *Proverbs 24: 10*

Though the Lord give you the bread of adversity, and the water of affliction.

Old Testament: *Isaiah 30: 20*

We ought as much to pray for a blessing upon our daily rod as upon our daily bread.

John Owen

I never met with a single instance of adversity which I have not in the end seen was for my good.—I have never heard of a Christian on his deathbed complaining of his afflictions.

Alexander M. Proudfit

Behold a worthy sight, to which the God . . . may direct his gaze. Behold a thing worthy of a God, a brave man matched in conflict with adversity.

Seneca: *De Providentia,* IV

Gold is tried in fire, and acceptable men in the furnace of adversity.

Seneca: *De Providentia,* V

A wise man struggling with adversity is said by some heathen writer to be a spectacle on which the gods might look down with pleasure.

Sydney Smith: *Sermon on the Duties of the Queen*

For a man to rejoice in adversity is not grievous to him who loves; for so to joy is to joy in the cross of Christ.

Thomas à Kempis: *The Imitation of Christ*

AFFLICTION

Come then, affliction, if my Father wills, and be my frowning friend. A friend that frowns is better than a smiling enemy.

Anonymous

Afflicted, or distressed, in mind, body or estate.

Book of Common Prayer: A Prayer for All Conditions of Men

Now let us thank th' eternal power, convinc'd
That Heaven but tries our virtue by affliction:

That oft the cloud which wraps the present hour,
Serves but to brighten all our future days!

John Brown: *Barbarossa,* Act V, sc. 3

God measures out affliction to our need.

St. John Chrysostom: *Homily* IV

Afflictions sent by providence melt the constancy of the noble minded, but confirm the obduracy of the vile, as the same furnace that liquifies the gold, hardens the clay.

Charles Caleb Colton

The only way to meet affliction is to pass through it solemnly, slowly, with humility and faith, as the Israelites passed through the sea. Then its very waves of misery will divide, and become to us a wall, on the right side and on the left, until the gulf narrows before our eyes, and we land safe on the opposite shore.

Dinah Maria Mulock Craik

Count each affliction, whether light or grave, God's messenger sent down to thee.

Aubrey Thomas De Vere: *Sorrow*

Extraordinary afflictions are not always the punishment of extraordinary sins, but sometimes the trial of extraordinary graces.—Sanctified afflictions are spiritual promotions.

Matthew Henry

Pulpits and Sundays, sorrow dogging sin,
Afflictions sorted, anguish of all sizes,
Fine nets and stratagems to catch us in,
Bibles laid open, millions of surprises.

George Herbert: *The Temple*

God ne'er afflicts us more than our desert,
Though He may seem to over-act His part:
Sometimes He strikes us more than flesh can bear;
But yet still less than grace can suffer here.

Robert Herrick: *Noble Numbers*

Let us be patient! These severe afflictions
Not from the ground arise,

But oftentimes celestial benedictions
  Assume this dark disguise.

> Henry Wadsworth Longfellow:
> *Resignation*

Affliction is God's shepherd dog to drive us
back to the fold.

> *Megiddo Message*

The bread of affliction.

> *Old Testament: Deuteronomy 16: 3*

Feed him with bread of affliction and with
water of affliction.

> *Old Testament: I Kings 22: 27,*
> *II Chronicles 18: 26*

Although affliction cometh not forth of the
dust, neither doth trouble spring out of the
ground; yet man is born unto trouble, as the
sparks fly upward.

> *Old Testament: Job 5: 6–7*

Many are the afflictions of the righteous: but
the Lord delivereth him out of them all.

> *Old Testament: Psalms 34: 19*

Before I was afflicted I went astray: but now
I have kept thy word.

> *Old Testament: Psalms 119: 67*

I have chosen thee in the furnace of affliction.

> *Old Testament: Isaiah 48: 10*

He was afflicted, yet he opened not his
mouth: he is brought as a lamb to the
slaughter, and as a sheep before her shearers
is dumb, so he openeth not his mouth.

> *Old Testament: Isaiah 53: 7*

Believe me, the gods spare the afflicted, and
do not always oppress those who are unfortunate.

> Ovid: *Epistolae Ex Ponto*, III, 6, 21

By afflictions God is spoiling us of what
otherwise might have spoiled us.—When he
makes the world too hot for us to hold, we
let it go.

> Sir John Powell

Affliction is not sent in vain, young man,
From that good God, who chastens whom
  he loves.

> Robert Southey: *Madoc in Wales*,
> III, l. 176

The Lord gets his best soldiers out of the
highlands of affliction.

> Charles Haddon Spurgeon: *Gleanings*
> *Among the Sheaves. Sorrow's*
> *Discipline*

As sure as God puts his children into the
furnace of affliction, he will be with them
in it.

> Charles Haddon Spurgeon

Affliction is a divine diet which though it be
not pleasing to mankind, yet Almighty God
hath often imposed it as a good, though
bitter, physic, to those children whose souls
are dearest to him.

> Izaak Walton

With silence only as their benediction,
  God's angels come
Where in the shadow of a great affliction,
  The soul sits dumb!

> John Greenleaf Whittier: *To my Friend*
> *on the Death of his Sister*

ALMS

The word "alms" has no singular, as if to
teach us that a solitary act of charity scarcely
deserves the name.

> Anonymous

Water will quench a flaming fire; and alms
maketh an atonement for sins.

> *Apocrypha: Ecclesiasticus 3: 30*

If thou hast abundance, give alms accord-
ingly; if thou have but little, be not afraid
to give according to that little.

> *Apocrypha: Tobit 4: 8*

Even the beggar who lives on alms should
himself bestow alms.

> *Babylonian Talmud: Gittin*, fo. 7b

Alms delivereth from death.

Babylonian Talmud: Shabbuth, fo. 156b

A householder, by giving alms, gains the same reward in heaven as a student who presents a cow to his teacher.

The Code of Manu: 3

Alms are but the vehicles of prayer.

John Dryden

Give no bounties: make equal laws: secure life and prosperity and you need not give alms.

Ralph Waldo Emerson: *Wealth*

The little alms are the best alms.

French Proverb

He that hath a good memory giveth few alms.

Thomas Fuller: *Worthies of England*

Steal the hog, and give the feet for alms.

George Herbert: *Jacula Prudentum*

Alms never make poor.

George Herbert: *Outlandish Proverbs*

Give, if thou canst, an alms; if not, afford,
Instead of that, a sweet and gentle word.

Robert Herrick: *Alms*

Be constant in prayer and give alms, and what good ye have sent before for your souls ye shall find it with God.

The Koran: II

The gift without the giver is bare;
Who gives himself with his alms feeds three,—
Himself, his hungering neighbor, and me.

James Russell Lowell: *The Vision of Sir Launfal,* Pt. II, st. 8

A man's giving in alms one piece of silver in his lifetime is better than giving one hundred when about to die.

Mohammed

I had much rather live not at all, than to live by alms.

Michel Eyquem de Montaigne: *Essays,* Bk. III, ch. 5

When thou doest alms, let not thy left hand know what thy right hand doeth.

New Testament: Matthew 6: 3

Sell that ye have, and give alms.

New Testament: Luke 12: 33

The greatest of almsgivers is cowardice.

Friedrich Wilhelm Nietzsche: *Human All-too-Human*

I do not give alms: I am not poor enough for that.

Friedrich Wilhelm Nietzsche: *Thus Spake Zarathustra,* Intro., 1885

. . . prayers, which are old age's alms.

George Peele: *Polyhymnia. The Aged-Men-at-Arms,* st. 2

Steal the goose and give the giblets in alms.

John Ray: *English Proverbs*

Time hath, my lord, a wallet at his back,
Wherein he puts alms for oblivion,
A great-sized monster of ingratitudes:
These scraps are good deeds past; which are devour'd
As fast as they are made, forgot as soon
As done.

William Shakespeare: *Troilus and Cressida,* Act III, sc. 3, l. 171

His alms were money put to interest
In the other world.

Robert Southey: *The Alderman's Funeral*

The noblest charity is to prevent a man from accepting charity; and the best alms are to show and to enable a man to dispense with alms.

The Talmud

I must be dunned for alms, and do not scramble over hedges and ditches in searching for opportunities of flinging away my money on good works.

Horace Walpole: Letter to Hannah J. More, February 20, 1790

ANGELS

How many angels can dance upon the point of a needle?

Ascribed to various medieval theologians

We should pray to the angels, for they are given to us as guardians.

St. Ambrose: *On Bereavement*

But men must know, that in this theater of man's life it is reserved only for God and the angels to be lookers on.

Sir Francis Bacon: *Advancement of Learning*

I want to be an angel,
  And with the angels stand,
A crown upon my forehead,
  A harp within my hand.

Urania Bailey: *I Want to be an Angel*

There's not much practical Christianity in the man who lives on better terms with angels and seraphs, than with his children, servants and neighbors.

Henry Ward Beecher

We not only live among men, but there are airy hosts, blessed spectators, sympathetic lookers-on, that see and know and appreciate our thoughts and feelings and acts.

Henry Ward Beecher: *Royal Truths*

Like those of angels, short visits and far between.

Robert Blair: *The Grave*, II

I have always found that angels have the vanity to speak of themselves as the only wise; this they do with a confident insolence sprouting from systematic reasoning.

William Blake: *The Marriage of Heaven and Hell*

Between creatures of mere existence and things of life there is a large disproportion of nature: between plants and animals, or creatures of sense, a wider difference: between them and man a far greater: and if the proportion hold on, between man and angels there should be yet a greater.

Sir Thomas Browne: *Religio Medici*, I

'Tis only when they spring to Heaven that angels
Reveal themselves to you.

Robert Browning: *Paracelsus*, Pt. V

The more materialistic science becomes, the more angels shall I paint: their wings are my protest in favor of the immortality of the soul.

E. C. Burne-Jones: *To Oscar Wilde*

Every man hath a good and a bad angel attending on him in particular, all his life long.

Robert Burton: *Anatomy of Melancholy*, Pt. I, sec. 2, mem. 1, subs. 2

The angels all were singing out of tune,
  And hoarse with having little else to do,
Excepting to wind up the sun and moon,
  Or curb a runaway young star or two.

George Gordon, Lord Byron: *The Vision of Judgment*, st. 2

The angels are the dispensers and administrators of the Divine beneficence toward us; they regard our safety, undertake our defense, direct our ways, and exercise a constant solicitude that no evil befall us.

John Calvin: *Institutes of the Christian Religion*, I

What though my winged hours of bliss have been
Like angel-visits, few and far between?

Thomas Campbell: *Pleasures of Hope*, Pt. II, l. 377

Music is well said to be the speech of angels.

Thomas Carlyle

The angels may have wider spheres of action and nobler forms of duty than ourselves, but truth and right to them and to us are one and the same thing.

Edwin Hubbell Chapin

This world has angels all too few,
And heaven is overflowing.

Samuel Taylor Coleridge:
To a Young Lady

Hold the fleet angel fast until he bless thee.

Nathaniel Cotton: *To-morrow*, l. 36

When one that holds communion with the skies
Has fill'd his urn where these pure waters rise,
And once more mingles with us meaner things,
'Tis ev'n as if an angel shook his wings.

William Cowper: *Charity*, l. 435

We are ne'er like angels till our passion dies.

Thomas Dekker: *The Honest Whore*,
Pt. II, Act I, sc. 2

We trust, in plumed procession,
For such the angels go,
Rank after rank, with even feet
And uniforms of snow.

Emily Dickinson: *Poems*, Pt. I, no. 16

What is the question now placed before society with the glib assurance which to me is most astonishing? That question is this: Is man an ape or an angel? I, my lord, I am on the side of the angels. I repudiate with indignation and abhorrence those new fangled theories.

Benjamin Disraeli: *Speech at Oxford
Diocesan Conference*, November 25, 1864

That science ranks as monstrous things
Two pairs of upper limbs; so wings—
E'en Angel's wings!—are fictions.

Henry Austin Dobson: *A Fairy Tale*,
Oxford University Press

Let old Timotheus yield the prize
Or both divide the crown;
He rais'd a mortal to the skies
She drew an angel down.

John Dryden: *Alexander's Feast*

God hath chosen her as a pattern for the other angels.

Epitaph in West Moulsey
churchyard, England

Make yourself familiar with the angels, and behold them frequently in spirit; for without being seen, they are present with you.

St. Francis de Sales: *Introduction
to the Devout Life*, XV

A young angel, an old devil.

French Proverb

What's impossible to all humanity may be possible to the metaphysics and physiology of angels.

Joseph Glanvill: *The Vanity of
Dogmatizing*

Not Angles, but Angels!

Pope Gregory the Great

There are nine orders of angels, to wit, angels, archangels, virtues, powers, principalities, dominations, thrones, cherubim, and seraphim.

Pope Gregory the Great: *Homilies*,
XXXIV

When a man dies they who survive him ask what property he has left behind. The angel who bends over the dying man asks what good deeds he has sent before him.

The Koran

Praise be to Allah, the creator of the heavens and earth, who maketh the angels his messengers, and giveth them two, three, or four pairs of wings.

Ibid.

Whether God loves a lying angel better than a true man.

Charles Lamb: Proposition submitted (satirically) to S. T. Coleridge for debate "at Leipsic or Gootingen," 1798

The better angels of our nature.

Abraham Lincoln: *First Inaugural Address*, March 4, 1861

There are two angels, that attend unseen
Each one of us, and in great books record
Our good and evil deeds. He who writes down
The good ones, after every action closes
His volume, and ascends with it to God.
The other keeps his dreadful day-book open
Till sunset, that we may repent; which doing,
The record of the action fades away,
And leaves a line of white across the page.

Henry Wadsworth Longfellow: *Christus,
Pt. II, The School of Salerno*

But all God's angels come to us disguised:
Sorrow and sickness, poverty and death,
One after other lift their frowning masks,
And we behold the Seraph's face beneath,
All radiant with the glory and the calm
Of having looked upon the front of God.

James Russell Lowell: *On the Death of
a Friend's Child*

An angel is a spiritual creature created by God without a body, for the service of Christendom and of the Church.

Martin Luther: *Table Talk*

In this dim world of clouding cares,
  We rarely know, till 'wildered eyes
  See white wings lessening up the skies,
The angels with us unawares.

Gerald Massey: *Ballad of
Babe Christabel*

Millions of spiritual creatures walk the earth unseen, both when we sleep and when we awake.

John Milton

The helmed Cherubim,
And sworded Seraphim,

Are seen in glittering ranks with wings display'd.

John Milton: *Hymn on the
Nativity*, l. 112

Look homeward, Angel, now, and melt with ruth.

John Milton: *Lycidas*, l. 163

As far as angel's ken.

John Milton: *Paradise Lost,
Bk. I*, l. 59

For God will deign
To visit oft the dwellings of just men
Delighted, and with frequent intercourse
Thither will send his winged messengers
On errands of supernal grace.

John Milton: *Paradise Lost,
Bk. VII*, l. 569

Be not forgetful to entertain strangers: for thereby some have entertained angels unawares.

New Testament: Hebrews 13: 2

God spared not the angels that sinned, but cast them down to hell, and delivered them into chains of darkness.

New Testament: II Peter 2: 4

And with the morn those angel faces smile Which I have loved long since, and lost awhile.

Cardinal John Henry Newman: *The
Pillar of the Cloud*

Angels, as 'tis but seldom they appear,
So neither do they make long stay;
They do but visit and away.

John Norris: *To the Memory of
His Niece*

And he [the angel] said, Let me go, for the day breaketh. And he [Jacob] said, I will not let thee go, except thou bless me.

Old Testament: Genesis 32: 26

Angels may become men or demons, and again from the latter they may rise to be men or angels.

Origen: *De Principiis*

Man is neither angel nor brute, and the unfortunate thing is that he who would act the angel acts the brute.

Blaise Pascal

In these days you must go to Heaven to find an angel.

Polish Proverb

Men would be angels, angels would be gods.
Alexander Pope: *Essay on Man*,
Epis. I, l. 126

The guardian angels of life sometimes fly so high as to be beyond our sight, but they are always looking down upon us.

Jean Paul Richter

If some people really see angels where others see only empty space, let them paint the angels; only let not anybody else think they can paint an angel too, on any calculated principles of the angelic.

John Ruskin: *Modern Painters*

All angel now, and little less than all,
While still a pilgrim in this world of ours.
Sir Walter Scott: *Lord of the Isles*
(referring to Harriet, Duchess
of Buccleugh)

Angels are bright still, though the brightest fell.

William Shakespeare: *Macbeth*,
Act IV, sc. 3, l. 22

A ministering angel shall my sister be.
William Shakespeare: *Hamlet*,
Act V, sc. 1, l. 264

I guess one angel in another's hell:
The truth I shall not know, but live in doubt,
Till my bad angel fire my good one out.
William Shakespeare: *The Passionate
Pilgrim*, l. 26

And flights of angels sing thee to thy rest!
William Shakespeare: *Hamlet*,
Act V, sc. 2, l. 371

Weak men must fall, for heaven still guards the right.

William Shakespeare: *Richard II*,
Act III, sc. 2, l. 62

To equip a dull, respectable person with wings would be but to make a parody of an angel.

Robert Louis Stevenson: *Virginibus
Puerisque: Crabbed Age and Youth*

Around our pillows golden ladders rise,
And up and down the skies,
With winged sandals shod,
The angels come, and go, the Messengers of
God!
Richard Henry Stoddard: *Hymn to the
Beautiful*

Sweet souls around us watch us still,
Press nearer to our side;
Into our thoughts, into our prayers,
With gentle helpings glide.
Harriet Beecher Stowe: *The
Other World*

I have seen a thousand times that angels are human forms, or men, for I have conversed with them as man to man, sometimes with one alone, sometimes with many in company.

Emanuel Swedenborg: *Arcana Coelestia*

While shepherds watched their flocks by
night,
All seated on the ground,
The angel of the Lord came down,
And glory shone around.

Nahum Tate: *While Shepherds
Watched*

Beauty is not necessary to God's angels.
Tertullian: *Women's Dress*

Like outcast spirits who wait,
And see, through Heaven's gate,
Angels within it.
William Makepeace Thackeray: *The
Church Porch*

I have no angels left
Now, Sweet, to pray to:

ANTICHRIST

Where you have made your shrine
   They are away to.
They have struck Heaven's tent,
   And gone to cover you:
Whereso you keep your state
   Heaven is pitched over you.

     Francis Thompson: *A Carrier Song*, st. 4

Calm as a child to slumber soothed,
As if an Angel's hand had smoothed
The still, white features into rest.

     John Greenleaf Whittier

What know we of the Blest above
But that they sing, and that they love?

     William Wordsworth: *Scene on
     the Lake of Brienz* (quoted
     from Waller)

Angels from friendship gather half their joy.

     Edward Young: *Night Thoughts*,
     Night II

Who does the best his circumstance allows
Does well, acts nobly; angels could do no
   more.

     Ibid.

ANTICHRIST

Antichrist is the Pope and the Turk together.
A beast full of life must have a body and soul.
The spirit or soul of Antichrist is the Pope,
his flesh and body the Turk.

     Martin Luther: *Table Talk*

And if Antichrist is like Christ, Christ I suppose is like Antichrist.

     Cardinal John Henry Newman

Even now there are many antichrists.

     New Testament: I John 2: 18

He is antichrist, that denieth Father and
Son.

     New Testament: I John 2: 22

ASPIRATION

Whoever refuses to confess that Jesus Christ
is come in the flesh is Antichrist.

     St. Polycarp: *Epistle to the Philippians*

ASPIRATION

To bliss unknown my lofty soul aspires,
My lot unequal to my vast desires.

     John Arbuthnot: *Gnothi Seaton*, l. 3

By aspiring to a similitude of God in goodness or love, neither man nor angel ever
transgressed, or shall transgress.

     Sir Francis Bacon: *Advancement of
     Learning*, Bk. II

There is not a heart but has its moments
of longing, yearning for something better,
nobler, holier than it knows now.

     Henry Ward Beecher

We are not to make the ideas of contentment
and aspiration quarrel, for God made them
fast friends.—A man may aspire, and yet be
quite content until it is time to rise; and both
flying and resting are but parts of one contentment. The very fruit of the gospel is
aspiration. It is to the heart what spring is
to the earth, making every root, and bud,
and bough desire to be more.

     Henry Ward Beecher

Ah, but a man's reach should exceed his
   grasp,
Or what's a Heaven for?

     Robert Browning: *Andrea del Sarto*

Faith is love taking the form of aspiration.

     William Ellery Channing

'Tis immortality to die aspiring.

     George Chapman: *The Conspiracy
     of Byron*, I

Strong souls
Live like fire-hearted suns; to spend their
   strength
In furthest striving action.

     George Eliot: *The Spanish Gypsy*

A good man, through obscurest aspirations,
Has still an instinct of the one true way.

> Johann Wolfgang von Goethe: *Faust,*
> *Prolog im Himmel,* Der Herr, l. 88

God, give me hills to climb,
And strength for climbing!

> Arthur Guiterman: "Hills," *Death*
> *and General Putnam and 101*
> *Other Poems,* E. P. Dutton &
> Co., Inc.

This world has too low a ceiling for aspiring
man!

> J. Wallace Hamilton

Aspirations after the holy—the only aspirations in which the soul can be assured it will
never meet with disappointment.

> Maria McIntosh

Execrable son! so to aspire
Above his brethren, to himself assuming
Authority usurp'd, from God not given.

> John Milton: *Paradise Lost,*
> Bk. XII, l. 64

It is impossible that the church should ever
unconditionally identify itself with human
aspirations; it must retain the integrity of
its judgment and yet be recognized as the
champion of all that is good and true in the
changing life of men.

> Stephen C. Neill

Thy destiny is only that of man, but thy
aspirations may be those of a god.

> Ovid: *Metamorphoses,* II

I have Immortal longings in me.

> William Shakespeare: *Antony and*
> *Cleopatra,* Act V, sc. 2, l. 282

He rises on the toe: that spirit of his
In aspiration lifts him from the earth.

> William Shakespeare: *Troilus and*
> *Cressida,* Act IV, sc. 5, l. 15

It is not for man to rest in absolute contentment.—He is born to hopes and aspirations

as the sparks fly upward, unless he has brutified his nature and quenched the spirit of
immortality which is his portion.

> Robert Southey

The heavens are as deep as our aspirations
are high.

> Henry David Thoreau

God has never ceased to be the one true aim
of all right human aspiration.

> Alexandre Vinet

Selfishness is the only real atheism; aspiration, the only real religion.

> Israel Zangwill: *Children of the*
> *Ghetto,* Bk. II, ch. 16

ATHEISM

Atheism is the death of hope, the suicide of
the soul.

> Anonymous

You can't climb to salvation on atheistic
steppes.

> Anonymous

A little philosophy inclineth a man's mind
to atheism; but depth in philosophy bringeth men's minds to religion.

> Sir Francis Bacon: *Essays,* XVI

Atheism is rather in the lip than in the heart
of man.

> Sir Francis Bacon: *Essays: Of Atheism*

Atheism is the folly of the metaphysician,
not the folly of human nature.

> George Bancroft

An atheist is a man who looks through a
telescope and tries to explain what he can't
see.

> O. A. Battista: *Power to Influence People,*
> Copyright 1959 by O. A. Battista

An irreligious man, a speculative or a practical atheist, is as a sovereign, who voluntarily takes off his crown and declares himself unworthy to reign.

John Stuart Blackie

An atheist-laugh's a poor exchange
For Deity offended!

Robert Burns: *Epistle to a
Young Friend*

God knows, I'm not the thing I should be,
Nor am I even the thing I could be.
But twenty times I rather would be
  An atheist clean,
Than under gospel colours hid be
Just for a screen.

Robert Burns: *Epistle to
Reverend John McBath*

Who seeks perfection in the art
Of driving well an ass and cart,
Or painting mountains in a mist,
Seeks God although an Atheist.

Francis Carlin: Perfection. From *My
Ireland* by Francis Carlin (James
Francis Carlin MacDonnell). All
rights reserved. Reprinted by permission of Holt, Rinehart and
Winston, Inc.

You don't find atheists in the country; you can't watch a field of wheat ripple and ripen without deep beliefs and without feeling that you're a small part of something pretty big and lasting. No man grows roses and cabbages for himself alone. You have to share to enjoy.

Chester Charles: *Farm Quarterly*

Forth from his dark and lonely hiding-place,
(Portentous sight!) the owlet Atheism,
Sailing on obscene wings athwart the noon,
Drops his blue-fringed lids, and holds them close,
And hooting at the glorious sun in Heaven,
Cries out, "Where is it?"

Samuel Taylor Coleridge: *Fears in
Solitude*

Atheism, if it exists, is the result of ignorance and pride, of strong sense and feeble reason, of good eating and ill living. It is the plague of society, the corrupter of morals, and the underminer of property.

Jeremy Collier

The three great apostles of practical atheism, that make converts without persecuting, and retain them without preaching, are wealth, health and power.

Charles Caleb Colton: *Lacon*

There are no atheists in foxholes.

William T. Cummings: Sermons on
Bataan, March 1942

Virtue in distress, and vice in triumph, make atheists of mankind.

John Dryden

Here Lies an Atheist: All Dressed Up and No Place to Go.

Epitaph

He only is a true atheist to whom the predicates of the Divine Being—for example, love, wisdom and justice—are nothing.

Ludwig Andreas Feuerbach: *Das Wesen
des Christentums*

Atheism is a theoretical formulation of the discouraged life.

Harry Emerson Fosdick

Some are atheists only in fair weather.

Thomas Fuller: *Gnomologia*

An atheist is got one point beyond the Devil.

Ibid.

Only in Atheism does the spring rise higher than the source, the effect exist without the cause, life come from a stone, blood from a turnip, a silk purse from a sow's ear, a Beethoven Symphony or a Bach Fugue from a kitten's walking across the keys.

James M. Gillis: *On Almost Everything.*

11

The real heretic of our time is not the atheist or the agnostic (who are often good and decent people with a respect for reality and human dignity) but the faith-in-faith fanatics who murmur, 'It doesn't matter what you believe, as long as it makes you feel good.' This turns religion into a wholly subjective matter, like taste in food or furnishings, and thus robs theology of its claim to ultimate truth.

Sydney J. Harris, in Chicago
Daily News

Atheism is the last word of theism.

Heinrich Heine: *MS. Papers*

The devil divides the world between atheism and superstition.

George Herbert: *Jacula Prudentum*

It is atheism and blasphemy to dispute what God can do: good Christians content themselves with His will revealed in His Word.

James I: *Speech in the Star Chamber*

There are so few atheists in the world because it takes more credulity to accept the atheistic position than most men can muster.

Gerald Kennedy

The Kingdom that is infested by atheists is beset by famine and disease, and soon perishes.

Code of Manu: 8

In agony or danger, no nature is atheist. The mind that knows not what to fly to, flies to God.

Henry More

Atheism shows strength of mind, but only to a certain degree.

Blaise Pascal

Few men are so obstinate in their atheism, that a pressing danger will not compel them to the acknowledgment of a divine power.

Plato

Atheism is a disease of the soul before it becomes an error of understanding.

Plato

No one has ever died an atheist.

Plato: *Laws*, X

Atheists put on a false courage in the midst of their darkness and misapprehensions, like children who, when they fear to go in the dark, will sing or whistle to keep up their courage.

Alexander Pope

An atheist is one who prays when he can think of no other way out of his trouble.

Prison Mirror

Atheists brag that they can get along without God; this is hardly a distinction in an era where very, very few pay the Lord more than a Sunday call.

Dagobert D. Runes: *Dictionary of Thought*

O Reader! hast thou ever stood to see
   The Holly-tree?
The eye that contemplates it well perceives
   Its glossy leaves
Ordered by an Intelligence so wise
As might confound the Atheist's sophistries.

Robert Southey: *The Holly-Tree*

Fervid atheism is usually a screen for repressed religion.

Wilhelm Stekel: *Autobiography*, 1950,
Liveright Publishing Corp.

All atheists are rascals, and all rascals are atheists.

August Strindberg: *Zones of the Spirit*

There are some spirits so atheistical that they . . . search their houses with a sunbeam, that they may be instructed in all the corners of nastiness.

Jeremy Taylor: *Holy Living*, ch. 2, sec. 3

An atheist is a disbeliever who prefers to raise his children in a Christian community.

Phil H. Tuseth

All revolutions run into extremes: the bigot makes the boldest atheist.

Sir John Vanbrugh: *The Provok'd Wife*, V

An atheist's most embarrassing moment is when he feels profoundly thankful for something, but can't think of anybody to thank for it.

Mary Ann Vincent

Atheism is the vice of a few intelligent people.

Voltaire

The atheists are for the most part impudent and misguided scholars who reason badly, and who, not being able to understand the Creation, the origin of evil, and other difficulties, have recourse to the hypothesis of the eternity of things and of inevitability.

Voltaire: *Philosophical Dictionary*

The religion of the atheist has a God-shaped blank at its heart.

H. G. Wells

Atheism thrives where religion is most debated.

Welsh Proverb

Some are atheists by neglect; others are so by affectation; they that think there is no God at some times do not think so at all times.

Benjamin Whichcote: *Moral and Religious Aphorisms*

By night, an atheist half-believes in God.

Edward Young: *Night Thoughts, Night* V, l. 176

ATONEMENT

By Thine agony and bloody sweat; by Thy cross and passion; by Thy precious death and burial; by Thy glorious resurrection and ascension; and by the coming of the Holy Ghost, good Lord, deliver us.

The Book of Common Prayer: The Litany

When we think of the atonement we are apt to think only of what man gains. We must remember what it cost God and what it costs him now when men refuse his love.

Frank Fitt

In the cross, God descends to bear in his own heart the sins of the world. In Jesus, he atones at unimaginable cost to himself.

Woodrow A. Geier: *Religion in Life*

It is part of the Jewish High Holidays that you cannot face the new year without having something deep and important take place inside you, a psychological process that religion has called atonement. Too many people are seeking a sense of "at-one-ment" with God without paying the price of atonement for their thoughtless, selfish and often wicked deeds. They cry out in anguish for peace—peace of mind, peace of soul, world peace—without understanding that these are not goals to be sought in and for themselves, but rather the by-products of just and righteous living.

Donald Harrington

Let us not forget that the crucifixion of Christ was, and was intended to be to all the intelligences of the universe, the most significant exhibition of the love of God. "Herein was love."

J. Gilchrist Lawson

I must die or get somebody to die for me. If the Bible doesn't teach that, it doesn't teach anything. And that is where the atonement of Jesus Christ comes in.

Dwight L. Moody

For if, when we were enemies, we were reconciled to God by the death of his Son, much more, being reconciled, we shall be saved by his life. And not only so, but we also joy in God through our Lord Jesus Christ, by whom we have now received the atonement.

New Testament: Romans 5: 10, 11

The blood of Jesus Christ his Son cleanseth us from all sin.

New Testament: I John 1: 7

On the tenth day of this seventh month there shall be a day of atonement: it shall be an holy convocation unto you; and ye shall afflict your souls, and offer an offering made by fire unto the Lord.

Old Testament: Leviticus 23: 27

When God pardons, he consigns the offense to everlasting forgetfulness.

Merv Rosell

The atonement, for which the cross is but the symbol, is wholly ethical in its implications; for in the cross . . . mercy and truth met together, righteousness and peace embraced each other. . . .

Miles W. Smith: *Adult Class*

On the Day of Atonement it is forbidden to eat or to drink, to wash, to anoint one's self, or to fasten the shoes. Whoever eats food to the size of a large date, or drinks as much as a mouthful, is guilty.

The Talmud: Yomah, VIII

He left His Father's throne above,
  (So free, so infinite His grace!)
Emptied Himself of all but love,
  And bled for Adam's helpless race.

Charles Wesley: *Free Grace*

B

BAPTISM

Being by nature born in sin, and the children of wrath, we are hereby made the children of grace.

*Book of Common Prayer:
The Catechism*

This sacrament of the Christian Church dates back in one form or another to pre-apostolic times. *Baptism for the dead* was the baptism of a living person instead of and for the sake of one who had died unbaptized. *Baptism of blood* was martyrdom for the sake of Christ and supplied the place of the sacrament if the martyr was unbaptized. *Baptism of desire* is the virtue or grace of baptism acquired by one who dies earnestly desiring baptism before he can receive it. *Baptism of fire* is really martyrdom, but the phrase was misapplied by Napoleon to one who went under fire in battle for the first time.

*Brewer's Dictionary of Phrase
and Fable*

I think the baptismal service almost perfect. I never could attend a christening without tears bursting forth at the sight of the helpless infant in a pious clergyman's arms.

Samuel Taylor Coleridge: *Table Talk,*
August 9, 1832

When the Church baptizes a child, that action concerns me, for that child is thereby connected to that which is my head too, and ingrafted into that body whereof I am a member.

John Donne

The strength of baptism, that's within;
It saves the soul from drowning sin.

Robert Herrick: *Noble Numbers*

Fall on me like a silent dew,
  Or like those maiden showers,
Which, by the peep of day, do strew
  A baptism o'er the flowers.

Robert Herrick: *To Music, to Becalm
His Fever*

A part of the act of baptism in the Church of India is for the candidate to place his own hand on his head and say, "Woe is me if I preach not the gospel." This is part of the baptismal service of new members, not the ordination of ministers!

E. Paul Hovey

When a Baptist was asked about baptism he replied, "It's all right, but you mustn't hang around the river too long."

E. Stanley Jones: *The Way,*
Abingdon Press

The church I belong to is torn in a fierce dispute. One section says that baptism is *in* the name of the Father, and the other that it is *into* the name of the Father. I belong to one of these parties. I feel most strongly about it. I would die for it in fact—but I forget which it is!

David Lloyd-George

(Baptism) signifies that the old Adam in us is to be drowned by daily sorrow and repentance, and perish with all sins and evil lusts; and that the new man should daily come forth again and rise, who shall live

15

before God in righteousness and purity forever.

Luther's Small Catechism

In the sacrament of Baptism, the congregation expresses its objectivity by taking up the child into its life much as a mother embraces an infant. The baptismal act is the Church's affirmation of its maternal responsibility, a profession of its existence as a congregation.

Carl Michalson: "Why Methodists Baptize," *New Christian Advocate,* June, 1958

The baptism of the Christians is an emblem of our Moslem ablutions. Their only error consists in ascribing to one ablution an efficacy which permits them to omit all others.

Charles Louis de Secondat Montesquieu: *Persian Letters,* XXXV

Go ye therefore, and teach all nations, baptizing them in the name of the Father, and of the Son, and of the Holy Ghost.

New Testament: Matthew 28: 19

Repent, and be baptized every one of you in the name of Jesus Christ for the remission of sins, and ye shall receive the gift of the Holy Ghost.

New Testament: Acts 2: 38

One Lord, one faith, one baptism.

New Testament: Ephesians 4: 5

In baptism, the Christian is born. His old self is buried and the new self emerges. Whether in the case of infants or adults, baptism signifies this more as a promise than as an actually fulfilled fact. The direction is indicated rather than the arrival.

Friedrich Rest: *Pulpit Preaching*

The efficacy of baptism is not tied to that moment of time wherein it is administered. . . .

The Westminster Confession of Faith: ch. 28

16

BELIEF, BELIEVING

If life is a comedy to him who thinks and a tragedy to him who feels, it is a victory to him who believes.

Anonymous

There are many great truths which we do not deny, and which nevertheless we do not fully believe.

James W. Alexander

I believe without bother
In This, That, and T'other;
   Whatever is current, no matter.

I believe in Success,
And in Comfort no less;
   I believe all the rest is but patter.

William Allingham: *Blackberries*

A belief is not true because it is useful.

Henri Frédéric Amiel: *Journal*

I'm a believer in God and the ultimate goodness.

Marian Anderson

For I do not seek to understand that I may believe, but I believe in order to understand. For this I believe—that unless I believe, I should not understand.

St. Anselm: *Proslogium,* I

It is forbidden to decry other sects; the true believer gives honor to whatever in them is worthy of honor.

Asoka: *Decree*

If the thing believed is incredible, it is also incredible that the incredible should have been so believed.

St. Augustine: *The City of God,* XXII, 427

Man prefers to believe what he prefers to be true.

Sir Francis Bacon: *Aphorisms,* no. 49

Strong beliefs win strong men, and then make them stronger.

Walter Bagehot

It is a singular fact that many men of action incline to the theory of fatalism, while the greater part of men of thought believe in a divine providence.

Honoré de Balzac

What a man accomplishes depends on what he believes.

Bankers Bulletin

Freedom of belief is pernicious; it is nothing but the freedom to be wrong.

St. Robert Bellarmine

Man is made by his belief. As he believes, so he is.

Bhagavad-Gita

Every thing possible to be believ'd is an image of truth.

William Blake: *The Marriage of Heaven and Hell*

Believing hath a core of unbelieving.

Robert Williams Buchanan: *Songs of Seeking*

Believe nothing, O monks, merely because you have been told it . . . or because it is traditional, or because you yourselves have imagined it. Do not believe what your teacher tells you merely out of respect for the teacher. But whatsoever, after due examination and analysis, you find to be conducive to the good, the benefit, the welfare of all beings—that doctrine believe and cling to, and take it as your guide.

Gautama Buddha

In belief lies the secret of all valuable exertion.

John Bulwer

It is always easier to believe than to deny. Our minds are naturally affirmative.

John Burroughs: *The Light of Day*, Houghton Mifflin Company

It is believable because unbelievable.

Robert Burton: *Anatomy of Melancholy* (quoting Tertullian)

For fools are stubborn in their way,
As coins are harden'd by th' allay;
And obstinacy's ne'er so stiff
As when 'tis in a wrong belief.

Samuel Butler: *Hudibras*, Pt. III, Canto II, l. 481

Men willingly believe what they wish.

Gaius Julius Caesar: *De Bello Gallico*

No iron chain, or outward force of any kind, could ever compel the soul of man to believe or to disbelieve: it is his own indefeasible light, that judgment of his; he will reign and believe there by the grace of God alone!

Thomas Carlyle: *Heroes and Hero-Worship*

A man lives by believing something; not by debating and arguing about many things.

Ibid.

We do everything by custom, even believe by it; our very axioms, let us boast of free-thinking as we may, are oftenest simply such beliefs as we have never heard questioned.

Thomas Carlyle: *Sartor Resartus*

One does not have to believe everything one hears.

Cicero: *De Divinatione*, Bk. II, ch. 13, sec. 31

He that will believe only what he can fully comprehend must have a very long head or a very short creed.

Charles Caleb Colton

Each man's belief is right in his own eyes.

William Cowper: *Hope*

Believe only half of what you see and nothing that you hear.

Dinah Maria Mulock Craik: *A Woman's Thoughts*

If you believe in the Lord, He will do half the work—but the last half. He helps those who help themselves.

Cyrus K. Curtis

We believe whatever we want to believe.

Demosthenes: *Third Olynthiac*

"I make it a rule only to believe what I understand," replied Proserpine.

Benjamin Disraeli: *The Infernal Marriage*, Pt. I, ch. 4

Our beliefs in a rich future life are of little importance unless we coin them into a rich present life.

Thomas Dreier

All progress is made by men of faith who believe in what is right and, what is more important, actually do what is right in their own private affairs. You cannot add to the peace and good will of the world if you fail to create an atmosphere of harmony and love right where you live and work.

Thomas Dreier

With how much ease believe we what we wish!

John Dryden: *All for Love*, Act IV, sc. 1

Who can believe what varies every day,
Nor ever was, nor will be at a stay?

John Dryden: *The Hind and The Panther*, Pt. II, l. 36

Christianity is not believing the impossible, but doing the incredible.

Sherwood Eddy

We are all apt to believe what the world believes about us.

George Eliot

What is your religion? I mean—not what you know about religion but the belief that helps you most?

George Eliot

'Twas God the word that spake it,
He took the Bread and brake it;
And what the word did make it;
That I believe, and take it.

Queen Elizabeth I

A man must not swallow more beliefs than he can digest.

Havelock Ellis: *The Dance of Life*

We are born believing. A man bears beliefs, as a tree bears apples.

Ralph Waldo Emerson: *Conduct of Life: Worship*

Belief consists in accepting the affirmations of the soul; unbelief, in denying them.

Ralph Waldo Emerson: *Representative Men*

Great believers are always reckoned infidels, impracticable, fantastic, atheistic and really men of no account. . . . He had rather stand charged with the imbecility of scepticism, than with untruth.

Ralph Waldo Emerson: *Representative Men*

All ages of belief have been great; all of unbelief have been mean.

Ralph Waldo Emerson: *The Sovereignty of Ethics*

When faith is in the mouth rather than in the heart, when the solid knowledge of Sacred Scripture fails us, nevertheless by terrorization we drive men to believe what they do not believe, to love what they do not love, to know what they do not know. That which is forced cannot be sincere, and that which is not voluntary cannot please Christ.

Desiderius Erasmus: from Roland H. Bainton's *Hunted Heretic*

To accomplish great things, we must not only act but also dream, not only plan but also believe.

Anatole France

To die for an idea is to place a pretty high price upon conjecture.

Anatole France: *The Revolt of the Angels*

The practical test of a belief is the real test of its soundness.

James Anthony Froude

He does not believe that does not live according to his belief.

Thomas Fuller: *Gnomologia*

And as with guns we kill the crow,
    For spoiling our relief,
The devil so must we o'erthrow,
    With gunshot of belief.

George Gascoigne: *Good-morrow*

In this tendency to accept what we find, to believe what we are told, is at once good and evil. It is this which makes social advance possible; it is this which makes it so slow and painful. It is thus tyranny is maintained and superstition perpetuated.

Henry George: *Social Problems*

The mob that would die for a belief seldom hesitates to inflict death upon any opposing heretical group.

Ellen Glasgow: *I Believe*

Maturity of mind is best shown in slow belief.

Baltasar Gracián y Morales

Quick believers need broad shoulders.

George Herbert: *Jacula Prudentum*

He that believes all, misseth; he that believes nothing, hits not.

George Herbert: *Outlandish Proverbs*

Fields are won by those who believe in the winning.

Thomas Wentworth Higginson:
Americanism in Literature

A man is shaped to beliefs long held however uncritically—as the roots of a tree that has grown in the crevices of a rock.

Justice Oliver Wendell Holmes, Jr.,
Harvard University Press

People automatically believe in books. Messages come from behind the controlled and censored areas of the world and they do not ask for radios, for papers and pamphlets. They invariably ask for books. They believe books when they believe nothing else.

E. Paul Hovey

What we call rational grounds for our beliefs are often extremely irrational attempts to justify our instincts.

Thomas Henry Huxley: *On the Natural Inequality of Man*

In the matter of belief, we are all extreme conservatives.

William James: *Pragmatism,* courtesy of David McKay Co. Inc., and Paul R. Reynolds & Son

Faith means belief in something concerning which doubt is theoretically possible.

William James (permission to reprint granted by Paul R. Reynolds & Son)

Be not afraid of life. Believe that life *is* worth living, and your belief will help create the fact.

William James (permission to reprint granted by Paul R. Reynolds & Son)

Ignorance is preferable to error; and he is less remote from truth who believes nothing, than he who believes what is wrong.

Thomas Jefferson: *Writings,* Vol. II, p. 43

Every man who attacks my belief diminishes in some degree my confidence in it, and therefore makes me uneasy, and I am angry with him who makes me uneasy.

Samuel Johnson

The things a man believes most profoundly are rarely on the surface of his mind or on the tip of his tongue. Newly acquired notions, formulas learned by rote from books, decisions based on expediency, the fashionable ideas of the moment—these are right on top of the pile, ready to be sampled and displayed in bright after-dinner conversation. But the ideas that make up a man's philosophy of life are somewhere way down below.

> Eric Johnston: *America Unlimited*. Copyright 1942, 1943, 1944 by Eric Johnston. Reprinted by permission of Doubleday & Company, Inc.

Better trust all and be deceived,
    And weep that trust, and that deceiving,
Than doubt one heart, that, if believed,
    Had blessed one's life with true believing.

> Fanny Kemble

He who expects men to be always as good as their beliefs, indulges in a groundless hope; and he who expects men to be always as bad as their beliefs, vexes himself with a needless fear.

> J. S. Kieffer

Everyone believes very easily whatever he fears or desires.

> Jean de La Fontaine: *Fables,* XI

Credulity is the man's weakness, but the child's strength.

> Charles Lamb

Believe nothing and be on guard against everything.

> Latin Proverb

Believe you have it, and you have it.

> Latin Proverb

There is a great difference between believing a thing and not being able to believe the contrary. I often come to believe in things without being able to prove them, and to disbelieve in others without being able to disprove them.

> Georg Christoph Lichtenberg: *Reflections*

Many a time I have wanted to stop talking and find out what I really believed.

> Walter Lippmann: *The London Observer,* March 27, 1938

Toward no crimes have men shown themselves so cold-bloodedly cruel as in punishing differences of belief.

> James Russell Lowell: *Witchcraft,* Vol. II, p. 374

O thou, whose days are yet all spring,
    Faith, blighted once, is past retrieving;
Experience is a dumb, dead thing;
    The victory's in believing.

> James Russell Lowell: *To ——*

It is easier to believe than to doubt.

> Everett Dean Martin: *The Meaning of a Liberal Education,* ch. 5

A well-bred man keeps his beliefs out of his conversation.

> André Maurois

Believe that you may understand.

> Medieval Latin Saying

We are the personification of the things we really believe in.

> *Megiddo Message*

One person with a belief is equal to a force of ninety-nine who have only interests.

> John Stuart Mill

That man will go far; he believes all he says.

> Honoré de Riquetti Mirabeau (of Robespierre)

We believe nothing so firmly as what we least know.

> Michel Eyquem de Montaigne: *Essays*

Some impose upon the world that they believe that which they do not; others, more in number, make themselves believe that they believe, not being able to penetrate into that which is to believe.

Michel Eyquem de Montaigne: *Apology for Raimond Sebond*

It is as absurd to argue men, as to torture them, into believing.

Cardinal John Henry Newman

Whosoever shall offend one of these little ones that believe in me, it is better for him that a millstone were hanged about his neck, and he were cast into the sea.

New Testament: Mark 9: 42

He that believeth not shall be damned.

New Testament: Mark 16: 16

Jesus saith unto him, Thomas, because thou hast seen me, thou hast believed: blessed are they that have not seen, and yet have believed.

New Testament: John 20: 29

Charity . . . believeth all things. . . .

New Testament: I Corinthians 13: 7

I know whom I have believed.

New Testament: II Timothy 1: 12

Believe! No storm harms a man who believes.

Ovid: *Amores*, Bk. II, eleg. 11, l. 22

Do not believe hastily.

Ovid: *Ars Amatoria*, Bk. III, l. 685

Where belief is painful, we are slow to believe.

Ovid: *Heroides*, Epis. II, l. 9

An honest belief, while hard to come by, is humanity's main asset and hope.

Peabody Journal of Education

I will utter what I believe today, if it should contradict all I said yesterday.

Wendell Phillips

Remember that what you believe will depend very much upon what you are.

Noah Porter

Never tell all that you know, or do all that you can, or believe all that you hear.

Portuguese Proverb

And when religious sects ran mad,
  He held, in spite of all his learning,
That if a man's belief is bad,
  It will not be improved by burning.

Winthrop Mackworth Praed: *Poems of Life and Manners*, Pt. II, The Vicar, st. 9

When civilizations fail, it is always man who has failed—not in his body, not in his fundamental equipment and capacities, but in his will, spirit and mental habits. Men and civilizations live by their beliefs and die when their beliefs pass into doubt.

Philip Lee Ralph: *The Story of Our Civilization, 1954*, E. P. Dutton & Co., Inc.

To believe is to be strong. Doubt cramps energy. Belief is power.

Frederick William Robertson

Unfounded beliefs are the homage which impulse pays to reason.

Bertrand Russell, Liveright Publishing Corp.

The people would not believe in God at all if they were not permitted to believe wrong in Him.

Sir George Savile, Lord Halifax

Tell that to the marines—the sailors won't believe it.

Sir Walter Scott: *Redgauntlet*, ch. 13

It is equally an error to believe all men or no man.

Seneca

What the wretched wish for intensely, that they easily believe.

Seneca: *Hercules Furens*, l. 313

People who believe that man is a happenstance evolution out of matter impelled by blind force are too naïve to live in a world which long ago discovered that magic doesn't work.

S. F. C. Spotlight

Stands not within the prospect of belief.

William Shakespeare: *Macbeth*,
Act I, sc. 3, l. 74

Know you what it is to be a child? . . . It is to have a spirit yet streaming from the waters of baptism; it is to believe in love, to believe in loveliness, to believe in belief.

Percy Bysshe Shelley

I believe because I do believe.

Percy Bysshe Shelley: *Letter to
T. J. Hogg*

Belief is a passion, or involuntary operation of the mind, and like other passions, its intensity is precisely proportionate to the degrees of excitement.

Percy Bysshe Shelley: *Queen Mab*

I am not afraid of those tender and scrupulous consciences who are ever cautious of professing and believing too much; if they are sincerely wrong, I forgive their errors and respect their integrity.—The men I am afraid of are those who believe everything, subscribe to everything, and vote for everything.

William Davies Shipley

Birds sing on a bare bough;
O believer, canst not thou?

Charles Haddon Spurgeon: *Salt-Cellars*

The want of belief is a defect that ought to be concealed when it cannot be overcome.

Jonathan Swift: *Thoughts on Religion*

Nor can belief touch, kindle, smite, reprieve
His heart who has not heart to disbelieve.

Algernon Charles Swinburne:
In the Bay, st. 31

Who . . . has ever seen an idea? . . . Who has ever seen love? . . . Who has ever seen faith? . . . The real things in the world are the invisible spiritual realities. Is it so difficult, then, to believe in God?

Charles Templeton: *Life Looks Up*,
Harper & Row, Publishers, Inc.

Believing where we cannot prove.

Alfred, Lord Tennyson: *In Memoriam:
Introduction*, st. 1

You believe easily that which you hope for earnestly.

Terence

I believe because it is impossible.

Tertullian: *De Carne Christi*

While men believe in the infinite, some ponds will be thought to be bottomless.

Henry David Thoreau

To believe in God for me is to feel that there is a God, not a dead one, or a stuffed one, but a living one, who with irresistible force urges us towards more loving.

Vincent van Gogh

Conviction is the Conscience of the Mind.

Mary Augusta Ward: *Robert Elsmere*,
Bk. IV, ch. 26

Belief means that the truth has made a conquest in personality.

Leslie D. Weatherhead, *This Is
The Victory*, Abingdon Press

The opposite of joy is not sorrow. It is unbelief.

Ibid.

Believe things, rather than men.

Benjamin Whichcote: *Moral and
Religious Aphorisms*

Man can believe the impossible, but man can never believe the improbable.

Oscar Wilde: *The Decay of Lying*

There littleness was not; the least of things
Seemed infinite; and there his spirit shaped
Her prospects, nor did he believe,—He *saw*.

William Wordsworth: *The Excursion*,
Bk. I, st. 12

BENEVOLENCE

Rare benevolence! the minister of God.

Thomas Carlyle

There cannot be a more glorious object in
creation than a human being replete with
benevolence, meditating in what manner he
may render himself most acceptable to the
Creator by doing good to his creatures.

Henry Fielding

It is the glory of the true religion that it in-
culcates and inspires a spirit of benevolence.
—It is a religion of charity, which none other
ever was.—Christ went about doing good;
he set the example to his disciples, and they
abounded in it.

Thomas Fuller

Benevolence is allied to few vices; selfishness
to fewer virtues.

Henry Home

Beneficence is a duty; and he who frequently
practices it and sees his benevolent intentions realized, at length comes to love him
to whom he has done good.

Immanuel Kant

Benevolence is the distinguishing characteristic of man. As embodied in man's conduct,
it is called the path of duty.

Mencius: *Discourses*, VII

Benevolent feeling ennobles the most trifling
actions.

William Makepeace Thackeray

BIBLE

Many things in the Bible I cannot understand; many things in the Bible I only think

I understand; but there are many things in
the Bible I cannot misunderstand.

Anonymous

The Bible is the only Book by which you
may know certainly the future; it is the
only Book that satisfactorily answers the
questions, Where did I come from? Why am
I here? Where am I going?

Anonymous

The devil is not afraid of the Bible that has
dust on it.

Anonymous

So great is my veneration for the Bible that
the earlier my children begin to read it, the
more confident will be my hope that they
will prove useful citizens to their country,
and respectable members of society.

John Quincy Adams

There are ten men who will fight for the
Bible to one who will read it.

L. R. Akers: *Eighth Fear and other
Sermons*, Abingdon Press

There can be no falsehood anywhere in the
literal sense of Holy Scripture.

St. Thomas Aquinas: *Summa
theologica I*

I am a man of one book.

St. Thomas Aquinas

To the Bible men will return, and why?
Because they cannot do without it.

Matthew Arnold

The reason people are down on the Bible is
that they're not up on the Bible.

William Ward Ayer

It may be truly affirmed that there was never
any philosophy, religion, or other discipline,
which did so plainly and highly exalt the
good which is communicative, and depress
the good which is private and particular, as
the Holy Faith.

Sir Francis Bacon: *The Advancement of
Learning*, II, 20, 7

The Bible rose to the place it now occupies because it deserved to rise to that place, and not because God sent anybody with a box of tricks to prove its divine authority.

> From *The Man and The Book Nobody Knows* by Bruce Barton, copyright © 1959 by the Bobbs-Merrill Company, Inc., reprinted by permission of the publishers

The word of God tends to make large-minded, noble-hearted men.

> Henry Ward Beecher

The Bible is God's chart for you to steer by, to keep you from the bottom of the sea, and to show you where the harbour is, and how to reach it without running on rocks and bars.

> Henry Ward Beecher

Sink the Bible to the bottom of the ocean, and man's obligations to God would be unchanged. He would have the same path to tread, only his lamp and his guide would be gone; he would have the same voyage to make, only his compass and chart would be overboard.

> Henry Ward Beecher

Almost any fool can prove the Bible ain't so—it takes a wise man to believe it.

> Josh Billings

On the day before the last he (Strindberg) called for his Bible, which he always kept within easy reach. Placing his hand on it, he said quietly, "Everything personal is now wiped out. I have settled with life. My balance has been struck. This book alone is right."

> Edwin Björkman: *Voices of Tomorrow:* August Strindberg

The Bible has always been regarded as part of the Common Law of England.

> Sir William Blackstone: *Commentaries on the Laws of England*

No nation is better than its sacred book. In that book are expressed its highest ideals of life, and no nation rises above those ideals. No nation has a sacred book to be compared with ours. This American nation from its first settlement at Jamestown to the present hour is based upon and permeated by the principles of the Bible. The more this Bible enters into our national life the grander and purer and better will that life become.

> David Josiah Brewer

This is a work too hard for the teeth of time, and cannot perish but in the general flames, when all things shall confess their ashes.

> Sir Thomas Browne: *Religio Medici,* I

The Bible holds up before us ideals that are within sight of the weakest and the lowliest, and yet so high that the best and the noblest are kept with their faces turned ever upward. It carries the call of the Saviour to the remotest corners of the earth; on its pages are written the assurances of the present and our hopes for the future.

> William Jennings Bryan

Alone at nights,
I read my Bible more and Euclid less.

> Robert Williams Buchanan: *An Old Dominie's Story*

I have sometimes seen more in a line of the Bible than I could well tell how to stand under, and yet at another time the whole Bible hath been to me as dry as a stick.

> John Bunyan: *Grace Abounding to the Chief of Sinners*

Holy Bible, book divine,
Precious treasure, thou art mine;
Mine to teach me whence I came,
Mine to teach me what I am.

> John Burton: *Holy Bible, Book Divine*

All history . . . is an inarticulate Bible.

> Thomas Carlyle: Quoted in Froude's *Early Life of Carlyle*

What built St. Paul's Cathedral? Look at the heart of the matter, it was that divine Hebrew Book,—the word partly of the man Moses, an outlaw tending his Midianitish herds, four thousand years ago, in the wilderness of Sinai! It is the strangest of things, yet nothing is truer.

> Thomas Carlyle: *Heroes and Hero-Worship; The Hero as Man of Letters*

Oh, that pestilent book! Never more on it look—
I wish I could sing it out louder—
It has done men more harm, I dare boldly affirm,
Than th' invention of guns and of powder.

> *The Catholick Ballad*

Time can take nothing from the Bible. It is the living monitor. Like the sun, it is the same in its light and influence to man this day which it was years ago. It can meet every present inquiry and console every present loss.

> Richard Cecil

The history of all the great characters of the Bible is summed up in this one sentence: They acquainted themselves with God, and acquiesced in His will in all things.

> Richard Cecil

The Bible resembles an extensive garden, where there is a vast variety and profusion of fruits and flowers, some of which are more essential or more splendid than others; but there is not a blade suffered to grow in it which has not its use and beauty in the system.

> Richard Cecil: *Remains*

The incongruity of the Bible with the age of its birth; its freedom from earthly mixtures; its original, unborrowed, solitary greatness; the suddenness with which it broke forth amidst the general gloom; these, to me, are strong indications of its Divine descent: I cannot reconcile them with a human origin.

> William Ellery Channing

The Bible only is the religion of Protestants.

> William Chillingworth: *The Religion of Protestants a Safe Way to Salvation*

No lawyer can afford to be ignorant of the Bible.

> Rufus Choate

My Bible tells me how to go to heaven, not how the heavens go.

> J. R. Cohu: *The Bible and Modern Thought*, V

Beside our own standards, the Old Testament is lusty and free; some of its contents would be banned in Boston were they published under less sacred auspices.

> William Graham Cole: *Ladies' Home Journal*, October, 1959

For more than a thousand years the Bible, collectively taken, has gone hand in hand with civilization, science, law—in short, with the moral and intellectual cultivation of the species, always supporting and often leading the way.

> Samuel Taylor Coleridge

Good and holy men, and the best and wisest of mankind, and kingly spirits of history, enthroned in the hearts of mighty nations, have borne witness to its influences, have declared it to be beyond compare the most perfect instrument of humanity.

> Samuel Taylor Coleridge

To give the history of the Bible as a *book*, would be little less than to relate the origin or first excitement of all the literature and science, that we now possess.

> Samuel Taylor Coleridge: *Biographia Literaria*, II

Do you know a book that you are willing to put under your head for a pillow when you are dying? Very well; that is the book you want to study when you are living. There is only one such book in the world.

> Joseph Cook

A glory gilds the sacred page,
Majestic like the sun;
It gives a light to every age,—
It gives, but borrows none.

The hand that gave it still supplies
  The gracious light and heat;
His truths upon the nations rise,—
  They rise, but never set.

> William Cowper: *The Light and
> Glory of the World*

And of all arts sagacious dupes invent,
To cheat themselves and gain the world's
  assent,
The worst is—Scripture warp'd from its
  intent.

> William Cowper: *The Progress of
> Error*, l. 435

Just knows, and knows no more, her Bible
  true . . .
And in that charter reads, with sparkling
  eyes,
Her title to a treasure in the skies.

> William Cowper: *Truth*, l. 327

The Bible has often been treated as if it
were a wax nose which may be twisted at
the whim of the interpreter.

> Clarence Tucker Craig: *The Beginnings
> of Christianity*, Abingdon Press

Lo, here a little volume, but great book!
(Fear it not, sweet, It is no hypocrite),
Much larger in itself than in its look.

> Richard Crashaw: *Prayer Prefixed
> to a Little Prayer-Book*, I, 1

It is an armoury of light;
Let constant use but keep it bright,
  You'll find it yields
To holy hands and humble hearts,
  More swords and shields
Than sin hath snares, or hell hath darts.

> Richard Crashaw: *Prayer Prefixed
> to a Little Prayer-Book*, I, 24

There is one Book, and only one, which embraces all the heights and depths of human
nature. The Bible belongs to those elemental
things—like the sky and the wind and the
sea, like bread and wine, like the kisses of
little children and tears shed beside the grave
—which can never grow stale or out of date,
because they are the common heritage of
mankind.

> T. H. Darlow: *The Greatest Book
> in the World*

Other books were given for our information,
the Bible was given for our transformation.

> *The Defender*

Men do not reject the Bible because it contradicts itself but because it contradicts
them.

> *Ibid.*

The greatest source of material for motion
pictures is the Bible, and almost any chapter
in the Bible would serve as a basic idea for
a motion picture.

> Cecil B. DeMille

After more than sixty years of almost daily
reading of the Bible, I never fail to find it
always new and marvellously in tune with
the changing needs of every day.

> Cecil B. DeMille

The New Testament is the best book the
world has ever known or will know.

> Charles Dickens

There is a small book: one can put it in one's
pocket, and yet all the libraries of America,
numerous as they are, would hardly be large
enough to hold all the books which have
been inspired by this one little volume. The
reader will know what I am speaking of; it
is the Bible, as we are used to call it—the
Book, the book of mankind, as it has properly been called.

> Ernest von Dobschutz: *The Influence
> of the Bible on Civilization*

Of all commentaries upon the Scriptures,
good examples are the best and the liveliest.

> John Donne: *Sermon Preached
> at a Marriage*

You rule the Scripture, not the Scripture
you.

> John Dryden: *The Hind and the Panther*,
> Pt. II, l. 187

And that the Scriptures, though not every-
where
Free from corruption, or entire, or clear,
Are uncorrupt, sufficient, clear, entire
In all things which our needful faith require.

John Dryden: *Religio Laici*

Whence, but from heaven could men, un-
skilled in arts,
In several ages born, in several parts,
Weave such agreeing truths? Or how, or why
Should all conspire to cheat us with a lie?
Unasked their pains, ungrateful their advice,
Starving their gain, and martyrdom their
price.

Ibid.

The Bible is a window in this prison world,
through which we may look into eternity.

Timothy Dwight

The Old Testament prophets and the New
Testament writers denounce the exclusive
privileges of the rich and the usurpation of
the rights of the poor, and strenuously en-
force their demands for righteous dealings
among men. The Bible, like an unfailing
arsenal, has supplied the ammunition for the
agelong struggle for liberty.

Charles David Eldridge: *Christianity's
Contribution to Civilization*, II, 11

The vice of our theology is seen in the claim
that the Bible is a closed book and that the
age of inspiration is past.

Ralph Waldo Emerson

Nor can the Bible be closed until the last
great man is born.

Ralph Waldo Emerson: *Representative
Men: Uses of Great Men*

The Bible is like an old Cremona; it has been
played upon by the devotion of thousands of
years until every word and particle is public
and tunable.

Ralph Waldo Emerson: *Letters
and Social Aims: Quotation
and Originality*

The word unto the prophet spoken
Was writ on tablets yet unbroken:
The word by seers or sibyls told,
In groves of oak or fanes of gold,
Still floats upon the morning wind,
Still whispers to the willing mind.

Ralph Waldo Emerson: *The Problem*

Out from the heart of nature rolled
The burdens of the Bible old.

Ibid.

All the distinctive features and superiority
of our republican institutions are derived
from the teachings of Scripture.

Edward Everett

The dog is mentioned in the Bible 18 times
—the cat not even once.

W. E. Farbstein, quoted in *Reader's
Digest*, August, 1935, issue

No student can historically understand the
Bible until he is ready to lay aside all prior
considerations, and examine it analytically,
arriving by induction at a real knowledge
as to its claims and character. . . . We must
never lose sight of the fact that the Bible is
not a single nor even a homogeneous book.
The Bible is, strictly speaking, not a book
but a library.

Frederic William Farrar: *The Bible*

Men have misused Scripture just as they
misuse light or food.

Ibid.

The Scriptures teach us the best way of
living, the noblest way of suffering, and the
most comfortable way of dying.

John Flavel

The Word of God is in the Bible as the soul
is in the body.

Peter Taylor Forsyth

The Bible thoroughly known is a literature
of itself—the rarest and richest in all de-
partments of thought or imagination which
exists.

James Anthony Froude, in his sketch of
the life of John Bunyan

Jest not with the two-edged sword of God's word.

Thomas Fuller: *The Holy State and the Profane State*

This is the cannon that will make Italy free.

Giuseppe Garibaldi, on the Bible

It is supremacy, not precedence, that we ask for the Bible; it is contrast, as well as resemblance, that we must feel compelled to insist on. The Bible is stamped with specialty of origin, and an immeasurable distance separates it from all competitors.

William Ewart Gladstone

It is not the Bible that produced religion and morals, but religion and morals that produced the Bible.

William Ewart Gladstone

The Bible grows more beautiful, as we grow in our understanding of it.

Johann Wolfgang von Goethe

It has been truly said that any translation of the masterpiece (the Bible) must be a failure.

Edgar J. Goodspeed; University of Chicago Press

Hold fast to the Bible as the sheet-anchor of your liberties; write its precepts in your hearts, and practice them in your lives. To the influence of this book we are indebted for all the progress made in true civilization, and to this we must look as our guide in the future. "Righteousness exalteth a nation; but sin is a reproach to any people."

Ulysses S. Grant

It is impossible to mentally or socially enslave a Bible-reading people.

Horace Greeley

Holy Scripture is a stream of running water, where alike the elephant may swim, and the lamb walk without losing its feet.

Pope Gregory the Great

The highest earthly enjoyments are but a shadow of the joy I find in reading God's word.

Lady Jane Grey

No one ever graduates from Bible study until he meets the Author face to face.

Everett T. Harris, quoted in *Christian Herald*

It is a plain old book, modest as nature itself, and as simple, too; a book of an unpretending work-day appearance, like the sun that warms or the bread that nourishes us . . . And the name of this book is simply—the Bible.

Heinrich Heine: *Scintillations: Religion*

There is a Book worth all other books which were ever printed.

Patrick Henry

Stars are poor books, and oftentimes do miss: This book of stars lights to eternal bliss.

George Herbert: *The Holy Scriptures*, Sonnet II

The book of books, the storehouse and magazine of life and comfort, the Holy Scriptures.

George Herbert: *A Priest of the Temple*, ch. 4

The Bible? That's the Book. The Book indeed,
 The Book of books;
 On which who looks,
As he should do, aright, shall never need
 Wish for a better light
 To guide him in the night.

George Herbert: *The Synagogue: The Bible*

Bibles laid open, millions of surprises.

George Herbert: *The Temple*

The best evidence of the Bible's being the word of God is found between its covers.

Charles Hodge

What you bring away from the Bible depends to some extent on what you carry to it.

Oliver Wendell Holmes, Sr.

No book has been read more widely, more carefully, more sympathetically, more critically. Yet no book has been subject to greater variety of interpretations, many of them mutually incompatible.

Sidney Hook: *Education for Modern Man*

The Bible is common-sense inspired.

Rees Howells

England has two books, the Bible and Shakespeare. England made Shakespeare, but the Bible made England.

Victor Hugo

The New Testament holds up a strong light by which a man can read even the small print of his soul.

John A. Hutton

The dogma of the infallibility of the Bible is no more self-evident than is that of the infallibility of the Popes.

Thomas Henry Huxley: *Essays Upon Some Controverted Questions*

The Bible has been the *Magna Charta* of the poor and of the oppressed.

Ibid.

There's a big difference between the books that men make and the Book that makes men.

In A Nutshell

If you Christians in India, in Britain, or in America, were like your book, you would conquer India in five years.

An Indian Brahman to a Missionary

I have always said, I always say, that the studious perusal of the sacred volume will make better citizens, better fathers, and better husbands.

Thomas Jefferson

Not versions, but perversions.

St. Jerome, of the versions of the Bible current in his day

The Scriptures contain independently of a divine origin, more true sublimity, more exquisite beauty, purer morality, more important history, and finer strains of both poetry and eloquence than could be collected, within the same compass from all other books that were ever composed in any age or in any language.

Sir William Jones: *Address,* February, 1792

The Bible is the Iliad of religion.

Joseph Joubert

When you start a Bible movement, it means revolution—a quiet revolution against darkness and crime.

Toyohiko Kagawa: *Behold the Man,* Harper & Row, Publishers, Inc.

The Bible is the greatest benefit which the human race has ever experienced.

Immanuel Kant

A single line in the Bible has consoled me more than all the books I ever read besides.

Immanuel Kant

There is a book, who runs may read,
  Which heavenly truth imparts,
And all the lore its scholars need,
  Pure eyes and Christian hearts.

John Keble: *The Christian Year: Septuagesima*

A man may learn from his Bible to be a more thorough gentleman than if he had been brought up in all the drawing-rooms in London.

Charles Kingsley: *The Water Babies*

Break Thou the bread of life, dear Lord, to me,
As Thou didst break the loaves beside the sea;
Beyond the sacred page I seek Thee, Lord;
My spirit pants for Thee, O living Word.

Mary A. Lathbury

The Bible is a book in comparison with which all others in my eyes are of minor importance; and which in all my perplexities and distresses has never failed to give me light and strength.

Robert E. Lee

The Bible continues to be the best selling book; it is regarded as the most economical of all fire-escapes.

Lexington (Ky.) *Leader*

Read this book for what on reason you can accept and take the rest on faith, and you will live and die a better man.

Abraham Lincoln

This great book . . . is the best gift God has given to man. . . . But for it we could not know right from wrong.

Abraham Lincoln

All that I am I owe to Jesus Christ, revealed to me in His divine Book.

David Livingstone

The Bible is one of the greatest blessings bestowed by God on the children of men.— It has God for its author, salvation for its end, and truth without any mixture for its matter.—It is all pure, all sincere; nothing too much; nothing wanting.

John Locke

So *we're* all right, an' I, for one,
  Don't think our cause'll lose in vally
By rammin' Scriptur' in our gun,
  An' gittin' Natur' for an ally.

James Russell Lowell: *The Biglow Papers, Second Series*, no. 7, st. 17

Christ is the Master; the Scriptures are only the servant. The true way to test all the Books is to see whether they work the will of Christ or not. No Book which does not preach Christ can be apostolic, though Peter or Paul were its author. And no Book which does preach Christ can fail to be apostolic, though Judas, Ananias, Pilate or Herod were its author.

Martin Luther: Introduction to his German trans. of the New Testament

No word or words of man can ever for all time confine the meaning of the Bible, for the Bible is a living book, and therefore, an ever-enlarging book.

James G. K. McClure: *The Supreme Book of Mankind*, VI

The book to read is not the one which thinks for you, but the one which makes you think. No book in the world equals the Bible for that.

James McCosh: *The Laws of Discursive Thought*

What Dryden said about Chaucer applies in infinitely greater degree to the Bible: "Here is God's plenty."

Robert J. McCracken: *The Making of the Sermon*, Harper & Row Publishers, Inc.

The English Bible (is) a book which, if everything else in our language should perish, would alone suffice to show the whole extent of its beauty and power.

Thomas Babington Macaulay: *John Dryden (Edinburgh Review*, January, 1828)

My way of learning a language is always to begin with the Bible, which I can read without a dictionary.

Thomas Babington Macaulay: *Letter to Macvey Napier*

The foundation, the state, the perfection of wisdom is knowledge of the Holy Scriptures.

Rabanus Maurus, Archbishop of Mainz

What is a home without a Bible?
  'Tis a home where daily bread
For the *body* is provided,
  But the *soul* is never fed.

Charles Delucena Meigs: *Home Without a Bible*

The mystery of the Bible should teach us, at one and the same time, our nothingness and our greatness, producing humility and animating hope.

Henry Melville

The morality of the Bible is, after all, the safety of society.

Francis Cassette Monfort

Sin will keep you from this Book. This Book will keep you from sin.

Dwight L. Moody

I know the Bible is inspired because it inspires me.

Dwight L. Moody

The question of the authority of the Bible need not trouble the humblest reader. It is not "a code which fell from the sky, guaranteed by an ecclesiastical imprimatur," but a collection of writing which breathes upon us the only authority that is worth regarding —the authority of the power of the Spirit.

Frank W. Moyle in *Watchman-Examiner*

I read my Bible to know what people ought to do, and my newspaper to know what they are doing.

Cardinal John Henry Newman

Its light is like the body of heaven in its clearness; its vastness like the bosom of the sea; its variety like scenes of nature.

Cardinal John Henry Newman: *Tracts for the Times*, no. 87

Search the scriptures.

New Testament: John 5: 39

Wot ye not what the scripture saith?

New Testament: Romans 11: 2

What saith the scripture?

New Testament: Galatians 4: 30
(also in *Romans 4: 3*)

All scripture is given by inspiration of God, and is profitable for doctrine, for reproof, for correction, for instruction in righteousness.

New Testament: II Timothy 3: 16

But the word of the Lord endureth for ever.

New Testament: I Peter 1: 25

. . . no prophecy of the scripture is of any private interpretation. For the prophecy came not in old time by the will of man: but holy men of God spake as they were moved by the Holy Ghost.

New Testament: II Peter 1: 20–21

We account the Scriptures of God to be the most sublime philosophy. I find more sure marks of authority in the Bible than in any profane history whatever.

Sir Isaac Newton

No sciences are better attested than the religion of the Bible.

Sir Isaac Newton

The history of every individual man should be a Bible.

Novalis: *Christianity or Europe*
(Carlyle, trans.)

If all the neglected Bibles were dusted simultaneously, we would have a record dust storm and the sun would go into eclipse for a whole week.

David F. Nygren, in *Watchman-Examiner*

It has been well said that upsetting the Bible is like upsetting a solid cube of granite; it is just as big one way as the other, and when you have upset it, it is right side up, and when you overturn it again, it is right side up still.

Ibid.

This little book—it has said everything there is to be said. Everything is implied and anticipated in it. Whatever one should like to put into words has already been said in it.

Mordecai Obadiah: *Mipee Bialik*, p. 37

Thy word is a lamp unto my feet, and a light unto my path.

Old Testament: Psalms 119: 105

You cannot name any example in any heathen author but I will better it in Scripture.

Sir Thomas Overbury: Crumms Fal'n from the King James's Table, X

God's Road Map—the Bible.

Kenyon A. Palmer

The Bible goes equally to the cottage of the peasant, and the palace of the king.—It is woven into literature, and colors the talk of the street.—The bark of the merchant cannot sail without it; and no ship of war goes to the conflict but it is there.—It enters men's closets; directs their conduct, and mingles in all the grief and cheerfulness of life.

Theodore Parker

Most wondrous book! bright candle of the
Lord!
Star of Eternity! The only star
By which the bark of man could navigate
The sea of life, and gain the coast of bliss
Securely.

Robert Pollok: The Course of Time,
Bk. II, l. 270

Fresh light shall yet break out from God's Word.

John Robinson

I must confess to you that the majesty of the Scriptures astonishes me; the holiness of the Evangelists speaks to my heart and has such striking characters of truth, and is, moreover, so perfectly inimitable, that if it had been the invention of men, the inventors would be greater than the greatest heroes.

Jean Jacques Rousseau

My mother's influence in molding my character was conspicuous. She forced me to learn daily long chapters of the Bible by heart. To that discipline and patient, accurate resolve I owe not only much of my general power of taking pains, but of the best part of my taste for literature.

John Ruskin

The Bible is the one Book to which any thoughtful man may go with any honest question of life or destiny and find the answer of God by honest searching.

John Ruskin

Within that awful volume lies
The mystery of mysteries!
Happiest they of human race,
To whom God has granted grace
To read, to fear, to hope, to pray,
To lift the latch, and force the way:
And better had they ne'er been born,
Who read to doubt, or read to scorn.

Sir Walter Scott: The Monastery, ch. 12

No book presents morals in such inextricable union with politics as the Bible.

Sir John Robert Seeley: The Growth of
British Policy

The whole hope of human progress is suspended on the ever-growing influence of the Bible.

William H. Seward

The devil can cite Scripture for his purpose.
An evil soul producing holy witness
Is like a villain with a smiling cheek,
A goodly apple rotten at the heart:
O, what a goodly outside falsehood hath!

William Shakespeare: The Merchant
of Venice, Act I, sc. 3, l. 99

But then I sigh; and, with a piece of Scripture,
Tell them that God bids us to do good for evil:
And thus I clothe my naked villany
With old odd ends stolen out of holy writ,
And seem a saint when most I play the devil.

William Shakespeare: Richard III,
Act I, sc. 3, l. 334

. . . My Bible, which is a vast Holy Land.

James Smetham: Letter to Mrs. T.

What makes the difference is not how many times you have been through the Bible, but how many times and how thoroughly the Bible has been through you.

Gipsy Smith

The books of men have their day and grow obsolete. God's Word is like Himself, "the same yesterday, today and forever."

Robert Payne Smith

Democracy is nothing but an attempt to apply the principles of the Bible to a human society.

Wallace C. Speers: *Laymen Speaking,* Association Press

Never, with the Bible in our hands, can we deny rights to another, which, under the same circumstances, we could claim for ourselves.

Gardiner Spring: *The Obligations of the World to the Bible,* p. 91

In God's word we have a perfect standard both of duty and character, that by the influence of both, appealing to the best principles of our nature, we may be roused to the noblest and best efforts.

Samuel Spring

Nobody ever outgrows Scripture; the Book widens and deepens with our years.

Charles Haddon Spurgeon

Even the style of the Scriptures is more than human.

Sir Richard Steele

The Bible is a telescope between man and God; it is the rending of a veil.

Augustus H. Strong: *American Poets and Their Theology,* 11, 2; Judson Press (used by permission)

The real influence of the Bible cannot be measured; it is reckoned only in terms of hearts that have been lifted up, decisions that have been changed, the men and women who, in response to its impervious demands, have done justice and loved kindness and walked humbly with God.

Taken from *The Book God Made* by J. Carter Swaim, © 1959 by Hawthorn Books, Inc.

The Scripture, in time of disputes, is like an open town in time of war, which serves indifferently the occasions of both parties.

Jonathan Swift: *Thoughts on Various Subjects*

There are only two things at work,—the very word of God as it is transmitted by Scripture, and the emotions of the heart of man, as the word of God excites and maintains them.

Henri A. Taine: *History of English Literature,* II, 5

The deathless Book has survived three great dangers: the negligence of its friends; the false systems built upon it; the warfare of those who have hated it.

Isaac Taylor

The man of one book is always formidable; but when that book is the Bible he is irresistible.

William Mackergo Taylor

The Scriptures of God, whether belonging to Christian or Jew, are much more ancient than any secular literature.

Tertullian: *The Testimony of the Christian Soul*

The thing is, that the Bible, whether you consider it as a collection of fables, transmuted through the golden mists of an elder time, or as a system of ethics, or as a profession of faith, is the most convincing and comprehensive record of human experience and aspiration that exists in our world.

John W. Thomason, Jr.: "The Best Best-Seller," *American Mercury,* January, 1937

Be careful how you live; you may be the only Bible some person ever reads.

W. J. Toms: *Detroit News*

Most people are bothered by those passages in Scripture which they cannot understand; but as for me, I always noticed that the passages in Scripture which trouble me most are those which I do understand.

> Mark Twain

Tell your prince that this book (the Bible) is the secret of England's greatness.

> Queen Victoria to an African Prince

If we would destroy the Christian religion, we must first of all destroy man's belief in the Bible.

> Voltaire

Every hour
I read you kills a sin,
Or lets a virtue in
To fight against it.

> Izaak Walton

Jesus loves me—this I know,
For the Bible tells me so.

> Susan Bogert Warner: *The Love of Jesus*

How glad the heathens would have been,
    That worship idols, wood and stone,
If they the book of God had seen.

> Isaac Watts: *Praise for the Gospel*

Dear Lord, this Book of thine
    Informs me where to go,
For grace to pardon all my sin,
    And make me holy too.

> Isaac Watts: *Praise to God for
> Learning to Read*

The stars, that in their courses roll,
    Have much instruction given;
But thy good Word informs my soul
    How I may climb to heaven.

> Isaac Watts: *The Excellency of
> the Bible*

I believe that the Bible is to be understood and received in the plain and obvious meaning of its passages; since I cannot persuade myself that a book intended for the instruction and conversion of the whole world, should cover its true meaning is such mystery and doubt, that none but critics and philosophers can discover it.

> Daniel Webster: *Confession of Faith*

The Bible is a book of faith, and a book of doctrine, and a book of morals, and a book of religion, of especial revelation from God.

> Daniel Webster

Sir, if the Bible be not true, I am as very a fool and madman as you can conceive; but if it be of God I am sober-minded.

> John Wesley: To a friend, on sailing
> for Georgia, 1735

I am a Bible-bigot. I follow it in all things, both great and small.

> John Wesley: *Journal,* June 2, 1766

Fear is the denomination of the Old Testament; belief is the denomination of the New.

> Benjamin Whichcote: *Moral and
> Religious Aphorisms*

Nothing is of faith that is not in Scripture.

> *Ibid.*

"O Bible," say I, "What follies and monstrous barbarities are defended in *thy* name."

> Walt Whitman, paraphrasing
> Madame Roland

Foul shame and scorn be on ye all
    Who turn the good to evil,
And steal the Bible from the Lord
    And give it to the Devil.

> John Greenleaf Whittier: *A Sabbath
> Scene*

We search the world for truth; we cull
The good, the pure, the beautiful,
From all old flower fields of the soul;
And, weary seekers of the best,
We come back laden from our quest,
To find that all the sages said
Is in the Book our mothers read.

> John Greenleaf Whittier: *Miriam*

The only objection against the Bible is a bad life.

> John Wilmot, Earl of Rochester:
> *Last Words*

This Bible is for the government of the people, by the people, and for the people.

Preface to translation of the Bible by Wycliffe and Hereford

BISHOPS

No bishop, no king.

James I

A bishop should die preaching.

John Jewell

The bishop is in the nature of an ecclesiastical sheriff.

Francis North

A bishop ought to die on his legs.

John Woolton

BLESSING(S)

Blessed is the man who is too busy to worry in the daytime and too sleepy to worry at night.

Anonymous

A year of self-surrender will bring larger blessings than fourscore years of selfishness.

Anonymous

God bless me and my son Jim—
Me and my wife, Jim and his wife,
Us four, and no more.

Anonymous

'Tis not for mortals always to be blest.

John Armstrong: *Art of Preserving Health*, Bk. IV, l. 260

Blessedness consists in the accomplishment of our desires, and in our having only regular desires.

St. Augustine

Blessed is the man who has a skin of the right thickness. He can work happily in spite of enemies and friends.

Henry T. Bailey

Bless me in this life with but peace of my conscience, command of my affections, the love of Thyself and my dearest friends, and I shall be happy enough to pity Caesar.

Sir Thomas Browne: *Religio Medici*, Pt. II, conclusion

Blessed are the valiant that have lived in the Lord.

Thomas Carlyle: *Cromwell's Letters and Speeches*, Vol. V, Pt. 10

There is in man a higher than love of happiness; he can do without happiness, and instead thereof seek blessedness.

Thomas Carlyle: *Sartor Resartus*, II

Reflect upon your present blessings, of which every man has many; not on your past misfortunes, of which all men have some.

Charles Dickens

Make no mistake about it, responsibilities toward other human beings are the greatest blessings God can send us.

Dorothy Dix

Good when He gives, supremely good,
   Nor less when He denies.
E'en crosses from His sovereign hand
   Are blessings in disguise.

Old Hymn

Will God's blessing make my pot boil?

James Kelly: *Complete Collection of Scotch Proverbs*

Praise God from whom all blessings flow!

Thomas Ken: *Morning and Evening Hymn*, st. 10

Never undertake anything for which you wouldn't have the courage to ask the blessings of Heaven.

Georg Christoph Lichtenberg

I am a confirmed believer in blessings in disguise. I prefer them undisguised when I myself happen to be the person blessed; in fact, I can scarcely recognize a blessing in disguise except when it is bestowed upon someone else.

Robert Lynd

Wherefore, Christian men, be sure,
  Wealth or rank possessing,
Ye who now do bless the poor
  Shall yourselves find blessing.

John Mason Neale: Good King
Wenceslas, st. 5

Blessed is he that cometh in the name of the Lord.

New Testament: Matthew 23: 39

Out of the same mouth proceedeth blessing and cursing.

New Testament: James 3: 10

He whom thou blessest is blessed, and he whom thou cursest is cursed . . . Blessed is he that blesseth thee, and cursed is he that curseth thee.

Old Testament: Numbers 22: 6, 24: 9

Blessed shall be thy basket and thy store.

Old Testament: Deuteronomy 28: 5

The Lord gave, and the Lord hath taken away; blessed be the name of the Lord.

Old Testament: Job 1: 21

Bless the Lord, O my soul: and all that is within me, bless his holy name.

Old Testament: Psalms 103: 1

A double blessing is a double grace.

William Shakespeare: Hamlet,
Act I, sc. 3, l. 53

I had most need of blessing, and 'Amen'
Stuck in my throat.

William Shakespeare: Macbeth,
Act II, sc. 2, l. 32

Thrice blest whose lives are faithful prayers,
  Whose loves in higher love endure;
What souls possess themselves so pure,
Or is there blessedness like theirs?

Alfred, Lord Tennyson: In Memoriam,
Pt. XXXII, st. 4

Hush, my dear, lie still and slumber.
  Holy angels guard thy bed.
Heavenly blessings without number
  Gently falling on thy head.

Isaac Watts: A Cradle Hymn

It is generally true that all that is required to make men unmindful of what they owe to God for any blessing, is, that they should receive that blessing often and regularly.

Richard Whately

God blesses still the generous thought,
  And still the fitting word He speeds;
And truth at His requiring taught
  He quickens into deeds.

John Greenleaf Whittier

He who blesses most is blest.

John Greenleaf Whittier: Lines for the
Agricultural Exhibition at Amesbury

BROTHERHOOD

If any lift of mine may ease
  The burden of another,
God give me love and care and strength
  To help my ailing brother.

Anonymous: If Any Little Word of
Mine, st. 2

I sought my soul—but my soul I could not see; I sought my God—but my God eluded me; I sought my brother—and found all three.

Anonymous

I met a little maid
  A rosy burden bearing;
"Is he not heavy?" I said
  As past me she was hurrying.

She looked at me with grave, sweet eyes,
 This fragile little mother,
And answered in swift surprise:
 "Oh, no Sir, he's my brother."

Anonymous

The time shall come
When man to man shall be a friend and
brother.

William Allingham

We are they who will not take
 From palace, priest, or code,
A meaner Law than "Brotherhood"—
 A lower Lord than God.

Sir Edwin Arnold: Armageddon:
A War Song of the Future, st. 4

Men exist for the sake of one another. Teach
them then or bear with them.

Marcus Aurelius: Meditations

You can't spell "brothers" and not spell
"others."

Baptist Standard

When people universally realize that all are
united by the common bond of mortality
and by the basic needs . . . the need to
worship and to love, to be housed and fed,
to work and play—perhaps we will have
learned to understand—which is to love
spiritually, and there will be peace and
brotherhood on earth. Without brotherhood, peace is not possible.

Faith Baldwin: The Presbyterian
Outlook

Dostoevski causes one of his characters to
(say): "I am X in an indeterminate equation.
I am a sort of phantom in life who has lost
all beginning and end, who has forgotten his
own name." The affirmation that we find in
the Gospel causes us to confront every man
with the word, "I know your real name. You
are not an X in an indeterminate equation
or a phantom in life, you are a child of God,
you are a brother of mine in Christ."

Harold A. Bosley: Religion in Life

Blow wind of God and set us free
 from hate and want of charity;
Strip off the trappings of our pride,
 and give us to our brother's side.

William Charles Braithwaite

Christians may not see eye to eye, but they
can walk arm in arm.

Brotherhood Journal

Brotherhood is not just a Bible word. Out
of comradeship can come and will come the
happy life for all. The underdog can and
will lick his weight in the wildcats of the
world.

Heywood Broun

I think, am sure, a brother's love exceeds
All the world's loves in its unworldliness.

Robert Browning: A Blot on the
'Scutcheon, Act II, sc. 1

Then let us pray that come it may,
 As come it will for a' that,
That sense and worth, o'er a' the earth,
 May bear the gree and a' that.
 For a' that, and a' that,
 It's comin' yet, for a' that,
When man to man, the world o'er,
 Shall brithers be for a' that.

Robert Burns: Is There for Honest
Poverty

Affliction's sons are brothers in distress;
A brother to relieve, how exquisite the bliss!

Robert Burns: Winter Night

Of a truth men are mystically united; a mysterious bond of brotherhood makes all men
one.

Thomas Carlyle

Let us no more be true to boasted race or
 clan,
But to our highest dream, the brotherhood
 of man.

Thomas Curtis Clark: The New
Loyalty, Harper & Row, Pub-
lishers, Inc.

Brotherhood makes good sense, good religion, and good democracy.

Everett R. Clinchy

What is brotherhood? Brotherhood is giving to others the rights you want to keep for yourself . . . giving to the individual in another group the same dignity, the same full appreciation that you want to have yourself.

Everett R. Clinchy

Our doctrine of equality and liberty and humanity comes from our belief in the brotherhood of man, through the fatherhood of God.

Calvin Coolidge

Brotherhood must have a religious basis if it is to have any real significance. Without faith in the fatherhood of God, as Jesus and the prophets preached it, people have a pretty hard time being brotherly. They drift off into hate societies, or more often, into the society of the indifferent.

Edwin T. Dahlberg

The world is now too dangerous for anything but the truth, too small for anything but brotherhood.

A. Powell Davies: *Ethical Outlook*

While there is a lower class, I am in it. While there is a criminal class I am of it. While there is a soul in prison I am not free.

Eugene V. Debs: *Labor and Freedom*

Until you have become really, in actual fact, as brother of every one, brotherhood will not come to pass.

Feodor Dostoevski: *The Brothers Karamazov*

The universe is but one great city, full of beloved ones, divine and human by nature, endeared to each other.

Epictetus

The people who make no roads are ruled out from intelligent participation in the world's brotherhood.

Michael Fairless: *The Roadmender*, l. 5

There is no brotherhood of man without the fatherhood of God.

Henry Martyn Field

We yearn for world brotherhood so passionately we can't wait to spend $300 on a television set to see some brother get beaten up good in a fast ten rounds.

Fine Paper Salesman

Yes, you'd know him for a heathen
If you judged him by the hide,
But bless you, he's my brother,
For he's just like me inside.

Robert Freeman: *The Heathen*

Jesus throws down the dividing prejudices of nationality, and teaches universal love, without distinction of race, merit, or rank. —A man's neighbor is every one that needs help.

John Cunningham Geikie

Where'er I roam, whatever realms to see,
My heart untravell'd fondly turns to thee;
Still to my brother turns with ceaseless pain,
And drags at each remove a lengthening chain.

Oliver Goldsmith: *The Traveler*

If you really believe in the brotherhood of man, and you want to come into its fold, you've got to let everyone else in too.

Oscar Hammerstein

Brotherhood doesn't come in a package. It is not a commodity to be taken down from the shelf with one hand—it is an accomplishment of soul-searching prayer and perseverance.

Oveta Culp Hobby

Science can make a neighborhood of the nations, but only Christ can make the nations into a Brotherhood.

John Holland: *Prairie Farmer*

If we do not go out into the world and call every man our brother, there are those who will go out and call him comrade.

E. Paul Hovey

It is through fraternity that liberty is saved.

Victor Hugo

Write me as one that loves his fellowmen.

Leigh Hunt: *Abou Ben Adhem*

When I was small,
I knew no color, or creed at all.
Since then, of course, I grew:
Now I know Negro, Gentile and Jew.
Please dear Lord, let me always be
Small, that I may never see
Color, or creed at all.

James G. Johnson: *Watchman-Examiner*

We talk about building bridges of brotherhood around the world in answer to the communist pretensions, and that's a splendid vision. But brotherhood begins on a man-to-man basis across the oceans. Without that footing it is idle talk and an empty vision.

Eric Johnston, Copyright 1942, 1943, 1944 by Eric Johnston. Reprinted by permission of Doubleday & Company, Inc.

The answer to the question, "Am I my brother's keeper?" must always be "No—! I am my brother's brother."

Dr. Paul Klapper in *Live a New Life,* by David Guy Powers, Doubleday & Co.

If God is thy father, man is thy brother.

Alphonse de Lamartine

The amiable age when man said to man,
Let us be brothers—or I'll knock you on the head.

Ecouchard Lebrun-Pindare: *Sur la Fraternité ou la Morte*

A brother is a friend given by nature.

Jean Baptiste Legouvé

All your strength is in your union;
All your danger in discord
Therefore be at peace henceforward
And as brothers live together.

Henry Wadsworth Longfellow

Brotherhood, once a dream and a vision, has now become a dire necessity.

Louis L. Mann

One language builds a fence. Two languages can construct a gate.

Boyd A. Martin

The best way to prove to yourself that you're not superior to a brother man of different color or creed is to get acquainted with him.

Mason City (Iowa) *Globe Gazette*

Fellowship is heaven, and lack of fellowship is hell; fellowship is life, and lack of fellowship is death; and the deeds that ye do upon the earth, it is for fellowship's sake that ye do them.

William Morris: *A Dream of John Ball,* ch. 4

Whosoever is angry with his brother without a cause shall be in danger of the judgment.

New Testament: Matthew 5: 22

Be kindly affectioned one to another with brotherly love: in honor preferring one another.

New Testament: Romans 12: 10

Why dost thou judge thy brother?

New Testament: Romans 14: 10

The right hands of fellowship.

New Testament: Galatians 2: 9

Let brotherly love continue.

New Testament: Hebrews 13: 1

If a man says, I love God, and hateth his brother, he is a liar.

New Testament: I John 4: 20

Help thy brother's boat across, and lo! thine own has reached the shore.

Old Hindu Proverb

Am I my brother's keeper?

Old Testament: Genesis 4: 9

Behold, how good and how pleasant it is for brethren to dwell together in unity!

Old Testament: Psalms 133: 1

A brother offended is harder to be won than a strong city.

Old Testament: Proverbs 18: 19

The only brotherhood nobody has tried to organize lately is the Brotherhood of Man.

Parade

Just the thought of brotherhood has a sobering effect on me, for it reminds me that I am only a transitory member of a very large family called Humanity.

Bellamy Partridge

We must not only affirm the brotherhood of man; we must live it.

Henry Codman Potter

It would be much better to have the one week in fifty-two dedicated to hate, a week when we would all be able to get the hate out of our systems, treat one another as badly as we know how, and then observe the remaining fifty-one weeks as Brotherhood Weeks.

Rabbi Samuel Price: *Arkansas Baptist*

There will never be a brotherhood of mankind as long as there is a need for burglar alarms.

Publishers' Syndicate

The race of mankind would perish from the earth did they cease to aid each other.

Sir Walter Scott

However wretched a fellow mortal may be, he is still a member of our common species.

Seneca

We are members of one great body, planted by nature in a mutual love, and fitted for a social life. We must consider that we were born for the good of the whole.

Seneca

Dogs are born loving people. If only men were too!

S. F. C. Spotlight

We must love men ere they will seem worthy of our love.

William Shakespeare

No one can be perfectly free till all are free; no one can be perfectly moral till all are moral; no one can be perfectly happy till all are happy.

Herbert Spencer: *Social Statics,* Pt. IV, ch. 30, sec. 16

A peaceful world depends upon better understanding and respect for each other in a spirit of brotherhood and adherence to ethical principles. If these are lost, civilization gradually disappears.

Herman W. Steinkraus, Bridgeport Brass Co., quoted in *Chaplain*

The world is now too dangerous for anything but the truth, too small for anything but brotherhood.

Adlai Stevenson: *Saturday Review,* February 7, 1959

There is a fellowship more quiet even than solitude, and which, rightly understood, is solitude made perfect.

Robert Louis Stevenson: *Travels with a Donkey: A Night Among the Pines*

And when with grief you see your brother stray,
Or in a night of error lose his way,
Direct his wandering and restore the day . . .
Leave to avenging Heaven his stubborn will.
For, O, remember, he's your brother still.

Jonathan Swift: *The Swan Tripe Club in Dublin*

Slav, Teuton, Kelt, I count them all
My friends and brother souls,
With all the peoples, great and small,
That wheel between the poles.

Alfred, Lord Tennyson: *The Charge of the Heavy Brigade: Epilogue*

BROTHERHOOD

The sixteenth century said, "Responsibility to God."—The present nineteenth says, "The brotherhood of man."

Charles Lemuel Thompson

We cannot hope to command brotherhood abroad unless we practice it at home.

Harry S Truman

Throw out the life-line across the dark wave,
There is a brother whom someone must save.

Edward Smith Ufford: *Throw Out the Life-Line*

You can't hold a man down without staying down with him.

Booker T. Washington

Am I not a man and brother?

Josiah Wedgwood: *On a Medallion*

Lo, soul! seest thou not God's purpose from the first?
The earth to be spann'd, connected by network,
The people to become brothers and sisters,
The races, neighbors, to marry and be given in marriage,
The oceans to be cross'd, the distant brought near,
The lands to be welded together.

Walt Whitman: *Passage to India*

Whoever degrades another degrades me,
And whatever is done or said returns at last to me.

Walt Whitman: *Song of Myself*

God, what a world if man in street and mart,
Felt that same kinship of the human heart
Which makes them, in the face of fire and flood,
Rise to the true meaning of Brotherhood.

Ella Wheeler Wilcox, Rand McNally & Co.

The churches will take longer to achieve integration because they are undertaking a much greater accomplishment. Worshiping together is a more personal thing than riding trains or attending movies together. Tolerance is not enough; it must be real brotherhood or nothing.

Frank T. Wilson

The opportunity to practice brotherhood presents itself every time you meet a human being.

Jane Wyman

The working man must not lose sight of the fact that the principles of brotherhood are applicable to all men, regardless of capital or poverty.

John Lewis Zacker

BURDEN(S)

Life has burdens that no one can escape. Christianity does not remove the load: it teaches us how best to bear the burdens that fall rightfully to us.

Anonymous

I do not pray for a lighter load, but for a stronger back.

Phillips Brooks

God had made the back to the burden.

William Cobbett: *Rural Rides*

God giveth the shoulder according to the burden.

German Proverb

For other things mild Heav'n a time ordains,
And disapproves that care, though wise in show,
That with superfluous burden loads the day,
And, when God sends a cheerful hour, refrains.

John Milton: *Sonnet XI, To Cyriack Skinner*

41

Prayer is the burden of a sigh,
  The falling of a tear;
The upward glancing of an eye,
  When none but God is near.

> James Montgomery: *What is Prayer?*, st. 2

For my yoke is easy, and my burden is light.

> *New Testament: Matthew 11: 30*

[We] have borne the burden and heat of the day.

> *New Testament: Matthew 20: 12*

Bear ye one another's burdens.

> *New Testament: Galatians 6: 2*

Every man shall bear his own burden.

> *New Testament: Galatians 6: 5*

Cast thy burden upon the Lord, and he shall sustain thee: he shall never suffer the righteous to be moved.

> *Old Testament: Psalms 55: 22*

The almond tree shall flourish, and the grasshopper shall be a burden, and desire shall fail: because man goeth to his long home, and the mourners go about the streets.

> *Old Testament: Ecclesiastes 12: 5*

The burden of long living. Thou shalt fear
Waking, and sleeping mourn upon thy bed;
And say at night "Would God the day were
    here,"
And say at dawn, "Would God the day were
    dead."

> Algernon Charles Swinburne: *A Ballad of Burdens*, st. 4

C

CHARITY

The trouble is that too often charity not only begins but *ends* at home.

Anonymous

Charity is injurious unless it helps the recipient to become independent of it.

Anonymous

Charity excuseth not cheating.

Anonymous

The poor man's charity is to wish the rich man well.

Anonymous

Definition of an old-timer: one who remembers when charity was a virtue and not an organization.

Anonymous

Giving until it hurts is not a true measure of charity. Some are more easily hurt than others.

Anonymous

In charity to all mankind, bearing no malice or ill-will to any human being, and even compassionating those who hold in bondage their fellow-men, not knowing what they do.

John Quincy Adams: *Letter to A. Bronson,* July 30, 1838

Charity is a virtue of the heart, and not of the hands.

Joseph Addison: *The Guardian,* no. 166

Charity is faith in what is alike. It is not put off by contrary evidence; therefore it pays homage to humanity in the fool, the idiot, the criminal, the unhappy; but also in the rich, the powerful, the frivolous, the unjust, the drunkard, the brute, the jealous, the envious; it reaches across to decide in their favor, to help them, above all, to love them.

Chartier Alain

The living need charity more than the dead.

George Arnold: *The Jolly Old Pedagogue*

He that defers his charity until he is dead is, if a man weighs it rightly, rather liberal of another man's than of his own.

Sir Francis Bacon: *Collection of Sentences,* no. 55

The desire of power in excess caused the angels to fall; the desire of knowledge in excess caused man to fall; but in charity there is no excess, neither can angel or man come in danger by it.

Sir Francis Bacon: *Essays: Of Goodness*

In necessary things, unity; in doubtful things, liberty; in all things, charity.

Motto of Richard Baxter

Be charitable before wealth make thee covetous, and lose not the glory of the mite.

Sir Thomas Browne: *Christian Morals,* Pt. I, sec. 5

True charity is sagacious, and will find out hints for beneficence.

Sir Thomas Browne: *Christian Morals,* Pt. I, sec. 6

For this I think charity, to love God for himself, and our neighbour for God.

Sir Thomas Browne: *Religio Medici,* Pt. II, sec. 14

He who bestows his goods upon the poor,
Shall have as much again, and ten times
more.

> John Bunyan: *The Pilgrim's
> Progress,* Pt. II

No sound ought to be heard in the church
but the healing voice of Christian charity.

> Edmund Burke: *Reflections on the
> Revolution in France*

Never to judge rashly; never to interpret the
actions of others in an ill-sense, but to compassionate their infirmities, bear their burdens, excuse their weaknesses, and make up
for their defects—to hate their imperfections,
but love themselves, this is the true spirit of
charity.

> Nicolas Caussin

Christian charity knows no iron curtain.

> Copyright 1949 Christian Century
> Foundation. Reprinted by per-
> mission from the *Christian
> Century*

Charity is the scope of all God's commands.

> St. John Chrysostom

Charity is, indeed, a great thing, and a gift
of God, and when it is rightly ordered, likens
us to God himself, as far as that is possible;
for it is charity which makes the man.

> St. John Chrysostom: *True Almsgiving*

Posthumous charities are the very essence of
selfishness when bequeathed by those who,
even alive, would part with nothing.

> Charles Caleb Colton

Did universal charity prevail, earth would
be a heaven, and hell a fable.

> Charles Caleb Colton: *Lacon,*
> Vol. I, no. 160

True Charity, a plant divinely nurs'd.

> William Cowper: *Charity,* l. 573

Did charity prevail, the press would prove
A vehicle of virtue, truth and love.

> William Cowper: *Charity,* l. 624

Ambition, malice, rage and hate
Are strangers to my soul;
But peace and joy possess the parts,
And charity the whole.

> Daniel Defoe: *A Review of the Affairs
> of France and of all Europe,* VIII

This only is charity, to do all, all that we can.

> John Donne

First daughter to the love of God, is charity
to man.

> William Drennan

There are two kinds of charity, remedial, and
preventive.—The former is often injurious
in its tendency; the latter is always praise-
worthy and beneficial.

> Tryon Edwards

The worst of charity is, that the lives you are
asked to preserve are not worth preserving.

> Ralph Waldo Emerson: *Conduct of
> Life: Considerations by the Way*

As cold as charity.

> English Phrase

What is faith? What you do not see.
What is hope? A great thing.
What is charity? A great rarity.

> *Facetiae Cantabrigiensis*

A rich man without charity is a rogue; and
perhaps it would be no difficult matter to
prove that he is also a fool.

> Henry Fielding

There is much truth in the observation that
charity eases the conscience of the rich more
often than it eases the condition of the poor.

> Irving H. Flamm: *An Economic Pro-
> gram for a Living Democracy*

True virtue has no limits, but goes on and
on, and especially holy charity, which is

the virtue of virtues, and which, having an infinite object, would become infinite if it could meet with a heart capable of infinity.

St. Francis de Sales: *Introduction to the Devout Life,* I

He that feeds upon charity has a cold dinner and no supper.

Thomas Fuller: *Gnomologia*

Charity and pride have different aims, yet both feed the poor.

Ibid.

Charity is indeed a noble and beautiful virtue, grateful to man, and approved by God. But charity must be built on justice. It cannot supersede justice.

Henry George: *The Condition of Labor,* p. 92

Charity sees the need; not the cause.

German Proverb

Charity gives itself rich; covetousness hoards itself poor.

German Proverb

Charity, like nature, abhors a vacuum. Next to putting it into the bank, men like to squander their superfluous wealth on those to whom it is sure of doing the least possible good.

William Hazlitt: *Butts of Different Sorts*

Charity is the spice of riches.

Hebrew Proverb

Charity is the sterilized milk of human kindness.

Oliver Herford

There can be no greater argument to a man of his own power than to find himself able not only to accomplish his own desires, but also to assist other men in theirs; and this is that conception wherein consisteth charity.

Thomas Hobbes: *On Human Nature,* IX

Alas! for the rarity, of Christian charity
Under the sun!

Thomas Hood: *The Bridge of Sighs*

The charity that hastens to proclaim its good deeds, ceases to be charity, and is only pride and ostentation.

William Hutton

The best form of charity is extravagance . . . the prodigality of the rich is the providence of the poor.

Robert Green Ingersoll: *Hard Times and the Way Out*

I deem it the duty of every man to devote a certain portion of his income for charitable purposes; and that it is his further duty to see it so applies and to do the most good of which it is capable. This I believe to be best insured by keeping within the circle of his own inquiry and information the subjects of distress to whose relief his contributions should be applied.

Thomas Jefferson

You are much surer that you are doing good when you *pay* money to those who work, as the recompense of their labor, than when you *give* money merely in charity.

Samuel Johnson

Be charitable and indulgent to every one but thyself.

Joseph Joubert

Charity is a debt of honor.

Immanuel Kant: Lecture at Königsberg

It is good to be charitable—but to whom?

Jean de La Fontaine: *Fables,* VI

Help thy kin, Christ biddeth, for there beginneth Charity.

William Langland: *Piers Plowman,* Passus, XVIII, l. 61

We have made the slogan "Charity begins at home" a part of our religion—although it was invented by a Roman pagan, and is directly contrary to the story of the Good Samaritan. Charity begins where the need is greatest and the crisis is most dangerous.

Frank C. Laubach: *Thirty Years With the Silent Billion*

Where has the Scripture made merit the rule or measure of charity?

William Law: *A Serious Call to a Devout and Holy Life,* VIII

The law of mutual charity perfects the law of justice.

Pope Leo XIII: *Graves de communi,* January 18, 1901

Justice forbids us to use slander or libel. Charity goes still further: it orders us to defend absent persons against slander or libel.

L'Etoile

With malice toward none; with charity for all.

Abraham Lincoln: *Second Inaugural Address,* March 4, 1865

Here lies Estella, who transported a large fortune to Heaven in acts of charity, and has gone thither to enjoy it.

H. J. Loring: *Epitaphs Quaint, Curious and Elegant*

Charity has in it sometimes, perhaps often, a savor of superiority.

James Russell Lowell: Speech in Westminster Abbey, December 13, 1881

Anticipate charity by preventing poverty; assist the reduced fellowman, either by a considerable gift, or a sum of money, or by teaching him a trade, or by putting him in the way of business, so that he may earn an honest livelihood, and not be forced to the dreadful alternative of holding out his hand for charity. This is the highest step and the summit of charity's golden ladder.

Moses Maimonides: *Charity's Eight Degrees*

I would have none of that rigid and circumspect charity which is never exercised without scrutiny, and which always mistrusts the reality of the necessities laid open to it.

Jean Baptiste Massilon

In things essential, unity; in doubtful, liberty; in all things, charity.

Rupertus Meldenius

Charity is never lost: it may meet with ingratitude, or be of no service to those on whom it was bestowed, yet it ever does a work of beauty and grace upon the heart of the giver.

Conyers Middleton

As for charity, it is a matter in which the immediate effect on the persons directly concerned, and the ultimate consequence to the general good, are apt to be at complete war with one another.

John Stuart Mill: *The Subjection of Women,* IV

In this cold world where Charity lies bleating Under a thorn, and none to give him greeting.

Edna St. Vincent Millay: "Sonnet CXXIX" from *Collected Poems,* Harper & Row, Publishers, copyright 1939 by Edna St. Vincent Millay, used by permission of Norma Millay

Though I speak with the tongues of men and of angels, and have not charity, I am become as sounding brass, or a tinkling cymbal.

New Testament: I Corinthians 13: 1

And though I have the gift of prophecy, and understand all mysteries, and all knowledge; and though I have all faith, so that I could remove mountains, and have not charity, I am nothing.

New Testament: I Corinthians 13: 2

And though I bestow all my goods to feed the poor, and though I give my body to be burned, and have not charity, it profiteth me nothing.

New Testament: I Corinthians 13: 3

Charity suffereth long, and is kind; charity envieth not; charity vaunteth not itself, is not puffed up.

New Testament: I Corinthians 13: 4

Charity never faileth.

New Testament: I Corinthians 13: 8

Now abideth faith, hope, charity, these three; but the greatest of these is charity.

New Testament: I Corinthians 13: 13

Put on charity, which is the bond of perfectness.

New Testament: Colossians 3: 14

Charity shall cover the multitude of sins.

New Testament: I Peter 4: 8

Organized charity, scrimped and iced,
In the name of a cautious, statistical Christ.

John Boyle O'Reilly: *In Bohemia*

Charity cannot take the place of justice unfairly withheld.

Pope Pius XI: *Quadragesimo anno*,
May 15, 1931

A strong argument for the religion of Christ is this—that offences against charity are about the only ones which men on their deathbeds can be made—not to understand —but to feel—as crimes.

Edgar Allan Poe: *Marginalia*

For forms of government let fools contest;
Whate'er is best adminster'd is best;
For modes of faith let graceless zealots fight;
His can't be wrong whose life is in the right.
In faith and hope the world will disagree,
But all mankind's concern is charity.

Alexander Pope: *Essay on Man*,
Epis. III, l. 303

Charity, decent, modest, easy, kind,
Softens the high, and rears the abject mind;
Knows with just reins, and gentle hand to
    guide,
Betwixt vile shame and arbitrary pride.

Matthew Prior: *Charity*

Flatter not thyself in thy faith to God, if thou lackest in charity to thy neighbor; and think not thou hast charity for thy neighbor if thou fail in faith to God.

Francis Quarles

Charity is a naked child, giving honey to a bee without wings.

Francis Quarles: *Encheiridion*

The charitable give out at the door, and God puts in at the window.

John Ray: *English Proverbs*

How often it is difficult to be wisely charitable—to do good without multiplying the sources of evil. To give alms is nothing unless you give thought also. It is written, not "blessed is he that feedeth the poor," but "blessed is he that considereth the poor." A little thought and a little kindness are often worth more than a great deal of money.

John Ruskin

Charity begins at hame, but shouldna end there.

Scottish Proverb

A tear for pity and a hand
Open as day for melting charity.

William Shakespeare: *Henry IV, Part II*,
Act IV, sc. 4, l. 31

Charity itself fulfills the law,
And who can sever love from charity?

William Shakespeare: *Love's Labour's
Lost*, Act IV, sc. 3, l. 364

Charity,
Which renders good for bad, blessings for curses.

William Shakespeare: *Richard III*,
Act I, sc. 2, l. 68

As frozen as charity.

Robert Southey: *The Soldier's
Wife*, st. 4

True charity is the desire to be useful to others without thought of recompense.

Emanuel Swedenborg: *Arcana Coelestia*,
sec. 3419

Charity is to will and do what is just and right in every transaction.

> Emanuel Swedenborg: *Heaven and Hell*

He who has never denied himself for the sake of giving, has but glanced at the joys of charity.

> Madam Anne Soymanov Swetchine

I hate nobody; I am in charity with the world.

> Jonathan Swift: *Polite Conversation*

Loving kindness is greater than laws; and the charities of life are more than all ceremonies.

> *The Talmud*

The noblest charity is to prevent a man from accepting charity; and the best alms are to show and to enable a man to dispense with alms.

> *The Talmud*

Charity begins at home.

> Terence: *Andria*, l. 635

He is truly great who hath a great charity.

> Thomas à Kempis: *Imitation of Christ*, Pt. I, ch. 3

I rather think there is an immense shortage of Christian charity among so-called Christians.

> Harry S Truman

Simple rules for saving money: To save half, when you are fired by an eager impulse to contribute to a charity, wait and count forty. To save three-quarters, count sixty. To save it all, count sixty-five.

> Mark Twain

Behold, I do not give lectures or a little charity,
When I give I give myself.

> Walt Whitman: *Leaves of Grass: Song of Myself*, XL

Melt not in an acid sect
The Christian pearl of charity.

> John Greenleaf Whittier: *Snow-Bound*

Charity beginneth first at itself.

> Thomas Wilson: *Discourse Upon Usury*, l. 235

The charities that soothe and heal and bless
Are scattered at the feet of Man—like flowers.

> William Wordsworth: *The Excursion*, Bk. IX, l. 239

Charity should begin at himself.

> John Wycliffe: *Works*, p. 76

CHRIST

Whenever Christianity has struck out a new path on her journey it has been because the personality of Jesus has again become living, and a ray from His Being has once more illuminated the world.

> Anonymous

They borrowed a bed to lay His head
 When Christ the Lord came down;
They borrowed an ass in the mountain pass
 For Him to ride to town;
But the crown He wore and the cross He bore
 Were His own—
 The cross was His own.

> Anonymous

In trouble then and fear I sought
 The Man who taught in Galilee;
And peace unto my soul was brought,
 And all my faith came back to me.

> Anonymous

Matthew presents Jesus as the Royal Saviour; Mark, as the Servant of man; Luke, as the Son of man; John, as Son of God.

> Anonymous

It is queer how incredulously people, Christian as well as irreligious, listen to old Thomas Dekker's famous saying about Jesus: "*The first true gentleman that ever breathed.*"

> Anonymous

The name of Jesus is the one lever that lifts the world.

Anonymous

For two thousand years Jesus Christ has been the one central character of human history.

Anonymous

Yesterday, today, forever,
  Jesus is the same;
All may change, but Jesus never,
  Glory to His Name.

Anonymous

Commander-in-chief of the Celestial Army, King of Zion, Eternal Emperor, Pontifex Maximus of the Christian Church, Archbishop of All Souls, Elector of Truth, Archduke of Glory, Duke of Life, Prince of Peace, Defender of the Gates of Hell, Conqueror of Death, Hereditary Lord of All Nations, Lord of Justice, and Head of the Sacred Council of the Heavenly Father.

Anonymous

Take, then, your paltry Christ,
  Your gentleman God.
We want the carpenter's son,
  With his saw and hod.

Francis Adams

The manger is Heaven, yes, greater than Heaven. Heaven is the handiwork of this child.

Agathias Scholasticus: *On the Birth
of Christ*

Trumpets! Lightnings! The earth trembles! But into the Virgin's womb thou didst descend with noiseless tread.

Ibid.

All my theology is reduced to this narrow compass—Christ Jesus came into the world to save sinners.

Archibald Alexander

There is a green hill far away,
  Without a city wall,

Where the dear Lord was crucified,
  Who died to save us all.

Cecil Frances Alexander: Hymn,
There Is a Green Hill

As the print of the seal on the wax is the express image of the seal itself, so Christ is the express image—the perfect representation of God.

St. Ambrose

Try all the ways to peace and welfare you can think of, and you will find that there is no way that brings you to it except the way of Jesus. But this way does bring it to you.

Matthew Arnold

Jesus Christ and his precepts are found to hit the moral experience of mankind; to hit it in the critical points; to hit it lastingly; and when doubts are thrown upon their really hitting it, then to come out stronger than ever.

Matthew Arnold

Nothing will do except righteousness; and no other conception of righteousness will do except Christ's conception of it.

Matthew Arnold

Now he is dead, far hence he lies
  In the lorn Syrian town;
And on his grave, with shining eyes,
  The Syrian stars look down.

Matthew Arnold: *Obermann Once
More*

Jesus Christ is the outstanding personality of all time. . . . No other teacher—Jewish, Christian, Buddhist, Mohammedan—is *still* a teacher whose teaching is such a guidepost for the world we live in. Other teachers may have something basic for an Oriental, an Arab, or an Occidental; but every act and word of Jesus has value for all of us. He became the Light of the World. Why shouldn't I, a Jew, be proud of that?

Sholem Asch: "I Had to Write These
Things," in *Christian Herald*

Christ is not valued at all unless he be valued above all.

St. Augustine

I have read in Plato and Cicero sayings that are very wise and very beautiful; but I never read in either of them: "Come unto me all ye that labour and are heavy laden."

St. Augustine

God be thanked for that good and perfect gift, the gift unspeakable: His life, His love, His very self in Christ Jesus.

Maltbie D. Babcock

The name of Christ—the one great word —well worth all the languages in earth or heaven.

Samuel Bailey

The King of love my Shepherd is,
    Whose goodness faileth never;
I nothing lack if I am His
    And He is mine forever.

Sir Henry William Baker

I find the name of Jesus Christ written on the top of every page of modern history.

George Bancroft

He spake of lilies, vines and corn,
The sparrow and the raven,
And the words so natural yet so wise
Were on men's hearts engraven;

And yeast and bread and flax and cloth
And eggs and fish and candles.
See how the most familiar world
He most divinely handles.

George A. Barton

Take the name of Jesus with you,
    Child of sorrow and of woe;
It will joy and comfort give you;
    Take it, then, where'er you go.

Lydia Baxter

If Christ is not divine, every impulse of the Christian world falls to a lower octave, and light and love and hope decline.

Henry Ward Beecher

If Christ is the wisdom of God and the power of God in the experience of those who trust and love Him, there needs no further argument of His divinity.

Henry Ward Beecher

Hail, O bleeding Head and wounded,
With a crown of thorns surrounded,
Buffeted, and bruised and battered,
Smote with reed by striking shattered,
    Face with spittle vilely smeared!
Hail, whose visage sweet and comely,
Marred by fouling stains and homely,
Changed as to its blooming color,
All now turned to deathly pallor,
    Making heavenly hosts affeared!

St. Bernard of Clairvaux

Jesus, Thou Joy of loving hearts!
    Thou Fount of life! Thou Light of men!
From the best bliss that earth imparts,
    We turn unfilled to Thee again.

St. Bernard of Clairvaux

A man who can read the New Testament and not see that Christ claims to be more than a man, can look all over the sky at high noon on a cloudless day and not see the sun.

William E. Biederwolf

Art is the Tree of Life. Science is the Tree of Death. God is Jesus.

William Blake

Feed on Christ, and then go and live your life, and it is Christ in you that lives your life, that helps the poor, that tells the truth, that fights the battle, and that wins the crown.

Phillips Brooks

Never be afraid to bring the transcendent mysteries of our faith, Christ's life and death and resurrection, to the help of the humblest and commonest of human wants.

Phillips Brooks

Jesus Christ, the condescension of divinity, and the exaltation of humanity.

Phillips Brooks

In the best sense of the word, Jesus was a radical. . . . His religion has been so long identified with conservatism—often with conservatism of the obstinate and unyielding sort—that it is almost startling for us sometimes to remember that all of the conservatism of his own times was against him; that it was the young, free, restless, sanguine, progressive part of the people who flocked to him.

Phillips Brooks

Never does human nature seem so courageous and so wicked all at once as when we stand before the cross of Jesus! The most enthusiastic hopes, the most profound humiliation, have found their inspiration there.

Phillips Brooks

Speak low to me, my Saviour, low and sweet
From out the hallelujahs, sweet and low,
Lest I should fear and fall, and miss Thee so
Who art not missed by any that entreat.

Elizabeth Barrett Browning: *Comfort*

All outside is lone field, moon and such
    peace,
Flowing in, filling up, as with a sea,
Whereupon comes Someone, walks fast on
    the white,
Jesus Christ's self . . .
To meet me and calm all things back again.

Robert Browning

In every pang that rends the heart
The Man of Sorrows has a part.

Michael Bruce: *Christ Ascended*

Perhaps the Christian volume is the theme,
    How guiltless blood for guilty man was
    shed,
How He who bore in heaven the second
    name
    Had not on earth whereon to lay His head.

Robert Burns

Jesus cannot be our Savior unless he is first our Lord.

Hugh C. Burr

Jesus gave history a new beginning. In every land He is at home: everywhere men think His face is like their best face—and like God's face. His birthday is kept across the world. His death-day has set a gallows against every city skyline. Who is He?

George A. Buttrick, in *Life Magazine*

If ever man was God or God man, Jesus Christ was both.

George Gordon, Lord Byron

If Jesus Christ were to come today people would not even crucify him. They would ask him to dinner, and hear what he has to say, and make fun of it.

Thomas Carlyle

The difference between Socrates and Jesus Christ? The great Conscious; the immeasurably great Unconscious.

Thomas Carlyle: *Journal*

The sages and heroes of history are receding from us, and history contracts the record of their deeds into a narrower and narrower page. But time has no power over the name and deeds and words of Jesus Christ.

William Ellery Channing

I know of no sincere enduring good but the moral excellency which shines forth in Jesus Christ.

William Ellery Channing

I know of a world that is sunk in shame,
    Where hearts oft faint and tire;
But I know of a Name, a precious Name,
    That can set that world on fire:
Its sound is sweet, its letters flame.
I know of a Name, a precious Name,
        'Tis Jesus.

J. Wilbur Chapman

Still as of old
Men by themselves are priced—
For thirty pieces Judas sold
Himself, not Christ.

Hester H. Cholmondeley

He changed sunset into sunrise.

Clement of Alexandria

Lovely was the death
Of Him whose life was Love! Holy with
power,
He on the thought-benighted Skeptic beamed
Manifest Godhead.

Samuel Taylor Coleridge:
Religious Musings

The Christian faith is firmly rooted in the
incarnation, in the conviction that, "God was
in Christ, reconciling the world unto himself." To believe in Christ is to believe that
God has come to earth to dwell with men.
. . . In Jesus, we meet the living. Jesus is
more than a religious genius or a holy man
or a spiritual pioneer. To believe in Christ
is to believe that the living God has come.

Earle W. Crawford: "God Is With Us,"
Pulpit Preaching.

The best of men
That e'er wore earth about Him was a
Sufferer,
A soft, meek, patient, humble, tranquil
spirit;
The first true gentleman that ever breathed.

Thomas Dekker

God clothed himself in vile man's flesh so
He might be weak enough to suffer woe.

John Donne: *Holy Sonnets*

Every character has an inward spring; let
Christ be that spring. Every action has a
keynote; let Christ be that note, to which
your whole life is attuned.

Henry Drummond

Your Saviour comes not with gaudy show,
Nor was His kingdom of the world below;
The crown He wore was of the pointed
thorn,
In purple He was crucified, not born.

John Dryden

The dying Jesus is the evidence of God's
anger toward sin; but the living Jesus is the
proof of God's love and forgiveness.

Lorenz Eifert

Christ was the word that spake it;
He took the bread and brake it;
And what that word did make it,
That I believe and take it.

Attributed to Queen Elizabeth I

Just as I am, without one plea
But that Thy blood was shed for me,
And that Thou bid'st me come to Thee,
O Lamb of God, I come!

Charlotte Elliott: Hymn, *Just As I Am*

The unique impression of Jesus upon mankind—whose name is not so much written
as ploughed into the history of the world—
is proof of the subtle virtue of this infusion.
Jesus belonged to the race of prophets. He
saw with open eyes the mystery of the soul.
One man was true to what is in you and me.
He, as I think, is the only soul in history
who has appreciated the worth of man.

Ralph Waldo Emerson

Jesus is the most perfect of all men that have
yet appeared.

Ralph Waldo Emerson

Jesus astonishes and overpowers sensual
people. They cannot unite Him to history
or reconcile Him with themselves.

Ralph Waldo Emerson

An era in human history is the life of Jesus,
and its immense influence for good leaves
all the perversion and superstition that has
accrued almost harmless.

Ralph Waldo Emerson: *Uncollected
Lectures*

Had Christ the death of death to death
Not given death by dying,
The gates of life had never been
To mortals open lying.

Epitaph

By a Carpenter mankind was made, and only
by that Carpenter can mankind be remade.

Desiderius Erasmus

Earth grows into heaven, as we come to
live and breathe in the atmosphere of the

incarnation. Jesus makes heaven wherever He is.

Frederick William Faber

Jesus came, not to hush the natural music of men's lives, nor to fill it with storm and agitation, but to retune every silver chord in that "harp of a thousand strings" and to make it echo with the harmonies of heaven.

Frederic W. Farrar

No man can follow Christ and go astray.

William H. P. Faunce

Blest be the tie that binds
Our hearts in Christian love.

John Fawcett: *Blest Be the Tie
That Binds*

He is a path, if any be misled;
He is a robe, if any naked be;
If any chance to hunger, he is bread;
If any be a bondman, he is free;
If any be but weak, how strong is he!
To dead men life is he, to sick men health;
To blind men sight, and to the needy wealth;
A pleasure without loss, a treasure without
stealth.

Giles Fletcher: *Excellency of Christ*

Jesus did not spend His time guarding the customs; He was sent to His death by the men who did.

Kenneth J. Foreman, *The Presbyterian
Outlook*

It is not difficult to see one vital significance of Jesus Christ: He has given us the most glorious interpretation of life's meaning that the sons of men have ever had. The fatherhood of God, the friendship of the Spirit, the sovereignty of righteousness, the law of love, the glory of service, the coming of the kingdom, the eternal hope—there never was an interpretation of life to compare with that.

Harry Emerson Fosdick in *Christianity
and Progress*

The most perfect being who has ever trod the soil of this planet was called the Man of Sorrows.

James Anthony Froude

I love and venerate the religion of Christ, because Christ came into the world to deliver humanity from slavery, for which God had not created it.

Giuseppe Garibaldi

If Jesus Christ is a man—
And only a man,—I say
That of all mankind I cleave to Him
And to Him will I cleave alway.

If Jesus Christ is a god—
And the only God,—I swear
I will follow Him through heaven and hell,
The earth, the sea, and the air!

Richard Watson Gilder in *The Song
of a Heathen*

The Son of God goes forth to war,
A kingly crown to gain;
His blood-red banner streams afar!
Who follows in His train?

Reginald Heber: *The Son of God*

Jesus Christ is in the noblest and most perfect sense the realized ideal of humanity.

Johann Gottfried von Herder

God bought men here with His heart's blood
expense;
And man sold God here for base thirty pence.

Robert Herrick: *God's Price and
Man's Price*

More about Jesus I would know,
More of His graces to others show;
More of His saving fulness see,
More of His love who died for me.

E. E. Hewitt

No revolution that has ever taken place in society can be compared to that which has been produced by the words of Jesus Christ.

Mark Hopkins

Mine eyes have seen the glory of the coming
of the Lord;
He is trampling out the vintage where the
grapes of wrath are stored;

He hath loosed the fateful lightning of His
 terrible swift sword;
　His truth is marching on.

> Julia Ward Howe: *Battle-
> Hymn of the Republic*

The great Physician now is near,
　The sympathizing Jesus;
He speaks the drooping heart to cheer,
Oh, hear the voice of Jesus.

> William Hunter

Thou canst not comprehend it, thou who
hast never been under the power of the God-
man. It is more than teaching that he spreads
over the earth: it is witchcraft that takes the
mind captive. They who have been under
Him, I believe, can never get free.

> Henrik Ibsen: Julian the Apostate in
> *Emperor and Galilean*

Man's ultimate destiny depends not on
whether he can learn new lessons or make
new discoveries and conquests, but on his
acceptance of the lesson taught him close
upon two thousand years ago.

> Inscription at the Eastern Entrance of
> Rockefeller Center, in New York City

The highest service may be prepared for
and done in the humblest surroundings. In
silence, in waiting, in obscure, unnoticed
offices, in years of uneventful, unrecorded
duties, the Son of God grew and waxed
strong.

> Inscription in the Chapel of Stanford
> University

When Jesus comes, the shadows depart.

> Inscription on the Wall of a Castle
> in Scotland

The strange thing about Jesus is that you
can never get away from Him.

> Japanese Student

His parentage was obscure; His condition
poor; His education null; His natural endowments great; His life correct and innocent;

He was meek, benevolent, patient, firm, dis-
interested, and of the sublimest eloquence.

> Thomas Jefferson

I hold the precepts of Jesus as delivered by
himself, to be the most pure, benevolent, and
sublime which have ever been preached to
man. I adhere to the principles of the first
age; and consider all subsequent innovations
as corruptions of this religion, having no
foundation in what came from him.

> Thomas Jefferson

I have prayed in her fields of poppies,
　I have laughed with the men who died—
But in all my ways and through all my days
　Like a friend He walked beside.
I have seen a sight under Heaven
　That only God understands,
In the battle's glare I have seen Christ there
　With the Sword of God in His Hand.

> Gordon Johnstone: *On the Fields of
> Flanders*

Thou hast conquered, Galilean.

> Julian the Apostate

One Name above all glorious names
　With its ten thousand tongues
The everlasting sea proclaims,
　Echoing angelic songs.

> John Keble: *The Christian Year*

Sun of my soul! Thou Saviour dear,
It is not night if Thou be near.

> *Ibid.*

The head that once was crowned with thorns
Is crowned with glory now.

> Thomas Kelley: *Hymn*

In an unpermissible and unlawful way
people have become *knowing* about Christ,
for the only permissible way is to be
believing.

> Sören Kierkegaard

　　He that lends
To Him, need never fear to lose his venture.

> Charles Kingsley: *The Saint's
> Tragedy*

Today the greatest single deterrent to knowledge of Jesus is his familiarity. Because we think we know him, we pass him by.

Winifred Kirkland

If Christians had ever been brave enough to make Christ alive, nobody would now be saying that Christianity is dead.

Winifred Kirkland

If Shakespeare should come into this room, we would all rise; but if Jesus Christ should come in, we would all kneel.

Charles Lamb

But Thee, but Thee, O sovereign Seer of time,
But Thee, O poets' Poet, Wisdom's Tongue,
But Thee, O man's best Man, O love's best Love,
O perfect life in perfect labor writ,
O all men's Comrade, Servant, King, or Priest,—
Oh, what amiss may I forgive in Thee,
Jesus, good Paragon, thou Crystal Christ?

Sidney Lanier: *The Crystal*

Into the woods my Master went,
Clean forspent, forspent,
Into the woods my Master came,
Forspent with love and shame.
But the olives they were not blind to Him,
The little gray leaves were kind to Him,
The thorn-tree had a mind to Him,
When into the woods He came.

Sidney Lanier: *A Ballad of Trees
and the Master*

If Christianity were taught and understood conformable to the spirit of its Founder, the existing social organism could not exist a day.

Emile Louis Victor de Lavelaye

I am of the opinion that we should endeavor with all possible zeal to obtain an exact understanding of the great personality of Jesus and to reclaim him for Judaism.

Moritz Lazarus

The well-spring of whatever is best and purest in human life. The first trustworthy and practical teacher of the Immortality of the Soul.

Gotthold Ephraim Lessing

"Isn't this Joseph's son?"—ay, it is He;
Joseph the carpenter—same trade as me.

Catherine C. Liddell: *Jesus the
Carpenter*

I will place no value on anything I have or may possess except in relation to the Kingdom of Christ.

David Livingstone

God had only one Son, and he was a missionary and a physician.

David Livingstone

Anything that one imagines of God apart from Christ is only useless thinking and vain idolatry.

Martin Luther

In his life, Christ is an example, showing us how to live; in his death, he is a sacrifice, satisfying for our sins; in his resurrection, a conqueror; in his ascension, a king; in his intercession, a high priest.

Martin Luther

When Jesus Christ utters a word, He opens His mouth so wide that it embraces all Heaven and earth, even though that word be but in a whisper.

Martin Luther

Christ will remain a priest and king, though He was never consecrated by any papist bishop or greased by any of those shavelings; but He was ordained and consecrated by God Himself, and by Him anointed.

Martin Luther

God never gave man a thing to do concerning which it were irreverent to ponder how the Son of God would have done it.

George Macdonald

If I could hear Christ praying for me in the next room, I would not fear a million enemies. Yet distance makes no difference. He is praying for me.

Robert M. McCheyne

Christ is the bread for men's souls. In Him the Church has enough to feed the whole world.

Ian Maclaren

Son of Man, whenever I doubt of life I think of thee. Thou never growest old to me. Last century is old. Last year is obsolete fashion, but thou art not obsolete. Thou art abreast of all the centuries, and I have never come up to thee, modern as I am.

Prayer of George Matheson

Belief in the resurrection of Jesus is the motive power of all Christian mankind. From what did this faith spring? From five or six remarkably vivid hallucinations. To think so is just as absurd as to suppose that five or six sparks would make water boil in a huge caldron.

Dimitrii Merezhkovski, in *Jesus Manifest.* © 1936, Charles Scribner's Sons

Lo! Christ himself chose only twelve,
Yet one of these turned out a thief.

Joaquin Miller: *A Song of the South*

The hands of Christ seem very frail,
For they were broken by a nail.
But only they reach Heaven at last
Whom these frail, broken hands hold fast.

John Richard Moreland:
His Hands

Love cannot die, nor truth betray;
Christ rose upon an April day.

John Richard Moreland: *Resurgam*

Christ is the key to the history of the world. Not only does all harmonize with the mission of Christ, but all is subordinate to it.

Johannes von Müller

I know men; and I tell you that Jesus Christ is no mere man. Between him and every other person in the world there is no possible term of comparison. Alexander, Caesar, Charlemagne, and I have founded empires. But on what did we rest the creations of our genius? Upon force. Jesus Christ founded his empire upon love; and at this hour millions of men would die for him.

Napoleon Bonaparte

The nature of Christ's existence is mysterious, I admit; but this mystery meets the wants of man.—Reject it and the world is an inexplicable riddle; believe it, and the history of our race is satisfactorily explained.

Napoleon Bonaparte

Life passes, riches fly away, popularity is fickle, the senses decay, the world changes. One alone is true to us; One alone can be all things to us; One alone can supply our need.

Cardinal John Henry Newman

The foxes have holes, and the birds of the air have nests; but the Son of man hath not where to lay his head.

New Testament: Matthew 8: 20

Lo, I am with you alway, even unto the end of the world.

New Testament: Matthew 28: 20

For God so loved the world, that he gave his only begotten Son, that whosoever believeth in him should not perish, but have everlasting life.

New Testament: John 3: 16

Then came Jesus forth, wearing the crown of thorns, and the purple robe. And Pilate saith unto them, Behold the man! [*Ecce Homo.*]

New Testament: John 19: 5

But we preach Christ crucified, unto the Jews a stumblingblock, and unto the Greeks foolishness.

New Testament: I Corinthians 1: 23

Thanks be unto God for his unspeakable gift.

New Testament: II Corinthians 9: 15

And are built upon the foundation of the apostles and prophets, Jesus Christ himself being the chief corner stone.

New Testament: Ephesians 2: 20

Christ is all, and in all.

New Testament: Colossians 3: 11

. . . Jesus. . . was made a little lower than the angels. . . .

New Testament: Hebrews 2: 9

Jesus Christ the same yesterday, and to day, and for ever.

New Testament: Hebrews 13: 8

How sweet the name of Jesus sounds
    In a believer's ear;
It soothes his sorrows, heals his wounds,
    And drives away his fear.

John Newton

Jesus died too soon. He would have repudiated His doctrine if He had lived to my age.

Friedrich Wilhelm Nietzsche

If Christ comes to rule in the hearts of men, it will be because we take him with us on the tractor, behind the desk, when we're making a sale to a customer, or when we're driving on the road.

Alexander Nunn in Houston (Texas)
Times, All-Church Press

They gave him a manger for a cradle, a carpenter's bench for a pulpit, thorns for a crown, and a cross for a throne. He took them and made them the very glory of his career.

W. E. Orchard: *The Temple*,
E. P. Dutton & Company,
Inc., and J. M. Dent & Sons,
Ltd.

Near, so very near to God,
    Nearer I cannot be;
For in the person of his Son
    I am as near as he.

Catesby Paget: *Hymn*

After reading the doctrines of Plato, Socrates or Aristotle, we feel the specific difference between their words and Christ's is the difference between an inquiry and a revelation.

Joseph Parker

Only a Christ could have conceived a Christ.

Joseph Parker: *Ecce Deus*

Jesus Christ is a God to whom we can approach without pride, and before whom we may abase ourselves without despair.

Blaise Pascal

Jesus Christ is the centre of all, and the goal to which all tends.

Blaise Pascal

All hail the power of Jesus' name!
    Let angels prostrate fall;
Bring forth the royal diadem,
    To crown Him Lord of all!

Edward Perronet: *Coronation*

He who was foretold and foreshadowed by the holy religion of Judea, which was designed to free the universal aspiration of mankind from every impure element, he has come to instruct, to obey, to love, to die, and by dying to save mankind.

Edmond de Pressensé

Jesus was the greatest religious genius that ever lived. His beauty is eternal, and his reign shall never end. Jesus is in every respect unique, and nothing can be compared with him.

Joseph Ernest Renan

All history is incomprehensible without Christ.

Joseph Ernest Renan

Two thousand years ago there was One here on this earth who lived the grandest life that ever has been lived yet.—a life that every thinking man, with deeper or shallower meaning, has agreed to call divine.

Frederick William Robertson

What can I give Him
Poor as I am?
If I were a shepherd,
I would give Him a lamb;
If I were a wise man,
I would do my part,—
But what can I give Him,
Give my heart.

Christina Georgina Rossetti: *What Can I Give Him?*

My advice to you is, take a house next door to the Physician, for it will be very singular if you should prove to be the very first he ever turned away unhealed.

Samuel Rutherford

Without Christ life is as the twilight with dark night ahead; with Christ it is the dawn of morning with the light and warmth of full day ahead.

Philip Schaff

I am no more of a Christian than Pilate was, or you are, gentle hearer; and yet, like Pilate, I greatly prefer Jesus of Nazareth to Amos or Caiaphas; and I am ready to admit that I see no way out of the world's misery but the way which would have been found by his will.

George Bernard Shaw

The face of Christ does not indeed show us everything, but it shows us the one thing we need to know—the character of God. God is the God who sent Jesus.

P. Carnegie Simpson

The Carpenter of Galilee
Comes down the street again,
In every land, in every age,
He still is building men.
On Christmas Eve we hear him knock;
He goes from door to door:

"Are any workmen out of work?
The Carpenter needs more."

Hilda W. Smith, in "The Carpenter of Galilee"

You never get to the end of Christ's words. There is something in them always behind. They pass into proverbs; they pass into laws; they pass into doctrines; they pass into consolations; but they never pass away, and after all the use that is made of them they are still not exhausted.

Arthur P. Stanley

When Christ came into my life, I came about like a well-handled ship.

Robert Louis Stevenson.

As little as humanity will ever be without religion, as little will it be without Christ.

David F. Strauss

Thou hast conquered, O pale Galilean!
The world has grown grey from Thy breath.

Algernon Charles Swinburne: *Hymn to Proserpine*

If Christ be not divine, every impulse of the Christian world falls to a lower octave, and light and love and hope alike decline.

David Swing

Men overlooked a baby's birth
When love unnoticed came to earth;
And later, seeking in the skies,
Passed by a man in workman's guise.
The only children paused to stare
While God Incarnate made a chair.

Mary Tatlow

He went about, he was so kind,
To cure poor people who were blind;
And many who were sick and lame,
He pitied them and did the same.

Ann and Jane Taylor: *About Jesus Christ*

He wakes desires you never may forget;
He shows you stars you never saw before;
He makes you share with Him forevermore
The burden of the world's divine regret.

Alfred, Lord Tennyson

Our fair father Christ.

Alfred, Lord Tennyson

The Lord from Heaven,
Born of a village girl, carpenter's son,
Wonderful, Prince of Peace, the mighty God.

Alfred, Lord Tennyson

Ring in the valiant man and free,
    The larger heart, the kindlier hand!
    Ring out the darkness of the land,
Ring in the Christ that is to be!

Alfred, Lord Tennyson: *In Memoriam*

They should have known that he was God.
His patience should have proved that to
them.

Tertullian

All His glory and beauty come from within,
and there He delights to dwell, His visits
there are frequent, His conversation sweet,
His comforts refreshing; and His peace passing all understanding.

Thomas à Kempis: *Imitation of Christ*

Little Jesus, was Thou shy
Once, and just so small as I?
And what did it feel like to be
Out of Heaven, and just like me?

Francis Thompson: *Ex Ore Infantium*

After six years given to the impartial investigation of Christianity, as to its truth or
falsity, I have come to the deliberate conclusion that Jesus Christ was the Messiah of
the Jews, the Saviour of the world, and my
personal Saviour.

Lew Wallace

His love at once, and dread, instruct our
    thought;
As man He suffer'd, and as God He taught.

Edmund Waller: *Of Divine Love*

The man, the Christ, the soldier.
Who from his cross of pain
Cried to the dying comrade,
"Lad, we shall meet again."

Willard Austin Wattles: *Comrades of
the Cross,* from the book *Lanterns
in Gethsemane* by Willard Wattles.
Copyright, 1918 by E. P. Dutton &
Co., Inc. Reprinted by permission
of the publishers

Jesus shall reign where e'er the sun
Doth his successive journeys run;
His kingdom stretch from shore to shore
Till moons shall wax and wane no more.

Isaac Watts: *The Psalms of David*

If I might comprehend Jesus Christ, I could
not believe on Him. He would be no greater
than myself. Such is my consciousness of sin
and inability that I must have a superhuman
Saviour.

Daniel Webster

Is it any wonder that to this day this Galilean
is too much for our small hearts?

H. G. Wells: *Outline of History*

Jesus! the name high over all,
In hell, or earth, or sky;
Angels and men before it fall,
And devils fear and fly.

Charles Wesley: *Hymn*

The holiest of men still need Christ as
their Prophet, as "the light of the world."
For he does not give them light but from
moment to moment; the instant He withdraws, all is darkness. They still need Christ
as their King, for God does not give them
a stock of holiness. But unless they receive
a supply every moment, nothing but un-
holiness would remain. They still need
Christ as their Priest, to make atonement
for their holy things. Even perfect holiness
is acceptable to God only through Jesus
Christ.

John Wesley: *Christian Perfection*

I lift my arms beyond the night, and see
Above the banners of Man's hate unfurled,
The holy figure that on Calvary
Stretched arms out wide enough for all the
    world.

John Hall Wheelock, in *The Black
Panther,* by permission of Charles
Scribner's Sons

Christ is clothed with human nature.

Benjamin Whichcote

All we want in Christ, we shall find in Christ. If we want little, we shall find little. If we want much, we shall find much; but if, in utter helplessness, we cast our all on Christ, He will be to us the whole treasury of God.

Henry Benjamin Whipple

In darkness there is no choice. It is light that enables us to see the differences between things; and it is Christ that gives us light.

Mrs. C. T. Whitmell: *Christ in Flanders*

We faintly hear, we dimly see,
  In differing phrase we pray;
But dim or clear, we own in Him
  The life, the truth, the way.

John Greenleaf Whittier

Only once did God choose a completely sinless preacher.

Alexander Whyte

The Sermon on the Mount is Christ's biography. Every syllable He had already written down in deeds. The sermon merely translated His life into language.

Thomas Wright

Do you think it was self-denial for the Lord Jesus to come down from heaven to rescue a world: Was it self-denial? No, it was love —love that swallows up everything, and first of all self.

Nikolaus Ludvig von Zinzendorf to John Wesley

CHRISTIAN(S),
CHRISTIANITY

The religion of Jesus begins with the verb "follow" and ends with the word "go."

Anonymous

Christianity teaches a man to spend the best part of his life preparing for the worst.

Anonymous

Christianity is the science of character building, the philosophy of immortality, the logic of earth and heaven contacts, the solution of the riddle of existence.

Anonymous

Christianity is the spirit of Jesus Christ at work in the world.

Anonymous

I have sent for you that you may see how a Christian can die.

Joseph Addison: On his death-bed, to his step-son

I hold that the Christian religion is the best yet promulgated, but do not thence infer that it is not susceptible of improvement; nor do I wish to confound its doctrines with its founder, and to worship one of my fellow-beings.

Amos Bronson Alcott: *Diary*

The Christian is not one who has gone all the way with Christ. None of us has. The Christian is one who has found the right road.

Charles L. Allen: *When the Heart is Hungry*

In order to see Christianity, one must forget almost all the Christians.

Henri Frédéric Amiel: *Journal*

The Christians do not commit adultery. They do not bear false witness. They do not covet their neighbor's goods. They honor father and mother. They love their neighbors. They judge justly. They avoid doing to others what they do not wish done to them. They do good to their enemies. They are kind.

St. Aristides: *Apology for the Christian Faith*

Protestantism has the method of Jesus with His secret too much left out of mind; Catholicism has His secret with His method too much left out of mind; neither has His unerring balance, His intuition, His sweet reasonableness. But both have hold of a great truth, and get from it a great power.

Matthew Arnold: *Literature and Dogma*, X

The distinction between Christianity and all other systems of religion consists largely in this, that in these others, men are found seeking after God, while Christianity is God seeking after men.

Thomas Arnold

There was never law or sect, or opinion did so much magnify goodness, as the Christian religion doth.

Sir Francis Bacon: *Essays: Of Goodness*

It does not require great learning to be a Christian and to be convinced of the truth of the Bible. It requires only an honest heart and a willingness to obey God.

William Barnes

No nations are more warlike than those which profess Christianity.

Pierre Bayle: *Pensées sur la Comète*

If a man cannot be a Christian in the place where he is, he cannot be a Christian anywhere.

Henry Ward Beecher: *Life Thoughts*

Christians and camels receive their burdens kneeling.

Ambrose Bierce: *The Devil's Dictionary*, published by Dover Publications, Inc., New York, N.Y.

Christian: One who believes that the New Testament is a divinely inspired book admirably suited to the spiritual needs of his neighbor.

Ibid.

Infidel: In New York, one who does not believe in the Christian religion; in Constantinople, one who does.

Ibid.

A Christian is one who rejoices in the superiority of a rival.

Edwin Booth

Christianity is not "an idea in the air." It is feet on the ground going God's way.

Frederick W. Brink: *This Man and This Woman*, Association Press

I dare without usurpation assume the honourable style of a Christian.

Sir Thomas Browne: *Religio Medici*, Pt. I, 1

We all have known . . .
Good popes who brought all good to
jeopardy,
Good Christians who sat still in easy chairs,
And damned the general world for standing up.

Elizabeth Barrett Browning: *Aurora Leigh*, Bk. IV, l. 498

How very hard it is to be
A Christian!

Robert Browning: *Easter Day*

The egg's no chick by falling from the hen,
Nor man a Christian till he's born again.

John Bunyan: *A Book for Boys and Girls*

Christianity is a scheme quite beyond our comprehension.

Joseph Butler: *The Analogy of Religion*

After all, what is the essence of Christianity? What is the kernel of the nut? Surely common sense and cheerfulness, with unflinching opposition to the charlatanisms and Pharisaisms of a man's own times.

Samuel Butler

People in general are equally horrified at hearing the Christian religion doubted, and at seeing it practised.

Samuel Butler

Christianity is intensely practical. She has no trait more striking than her common sense.

Charles Buxton

Christianity has not failed. It is simply that nations have failed to try it. There would be no war in a God-directed world.

Rear-Admiral Richard E. Byrd,
G. P. Putnam's Sons

Christians have burnt each other, quite persuaded
That all the Apostles would have done as they did.

George Gordon, Lord Byron: *Don Juan,*
Canto I, st. 83

Some Christians have a comfortable creed.

George Gordon, Lord Byron: *Don Juan,*
Canto II, st. 86

On all sides there are signs of decay of the faith. People do not go to church, or if they go, it is for the sake of the music, or for some non-religious motive. The evidence is overwhelming that the doctrines of Christianity have passed into the region of doubt.

Lord Hugh Cecil: Speech in the
House of Commons

The purpose of Christianity is not to avoid difficulty, but to produce a character adequate to meet it when it comes. It does not make life easy; rather it tries to make us great enough for life.

James L. Christensen

An alarming weakness among Christians is that we are producing Christian activities faster than we are producing Christian experience and Christian faith.

Church Management

The flame of Christian ethics is still our highest guide.

Sir Winston Churchill: Speech at the Mid-Century Convocation at M.I.T., March 31, 1949, Houghton Mifflin Company

Christianity is not a theory or speculation, but a life; not a philosophy of life, but a living presence.

Samuel Taylor Coleridge

The greatest of all blessings, and the most ennobling of all privileges, is to be indeed a Christian.

Samuel Taylor Coleridge

He who begins by loving Christianity better than Truth will proceed by loving his own sect or church better than Christianity, and end in loving himself better than all.

Samuel Taylor Coleridge: *Aids to
Reflection: Aphorisms*

Nobody can teach you how to be a Christian —you learn it on the job.

Reprinted from *The Country Parson,* by Frank A. Clark, by permission of The Register-Tribune Syndicate

The Christian religion is a constant living with God.

Samuel S. Curry

His Christianity was muscular.

Benjamin Disraeli: *Endymion,* ch. 14

Give us a genuine Christianity that may provoke persecution but will not provoke contempt.

Amzi Clarence Dixon

In every Christian
Hourly tempestuous persecutions grow.
Temptations martyr us alive. A man
Is to himself a Diocletian.

John Donne: *The Litany*

Christ built no church, wrote no book, left no money, and erected no monuments; yet show me ten square miles in the whole earth without Christianity, where the life of man and the purity of women are respected and I will give up Christianity.

Henry Drummond

There is no leveler like Christianity, but it levels by lifting all who receive it to the lofty table-land of a true character and of undying hope both for this world and the next.

Jonathan Edwards

Every Stoic was a Stoic; but in Christendom where is the Christian?

Ralph Waldo Emerson: *Self-Reliance*

Two inestimable advantages Christianity has given us: first, the Sabbath, the jubilee of the whole world; . . . and secondly, the institution of preaching.

Ralph Waldo Emerson: *Nature, Addresses, and Lectures: Address*

Saints are made but Christians are born.

George E. Failing: *The Wesleyan Methodist*

The religion of Christ has made a Republic like ours possible; and the more we have of this religion the better the Republic.

Henry Martyn Field

Philosophy makes us wiser, but Christianity makes us better men.

Henry Fielding: *Tom Jones,* Bk. VIII, ch. 13

It is not the business of Christianity to provide an organization for the world but to infuse the spirit of Christ into the organizations of the world.

Fred Fisher

A Christian in this world is but gold in the ore; at death, the pure gold is smelted out and separated and the dross cast away and consumed.

John Flavel

Christianity might be described as the religion of the second mile; duty demands that you go one mile, Christ says you must go two.

Faith Forsyte: *Tit-Bits*

Christians are supposed not merely to endure change, nor even to profit by it, but to cause it.

Harry Emerson Fosdick

A good Christian would rather be robbed than rob others—rather be murdered than murderer—martyred than tyrant.

Ascribed to St. Francis de Sales

He who shall introduce into public affairs the principles of primitive Christianity will change the face of the world.

Benjamin Franklin: Letter to the French ministry

When we were watching the distribution of clothing in Jordan, I found myself wondering what it would be like to be wearing the clothes of someone else; how it would be like always in someone else's shoes. Then it occurred to me that this is precisely what Christianity means—eternally being in someone else's shoes.

R. Paul Freed

A Christian is the keyhole through which other folk see God.

Robert E. Gibson

A local thing called Christianity.

Thomas Hardy: *The Dynasts: Spirit of the Years,* sc. 6

A Christian is God Almighty's gentleman.

Augustus William and Julius Charles Hare: *Guesses at Truth*

The missionaries are right. The world needs more than policy. It needs healing and practical instruction and an appreciation of other people which is the essence of applied Christianity.

Brooks Hays

I reckon him a Christian indeed who is not ashamed of the Gospel, nor a shame to it.

Matthew Henry

For one who rejects Christianity because he misunderstands it, ten reject it because they understand it too well—because they know it is a call to the selfless and sacrificial life.

E. Herman

It is a matter of surprise that men whose Christian honesty, purity, and self-devotedness are conceded on every hand, are often men with whom we do not like to associate.

Josiah Gilbert Holland: *Everyday Topics*

A man may carry the whole scheme of Christian truth in his mind from boyhood to old age without the slightest effect upon his character and aims. It has less influence than the multiplication table.

Josiah Gilbert Holland: *Everyday Topics*

Christianity is the greatest civilizing, moulding, uplifting power on this globe.

Mark Hopkins

To make one a complete Christian he must have the works of a Papist, the words of a Puritan, and the faith of a Protestant.

James Howell: *Familiar Letters*

No Christian can be a pessimist, for Christianity is a system of radical optimism.

William R. Inge: *Obituary editorial, Manchester Guardian,* February 27, 1954

Of all the systems of morality, ancient and modern, which have come under my observation, none appear so pure to me as that of Jesus.

Thomas Jefferson

To the corruptions of Christianity I am indeed, opposed; but not to the genuine precepts of Jesus himself. I am a Christian in the only sense in which he wished any one to be; sincerely attached to his doctrines in preference to all others; ascribing to himself every human excellence; and believing he never claimed any other.

Thomas Jefferson: *Writings,* Vol. X, p. 379

Millions of innocent men, women and children, since the introduction of Christianity, have been burned, tortured, fined and imprisoned, yet we have not advanced one inch toward uniformity. What has been the effect of coercion? To make one-half of the world fools and the other half hypocrites.

Thomas Jefferson: *Notes on Virginia*

I think all Christians, whether papists or Protestants, agree in the essential articles, and that their differences are trivial, and rather political than religious.

Samuel Johnson

Christianity is the highest perfection of humanity.

Ibid.

The measure of a Christian is not in the height of his grasp but in the depth of his love.

Clarence Jordan

Look in, and see Christ's chosen saint
  In triumph wear his Christ-like chain;
No fear lest he should swerve or faint;
  "His life is Christ, his death is gain."

John Keble: *Christian Year, St. Luke: The Evangelist*

Not until man has become so utterly unhappy, or has grasped the woefulness of life so deeply that he is moved to say, and mean it: Life for me has no value—not till then is he able to make a bid for Christianity.

Sören Kierkegaard

Most people believe that the Christian commandments are intentionally a little too severe—like setting a clock half an hour ahead to make sure of not being late in the morning.

Sören Kierkegaard

Christianity can never come to us as a bargain; it can never be had at a wholesale price. We must be willing to pay the full price of surrender and trust.

William L. Krutza: *The Alliance Witness*

A wise man will always be a Christian, because the perfection of wisdom is to know where lies tranquillity of mind, and how to attain it, which Christianity teaches.

Walter Savage Landor: *Imaginary Conversations: Marvell and Parker*

What was invented two thousand years ago was the spirit of Christianity.

Gerald Stanley Lee: *Crowds,* Bk. II, ch. 18

Civil society was renovated in every part by the teachings of Christianity. In the strength of that renewal the human race was lifted up to better things. Nay, it was brought back from death to life.

> Pope Leo XIII: *Rerum novarum*,
> May 15, 1891

In a sermon by a notable American preacher a few years ago these words appeared: "Christianity has grown soft, sentimental, saccharine; it has become too much flute and too little trumpet."

> Halford E. Luccock: *Christian Herald*

The Christians are unhappy men who are persuaded that they will survive death and live forever; in consequence, they despise death and are willing to sacrifice their lives to their faith.

> Lucian: *On the Death of Peregrinus*

Christianity is both science and art. Science is to know; art is to do. What we know is incomplete until fulfilled in the act. The most practical of all religions is Christianity, because it demands that the act accompany the thought.

> Richard Lynch: *Good Business*

True Christianity is love in action.

> David O. McKay

The real security of Christianity is to be found in its benevolent morality; in its exquisite adaptation to the human heart; in the facility with which its scheme accommodates itself to the capacity of every human intellect; in the consolation which it bears to the house of mourning; in the light with which it brightens the great mystery of the grave.

> Thomas Babington Macaulay

A Christian is commanded, under the strongest sanctions, to be just in all his dealings. Yet to how many of the twenty-four millions of professing Christians in these islands would any man in his senses lend a thousand pounds without security?

> Thomas Babington Macaulay: *Civil Disabilities of the Jews* (Edinburgh Review, January, 1831)

Many of us who profess to be Christians are so busy with the mechanics of our religion that we have no time left for the spiritual part of it.

> William B. Martin

A church membership does not make a Christian any more than owning a piano makes a musician.

> Douglas Meador: *These Times*

To pretend that Christianity was intended to stereotype existing forms of government and society, and protect them against change, is to reduce it to the level of Islamism and Brahminism. It is precisely because Christianity has not done this that it has been the religion of the progressive portion of mankind.

> John Stuart Mill: *The Subjection of Women*

He that can apprehend and consider vice with all her baits and seeming pleasures, and yet abstain, and yet distinguish and prefer that which is truly better, he is the true warfaring Christian.

> John Milton: *Areopagitica*

Men of simple understanding, little inquisitive and little instructed, make good Christians.

> Michel Eyquem de Montaigne: *Essays*

Christianity is the power of God in the soul of man.

> Robert Boyd Munger

The religion of Jesus is a threat, that of Mohammed is a promise.

> Napoleon Bonaparte

And the disciples were called Christians first in Antioch.

> *New Testament: Acts 11: 26*

Then Agrippa said unto Paul, Almost thou persuadest me to be a Christian.

> *New Testament: Acts 26: 28*

The Christian is like the ripening corn: the riper he grows the more lowly he bends his head.

North Carolina *Christian Advocate*

As to the Christian system of faith, it appears to me as a species of atheism—a sort of religious denial of God. It professes to believe in a man rather than a God. It is a compound made up chiefly of manism with but little deism, and is as near to atheism as twilight is to darkness.

Thomas Paine: *The Age of Reason,* I

Silence the voice of Christianity, and the world is well-nigh dumb, for gone is that sweet music which kept in order the rulers of the people, which cheers the poor widow in her lonely toil, and comes like light through the windows of morning to men who sit stooping and feeble, with failing eyes and a hungering heart.

Theodore Parker: *Critical and Miscellaneous Writings: A Discourse of the Transient and Permanent in Christianity*

Let not it be imagined that the life of a good Christian must be a life of melancholy and gloominess; for he only resigns some pleasures to enjoy others infinitely better.

Blaise Pascal

The Christian religion teaches me two points —that there is a God whom men can know, and that their nature is so corrupt that they are unworthy of Him.

Blaise Pascal: *Pensées,* VIII

To be like Christ is to be a Christian.

William Penn: *Last Words*

Christianity is a battle—not a dream.

Wendell Phillips

A federation of Christians is inconceivable in which each member retains his own opinions and private judgment in matters of faith.

Pope Pius XI: *Mortalium animos,* January 6, 1928

Christianity is the least concerned about religion of any of the world's faith. It is primarily concerned about life.

T. D. Price

Christianity is not a puzzle to be solved, but a way of life to be adopted. It is not a creed to be memorized, but a Person to follow.

Quick Quotes

You are Christians of the best edition, all picked and culled.

François Rabelais: *Works,* Bk. IV, ch. 50

Christianity is like electricity. It cannot enter a person unless it can pass through.

Richard C. Raines

It does not take a great mind to be a Christian, but it takes all the mind a man has.

Richard C. Raines

The only truly happy men I have ever known were Christians.

John Randolph

It is through Christianity that Judaism has really conquered the world. Christianity is the masterpiece of Judaism, its glory and the fullness of its evolution.

Joseph Ernst Renan: *History of Israel*

The true Christian is the true citizen, lofty of purpose, resolute in endeavor, ready for a hero's deeds, but never looking down on his task because it is cast in the day of small things; scornful of baseness, awake to his own duties as well as to his rights, following the higher law with reverence, and in this world doing all that in his power lies, so that when death comes he may feel that mankind is in some degree better because he lived.

Theodore Roosevelt: Speech in New York, December 30, 1900

In the ethic of Christianity, it is the relation of the soul to God that is important, not the relation of man to his fellow man.

Bertrand Russell: *Marriage and Morals,* p. 175, Liveright Publishing Corp.

Christianity is the world's monumental fraud if there be no future life.

Martin J. Scott: *Religion and Commonsense*, p. 120

Neither having the accent of Christians, nor the gait of Christian, pagan or man.

William Shakespeare: *Hamlet*, Act III, sc. 2, l. 23

How like a fawning publican he looks!
I hate him for he is a Christian.

William Shakespeare: *Merchant of Venice*, Act I, sc. 3, l. 42

O father Abram, what these Christians are,
Whose own hard dealings teaches them suspect
The thoughts of others.

William Shakespeare: *Merchant of Venice*, Act I, sc. 3, l. 161

This making of Christians will raise the price of hogs: if we grow all to be pork-eaters, we shall not shortly have a rasher on the coals for money.

William Shakespeare: *Merchant of Venice*, Act III, sc. 5, l. 25

For in converting Jews to Christians, you raise the price of pork.

William Shakespeare: *Merchant of Venice*, Act III, sc. 5, l. 38

Methinks sometimes I have no more wit than a Christian.

William Shakespeare: *Twelfth Night*, Act I, sc. 3, l. 89

Why not give Christianity a trial? The question seems a hopeless one after 2000 years of resolute adherence to the old cry of "Not this man, but Barrabbas." . . . "This man" has not been a failure yet, for nobody has ever been sane enough to try his way.

George Bernard Shaw: *Preface, Androcles and the Lion*

As to the Christian creed, if true
Or false, I never questioned it;
I took it as the vulgar do.

Percy Bysshe Shelley: *Rosalind and Helen*, l. 512

The central problem of Christianity is: if the Messiah has come why is the world so evil? For Judaism, the problem is: if the world is so evil, why does the Messiah not come?

Seymour Siegel: *Saturday Review*, March 28, 1959

Many Christians are like chestnuts—very pleasant nuts, but enclosed in very prickly burrs, which need various dealings of Nature and her grip of frost before the kernel is disclosed.

Horatio Smith: *The Tin Trumpet: Christians*

Christianity will gain by every step that is taken in the knowledge of man.

Johann Kaspar Spurzheim

A wise person truly said, "It ought to be as impossible to forget that there is a Christian in the house as it is to forget that there is a ten-year-old boy in it."

Roger J. Squire: *Church Management*

The Christian church is not a congregation of righteous people. It is a society of those who know they are not good.

Dwight E. Stevenson

There are many in the Church as well as out of it who need to learn that Christianity is neither a creed nor a ceremonial, but a life vitally connected with a loving Christ.

Josiah Strong

Christians are found almost everywhere, but they are not necessarily found anywhere; sometimes they are found in church, but not all persons in churches are Christians. What persons do outside the churches is the test.

James E. Sweaney, *Progress*. Unity School of Christianity

CHRISTIAN(S), CHRISTIANITY

A man becomes a Christian; he is not born one.

Tertullian: *The Testimony of the Christian Soul*

"See," they say, "how these Christians love one another," for themselves hate one another; "and how they are ready to die for each other," for themselves will be readier to kill each other.

Tertullian: *Apologeticus*, ch. 39, sec. 7

Christianity is the companion of liberty in all its conflicts—the cradle of its infancy, and the divine source of its claims.

Alexis de Tocqueville

The Christian cannot promise to do or not do a given thing at a given time, for he cannot know what the law of love, which is the commanding principle of his life, will demand of him at that time.

Leo Tolstoy: *The Kingdom of God is Within You*

Christianity, with its doctrine of humility, of forgiveness, of love, is incompatible with the state, with its haughtiness, its violence, its punishment, its wars.

Ibid.

The world is equally shocked at hearing Christianity criticized and seeing it practiced.

D. Elton Trueblood

Christians have been the most intolerant of all men.

Voltaire: *Philosophical Dictionary*

Christianity can be condensed into four words: Admit, Submit, Commit and Transmit.

Samuel Wilberforce

You say that you believe the Gospel; you live as if you were sure not one word of it is true.

Thomas Wilson: *Maxims of Piety*, p. 44

A Christian is the highest style of man.

Edward Young: *Night Thoughts*, Night IV, l. 788

Scratch the Christian and you find the pagan —spoiled.

Israel Zangwill: *Children of the Ghetto*, Bk. II, ch. 6

CHRISTMAS

Christmas is a time for "giving up" sin, bad habits, and selfish pleasures. Christmas is a time for "giving in" surrender to Christ, acceptance of Him as King. Christmas is a time for "giving out" real giving, not swapping.

Anonymous

The message of Christmas is that the visible material world is bound to the invisible spiritual world.

Anonymous

Selfishness makes Christmas a burden: love makes it a delight.

Anonymous

The universal joy of Christmas is certainly wonderful. We ring the bells when princes are born, or toll a mournful dirge when great men pass away. Nations have their red-letter days, their carnivals and festivals, but once in the year and only once, the whole world stands still to celebrate the advent of a life. Only Jesus of Nazareth claims this worldwide, undying remembrance. You cannot cut Christmas out of the calendar, nor out of the heart of the world.

Anonymous

So remember while December
Brings the only Christmas day,
In the year let there be Christmas
In the things you do and say;
Wouldn't life be worth the living
Wouldn't dreams be coming true
If we kept the Christmas spirit
All the whole year through?

Anonymous: "The Whole Year Through"

It is Christmas in the mansion,
  Yule-log fires and silken frocks;
It is Christmas in the cottage,
  Mother's filling little socks.

It is Christmas on the highway,
  In the thronging, busy mart;
But the dearest, truest Christmas
Is the Christmas in the heart.

> Anonymous: "Christmas in the Heart"

Christmas is over and Business is Business.

> Franklin Pierce Adams: "For the Other 364 Days," from *FPA's Book of Quotations,* Funk & Wagnalls Co., Inc.

I have often thought, says Sir Roger, it happens very well that Christmas should fall out in the middle of winter.

> Joseph Addison: *The Spectator,* no. 269

The world is large and complex, and sometimes there seems to be no sacred ground. But in tent and palace, in adobe hut and castle, in barrack prison and under lighted trees across the lands, the language of Christmas is universal.

> Marcus Bach: *Weekly Unity*

Christmas is coming, the geese are getting fat,
Please to put a penny in the old man's hat;
If you haven't got a penny, a ha'penny will do,
If you haven't got a ha'penny, God bless you!

> Beggar's Rhyme

Christmas itself may be called into question
If carried so far it creates indigestion.

> Ralph Bergengren: *The Unwise Christmas*

Come, all ye faithful, joyful and triumphant;
Come ye, come ye to Bethlehem;
Come and behold Him, born the king of angels;
Come and adore Him, come and adore Him,
Come and adore the Lord.

> Attributed to St. Bonaventure

The feet of the humblest may walk in the fields
Where the feet of the holiest have trod.
This, this is the marvel to mortals revealed,
When the silvery trumpets of Christmas have pealed,
That mankind are the children of God.

> Phillips Brooks

Then let every heart keep Christmas within.
  Christ's pity for sorrow,
  Christ's hatred for sin,
  Christ's care for the weakest,
  Christ's courage for right.
Everywhere, everywhere, Christmas tonight!

> Phillips Brooks

The character of the Creator cannot be less than the highest He has created, and the highest is that babe born to Mary on that first Christmas morning.

> A. Ian Burnett: *Lord of All Life*

Christians awake, salute the happy morn
Whereon the Saviour of the world was born.

> John Byrom: *Hymn for Christmas Day*

Christmas is not a date. It is a state of mind.

> Mary Ellen Chase, copyright by the N. Y. Times. Reprinted by permission

You can't escape Christmas; you can only escape yourself.

> John Cogley: *The Commonweal*

God rest ye, little children; let nothing you affright,
For Jesus Christ, your Saviour, was born this happy night;
Along the hills of Galilee the white flocks sleeping lay,
When Christ, the child of Nazareth was born on Christmas Day.

> Dinah Maria Mulock Craik: *Christmas Carol,* st. 2

I have always thought of Christmas time, when it has come round, as a good time; a

kind, forgiving, charitable time; the only
time I know of, in the long calendar of the
year, when men and women seem by one
consent to open their shut-up hearts freely,
and to think of people below them as if they
really were fellow passengers to the grave,
and not another race of creatures bound on
other journeys. . . . And so as Tiny Tim
said: "A merry Christmas to us all, my dears.
God bless us, every one."

Charles Dickens

It is good to be children sometimes, and
never better than at Christmas, when its
mighty Founder was a child Himself.

Charles Dickens

Many merry Christmases, friendships, great
accumulation of cheerful recollections, affection on earth, and Heaven at last for all
of us.

Charles Dickens

The night that erst no name had worn,
   To it a happy name is given;
For in that stable lay new-born
   The peaceful Prince of Earth and Heaven,
In the solemn midnight Centuries ago.

Alfred Domett: *A Christmas Hymn*

Blest Christmas morn, though murky clouds
   Pursue thy way,
Thy light was born where storm enshrouds
   Nor dawn nor day!

Mary Baker Eddy: "Christmas Morn,"
st. 1, *Poems,* p. 29

They err who think Santa Claus comes down
the chimney; he really enters through the
heart.

Mrs. Paul M. Ell

It is Christmas in the heart that puts Christmas in the air.

W. T. Ellis

Instead of being a time of unusual behavior,
Christmas is perhaps the only time in the
year when people can obey their natural

impulses and express their true sentiments
without feeling self-conscious and, perhaps,
foolish. Christmas in short, is about the only
chance a man has to be himself.

Francis C. Farley: *West Virginia Oil
News*

'Most all the time, the whole year round,
   there ain't no flies on me,
But jest 'fore Christmas I'm as good as I
   kin be!

Eugene Field: *Jest 'fore Christmas*

There was a gift for each of us left under
the tree of life 2000 years ago by Him whose
birthday we celebrate today. The gift was
withheld from no man. Some have left the
packages unclaimed. Some have accepted the
gift and carry it around, but have failed to
remove the wrappings and look inside to discover the hidden splendour. The packages
are all alike: in each is a scroll on which is
written, "All that the Father hath is thine."
Take and live!

First Baptist Church Bulletin,
Syracuse, New York

A green Christmas is neither handsome nor
healthful.

Thomas Fuller: *Holy State: Of
Time-Serving*

How bless'd, how envied, were our life,
Could we but 'scape the poulterer's knife!
But man, curs'd man, on Turkeys preys,
And Christmas shortens all our days:
Sometimes with oysters we combine,
Sometimes assist the savory chine;
From the low peasant to the lord,
The Turkey smokes on every board.

John Gay: *Fables: The Turkey and
the Ant*

Green Christmas, white Easter.

German Proverb

I sometimes think we expect too much of
Christmas Day. We try to crowd into it the
long arrears of kindliness and humanity of
the whole year. As for me, I like to take my

Christmas a little at a time, all through the year. And thus I drift along into the holidays—let them overtake me unexpectedly—waking up some fine morning and suddenly saying to myself: "Why, this is Christmas Day!"

> David Grayson: *Adventures in Friendship,* Doubleday & Company

They talk of Christmas so long that it comes.

> George Herbert: *Jacula Prudentum*

Come, bring with a noise,
My merry, merry boys,
The Christmas log to the firing;
While my good dame, she
Bids ye all be free;
And drink to your hearts' desiring.

> Robert Herrick: *Ceremonies for Christmas*

The best of all gifts around any Christmas tree: the presence of a happy family all wrapped up in each other.

> Burton Hillis: *Better Homes and Gardens,* c/r Meredith Publishing Co.

There's a song in the air!
There's a star in the sky!
There's a mother's deep prayer
And a Baby's low cry!
And the star rains its fire where the Beautiful sing,
For the manger of Bethlehem cradles a King.

> Josiah Gilbert Holland: *A Christmas Carol*

Christmas is the season for kindling the fire of hospitality in the hall, the genial flame of charity in the heart.

> Washington Irving

As I sat on a sunny bank
On Christmas day in the morning
I spied three ships come sailing in.

> Washington Irving: *Sketch Book. The Sunny Bank*

When mother-love makes all things bright,
When joy come with the morning light,

When children gather round their tree,
Thou Christmas Babe, we sing of thee!

> Tudor Jenks: *A Christmas Song*

The joy of brightening other lives, bearing each others' burdens, easing others' loads and supplanting empty hearts and lives with generous gifts becomes for us the magic of Christmas.

> W. C. Jones

Now the essence, the very spirit of Christmas, is this: that we first make believe a thing is so and lo! it presently turns out to be so.

> Stephen Butler Leacock

A Christmas candle is a lovely thing;
It makes no noise at all,
But softly gives itself away;
While quite unselfish, it grows small.

> Eva K. Logue

Shepherds at the grange,
Where the Babe was born,
Sang with many a change,
Christmas carols until morn.

> Henry Wadsworth Longfellow: *By the Fireside, A Christmas Carol*

I heard the bells on Christmas Day
Their old, familiar carols play,
And wild and sweet
The words repeat
Of peace on earth, good-will to men!

> Henry Wadsworth Longfellow: *Christmas Bells*

The whole, wide world: turned selfless for a day,
Lays down its gifts beneath the Christmas fir,
And strangely, touched by memory of a star,
Each gift is gold and frankincense and myrrh.

> Adelaide Love: "Alchemy" in *Poems for the Great Days*

"What means this glory round our feet,"
The Magi mused, "more bright than morn!"
And voices chanted clear and sweet,
"To-day the Prince of Peace is born."

> James Russell Lowell: *Christmas Carol*

There are some of us . . . who think to our-selves, "If I had only been there! How quick I would have been to help the Baby. I would have washed His linen. How happy I would have been to go with the shepherds to see the Lord lying in the manger!" Yes, we would. We say that because we know how great Christ is, but if we had been there at that time, we would have done no better than the people of Bethlehem. . . . Why don't we do it now? We have Christ in our neighbor.

Martin Luther.

This is Christmas: not the tinsel, not the giving and receiving, not even the carols, but the humble heart that receives anew the wondrous gift, the Christ.

Frank McKibben

While rich men sigh and poor men fret,
Dear me! we can't spare Christmas yet!

Edward S. Martin: *Christmas, 1898*

I wish we could put up some of the Christmas spirit in jars and open a jar of it every month.

Harlan Miller: *Better Homes and Gardens,* c/r Meredith Publish-ing Co.

Probably the reason we all go so haywire at Christmas time with the endless unrestrained and often silly buying of gifts is that we don't quite know how to put our love into words.

Ibid.

The outdoor Christmas lights, green and red and gold and blue and twinkling, remind me that most people are that way all year round—kind, generous, friendly and with an occasional moment of ecstasy. But Christmas is the only time they dare reveal themselves.

Ibid.

What a blessing Christmas is! What it does for friendship! Why, if there were no Christ-mas, as Channing Pollock put it, we'd have to invent one, for it is the one season of the year when we can lay aside all gnawing worry, indulge in sentiment without censure,

assume the carefree faith of childhood, and just plain "have fun." Whether they call it Yuletide, Noel, Weinachten, or Christmas, people around the earth thirst for its refresh-ment as the desert traveller for the oasis.

D. D. Monroe: *Rotarian*

'Twas the night before Christmas, when all
through the house
Not a creature was stirring,—not even a
mouse:
The stockings were hung by the chimney
with care,
In hopes that St. Nicholas soon would be
there.

Clement Clarke Moore: *A Visit from St. Nicholas*

Just for a few hours on Christmas Eve and Christmas Day the stupid, harsh mechanism of the world runs down, and we permit ourselves to live according to untrammeled common sense, the unconquerable efficiency of good will.

"Just for a few hours on Christmas Eve . . ." from Essays by Christopher Morley. Copyright, 1918, 1946 by Christopher Morley. Published by J. B. Lippincott Company

Let Christmas not become a thing
Merely of merchant's trafficking,
Of tinsel, bell and holly wreath
And surface pleasure, but beneath
The childish glamour, let us find
Nourishment for soul and mind.
Let us follow kinder ways
Through our teeming human maze,
And help the age of peace to come
From a Dreamer's martyrdom.

Madeline Morse: *Dairymen's League News*

God rest you merry, gentlemen,
Let nothing you dismay,
For Jesus Christ, our Saviour,
Was born upon this day.

Old Carol

As many mince pies as you taste at Christmas,
so many happy months will you have.

Old English Saying

Christmas is not just a day, an event to be
observed and speedily forgotten. It is a spirit
which should permeate every part of our
lives. To believe that the spirit of Christmas
does change lives and to labor for the realization of its coming to all men is the essence
of our faith in Christ.

William Parks: *Missions*

Christmas is not in tinsel and lights and out-
ward show . . .
The secret lies in an inner glow.
It's lighting a fire inside the heart . . .
Good Will and Joy a vital part.
It's higher thought and a greater plan.
It's glorious dream in the soul of man.
Christmas begins deep down inside . . .
Then engulfs the world like a mighty tide!

Wilfred A. Peterson: *The Art of Living,*
Simon & Schuster, Inc.

Until one feels the spirit of Christmas—there
is no Christmas. All else is outward display
—so much tinsel and decorations. For it isn't
the holly, it isn't the snow. It isn't the tree
nor the firelight's glow. It's the warmth that
comes to the hearts of men when the Christmas spirit returns again.

Pipefuls

After a Christmas comes a Lent.

John Ray: *English Proverbs*

Christmas began in the heart of God. It is
complete only when it reaches the heart of
man.

Religious Telescope

The Christmas tree has taken the place of
the altar in too much of our modern Christmas observance.

Earl Riney: *Church Management*

It is not even the beginning of Christmas
unless it is Christmas in the heart.

Richard Roberts: *Contemporary Christ*

Christmas, my child, is love in action. . . .
When you love someone, you give to them,
as God gives to us. The greatest gift He ever
gave was the Person of His Son, sent to us in
human form so that we might know what
God the Father is really like! Every time we
love, every time we give, it's Christmas.

Dale Evans Rogers

For most of us it can be a Happy Christmas
if by happiness we mean that we have done
with doubts, that we have set our hearts
against fear, that we still believe in the
Golden Rule for all mankind.

Franklin D. Roosevelt

At Christmas-tide the open hand
Scatters its bounty o'er sea and land,
And none are left to grieve alone.
For love is heaven and claims its own.

Margaret E. Sangster

England was merry England when
Old Christmas brought his sports again.
'Twas Christmas broach'd the mightiest ale;
'Twas Christmas told the merriest tale;
A Christmas gambol oft could cheer
The poor man's heart through half the year.

Sir Walter Scott: *Marmion*, Canto VI,
Introduction

Heap on more wood!—the wind is chill;
But let it whistle as it will,
We'll keep our Christmas merry still.

Ibid.

Some say that ever 'gainst that season comes
Wherein our Saviour's birth is celebrated,
The bird of dawning singeth all night long;
And then, they say, no spirit dares stir
abroad;
The nights are wholesome; then no planets
strike,
No fairy takes, nor witch hath power to
charm,
So hallow'd and so gracious is the time.

William Shakespeare: *Hamlet*, Act I,
sc. 1, l. 158

Tho Christ a thousand times
In Bethlehem be born,
If He's not born in thee
Thy soul is still forlorn.

Angelus Silesius

Every little child in all the world has been a little safer since the coming of the Child of Bethlehem.

Roy L. Smith: *The Methodist Story*

A good many people with houses half empty on Christmas Eve have blamed the little inn-keeper of Bethlehem because his place was full.

Ibid.

The hinge of history is on the door of a Bethlehem stable.

Ralph W. Sockman

Life is much like Christmas—you are more apt to get what you expect than what you want.

South African Bulletin

The antiquarians have disputed much and long about whether the event which Christmas commemorates can have taken place late in the month we call December. We have been told that this is the very height of the rainy season in Palestine, when it would be most unlikely to find either flocks or shepherds at night in the fields near Bethlehem. But it makes no difference to the solemn suggestiveness of the season, whether the exact date is right or wrong.

Herbert Leslie Stewart: *National Home Monthly* (Canada)

A hot Christmas makes a fat churchyard.

John Swan: *Speculum Mundi*, CLXI

Coming! ay, so is Christmas.

Jonathan Swift: *Polite Conversation*, Dial. I

The family, the story, the carol and the gift. These four when divested of their present secularistic trappings give us the pure Christian element of Christmas. I do believe that quite a case can be made for a thoroughly enjoyable Christmas with every whit as much spirit and color using only these four ingredients.

John D. Tate: "For a Christian Christmas," *Christian Century*, November 23, 1949

The time draws near the birth of Christ:
The moon is hid; the night is still;
The Christmas bells from hill to hill
Answer each other in the mist.

Alfred, Lord Tennyson: *In Memoriam*, XXVIII

As fits the holy Christmas birth,
Be this, good friends, our carol still—
Be peace on earth, be peace on earth,
To men of gentle will.

William Makepeace Thackeray: *The End of the Play*

Christmas is here:
Winds whistle shrill,
Icy and chill,
Little care we:
Little we fear
Weather without,
Sheltered about
The Mahogany-Tree

William Makepeace Thackeray: *The Mahogany-Tree*

For centuries men have kept an appointment with Christmas. Christmas means fellowship, feasting, giving and receiving, a time of good cheer, home.

W. J. Ronald Tucker: *Pulpit Preaching*

At Christmas play and make good cheer,
For Christmas comes but once a year.

Thomas Tusser: *Hundreth Good Pointes of Husbandrie*, ch. 12

The Light that shines from the humble manger is strong enough to lighten our way to the end of our days.

Vita-Rays

They keep Christmas all the year.

Edward Walker: *Paraemiologia*

After all, Christmas is but a big love affair to remove the wrinkles of the year with kindly remembrances.

John Wanamaker

Life still hath one romance that naught can
bury—
Not Time himself, who coffins Life's
romances—
For still will Christmas gild the year's
mischances,
If Childhood comes as here, to make him
merry.

Walter Theodore Watts-Dunton: *The
Christmas Tree*

Christmas is for children. But it is for grown-ups too. Even if it is a headache, a chore, and nightmare, it is a period of necessary defrosting of chill and hide-bound hearts.

Lenora Mattingly Weber: *Extension*

Take Christ out of Christmas, and December becomes the bleakest and most colorless month of the year.

A. F. Wells: *Link*

I love the Christmas-tide, and yet,
I notice this, each year I live;
I always like the gifts I get,
But how I love the gifts I give!

Carolyn Wells: *A Thought*

Thus we can always know that men could live with goodwill and understanding for each other, because one day in each year the little Divine Prince of Peace still compels them to do it.

Charles Jeremiah Wells

CHURCH

This was posted on a Bronx, New York, church bulletin board: "Do come in—Trespassers will be forgiven."

Anonymous

God sends no churches from the skies,
Out of our *hearts* they must arise.

Anonymous

And whether it be a rich church
Or a poor church anywhere,
Truly it is a great church
It God is worshipped there.

Anonymous

The Church has many critics but no rivals.

Anonymous

It is not the function of the Christian Church to create a new civilization; it is the Church's function to create the creators of a new civilization.

Anonymous

The Church faces a generation which is trying to drink its way to prosperity, war its way to peace, spend its way to wealth and enjoy its way to heaven.

Anonymous

The church is never a place, but always a people; never a fold but always a flock, never a sacred building but always a believing assembly. The church is you who pray, not where you pray. A structure of brick or marble can no more be a church than your clothes of serge or satin can be you. There is in this world nothing sacred but man, no sanctuary of God but the soul.

Anonymous

A Church exists for the double purpose of gathering in and *sending out*.

Anonymous

When we walk softly into the church,
We feel upon the air
A summons that is like a hymn,
A call that tells of prayer.

Anonymous

The church has suffered from putting too high a premium on orthodoxy in words and too little emphasis upon superiority in deeds and character.

Advance

A room of quiet . . . a temple of peace.
The home of faith . . . where doubtings cease.

A house of comfort . . . where hope is given;
A source of strength . . . to make earth
heaven.
A shrine of worship . . . a place to pray—
I found all this . . . in my church today.

Cyrus E. Albertson

He cannot have God for his father who refuses to have the church for his mother.

St. Augustine: *De Symbolo*

The church with no great anguish on its
heart has no great music on its lips.

Karl Barth

It is a law of human nature that the Church
should wish to do everything and be everything.

Charles Baudelaire

We must stop giving the impression that the
church is surrounded by a wall, fighting for
its existence against a world that is trying
to destroy it; instead, we must realize that
the church is a force pushing out into the
world.

Isaac K. Beckes

For commonly, wheresoever God buildeth a
church, the devil will build a chapel just by.

Thomas Becon: *Catechism*

The Church is not a gallery for the exhibition of eminent Christians, but a school for
the education of imperfect ones.

Henry Ward Beecher

It is always dangerous to go to church, for
there is always a chance that God's word will
break through the protecting shell Americans have built up.

Eugene Carson Blake

Unless there are people who are responding
to the love of God as revealed in Christ and
so are worshipping Him, the Church is not
very important.

Eugene Carson Blake

The Christian church does not need more
popular preaching, but more unpopular
preaching.

Walter Russell Bowie

The world is too strong for a divided church.

Charles H. Brent

The Church cannot be content to live in its
stained-glass house and throw stones thru
the picture windows of modern culture.

From *The Significance of the Church* by
Robert McAfee Brown. Copyright,
W. L. Jenkins. The Westminster
Press. Used by permission

They build not castles in the air who would
build churches on earth: and though they
leave no such structures here, may lay good
foundations in Heaven.

Sir Thomas Browne: *To a Friend*, sec. 23

Life treads on life, and heart on heart;
We press too close in church and mart
To keep a dream or grave apart.

Elizabeth Barrett Browning: *A Vision of
Poets. Conclusion*, l. 820

The Church that compromises Truth today
will compromise Morals tomorrow.

H. D. Bruce

The greatest sin of the church is that it holds
the gospel from itself and from the world.

Emil Brunner, The Westminster Press.
Used by permission

A church exists by mission as fire exists by
burning.

Ibid.

Persecution has not crushed the church;
power has not beaten it back; time has not
abated its forces; and what is most wonderful
of all, the abuses of its friends have not
shaken its stability.

Horace Bushnell

The church must be a very strong and righteous thing, for it has survived every enemy it ever had.

Eddie Cantor

We are ready to proclaim in Italy this principle. A free church in a free state.

Camillo Benso, Conte di Cavour: *Speech*

Man is a religious animal, and if he holds aloof from public worship he starves and stunts his highest instincts. If a man is to come to his full stature, he must come to it inside the church.

James W. Clarke: *Newsletter to Presbyterian Men*

An instinctive taste teaches men to build their churches in flat countries with spire-steeples, which, as they cannot be referred to any other object, point as with silent finger to the sky and stars.

Samuel Taylor Coleridge: *The Friend*, sec. 1, no. 14

Certainly, by every test but that of influence, the church has never been stronger. . . . Its membership is growing more rapidly than the population. The increase in wealth and in social activities is even more impressive. Never before has the church been materially more powerful, or spiritually less effective.

Henry Steele Commager: *The American Mind*

The Church consists principally of two parts, the one called Church triumphant, and the other the Church militant.

Council of Trent: *Catechism*, I

What is a church?—Our honest sexton tells, " 'Tis a tall building, with a tower and bells."

George Crabbe: *The Borough*

"What is a church?" Let truth and reason speak;
They would reply—"The faithful, pure and meek,

From Christian folds, the one selected race,
Of all professions, and in every place."

Ibid.

Wherever God erects a house of prayer,
The Devil always builds a chapel there;
And 'twill be found, upon examination,
The latter has the largest congregation.

Daniel Defoe: *The True-Born Englishman*

I love thy Church, O God!
Her walls before Thee stand,
Dear as the apple of Thine eye,
And graven on Thy hand.

Timothy Dwight

A church should be a power-house, where sluggish spirits can get recharged and re-animated.

Samuel A. Eliot

The multitude of false churches accredits the true religion.

Ralph Waldo Emerson: *Essays, Second Series: Nature*

If I should go out of church whenever I hear a false sentiment I could never stay there five minutes. But why come out? The street is as false as the church.

Ralph Waldo Emerson: *Essays, Second Series: New England Reformers*

Accepts the village church as part of the sky.

Ralph Waldo Emerson: *Journals*

Some people go to church to see who didn't.

Employment Counselor

The church is an anvil that has worn out many hammers.

English Proverb, not recorded before the 19th century

The church is the family of God. It is seen in miniature in each family.

John Ferguson: *Christian Faith for Today*

A good newspaper and Bible in every house, a good schoolhouse in every district, and a church in every neighborhood, all appreciated as they deserve, are the chief support of virtue, morality, civil liberty, and religion.

Benjamin Franklin

The church always defaces itself, it always denies God when it seeks to set itself apart from the world in which it exists; when it makes itself a place of refuge, a citadel with high walls inside of which men can hide; when it shuts doors to close out any part of the life of man.

Dr. Franklin Clark Fry: in address, "The Ministry of the Laity in Economic Life"

The church alone beyond all question,
Has for ill-gotten goods the right digestion.

Johann Wolfgang von Goethe:
Faust, Pt. I, sc. 9, l. 35

Leave the matter of religion to the family altar, the church, and the private school, supported entirely by private contributions. Keep the church and the State for ever separate.

Ulysses S. Grant: Speech at Des Moines,
Iowa

A Church to me is the symbol of faith in the life eternal; it typifies decency, kindliness and fair dealing; it offers comfort to the sorrowing. With the golden rule it would make neighbors of us all.

Edgar A. Guest

The Church of Christ is the world's only social hope and the sole promise of world peace.

Sir Douglas Haig

I think all churches are like the spokes of a wheel, all leading into the same goal.

Esther Hartman

The poorer the church, the purer the church.

William Hazlitt: English Proverbs

The chief trouble with the church is that you and I are in it.

Charles H. Heimsath: Sermons on the
Inner Life, Abingdon Press

The way to preserve the peace of the church is to preserve its purity.

Matthew Henry

Kneeling ne'er spoiled silk stocking: quit thy
state.
All equal are within the church's gate.

George Herbert: The Church-Porch, st. 68

When once thy foot enters the church, be
bare;
God is more there than thou.

Ibid.

Nothing last but the Church.

George Herbert: Jacula Prudentum

The nearer the church, the farther from God.

John Heywood: Proverbs, Pt. I, ch. 9

If you go to church, and like the singing better than the preaching that's not orthodox.

Edgar Watson Howe

A church is God between four walls.

Victor Hugo: Ninety-Three, Pt. II,
Bk. III, ch. 2

The only place a new hat can be carried into with safety is a church, for there is plenty of room there.

Leigh Hunt

There is little piety in big churches.

Italian Proverb

God bless the little church around the corner.

Joseph Jefferson, in George MacAdam:
The Little Church Around the
Corner

Campbell is a good man, a pious man. I am afraid he has not been in the inside of a church for many years, but he never passes a church without pulling off his hat. This shows that he has good principles.

Samuel Johnson

To be of no church is dangerous. Religion, of which the rewards are distant, and which is animated only by faith and hope, will glide by degrees out of the mind, unless it be invigorated and reimpressed by external ordinances and by stated calls to worship.

Samuel Johnson

God pity the nation whose factory chimneys rise higher than her church spires.

John Kelman

The Church cannot be restricted to the sanctuary. The Church isn't just a preaching Church, a sacramental Church, but is involved in the total life of the human being, which is another way of saying religion has implications in society.

Francis J. Lally: Interview with Mike Wallace, 1958

The average man goes to church six times a year and has attended Sunday School for two afternoons and can sing half a hymn.

Stephen Butler Leacock: *Winnowed Wisdom*

The Church does not die.

Legal Maxim

The Church is the mansion-house of the Omnipotent God.

Legal Maxim

The real unity of the church must not be organized, but exercised.

Johannes Lilje

Bless all the churches, and blessed be God, who, in this our great trial, giveth us the churches.

Abraham Lincoln

A minister addressing a conference of preachers said that too many of our churches are like "a middle-class solarium where tired old spiritual limbs are warmed a bit from week to week."

Halford E. Luccock: *Christian Herald*

It is impossible for the Christian and true church to subsist without the shedding of blood, for her adversary, the Devil, is a liar and a murderer. The church grows and increases through blood; she is sprinkled with blood.

Martin Luther: *Table Talk*

A church is disaffected when it is persecuted, quiet when it is tolerated, and actively loyal when it is favored and cherished.

Thomas Babington Macaulay: *Hallam*

A beggarly people. A church and no steeple.

Edmund Malone

If the growth of modern science has taught anything to religion and to the modern world, it is that the method of progress is the method of evolution, not the method of revolution. Let every man reflect well on these things before he assists in stabbing to death, or in allowing to starve to death, organized religion in the United States.

Robert Andrews Millikan: *Time, Matter, and Values*, The University of North Carolina Press, 1932

The Christian Church belongs to God and not to man; the church cannot become a tool of any social order, whether it be imperialist, capitalist, or communist.

Samuel Moffett: *Missions*

The difference between listening to a radio sermon and going to church, someone has said, is almost like the difference between calling your girl on the telephone and spending an evening with her.

Moody Monthly

When the early church fathers came together, they talked about their powers; when modern churchmen come together, they talk about their problems.

Arthur J. Moore

The Christian church is a society of sinners. It is the only society in the world, membership in which is based upon the single qualification that the candidate shall be unworthy of membership.

Charles Clayton Morrison: *What Is Christianity?*, Harper & Row, Publishers, Inc.

Burned but not consumed.

Motto of the Church of Scotland

The church is not to be judged by the frailties or failures of its members. The Church is to be judged for what it can do for a person, and what it offers in its ideals, its resources, and not by those who have let the church down.

Robert Boyd Munger: *What Jesus Says*

As, like a church and an ale-house, God and the Devil they many times dwell near to either.

Thomas Nashe: *Have with You to Saffron-Walden*

And I say also unto thee, That thou art Peter, and upon this rock I will build my church; and the gates of hell shall not prevail against it.

New Testament: Matthew 16: 18

Feed the church of God, which he hath purchased with his own blood.

New Testament: Acts 20: 28

Other foundation can no man lay than that is laid, which is Jesus Christ.

New Testament: I Corinthians 3: 11

Christ . . . loved the church, and gave himself for it; That he might sanctify and cleanse it with the washing of water by the word, That he might present it to himself a glorious church, not having spot, or wrinkle, or any such thing; but that it should be holy and without blemish.

New Testament: Ephesians 5: 25b–27

Our business is not to do something *for* the church, but to do something *with* it.

Joseph Fort Newton

How amiable are thy tabernacles, O Lord of hosts!
Blessed are they that dwell in thy house . . .
I had rather be a doorkeeper in the house of my God,
Than to dwell in the tents of wickedness.

Old Testament: Psalms 84: 1, 4, 10

I was glad when they said unto me,
Let us go into the house of the Lord.

Old Testament: Psalms 122: 1

Without the church no one is saved.

Origen: *De Principiis*

The adulterous connection of church and state.

Thomas Paine: *The Age of Reason*

The world does not take the church seriously because the church is not serious. The world is suing us for divorce because of nonsupport. Religion is more complicated than mathematics.

Paul Calvin Payne

It were better to be of no church than to be bitter for any.

William Penn

We must revolutionize ourselves as a church and get down where the people live. And we must realize that there is no longer such a thing as a Christian West. Can we deny that our god and our idol is our standard of living?

James A. Pike

Christians for decades have been singing, "Like a Mighty Army Moves the Church of God." This is still poetic fancy.

Daniel A. Poling

I ought to join the church because I ought to be better than I am.

Daniel A. Poling: *The Call of the Church*

Some to church repair
Not for the doctrine, but the music there.

Alexander Pope: *Essay on Criticism*, Pt. II, l. 142

Who builds a church to God, and not to
fame,
Will never mark the marble with his name.
> Alexander Pope: *Moral Essays*, Epis. III,
> l. 285

Who taught that heaven-directed spire to
rise?
> Alexander Pope: *Moral Essays*, Epis. III,
> l. 261

Many come to bring their clothes to church
rather than themselves.
> Proverb

The business of the Christian Church is to
lead men up and up. If she persists in saying
that religion only (in its narrow sense) is
her business, men of sense and sympathy will
leave her.
> William S. Rainsford

Go tell the Church it shows
What's good, and doth no good.
> Sir Walter Raleigh: *The Lie*

Our houses of worship have become places
for the social climbers and our congregations
have become just crowds, like the patrons of
a movie theater. . . . The church should be
a chamber of commerce in reverse and point
up what is wrong in a community. The great
sin of the church is to be so interested in
serving those within it that it cannot serve
the needs of those without.
> Albert T. Rasmussen: *Christian Social
> Ethics*, © 1956 Prentice-Hall

The church is with her back to the wall, you
would think, to hear many church folks talk.
But I think she has her face to the weeping
wall when really she ought to have her back
to the wall and her face toward God.
> W. Quay Rossell

The church has lower standards for membership than those for getting on a bus.
> Harry R. Rudin: *Christian Century*,
> June 4, 1952, p. 665

A Christian church is a body or collection
of persons, voluntarily associated together,
professing to believe what Christ teaches,
to do what Christ enjoins, to imitate his
example, cherish his spirit, and make known
his gospel to others.
> Robert Fleming Sample

If to do were as easy as to know what were
good to do, chapels had been churches, and
poor men's cottages princes' palaces.
> William Shakespeare: *The Merchant of
> Venice*, Act I, sc. 2, l. 13

An I have not forgotten what the inside of
a church is made of, I am a peppercorn.
> William Shakespeare: *Henry IV,
> Part I*, Act III, sc. 3, l. 9

The Churches must learn humility as well
as teach it.
> George Bernard Shaw: *Saint Joan:
> Preface*

If the Christian Church were a pillar of fire
leading the peoples of the world, instead of
an ambulance corps bringing up the rear as
it so often seems to be, communism probably
would never have been born.
> Helen Shoemaker: *The Secret of
> Effective Prayer*

A sparrow fluttering about the church is
an antagonist which the most profound
theologian in Europe is wholly unable to
overcome.
> Sydney Smith

The holiest moment of the church service is
the moment when God's people—strengthened by preaching and sacrament—go out
of the church door into the world *to be the
Church*. We don't *go* to church; we *are* the
Church.
> Ernest Southcott: quoted in *Christian
> Herald*

The church should be the Society of the Forgiven and Forgiving.

William George Spencer

We cannot be good churchmen and bad citizens. Nor can we ever be good citizens and bad churchmen.

A. Steimle

I never weary of great churches. It is my favourite kind of mountain scenery. Mankind was never so happily inspired as when it made a cathedral.

Robert Louis Stevenson: *An Island Voyage*

Went to church today, and was not greatly depressed.

Robert Louis Stevenson: *Journal*

The bars of the church are sometimes so low that any old hog with two or three suits of clothes and a bankroll can crawl through.

W. A. ("Billy") Sunday

Love your enemy, bless your haters,
  said the Greatest of the great;
Christian love among the Churches,
  looked the twin of heathen hate.

Alfred, Lord Tennyson: *Locksley Hall Sixty Years After*

The churches have killed their Christ.

Alfred, Lord Tennyson: *Maud*

Where three are gathered together, there is a church, even though they be laymen.

Tertullian

Churches: Soulariums.

P. K. Thomajan: *Phoenix Flame*

The Church is a religious home, a sanctuary for worship, a school for religious instruction, a fighting unit for the new world that is building. It is a social center of the highest type, since it gathers into relations of mutual helpfulness people of every age and condition, and since it adds to the attractions of the ordinary club the power of religion and the generous sympathies of the altruistic impulse. The Church is the most broadening and catholic organization among men, since its vision is to the ends of the world whither the gospel is being carried, and since its citizenship is in heaven as well as in the earth.

Worth M. Tippy

The primary duty of the church is to *be* the Christian community.

Willem Adolf Visser T'Hooft: *None Other Gods*, Harper & Row, Publishers Inc.

See the Gospel Church secure,
  And founded on a Rock!
All her promises are sure;
  Her bulwarks who can shock?

Charles Wesley: *The Church*, st. 9

The itch of disputation will prove the scab of the Church.

Sir Henry Wotton: *Panegyric to King Charles*

To some people religious freedom means the choice of churches which they may stay away from.

York Trade Compositor

How the tall temples, as to meet their gods, Ascend the skies!

Edward Young: *Night Thoughts; Night VI, l. 781*

CONFESSION

Open confession, open penance.

Robert Armin: *A Nest of Ninnies*

Confession of sin comes from the offer of mercy. Mercy displayed causes confession to flow, and confession flowing opens the way to mercy. If I have not a contrite heart, God's mercy will never be mine; but if God had not manifested His mercy in Christ, I could never have a contrite heart.

William D. Arnot

The confession of evil works is the first beginning of good works.
St. Augustine

Confess your sins to one another.
The Venerable Bede: *Commentary on the Epistle of James*

Confess your sins to the Lord and you will be forgiven: confess them to man and you will be laughed at.
Josh Billings

The Scripture moveth us, in sundry places to acknowledge and confess our manifold sins and wickedness.
Book of Common Prayer: Morning Prayer

Full sweetly heard he confession,
And pleasant was his absolution.
Geoffrey Chaucer: *Canterbury Tales: Prologue*

Come, now again thy woes impart,
Tell all thy sorrows, all thy sin;
We cannot heal the throbbing heart,
Till we discern the wounds within.
George Crabbe: *The Hall of Justice, Pt. II, l. 1*

There are two confessionals, in one or the other of which we must be shriven.
Ralph Waldo Emerson: *Essays, First Series: Self-Reliance*

Confession is the first step to repentance.
English Proverb

It is an abuse to confess any kind of sin, whether mortal or venial, without a will to be delivered from it, since confession was instituted for no other end.
St. Francis de Sales: *Introduction to the Devout Life, XIX*

Of all unhappy sinners, I'm the most unhappy one!

The padre said, "Whatever have you been and gone and done?"
Sir William Schwenk Gilbert: *Gentle Alice Brown*

A general confession is good, but in it lurks the danger of "acknowledging and bewailing" humanity's sins and not our own.
Georgia Harkness: *Religious Living* (A Reflection Book), Association Press

Deceive not thy physician, confessor, nor lawyer.
George Herbert: *Jacula Prudentum*

People think the confessional is unknown in Protestant churches. It is a great mistake. The principal change is, that there is no screen between the penitent and the father confessor.
Oliver Wendell Holmes, Sr.: *The Guardian Angel*, XIII

Open confession is good for the soul.
James Kelly: *Complete Collection of Scottish Proverbs*

It is the duty of nations as well as of men to confess their sins and transgressions in humble sorrow, yet with assured hope that genuine repentance will lead to mercy and pardon.
Abraham Lincoln: Proclamation, March 30, 1863

Under seal of the confessional.
Medieval Latin Phrase

They shall confess their sin which they have done.
Old Testament: Numbers 5: 7

He's half absolv'd who has confessed.
Matthew Prior: *Alma*, Canto II, l. 22

Confess yourself to heaven;
Repent what's past; avoid what's to come.
William Shakespeare: *Hamlet, Act III, sc. 4, l. 149*

It is the confession, not the priest, that gives absolution.

Oscar Wilde

CONSCIENCE

When you have taken out your conscience and turned it over to Christ you cannot do with your conscience what you will.

Anonymous

Conscience is condensed character.

Anonymous

A bad conscience embitters the sweetest comforts; a good one sweetens the bitterest crosses.

Anonymous

It is a beautiful idea that every man has within a Guardian Angel; and that it is true, too, for Conscience is ever on the watch, ever ready to warn us of danger.

Anonymous

It is not difficult to get away into retirement, and there live upon your own conviction; nor is it difficult to mix with men and follow their convictions; but to enter into the world, and there live firmly and fearlessly according to your own conscience, that is Christian greatness.

Anonymous

A good conscience is the palace of Christ; the temple of the Holy Ghost; the paradise of delight, the standing Sabbath of the saints.

St. Augustine

Conscience and reputation are two things. Conscience is due to yourself, reputation to your neighbor.

St. Augustine: *Works,* Vol. XXI

Conscience is the perfect interpreter of life.

Karl Barth: *The Word of God and the Word of Man* translated by Douglas Horton, Harper & Row, Publishers, Inc.

Conscience is God's vicegerent on earth, and, within the limited jurisdiction given to it, it partakes of his infinite wisdom and speaks in his tone of absolute command. It is a revelation of the being of a God, a divine voice in the human soul, making known the presence of its rightful sovereign, the author of the law of holiness and truth.

Francis Bowen

The great beacon light God sets in all,
The conscience of each bosom.

Robert Browning: *Strafford,* Act IV, sc. 2

Those whom God forsakes, the devil by his permission lays hold on. Sometimes he persecutes them, with that worm of conscience, as he did Judas, Saul, and others. The poets call it Nemesis.

Robert Burton: *Anatomy of Melancholy,* Pt. III, sec. 4, mem. 2, subs. 3

It is astonishing how soon the whole conscience begins to unravel if a single stitch drops.—One single sin indulged in makes a hole you could put your head through.

Charles Buxton

Yet still there whispers the small voice within,
Heard through Gain's silence, and o'er Glory's din;
Whatever creed be taught or land be trod,
Man's conscience is the oracle of God.

George Gordon, Lord Byron: *The Island,* Canto I, st. 6

A sleeping pill will never take the place of a clear conscience.

Eddie Cantor

To endeavour to domineer over conscience, is to invade the citadel of heaven.

Charles V

The still small voice.

William Cowper: *The Task,* V

No hell like a bad conscience.

John Crowne: *The Ambitious Statesman,* Act V, sc. 3

Conscience is merely our own judgment of the right or wrong of our actions, and so can never be a safe guide unless enlightened by the word of God.

Tryon Edwards

A good conscience is a continual Christmas.

Benjamin Franklin: *Poor Richard*

Conscience, true as the needle to the pole points steadily to the pole-star of God's eternal justice, reminding the soul of the fearful realities of the life to come.

Ezra Hall Gillett

The church is the only conscience the government has. When a church is silent, the state can have no conscience.

Edward W. Grant

There is always a voice saying the right thing to you somewhere, if you'll only listen for it.

Thomas Hughes

There is a spectacle more grand than the sea; it is heaven; there is a spectacle more grand than heaven; it is the conscience.

Victor Hugo: *Les Misérables: Fantine,*
Bk. VII, ch. 3

Every man, however good, has a yet better man within him. When the outer man is unfaithful to his deeper convictions, the hidden man whispers a protest. The name of this whisper in the soul is conscience.

Friedrich Heinrich Alexander Von
Humboldt

Churches come and go, but there has ever been but one religion. The only religion is conscience in action.

Henry Demarest Lloyd

In vain we call old notions fudge,
    And bend our conscience to our dealing;
The Ten Commandments will not budge,
    And stealing *will* continue stealing.

James Russell Lowell

Conscience is a God to all mortals.

Menander: *Monostikoi*, no. 564

Conscience is a walkie-talkie set by which God speaks to us.

James J. Metcalf: *The Expositor*

Help us to save free conscience from the paw
Of hireling wolves, whose gospel is their maw.

John Milton: *Sonnet: To Cromwell*

Conscience, the bosom-hell of guilty man!

James Montgomery: *Pelican Island,*
Canto V, l. 127

Conscience is the true vicar of Christ in the soul; a prophet in its information; a monarch in its peremptoriness; a priest in its blessings or anathemas, according as we obey or disobey it.

Cardinal John Henry Newman

Herein do I exercise myself, to have always a conscience void of offence toward God, and toward men.

New Testament: Acts 24: 16

The wicked flee when no man pursueth.

Old Testament: Proverbs 28: 1

I owe my conscience to no mortal man.

William Penn

Conscience has nothing to do as law-giver or judge, but is a witness against me if I do wrong, and which approves if I do right.—To act against conscience is to act against reason and God's law.

Austin Phelps

What Conscience dictates to be done,
    Or warns me not to do;
This teach me more than Hell to shun,
    That more than Heav'n pursue.

Alexander Pope: *Universal Prayer*

Cowardice asks, Is it safe? Expediency asks, Is it politic? Vanity asks, Is it popular? but Conscience asks, Is it right?

William Morley Punshon

Conscience is the voice of the soul, the passions are the voice of the body.

Jean Jacques Rousseau: *Emile,* Bk. IV

The worm of conscience consorts with the owl.
Sinners and evil spirits shun the light.

Johann Christoph Friedrich von Schiller:
Kabale und Liebe, Act V, sc. 1

Live with men as if God saw you; converse with God as if men heard you.

Seneca: *Epistolae Ad Lucilium*

Thus conscience does make cowards of us all.

William Shakespeare: *Hamlet,*
Act III, sc. 1, l. 83

I know thou art religious,
And hast a thing within thee called conscience,
With twenty popish tricks and ceremonies,
Which I have seen thee careful to observe.

William Shakespeare: *Titus Andronicus,*
Act V, sc. 1, l. 74

My conscience is my crown,
Contented thoughts my rest;
My heart is happy in itself;
My bliss is in my breast.

Robert Southwell: *Content and Rich*

And I know of the future judgment
How dreadful so'er it be
That to sit alone with my conscience
Would be judgment enough for me.

Charles William Stubbs: *Alone with
my Conscience*

Conscience is that still, small voice
That quells a wicked thought
Then adds this sequence,
'Besides, you might get caught.'

Supervision

Conscience is God's presence in man.

Emanuel Swedenborg: *Arcana Coelestia,*
sec. 4299

Liberty of conscience is nowadays not only understood to be the liberty of believing

what men please, but also of endeavoring to propagate that belief as much as they can.

Jonathan Swift: *Sermon on the
Testimony of Conscience*

There is a difference between him who does no misdeeds because of his own conscience and him who is kept from wrong-doing because of the presence of others.

The Talmud

He will easily be content and at peace whose conscience is pure.

Thomas à Kempis

Conscience tells us that we ought to do right, but it does not tell us what right is—that we are taught by God's word.

Henry Clay Trumbull

Labor to keep alive in your breast that little spark of celestial fire, called Conscience.

George Washington: *Moral Maxims:
Conscience*

A conscience void of offence before God and man is an inheritance for eternity.

Daniel Webster

CONSECRATION

Consecration is not wrapping one's self in a holy web in the sanctuary and then coming forth after prayer and twilight meditation and saying, "There, I am consecrated." Consecration is going out into the world where God Almighty is and using every power for his glory. It is taking all advantages as trust funds—as confidential debts owed to God. It is simply dedicating one's life, in its whole flow, to God's service.

Henry Ward Beecher

Our reservations are the damnation of our consecrations.

General William Booth

It does not take great men to do great things; it only takes consecrated men.

Phillips Brooks

A picket frozen on duty—
   A mother starved for her brood—
Socrates drinking the hemlock,
   And Jesus on the rood;
And millions who, humble and nameless,
   The straight, hard pathway trod—
Some call it Consecration,
   And others call it God.

> William Herbert Carruth: *Each in His*
> *Own Tongue*

Loyalty that will do anything, that will endure anything, that will make the whole being consecrate to Him, is what Christ wants. Anything else is not worthy of Him.

> Burdett Hart

Take my life, and let it be
Consecrated, Lord, to Thee . . .
Take my hands, and let them move
At the impulse of Thy love.

> Frances Ridley Havergal

From henceforth thou shalt learn that there
   is love
To long for, pureness to desire, a mount
Of consecration it were good to scale.

> Jean Ingelow: *A Parson's Letter to*
> *a Young Poet*, Pt. II, l. 55

Consecration is handing God a blank sheet to fill in with your name signed at the bottom.

> M. H. Miller

My body, soul and spirit thus redeemed,
Sanctified and healed I give, O Lord, to
   Thee,
A consecrated offering, Thine evermore to
   be.
That all my powers with all their might
In thy sole glory may unite.

> Henry Wilson

The light that never was, on sea or land,
The consecration, and the Poet's dream.

> William Wordsworth: *Elegiac Stanzas,*
> *Suggested by a Picture of Peele Castle*
> *in a Storm*, l. 15

The consecrated, one-talent man or woman has promise of a larger influence than any intellectual genius who has not met the Master.

> Samuel M. Zwemer

CONTENTMENT

A contented mind is the greatest blessing a man can enjoy in this world; and if, in the present life, his happiness arises from the subduing of his desires, it will rise to the next from the gratification of them.

> Joseph Addison

Contentment is a pearl of great price, and whoever procures it at the expense of ten thousand desires makes a wise and a happy purchase.

> John Balguy

There is a sense in which a man looking at the present in the light of the future, and taking his whole being into account, may be contented with his lot: that is Christian contentment.—But if a man has come to that point where he is so content that he says, "I do not want to know any more, or do any more, or be any more," he is in a state in which he ought to be changed into a mummy!

> Henry Ward Beecher

I was too ambitious in my deed,
And thought to distance all men in success,
Till God came to me, marked the place, and
   said,
"Ill doer, henceforth keep within this line,
Attempting less than others"—and I stand
And work among Christ's little ones, content.

> Elizabeth Barrett Browning: *Content*
> *in Service*

God hath made none (that all might be) contented.

> George Chapman: *The Tears of Peace,*
> l. 370

We'll therefore relish with content,
Whate'er kind Providence has sent,
   Nor aim beyond our pow'r;

For, if our stock be very small,
'Tis prudent to enjoy it all,
Nor lose the present hour.
Nathaniel Cotton: *The Fireside,* st. 10

I am always content with what happens; for
I know that what God chooses is better than
what I choose.
Epictetus

Resign every forbidden joy; restrain every
wish that is not referred to God's will; banish
all eager desires, all anxiety; desire only the
will of God; seek him alone and supremely,
and you will find peace.
François de Salignac de La Mothe
Fénelon

An ounce of contentment is worth a pound
of sadness, to serve God with.
Thomas Fuller

Contentment consisteth not in adding more
fuel, but in taking away some fire; not in
multiplying of wealth, but in subtracting
men's desires.
Thomas Fuller: *The Holy State*

My God, give me neither poverty nor riches,
but whatsoever it may be the will to give,
give me, with it, a heart that knows humbly
to acquiesce in what is thy will.
Gotthold (Christian Scriver)

Whatever comes, let's be content withall:
Among God's blessings there is no one small.
Robert Herrick: *Welcome What Comes*

It is right to be contented with what we have,
but never with what we are.
Sir James Mackintosh

They that deserve nothing should be content
with anything. Bless God for what you have,
and trust God for what you want. If we cannot bring our condition to our mind, we
must bring our mind to our condition; if a
man is not content in the state he is in, he
will not be content in the state he would
be in.
Erskine Mason

I have learned, in whatsoever state I am,
therewith to be content.
New Testament: Philippians 4: 11

Be content with such things as ye have.
New Testament: Hebrews 13: 5

My cup runneth over.
Old Testament: Psalms 23: 5

If you are wise, be wise; keep what goods the
gods provide you.
Titus Maccius Plautus: *Rudens,* Act IV,
sc. 7, l. 1229

I earn that I eat, get that I wear, owe no man
hate, envy no man's happiness; glad of other
men's good, content with my harm.
William Shakespeare: *As You Like It,*
Act III, sc. 2, l. 77

Then be content, poor heart!
God's plans, like lilies pure and white, un-
fold:
We must not tear the close-shut leaves
apart—
Time will reveal the calyxes of gold!
May Louise Riley Smith: *Sometime*

No chance is evil to him that is content.
Jeremy Taylor: *Holy Living:
Of Contentedness*

Submission is the only reasoning between a
creature and its maker and contentment in
his will is the best remedy we can apply to
misfortunes.
Sir William Temple

Dear little head, that lies in calm content
Within the gracious hollow that God
made
In every human shoulder, where He meant
Some tired head for comfort should be
laid.
Celia Laighton Thaxter: *Song*

An elegant, Sufficiency, Content,
Retirement, rural Quiet, Friendship, Books,
Ease and alternate Labor, useful Life,
Progressive Virtue, and approving Heaven!
James Thomson: *Seasons. Spring,* i. 1159

There is a jewel which no Indian mines can
    buy,
  No chymic art can counterfeit;
It makes men rich in greatest poverty,
    Makes water wine; turns wooden cups to
    gold;
  The homely whistle to sweet music's
    strain,
Seldom it comes;—to few from Heaven sent,
That much in little, all in naught, *Content.*

      John Wilbye: *Madrigales. There Is
      a Jewel*

CONVERSION

Conversion is no repairing of the old building; but it takes all down and erects a new
structure. The sincere Christian is quite a
new fabric, from the foundation to the top-
stone all new.

      Joseph Alleine

Conversion is a deep work—a heart-work. It
goes throughout the man, throughout the
mind, throughout the members, throughout
the entire life.

      Joseph Alleine

Where there is a sound conversion, then a
man is wholly given unto God, body, soul,
and spirit. He regards not sin in his heart,
but hath a respect to all God's commandments.

      Robert Bolton

Conversion is but the first step in the divine
life.—As long as we live we should more and
more be turning from all that is evil, and to
all that is good.

      Tryon Edwards

As to the value of conversions, God can only
judge.—He alone can know how wide are
the steps which the soul has to take before
it can approach to a community with him,
to the dwelling of the perfect, or to the intercourse and friendship of higher natures.

      Johann Wolfgang von Goethe

A man who is converted from Protestantism
to popery parts with nothing; he is only
superadding to what he already had. But a
convert from popery to Protestanism gives
up as much of what he has held sacred as
anything that he retains.

      Samuel Johnson

The time when I was converted was when
religion became no longer a mere duty, but
a pleasure.

      John L. Lincoln

To go through life without ever being
converted to anything seems a mark of in-
sensitiveness. The ideal world would be a
world in which everybody was capable of
conversion and in which at the same time
the converts would admit the possibility that
they might be mistaken.

      Robert Lynd

Except ye be converted, and become as little
children, ye shall not enter into the kingdom
of heaven.

      New Testament: Matthew 18: 3

Men often take their imagination for their
heart; and they believe they are converted
as soon as they think of being converted.

      Blaise Pascal

I went to America to convert the Indians;
now who will convert me?

      John Wesley

COVETOUSNESS

Nothing lies on our hands with such uneasiness as time. Wretched and thoughtless
creatures! In the only place where covetousness were a virtue we turn prodigals.

      Joseph Addison

After hypocrites, the greatest dupes the devil
has are those who exhaust an anxious existence in the disappointments and vexations
of business, and live miserably and meanly
only to die magnificently and rich.—They

serve the devil without receiving his wages, and for the empty foolery of dying rich, pay down their health, happiness, and integrity.

Charles Caleb Colton

When all sins are old in us and go upon crutches, covetousness does but then lie in her cradle.

Thomas Dekker

A covetous man does nothing well till he dies.

Thomas Fuller: *Gnomologia*, no. 51

The covetous man never has money; the prodigal will have none shortly.

Ben Jonson

Take heed, and beware of covetousness: for a man's life consisteth not in the abundance of the things which he possesseth.

New Testament: Luke 12: 15

Thou shall not covet thy neighbour's house, thou shalt not covet thy neighbour's wife, nor his manservant, nor his maidservant, nor his ox, nor his ass, nor any thing that is thy neighbour's.

Old Testament: Exodus 20: 17

Abundance consists not so much in material possessions, but in an uncovetous spirit.

John Selden

Desire of having is the sin of covetousness.

William Shakespeare

I am not covetous for gold,
Nor care I who doth feed upon my cost;
It yearns me not if men my garments wear;
Such outward things dwell not in my desires:
But if it be a sin to covet honour,
I am the most offending soul alive.

William Shakespeare: *Henry V*,
Act IV, sc. 3, l. 24

Covetousness is both the beginning and end of the devil's alphabet—the first vice in corrupt nature that moves, and the last which dies.

Robert South

Covetousness is the root of all evil, the ground of all vice.

Leonard Wright: *Display of Dutie*, X

I have heard thousands of confessions, but never one of covetousness.

St. Francis Xavier

CREED, CREEDS

Faithfully faithful to every trust,
  Honestly honest in every deed,
Righteously righteous and justly just;
  This is the whole of the good man's
    creed.

Anonymous

Thou waitest for the spark from heaven!
  and we,
Light half-believers in our casual creeds . . .
Who hesitate and falter life away,
And lose tomorrow the ground won today.

Matthew Arnold: *The Scholar Gypsy*,
st. 18

Brother, the creed would stifle me
That shelters you.

Karle Wilson Baker: *Creeds*, st. 2

The best creed we can have is charity toward the creeds of others.

Josh Billings

Think truly, and thy thoughts
  Shall the world's famine feed.
Speak truly, and each word of thine
  Shall be a fruitful seed.
Live truly, and thy life shall be
  A great and noble creed.

Horatius Bonar: *Hymns of Faith and
Hope*, p. 113

If you have a Bible creed, it is well; but is it filled out and inspired by Christian love?

J. F. Brodie

Where I may see saint, savage, sage,
Fuse their respective creeds in one,
Before the general Father's throne.

> Robert Browning: *Christmas Eve,*
> Pt. XIX

Sapping a solemn creed with solemn sneer.

> George Gordon, Lord Byron: *Childe*
> *Harold's Pilgrimage,* Canto III,
> st. 107

I speak not of men's creeds—they rest between
Man and his Maker.

> George Gordon, Lord Byron: *Childe*
> *Harold's Pilgrimage,* Canto IV,
> st. 95

In politics, as in religion, we have less charity for those who believe the half of our creed, than for those who deny the whole of it.

> Charles Caleb Colton

A good creed is a gate to the city that hath foundations; a misleading creed may be a road to destruction, or if both misleading and alluring it may become what Shakespeare calls a primrose path to the eternal bonfire.

> Joseph Cook

The Athanasian Creed is the most splendid ecclesiastical lyric ever poured forth by the genius of man.

> Benjamin Disraeli: *Endymion,* ch. 52

There you will find what
        Every man needs,
Wild religion
        Without any creeds.

> Louise Driscoll: *Spring Market,* st. 5

Go put your creed into your deed,
Nor speak with double tongue.

> Ralph Waldo Emerson: *Ode,* st. 5

Uncursed by doubt our earliest creed we take;
We love the precepts for the teacher's sake.

> Oliver Wendell Holmes, Sr.: *A Rhymed*
> *Lesson,* l. 191

He knew
Behind all creeds the Spirit is One.

> Andrew Lang: "Herodotus in Egypt,"
> *The Poetical Works of Andrew*
> *Lang,* Longmans, Green & Co. Ltd.

Righteousness is nonsectarian. No man's creed is wrong whose deed is right.

> Gotthold Ephraim Lessing

The weakest part of a man's creed is that which he holds for himself alone; the strongest is that which he holds in common with all Christendom.

> John McVickar

Shall I ask the brave soldier, who fights by my side
In the cause of mankind, if our creeds agree?

> Thomas Moore: *Come, Send Round*
> *the Wine,* st. 2

What is fanaticism today is the fashionable creed tomorrow, and trite as the multiplication table a week after.

> Wendell Phillips

We have a Calvinistic creed, a Popish liturgy, and an Arminian clergy.

> William Pitt: See *Prior's Life of Burke,*
> ch. 10

Necessity is the argument of tyrants; it is the creed of slaves.

> William Pitt: *Speech on the India Bill*

At the muezzin's call for prayer,
The kneeling faithful thronged the square,
And on Pushkara's lofty height
The dark priest chanted Brahma's might.
Amid a monastery's weeds
An old Franciscan told his beads;
While to the synagogue there came
A Jew to praise Jehovah's name.
The one great God looked down and smiled
And counted each His loving child;
For Turk and Brahmin, monk and Jew
Had reached Him through the gods they knew.

> Harry Romaine: "Ad Caelum" (*Munsey's*
> *Magazine*), January, 1895

91

So at the end of the long journey I have come
to this: the first article of my creed is that I
am a moral personality under orders.

William L. Sullivan

A creed is a rod,
   And a crown is of night;
But this thing is God,
   To be man with thy might,
To grow straight in the strength of thy spirit,
   and to live out thy life as the light.

Algernon Charles Swinburne: Hertha,
st. 15

And so the Word had breath, and wrought
   With human hands the creed of creeds
   In loveliness of perfect deeds,
More strong than all poetic thought.

Alfred, Lord Tennyson: In Memoriam

The Shadow cloak'd from head to foot,
Who keeps the keys of all the creeds.

Ibid.

There lives more faith in honest doubt,
Believe me, than in half the creeds.

Ibid.

Truth has never been, can never be, contained in any one creed.

Mary Augusta Ward: Robert Elsmere,
Bk. VI, ch. 38

Human hopes and human creeds
Have their root in human needs.

Eugene Fitch Ware: The Rhymes of
Ironquill. Preface. © 1940 by
G. P. Putnam's Sons

How pitiful are little folk—
   They seem so very small;
They look at stars, and think they are
   Denominational.

Willard Austin Wattles: Creeds, from the
book Lanterns in Gethsemane by
Willard Wattles. Copyright, 1918,
by E. P. Dutton & Co., Inc. Re-
printed by permission of the
publisher

The only creed that is worth twopence to
you is not a creed that you tried to take over
from your grandfather. The only creed that
is going to be worth anything to you is the
creed you built up out of your own experience of Christ. Start with the friendship and
let your creed make itself.

Leslie D. Weatherhead: Jesus and
Ourselves, Abingdon Press

Creeds and schools in abeyance.

Walt Whitman: Song of Myself, I

The world has a thousand creeds, and never
   a one have I;
Nor church of my own, though a million
   spires are pointing the way on high.
But I float on the bosom of faith, that bears
   me along like a river;
And the lamp of my soul is alight with love,
   for life, and the world, and the Giver.

Ella Wheeler Wilcox: Heresy,
Rand McNally & Co.

Great God! I'd rather be
A Pagan suckled in a creed outworn;
So might I, standing on this pleasant lea,
Have glimpses that would make me less for-
   lorn;
Have sight of Proteus rising from the sea;
Or hear old Triton blow his wreathed horn.

William Wordsworth: The World
Is Too Much With Us

THE CROSS, CROSSES

The cross is "I" crossed out.

Anonymous

We bring the atoms of sin to the cross where
they are smashed.

Anonymous

If o'er the dial glides a shade, redeem
The time for lo! it passes like a dream:

But if 'tis all a blank, than mark the loss
Of hours unblest by shadows from the cross.

> On a Sun Dial in a churchyard at
> Shenstone, England

To repel one's cross is to make it heavier.

> Henri Frédéric Amiel

Onward, Christian soldiers,
  Marching as to war,
With the Cross of Jesus
  Going on before.

> Sabine Baring-Gould: *Onward,*
> *Christian Soldiers*

The cross is the only ladder high enough to touch Heaven's threshold.

> George Dana Boardman

You shall not press down upon the brow of labor this crown of thorns—you shall not crucify mankind upon a cross of gold!

> William Jennings Bryan

Behind the cross there's the devil.

> Miguel de Cervantes: *Don Quixote,*
> Pt. I, ch. 6

Through this sign thou shalt conquer.

> Constantine the Great

The Cross!
There, and there only (though the deist rave,
And atheist, if Earth bears so base a slave);
There and there only, is the power to save.

> William Cowper: *The Progress*
> *of Error,* l. 613

The cross is the ladder of heaven.

> Thomas Draxe: *Biblioth, Scholas,*
> Instr. 36

There is no comma after cross; the cross is a continuous affair.

> Evert F. Ellis

No cross, no crown.

> English Proverb

The greatest of all crosses is self—If we die in part every day, we shall have but little to do on the last.—These little daily deaths will destroy the power of the final dying.

> François de Salignac de La Mothe
> Fénelon

The cross on the breast and the devil in the heart.

> Thomas Fuller: *Gnomologia,*
> no. 4462

In the Cross, God descends to bear in his own heart the sins of the world. In Jesus, he atones at unimaginable cost to himself.

> Woodrow A. Geier: *Religion in Life*

We do not attach any intrinsic value to the Cross; this would be sinful and idolatrous. Our veneration is referred to Him who died upon it.

> James, Cardinal Gibbons: *The Faith*
> *of our Fathers*

Though good things answer many good
  intents,
Crosses do still bring forth the best events.

> Robert Herrick: *Crosses*

Sorrows our portion are: ere hence we go,
Crosses we must have; or, hereafter, woe.

> Robert Herrick: *Sorrows*

By the Cross, on which suspended,
With his bleeding hands extended,
  Hung that Son she so adored,
Stood the mournful Mother weeping,
She whose heart, its silence keeping,
  Grief had cleft as with a sword.

> Jacapone da Todi: *Stabat Mater*

Many commit the same crime with a very different result. One bears a cross for his crime; another a crown.

> Juvenal: *Satires,* XIII, 103

Golgotha is dreadfully real: as real as suffering, as real as hard work and sacrifice, as real as failure, as real as persecution.

> V. A. Kraft

Jesus Christ is risen today,
Our triumphant holy day;
Who did once upon the cross
Suffer to redeem our loss.
  Hallelujah!

Jesus Christ is Risen Today
(from a Latin hymn)

They, the holy ones and weakly,
  Who the cross of suffering bore,
Folded their pale hands so meekly,
  Spake with us on earth no more!

Henry Wadsworth Longfellow:
Footsteps of Angels, st. 5

No man ought to lay a cross upon himself, or to adopt tribulation, as is done in popedom; but if a cross or tribulation come upon him, then let him suffer it patiently, and know that it is good and profitable for him.

Martin Luther: *Table Talk*

The cross has been carried forward on the hilt of the sword.

E. M. Macdonald: *The Truth Seeker*

The way of the Cross is the way of light.

Medieval Latin Proverb

Every bird that upwards swings
Bears the Cross upon its wings.

John Mason Neale

He that taketh not his cross, and followeth after me, is not worthy of me.

*New Testament: Matthew 10: 38;
Luke 14: 27*

Whosoever will come after me, let him deny himself, and take up his cross, and follow me.

*New Testament: Mark 8: 34;
Matthew 16: 24; Luke 9: 23*

But God forbid that I should glory, save in the cross of our Lord Jesus Christ.

New Testament: Galatians 6: 14

The cross is central. It is struck into the middle of the world, into the middle of time, into the middle of destiny. The cross is struck into the heart of God.

Frederick W. Norwood: *Today is Mine,*
T. C. Clark, ed., Harper & Row,
Publishers, Inc.

It may take a crucified church to bring a crucified Christ before the eyes of the world.

W. E. Orchard: *The Temple*, E. P.
Dutton & Co., Inc. and J. M. Dent
& Sons, Ltd.

The way to bliss lies not on beds of down,
And he that has no cross deserves no crown.

Francis Quarles: *Esther*

We go to Calvary to learn how we may be forgiven, and to learn how to forgive others, to intercede on their behalf, to join the noble band of intercessors.

S. J. Reid: *The Seven Windows*

The cross of Christ is the sweetest burden that I ever bore; it is such a burden as wings are to a bird, or sails to a ship, to carry me forward to my harbor.

Samuel Rutherford

The cross of Christ, on which he was extended, points, in the length of it, to heaven and earth, reconciling them together; and in the breadth of it, to former and following ages, as being equally salvation to both.

Samuel Rutherford

Not he who scorns the Saviour's yoke
Should wear his cross upon the heart.

Johann Christoph Friedrich von Schiller:
The Fight With the Dragon, st. 24

It has been the cross which has revealed to good men that their goodness has not been good enough.

Johann Hieronymus Schroeder

In the presence of the cross man dares not speculate about the degree of his goodness;

rather he is at once cast down by his sin and overwhelmed by the joyous insight that God is the kinsman of the way.

Johann Hieronymus Schroeder

Crosses are the ladders that lead to heaven.

Samuel Smiles: *Self-Help,* p. 341

And all through life I see a cross—
    Where sons of God yield up their
        breath;
There is no gain except by loss;
    There is no life except by death;
    There is no vision but by faith.

Walter Chalmers Smith: *Olrig Grange,*
Bk. VI

There are no crown-wearers in heaven who were not cross-bearers here below.

Charles Haddon Spurgeon: *Gleanings
among the Sheaves. Cross-Bearers*

In all our actions, when we come in or go out, when we dress, when we wash, at our meals, before retiring to sleep, we make on our foreheads the sign of the cross. These practices are not commited by a formal law of Scripture, but tradition teaches them, custom confirms them, faith observes them.

Tertullian: *De Corona,* III

Carry the cross patiently, and with perfect submission; and in the end it shall carry you.

If you bear the cross unwillingly, you make it a burden, and load yourself more heavily; but you must needs bear it. If you cast away one cross, you will certainly find another, and perhaps a heavier.

Thomas à Kempis

Salvation by the cross.

Thomas à Kempis: *Imitation of Christ,*
II, 2

In the cross there is safety.

Thomas à Kempis: *Imitation of Christ,*
II, 12

Christianity without the Cross is nothing. The Cross was the fitting close of a life of rejection, scorn, and defeat. But in no true sense have these things ceased or changed. Jesus is still He whom man despiseth, and the rejected of men.

James Thomson: *The Great Argument*

Nothing in my hand I bring,
Simply to Thy cross I cling.

Augustus M. Toplady: Hymn:
Rock of Ages

The sweetest joys a heart can hold
Grow up between its crosses.

Nixon Waterman: *Recompense*

D

DAMNATION

From all evil and mischief; from sin; from
the crafts and assaults of the Devil; from
Thy wrath, and from everlasting damnation,
Good Lord, deliver us.

>   *The Book of Common Prayer:*
>   *The Litany*

The idea of damnation is anything but dis-
agreeable to some people; it gives them a
kind of gloomy consequence in their own
eyes. We must be something particular, they
think, or God would hardly think it worth
His while to torment us for ever.

>   George Borrow: *Wild Wales*, XLVII

When a damned soul shall have shed tears
enough to fill all the rivers of the world,
even if he should have shed but one a century, he will be no nearer deliverance after
so many millions of years; he will only have
begun to suffer.

>   Dominique Bouhours: *Pensées*
>   *chrétiennes*

There's a great text in Galatians,
  Once you trip on it, entails
Twenty-nine distinct damnations,
  One sure, if another fails.

>   Robert Browning: *Soliloquy in a*
>   *Spanish Cloister*

God foreordained for His own glory and
the display of His attributes of mercy and
justice, a part of the human race, without
any merit of their own, to eternal salvation,
and another part, in just punishment of their
sin, to eternal damnation.

>   John Calvin: *Institutes of the Christian*
>   *Religion*

What do the damned endure, but to despair?

>   William Congreve: *The Mourning*
>   *Bride,* Act III, sc. 1

You can and you can't—You shall and you
shan't—You will and you won't—You'll be
damned if you do—And you'll be damned if
you don't.

>   Lorenzo Dow: *Reflections on the*
>   *Love of God*

All children are by nature children of wrath,
and are in danger of eternal damnation in
Hell.

>   Jonathan Edwards: *Sermon to Children*

The damned are in the abyss of Hell, as
within a woeful city, where they suffer unspeakable torments in all their senses and
members, because as they have employed all
their senses and their members in sinning, so
shall they suffer in each of them the punishment due to sin.

>   St. Francis de Sales: *Introduction to the*
>   *Devout Life,* XV

Just prophet, let the damn'd one dwell
Full in the sight of Paradise,
Beholding heaven and feeling hell.

>   Thomas Moore: *Lalla Rookh, Fire*
>   *Worshippers*

Die and be damned.

>   Thomas Mortimer

Ye serpents, ye generation of vipers, how can
ye escape the damnation of hell?

>   *New Testament: Matthew 23: 33*

I think the Devil will not have me damned,
lest the oil that is in me should set Hell on
fire.

> William Shakespeare: *The Merry
> Wives of Windsor*, Act V, sc. 5, l. 38

All are damnable and damned;
Each one damning, damns the other;
They are damned by one another.

> Percy Bysshe Shelley: *Peter Bell
> the Third*, III

I had rather be damned with Plato and Lord
Bacon than go to Heaven with Paley and
Malthus.

> Percy Bysshe Shelley: *Prometheus
> Unbound*

A man may be damned for despairing to be
saved.

> Jeremy Taylor: *Holy Living*, p. 259

Forgive me if, midst all Thy works
No hint I see of damning;
And think there's faith among the Turks,
And hope for e'en the Brahmin.

> William Makepeace Thackeray:
> *Jolly Jack*

Were't not for gold and women, there would
be no damnation.

> Cyril Tourneur: *The Revenger's
> Tragedy*, I

DEATH

Come gentle death, the ebb of care;
The ebb of care, the flood of life.

> Anonymous

The universe is God's house. In His house
are many rooms. Death pushes aside the
portiere that we may pass from one room to
another.

> Anonymous

The tomb is not an endless night—
  It is a thoroughfare, a way

That closes in a soft twilight
And opens in eternal day.

> Anonymous

Death and Love are two wings which bear
men from earth to heaven.

> Anonymous

Some day the bell will sound,
Some day my heart will bound,
As with a shout
That school is out
And lessons done,
I homeward run.

> Anonymous

Some die without having really lived, while
others continue to live, in spite of the fact
that they have died.

> Anonymous

Passed on, beyond our mortal vision,
  But now the thought is robbed of gloom,
Within the Father's many mansions
  Still dwelling in another room.

The one whose going left us lonely
  Is scaling heights undreamed of yore,
And guided on by Love's unfolding,
  Has gone upstairs and shut the door.

> Anonymous

In the democracy of the dead, all men are
equal. The poor man is as rich as the richest,
and the rich man as poor as the pauper. The
creditor loses his usury, and the debtor is
acquitted of his obligation. There the proud
man surrenders his dignity; the politician
his honors; the wordling his pleasures; the
invalid needs no physician; the laborer rests
from toil. The wrongs of time are redressed;
injustice is expiated, and the irony of fate is
refuted.

> Anonymous

The epitaph on the grave in Canterbury,
England, of Henry Alford, writer of the
hymn, "Ten Thousand Times Ten Thousand," is: "The inn of a pilgrim journeying
to Jerusalem."

Death is a black camel, which kneels at the gates of all.

Abd-El-Kader: *Rappel à l'Intelligent*

Death is the opening of a more subtle life. In the flower, it sets free the perfume; in the chrysalis, the butterfly; in man, the soul.

Juliette Adam (pseudonym—Comte Paul Vasili)

The thought of death leaves me completely calm because I have the firm conviction that our spirit is a being of an indestructible nature, continuing from eternity to eternity; it is similar to the sun, which seems to set each night for us mortals, but which actually never sets, instead continues to shine uninterruptedly.

Aerzté-Kalendar, Germany (*Quote* translation)

We have loved the stars too fondly to be fearful of the night.

Inscription in the crypt of Allegheny Observatory, University of Pittsburgh

Virtue and vice are the only things in this world, which, with our souls, are capable of surviving death.

Ethan Allen: *Reason the Only Oracle of Man*, p. 473

We're here today and gone tomorrow.

American Proverb

When death is imminent, we open our hearts quickly and wide. How much more Christian love there would be if we didn't wait for death to release our reserves!

Hazel Beck Andre: "My Last Best Days on Earth," *Reader's Digest*, October, 1956

Judge none blessed before his death.

Apocrypha: Ecclesiasticus 11: 28

God made no Death: neither hath he pleasure in the destruction of the living.

Apocrypha: Wisdom of Solomon

Death rides a fast camel.

Arab Proverb

The end of birth is death; the end of death is birth: this is ordained!

Sir Edwin Arnold: *The Song Celestial*, ch. 2

Truth sits upon the lips of dying men.

Matthew Arnold

Death to the Christian is the funeral of all his sorrows and evils, and the resurrection of all his joys.

Aughey

It is as natural to die as to be born; and to a little infant, perhaps, the one is as painful as the other.

Sir Francis Bacon: *Essays: Of Death*

Life! We've been long together
Through pleasant and through cloudy weather;
'Tis hard to part when friends are dear—
Perhaps 'twill cost a sigh, a tear;
Then steal away, give little warning,
Choose thine own time;
Say not good-night,—but in some brighter clime
Bid me good-morning.

Anna Letitia Barbauld: *Ode to Life*

I shall hear in heaven.

Ludwig von Beethoven, referring to his deafness

Death the gate of life.

St. Bernard of Clairvaux: *In Transitu S. Malachi*, Sermon I, sec. 4, ad fin.

Beyond the shining and the shading
I shall be soon.
Beyond the hoping and the dreading
I shall be soon.
Love, rest and home—
Lord! tarry not, but come.

Horatius Bonar: *Beyond the Smiling and the Weeping*

In the midst of life we are in death

> Book of Common Prayer: Burial of
> the Dead

They rest from their labours.

> Ibid.

Irrevocable as death.

> Charlotte Brontë

Death . . . pale priest of the mute people.

> Robert Browning: Balaustion's
> Adventure, l. 303

The grand Perhaps!

> Robert Browning: Bishop Blougram's
> Apology

O thou soul of my soul! I shall clasp thee
again,
And with God be the rest!

> Robert Browning: Prospice

Christ has made of death a narrow, starlit
strip between the companionships of yesterday and the reunions of tomorrow.

> William Jennings Bryan

Raise then, the hymn to Death, Deliverer!
God hath anointed thee to free the oppressed
And crush the oppressor.

> William Cullen Bryant: Hymn to Death

My sword I give to him that shall succeed
me in my pilgrimage, and my courage and
skill to him that can get it. My marks and
scars I carry with me, to be a witness for me
that I have fought his battles who now will
be my rewarder. When the day that he must
go hence was come, many accompanied him
to the riverside, into which as he went he
said: "Death, where is thy sting?" And as he
went down deeper, he said: "Grave, where
is thy victory?" So he passed over, and all the
trumpets sounded for him on the other side.

> John Bunyan: The Pilgrim's Progress,
> Pt. II

The fear of death is worse than death.

> Robert Burton: Anatomy of Melancholy

The Way of All Flesh.

> Samuel Butler the Younger: Title of
> posthumous novel published in 1903

Heaven gives its favorites—early death.

> George Gordon, Lord Byron

Oh God! it is a fearful thing
To see the human soul take wing
In any shape, in any mood.

> George Gordon, Lord Byron: The
> Prisoner of Chillon, Pt. VIII

To live in hearts we leave behind,
Is not to die.

> Thomas Campbell: Hallowed Ground,
> st. 6

If a man was great while living, he becomes
tenfold greater when dead.

> Thomas Carlyle: Heroes and Hero-
> Worship

Even for the dead, I will not bind
My soul to grief, death cannot long divide;
For is it not as if the rose that climbed
My garden wall had bloomed the other
side?

> Alice Cary

Death comes not to the living soul,
Nor age to the loving heart.

> Phoebe Cary

My God, my Father and my Friend
Do not forsake me in the end.

> Thomas di Celano: Dies Irae

I go from a corruptible to an incorruptible
crown, where no disturbance can have place.

> Charles I of England, on the scaffold

I depart from life as from an inn, and not
as from my home.

> Cicero: De Senectute

The divinity who rules within us, forbids us
to leave this world without his command.

> Cicero: Tusculanarum Disputationum

Death, to a good man, is but passing through a dark entry, out of one little dusky room of his Father's house into another that is fair and large, lightsome and glorious, and divinely entertaining.

McDonald Clarke

Death is like thunder in two particulars: we are alarmed at the sound of it, and it is formidable only from that which preceded it.

Charles Caleb Colton

When I am dying I want to know that I have a similarity to God, so that my will is the same as his will, and that I love and hate and wish what he does.

Joseph Cook

Death comes with a crawl, or comes with a
    pounce,
And whether he's slow or spry,
It isn't the fact that you're dead that counts,
But only, how did you die?

Edmund Vance Cooke: *How
Did You Die?*

Far happier are the dead, methinks, than
    they
Who look for death, and fear it every day.

William Cowper: *On Invalids*

Death be not proud, though some have called
    thee
Mighty and dreadful, for, thou art not so,
For, those, whom thou think'st, thou dost
    overthrow,
Die not, poor death, nor yet canst thou kill
    me . . .
One short sleep past, we wake eternally,
And death shall be no more; death, thou
    shalt die.

John Donne: *Holy Sonnets,* no. 10

No man is an island, intire of it self; every man is a piece of the continent, a part of the main; if a clod be washed away by the sea, Europe is the less, as well as if a promontory were, as well as if a manor of thy friends or of thine own were. Any man's death diminishes me, because I am involved in mankind. And

therefore never send to know for whom the bell tolls; it tolls for thee.

John Donne: *Devotions upon Emergent
Occasions*

Sleep on, beloved, sleep, and take thy rest;
Lay down thy head upon thy Saviour's breast
We love thee well, but Jesus loves thee best—
Good-night! Good-night! Good-night!

Sarah Doudney: *The Christian's
Good-Night.* Ira D. Sankey
wrote the music for this hymn
which was sung at the funeral
of Dr. Charles H. Spurgeon

Obstinate as death.

John Dryden

Death is a law, not a punishment.

Jean-Baptiste Dubos

Death has nothing terrible which life has not made so. A faithful Christian life in this world is the best preparation for the next.

Tryon Edwards

This world is the land of the dying; the next is the land of the living.

Tryon Edwards

When death, the great reconciler, has come, it is never our tenderness that we repent of, but our severity.

George Eliot

Worldly faces never look so worldly as at a funeral.

George Eliot

Father in thy gracious keeping
Leave me now thy servant sleeping.

John Lodge Ellerton: *Now the
Laborer's Task is O'er*

The buried are not lost, but gone before.

Ebenezer Elliott: *The Excursion*

Dead men tell no tales.

English Proverb traced by Apperson
to 1664

"Who gathered this flower?" The gardener answered, "The Master." And his fellow-servant held his peace.

Epitaph, Budock Churchyard and elsewhere

The dead have no tears, and forget all sorrow.

Euripides: *The Troades*

Death is not, to the Christian, what it has often been called, "Paying the debt of nature." No, it is not paying a debt; it is rather like bringing a note to a bank to obtain solid gold in exchange for it. You bring a cumbrous body which is nothing worth, and which you could not wish to retain long; you lay it down, and receive for it, from the eternal treasures, liberty, victory, knowledge, and rapture.

John Foster

Death is as necessary to the constitution as sleep: we shall rise refreshed in the morning.

Benjamin Franklin

Life is a state of embryo, a preparation for life. A man is not completely born until he has passed through death.

Benjamin Franklin

There is no better armor against the shafts of death than to be busied in God's service.

Thomas Fuller

To die is landing on some silent shore;
Where billows never break nor tempests roar;
Ere well we feel the friendly stroke 'tis o'er.

Sir Samuel Garth: *The Dispensary*, III

When death comes to me it will find me busy, unless I am asleep. If I thought I was going to die tomorrow, I should nevertheless plant a tree today.

Stephen Girard

I never think he is quite ready for another world who is altogether weary of this.

Hugh Hamilton

The ancients dreaded death: the Christian can only fear dying.

Augustus William and Julius Charles Hare: *Guesses at Truth*

And I hear from the outgoing ship in the bay
The song of the sailors in glee:
So I think of the luminous footprints that bore
The comfort o'er dark Galilee,
And wait for the signal to go to the shore,
To the ship that is waiting for me.

Francis Bret Harte: *The Two Ships*

Grieve not that I die young. Is it not well
To pass away ere life hath lost its brightness?

Flora Elizabeth Hastings: *Swan Song*

We sometimes congratulate ourselves at the moment of waking from a troubled dream; it may be so the moment after death.

Nathaniel Hawthorne

Death keeps no calendar.

George Herbert: *Outlandish Proverbs*

He that fears death lives not.

George Herbert: *Jacula Prudentum*

Those that God loves, do not live long.

Ibid.

Death is as the foreshadowing of life. We die that we may die no more.

Herman Hooker

Pale Death, with impartial step, knocks at the poor man's cottage and at the palaces of kings.

Horace: *Odes*, Bk. I, ode 4, l. 13

And if there be no meeting past the grave,
If all is darkness, silence, yet 'tis rest.
Be not afraid, ye waiting hearts that weep,
For still He giveth His beloved sleep,
And if an endless sleep He wills, 'tis best.

Mrs. Thomas Henry Huxley: *Lines*, on the grave of Thomas Henry Huxley

When death comes, he respects neither age nor merit. He sweeps from this earthly existence the sick and the strong, the rich and the poor, and should teach us to live to be prepared for death.

> Andrew Jackson: *Letter: My Dear E.*

Oh, write of me not "Died in bitter pains," But "Emigrated to another star!"

> Helen Hunt Jackson: *Emigravit*

We are but tenants, and . . . shortly the great Landlord will give us notice that our lease has expired.

> Joseph Jefferson: *Inscription*, on his monument at Sandwich, Cape Cod, Mass.

To neglect, at any time, preparation for death, is to sleep on our post at a siege; to omit it in old age, is to sleep at an attack.

> Samuel Johnson

Death is the beginning of life. After taps, comes reveille.

> *Journal of the American Judicature Society*

'Tis sweet, as year by year we lose Friends out of sight, in faith to muse How grows in Paradise our store.

> John Keble: *Burial of the Dead*

Gone before, To that unknown and silent shore.

> Charles Lamb: *Hester*

Death stands above me, whispering low I know not what into my ear; Of this strange language all I know Is, there is not a word of fear.

> Walter Savage Landor: *Death Stands Above Me*

He has joined the majority.

> Latin Saying

Let the tent be struck.

> Robert E. Lee

Death is not a foe, but an inevitable adventure.

> Sir Oliver Lodge

There is no Death! What seems so is transition; This life of mortal breath Is but a suburb of the life elysian, Whose portal we call Death.

> Henry Wadsworth Longfellow: *Resignation*

The long, mysterious Exodus of Death.

> Henry Wadsworth Longfellow: *The Jewish Cemetery at Newport*

The gods conceal from men the happiness of death, that they may endure life.

> Lucan

Why shed tears that thou must die? For if thy past life has been one of enjoyment, and if all thy pleasures have not passed through thy mind, as through a sieve, and vanished, leaving not a rack behind, why then dost thou not, like a thankful guest, rise cheerfully from life's feast, and with a quiet mind go take thy rest.

> Lucretius: *De rerum natura,* III

We should teach our children to think no more of their bodies when dead than they do of their hair when cut off, or of their old clothes when they have done with them.

> George Macdonald: *Annals of a Quiet Neighborhood*

There is no such thing as death. In nature nothing dies. From each sad remnant of decay Some forms of life arise.

> Charles Mackay: *There is No Such Thing as Death*

We picture death as coming to destroy; let us rather picture Christ as coming to save. We think of death as ending; let us rather think of life as beginning, and that more abundantly. We think of losing; let us think of gaining. We think of parting, let us think

of meeting. We think of going away; let us
think of arriving. And as the voice of death
whispers "You must go from earth," let us
hear the voice of Christ saying, "You are but
coming to Me!"

> Norman Macleod

There is no death! the stars go down
   To rise upon some other shore,
And bright in Heaven's jeweled crown,
   They shine for ever more.

> John Luckey McCreery: *There Is No*
> *Death*

"God help the fools who count on death for
gain."

> Frank T. Marzials: *Death as the Fool*

The transition between life and death must
be gentle in the winter of life. Death must
be invested with a certain grandeur and
poetry, if it comes to a man who has completed his mission. He has nothing to fear,
nothing to dread.

> Rudolph Matas

Whom the gods love dies young.

> Menander: *Dis Exapaton*, frag. 125

Every man faces two deaths and not just
one. There is the biological event marked
by mortuaries and monuments. But there is
also the personal event, the spiritual death,
which often goes unnoticed.

> Carl Michalson: *Faith for Personal*
> *Crises*, Charles Scribners Sons

The Pilot of the Galilean lake,
Two massy keys he bore of metals twain
(The golden opes, the iron shuts amain).

> John Milton: *Lycidas*, l. 109

They eat, they drink, and in communion
   sweet
Quaff immortality and joy.

> John Milton: *Paradise Lost*, Bk. V, l. 637

From out the throng and stress of lies,
From out the painful noise of sighs,
One voice of comfort seems to rise:
"It is the meaner part that dies."

> William Morris: *Comfort*

Out of the finite darkness,
Into the infinite light.

> Louise Chandler Moulton

Let the dead bury their dead.

> *New Testament: Matthew 8: 22*

She is not dead, but sleepeth.

> *New Testament: Luke 8: 52*

Passed from death unto life.

> *New Testament: John 5: 24*

He that is dead is freed from sin.

> *New Testament: Romans 6: 7*

Who shall deliver me from the body of this
death?

> *New Testament: Romans 7: 24*

To be carnally minded is death.

> *New Testament: Romans 8: 6*

The last enemy that shall be destroyed is
death.

> *New Testament: I Corinthians 15: 26*

O death, where is thy sting? O grave, where
is thy victory?

> *New Testament: I Corinthians 15: 55*

And I looked, and behold a pale horse: and
his name that sat on him was Death.

> *New Testament: Revelation 6: 8*

Blessed are the dead which die in the Lord
from henceforth: Yea, saith the Spirit, that
they may rest from their labours; and their
works do follow them.

> *New Testament: Revelation 14: 13*

This much, and this is all, we know,
   They are supremely blest,
Have done with sin, and care, and woe,
   And with their Saviour rest.

> John Newton: *Olney Hymns*

On fame's eternal camping-ground
   Their silent tents are spread,

And glory guards with solemn round,
  The bivouac of the dead.
> Theodore O'Hara: *The Bivouac of the
>   Dead*

For dust thou art, and unto dust shalt thou
return.
> *Old Testament: Genesis 3: 19*

There the wicked cease from troubling; and
there the weary be at rest.
> *Old Testament: Job 3: 17*

Thou shalt come to thy grave in a full age,
like as a shock of corn cometh in in his
season.
> *Old Testament: Job 5: 26*

Before I go whence I shall not return, even
to the land of darkness and the shadow of
death.
> *Old Testament: Job 10: 21*

The king of terrors.
> *Old Testament: Job 18: 14*

The sorrows of death compassed me.
> *Old Testament: Psalms 18: 4*

I have said, Ye are gods; . . . But ye shall
die like men.
> *Old Testament: Psalms 82: 6, 7*

Yet a little sleep, a little slumber, a little
folding of the hands to sleep.
> *Old Testament: Proverbs 6: 10*

The righteous hath hope in his death.
> *Old Testament: Proverbs 14: 32*

One event happeneth to them all.
> *Old Testament: Ecclesiastes 2: 14*

There is no discharge in that war.
> *Old Testament: Ecclesiastes 8: 8*

We have made a covenant with death.
> *Old Testament: Isaiah 28: 15*

We all do fade as a leaf.
> *Old Testament: Isaiah 64: 6*

Death is the scion of the house of hope.
> Dorothy Parker: *Death,*
>   The Viking Press

Death's but a path that must be trod,
If man would ever pass to God.
> Thomas Parnell: *A Night-Piece
>   on Death,* l. 67

They that love *beyond* the *world,* cannot be
separated. Death cannot kill what *never* dies.
Nor can Spirits ever be divided that love and
live in the *same* Divine Principle; the Root
and Record of their *Friendship.* Death is but
crossing the *world,* as Friends do the Seas,
they live in one another still.
> William Penn: *Fruits of Solitude,* Pt. II

A good death does honor to a whole life.
> Petrarch: *Canzoniere,* XVI

And the fever called "Living"
  Is conquered at last.
> Edgar Allan Poe: *For Annie*

The world recedes; it disappears;
Heav'n opens on my eyes; my ears
  With sound seraphic ring:
Lend, lend your wings! I mount! I fly!
O Grave! where is thy victory?
  O Death! where is thy sting?
> Alexander Pope: *The Dying Christian
>   to His Soul*

If thou expect death as a friend, prepare to
entertain him; if as an enemy, prepare to
overcome him.—Death has no advantage
except when he comes as a stranger.
> Francis Quarles

She slept the sleep of the just.
> Jean Baptiste Racine: *Abrege de
>   L'Histoire de Port Royal,*
>   Vol. IV, l. 517

O eloquent, just, and mighty death! whom
none could advise, thou hast persuaded:

what none hath dared, thou hast done; and whom all the world hath flattered, thou only hast cast out of the world and despised: thou hast drawn together all the far stretched greatness, all the pride, cruelty and ambition of man, and covered it all over with these two narrow words, Hic jacet!

Sir Walter Raleigh

On death and judgment, heaven and hell, who oft doth think, must needs die well.

Sir Walter Raleigh

If Socrates died like a philosopher, Jesus Christ died like a God.

Jean Jacques Rousseau

Out of the chill and shadow,
 Into the thrill and the shine;
Out of the dearth and famine,
 Into the fulness divine.

Margaret E. Sangster: *Going Home*

Make thine account with Heaven, governor,
Thou must away, thy sand is run.

Johann Christoph Friedrich von Schiller:
Wilhelm Tell, Act IV, sc. 3

Is death the last sleep? No, it is the last and final awakening.

Sir Walter Scott

Death is sometimes a punishment, often a gift; to many it has been a favor.

Seneca: *Hercules Œtaeus*

He that dies pays all debts.

William Shakespeare: *The Tempest*,
Act III, sc. 2, l. 140

Out of the jaws of death.

William Shakespeare: *Twelfth Night*,
Act III, sc. 4, l. 394

The undiscover'd country from whose bourn
No traveller returns.

William Shakespeare: *Hamlet*,
Act III, sc. 1, l. 79

A man can die but once: we owe God a death.

William Shakespeare: *Henry IV, Part II*,
Act III, sc. 2, l. 251

And, to add greater honours to his age
Than man could give him, he died fearing
 God.

William Shakespeare: *Henry VIII*,
Act IV, sc. 2, l. 68

Tomorrow, and tomorrow, and tomorrow,
Creeps in this petty pace from day to day
To the last syllable of recorded time,
And all our yesterdays have lighted fools
The way to dusty death.

William Shakespeare: *Macbeth*,
Act V, sc. 5, l. 19

I am borne darkly, fearfully, afar;
Whilst, burning through the inmost veil of
 Heaven,
The soul of Adonais, like a star,
Beacons from the abode where the Eternal
 are.

Percy Bysshe Shelley: *Adonais*, st. 55

Whate'er thou lovest, man, that, too,
 become thou must—
God, if thou lovest God; dust, if thou
 lovest dust.

Angelus Silesius: *The Cherubic Pilgrim*

Yes, 'twill only be a sleep:
When, with songs and dewy light,
Morning blossoms out of Night,
She will open her blue eyes
'Neath the palms of Paradise,
While we foolish ones shall weep.

Edward Rowland Sill: *Sleeping*

What may we take into the vast Forever?
 That marble door
Admits no fruit of all our long endeavor,
 No fame-wreathed crown we wore,
 No garnered lore.

Edward Rowland Sill: *The Future*

Be of good cheer about death, and know this of a truth, that no evil can happen to a good man, either in life or after death.

Socrates: *Plato's Apology*

To fear death, gentlemen, is nothing other than to think oneself wise when one is not; for it is to think one knows what one does not know. No man knows whether death may not even turn out to be the greatest of blessings for a human being; and yet people fear it as if they knew for certain that it is the greatest of evils.

Socrates: *Plato's Apology*

The wicked is driven away in his wickedness: but the righteous hath hope in his death.

Solomon

Say nothing but good of the dead.

Ascribed to Solon

Home is the sailor,
Home from the sea,
And the hunter home from the hill.

Robert Louis Stevenson: *Requiem*

When sinks the soul, subdued by toil, to slumber,
  Its closing eye looks up to Thee in prayer;
Sweet the repose beneath Thy wings o'er-
  shading,
  But sweeter still to wake and find Thee
    there.

Harriet Beecher Stowe

Men fear death because they refuse to understand it. But the manner of death is more important than death itself. Fine dying is a man's privilege, for that man can himself control. We cannot influence death but we can influence the style of our departure. Men surprise themselves by the fashion in which they face this death: some more proudly and more valiantly than ever they dared imagine; and some in abject terror.

Cyrus L. Sulzberger: *My Brother Death*, Harper & Row, Publishers, Inc.

It is impossible that anything so natural, so necessary, and so universal as death, should ever have been designed by Providence as an evil to mankind.

Jonathan Swift

Sunset and evening star,
  And one clear call for me!
And may there be no moaning at the bar
  When I put out to sea . . .
For tho' from out our bourne of Time and
  Place
  The flood may bear me far,
I hope to see my Pilot face to face
  When I have crost the bar.

Alfred, Lord Tennyson:
Crossing the Bar

God's finger touched him, and he slept.

Alfred, Lord Tennyson: *In Memoriam*,
Pt. LXXXV, st. 5

And the wicked cease from troubling, and the weary are at rest.

Alfred, Lord Tennyson: *The May
Queen,* last line

Death's truer name
Is "Onward," no discordance in the roll
And march of that Eternal Harmony
Whereto the world beats time.

Alfred, Lord Tennyson: *Unpublished
Sonnet (Life,* vol. I)

His maker kissed his soul away,
  And laid his flesh to rest.

Isaac Watts: *The Presence of God*

I saw him now going the way of all flesh.

John Webster: *Westward Hoe* [1607]
(in collaboration with Dekker),
Act II, sc. 2

Nothing can happen more beautiful than death.

Walt Whitman: *Starting from Paumanok*

God calls our loved ones,
  But we lose not wholly
    What He hath given;
They live on earth
  In thought and deed
    As truly as in His heaven.

John Greenleaf Whittier

Ah well! for us all some sweet hope lies
Deeply buried from human eyes;
And, in the hereafter, angels may
Roll the stone from its grave away!

    John Greenleaf Whittier: *Maud Muller*

Henceforward, listen as we will,
The voices of that hearth are still;
Look where we may, the wide earth o'er
Those lighted faces smile no more . . .
Yet Love will dream, and Faith will trust
(Since He who knows our need is just)
That somehow, somewhere, meet we must.

    John Greenleaf Whittier: *Snow-Bound*,
                    l. 187

It is infamy to die and not be missed.

                Carlos Wilcox

It is but crossing with a bated breath,
A white, set face, a little strip of sea—
To find the loved one waiting on the shore,
More beautiful, more precious than before.

    Ella Wheeler Wilcox: *The Crossing*
    (inscribed upon a wreath sent by
    Queen Alexandra, to be laid on
    the coffin of Mrs. William Ewart
    Gladstone), Rand McNally & Co.

Death is an angel with two faces;
To us he turns
A face of terror, blighting all things fair;
The other burns
With glory of the stars, and love is there.

    Theodore Chickering Williams:
    A Thanatopsis, Houghton
    Mifflin Co.

How beautiful it is for man to die
Upon the walls of Zion! to be called,
Like a watch-worn and weary sentinel
To put his armor off and rest—in heaven!

    Nathaniel Parker Willis: *On the Death
    of a Missionary*

But when the great and good depart,
What is it more than this—
That Man, who is from God sent forth,
Doth yet again to God return?—
Such ebb and flow must ever be,
Then wherefore should we mourn?

    William Wordsworth: *Lines on the
    Expected Dissolution of Mr Fox*

Absence and death, how differ they? and how
Shall I admit that nothing can restore
What one short sigh so easily removed?
Death, life, and sleep, reality and thought—
Assist me, God, their boundaries to know,
O teach me calm submission to thy Will!

    William Wordsworth: *Maternal Grief*,
                    l. 8

Death gives us more than was in Eden lost.
This king of terrors is the prince of peace.

    Edward Young: *Night Thoughts*,
           Night III, l. 534

Nothing is dead, but that which wished to
    die;
Nothing is dead, but wretchedness and pain.

    Edward Young: *Night Thoughts*,
           Night VI, l. 41

DEVIL, THE

The devil was sick, the devil a monk would
    be;
The devil was well, the devil a monk was he.

                Anonymous

God made bees, and bees made honey,
God made man, and man made money,
Pride made the devil, and the devil made
    sin;
So God made a coal-pit to put the devil in.

                Anonymous

Talk of devils being confined to hell, or
hidden by invisibility!—We have them by
shoals in the crowded towns and cities of the
world.—Talk of raising the devil!—What
need for that, when he is constantly walking
to and fro in our streets, seeking whom he
may devour.

                Anonymous

The devil is no idle spirit, but a vagrant,
runagate walker, that never rests in one
place.—The motive, cause, and main intention of his walking is to ruin man.

              Thomas Adams

The Devil often transforms himself into an angel to tempt men, some for their instruction and some for their ruin.

> St. Augustine: *The City of God*, XV

The devil may also make use of morality.

> Karl Barth: *The Word of God and the Word of Man* (translated by Douglas Horton), Harper & Row, Publishers, Inc.

The devil take the hindmost!

> Francis Beaumont and John Fletcher: *Philaster*, Act V

How the devil rebukes sin!

> Aphra Behn: *Roundheads*, Act V, sc. 2

If two New Hampshiremen aren't a match for the devil, we might as well give the country back to the Indians.

> Stephen Vincent Benét: *The Devil and Daniel Webster*

The Devil entangles youth with beauty, the miser with gold, the ambitious with power, the learned with false doctrine.

> Henry George Bohn: *Handbook of Proverbs*

Renounce the devil and all his works.

> *Book of Common Prayer: Baptism of Infants*

Grant that he may have power and strength to have victory, and to triumph, against the devil, the world, and the flesh. Amen.

> *Ibid.*

The devil's ever kind to his own.

> Alexander Brome: *New Montebank*

The heart of man is the place the devil dwells in: I feel sometimes a hell within myself.

> Sir Thomas Browne: *Religio Medici*, Pt. I, sec. 51

The devil's most devilish when respectable.

> Elizabeth Barrett Browning: *Aurora Leigh*, Bk. VII, l. 105

The Devil that old stager . . . who leads Downward, perhaps, but fiddles all the way!

> Robert Browning: *Red Cotton Night-Cap Country*, Pt. II, l. 264

Every man for himself, his own ends, the Devil for all.

> Robert Burton: *Anatomy of Melancholy*, Pt. III, sec. 1

The Devil himself, which is the author of confusion and lies.

> Robert Burton: *Anatomy of Melancholy*, Pt. III, sec. 4

An apology for the Devil: It must be remembered that we have only heard one side of the case. God has written all the books.

> Samuel Butler: *Note Books. Higgledy-Piggledy: An Apology for the Devil*

The Devil hath not in all his quiver's choice, An arrow for the heart like a sweet voice.

> George Gordon, Lord Byron: *Don Juan*, Canto XV, st. 13

And them all the Lord transformed to devils, Because they His deed and word Would not revere.

> Caedmon: *Creation. The Fall of the Rebel Angels*

Sarcasm I now see to be, in general, the language of the Devil; for which reason I have, long since, as good as renounced it.

> Thomas Carlyle: *Sartor Resartus*

Here's the devil-and-all to pay.

> Miguel de Cervantes: *Don Quixote*

One devil is like another.

> *Ibid.*

The Devil is good when he is pleased.

> John Clarke: *Paraemiologia*
> *Anglo-Latina*

'Tis an ill company where the Devil bears
the banner.

> *Ibid.*

Talk of the devil, and his horns appear, says
the proverb.

> Samuel Taylor Coleridge: *Biographia*
> *Literaria*, ch. 23

If I were a painter I would draw the Devil
like an idiot, a driveller with a bib and bells:
a man should have his head and horns, and
woman the rest of him.

> William Congreve: *The Way of the*
> *World*, III

The devil knoweth his own, and is a particular bad paymaster.

> Francis Marion Crawford

The Devil is kind to (or takes care of) his
own.

> John Day: *The Isle of Gulls*, II

His laws are easy, and his gentle sway
Makes it exceeding pleasant to obey.

> Daniel Defoe: *The True-Born*
> *Englishman*, I

Every devil has not a cloven hoof.

> Daniel Defoe: *History of the Devil*,
> Pt. II, ch. 6

It is become a proverb, *as great as the devil*
and Dr. Foster.

> *Ibid.*

Go, and catch a falling star,
    Get with child a mandrake root,
Tell me, where all past years are,
    Or who cleft the Devil's foot.

> John Donne: *Song*, st. 1

Better sit still, than rise to meet the devil.

> Michael Drayton: *The Owl*

When to sin our bias'd nature leans,
The careful devil is still at hand with means.

> John Dryden: *Absalom and*
> *Achitophel*, Pt. I, l. 79

Never was hood so holy but the Devil could
get his head in it.

> Dutch Proverb

The Devil has his marytrs among men.

> Dutch Proverb

When the Devil gets himself into the church,
he seats himself on the altar.

> Dutch Proverb

The devil has at least one good quality,
that he will flee if we resist him.—Though
cowardly in him, it is safety for us.

> Tryon Edwards

A religion can no more afford to degrade
its Devil than to degrade its God.

> Havelock Ellis: *Impressions and*
> *Comments*, Ser. I, p. 33

If I am the Devil's child, I will live then from
the Devil.

> Ralph Waldo Emerson: *Essays, First*
> *Series: Self-Reliance*

All the devils respect virtue.

> Ralph Waldo Emerson: *Essays, First*
> *Series: Spiritual Laws*

Every man before he dies shall see the Devil.

> English Proverb

The Devil is dead.

> English Proverb

The Devil is God's ape.

> English Proverb

The Devil hates holy water.

> English Proverb

Talk of the devil and he'll appear.

> Desiderius Erasmus: *Adagia*, XVII

'Tis an easier matter to raise the devil than to lay him.

Desiderius Erasmus: *Adagia,* CCII

The Devil is a busy bishop in his own diocese.

David Fergusson: *Scottish Proverbs*

What a silly fellow must he be who would do the devil's work for nothing.

Henry Fielding: *Joseph Andrews,* Bk. II, ch. 16

What the devil and Doctor Faustus, shan't I do what I will with my own daughter?

Henry Fielding: *Tom Jones,* Bk. XVIII, ch. 8

The Devil paints himself black, but we see him rose-colored.

Finnish Proverb

O woman, perfect woman! what distraction Was meant to mankind when thou wast made a devil!

John Fletcher: *Monsieur Thomas,* Act III, sc. 1

Speak boldly, and speak truly, Shame the devil.

John Fletcher: *Wit Without Money,* Act IV

Each man for himself and the Devil for all.

John Florio: *First Fruites,* fo. 33

Of three things the Devil makes his mess; Of lawyers' tongues, of scriveners' fingers— you the third may guess.

John Florio: *Second Fruites*

Better keep the devil at the door than turn him out of the house.

Thomas Fuller: *Gnomologia*

If the devil catch a man idle, he'll set him at work.

Ibid.

You would do little for God if the Devil were dead.

Ibid.

Where the Devil can't go he sends his grandmother.

German Proverb

Set a beggar on horseback, and he'll outride the Devil.

German Proverb

The devil is an egotist.

Johann Wolfgang von Goethe: *Faust,* Act I, sc. 4, l. 124

'Gainst the logic of the devil Human logic strives in vain.

Adam Lindsay Gordon: *The Wayside House*

Why do I believe in the Devil? *For three reasons.*
1. Because the Bible plainly says he exists.
2. Because I see his work everywhere.
3 Because great scholars have recognized his existence.

William F. ("Billy") Graham: *This Week,* March 2, 1958

We must not so much as taste of the devil's broth, lest at last he bring us to eat of his beef.

Thomas Hall: *Funebria Florae,* XII

The hypothesis of a personal Devil has many advantages. It explains the whole of the facts; it avoids the postulation of two first causes; it vindicates the moral perfection of the Diety; and it allows the optimistic hope to be entertained that in the end good will triumph over evil.

Charles Harris: *A Text-Book of Apologetics*

I call'd the devil, and he came
    And with wonder his form did I closely
        scan;
He is not ugly, and is not lame,
    But really a handsome and charming
        man.

A man in the prime of life is the devil,
    Obliging, a man of the world, and civil;
A diplomatist too, well skill'd in debate,
He talks quite glibly of church and state.

> Heinrich Heine: *Pictures of Travels.*
> *The Return Home*

Why should the Devil have all the good tunes?

> Rowland Hill: *Sermons* (quoted
> in Broome Life)

One of the principal objects of American reverence is the Devil. There are multitudes who are shocked to hear his name mentioned lightly, and who esteem such mention profanity.

> Josiah Gilbert Holland: *Everyday Topics*

The world is all the richer for having a devil in it, *so long as we keep our foot upon his neck.*

> William James (Permission to reprint
> granted by Paul R. Reynolds & Son)

The Devil can equivocate as well as a shopkeeper.

> Ben Jonson: *Bartholomew Fair,* I

The Devil is an ass, I do acknowledge it.

> Ben Jonson: *The Devil is an Ass,*
> Act IV, sc. 1

The Devil's cow calves twice a year.

> James Kelly: *Complete Collection
> of Scottish Proverbs*

The Dee'l is no worse than he's called.

> *Ibid.*

The Devil bides his day.

> *Ibid.*

When you close your eyes to the devil, be sure that it is not a wink.

> John C. Kulp

Who is the most diligent bishop and prelate in England? . . . I will tell you. It is the devil . . . He is never out of his diocese . . . The devil is diligent at his plough.

> Hugh Latimer: *Sermon on Ploughers*

When the Devil preaches the world's near an end.

> Sir Roger L'Estrange: *Sueños*

And the Devil said to Simon Legree:
"I like your style, so wicked and free."

> Vachel Lindsay: "A Negro Sermon,"
> *The Chinese Nightingale and
> Other Poems,* copyright by the
> Macmillan Company. Renewed
> 1947 by Elizabeth C. Lindsay

Devils are not so black as they are painted.

> Thomas Lodge: *A Margarite
> of America,* p. 57

Tell your master that if there were as many devils at Worms as tiles on its roofs, I would enter.

> Martin Luther: *On approaching Worms*

For where God built a church, there the Devil would also build a chapel.

> Martin Luther: *Table Talk*

The Devil has two manner of shapes or forms, wherein he disguises himself; he either appears in the shape of a serpent, to affright and kill; or else in the form of a silly sheep, to lie and deceive; these are his two court colors.

> *Ibid.*

For it is often said of him that yet lives,
He must needs go that the devil drives.

> John Lydgate: *Assembly of Gods,* III, 2

That there is a Devil is a thing doubted by none but such as are under the influences of the Devil. For any to deny the being of a Devil must be from an ignorance or profaneness worse than diabolical.

> Cotton Mather: *A Discourse on the
> Wonders of the Invisible World*

It is the devil's masterstroke to get us to accuse him.

> George Meredith

Satan, so call him now, his former name
Is heard no more in heav'n.

> John Milton: *Paradise Lost,* Bk. V, l. 655

Abash'd the Devil stood,
And felt how awful goodness is, and saw
Virtue in her shape how lovely; saw, and
    pin'd
His loss.

John Milton: *Paradise Lost,* Bk. IV, l. 846

Get thee behind me, Satan.

New Testament: Mark 8: 33

Resist the devil, and he will flee from you.

New Testament: James 4: 7

Be sober, be vigilant; because your adversary
the devil, as a roaring lion, walketh about,
seeking whom he may devour.

New Testament: I Peter 5: 8

How art thou fallen from heaven, O Lucifer,
son of the morning!

Old Testament: Isaiah 14: 12

When men grow virtuous in their old age,
they only make a sacrifice to God of the
devil's leavings.

Alexander Pope: *Thoughts on Various
Subjects*

What is got over the Devil's back is spent
under the belly.

François Rabelais: *Works,* Book V,
Author's Prologue, ch. 11

Never hold a candle to the devil.

John Ray: *English Proverbs*

Here's the devil to pay.

Samuel Richardson: *Clarissa Harlowe,*
Bk. VI, 87

When the priest's away the Devil will play.

Russian Proverb

The Devil and me, we don't agree;
I hate him; and he hates me.

Salvation Army Hymn

Accursed be he who plays with the devil.

Johann Christoph Friedrich von Schiller:
Wallenstein's Death, I, 3, 64

Casting out the devils is mere juggling; they
never cast out any but what they first cast in.

John Selden: *Table Talk: Devils*

. . . that devil's madness—War.

Robert William Service: *Michael,*
Ryerson Press

He must have a long spoon that shall eat
with the devil.

William Shakespeare: *Comedy of
Errors,* Act IV, sc. 3, l. 65

One sees more devils than vast hell can hold.

William Shakespeare: *A Midsummer-
Night's Dream,* Act V, sc. 1, l. 9

The spirit that I have seen
May be the devil: and the devil hath power
To assume a pleasing shape.

William Shakespeare: *Hamlet,*
Act II, sc. 2, l. 627

The devil shall have his bargain; for he was
never yet a breaker of proverbs.

William Shakespeare: *Henry IV, Part I,*
Act I, sc. 2, l. 131

He will give the devil his due.

William Shakespeare: *Henry IV, Part I,*
Act I, sc. 2, l. 132

The devil rides upon a fiddlestick.

William Shakespeare: *Henry IV, Part I,*
Act II, sc. 4, l. 534

The prince of darkness is a gentleman.

William Shakespeare: *King Lear,*
Act III, sc. 4, l. 148

'tis the eye of childhood
That fears a painted devil.

William Shakespeare: *Macbeth,*
Act II, sc. 2, l. 54

No man means evil but the devil, and we
shall know him by his horns.

William Shakespeare: *Merry Wives of
Windsor,* Act V, sc. 2, l. 15

Sometimes we are devils to ourselves
When we will tempt the frailty of our
    powers,
Presuming on their changeful potency.
> William Shakespeare: *Troilus and
>   Cressida*, Act IV, sc. 4, l. 97

What, man! defy the devil: consider, he's an
enemy to mankind.
> William Shakespeare: *Twelfth Night*,
>   Act III, sc. 4, l. 108

He who would fight the devil with his own
weapons, must not wonder if he finds him
an overmatch.
> Robert South

From his brimstone bed at break of day
A-walking the Devil is gone,
To look at his little snug farm of the world,
And see how his stock went on . . .
His coat was red and his breeches were blue,
And there was a hole where his tail came
    through.
> Robert Southey: *The Devil's Walk*,
>   sts. 1, 3

Go, poor devil, get thee gone! Why should
I hurt thee? This world surely is wide enough
to hold both thee and me.
> Laurence Sterne: *Tristram Shandy*,
>   Bk. II, ch. 12

The Devil comes where money is; where it
is not he comes twice.
> Swedish Proverb

The devil is good when he is pleased.
> Jonathan Swift: *Polite Conversation*,
>   Dial. II

The devil does not tempt unbelievers and
sinners who are already his own.
> Thomas à Kempis

The Devil is subtle, yet weaves a coarse web.
> Richard Chenevix Trench: *Lessons in
>   Proverbs*

All religions issue Bibles against Satan, and
say the most injurious things against him,
but we never hear his side.
> Mark Twain

You must have the devil in you to succeed
in any of the arts.
> Voltaire

The Devil has three children: pride, falsehood and envy.
> Welsh Proverb

All the works of our evil nature are the work
of the devil.
> John Wesley

The bane of all that dread the Devil!
> William Wordsworth: *The Idiot Boy*,
>   st. 67

The devil will take his own.
> Thomas Wright: *Essays on the
>   Middle Ages*, Vol. I, p. 146

DEVOTION

Compar'd with this, how poor Religion's
    pride,
In all the pomp of method and of art,
When men display to congregations wide,
    Devotion's ev'ry grace, except the heart!
> Robert Burns: *The Cotter's
>   Saturday Night*

A man cannot make a pair of shoes rightly
unless he do it in a devout manner.
> Thomas Carlyle: *Letter to
>   Thomas Erskine*

Solid devotions resemble the rivers which
run under the earth—they steal from the
eyes of the world to seek the eyes of God;
and it often happens that those of whom
we speak least on earth, are best known in
heaven.
> Nicolas Caussin

Devotion is simply the promptitude, fervor, affection, and agility which we have in the service of God: and there is a difference between a good man and a devout man; for he is a good man who keeps the commandments of God, although it be without great promptitude or fervor; but he is devout who not only observes them but does so willingly, promptly, and with a good heart.

St. Francis de Sales

Satan rocks the cradle when we sleep at our devotions.

Joseph Hall

As down in the sunless retreats of the ocean,
  Sweet flowers are springing no mortal can see,
So deep in my soul the still prayer of devotion
  Unheard by the world, rises silent to Thee.

Thomas Moore: *As Down in the Sunless Retreats*

The secret heart is devotion's temple; there the saint lights the flame of purest sacrifice, which burns unseen but not unaccepted.

Hannah More

When I am with God
My fear is gone
In the great quiet of God.
My troubles are as the pebbles on the road,
My joys are like the everlasting hills.

Walter Rauschenbusch: *The Little Gate to God*

'Tis too much proved—that with devotion's visage
And pious action we do sugar o'er
The devil himself.

William Shakespeare: *Hamlet*, Act III, sc. 1, l. 47

The devotion of the moth for the star,
  Of the night for the morrow,
The devotion to something afar
  From the sphere of our sorrow.

Percy Bysshe Shelley: *To ——. One Word is too Often Profaned*

Devotion is not a thing which passes, which comes and goes, as it were, but it is something habitual, fixed, permanent, which extends over every instant of life and regulates all our conduct.

Douglas V. Steere: *Prayer and Worship*

The private devotions and secret offices of religion are like the refreshing of a garden with the distilling and petty drops of a waterpot; but addressed from the temple, they are like rain from heaven.

Jeremy Taylor

Devotion! daughter of Astronomy!

Edward Young: *Night Thoughts*, Night IX, l. 769

DISCIPLES

We may be doing Jesus an injustice in stressing the fact that He so frequently said "Go . . . !" His first word to His disciples was not "Go" but "Come."

Anonymous

James the brother of Jesus and James the son of Zebedee preach and are killed by mobs in Jerusalem; Matthew is slain on a sword in Ethiopia; Philip is hanged in Phrygia; Bartholomew flayed alive in Armenia. Andrew is crucified in Achaia, Thomas is run through with a lance in East India, Thaddeus is shot to death with arrows, a cross goes up in Persia for Simon the Zealot, and another in Rome for Peter. Matthias is beheaded; only John escapes a martyr's grave.

Frank S. Mead: *The March of Eleven Men*

The disciple is not above his master, nor the servant above his lord.

New Testament: Matthew 10: 24

If any man come to me, and hate not his father, and mother, and wife, and children, and brethren, and sisters, yea, and his own life also, he cannot be my disciple.

New Testament: Luke 14: 26

DIVINITY

No true disciple of mine will ever be a Ruskinian; he will follow, not me, but the instincts of his own soul, and the guidance of its Creator.

John Ruskin: *St. Mark's Rest*

DIVINITY

Sacred and inspired divinity, the sabbath and port of all men's labours and peregrinations.

Sir Francis Bacon: *Advancement of Learning*, Bk. II

There is surely a piece of divinity in us, something that was before the elements, and owes no homage unto the sun.

Sir Thomas Browne: *Religio Medici*, Pt. II, sec. 11

No man was ever great without divine inspiration.

Cicero: *De Natura Deorum*, II, 66

What is there of the divine in a load of bricks? What is there of the divine in a barber's shop? Much. All.

Ralph Waldo Emerson: *Journal*

Not he that adorns but he that adores makes a divinity.

Baltasar Gracián y Morales

There's a divinity that shapes our ends, Rough-hew them how we will.

William Shakespeare: *Hamlet*, Act V, sc. 2, l. 10

The three black graces, Law, Physic, and Divinity.

Horatio and James Smith: *Punch's Holiday*

I hold that to need nothing is divine, and the less a man needs the nearer does he approach divinity.

Socrates: Quoted by Xenophon. *Men*, Bk. I, 6, 10

DOCTRINE

Every man is his own doctor of divinity, in the last resort.

Robert Louis Stevenson: *An Inland Voyage, Noyon*

DOCTRINE

Look to the essence of a thing whether it be a point of doctrine, of practice, or of interpretation.

Marcus Aurelius: *Meditations*, VIII, 22

Doctrine is nothing but the skin of truth set up and stuffed.

Henry Ward Beecher: *Life Thoughts*

Carried away with every blast of vain doctrine.

Book of Common Prayer: St. Mark's Day

No dogmas nail your faith.

Robert Browning: *Bishop Blougram's Apology*

A fundamental, and as many believe, the most essential part of Christianity, is its doctrine of reward and punishment in the world beyond; and a religion which had nothing at all to say about this great enigma we should hardly feel to be a religion at all.

Goldsworthy Lowes Dickinson: *The Greek View of Life*, ch. 1, sec. 11

Doctrine is the necessary foundation of duty; if the theory is not correct, the practice cannot be right.—Tell me what a man believes, and I will tell you what he will do.

Tryon Edwards

Pure doctrine always bears fruit in pure benefits.

Ralph Waldo Emerson

Doctrine is the framework of life—the skeleton of truth, to be clothed and rounded out by the living grace of a holy life.

Adoniram J. Gordon

Doctrines, as infections, fear,
Which are not steeped in vinegar.
> Matthew Green: *The Spleen,* l. 339

The question is not whether a doctrine is beautiful but whether it is true.—When we wish to go to a place, we do not ask whether the road leads through a pretty country, but whether it is the right road.
> Augustus William and Julius Charles Hare

Doctrines do not necessarily die from being killed.
> Thomas Henry Huxley: *Natural Rights and Political Rights*

Any doctrine that will not bear investigation is not a fit tenant for the mind of an honest man.
> Robert Green Ingersoll: *Intellectual Development*

What yesterday was fact, today is doctrine.
> Junius: *The Letters of Junius. Dedication To the English Nation*

He who receives
Light from above, from the Fountain of Light
No other doctrine needs, though granted true.
> John Milton: *Paradise Regained,* Bk. IV, l. 288

From the age of fifteen, dogma has been the fundamental principle of my religion. I know of no other religion; I cannot enter into the idea of any other sort of religion; religion, as a mere sentiment, is to me a dream and a mockery.
> Cardinal John Henry Newman: *Apologia pro Vita Sua,* ch. 2

Carried about with every wind of doctrine.
> *New Testament: Ephesians 4: 14*

Live to explain thy doctrine by thy life.
> Matthew Prior: *To Dr. Sherlock*

Say what men may, it is doctrine that moves the world. He who takes no position will not sway the human intellect.
> William Greenough Thayer Shedd

If you want a war, nourish a doctrine. Doctrines are the most fearful tyrants to which men ever are subject, because doctrines get inside of a man's own reason and betray him against himself. Civilized men have done their fiercest fighting for doctrines.
> William Graham Sumner: *War*

The doctrine that rectifies the conscience, purifies the heart, and produces love to God and man, is necessarily true, whether men can comprehend all its depths and relations or not.
> James Barr Walker

Better heresy of doctrine, than heresy of heart.
> John Greenleaf Whittier: *Mary Garvin,* st. 22

DOUBT

Doubt digs the grave of faith.
> Anonymous

Doubters invert the metaphor and insist that they need faith as big as a mountain in order to move a mustard seed.
> Anonymous

The man who speaks his positive convictions is worth a regiment of men who are always proclaiming their doubts and suspicions.
> Anonymous

Doubt is the accomplice of tyranny.
> Henri Frédéric Amiel: *Journal*

When men are in doubt, they always believe what is most agreeable.
> Flavius Arrianus: *The Anabasis of Alexander the Great*

Who never doubted, never half believed.
Where doubt there truth is—'tis her shadow.

> Philip James Bailey: *Festus:*
> *Sc. A Country Town*

He who shall teach the child to doubt
The rotting grave shall ne'er get out.

> William Blake: *Poems: Auguries*
> *of Innocence,* l. 77

He who doubts from what he sees
Will ne'er believe, do what you please.
If the sun and moon should doubt,
They'd immediately go out.

> William Blake: *Poems: Auguries*
> *of Innocence,* l. 97

You call for faith:
I show you doubt, to prove that faith exists.
The more of doubt, the stronger faith, I say,
If faith o'ercomes doubt.

> Robert Browning: *Bishop Blougram's*
> *Apology*

Who knows most, doubts most.

> Robert Browning

In the hands of unbelief half-truths are made
to do the work of whole falsehoods.—The
sowing of doubts is the sowing of dragon's
teeth, which ere long will sprout up into
armed and hostile men.

> Enoch Fitch Burr

Never be afraid of doubt, if only you have
the disposition to believe.

> Samuel Taylor Coleridge

Every step toward Christ kills a doubt. Every
thought, word, and deed for Him carries you
away from discouragement.

> Theodore Ledyard Cuyler

If you would be a real seeker after truth, it
is necessary that at least once in your life you
doubt, as far as possible, all things.

> René Descartes: *Principles of Philosophy*

They reckon ill who leave me out;
When me they fly, I am the wings;

I am the doubter and the doubt,
And I the hymn the Brahmin sings.

> Ralph Waldo Emerson: *May-Day and*
> *Other Pieces, Brahma*

For right is right, since God is God,
And right the day must win;
To doubt would be disloyalty,
To falter would be sin.

> Frederick William Faber

Doubt is hell in the human soul.

> Madam Gasparin

In the darkest night of the year,
When the stars have all gone out,
That courage is better than fear,
That faith is truer than doubt.

> Washington Gladden: *Ultima Veritas,*
> st. 4

Give me the benefit of your convictions, if
you have any, but keep your doubts to yourself, for I have enough of my own.

> Johann Wolfgang von Goethe

Why didn't someone tell me that I can
become a Christian and settle the doubts
afterward?

> William Rainey Harper

Man may doubt here and there, but mankind
does not doubt. The universal conscience is
larger than the individual conscience, and
that constantly comes in to correct and check
our own infidelity.

> Hugh Reginald Haweis: *Speech*
> *in Season,* Bk. III, 328

Knowledge of divine things is lost to us by
incredulity.

> Heraclitus

Doubt comes in at the window when inquiry
is denied at the door.

> Benjamin Jowett

The method which begins by doubting in
order to philosophize is just as suited to its
purpose as making a soldier lie down in a
heap in order to teach him to stand up
straight.

> Sören Kierkegaard

There is no doubt in this book.

The Koran, ch. 1

Then it is the brave man chooses, while the
coward stands aside,
Doubting in his abject spirit, till his Lord is
crucified.

James Russell Lowell: *The Present
Crisis,* st. 11

The man that feareth, Lord, to doubt,
In that fear doubteth thee.

George Macdonald: *Disciple,*
Pt. XXXII, st. 15

Let go the things in which you are in doubt
for the things in which there is no doubt.

Mohammed

Doubts are more cruel than the worst of
truths.

Jean Baptiste Molière: *Le Misanthrope,*
Act III, sc. 7

If you pray for bread and bring no basket
to carry it, you prove the doubting spirit
which may be the only hindrance to the
boon you ask.

Dwight L. Moody

O thou of little faith, wherefore didst thou
doubt?

New Testament: Matthew 14: 31

And he that doubteth is damned if he eat.

New Testament: Romans 14: 23

But the gods are dead—
Ay, Zeus is dead, and all the gods but Doubt,
And Doubt is brother devil to Despair!

John Boyle O'Reilly: *Prometheus. Christ*

Your doubts are the private detectives
Employed by your dislike, to make a case
Against change or choice.

William Robert Rodgers: *Words*

And better had they ne'er been born,
Who read to doubt, or read to scorn.

Sir Walter Scott: *The Monastery*

Where love is great, the littlest doubts are
fear;
When little fears grow great, great love grows
there.

William Shakespeare: *Hamlet,*
Act III, sc. 2, l. 181

Our doubts are traitors,
And make us lose the good we oft might win
By fearing to attempt.

William Shakespeare: *Measure for
Measure,* Act I, sc. 4, l. 78

Modest doubt is call'd
The beacon of the wise.

William Shakespeare: *Troilus and
Cressida,* Act II, sc. 2, l. 15

Beware of doubt—faith is the subtle chain
that binds us to the infinite.

Elizabeth Oakes Smith

It is never worth while to make rents in
a garment for the sake of mending them,
nor to create doubts in order to show how
cleverly we can quiet them.

Charles Haddon Spurgeon

To believe with certainty we must begin
with doubting.

Stanislas I (King of Poland): *Maxims
and Moral Sentences,* no. 61

Doubt feeds on faith. It cannot survive on
itself, for it degenerates into cynicism, which
is a parasite and destructive force.

A. M. Sullivan: *Spirit* Magazine

Cleave ever to the sunnier side of doubt,
And cling to Faith beyond the forms of
Faith.

Alfred, Lord Tennyson:
The Ancient Sage

Faith keeps many doubts in her pay. If I
could not doubt, I should not believe.

Henry David Thoreau

Talk faith. The world is better off without
Your uttered ignorance and morbid doubt.

Ella Wheeler Wilcox: *Speech,* st. 2,
Rand McNally & Co.

E

EASTER

May Easter Day
To thy heart say,
  "Christ died and rose for thee."
May Easter night
On thy heart write,
  "O Christ, I live to Thee."

Anonymous

The Easter message tells us that our enemies, sin, the curse and death, are beaten. Ultimately they can no longer start mischief. They still behave as though the game were not decided, the battle not fought; we must still reckon with them, but fundamentally we must cease to fear them any more.

Karl Barth: Dogmatics in Outline,
Harper & Row, Publishers, Inc.

The great Easter truth is not that we are to live newly after death—that is not the great thing—but that we are to be here and now by the power of the resurrection; not so much that we are to live forever as that we are to, and may, live nobly now because we are to live forever.

Phillips Brooks

Tomb, thou shalt not hold Him longer;
Death is strong, but Life is stronger;
Stronger than the dark, the light;
Stronger than the wrong, the right;
Faith and Hope triumphant say
Christ will rise on Easter Day.

Phillips Brooks: An Easter Carol

A kiss at Christmas and an egg at Easter.

Denham Tracts, II, 92

Their Lent is over, and their Easter won.

William Croswell Doane: Death

Hail, Day of days! in peals of praise
  Throughout all ages owned,
When Christ, our God, Hell's empire trod,
  And high o'er heaven was throned.

St. Venantius Fortunatus: Hail, Day of
Days

You keep Easter, when I keep Lent.

Thomas Fuller: Gnomologia, no. 5927

Rise, heart; thy Lord is risen. Sing His praise
  Without delays,
Who takes thee by the hand, that thou like-
  wise
  With Him mayst rise:
That, as His death calcined thee to dust,
His life may make thee gold, and much more,
  just.

George Herbert: The Church: Easter

On Easter Day the veil between time and eternity thins to gossamer.

Douglas Horton

I'll warrant you for an egg at Easter.

James Howell: Proverbs, 2

Easter so longed for is gone in a day.

James Howell: Proverbs, 20

One trouble with the churches is that too many people want to have Easter without Calvary.

Lawrence Pearsall Jacks

The day of resurrection! Earth, tell it out
  abroad:
The Passover of gladness, the Passover of
  God.
From death to life eternal, from this world
  to the sky,

Our Christ hath brought us over, with hymns
of victory.

St. John of Damascus: *The Day
of Resurrection*

Thou art the Sun of other days,
They shine by giving back thy rays.

John Keble: *The Christian Year:
Easter Days*

Come, ye saints, look here and wonder,
  See the place where Jesus lay;
He has burst His bands asunder;
  He has borne our sins away;
    Joyful tidings,
  Yes, the Lord has risen to-day.

Thomas Kelley: *Come, Ye Saints*

The story of Easter is the story of God's
wonderful window of divine surprise.

Carl Knudsen

At Easter let your clothes be new,
Or else be sure you will it rue.

Lean: *Collectanea,* Pt. I, p. 378

Easter is not a time for groping through
dusty, musty tomes or tombs to disprove
spontaneous generation or even to prove life
eternal. It is a day to fan the ashes of dead
hope, a day to banish doubts and seek the
slopes where the sun is rising, to revel in the
faith which transports us out of ourselves
and the dead past into the vast and inviting
unknown.

Lewiston (Idaho) *Tribune*

'Twas Easter Sunday. The full blossomed
  trees
Filled all the air with fragrance and with
  joy.

Henry Wadsworth Longfellow:
The Spanish Student,
Act I, sc. 3

O chime of sweet Saint Charity,
  Peal soon that Easter morn
When Christ for all shall risen be,
  And in all hearts new-born!

James Russell Lowell: *Godminster
Chimes,* st. 7

In the bonds of Death He lay
  Who for our offence was slain;
But the Lord is risen to-day,
  Christ hath brought us life again,
Wherefore let us all rejoice,
Singing loud, with cheerful voice,
  Hallelujah!

Martin Luther: *In the Bonds of Death*

In vain with stone the cave they barred;
In vain the watch kept ward and guard;
Majestic from the spoiled tomb,
In pomp of triumph Christ is come.

John Mason Neale: *Lift Up Your Voices*

The fasts are done; the Aves said;
  The moon has filled her horn
And in the solemn night I watch
  Before the Eastern morn.
So pure, so still the starry heaven,
  So hushed the brooding air,
I could hear the sweep of an angel's wings
  If one should earthward fare.

Edna Dean Proctor: *Easter Morning,*
Houghton Mifflin Company

I think of the garden after the rain;
  And hope to my heart comes singing,
"At morn the cherry blooms will be white,
  And the Easter bells be ringing!"

Edna Dean Proctor: *Easter Bells,*
Houghton Mifflin Company

He has but a short Lent that must pay money
at Easter.

Proverb

Spring bursts to-day,
For Christ is risen and all the earth's at play.

Christina Georgina Rossetti: *Easter Carol*

Angels, roll the rock away;
Death, yield up thy mighty prey:
See, He rises from the tomb,
Glowing with immortal bloom.
  Al-le-lu-ia! Al-le-lu-ia!
Christ the Lord is risen today!

Thomas Scott: *Easter Angels*

I can live forever with God. Trouble, illness,
and death may come but my real self—my

soul—will go on living in another existence with Almighty God. That is one of the plain meanings of Easter.

> From *Great Protestant Festivals* by Clarence Seidenspinner. By permission of Abelard-Schuman Ltd., New York, London and Toronto, all rights reserved. Copyright 1952

Didst thou not fall out with a tailor for wearing his new doublet before Easter?

> William Shakespeare: *Romeo and Juliet,* Act III, sc. 1, l. 30

Something happened on Easter Day which made Christ more alive on the streets of Jerusalem forty days after his crucifixion than on the day of His Triumphal Entry. A false report might last forty days but the church which was founded on a Risen Christ has lasted for nineteen centuries, producing generations of the race's finest characters and now including some six hundred million members.

> Ralph W. Sockman: *Pulpit Preaching*

God expects from men something more than at such times, and that it were much to be wished for the credit of their religion as well as the satisfaction of their conscience that their Easter devotions would in some measure come up to their Easter dress.

> Robert South: *Sermons,* Vol. XI, ser. 8

If Easter means anything to modern man it means that eternal truth is eternal. You may nail it to the tree, wrap it up in grave clothes, and seal it in a tomb; but "truth crushed to earth, shall rise again." Truth does not perish; it cannot be destroyed. It may be distorted; it has been silenced temporarily; it has been compelled to carry its cross to Calvary's brow or to drink the cup of poisoned hemlock in a Grecian jail, but with an inevitable certainty after every Black Friday dawns truth's Easter Morn.

> Donald Harvey Tippet: *Pastor*

Hail the day that sees Him rise
To His throne above the skies;

Christ, awhile to mortals given
Reascends His native Heaven.

> Charles Wesley: *Ascension*

Easter must be relived.
Where is the zeal that followed Easter's birth?
The faith that doomed the soulless gods of earth?
No shadow, lifeless spirit of repose
Prevailed that cloudless morn when Christ arose.
The Easter atmosphere cannot revive
A torpid faith that thinks itself alive.

> George W. Wiseman: *Expositor*

ERROR

It is human to err; it is devilish to remain wilfully in error.

> St. Augustine: *Sermons,* no. 164, sec. 14

The humblest citizen of all the land, when clad in the armor of a righteous cause, is stronger than all the hosts of Error.

> William Jennings Bryan: Speech at the National Democratic Convention, Chicago (1896)

Truth, crushed to earth, shall rise again;
Th' eternal years of God are hers;
But Error, wounded, writhes in pain,
And dies among his worshippers.

> William Cullen Bryant: *The Battle-Field,* st. 9

There will be mistakes in divinity while men preach, and errors in government while men govern.

> Sir Dudley Carleton

A man protesting against error is on the way toward uniting himself with all men that believe in truth.

> Thomas Carlyle: *Heroes and Hero-Worship*

Who errs and mends, to God himself commends.

Miguel de Cervantes

False doctrine does not necessarily make the
man a heretic, but an evil heart can make
any doctrine heretical.

Samuel Taylor Coleridge

We classify disease as error, which nothing
but Truth or Mind can heal, and this Mind
must be divine, not human.

Mary Baker Eddy: *Science and Health
with Key to the Scriptures,*
p. 483: 5–6

Truth is immortal; error is mortal.

Mary Baker Eddy: *Science and Health
with Key to the Scriptures,*
p. 466: 13

In its influence on the soul, error has been
compared to a magnet concealed near the
ship's compass.—As in the latter case, the
more favorable the winds, and the greater
the diligence and skill in working the ship,
the more rapidly will it be speeded on in
a wrong course; and so in the former, the
greater the struggle for safety, the more
speedy the progress to ruin.

Tryon Edwards

Errors of theory or doctrine are not so much
false statements, as partial statements. Half
a truth received, while the corresponding
half is unknown or rejected, is a practical
falsehood.

Tryon Edwards

Nothing is more harmful to a new truth than
an old error.

Johann Wolfgang von Goethe

While man's desires and aspirations stir,
He can not choose but err.

Johann Wolfgang von Goethe: *Faust,*
Pt. II

Dark Error's other hidden side is truth.

Victor Hugo: *The Legend of the Centuries*

Politics, like religion, hold up the torches of
martyrdom to the reformers of error.

Thomas Jefferson: *Letter to James Ogilvie*

Man-like it is to fall into sin,
Fiend-like it is to dwell therein;
Christ-like it is for sin to grieve,
God-like it is all sin to leave.

Friedrich von Logau: *Sinnegedichte*

The little I have seen of the world teaches me
to look upon the errors of others in sorrow,
not in anger. When I take the history of one
poor heart that has sinned and suffered, and
think of the struggles and temptations it has
passed through, the brief pulsations of joy,
the feverish inquietude of hope and fear, the
pressure of want, the desertion of friends, I
would fain leave the erring soul of my fellowman with Him from whose hands it came.

Henry Wadsworth Longfellow

So the last error shall be worse than the first.

New Testament: Matthew 27: 64

Who can understand his errors?

Old Testament: Psalms 19: 12

To err is human, to forgive divine.

Alexander Pope: *An Essay on
Criticism,* II

Shall error in the round of time
Still father Truth?

Alfred, Lord Tennyson: *Love and Duty*

ETERNITY

Eternity! thou pleasing dreadful thought!
Through what variety of untried being,
Through what new scenes and changes must
we pass!

Joseph Addison: *Cato,* Act V, sc. 1

Who can number the sand of the sea, and
the drops of rain, and the days of eternity?

Apocrypha: Ecclesiasticus 1: 2

Then gazing up 'mid the dim pillars high,
The foliaged marble forest where ye lie,
Hush, ye will say, it is eternity!'
This is the glimmering verge of heaven, and
there
The columns of the heavenly palaces.

> Matthew Arnold: *The Tomb*

The sole purpose of life in time is to gain
merit for life in eternity.

> St. Augustine: *Letter 130*

'Tis time unfolds Eternity.

> Philip James Bailey: *Festus: A Ruined
> Temple*

To see a world in a grain of sand
And a heaven in a wild flower,
Hold infinity in the palm of your hand
And eternity in an hour.

> William Blake: *Poems. Auguries
> of Innocence*, l. 1

Every tear from every eye
Becomes a babe in eternity.

> William Blake: *Poems. Auguries
> of Innocence*, l. 67

The created world is but a small parenthesis
in eternity.

> Sir Thomas Browne: *Works*

Eternity stands always fronting God; a stern
colossal image, with blind eyes, and grand
dim lips, that murmur evermore, "God—
God—God!"

> Elizabeth Barrett Browning

What we call eternity may be but an endless
series of the transitions which men call
deaths, abandonments of home, going ever
to fairer scenes and loftier heights.—Age
after age, the spirit—that glorious nomad—
may shift its tent, carrying with it evermore
its elements, activity and desire.

> Edward George Bulwer-Lytton

But there are wanderers o'er Eternity
Whose bark drives on and on, and anchor'd
ne'er shall be.

> George Gordon, Lord Byron: *Childe
> Harold*, Canto III, st. 70

Eternity forbids thee to forget.

> George Gordon, Lord Byron: *Lara*,
> Canto I, st. 23

He who has no vision of eternity has no hold
on time.

> Thomas Carlyle

Eternity looks grander and kinder if time
grows meaner and more hostile.

> Thomas Carlyle

There is, I know not how, in the minds of
men, a certain presage, as it were, of a future
existence, and this takes the deepest root, and
is most discoverable in the greatest geniuses
and most exalted souls.

> Cicero

Eternity! How know we but we stand
On the precipitous and crumbling verge
Of Time e'en now, Eternity below?

> Abraham Coles: *Eternity*

Eternity for bubbles proves at last
A senseless bargain.

> William Cowper: *The Task*, Bk. III, l. 175

Eternity is not an everlasting flux of time,
but time is as a short parenthesis in a long
period.

> John Donne: *Devotions*

All great natures delight in stability; all
great men find eternity affirmed in the very
promise of their faculties.

> Ralph Waldo Emerson

How vast is eternity!—It will swallow up
all the human race; it will collect all the
intelligent universe; it will open scenes and
prospects wide enough, great enough, and
various enough to fix the attention, and
absorb the minds of all intelligent beings
forever.

> Nathanael Emmons

Our object in life should be to accumulate a
great number of grand questions to be asked

and resolved in eternity.—Now we ask the sage, the genius, the philosopher, the divine, but none can tell; but we will open our queries to other respondents—we will ask angels, redeemed spirits and God.

John Foster

Eternity is not something that begins after you are dead. It is going on all the time. We are in it now.

Charlotte Perkins Gilman: *The Forerunner*

Let me dream that love goes with us to the shore unknown.

Felicia D. Hemans

In the presence of eternity, the mountains are as transient as the clouds.

Robert Green Ingersoll: *The Christian Religion*

It is eternity now. I am in the midst of it. It is about me in the sunshine; I am in it, as the butterfly in the light-laden air. Nothing has to come; it is now. Now is eternity; now is the immortal life.

Richard Jefferies: *The Story of My Heart*

Time is the image of eternity.

Diogenes Laertius: *Plato*, XLI

The horologe of Eternity
Sayeth this incessantly,—
   "Forever—never!
Never—forever!"

Henry Wadsworth Longfellow: *The Old Clock on the Stairs*, st. 9

The sum of all sums is eternity.

Lucretius: *De rerum natura*, III

But at my back I always hear
Time's winged chariot hurrying near;
And yonder all before us lie
Deserts of vast eternity.

Andrew Marvell: *To His Coy Mistress*

I leave eternity to Thee; for what is man that he should live out the lifetime of his God?

Herman Melville: *Moby Dick*, ch. 9

To have the sense of the eternal in life is a short flight for the soul. To have had it, is the soul's vitality.

George Meredith: *Diana of the Crossways*, ch. 1

Then shall be shown, that but in name
Time and eternity were both the same;
A point which life nor death could sever,
A moment standing still forever.

James Montgomery: *Time, a Rhapsody*

This speck of life in time's great wilderness,
This narrow isthmus 'twixt two boundless seas,
The past, the future, two eternities!

Thomas Moore: *Lalla Rookh, The Veiled Prophet of Khorassan*, st. 42

Eternity is a negative idea clothed with a positive name.—It supposes, in that to which it is applied, a present existence, and is the negation of a beginning or an end of that existence.

William Paley

The present's nothing: but eternity
Abides for those on whom all truth, all good,
Hath shone, in one entire and perfect light.

St. Paulinus of Nola

The time will come when every change shall cease,
This quick revolving wheel shall rest in peace:
No summer then shall glow, nor winter freeze;
Nothing shall be to come, and nothing past,
But an eternal now shall ever last.

Petrarch: *Triumph of Eternity*, l. 117

Every natural longing has its natural satisfaction. If we thirst, God has created liquids to gratify thirst. If we are susceptible of attachment, there are beings to gratify that love. If we thirst for life and love eternal, it is likely that there are an eternal life and an eternal love to satisfy that craving.

Frederick William Robertson

Learn to hold loosely all that is not eternal.
> A. Maude Royden

Eternity gives nothing back of what one leaves out of the minutes.
> Johann Christoph Friedrich von Schiller: *Resignation*, st. 18

Makes us heirs of all eternity.
> William Shakespeare: *Love's Labour's Lost*, Act I, sc. 1, l. 7

Or sells eternity to get a toy.
> William Shakespeare: *The Rape of Lucrece*, l. 144

Life, like a dome of many-coloured glass,
Stains the white radiance of eternity.
> Percy Bysshe Shelley: *Adonais*

The Pilgrim of Eternity, whose fame
Over his living head like Heaven is bent,
An early but enduring monument,
Came, veiling all the lightnings of his song
In sorrow.
> *Ibid*

If the human mind, by any future improvement of its sensibility, should become conscious of an infinite number of ideas in a minute, that minute would be eternity.
> Percy Bysshe Shelley: *Queen Mab*, notes

In time there is no present,
In eternity no future.
In eternity no past.
> Alfred, Lord Tennyson: *The "How" and the "Why"*

I saw Eternity the other night
Like a great ring of pure and endless light.
> Henry Vaughan: *The World*

The clock indicates the moment—but what does eternity indicate?
> Walt Whitman: *Song of Myself*, Pt. XLIV, l. 4

EVIL

To be free from evil thoughts is God's best gift.
> Aeschylus

There is nothing evil save that which perverts the mind and shackles the conscience.
> St. Ambrose: *Hexaem*, l. 31

For, were it not good that evil things should also exist, the omnipotent God would most certainly not allow evil to be, since beyond doubt it is just as easy for Him not to allow what He does not will, as it is for Him to do what He will.
> St. Augustine: *Enchiridion*

If men were basically evil, who would bother to improve the world instead of giving it up as a bad job at the outset?
> Van Wyck Brooks: *From a Writer's Notebook*

All that is necessary for the triumph of evil is that good men do nothing.
> Edmund Burke

This is a good universe. There is no permanent place in it for evil. Yea, it would seem as if God and man and the universe itself were opposed to evil. Evil may hide behind this fallacy and that, but it will be hunted from fallacy to fallacy until there is no more fallacy for it to hide behind.
> Thomas Carlyle

When God sends us evil, He sends with it the weapon to conquer it.
> Paul Vincent Carroll: "Shadow and Substance," in *Irish Stories and Plays*, published 1959 by The Devin-Adair Co.

Even in evil, that dark cloud that hangs over creation, we discern rays of light and hope, and gradually come to see, in suffering and temptation, proofs and instruments of the sublimest purposes of wisdom and love.
> William Ellery Channing

All evil, in fact, the very existence of evil, is inexplicable till we refer to the fatherhood of God. It hangs a huge blot in the universe till the orb of divine love rises behind it.—In that we detect its meaning.—It appears to us but a finite shadow, as it passes across the disk of infinite light.

> Edwin Hubbell Chapin

Although it be with truth thou speakest evil, this also is a crime.

> St. John Chrysostom: *Homilies*, III

As there is much beast and some devil in man, so there is some angel and some God in him.—The beast and devil may be conquered, but in this life are never destroyed.

> Samuel Taylor Coleridge

We are no more responsible for the evil thoughts that pass through our minds than a scarecrow for the birds which fly over the seedplot he has to guard. The sole responsibility in each case is to prevent them from settling.

> John Churton Collins: *Maxims and Reflections*

There are three modes of bearing the ills of life: by indifference, which is the most common; by philosophy, which is the most ostentatious; and by religion, which is the most effectual.

> Charles Caleb Colton

The belief in a supernatural source of evil is not necessary; men alone are quite capable of every wickedness.

> Joseph Conrad: *Under Western Eyes*, Pt. II, 4

We cannot do evil to others without doing it to ourselves.

> Joseph François Eduard Desmahis

Evil to him who thinks evil.

> Edward III—Motto of the Order of the Garter

The real problem is in the hearts and minds of men. It is not a problem of physics but of ethics. It is easier to denature plutonium than to denature the evil spirit of man.

> Albert Einstein

Every evil comes to us on wings and goes away limping.

> French Proverb

Our character is but the stamp on our souls of the free choices of good and evil we have made through life.

> John Cunningham Geikie

The Evil One has left, the evil ones remain.

> Johann Wolfgang von Goethe: *Faust*, Act I, sc. 6, l. 174

Know what is evil, no matter how worshipped it may be. Let the man of sense not mistake it, even when clothed in brocade, or at times crowned in gold, because it cannot thereby hide its hypocrisy, for slavery does not lose its infamy, however noble the master.

> Baltasar Gracián y Morales: *Gracián's Manual*

A beast is but like itself, but an evil man is half a beast and half a devil.

> Joseph Hall (Bishop of Norwich): *Meditations and Vows*, II

Evil is here in the world, not because God wants it or uses it here, but because he knows not how at the moment to remove it . . . Evil, therefore, is a fact not to be explained away, but to be accepted; and accepted not to be endured, but to be conquered. It is a challenge neither to our reason nor to our patience, but to our courage.

> John Haynes Holmes (Newton, *My Idea of God*, p. 119)

The lives of the best of us are spent in choosing between evils.

> Junius

No evil man is happy.

> Juvenal: *Satires*, Sat. IV, l. 8

We believe no evil till the evil's done.

> Jean de La Fontaine: *Fables*, Bk. I, fab. 8

Evil springs up, and flowers, and bears no
  seed,
And feeds the green earth with its swift
  decay,
Leaving it richer for the growth of truth.

James Russell Lowell: *Prometheus*

Evil into the mind of God or man
May come and go, so unapprov'd, and leave
No spot or blame behind.

John Milton: *Paradise Lost*, Bk. V, l. 117

Resist not evil.

New Testament: Matthew 5: 39

Sufficient unto the day is the evil thereof.

New Testament: Matthew 6: 34

Men loved darkness rather than light, because their deeds were evil.

New Testament: John 3: 19

Every one that doeth evil hateth the light.

New Testament: John 3: 20

Recompense to no man evil for evil.

New Testament: Romans 12: 17

Evil communications corrupt good manners.

New Testament: I Corinthians 15: 33

Abstain from all appearance of evil.

New Testament: I Thessalonians 5: 22

Many have puzzled themselves about the
origin of evil. I am content to observe that
there is evil, and that there is a way to escape
from it, and with this I begin and end.

John Newton

What is evil?—Whatever springs from weakness.

Frederich Wilhelm Nietzsche:
The Antichrist

The imagination of man's heart is evil from
his youth.

Old Testament: Genesis 8: 21

And unto man he said, Behold, the fear of
the Lord, that is wisdom; and to depart from
evil is understanding.

Old Testament: Job 28: 28

Yea, though I walk through the valley of
the shadow of death, I will fear no evil.

Old Testament: Psalm 23: 4

Fret not thyself because of evildoers, neither
be thou envious against the workers of
iniquity. For they shall soon be cut down
like the grass, and wither as the green herb.

Old Testament: Psalm 37: 1–2

I make peace, and create evil: I the Lord do
all these things.

Old Testament Isaiah 45: 7

Men never do evil so completely and cheerfully as when they do it from religious
conviction.

Blaise Pascal: *Pensées*

It is among the profound convictions of a
free society that the last word is never left
with evil, that God never gets in a blind
alley, and that even from the conspiracies
of malevolence some good may be drawn,
because importunity wins its consent even
against the most reluctant.

James H. Robinson: *Tomorrow Is Today*

Multitudes think they like to do evil; yet no
man ever really enjoyed doing evil since God
made the world.

John Ruskin: *Stones of Venice,*
Vol. I, ch. 11

There is some soul of goodness in things evil,
Would men observingly distil it out.

William Shakespeare: *Henry V,*
Act IV, sc. 1, l. 4

There is nothing either good or bad, but
thinking makes it so.

William Shakespeare: *Hamlet,*
Act II, sc. 2, l. 256

Never let a man imagine that he can pursue a good end by evil means, without sinning against his own soul.—The evil effect on himself is certain.

Robert Southey

He who is in evil, is also in the punishment of evil.

Emmanuel Swedenborg

Of two evils we should always choose the less.

Thomas à Kempis: *Imitation of Christ*

"Resist not evil" means "Do not resist the evil man," which is to say, "Never offer violence to another," which is to say, "Never commit an act that is contrary to love."

Leo Tolstoy: *On Life*

There are three all-powerful evils: lust, anger and greed.

Tulsī Dās: *Rāmāyan*

Evil is in antagonism with the entire creation.

Zschokke

F

FAITH

Without faith, we are as stained glass windows in the dark.

Anonymous

There are no miracles to men who do not believe in them.

Anonymous

It is not faith and works; it is not faith or works; it is faith that works.

Anonymous

Faith is the heart of the mind.

Anonymous

It is never a question with any of us of faith or no faith; the question always is, "In what or in whom do we put our faith?"

Anonymous

He who is small in faith will never be great in anything but failure.

Anonymous

Faith is the wire that connects you to grace, and over which grace comes streaming from God.

Anonymous

We need abounding faith that will cut all the t's off all the "Can'ts" and make them into "Cans."

Anonymous

Faith is, in the spiritual realm, what money is in the commercial realm.

Anonymous

The faith of the head is the faith that is dead;
The faith of the heart is better in part;
But the faith of the hand is the faith that will stand,
For the faith that will do must include the first two.

Anonymous

The great believers have been the unwearied waiters.

Anonymous

Faith never yet outstripped the bounty of the Lord.

Anonymous

Faith is believing what you know ain't so.

Anonymous

I need wide spaces in my heart
Where Faith and I can go apart
    And grow serene.
Life gets so choked by busy living,
Kindness so lost in fussy giving
    That Love slips by unseen.

Anonymous

It takes more than a soft pillow to insure sound sleep.

Anonymous

Faith is not merely praying
Upon our knees at night;
Faith is not merely straying
Through darkness into light;
Faith is not merely waiting
For glory that may be.
Faith is the brave endeavor,
The splendid enterprise,
The strength to serve, whatever
Conditions may arise.

Anonymous

129

Faith is kept alive in us, and gathers strength, more from practise than from speculations.

Joseph Addison: *The Spectator*

The cruse of oil and the barrel of meal overflow because the widow has firm faith.

Agathias Scholasticus: *On the Widow Who Fed Elijah*

Men can be attracted but not forced to the faith. You may drive people to baptism, (but) you won't move them one step further in religion.

Alcuin

Without faith a man can do nothing. But faith can stifle all science.

Henri Frédéric Amiel: *Journal*

Faith is a certitude without proofs. . . . Faith is a sentiment, for it is a hope; it is an instinct, for it precedes all outward instruction.

Ibid.

Faith has to do with things that are not seen, and hope with things that are not in hand.

St. Thomas Aquinas: *Summa theologica*

Faith is to believe, on the word of God, what we do not see, and its reward is to see and enjoy what we believe.

St. Augustine

For what is faith unless it is to believe what you do not see?

St. Augustine

Man must be arched and buttressed from within, else the temple wavers to the dust.

Marcus Aurelius

There never was found in any age of the world, either philosopher or sect, or law, or discipline which did so highly exalt the public good as the Christian faith.

Sir Francis Bacon

Give to faith the things which belong to faith.

Sir Francis Bacon: *Advancement of Learning*

Faith is a higher faculty than reason.

Philip James Bailey: *Festus*

I believe in the incomprehensibility of God.

Honoré de Balzac

They never fail who light
Their lamp of faith at the unwavering flame
Burnt for the altar service of the Race
Since the beginning.

Elsa Barker: *The Frozen Grail*

On the whole, more people are cheated by believing nothing than by believing too much.

P. T. Barnum

Inflexible in faith, invincible in arms.

James Beattie: *The Minstrel*

Faith and works are like the light and heat of a candle; they cannot be separated.

Faith without works is like a bird without wings; though she may hop about on earth, she will never fly to heaven.—But when both are joined together, then doth the soul mount up to her eternal rest.

Joseph Beaumont

If it weren't for faith, there would be no living in this world; we couldn't even eat hash.

Josh Billings

Live by faith until you have faith.

Peter Boehler to John Wesley

Christian faith is nothing else but the soul's venture. It ventures to Christ, in opposition to all legal terrors. It ventures on Christ in opposition to our guiltiness. It ventures for Christ, in opposition to all difficulties and discouragements.

William Bridges

Man is not naturally a cynic; he wants pitifully to believe, in himself, in his future, in his community and in the nation in which he is a part.

Louis Bromfield

If your faith in God is stronger for every humble task in which you need and get His aid, then that humble task is necessary to the fulness of your faith in God. It will make the music of your life more firm and solid.

Phillips Brooks

To believe only possibilities is not Faith, but mere Philosophy.

Sir Thomas Browne: *Religio Medici*

A little faith all undisproved.

Elizabeth Barrett Browning: *The Sleep*

'Tis well averred,
A scientific faith's absurd.

Robert Browning: *Easter Day*

Orthodoxy can be learned from others; living faith must be a matter of personal experience.

J. W. Buchsel

You can do very little with faith, but you can do nothing without it.

Samuel Butler the Younger: *Note-Books*

Faith is a knowledge of the benevolence of God toward us, and a certain persuasion of His veracity.

John Calvin: *Institutes of the Christian Religion*

Faith makes all evil good to us, and all good better; unbelief makes all good evil, and all evil worse. Faith laughs at the shaking of the spear; unbelief trembles at the shaking of a leaf, unbelief starves the soul; faith finds food in famine, and a table in the wilderness. In the greatest danger, faith says, "I have a great God." When outward strength is broken, faith rests on the promises. In the midst of sorrow, faith draws the sting out of every trouble, and takes out the bitterness from every affliction.

Robert Cecil

Skepticism has not founded empires, established principles, or changed the world's heart. The great doers of history have always been men of faith.

Edwin Hubbell Chapin

All the strength and force of man comes from his faith in things unseen. He who believes is strong; he who doubts is weak. Strong convictions precede great actions.

James Freeman Clarke

Faith is the daring of the soul to go farther than it can see.

William Newton Clarke

Faith is the ear of the soul.

Clement of Alexandria

Never yet did there exist a full faith in the divine word which did not expand the intellect while it purified the heart; which did not multiply the aims and objects of the understanding, while it fixed and simplified those of the desires and passions.

Samuel Taylor Coleridge

Faith makes the discords of the present the harmonies of the future.

Robert Collyer: *Things New and Old*

Faith and works are as necessary to our spiritual life as Christians, as soul and body are to our life as men; for faith is the soul of religion, and works, the body.

Arthur W. Colton

"Take courage, soul!
Hold not thy strength in vain!
With faith o'ercome the steeps
Thy God hath set for thee.
Beyond the Alpine summits of great pain
Lieth thine Italy."

Rose Terry Cooke: *Beyond*

Faith on a full stomach may be simply contentment—but if you have it when you're hungry, it's genuine.

Reprinted from *The Country Parson*, by Frank A. Clark, by permission of the Register-Tribune Syndicate

Faith needs her daily bread.

Dinah Maria Mulock Craik: *Fortune's Marriage*

I prefer a firm religious faith to every other blessing.—For it makes life a discipline of goodness; creates new hopes, when those of the world vanish; throws over the decay of life the most gorgeous of all lights; and awakens life even in death.

Sir Humphrey Davy

About 999 in 1000 believe everything; the other one believes nothing—except that it is a good thing for human society that the 999 believe everything.

Michael J. Dee: *Conclusions*

Faith is dead to doubt, dumb to discouragement, blind to impossibilities.

The Defender

No longer by implicit faith we err,
Whilst every man's his own interpreter.
Sir John Denham: *Progress of Human Learning*

To me, faith means not worrying.

John Dewey

Faith is a fine invention
  For gentlemen who see;
But Microscopes are prudent
  In an emergency.
Emily Dickinson: *Poems, Second Series*

Reason is our soul's left hand, Faith her right,
By these we reach divinity.
John Donne: *To the Countess of Bedford*

To take up half on trust, and half to try,
Name it not faith, but bungling bigotry.
John Dryden: *The Hind and the Panther*

Reason saw not, till Faith sprung the light.
John Dryden: *Religio Laici*

Who breaks his faith, no faith is held with him.
Guillaume de Salluste Du Bartas: *Devine Weekes and Workes*

Faith is a crusade—no weaklings need apply. No, I take that back. For we have here a regimen that makes weak men strong and cowards brave.

Henry M. Edmonds

Science has sometimes been said to be opposed to faith, and inconsistent with it. —But all science, in fact, rests on a basis of faith, for it assumes the permanence and uniformity of natural laws—a thing which can never be demonstrated.

Tryon Edwards

All I have seen teaches me to trust the Creator for all I have not seen.

Ralph Waldo Emerson

They can conquer who believe they can.

Ralph Waldo Emerson

The faith that stands on authority is not faith. The reliance on authority measures the decline of religion.

Ralph Waldo Emerson: *The Over-Soul*

Faith and love are apt to be spasmodic in the best minds. Men live on the brink of mysteries and harmonies into which they never enter, and with their hand on the door-latch they die outside.

Ralph Waldo Emerson: *Letter to Thomas Carlyle*, March 12, 1835

Religion is a life. Faith is only the fuse.

Et Cetera

Faith is not a sense, nor sight, nor reason, but taking God at His Word.

Arthur Benoni Evans

It is faith among men that holds the moral elements of society together, as it is faith in God that binds the world to his throne.

William Maxwell Evarts

Faith of our fathers, holy faith,
We will be true to thee till death.
Frederick William Faber: *Faith of Our Fathers*

There are three acts of faith; assent, acceptance, and assurance.

John Flavel

Unless there is within us that which is above us, we shall soon yield to that which is about us.

Peter Taylor Forsyth

Man cannot live without faith because the prime requisite in life's adventure is courage, and the sustenance of courage is faith.

Harry Emerson Fosdick

It is cynicism and fear that freeze life; it is faith that thaws it out, releases it, sets it free.

Harry Emerson Fosdick

In the affairs of this World, Men are saved, not by Faith, but by the want of it

Benjamin Franklin: Poor Richard

We cannot live on probabilities. The faith in which we can live bravely and die in peace must be a certainty, so far as it professes to be a faith at all, or it is nothing.

James Anthony Froude

Faith sees by the ears.

Thomas Fuller: Gnomologia

Doubters invert the metaphor and insist that they need faith as big as a mountain in order to move a mustard seed.

Webb B. Garrison

We lean on Faith; and some less wise have cried,
"Behold the butterfly, the seed that's cast!"
Vain hopes that fall like flowers before the blast!

Richard Watson Gilder: Love and Death, Houghton Mifflin Company

Epochs of faith, are epochs of fruitfulness; but epochs of unbelief, however glittering are barren of all permanent good.

Johann Wolfgang von Goethe

Faith in order, which is the basis of science, cannot reasonably be separated from faith in an ordainer, which is the basis of religion.

Asa Gray

Drop to your knees beside the wide road,
And pick up a stone to turn in your hand.
Now make one like it—seed of the earth—
Then if you succeed, tell me there's no God.
Take clay and dust, and fashion a child
With wistful brown eyes and breath in its lungs;
Make flesh-warm lips, a brain, and red blood—
Then, if you succeed, tell me there's no God.

Carrie Esther Hammill, in Denver Post

When false things are brought low,
And swift things have grown slow,
Feigning like froth shall go,
Faith be aye for aye.

Thomas Hardy: Between Us Now

Faith is not a stained-glass word reserved only for religious use, though it is essential to religion because it is essential to life. It is not something we can see on every streetcorner, but we dare not cross the street without it. . . . If faith were removed for one day, our whole way of life would collapse.

V. Carney Hargroves, in Quote

Christian faith is a grand cathedral, with divinely pictured windows.—Standing without, you can see no glory, nor can imagine any, but standing within every ray of light reveals a harmony of unspeakable splendors.

Nathaniel Hawthorne

Love asks faith and faith, firmness.

George Herbert: Jacula Prudentum

Faith is a thing that's four-square; let it fall this way or that, it not declines at all.

Robert Herrick: Hesperides

What here we hope for, we shall once inherit;
By Faith we walk here, not by the Spirit.

Robert Herrick: Faith

Faith is a gift of God which man can neither give nor take away by promise of rewards or menaces of torture.

Thomas Hobbes: *Leviathan*

Faith must have adequate evidence, else it is mere superstition.

Archibald Alexander Hodge

Faith, as an intellectual state, is self-reliance.

Oliver Wendell Holmes, Sr.: *The Professor at the Breakfast Table*

Wake in our breast the living fires,
The holy faith that warmed our sires.

Oliver Wendell Holmes: *Army Hymn*

Workless faith God never regards,
Faithless work God never rewards.

D. L. Hood

When men cease to be faithful to their God, he who expects to find them so to each other will be much disappointed.

George Horne

While reason is puzzling herself about the mystery, faith is turning it into her daily bread and feeding on it thankfully in her heart of hearts.

Frederic D. Huntington

Faith is an act of self-consecration, in which the will, the intellect, and the affections all have their place.

William R. Inge, in Marchant's *Wit and Wisdom of Dean Inge*, Longmans, Green & Co., Ltd., London

Faith is an act of rational choice which determines us to act as if certain things were true and in the confident expectation that they will prove to be true.

William R. Inge: *Labels and Libels*, p. 46, Harper & Row, Publishers, Inc.

It is not reason makes faith hard, but life.

Jean Ingelow: *A Pastor's Letter to a Young Poet*

Fear knocked at the door. Faith answered. No one was there.

Inscription at Hind's Head Inn, Bray, England

There is a limit where the intellect fails and breaks down, and this limit is where the questions concerning God, and freewill, and immortality arise.

Immanuel Kant

A simple, childlike faith in a Divine Friend solves all the problems that come to us by land or sea.

Helen Keller, Doubleday & Company, Inc.

And we shall be made truly wise if we be made content; content, too, not only with what we can understand, but content with what we do not understand—the habit of mind which theologians call—and rightly—faith in God.

Charles Kingsley: *Health and Education: On Bio-Geology*

Faith without works is nothing worth,
As dead as door-nail unless deeds follow.

William Langland: *Piers Plowman*

Defender of the Faith.

A Latin phrase, medieval, now used in title of English kings

Faith is the sister of justice.

Latin Proverb

Let us have faith that right makes might, and in that faith, let us to the end, dare to do our duty, as we understand it.

Abraham Lincoln: Speech in New York

The only faith that wears well and holds its color in all weathers, is that which is woven of conviction and set with sharp mordant of experience.

James Russell Lowell: *My Study Windows: Abraham Lincoln*

Yes, faith is a goodly anchor;
When skies are sweet as a psalm,

At the bows it lolls so stalwart
In its bluff, broad-shouldered calm . . .

But, after the shipwreck, tell me
What help in its iron thews,
Still true to the broken hawser,
Deep down among sea-weed and ooze?
James Russell Lowell: *After the Burial*

A capuchin says: wear a grey coat and a hood, a rope round thy body, and sandals on thy feet. A cordelier says: put on a black hood. An ordinary papist says: do this or that work, hear mass, pray, fast, give alms, etc. But a true Christian says: I am justified and saved only by faith in Christ, without any works or merits of my own. Compare these together, and judge which is the true righteousness.
Martin Luther: *Table Talk*

A perfect faith would lift us absolutely above fear.
George Macdonald: *Sir Gibbie*

The principal part of faith is patience.
George Macdonald: *Weighed and Wanting*

The Calvinistic people of Scotland, Switzerland, Holland, and New England, have been more moral than the same classes among other nations. Those who preached faith, or in other words a pure mind, have always produced more popular virtue than those who preached good acts, or the mere regulation of outward works.
Sir James Mackintosh

O welcome pure-eyed Faith, white-handed Hope,
Thou hovering angel, girt with golden wings!
John Milton: *Comus*

The faith that will shut the mouths of lions must be more than a pious hope that they will not bite.
Missionary Tidings

A little faith will bring your soul to heaven, but a lot of faith will bring heaven to your soul.
Dwight L. Moody

If faith produce no works, I see
That faith is not a living tree.
Thus faith and works together grow;
No separate life they e'er can know:
They're soul and body, hand and heart:
What God hath joined, let no man part.
Hannah More: *Dan and Jane*

The beginning of anxiety is the end of faith, and the beginning of true faith is the end of anxiety.
George Müller: *Signs of the Times*

The experience of life nearly always works towards the confirmation of faith.—It is the total significance of life that it reveals God to man; and life only can do this; neither thought, nor demonstration, nor miracle, but only life, weaving its threads of daily toil and trial and joy into a pattern on which, at last, is inscribed the name of "God."
Theodore T. Munger

Faith marches at the head of the army of progress.—It is found beside the most refined life, the freest government, the profoundest philosophy, the noblest poetry, the purest humanity.
Theodore T. Munger

All the scholastic scaffolding falls, as a ruined edifice, before one single word—faith.
Napoleon Bonaparte

If ye have faith as a grain of mustard seed, ye shall say unto this mountain, Remove hence to yonder place; and it shall remove; and nothing shall be impossible unto you.
New Testament: Matthew 17: 20

Blessed are they that have not seen, and yet have believed.
New Testament: John 20: 29

The just shall live by faith.
New Testament: Romans 1: 17

We walk by faith, not by sight.
New Testament: II Corinthians 5: 7

Fight the good fight of faith.

> *New Testament: I Timothy 6: 12*

I have fought a good fight, I have finished my course, I have kept the faith.

> *New Testament: II Timothy 4: 7*

Faith is the substance of things hoped for, the evidence of things not seen.

> *New Testament: Hebrews 11: 1*

For as the body without the spirit is dead, so faith without works is dead also.

> *New Testament: James 2: 26*

I . . . exhort you that ye should earnestly contend for the faith which was once delivered unto the saints.

> *New Testament: Jude 1: 3*

Belief is a truth held in the mind; faith is a fire in the heart.

> Joseph Fort Newton

If a man have a strong faith he can indulge in the luxury of scepticism.

> Frederich Wilhelm Nietzsche

I know that my redeemer liveth.

> *Old Testament: Job 19: 25*

My faith looks up to Thee,
Thou Lamb of Calvary,
  Saviour divine!

> Ray Palmer: *Hymn, The Lamb of God*

The truly religious man does everything as if everything depended upon himself, and then leaves everything as if everything depended on God.

> Joseph Parker

But give me, Lord, eyes to behold the truth;
A seeing sense that knows the eternal right;
A heart with pity filled, and gentlest truth;
A manly faith that makes all darkness light.

> Theodore Parker: *The Higher Good*

Faith is a kind of winged intellect. The great workmen of history have been men who believed like giants.

> Charles Henry Parkhurst: *Sermons: Walking by Faith*

Faith affirms what the senses do not affirm, but not the contrary of what they perceive. It is above, and not contrary to.

> Blaise Pascal: *Pensées*

In Faith and Hope the world will disagree.

> Alexander Pope: *Essay on Man*

He that has lost faith, what has he left to live on?

> Publilius Syrus: *Sententiae*

Lack of faith in God is the source of most of society's troubles.

> Albert E. Ribourg

Faith will beget in us three things: Vision, Venture, Victory.

> George W. Ridout: *The Wesleyan Methodist*

Faith is saying "Amen" to God.

> Merv Rosell

Faith is like a lily, lifted high and white.

> Christina Georgina Rossetti: *Hope*

The errors of faith are better than the best thoughts of unbelief.

> Thomas Russell

They live no longer in the faith of reason.

> Johann Christoph Friedrich von Schiller: *Wallenstein's Death*

In actual life every great enterprise begins with and takes its first forward step in faith.

> August Wilhelm von Schlegel

Faith is like love: It cannot be forced.

> Arthur Schopenhauer: *Parerga und Paralipomena*

Reason is the triumph of the intellect, faith of the heart.

> James Schouler: *History
> of the United States*

All work that is worth anything is done in faith.

> Albert Schweitzer: *Out of My Life
> and Thought*, Holt, Rinehart &
> Winston, Inc.

He wears his faith but as the fashion of his hat; it ever changes with the next block.

> William Shakespeare: *Much Ado
> About Nothing*, Act I, sc. 1, l. 75

There are no tricks in plain and simple faith.

> William Shakespeare: *Julius Caesar*,
> Act IV, sc. 2, l. 22

We believe the task ahead of us is never as great as the Power behind us.

> Sign on a Church Bulletin Board

The saddest thing that can befall a soul
Is when it loses faith in God and woman.

> Alexander Smith: *A Life Drama*

Faith is the subtle chain
Which binds us to the infinite; the voice
Of a deep life within, that will remain
Until we crowd it thence.

> Elizabeth Oakes Smith: *Faith*

To believe in something not yet proved and to underwrite it with our lives: it is the only way we can keep the future open. Man, surrounded by facts, permitting himself no surprise, no intuitive flash, no great hypothesis, no risk, is in a locked cell. Ignorance cannot seal the mind and imagination more securely.

> Lillian Smith: *The Journey*,
> The Cresset Press

It is always right that a man should be able to render a reason for the faith that is within him.

> Sydney Smith, in Lady Holland's *Memoir*

Faith is blended with the baby's first food.

> Ralph W. Sockman: *Sabbath Recorder*

Thy path is plain and straight,—that light
is given:
Onward in faith,—and leave the rest to
Heaven.

> Robert Southey: *The Retrospect*

Faith goes up the stairs that love has made and looks out of the windows which hope has opened.

> Charles Haddon Spurgeon

At the summit of every noble human endeavor, you will find a steeple pointing toward God.

> Mack Stokes: *The Argonaut*

Faith does nothing alone—nothing of itself, but everything under God, by God, through God.

> William Stoughton

Faith separate from love is not faith, but mere science, which in itself is void of spiritual life.

> Emanuel Swedenborg: *Heaven and Hell*

Christian, what of the night?—
I cannot tell; I am blind.
I halt and hearken behind
If haply the hours will go back
And return to the dear dead light,
To the watchfires and stars that of old
Shone where the sky now is black,
Glowed where the earth now is cold.

> Algernon Charles Swinburne: *A Watch
> in the Night*

Faith is a certain image of eternity. All things are present to it—things past, and things to come; it converses with angels, and antedates the hymns of glory. Every man that hath this grace is as certain there are glories for him, if he perseveres in duty, as if he had heard and sung the thanksgiving song for the blessed sentence of doomsday.

> Jeremy Taylor

Faith is the root of all blessings. Believe, and you shall be saved; believe, and you must needs be satisfied; believe, and you cannot but be comforted and happy.

> Jeremy Taylor

What can be more foolish than to think that all this rare fabric of heaven and earth could come by chance, when all the skill of science is not able to make an oyster.

Jeremy Taylor

And cling to Faith beyond the forms of Faith!

Alfred, Lord Tennyson:
The Ancient Sage

To persecute
Makes a faith hated, and is furthermore
No perfect witness of a perfect faith
In him who persecutes.

Alfred, Lord Tennyson: *Queen Mary*

Strong Son of God, immortal Love,
Whom we, that have not seen thy face,
By faith, and faith alone, embrace,
Believing where we cannot prove.

Alfred, Lord Tennyson: *In Memoriam*

We have but faith: we cannot know,
For knowledge is of things we see;
And yet we trust it comes from Thee,
A beam in darkness: let it grow.

Ibid.

Faith and unfaith can ne'er be equal powers;
Unfaith in aught is want of faith in all.

Alfred, Lord Tennyson: *Idylls of the
King: Merlin and Vivien*

The night is long and pain weighs heavily,
But God will hold His world above
despair;
Look to the East, where up the lucid sky
The morning climbs! The day shall yet be
fair.

Celia Laighton Thaxter: *Faith*

Faith is required of thee, and a sincere life, not loftiness of intellect, nor deepness in the mysteries of God.

Thomas à Kempis: *Imitation of Christ*

The mason asks but a narrow shelf to spring his brick from; man requires only an infinitely narrower one to spring his arch of faith from.

Henry David Thoreau: *Journal*

Despotism may govern without faith, but Liberty cannot.

Alexis de Tocqueville

Faith is the force of life.

Leo Tolstoy: *My Confessions*

An empty, meaningless faith may be worse than none.

D. Elton Trueblood

To believe that this terrible machine world is really from God, in God and unto God, and that through it and in spite of its blind fatality all works for good—that is faith in long trousers.

George Tyrrell

Under the influence of the blessed Spirit, faith produces holiness, and holiness strengthens faith. Faith, like a fruitful parent, is plenteous in all good works; and good works, like dutiful children, confirm and add to the support of faith.

Juan Valera

Faith in an all-seeing and personal God, elevates the soul, purifies the emotions, sustains human dignity, and lends poetry, nobility, and holiness to the commonest state, condition, and manner of life.

Juan Valera

Man needs faith in something he can trust to mend his troubles. For some it is the love of a good woman; for others, scotch tape.

Bill Vaughan: *Kansas City Star*

For they conquer who believe they can.

Virgil

Shew me thy faith by thy workes; if I have all faith and not luve, I am as sounding brass, or as a tinckling cymball; if faith workes, it workes by luve.

William Walwyn

Faith is raising the sail of our little boat until it is caught up in the soft winds above and picks up speed, not from anything within itself, but from the vast resources of the universe around us.

> Ralph W. Ward, Jr.: "Faith and the Third Dimension," in *Think*, April, 1955

Faith, mighty faith the promise sees
 And rests on that alone:
Laughs at impossibilities,
 And says it shall be done.

> Charles Wesley: *Hymns*, no. 360

A string of opinions is no more Christian faith, than a string of beads is Christian practice.

> John Wesley

As the flower is before the fruit, so is faith before good works.

> Richard Whately

Faith is the antiseptic of the soul.

> Walt Whitman: *Leaves of Grass*, Preface

Through this dark and stormy night
Faith beholds a feeble light
 Up the blackness streaking;
Knowing God's own time is best,
In a patient hope I rest
 For the full day-breaking!

> John Greenleaf Whittier: *Barclay of Ury*

A bending staff I would not break,
A feeble faith I would not shake,
Nor even rashly pluck away
The error which some truth may stay,
Whose loss might leave the soul without
A shield against the shafts of doubt.

> John Greenleaf Whittier: *Questions of Life*

We live by Faith; but Faith is not the slave
Of text and legend. Reason's voice and God's,
Nature's and Duty's, never are at odds.

> John Greenleaf Whittier: *Requirement*

Nothing before, nothing behind;
 The steps of faith
Fall on the seeming void, and find
 The rock beneath.

> John Greenleaf Whittier: *My Soul and I*

Faith is the root of works. A root that produceth nothing is dead.

> Thomas Wilson: *Maxims of Piety and of Christianity*

To believe on Christ is initial faith; to receive Him is appropriating faith; to understand Him is intelligent faith; to assimilate Him is active faith.

> Cornelius Woelfkin

Faith is the eye that sees Him, the hand that clings to Him, the receiving power that appropriates Him.

> Frederick James Woodbridge

'Tis hers to pluck the amaranthine flower
 Of Faith, and round the sufferer's temples bind
Wreaths that endure afflictions heaviest shower,
 And do not shrink from sorrow's keenest wind.

> William Wordsworth: *Weak is the Will of Man*

Through love, through hope, and faith's transcendent dower,
We feel that we are greater than we know.

> William Wordsworth: *The River Duddon*

The man without faith is a walking corpse.

> Pope Xystus I: *The Ring*

Faith is not reason's labor, but repose.

> Edward Young

Man is not made to question, but adore.

> Edward Young

Faith is not only a means of obeying, but a principal act of obedience; not only an altar on which to sacrifice, but a sacrifice itself, and perhaps, of all, the greatest. It is a submission of our understandings; an oblation of our idolized reason to God, which he requires so indispensably, that our whole will and affections, though seemingly a larger sacrifice, will not, without it, be received at his hands.

Edward Young

Some wish they did, but no man disbelieves.

Edward Young

Faith lights us through the dark to Deity; faith builds a bridge across the gulf of death, to break the shock that nature cannot shun, and lands thought smoothly on the farther shore.

Edward Young

FAMILY

Civilization varies with the family, and the family with civilization.—Its highest and most complete realization is found where enlightened Christianity prevails; where woman is exalted to her true and lofty place as equal with the man; where husband and wife are one in honor, influence, and affection, and where children are a common bond of care and love.—This is the idea of a perfect family.

William Aikman

It is a reverent thing to see an ancient castle or building not in decay: or to see a fair timber tree sound and perfect. How much more to behold an ancient and noble family which hath stood against the waves and weathers of time.

Sir Francis Bacon: *Essays*

A happy family is but an earlier heaven.

Sir John Bowring

A house without a roof would scarcely be a more different home, than a family unsheltered by God's friendship, and the sense of being always rested in His providential care and guidance.

Horace Bushnell

The ties of family and of country were never intended to circumscribe the soul. If allowed to become exclusive, engrossing, clannish, so as to shut out the general claims of the human race, the highest end of Providence is frustrated, and home, instead of being the nursery, becomes the grave of the heart.

William Ellery Channing

The family was ordained of God that children might be trained up for himself; it was before the church, or rather the first form of the church on earth.

Pope Leo XIII

A holy family, that make
Each meal a Supper of the Lord.

Henry Wadsworth Longfellow: *The Golden Legend*, Pt. I

The Christian home is the Master's workshop where the processes of character molding are silently, lovingly, faithfully and successfully carried on.

Richard Monckton Milnes

The son dishonoureth the father, the daughter riseth up against her mother, the daughter in law against her mother in law; a man's enemies are the men of his own house.

Old Testament: Micah 7: 6

The family is more sacred than the state, and men are begotten not for the earth and for time, but for Heaven and eternity.

Pope Pius XI: *Casti Connubii*

The three stages of modern family life are matrimony, acrimony, and alimony.

Virginian-Pilot

FASTING

When I am at Rome, I fast on a Saturday: when I am at Milan, I do not. Do the same. Follow the custom of the church where you are.

St. Ambrose

He who fasteth and doeth no good, saveth his bread, but loseth his soul.

> Henry George Bohn: *Handbook of Proverbs*

Whoso will pray, he must fast and be clean, And fat his soul, and make his body lean.

> Geoffrey Chaucer: *The Somnour's Tale*, l. 171

Fasting is better than prayer.

> St. Clement: *Second Epistle to the Corinthians*

Let not your fasts be with hypocrites, for they fast on Mondays and Thursdays, but do you fast on Wednesdays and Fridays.

> *The Didache*, or *Teachings of the Twelve Apostles*

The best of all medicines are resting and fasting.

> Benjamin Franklin

Noah the first was (as Tradition says) That did ordain the fast for forty days.

> Robert Herrick: *The Fast, Or Lent*

A fast is better than a bad meal.

> Irish Proverb

Who fast but does no other good saves his bread but goes to Hell.

> Italian Proverb

And join with thee calm Peace and Quiet, Spare Fast, that oft with gods doth diet.

> John Milton: *Il Penseroso*, l. 45

Moreover when ye fast, be not, as the hypocrites, of a sad countenance: for they disfigure their faces, that they may appear unto men to fast.

> *New Testament: Matthew 6: 16*

Feast to-day makes fast to-morrow.

> Titus Maccius Plautus: *Aulularia*

Surfeit is the father of much fast.

> William Shakespeare: *Measure for Measure*, Act I, sc. 2, l. 130

Feast, and your halls are crowded; Fast, and the world goes by.

> Ella Wheeler Wilcox: *Solitude*, Rand McNally & Co.

FATE

God overrules all mutinous accidents, brings them under his laws of fate, and makes them all serviceable to his purpose.

> Marcus Aurelius

We, in some unknown Power's employ, Move on a rigorous line; Can neither, when we will, enjoy; Nor, when we will, resign.

> Matthew Arnold

If by fate anyone means the will or power of God, let him keep his meaning but mend his language; for fate commonly means a necessary process which will have its way apart from the will of God and of men.

> St. Augustine: *The City of God*

Let those deplore their doom, Whose hope still grovels in this dark sojourn; But lofty souls, who look beyond the tomb, Can smile at fate, and wonder how they mourn.

> James Beattie: *The Minstrel*, Bk. I

The possession which the Creator has written on our forehead, be it small or great, we shall surely attain, even in the desert; and more than this we can never get, though we be on Mount Meru, whose sides are packed with gold.

> Bhartrihari: *The Vairagya Sataka*

Fate is not the ruler, but the servant of Providence.

> Edward George Bulwer-Lytton

Fate! there is no fate.—Between the thought and the success God is the only agent.

> Edward George Bulwer-Lytton

Eternal Deities
Who rule the World with absolute decrees,
And write whatever Time shall bring to pass
With pens of adamant on plates of brass.

John Dryden: *Palamon and Arcite*,
Bk. I, l. 470

All things are ordered by God, but his providence takes in our free agency, as well as his own sovereignty.

Tryon Edwards

Whatever limits us, we call Fate. . . . The limitations refine as the soul purifies, but the ring of necessity is always perched at the top.

Ralph Waldo Emerson: *Conduct of Life: Fate*

A strict belief in fate is the worst kind of slavery; on the other hand there is comfort in the thought that God will be moved by our prayers.

Epicurus

Though men determine, the gods do dispose: and oft times many things fall out betweene the cup and the lip.

Robert Greene: *Perimedes the Blacksmith*

'Tis writ on Paradise's gate,
"Woe to the dupe that yields to Fate!"

Hafiz (Shams-ud-Din Mohammed)

I do not know beneath what sky
   Nor on what seas shall be thy fate:
I only know it shall be high,
   I only know it shall be great.

Richard Hovey: *Unmanifest Destiny*, st. 7

That which God writes on thy forehead, thou wilt come to it.

The Koran

Fate holds the strings, and Men like children move
But as they're led: Success is from above.

Sir Henry Lansdowne: *Heroic Love*,
Act V, sc. 1

Let us, then, be up and doing,
   With a heart for any fate;

Still achieving, still pursuing,
   Learn to labour and to wait.

Henry Wadsworth Longfellow:
A Psalm Of Life, st. 9

Fate does not jest and events are not a matter of chance—there is no existence out of nothing.

Gamal Abdel Nasser: *The Philosophy of the Revolution*

He putteth down one, and setteth up another.

Old Testament: Psalms 75: 7

All things come alike to all: there is one event to the righteous, and to the wicked; to the good and to the clean, and to the unclean; to him that sacrificeth, and to him that sacrificeth not: as is the good, so is the sinner; and he that sweareth, as he that feareth an oath.

Old Testament: Ecclesiastes 9: 2

Yes, the first morning of creation wrote what the last dawn of reckoning shall read.

Omar Khayyám: *Rubáiyát*

Heaven from all creatures hides the book of fate.

Alexander Pope: *Essay on Man*,
Epis. I, l. 77

Fate has written a tragedy; its name is
   "The Human Heart."
The Theatre is the House of Life,
   Woman the mummer's part.
The Devil enters the prompter's box
   and the play is ready to start.

Robert William Service: *The Harpy*,
st. 12, Ryerson Press

O God! that one might read the book of fate!

William Shakespeare: *Henry IV, Part II*,
Act III, sc. 1, l. 45

I do not believe in that word Fate. It is the refuge of every self-confessed failure.

Andrew Soutar

For man is man and master of his fate.

Alfred, Lord Tennyson: *Idylls of the King, Geraint and Enid*, 1, l. 355

FEAR

Fear is the love that's due to gods and princes.

Anonymous

They that worship God merely from fear,
Would worship the devil too, if he appear.

Anonymous

He who fears God need fear nothing else,
and he who fears not God needs to fear everything else.

Anonymous

What governs men is the fear of truth.

Henri Frédéric Amiel: *Journal*

Fear is pain arising from the anticipation of evil.

Aristotle: *Rhetoric*, Bk. II

God planted fear in the soul as truly as he planted hope or courage.—It is a kind of bell or gong which rings the mind into quick life and avoidance on the approach of danger. —It is the soul's signal for rallying.

Henry Ward Beecher.

The fear of God kills all other fears.

Hugh Black

Christians had lost all fear of death. Since, therefore, the fear of death is the mother of all fear, when it has been destroyed, all other forms of fear are thereby vanquished.

John Sutherland Bonnell: *Heaven and Hell*

I learnt . . . to fear God, and to take my own part.

George Borrow: *Lavengro*, ch. 86

God made all the creatures, and gave them our love and our fear,

To give sign, we and they are his children, one family here.

Robert Browning: *Men and Women, Saul*, VI

The only sure way to take fear out of living is to keep a respectful fear of God in our lives, which means to maintain a reverent attitude toward His place and influence in the scheme of things. This brand of fear is a healthy ingredient, a deterrent to want, a spur to courage and confidence, an insurance against loss, a source of comfort and understanding at any age.

Eugene Asa Carr: *Freedom from Fear*

O praise not him who fears his God
But show me him who knows not fear!

James Fenimore Cooper: *Fate*

There's none but fears a future state; and when the most obdurate swear they do not, their trembling hearts belie their boasting tongues.

John Dryden

Fear not, then, thou child infirm,
There's no god dare wrong a worm.

Ralph Waldo Emerson: *May-Day and Other Pieces: Compensation, I*

Fear always springs from ignorance.

Ralph Waldo Emerson: *Nature, Addresses, and Lectures: The American Scholar*

One of the strange phenomena of the last century is the spectacle of religion dropping the appeal to fear while other human interests have picked it up.

Harry Emerson Fosdick

Those who loved to be feared, fear to be loved; they themselves are of all people the most abject; some fear them, but they fear every one.

St. Francis de Sales

Fear on guilt attends, and deeds of darkness; the virtuous breast ne'er knows it.

William Havard

Since fear is unreasonable, never try to reason with it. So-called "positive thinking" is no weapon against fear. Only positive faith can rout the black menace of fear and give life a radiance.

> Marion Hilliard: Quoted in *Digest of World Reading*, Melbourne, Australia

Fear knocked at the door. Faith answered. No one was there.

> Inscription over mantel of Hinds' Head Hotel, England

In morals, what begins in fear usually ends in wickedness; in religion, what begins in fear usually ends in fanaticism. Fear, either as a principle or a motive, is the beginning of all evil.

> Anna Brownell Jameson

Shame arise from the fear of men, conscience from the fear of God.

> Samuel Johnson: From Miss Reynolds— *Recollections of Johnson*

Our hearts, our hopes, are all with thee,
Our hearts, our hopes, our prayers, our tears,
Our faith triumphant o'er our fears,
Are all with thee,—are all with thee!

> Henry Wadsworth Longfellow: *The Building of the Ship*

Our greatest enemies are not wild beasts or deadly germs but fears that paralise thought, poison the mind, and destroy character. Our only protection against fear is faith.

> Ryllis Goslin Lynip: *Great Ideas of the Bible*, Harper and Row, Publishers, Inc.

Have you ever taken your fears to God, got the horizons of Eternity about them, looked at them in the light of His love and grace?

> Robert J. McCracken

Fear is faithlessness.

> George Macdonald

Neither fear, nor wish for, your last day.

> Martial: *Epigrams*, Bk. X, 47

Fear God. Honour the king.

> *New Testament: I Peter 2: 17*

In the morning thou shalt say, Would God it were even! and at even thou shalt say, Would God it were morning! for the fear of thine heart wherewith thou shalt fear, and for the sight of thine eyes which thou shalt see. . . .

> *Old Testament: Deuteronomy 28: 67*

One that feared God, and eschewed evil.

> *Old Testament: Job 1: 1*

The fear of the Lord is the beginning of wisdom.

> *Old Testament: Psalm 111: 10*

The fear of the Lord is the beginning of knowledge.

> *Old Testament: Proverbs 1: 7*

Happy is the man that feareth alway: but he that hardeneth his heart shall fall into mischief.

> *Old Testament: Proverbs 28: 14*

Let us hear the conclusion of the whole matter: fear God, and keep his commandments: for this is the whole duty of man.

> *Old Testament: Ecclesiastes 12: 13*

He that fleeth from the fear shall fall into the pit; and he that getteth up out of the pit shall be taken in the snare.

> *Old Testament: Jeremiah 48: 44*

There is a virtuous fear which is the effect of faith, and a vicious fear which is the product of doubt and distrust.—The former leads to hope as relying on God, in whom we believe; the latter inclines to despair, as not relying upon God, in whom we do not believe. Persons of the one character fear to lose God; those of the other character fear to find him.

> Blaise Pascal

One of the greatest artifices the devil uses to engage men in vice and debauchery, is to fasten names of contempt on certain virtues, and thus fill weak souls with a foolish fear of passing for scrupulous, should they desire to put them in practice.

Blaise Pascal

For fools rush in where angels fear to tread.

Alexander Pope: *Essay on Criticism,*
Pt. III, l. 66

The only thing we have to fear—is fear itself.

Franklin Delano Roosevelt

Fear is the tax that conscience pays to guilt.

George Sewell

Virtue is bold, and goodness never fearful.

William Shakespeare: *Measure for Measure,* Act III, sc. 1, l. 216

Truly, the souls of men are full of dread:
Ye cannot reason almost with a man
That looks not heavily and full of fear.

William Shakespeare: *Richard III,*
Act II, sc. 3, l. 39

Fear actually is related to love, as are all passions. Fear is the emotion that rises in us when there is a danger facing something or someone that we love, (such as) our good name, our children, our fortune. The catalogue of fears is the catalogue of loves. Love is an attraction for an object; fear is flight from it.

Bishop Fulton J. Sheen: *Life Is Worth Living,* McGraw-Hill Book Co., Inc.

Fear is two-fold; a fear of solicitous anxiety, such as makes us let go our confidence in God's providence, and a fear of prudential caution, whereby, from a due estimate of approaching evil, we endeavor our own security.—The former is wrong and forbidden; the latter not only lawful, but laudable.

Robert South

It was fear that first made gods in the world.

Publius Papinius Statius: *Thebais,*
Bk. III, l. 664

A great fear, when it is ill-managed, is the parent of superstition; but a discreet and well-guided fear produces religion.

Jeremy Taylor: *The Rule and Exercises of Holy Living*

As love, if love be perfect, casts out fear,
So hate, if hate be perfect, casts out fear.

Alfred, Lord Tennyson: *Idylls of the King: Merlin and Vivien,* l. 41

Some people are so afraid to die that they never begin to live.

Henry van Dyke

Three fears weaken the heart; fear of the truth, fear of poverty, and fear of the devil.

Welsh Proverb

No longer forward nor behind
I look in hope or fear;
But, grateful, take the good I find,
The best of now and here.

John Greenleaf Whittier: *My Psalm,* st. 3

It is only the fear of God that can deliver us from the fear of man.

John Witherspoon

FORGIVENESS

The happiest people are less forgetting and more forgiving.

Anonymous

A small boy, repeating the Lord's Prayer one evening prayed: "And forgive us our debts as we forgive those who are dead against us."

Anonymous

Every person should have a special cemetery lot in which to bury the faults of friends and loved ones.

Anonymous

The best way to get even is to forget.

Anonymous

A woman may consent to forget and forgive, but she never will drop the habit of referring to the matter now and then.

Anonymous

He who forgives ends the quarrel.

African Proverb

It is the prince's part to pardon.

Sir Francis Bacon

They who forgive most, shall be most forgiven.

Josiah W. Bailey

"I can forgive, but I cannot forget," is only another way of saying, "I cannot forgive."

Henry Ward Beecher: *Life Thoughts*

Life has taught me to forgive much, but to seek forgiveness still more.

Otto von Bismarck: In the autograph album of Count Enzenberg.

And throughout all eternity
I forgive you, you forgive me.

William Blake: *Poems from MSS.,* Untitled Poem, st. 14

Forgive us our trespasses as we forgive those who trespass against us.

Book of Common Prayer: The Lord's Prayer

Good to forget—
Best to forgive!

Robert Browning

Life that ever needs forgiveness has for its first duty to forgive.

Edward George Bulwer-Lytton

And if we do but watch the hour
There never yet was human power
Which could evade, if unforgiven,
The patient search and vigil long
Of him who treasures up a wrong.

George Gordon, Lord Byron

Nothing in this lost and ruined world bears the meek impress of the Son of God so surely as forgiveness.

Alice Cary

Never does the human soul appear so strong and noble as when it foregoes revenge, and dares to forgive an injury.

Edwin Hubbell Chapin

Wrongs are often forgiven; contempt never.

Philip Dormer Stanhope, Lord Chesterfield

Little, vicious minds abound with anger and revenge, and are incapable of feeling the pleasure of forgiving their enemies.

Philip Dormer Stanhope, Lord Chesterfield

It is more easy to forgive the weak who have injured us, than the powerful whom we have injured. That conduct will be continued by our fears which commenced in our resentment. He that has gone so far as to cut the claws of the lion will not feel himself quite secure until he has also drawn his teeth.

Charles Caleb Colton

He who forgives easily invites offense.

Pierre Corneille: *Cinna,* IV

The kindest and the happiest pair
Will find occasion to forbear;
And something, every day they live,
To pity, and perhaps forgive.

William Cowper: *Mutual Forbearance Necessary to the Happiness of the Married State*

It requires only an ounce of grace and a thimble full of brains to hold a grudge; but to entirely forget an injury is truly beautiful.

The Defender

May I tell you why it seems to me a good thing for us to remember wrong that has been done us? That we may forgive it.

Charles Dickens

But I forgive you . . . I do, and you can't help yourself.

Charles Dickens: *David Copperfield*, ch. 42

One always begins to forgive a place as soon as it's left behind.

Charles Dickens: *Little Dorrit*, Bk. I, ch. 2

Forgiveness to the injured doth belong,
But they ne'er pardon who have done the wrong.

John Dryden

She hugg'd the offender, and forgave the offence.

John Dryden: *Cymon and Iphigenia*

Reason to rule, mercy to forgive:
The first is law, the last prerogative.

John Dryden: *The Hind and the Panther*,
Pt. II, l. 261

God may forgive you, but I never can.

Queen Elizabeth I

God may forgive sins, he said, but awkwardness has no forgiveness in heaven or earth.

Ralph Waldo Emerson: *Society and Solitude*

Forgive and forget.

English Phrase in common use since the 14th century

Forgiveness is better than revenge; for forgiveness is the sign of a gentle nature, but revenge the sign of a savage nature.

Epictetus: *Fragments*, no. 68

Bear and forbear.

Epictetus (See Gellius, Bk. XVII, 6)

The noblest revenge is to forgive.

Thomas Fuller

Joy to forgive and joy to be forgiven
Hang level in the balances of Love.

Richard Garnett: *De Flagello Myrtéo*,
LXII

God will pardon me: that's his business.

Heinrich Heine

Forgiveness is the most necessary and proper work of every man; for, though, when I do not a just thing, or a charitable, or a wise, another man may do it for me, yet no man can forgive my enemy but myself.

Edward Herbert, Lord of Cherbury

He that cannot forgive others, breaks the bridge over which he himself must pass if he would ever reach heaven; for every one has need to be forgiven.

George Herbert

Pardon all but thyself.

George Herbert: *Jacula Prudentum*

The offender never pardons.

Ibid.

If you forgive people enough you belong to them, and they to you, whether either person likes it or not—squatter's rights of the heart.

James Hilton: *Time and Time Again*,
Atlantic-Little, Brown & Co. and John
Farquharson Ltd., 15 Red Lion
Square, London, W.C.1

It is in vain for you to expect, it is impudent for you to ask of God forgiveness for yourself if you refuse to exercise this forgiving temper as to others.

Benjamin Hoadly

It is right for him who asks forgiveness for his offenses to grant it to others.

Horace: *Satires*, I, 3, 74

Nobuddy ever fergits where he buried a hatchet.

From *Abe Martin's Broadcast*, by Kin
Hubbard, copyright 1930, 1958,
reprinted by permission of the
publishers, The Bobbs-Merrill
Co. Inc.

In the sphere of forgiveness, too many hatchets are buried alive.

Lem Hubbard, in the *Chicago Tribune*

Forgiving the unrepentant is like drawing pictures on water.

Japanese Proverb

A wise man will make haste to forgive, because he knows the true value of time, and will not suffer it to pass away in unnecessary pain.

Samuel Johnson: *The Rambler*

He who forgiveth, and is reconciled unto his enemy, shall receive his reward from God.

The Koran, XLII

It is hard for a haughty man ever to forgive one that has caught him in a fault, and whom he knows has reason to complain of him: his resentment never subsides till he has regained the advantage he has lost, and found means to make the other do him equal wrong.

Jean de La Bruyère

We forgive so long as we love.

François le La Rochefoucauld: *Maximes*

Forgive others often, but yourself never.

Latin Proverb

He who has not forgiven an enemy has never yet tasted one of the most sublime enjoyments of life.

Johann Kaspar Lavater

And unforgiving, unforgiven dies.

Lines on the Death of Queen Caroline

For 'tis sweet to stammer one letter
Of the Eternal's language;—on earth it
is called Forgiveness!

Henry Wadsworth Longfellow: *The Children of the Lord's Supper*, l. 214

We read that we ought to forgive our enemies; but we do not read that we ought to forgive our friends.

Cosimo de' Medici

Forgive what you can't excuse.

Mary Wortley Montagu: *Letter to James Stewart*

Blindness we may forgive, but baseness we will smite.

William Vaughn Moody: *An Ode in Time of Hesitation*, st. 9, Houghton Mifflin Co.

A Christian will find it cheaper to pardon than to resent. Forgiveness saves the expense of anger, the cost of hatred, the waste of spirits.

Hannah More

Love your enemies, bless them that curse you, do good to them that hate you, and pray for them which despitefully use you, and persecute you.

New Testament: Matthew 5: 44

Forgive us our debts, as we forgive our debtors.

New Testament: Matthew 6: 12

If ye forgive not men their trespasses, neither will your Father forgive your trespasses.

New Testament: Matthew 6: 15

Father, forgive them; for they know not what they do.

New Testament: Luke 23: 34

Be ye kind one to another, tenderhearted, forgiving one another, even as God for Christ's sake hath forgiven you.

New Testament: Ephesians 4: 32

If we confess our sins, he is faithful and just to forgive us our sins, and to cleanse us from all unrighteousness.

New Testament: I John 1: 9

Doing an injury puts you below your enemy; revenging one, makes you even with him; forgiving it sets you above him.

Nylic Review

Oh Thou, who man of baser Earth didst make,

And ev'n with Paradise devise the snake;
   For all the Sin wherewith the Face of man
Is blackened—man's forgiveness give and
   take.

> Omar Khayyám: *Rubáiyát*

It is only one step from toleration to forgiveness.

> Sir Arthur Wing Pinero: *The Second Mrs. Tanqueray,* Act III

A brave man thinks no one his superior who does him an injury; for he has it then in his power to make himself superior to the other by forgiving it.

> Alexander Pope

Forgive any sooner than thyself.

> Proverb

Forgive others many things, yourself nothing.

> Publilius Syrus: *Sententiae*

Hath any wronged thee?—Be bravely revenged.—Slight it, and the work is begun: forgive, and it is finished.—He is below himself that is not above an injury.

> Francis Quarles

Humanity is never so beautiful as when praying for forgiveness, or else forgiving another.

> Jean Paul Richter

When thou forgivest, the man who has pierced thy heart stands to thee in the relation of the sea-worm, that perforates the shell of the mussel, which straightway closes the wound with a pearl.

> Jean Paul Richter

We win by tenderness; we conquer by forgiveness.

> Frederick William Robertson

The narrow soul knows not the godlike glory of forgiving.

> Nicholas Rowe

The memory and conscience never did, nor ever will agree about forgiving injuries.

> Sir George Savile, Lord Halifax

To forgive all is as inhuman as to forgive none.

> Seneca

As you from crimes would pardon'd be,
Let your indulgence set me free.

> William Shakespeare: *The Tempest,* Epil.

I pardon him, as God shall pardon me.

> William Shakespeare: *Richard II,* Act V, sc. 3, l. 131

The truest joys they seldom prove,
   Who free from quarrels live;
'Tis the most tender part of love,
   Each other to forgive.

> John Sheffield (Duke of Buckingham)

There is a noble forgetfulness—that which does not remember injuries.

> Charles Simmons

Only the brave know how to forgive; it is the most refined and generous pitch of virtue that human nature can arrive at. A coward never forgave; it is not in his nature.

> Laurence Sterne: *Sermons*

If the injured one could read your heart, you may be sure he would understand and pardon.

> Robert Louis Stevenson: *Truth of Intercourse*

God forgives—forgives not capriciously, but with wise, definite, Divine pre-arrangement; forgives universally, on the grounds of an atonement and on the condition of repentance and faith.

> Richard Salter Storrs

We forgive too little; forget too much.

> Madam Anne Soymanov Swetchine

Pardon, not wrath, is God's best attribute.

> Bayard Taylor

149

There is nothing so advantageous to a man as a forgiving disposition.

Terence: *Adelphi,* V

Know all and you will pardon all.

Thomas à Kempis: *Imitation of Christ*

It is easier for the generous to forgive, than for the offender to ask forgiveness.

James Thomson

To be able to bear provocation is an argument of great reason, and to forgive it of a great mind.

John Tillotson

Forgiveness is the fragrance the violet sheds on the heel that has crushed it.

Mark Twain

Dear Lord and Father of mankind,
 Forgive our foolish ways;
Reclothe us in our rightful mind;
 In purer lives Thy service find,
In deeper reverence, praise.

John Greenleaf Whittier

The best of what we do and are,
 Just God, forgive!

William Wordsworth: *Thoughts Suggested on the Banks of Nith*

FREEDOM

Before God, there is neither Greek nor barbarian, neither rich nor poor, and the slave is as good as his master, for by birth all men are free; they are citizens of the universal commonwealth which embraces all the world, brethren of one family, and children of God.

Lord Acton: *The History of Freedom in Antiquity*

Oh, Lord, I want to be free, want to be free;
Rainbow round my shoulder, wings on my feet.

American Negro Song, quoted by Howard W. Odum: *Wings on My Feet,* IX

So long as Faith with Freedom reigns,
 And loyal Hope survives,
And gracious Charity remains
 To leaven lowly lives;
While there is one untrodden tract
 For intellect or will,
And men are free to think and act,
 Life is worth living still.

Alfred Austin: *Is Life·Worth Living?*

Freedom can be best understood ultimately as the freedom of the person who belongs wholly to no social group, who is a citizen of two cities, who is responsible to God. Christian faith provides not only the most adequate grounding for what is true in the common morality but also the motives for obedience which in the long run are most dependable.

John C. Bennett: *Christians and the State,* Charles Scribner's Sons

God has laid upon man the duty of being free, of safeguarding freedom of spirit, no matter how difficult that may be, or how much sacrifice and suffering it may require.

Nicholai Berdyaev

The cause of freedom is the cause of God.

William Lisle Bowles: *To Edmund Burke*

Freedom—no word was ever spoken that has held out greater hope, demanded greater sacrifice, needed more to be nurtured, blessed more the giver . . . or came closer to being God's will on earth.

Omar N. Bradley

Sound the loud timbrel o'er Egypt's dark sea!
Jehovah hath triumphed—his people are free.

George Gordon, Lord Byron: *Sacred Songs. Sound the Loud Timbrel*

Freedom is a need of the soul, and nothing else. It is in striving toward God that the soul strives continually after a condition of freedom. God alone is the inciter and guarantor of freedom. He is the only guarantor.

Whittaker Chambers: *Witness,* Random House, Inc.

But what is Freedom? Rightly understood,
A universal license to be good.

Hartley Coleridge: *Liberty*

Congress shall make no law respecting an establishment of religion, or prohibiting the free exercise thereof.

Constitution of the United States, Amendment I

To die for the truth is not to die merely for one's faith, or one's country; it is to die for the world.

Their blood is shed in confirmation of the noblest claim—the claim to feed upon immortal truth, to walk with God, and be divinely free.

William Cowper

The greatest gift which God in His bounty bestowed in creating, and the most conformed to His own goodness, and that which He prizes the most, was the freedom of the will, with which the creatures that have intelligence, they all and they alone, were and are endowed.

Alighieri Dante: *Divine Comedy, Paradiso,* Canto V, l. 19

Man is really free only in God, the source of his freedom.

Sherwood Eddy

If the truth be mighty, and God all-powerful, His children need not fear that disaster will follow freedom of thought.

François de Salignac de La Mothe Fénelon

The bulk of mankind by dint of feeling free become spiritually unemployed.

From *On Love: Aspects of a Single Theme,* by José Ortega y Gasset, translated by Tony Talbot; Meridian Books, The World Publishing Co., Cleveland and New York; copyright 1957 by The World Publishing Co. Used by permission

If we grant freedom to man, there is an end to the omniscience of God, for if the Divinity knows how I shall act, I must act so perforce.

Johann Wolfgang von Goethe: *Goethe to Eckerman*

Freedom, as we understand it in America, is not an economic discovery. It is not . . . even a political discovery. Freedom, in the last analysis, is a religious discovery.

William J. Grede, Board president, National Association of Manufacturers

Build thee more stately mansions, O my soul,
As the swift seasons roll!
Leave thy low-vaulted past!
Let each new temple, nobler than the last
Shut thee from heaven with a dome more vast,
'Till thou at length are free,
Leaving thine outgrown shell by life's unresting sea!

Oliver Wendell Holmes, Sr.: *The Chambered Nautilus*

In the beauty of the lilies Christ was born across the sea,
With a glory in his bosom that transfigures you and me;
As he died to make men holy, let us die to make men free,
While God is marching on.

Julia Ward Howe: *Battle Hymn of the Republic*

If some great Power would agree to make me think always what is true and do what is right on condition of being turned into a sort of clock, I would instantly close with the bargain. The only freedom I care about is the freedom to do right; the freedom to do wrong I am ready to part with.

Thomas Henry Huxley

The spirit of truth and the spirit of freedom —they are the pillars of society.

Henrik Ibsen: *Pillars of Society,* Act IV

Freedom of religion, freedom of the press, and freedom of person under the protection of the habeas corpus, these are principles that have guided our steps through an age of revolution and reformation.

Thomas Jefferson

Freedom has only the meaning with which men endow it. It is not enough to pay lip service to the concept of religious liberty. We must pay heart service to it, as well, else it remains an empty phrase instead of a living reality.

Kenneth B. Keating: *These Times*

There will be no true freedom without virtue, no true science without religion, no true industry without the fear of God and love to your fellow-citizens. Workers of England, be wise, and then you *must* be free, for you will be *fit* to be free.

Charles Kingsley: *Placard*

We reject the idea that any American is a "common man." No man is "common" and no man is "average" in the sight of God. This is the faith on which we base our . . . mission for human freedom.

Arthur B. Langlie

No person now or at any time hereafter living in this province who shall confess and acknowledge one Almighty God to be the Creator, Upholder and Ruler of the World, and who professes him or herself obliged in conscience to live peaceably and quietly under the civil government, shall in any case be molested or prejudiced for his or her conscientious persuasion or practise.

Law of Pennsylvania, December 10, 1682

The church is a revolutionary power, but the Christian revolution is not a revolt of violence; it is an inevitable and righteous revolution which demands that things be changed and man made free.

Charles T. Leber

. . . That this nation, under God, shall have a new birth of freedom.

Abraham Lincoln: *Gettysburg Address*

Those who deny freedom to others deserve it not for themselves, and, under a just God, cannot long retain it.

Abraham Lincoln: *Letter to H. L. Pierce*

If I have freedom in my love,
    And in my soul am free,
Angels alone, that soar above,
    Enjoy such liberty.

Richard Lovelace: *To Althea from Prison*

We on this continent should never forget that men first crossed the Atlantic not to find soil for their ploughs but to secure liberty for their souls.

Robert J. McCracken

No man who knows aught can be so stupid to deny that all men naturally were born free, being the image and resemblance of God Himself, and were, by privilege above all the creatures, born to command, and not to obey.

John Milton: *The Tenure of Kings and Magistrates*

If the Son therefore shall make you free, ye shall be free indeed.

New Testament: John 8: 36

With a great sum obtained I this freedom.

New Testament: Acts 22: 28

Paul said, But I was free born.

Ibid.

There is neither Jew nor Greek, there is neither bond nor free, there is neither male nor female: for ye are all one in Christ Jesus.

New Testament: Galatians 3: 28

Stand fast therefore in the liberty wherewith Christ hath made us free, and be not entangled again with the yoke of bondage.

New Testament: Galatians 5: 1

As free, and not using your liberty for a cloke of maliciousness, but as the servants of God.

New Testament: I Peter 2: 16

Not a man exists who talks bravely against the Church, but does not owe it to the Church that he can talk at all.

Cardinal John Henry Newman: *Historical Sketches*

The final contribution of religious faith to the whole problem of freedom is the freedom to confess our sins; the freedom to admit that we all stand under the ultimate judgment of God.

Ursula W. Niebuhr: *Man's Freedom Under God*

The union of faith and freedom is the essential genius of Protestantism.

Justin Wroe Nixon: *Advance* (Congregational)

God Almighty . . . has given to all men a natural right to be free, and they have it ordinarily in their power to make themselves so, if they please.

James Otis: *The Rights of the British Colonies Asserted and Proved*

Heaven knows how to put a proper price upon its goods; and it would be strange indeed, if so celestial an article as *Freedom* should not be highly rated.

Thomas Paine: *The American Crisis*, no. 1

. . . The American idea . . . a democracy, —that is, a government of all the people, by all the people, for all the people; of course, a government of the principles of eternal justice, the unchanging law of God: for shortness sake, I will call it the idea of Freedom.

Theodore Parker: *Speech*, Boston, May 20, 1850

In the Bible, and particularly in Jesus' spiritual concepts of God and man, all men can find the key to victory, not only one evil system, but in the greater crusade against all falsehood. Mankind, however, appears to come slowly to the realization that Freedom is not won and held solely by material means.

Admiral Arthur Radford: "Battle for Freedom," *Vital Speeches*

Oh, only a free soul will never grow old!

Jean Paul Richter: *Titan, Zykel*

We find freedom when we find God; we lose it when we lose Him.

Paul E. Scherer

Man is created free, and is free, even though born in chains.

Johann Christoph Friedrich von Schiller: *Die Worte des Glaubens*, st. 2

No man is free who is a slave to the flesh.

Seneca: *Epistolae Ad Lucilium*, XCII

Long may our land be bright
With freedom's holy light;
Protect us by Thy might,
  Great God, our King.

Samuel Francis Smith: *America*

Freedom is never a gift. It is the "pearl of great price" in anguish won.

The Theological Concept of Freedom

Every man, conducting himself as a good citizen, and being accountable to God alone for his religious opinions, ought to be protected in worshipping the Deity according to the dictates of his own conscience.

George Washington: *Letter to the United Baptist Chamber of Virginia*

God grants liberty only to those who love it, and are always ready to guard it.

Daniel Webster

FREE WILL

Only two possibilities exist: either one must believe in determinism and regard free will as a subjective illusion, or one must become a mystic and regard the discovery of natural laws as a meaningless intellectual game. Metaphysicians of the old schools have proclaimed one or the other of these doctrines, but ordinary people have always accepted the dual nature of the world.

Max Born: *Bulletin of the Atomic Scientists*, June, 1957

FREE WILL

Free will is but an illusion.

Anatole France

All theory is against freedom of the will; all experience for it.

Samuel Johnson

I confess that mankind has a free will, but it is to milk kine, to build houses, etc. and no further.

Martin Luther: *Table Talk*

On what pretense can man have interdicted marriage, which is a law of nature? 'Tis as though we were forbidden to eat, to drink, to sleep.

Ibid.

God is not willing to do everything, and thus take away our free will and that share of glory which belongs to us.

Niccolò Machiavelli: *The Prince*

God has so framed us as to make freedom of choice and action the very basis of all moral improvement, and all our faculties, mental and moral, resent and revolt against the idea of coercion.

William Matthews

Take heed lest passion sway
Thy judgment to do aught, which else free will
Would not admit.

John Milton: *Paradise Lost*, Bk. VIII, l. 634

He who *feels* that his will is not free is insane; he who *denies* it is foolish.

Friedrich Wilhelm Nietzsche

This also is clearly defined in the teaching of the Church, that every rational soul is possessed of freewill and volition; that it has a struggle to maintain with the devil and his angels, and opposing influences, because they strive to burden it with sins.

Origen: *De Principiis*, Proem 5

Without our faith in free will the earth would be the scene not only of the most horrible nonsense but also of the most intolerable boredom.

Arthur Schnitzler: *Buch der Sprueche und Bedenken*

There is no such thing as free will. The mind is induced to wish this or that by some cause, and that cause is determined by another cause, and so on back to infinity.

Benedict (Baruch) de Spinoza: *Ethics*

A horse that is hitched with others to a wagon is not free not to walk in front of the wagon; and if it will not draw, the wagon will strike its legs, and it will go whither the wagon goes, and will pull it involuntarily. But, in spite of this limited freedom, it is free itself to pull the wagon, or be dragged along by it. The same is true of man.

Leo Tolstoy

You must recognize as brothers and sisters all who live; and free to will, free to act, free to enjoy, you shall know the worth of existence.

Richard Wagner: *The Creative Force*

FRIEND, FRIENDSHIP

The Christian should never complain of his hard fortune while he knows that Christ is his friend.

Anonymous

Friendship is love without his wings.

Anonymous

Insomuch as any one pushes you nearer to God, he or she is your friend.

Anonymous

Before us is a future all unknown, a path untrod;
Beside us a friend well loved and known—
That friend is God.

Anonymous

Great souls by instinct to each other turn,
Demand alliance, and in friendship burn.

Joseph Addison: *The Campaign*

A faithful friend is a strong defense: and he that hath found such an one hath found a treasure.

Apocrypha: Ecclesiasticus 6: 14

Forsake not an old friend, for the new is not comparable unto him.

Apocrypha: Ecclesiasticus 9: 10

What is a friend? A single soul dwelling in two bodies.

Aristotle

The perfect friendship is that between good men, alike in their virtue.

Aristotle: *The Nicomachean Ethics,* VIII

I have loved my friends as I do virtue, my soul, my God.

Sir Thomas Browne: *Religio Medici,* II

Because discretion is always predominant in true friendship, it works and prevails least upon fools. Wicked men are often reformed by it, weak men seldom.

Edward Hyde, Lord Clarendon

My God, my Father, and my Friend,
Do not forsake me in my end.

Wentworth Dillon, Earl of Roscommon:
Translation of Dies Irae

Friendship is the gift of the gods, and the most precious boon to man.

Benjamin Disraeli: *Speech,* House of
Commons

Friendship, of itself a holy tie,
Is made more sacred by adversity.

John Dryden: *The Hind and the
Panther,* III

Friend more divine than all divinities.

George Eliot: *The Spanish Gypsy,*
Bk. IV, l. 8

God evidently does not intend us all to be rich, or powerful or great, but He does intend us all to be friends.

Ralph Waldo Emerson

We force no doors in friendship, but like the Christ in Revelation, we stand reverently at the door without, to knock. And only if the door be opened from within, may we welcome in to sup with our friend and he with us. The glory of Friendship is not the outstretched hand, nor the kindly smile, nor the joy of companionship; it is the spiritual inspiration that comes to one when he discovers that someone else believes in him and is willing to trust him with his friendship. My friends have come unsought. The great God gave them to me.

Ralph Waldo Emerson

God save me from my friends; I can take care of my enemies.

English Proverb

We ought to flee the friendship of the wicked, and the enmity of the good.

Epictetus: *Encheiridion*

No one can lay himself under obligation to do a wrong thing. Pericles, when one of his friends asked his services in an unjust cause, excused himself, saying, "I am a friend only as far as the altar."

Thomas Fuller

On the choice of friends
Our good or evil name depends.

John Gay

An English publication offered a prize for the best definition of a friend. Thousands of answers were received and the one that was given first prize was this: "A friend is the one who comes in when the whole world has gone out."

Grace Pulpit, Grace Methodist Church,
Atlanta, Georgia

Large was his bounty, and his soul sincere,
Heaven did a recompense as largely send:
He gave to mis'ry (all he had) a tear,
He gained from Heav'n ('twas all he wished)
a friend.

Thomas Gray: *Elegy in a Country
Churchyard, The Epitaph,* st. 2

Of all the heavenly gifts that mortal men
  commend,
What trusty treasure in the world can
  countervail a friend?

> Nicholas Grimald: *Of Friendship*

It is good to have some friends both in
Heaven and Hell.

> George Herbert: *Outlandish Proverbs*

But love is lost; the art of friendship's gone;
Though David had his Jonathan, Christ his
  John.

> George Herbert: *The Church-Porch*, st. 46

Friendship with the evil is like the shadow
in the morning, decreasing every hour; but
friendship with the good is like the evening
shadows, increasing till the sun of life sets.

> Johann Gottfried von Herder

Neither make thy friend equal to a brother.

> Hesiod: *Works and Days*, I

The difficulty is not so great to die for a
friend, as to find a friend worth dying for.

> Henry Home

Love seeks a guerdon; friendship is as God,
Who gives and asks no payment.

> Richard Hovey: *The Marriage of
  Guenevere*, Act I, sc. 1

Blessed are they who have the gift of making
friends, for it is one of God's best gifts. It involves many things, but above all, the power
of going out of one's self, and appreciating
whatever is noble and loving in another.

> Thomas Hughes

Friendship, peculiar boon of Heav'n,
  The noble mind's delight and pride,
To men and angels only giv'n,
  To all the lower world denied.

> Samuel Johnson: *Friendship: An Ode*

"A friend is the one who comes in when the
whole world has gone out." Even as David
thanked God for Jonathan and praised him
in well-remembered lines, so have we abundant reasons to thank God today for friends
and to resolve to keep these friendships in
constant repair.

> Edgar DeWitt Jones

He that hath no friend, and no enemy, is one
of the vulgar; and without talents, powers,
or energy.

> Johann Kaspar Lavater

I desire so to conduct the affairs of this
administration that if at the end, when I
come to lay down the reins of power, I have
lost every other friend on earth, I shall at
least have one friend left, and that friend
shall be down inside of me.

> Abraham Lincoln: Reply to Missouri
  Committee of Seventy

A friend of man was he, and thus, he was a
friend of God.

> Wilson MacDonald

To lose an old friend is as the loss of a bead
from life's rosary; or to drop a jewel into the
depths of a turbulent sea.

> Douglas Meador, in Matador (Texas)
  Tribune

We read that we ought to forgive our
enemies; but we do not read that we ought
to forgive our friends.

> Cosimo de' Medici

A friend of publicans and sinners.

> *New Testament: Matthew 11: 19*

Greater love hath no man than this, that a
man lay down his life for his friends.

> *New Testament: John 15: 13*

One God, no more,
But friends good store.

> Old English Rhyme

He that repeateth a matter separateth very
friends.

> *Old Testament: Proverbs 17: 9*

A man that hath friends must shew himself
friendly: and there is a friend that sticketh
closer than a brother.

Old Testament: Proverbs 18: 24

Faithful are the wounds of a friend.

Old Testament: Proverbs 27: 6

I was wounded in the house of my friends.

Old Testament: Zechariah 13: 6

The best way for a child to learn to fear God
is to know a real Christian. The best way for
a child to learn to pray is to live with a father
and mother who know a life of friendship
with God, and who truly pray.

Johann Heinrich Pestalozzi

The love of man to woman is a thing common and of course, and at first partakes more
of instinct and passion than of choice; but
true friendship between man and man is
infinite and immortal.

Plato

Never break off the friendship, rather untie
it, when those you become bound to appear
cheats. Hall says, "I will use my friend as
Moses did his rod: while it was a rod he
held it familiarly in his hand: When once
a serpent, he ran away from it."

James Puckle: *The Club*

Sudden friendship, sure repentance.

John Ray: *English Proverbs*

What is love? two souls and one flesh; friendship? two bodies and one soul.

Joseph Roux: *Meditations of a Parish
Priest*, Pt. IX, no. 31

Those friends thou hast, and their adoption
tried,
Grapple them to thy soul with hoops of steel;
But do not dull thy palm with entertainment
Of each new-hatched, unfledg'd comrade.

William Shakespeare: *Hamlet*,
Act I, sc. 3, l. 62

Be careful to make friendship the child and
not the father of virtue, for many are rather
good friends than good men; so, although
they do not like the evil their friend does,
yet they like him who does the evil; and
though no counselors of the offence, they yet
protect the offender.

Sir Philip Sidney

A true friend is the gift of God, and he only
who made hearts can unite them.

Robert South

By friendship you mean the greatest love, the
greatest usefulness, the most open communi-
cation, the noblest sufferings, the severest
truth, the heartiest counsel, and the greatest
union of minds of which brave men and
women are capable.

Jeremy Taylor

Nature and religion are the bands of friendship, excellence and usefulness are its great
endearments.

Jeremy Taylor

Some friendships are made by nature, some
by contract, some by interest, and some by
souls.

Jeremy Taylor

Hast thou a friend, as heart may wish at will?
Then use him so, to have his friendship still.
Wouldst have a friend, wouldst know what
friend is best?
Have God thy friend, who passeth all the
rest.

Thomas Tusser

The holy passion of Friendship is of so sweet
and steady and loyal and enduring a nature
that it will last through a whole life-time,
if not asked to lend money.

Mark Twain: *Pudd'nhead Wilson*

To God, thy country, and thy friend be true.

Henry Vaughan: *Rules and Lessons*, no. 8

Friendship, gift of Heaven, delight of great souls; friendship, which kings, so distinguished for ingratitude, are unhappy enough not to know.

> Voltaire: *La Henriade,* VIII

Friendship is the marriage of the soul; and this marriage is subject to divorce.

> Voltaire: *Philosophical Dictionary*

If I have not a friend, God sends me an enemy, that I may hear of my faults.

> Benjamin Whichcote: *Sermons*

I have *friends* in Spirit Land,—
Not shadows in a shadowy band,
Not *others* but *themselves* are they,
And still I think of them the same
As when the Master's summons came.

> John Greenleaf Whittier: *Lucy Hooper*

Who God doth late and early pray
  More of his grace than gifts to lend;
And entertains the harmless day
  With a religious book or friend.

> Sir Henry Wotton: *The Character of a Happy Life,* st. 5

Ceremony and great professing renders friendship as much suspect as it does religion.

> William Wycherley: *The Plain Dealer,* 1

Heaven gives us friends, to bless the present scene; resumes them to prepare us for the next.

> Edward Young

A foe to God was ne'er true friend to man,
Some sinister intent taints all he does.

> Edward Young: *Night Thoughts,* Night VIII, l. 704

G

GIFTS, GIVING

"Go break to the needy sweet charity's
  bread;
For giving is living," the angel said.
"And must I be giving again and again?"
My peevish and pitiless answer ran.
"Oh no," said the angel, piercing me
  through,
"Just give till the Master stops giving to
  you."

Anonymous

Give strength, give thought, give deeds, give
  wealth;
Give love, give tears, and give thyself.
Give, give, be always giving.
Who gives not is not living;
The more you give, the more you live.

Anonymous

He dropped a nickel in the plate,
  Then meekly raised his eyes;
Glad that his weekly rent was paid
  For a mansion in the skies.

Anonymous

It's not what you'd do with a million,
  If riches should e'er be your lot,
But what are you doing at present
  With the dollar and a quarter you've got?

Anonymous

Give to the world the best you have and the
best will come back to you.

Anonymous

"He's a man of generous impulses," is a
phrase of commendation sometimes heard.
It is a doubtful compliment. Generosity
should be a matter of discretion, not of
impulse.

Ernest Bourner Allen

If in carnal wealth, how much more in
spiritual does God love a cheerful giver?

St. Augustine: *Of the Catechizing of the
Unlearned*

The best thing to give to your enemy is
forgiveness; to an opponent, tolerance; to
a friend, your heart; to your child, a good
example; to a father, deference; to your
mother, conduct that will make her proud
of you; to yourself, respect; to all men,
charity.

Francis Maitland Balfour

Do we give according to our means, or
according to our meanness?

Bruce R. Baxter

Christians are never stingy.

Joseph F. Berry

Give and spend
And God will send.

Henry George Bohn: *Handbook of
Proverbs*

It is possible to give without loving, but it
is impossible to love without giving.

Richard Braunstein

God's gifts put man's best dreams to shame.

Elizabeth Barrett Browning: *Sonnets from
the Portuguese*, no. 26

That gift of his, from God descended.
Ah! friend, what gift of man's does not?

Robert Browning: *Christmas Eve*,
Canto XVI

A man there was, though some did count him
mad,
The more he cast away the more he had.

> John Bunyan: *The Pilgrim's Progress*,
> Pt. II

Gifts are as the gold which adorns the
temple; grace is like the temple that sanctifies
the gold.

> William Burkitt

Saints themselves will sometimes be,
Of gifts that cost them nothing free.

> Samuel Butler: *Hudibras, I*

Give plenty of what is given to you,
  And listen to pity's call;
Don't think the little you give is great
  And the much you get is small.

> Phoebe Cary: *A Legend of the Northland,*
> I, st. 8

It is not the weight of jewel or plate,
  Or the fondle of silk or fur;
'Tis the spirit in which the gift is rich,
  As the gifts of the Wise Ones were,
And we are not told whose gift was gold,
  Or whose was the gift of myrrh.

> Edmund Vance Cooke: *The Spirit of the
> Gift*

It was not an accident that seventeen of the
thirty-six parables of our Lord had to do
with property and stewardship.

> William James Dawson

Christian giving is God's divine plan to make
us like Himself; it reveals our religion and
bares our souls; it is prophetic and has to
do with the inner sensitiveness and gives a
keener vision to His work and plans.

> Warren H. Denison: *Stewardship
> Notebook*

It is said that gifts persuade even the gods.

> Euripides: *Medea*

The gifts of a bad man bring no good with
them.

> *Ibid.*

The true disciple of Jesus is neither a miser
nor a spendthrift, but a steward.

> William Hiram Foulkes: *Today*

That man may last, but never lives,
Who much receives, but nothing gives;
Whom none can love, whom none can thank,
Creation's blot, creation's blank.

> Thomas Gibbons

There is no charity in a man's leaving money
in his will; he has simply got to leave it. The
time to administer your trust is while you
are still living.

> William Ewart Gladstone

God has given us two hands—one to receive
with and the other to give with. We are not
cisterns made for hoarding; we are channels
made for sharing.

> Billy Graham

Give according to your means, or God will
make your means according to your giving.

> John Hall

Give not Saint Peter so much, to leave Saint
Paul nothing.

> George Herbert: *Jacula Prudentum*

Give unto all, lest he whom thou deny'st
May chance to be no other man but Christ.

> Robert Herrick: *Alms*

God loves a cheerful giver, but we settle for
a grudging one.

> Mildred McAfee Horton

We give Thee but Thine own,
  Whate'er the gift may be;
All that we have is Thine alone,
  A trust, O Lord, from Thee.

> William W. How

What you give to humanity you get back.
Bread cast upon the waters is much more
wholesome and nourishing than pie in the
sky.

> Melvin Jones: *Lion Magazine*

Give what you have. To someone it may be better than you dare to think.

> Henry Wadsworth Longfellow

The Holy Supper is kept, indeed,
In whatso we share with another's need;
Not what we give, but what we share,
For the gift without the giver is bare;
Who gives himself with his alms feeds three:
Himself, his hungering neighbor, and me.

> James Russell Lowell: *The Vision of Sir Launfal*

How blind men are to Heaven's gifts!

> Lucan: *De Bello Civili*, Bk. V, l. 528

Riches are the least worthy gifts which God can give man. What are they to God's word, to bodily gifts, such as beauty and health, or to the gifts of the mind, such as understanding, skill, wisdom! Yet men toil for them day and night, and take no rest. Therefore God commonly gives riches to foolish people, to whom he gives nothing else.

> Martin Luther

People do not care to give alms without some security for their money; and a wooden leg or a withered arm is a sort of draft upon heaven for those who choose to have their money placed to account there.

> Henry Mackenzie

Giving is most blessed and most acceptable when the donor remains completely anonymous.

> Moses Maimonides

Some people rob God when they give only a tenth, and others have no business to give even as much as that.

> G. Campbell Morgan: *This Was His Faith*

The world asks, How much does he give? Christ asks, Why does he give?

> John Raleigh Mott

Give to him that asketh thee, and from him that would borrow of thee turn not thou away.

> *New Testament: Matthew 5: 42*

Take heed that ye do not your alms before men, to be seen of them. . . . But when thou doest alms, let not thy left hand know what thy right hand doeth.

> *New Testament: Matthew 6: 1-3*

Freely ye have received, freely give.

> *New Testament: Matthew 10: 8*

Whosoever hath, to him shall be given, and he shall have more abundance: but whosoever hath not, from him shall be taken away even that he hath.

> *New Testament: Matthew 13: 12*

Give, and it shall be given unto you; good measure, pressed down, and shaken together, and running over.

> *New Testament: Luke 6: 38*

Silver and gold have I none; but such as I have give I thee.

> *New Testament: Acts 3: 6*

It is more blessed to give than to receive.

> *New Testament: Acts 20: 35*

God loveth a cheerful giver.

> *New Testament: II Corinthians 9: 7*

Every good gift and every perfect gift is from above, and cometh down from the Father of lights.

> *New Testament: James 1: 17*

All we can hold in our cold dead hands is what we have given away.

> Old Sanskrit Proverb

Thou shalt take no gift: for the gift blindeth the wise, and perverteth the words of the righteous.

> *Old Testament: Exodus 23: 8*

The liberal soul shall be made fat: and he that watereth shall be watered also himself.

> *Old Testament: Proverbs 11: 25*

A gift is as a precious stone in the eyes of him that hath it.

> *Old Testament: Proverbs 17: 8*

Every man is a friend to him that giveth gifts.

Old Testament: Proverbs 19: 6

He that giveth unto the poor shall not lack.

Old Testament: Proverbs 28: 27

A gift destroyeth the heart.

Old Testament: Ecclesiastes 7: 7

Let your portal be deaf to prayers, but wide to the giver.

Ovid: Amores, Bk. I, eleg. 8, l. 77

Do good with what thou hast; or it will do thee no good.

William Penn

What I kept, I lost,
What I spent, I had,
What I gave, I have.

Persian Proverb

Giving is the secret of a healthy life. Not necessarily money, but whatever a man has of encouragement and sympathy and understanding.

John D. Rockefeller, Jr.

There are three kinds of giving: grudge giving, duty giving, and thanksgiving. Grudge giving says, "I hate to," duty giving says, "I ought to," thanksgiving says, "I want to." The first comes from constraint, the second from a sense of obligation, the third from a full heart. Nothing much is conveyed in grudge giving since "the gift without the giver is bare." Something more happens in duty giving but there is no song in it. Thanksgiving is an open gate into the love of God.

Robert N. Rodenmayer: Thanks Be to God, Harper & Row, Publishers, Inc.

God has given some gifts to the whole human race, from which no one is excluded.

Seneca: De Beneficiis, Bk. IV, sec. 28

I have always been deeply impressed by an old Jewish proverb which says, "What you

give for the cause of charity in health is gold; what you give in sickness is silver; what you give after death is lead."

Nathan Straus: First paragraph of Will

He who gives when he is asked has waited too long.

Sunshine Magazine

As you give, so shall you receive. Contribute more and you will receive more. If you want a stronger rebound, throw the ball harder.

Sunshine Magazine

He who loves with purity considers not the gift of the lover, but the love of the giver.

Thomas à Kempis

You do not have to be rich to be generous. If he has the spirit of true generosity, a pauper can give like a prince.

Corinne U. Wells

Too often a cheerful giver is cheerful only because he's got away with giving as little as possible.

Wisconsin Journal of Education

Give all thou canst; high Heaven rejects the lore
Of nicely calculated less or more.

William Wordsworth: Ecclesiastical Sonnets, Pt. III, no. 43

GLORY

The glory of Him who moves everything penetrates through the universe, and is resplendent in one part more and in another less.

Alighieri Dante: Divine Comedy, Paradiso, Canto I, l. 1

To the greater glory of God.

Pope Gregory the Great: Dialogues, I

Glory, glory, hallelujah.

> Charles Sprague Hall: *John Brown's Body*

To lift up the hands in prayer gives God glory, but a man with a dungfork in his hand, a woman with a slop-pail, give him glory too. He is so great that all things give him glory if you mean they should. So then, my brethren, live.

> Gerard Manley Hopkins: *An Address on Saint Ignatius*

The glory of Him who
Hung His masonry pendant on naught, when the world He created.

> Henry Wadsworth Longfellow: *The Children of the Lord's Supper,* l. 177

To God be all the glory.

> Medieval Latin Phrase

To the greater glory of God.

> Motto of the Society of Jesus

Whether therefore ye eat, or drink, or whatever ye do, do all to the glory of God.

> *New Testament: I Corinthians 10: 31*

There is one glory of the sun, and another glory of the moon, and another glory of the stars: for one star differeth from another star in glory.

> *New Testament: I Corinthians 15: 41*

Who is this King of glory? The Lord of hosts, he is the King of glory.

> *Old Testament: Psalms 24: 10*

The hoary head is a crown of glory, if it be found in the way of righteousness.

> *Old Testament: Proverbs 16: 31*

Holy, holy, holy, is the Lord of hosts: the whole earth is full of his glory.

> *Old Testament: Isaiah 6: 3*

Like madness is the glory of this life.

> William Shakespeare: *Timon of Athens,* Act I, sc. 2, l. 139

O how quickly passes away the glory of the earth.

> Thomas à Kempis

Not in utter nakedness,
But trailing clouds of glory do we come.

> William Wordsworth: *Intimations of Immortality*

GOD

God may well be taken as a substitute for *everything*; but *nothing* can be taken as a substitute for God.

> Anonymous

The demand of the human understanding for causation requires but the one old and only answer, God.

> Anonymous

If God loved you as much as you love Him, where would you be?

> Anonymous

The only important decision we have to make is to live with God; He will make the rest.

> Anonymous

When God measures a man, He puts the tape around the heart instead of the head.

> Anonymous

God cannot please everybody.

> Anonymous

Every day God makes silk purses out of sows' ears.

> Anonymous

To most of us it would be very convenient if God were a rascal.

> Anonymous

Some people treat God like they do a lawyer; they go to Him only when they are in trouble.

> Anonymous

Some people talk about finding God—as if He could get lost.

Anonymous

A man, asked to explain what God is, replied, "I know if I'm not asked."

Anonymous

God has put up with a lot from most of us.

Anonymous

God is with those who persevere.

Anonymous

In God's will is our peace.

Anonymous

When I am operating, I feel the presence of God so real that I cannot tell where His skill ends and mine begins.

Anonymous (attributed to a famous surgeon)

The world we inhabit must have had an origin; that origin must have consisted in a cause; that cause must have been intelligent; that intelligence must have been supreme; and that supreme, which always was and is supreme, we know by the name of God.

Anonymous

The Mohammedans have ninety-nine names for God, but among them all they have not "our Father."

Anonymous

We should give God the same place in our hearts that He holds in the universe.

Anonymous

If we have God in all things while they are ours, we shall have all things in God when they are taken away.

Anonymous

God is great, and therefore He will be sought: He is good, and therefore He will be found.

Anonymous

In all His dispensations God is at work for our good. In prosperity He tries our gratitude; in mediocrity, our contentment; in misfortune, our submission; in darkness, our faith; under temptation, our steadfastness; and at all times, our obedience and trust in Him.

Anonymous

Most men forget God all day and ask Him to remember them at night.

Anonymous

Whosoever walks toward God one cubit, God runs toward him twain.

Anonymous

All the thousands and tens of thousands of gods are all but one God.

Anonymous

On U.S. coins is placed the motto: "In God We Trust." But this is not engraved upon any of our battleships or our bombs! Why?

George Matthew Adams

I believe in God and in His wisdom and benevolence.

John Adams: *Letter to Jefferson*

He sendeth sun, he sendeth shower,
Alike they're needful to the flower;
And joys and tears alike are sent
To give the soul fit nourishment.
As comes to me or cloud or sun,
Father! thy will, not mine, be done.
Sarah Flower Adams: *He Sendeth Sun,
He Sendeth Shower*

Nearer My God, to Thee—
Nearer to Thee—
E'en though it be a cross
That raiseth me;
Still all my song shall be
Nearer, my God, to Thee,
Nearer to Thee!
Sarah Flower Adams: *Nearer, my God,
to Thee!*

There is something very sublime, though very fanciful in Plato's description of God —"That truth his body, and light his shadow."

Joseph Addison

When all thy mercies, O my God,
　My rising soul surveys,
Transported with the view I'm lost,
　In wonder, love and praise.

Joseph Addison: *Hymn: With All Thy Mercies*

God loves to help him who strives to help himself.

Aeschylus: *Fragments*, frag. 223

Set God apart from mortal men, and deem not that he, like them, is fashioned out of flesh. Thou knowest him not; now he appeareth as fire, now as water, now as gloom; and he is dimly seen in the likeness of wild beasts, of wind, of cloud, of lightning, thunder, and of rain. All power hath he; lo, this is the glory of the Most High God.

Aeschylus: *Fragments*, frag. 239

To the man who strives earnestly, God also lends a helping hand.

Aeschylus: *Persae*, I, 742

God's mouth knows not to utter falsehood, but he will perform each word.

Aeschylus: *Prometheus Bound*, I, 1032

Even God cannot change the past.

Agathon

God is working His purpose out as year succeeds to year,
God is working His purpose out and the time is drawing near;
Nearer and nearer draws the time, the time that shall surely be,
When the earth shall be filled with the glory of God as the waters cover the sea.

Arthur Campbell Ainger: *God is Working His Purpose Out*

Man thinks, God directs.

Alcuin: *Epistles*

He who knows what it is to enjoy God will dread His loss; he who has seen His face will fear to see His back.

Richard Alleine

Man proposes, God disposes.

Ludovico Ariosto: *Orlando Furioso*, ch. 46, 35 (also, Thomas à Kempis)

God has many names though he is only one being.

Aristotle

God does not ask about our ability or our inability, but our availability.

The Arkansas Baptist

God's wisdom and God's Goodness!—Ah, but fools
Misdefine thee, till God knows them no more.
Wisdom and Goodness they are God!—what schools
Have yet so much as heard this simple lore.
This no Saint preaches, and this no Church rules:
'Tis in the desert, now and heretofore.

Matthew Arnold: *The Divinity*, st. 3

We, in some unknown Power's employ,
Move on a rigorous line:
Can neither, when we will, enjoy,
Nor, when we will, resign.

Matthew Arnold: *Stanzas in Memory of the Author of Obermann*, l. 133

A heathen philosopher once asked a Christian, "Where is God?" The Christian answered, "Let me first ask you, Where is He not?"

Aaron Arrowsmith

Thou hast made us for Thyself, and the heart of man is restless until it finds its rest in Thee.

St. Augustine: *Confessions*

God is best known in not knowing him.

St. Augustine: *De ordine*, II, 16

God is more truly imagined than expressed, and he exists more truly than is imagined.

St. Augustine: *De Trinitate*

We can know what God is not, but we cannot know what God is.

Ibid.

We are all dangerous folk without God's controlling hand.

William Ward Ayer

Back of the loaf is the snowy flour,
And back of the flour the mill;
And back of the mill is the wheat, and the shower,
And the sun, and the Father's will.

Maltbie D. Babcock: *Give Us This Day
Our Daily Bread*

Though a sharp sword be laid to thy throat, still pray to God for mercy.

Babylonian Talmud: *Berachoth*

God hangs the greatest weights upon the smallest wires.

Sir Francis Bacon

We cannot too often think, that there is a never sleeping eye that reads the heart, and registers our thoughts.

Sir Francis Bacon

It were better to have no opinion of God at all, than such an opinion as is unworthy of him: for the one is unbelief, the other is contumely.

Sir Francis Bacon: *Essays: Of Superstition*

The Ethiop gods have Ethiop lips,
Bronze cheeks and woolly hair;
The Grecian gods are like the Greeks,
As keen-eyed, cold, and fair.

Walter Bagehot: *Literary Studies: The
Ignorance of Man*

What men call accident is God's own part.

Gamaliel Bailey

There is nothing on earth worth being known, but God and our own souls.

Gamaliel Bailey

Naught but God
Can satisfy the soul.

Philip James Bailey: *Festus: Heaven*

Reason unaided by revelation can prove that God exists.

*Roman Catholic 1949 Revised Baltimore
Catechism*

At the foot of every page in the annals of nations may be written, "God reigns." Events as they pass away proclaim their original; and if you will but listen reverently, you may hear the receding centuries, as they roll into the dim distances of departed time, perpetually chanting "Te Deum Laudamus," with all the choral voices of the countless congregations of the age.

George Bancroft

A little girl repeating the twenty-third psalm said it this way: "The Lord is my shepherd, that's all I want."

Baraca-Philathea News

If the mind of God as discovered to us in His word and works is so vast and deep, what must His mind be in all its undisclosed resources in the infinity and eternity of its existence?

John Bate

God never made mouth but he made meat.

Thomas Becon: *Catechism*

God sits effulgent in heaven, not for a favoured few, but for the universe of life, and there is no creature so poor, or so low, that he may not look up with childlike confidence, and say, "My Father, Thou art mine."

Henry Ward Beecher

The very word "God" suggests care, kindness, goodness; and the idea of God in his infinity is infinite care, infinite kindness, infinite goodness.—We give God the name of good: it is only by shortening it that it becomes God.

Henry Ward Beecher

To some people, God is a peg to hang their troubles on.

Dan Bennett

In all parts of Nature's spacious sphere,
Of art ten thousand miracles appear;
And will you not the Author's skill adore
Because you think He might discover more?
You own a watch, the invention of the mind,
Though for a single motion 'tis designed,
As well as that which is with greater thought,
With various springs, for various motions
wrought.

Richard Blackmore: *The Creation*,
Bk. III

God appears and God is light
To those poor souls who dwell in night;
But does a human form display
To those who dwell in realms of day.

William Blake: *Auguries of Innocence*.

No worldly thing
Can a continuance have
Unless love back again it bring
Unto the cause which first the essence gave.

Boëthius: *Philosophiae Consolationis*,
Bk. IV, ch. 6, l. 46

God is not one thing because He is, and another thing because He is just; with Him to be just and to be God are one and the same.

Boëthius: *De Trinitate*, ch. 4, sec. 19

There is no door in my theatre through which God cannot see.

Edwin Booth

From Thee all human actions take their
springs,
The rise of empires, and the fall of kings.

Samuel Boyse: *The Deity*

But for the grace of God there goes John Bradford.

John Bradford, on seeing some criminals
taken to execution

I would rather walk with God in the dark than go alone in the light.

Mary Gardiner Brainard: *Not Knowing*

O Rock of Israel, Rock of Salvation, Rock struck and cleft for me, let those two streams of blood and water which once gushed out of thy side . . . bring down with them salvation and holiness into my soul.

Daniel Brevint: *Works*, p. 17

He made little, too, of sacraments and priests, because God was so intensely real to him. What should he do with lenses who stood thus full in the torrent of the sunshine.

Phillips Brooks: *Sermons, The Seriousness
of Life*

It never frightened a Puritan when you bade him stand still and listen to the speech of God. His closet and his church were full of reverberations of the awful, gracious, beautiful voice for which he listened.

Ibid.

God, as some cynic has said, is always on the side which has the best football coach.

Heywood Broun

The whole world is a phylactery, and everything we see is an item of the wisdom, power, or goodness of God.

Sir Thomas Browne

God is like a skillful geometrician.

Sir Thomas Browne: *Religio Medici*,
Pt. I, sec. 16

I fear God, yet am not afraid of him.

Sir Thomas Browne: *Religio Medici*,
Pt. I, sec. 52

Earth's crammed with heaven,
And every common bush afire with God.
And only he who sees takes off his shoes,
The rest sit round and pluck blackberries.

Elizabeth Barrett Browning: *Aurora
Leigh*, Bk. VII, l. 821

He testified this solemn truth, while phrenzy
    desolated,
Nor man nor nature satisfied whom only
    God created.

> Elizabeth Barrett Browning: *Cowper's
> Grave*, st. 8

God himself is the best Poet,
And the Real is his song.

> Elizabeth Barrett Browning: *The Dead
> Pan*, st. 36

But God has a few of us whom he
    whispers in the ear;
The rest may reason and welcome; 'tis
    we musicians know.

> Robert Browning: *Abt Vogler*

I say, the acknowledgment of God in Christ
Accepted by the reason, solves for thee
All questions in the earth and out of it.

> Robert Browning: *A Death in the Desert*

    If I stoop
Into a dark tremendous sea of cloud,
It is but for a time; I press God's lamp
Close to my breast; its splendour, soon or
    late,
Will pierce the gloom: I shall emerge one
    day.

> Robert Browning: *Paracelsus*

That we devote ourselves to God, is seen
In living just as though no God there were.

> *Ibid.*

God is the perfect poet,
Who in his person acts his own creations.

> *Ibid.*

In some time, His good time, we shall arrive;
He guides me and the bird in His good time.

> *Ibid.*

God! Thou art love! I build my faith on that.

> *Ibid.*

Be sure that God
Ne'er dooms to waste the strength he deigns
    impart.

> *Ibid.*

Of what I call God, and fools call Nature.

> Robert Browning: *The Ring and the
> Book:* The Pope, l. 1073

As the old Negro said, "Oh Lord, help me
to understand that You ain't gwine to let
nuthin' come my way, that You and me
together can't handle."

> Edgar White Burrill: *Science of Mind*

God makes; man shapes.

> Robert Burton: *The Anatomy of
> Melancholy*, III

It must be remembered that we have heard
only one side of the case. God has written
all the books.

> Samuel Butler: *Note-Books*

Doubtless God could have made a better
berry, but doubtless God never did.

> William Allen Butler: *Walton, the
> Compleat Angler*

We cannot get away from God, though we
can ignore Him.

> James Elliott Cabot

If thou knowest God, thou knowest that
everything is possible for God to do.

> Callimachus: *Fragmenta Incertae*, no. 27

A sense of Deity is inscribed on every heart.

> John Calvin

Oft have I heard, and now believe it true,
Who man delights in, God delights in too.

> Pons de Capdueil

Blessed be God's voice, for it is true, and
falsehoods have to cease before it!

> Thomas Carlyle

What this country needs is a man who knows
God other than by heresay.

> Thomas Carlyle

A picket frozen on duty—
    A mother starved for her brood—

Socrates drinking the hemlock,
  And Jesus on the rood;
And millions who, humble and nameless,
  The straight, hard pathway plod,—
Some call it Consecration,
  And others call it God.

William Herbert Carruth: *Each in His
                              Own Tongue*

God is a spirit, infinite, eternal, and un-
changeable in his being, wisdom, power,
holiness, justice, goodness, and truth.

Catechism

When God dawns he dawns for all.

Miguel de Cervantes: *Don Quixote,*
                        Pt. II, ch. 4

God who gives the wound gives the salve.

Miguel de Cervantes: *Don Quixote,*
                        Pt. II, ch. 19

God helps everyone with what is his own.

Miguel de Cervantes: *Don Quixote,*
                        Pt. II, ch. 26

Could we with ink the ocean fill,
  And were the heavens of parchment made,
Were every stalk on earth a quill,
  And every man a scribe by trade,
To write the love of God above
  Would drain the ocean dry,
Nor could the scroll contain the whole,
  Though stretch'd from sky to sky.

Chaldee Ode

The voice of the people is the voice of God.

Charlemagne

If this generation had more respect for divine
guidance it might have less need for guided
missiles.

Chilton (Wisconsin) *Times-Journal*

God the All-terrible! King, Who ordainest
Great winds Thy clarions, the lightnings
        Thy sword.

Henry Fothergill Chorley: *Hullah's Part
                                Music*

God has no grandchildren; either you know
Him firsthand or you do not know Him
at all.

Christian Life

An old mystic says somewhere, "God is an
unutterable sigh in the innermost depths of
the soul." With still greater justice, we may
reverse the proposition, and say the soul is
a never ending sigh after God.

Theodor Christlieb

There is something in the nature of things
which the mind of man, which reason, which
human power cannot effect, and certainly
that which produce this must be better than
man. What can this be but God?

Cicero

The celestial order and the beauty of the
universe compel me to admit that there
is some excellent and eternal Being, who
deserves the respect and homage of men.

Cicero: *De Divinatione,* Bk. II, ch. 72,
                                sec. 148

"God has not body, but a semblance of
body": what "a semblance of body" may
mean, in the case of God, I cannot understand; nor can you either, Velleius, only you
won't admit it.

Cicero: *De Natura Deorum,* Bk. I, ch. 24,
                                    sec. 68

There is nothing which God cannot effect.

Cicero: *De Natura Deorum,* Bk. III,
                        ch. 39, sec. 92

God is a sure paymaster.

John Clarke: *Paraemiologia Anglo-Latina*

Face to face with the universe, man will be
the sole evidence of his audacious dreams of
divinity, since the God he vainly sought is
himself.

Georges Clemenceau: *In the Evening of
                        My Thought,* p. 503

It fortifies my soul to know
That though I perish, truth is so;

169

That wheresoe'er I stray and range,
Whate'er I do, Thou dost not change.
I steadier step when I recall
That, if I slip, Thou dost not fall.

> Arthur Hugh Clough: *With Whom Is No Variableness*

Praise ye Jehovah, source of every blessing,
Before His gifts earth's richest boons are dim;
Resting in Him, His peace and joy possessing,
All things are ours, for we have all in Him.

> W. Cockburn-Campbell

God is to me that creative Force, behind and in the universe, who manifests Himself as energy, as life, as order, as beauty, as thought, as conscience, as love.

> Henry Sloane Coffin, in Newton: *My Idea of God*

God! sing, ye meadow-streams, with gladsome voice!
Ye pine groves, with your soft and soul-like sounds!
And they too have a voice, yon piles of snow.
And in their perilous fall shall thunder, God!

> Samuel Taylor Coleridge: *Hymn before Sunrise in the Vale of Chamouni*

Earth with her thousand voices, praises God.

> *Ibid.*

Even bein' Gawd ain't a bed of roses.

> Marc Connelly: *The Green Pastures,* Holt, Rinehart & Winston, and Delisle, Ltd.

There is a God in science, a God in history, and a God in conscience, and these three are one.

> Joseph Cook

To the bird's young ones he gives food.

> Pierre Corneille: *Athalie*

The servant of God hath a good master.

> Randle Cotgrave: *French-English Dictionary*

But who with filial confidence inspired,
Can lift to heaven an unpresumptious eye,
And smiling say, My Father made them all

> William Cowper: *Task,* Bk. V

Acquaint thyself with God, if thou would'st
taste
His works. Admitted once to his embrace,
Thou shalt perceive that thou wast blind
before:
Thine eye shall be instructed; and thine
heart
Made pure shall relish with divine delight
Till then unfelt, what hands divine have
wrought.

> *Ibid.*

God moves in a mysterious way
His wonders to perform;
He plants His footsteps in the sea
And rides upon the storm.

> William Cowper: *Hymn: Light Shining Out of Darkness*

The more I know of astronomy, the more I believe in God.

> Heber D. Curtis

There is a God! the sky his presence shares,
His hand upheaves the billows in their
mirth,
Destroys the mighty, yet the humble spares
And with contentment crowns the thought
of worth.

> Charlotte Cushman: *There is a God*

God honors no drafts where there are no deposits.

> *The Defender*

Love thy God and love Him only
And thy breast will ne'er be lonely.

> Aubrey Thomas DeVere: *The Waldenses*

One of the most convenient hieroglyphics of God is a circle; and a circle is endless; whom God loves, he loves to the end; and not for their own end, to their death, but to his end; and his end is that he might love them still.

> John Donne

God of the granite and the rose,
Soul of the sparrow and the bee,
The mighty tide of being flows
Thro' countless channels, Lord, from Thee.

Elizabeth Doten: *Reconciliation*

It isn't so urgent . . . whether you believe in God as whether he can believe in you. If you will conduct yourself in a manner that might encourage him to believe in you, the time may come when you feel that you should return the compliment.

Lloyd Douglas: *Invitation to Live,*
Houghton Mifflin Co.

God's love for poor sinners is very wonderful, but God's patience with ill-natured saints is a deeper mystery.

Henry Drummond

By tracing Heav'n his footsteps may be found:
Behold! how awfully he walks the round!
God is abroad, and wondrous in his ways
The rise of empires, and their fall surveys.

John Dryden: *Britannia Rediviva*

'Tis god-like God in his own coin to pay.
Ibid.

All love is lost but upon God alone.

William Dunbar: *The Merle and the
Nightingale*

Trying to build the brotherhood of man without the fatherhood of God is like trying to make a wheel without a hub.

Irene Dunne

The greatest question of our time is not communism versus individualism, not Europe versus America, not even the East versus the West: it is whether man can bear to live without God.

Will Durant

God is living, working still.

John S. Dwight

Too wise to err, too good to be unkind,
Are all the movements of the Eternal Mind.

John East: *Songs of My Pilgrimage*

If we seek God for our own good and profit, we are not seeking God.

Johannes Eckhart

Every law of matter or the body, supposed to govern man, is rendered null and void by the law of Life, God.

Mary Baker Eddy: *Science and Health,*
p. 380, 32–1

God is incorporeal, divine, supreme, infinite Mind, Spirit, Soul, Principle, Life, Truth, Love.

Mary Baker Eddy: *Science and Health,*
p. 465, 9–10

There is no life, truth, intelligence, nor substance in matter. All is infinite Mind and its infinite manifestation, for God is All-in-all. Spirit is immortal Truth; matter is mortal error.

Mary Baker Eddy: *Science and Health,*
p. 468, 9–12

A true love to God must begin with a delight in his holiness, and not with a delight in any other attribute; for no other attribute is truly lovely without this.

Jonathan Edwards: *A Treatise Concerning Religious Affections: Works,*
Vol. V, p. 143

He who has no friend has God.

Egyptian Proverb

God is a scientist, not a magician.

Albert Einstein

God is clever, but not dishonest.

Inscription over a fireplace in Fine Hall,
Princeton, N. J. (Albert Einstein)

The idea of God, and the sense of His presence, intensify all noble feeling and encourage all noble effort, pour new life into our languid love, and give firmness to our vacillating purpose.

George Eliot

God is an unutterable sigh in the human heart, said the old German mystic. And therewith said the last word.

Havelock Ellis: *Impressions and Comments,* Houghton Mifflin Co.

God may consent, but only for a time.

Ralph Waldo Emerson: *Conduct of Life: Fate*

Fear God, and where you go men will think they walk in hallowed cathedrals.

Ralph Waldo Emerson: *Conduct of Life: Worship*

The god of the cannibals will be a cannibal, of the crusaders a crusader, and of the merchant a merchant.

Ibid.

God enters by a private door into every individual.

Ralph Waldo Emerson: *Essays, First Series: Intellect*

To Be is to live with God.

Ralph Waldo Emerson: *Journals,* 1865

When the Master of the universe has points to carry in his government he impresses his will in the structure of minds.

Ralph Waldo Emerson: *Letters and Social Aims: Immortality*

As the bird alights on the bough, then plunges into the air again, so the thoughts of God pause but for a moment in any form.

Ralph Waldo Emerson: *Letters and Social Aims: Poetry and Imagination*

There is a crack in everything God has made.

Ralph Waldo Emerson: *Works*

God offers to every mind its choice between truth and repose.

Thomas Dunn English: *Essays*

God is where He was.

English Proverb

God comes with leaden feet, but strikes with iron hands.

English Proverb

When you have shut the doors and made a darkness within, remember never to say that you are alone; for you are not alone, but God is within.

Epictetus

Here lies the body of John Smith, who for forty years cobbled shoes in this village to the glory of God.

Epitaph

God tempers the cold to the shorn lamb.

Henri Estienne: *Premises*

Whom God would destroy he first makes mad.

Euripides

Try first thyself, and after call in God;
For to the worker God himself lends aid.

Euripides: *Hippolytus,* frag. 435

If I were God
And man made a mire
Of things: war, hatred,
Murder, lust, cobwebs,
Of infamy, entangling
The heart and soul
I would sweep him
To one side and start anew.
(I think I would.)
If I did this,
Would I be God?

The Evangelical Beacon

In form, the word "God" is small indeed, but in meaning it is infinite. It expresses the greatest thought that ever entered the heart of man. It is lisped by the children, read and known of all men; but also inscribed at the zenith of the universe, and shedding its glory on all below it.

Harry William Everest

) majesty unspeakable and dread!
Wert Thou less mighty than Thou art,
~hou wert, O Lord, too great for our belief,
Too little for our heart.
Frederick William Faber: *The Greatness of God*

do not believe in God, for that implies an
ffort of the will—I see God everywhere!
Jean Favre

Man moves himself, but God leads him.
François de Salignac de La Mothe
Fénelon: *Epiphany Sermon*

He is poor that God hates.
David Fergusson: *Scottish Proverbs*

Do as ye wald be done to.
Ibid.

The birth of every new baby is God's vote of
confidence in the future of man.
Imogene Fey

Paley's simile of the watch . . . must be
replaced by the simile of the flower. The
universe is not a machine but an organism
with an indwelling principle of life. It was
not made, but it has grown.
John Fiske, in Newton: *My Idea of God*

The way to God is by ourselves.
Phineas Fletcher: *The Purple Island: To the Reader*

Many roads lead to God. Travel any one
of them you like and I'm sure you'll come
within God's reach.
Claud H. Foster

God does well what He does.
French Proverb

God will know His own.
French Proverb

As the sensation of hunger presupposes
food to satisfy it, so the sense of dependence
on God presupposes His existence and
character.
Octavius Brookes Frothingham

Fellow-citizens: God reigns, and the Government at Washington lives!
James Abram Garfield: Speech on the
Assassination of Lincoln

Love is God's essence; Power but his attribute; therefore is his love greater than his
power.
Richard Garnett: *De Flagello Myrteo*, IV

God never made a tyrant, nor a slave.
William Lloyd Garrison: *Address*

I believe in God the Father Almighty because
wherever I have looked, through all that I
see around me, I see the trace of an intelligent mind, and because in natural laws, and
especially in the laws which govern the social
relations of men, I see, not merely the proofs
of intelligence, but the proofs of beneficence.
Henry George: *Speech*

This is well-nigh the greatest of discoveries
a man can make, that God is not confined
in churches, but that the streets are sacred
because His presence is there, that the
market-place is one of His abiding places,
and ought, therefore, to be a sanctuary. Any
moment in any place, the veil can suddenly
grow thin and God be seen.
R. C. Gillie, A. & C. Black, Ltd.

The Unknown Cause of the universe is Himself a Spirit, whose Word is perfect truth,
whose nature is perfect righteousness, whose
law is perfect love.
Washington Gladden

The task of statesmanship is to discover
where God Almighty is going during the
next fifty years.
William Ewart Gladstone

No one against God, except God himself.
Johann Wolfgang von Goethe:
Autobiography, Bk. XIX

As a man is, so is his God; therefore was God
so often an object of mockery.
Johann Wolfgang von Goethe: *Gedichte*

The promises of God are certain, but they do not all mature in 90 days.

Adoniram J. Gordon

A god from the machine (Deus ex Machina).

Greek Proverb

God's mills grind slow but sure.

Greek Proverb

You have to give God the benefit of the doubt.

Sacha Guitry

Who believes that equal grace
God extends in every place,
Little difference he scans
'Twixt a rabbit's God and man's.

Francis Bret Harte: *Battle Bunny: Envoi*

It is highly convenient to believe in the infinite mercy of God when you feel the need of mercy, but remember also his infinite justice.

Benjamin Robert Haydon: *Table Talk*

Sure, Lord, there is enough in thee to dry
Oceans of ink; for as the deluge did
Cover the earth, so doth thy majesty.
Each cloud distils thy praise, and doth forbid
Poets to turn it to another use.

George Herbert (Izaak Walton, *Life*, p. 325)

God strikes with his finger, and not with all his arm.

George Herbert: *Jacula Prudentum*

God gives his wrath by weight, and without weight his mercy.

Ibid.

God strikes not with both hands, for to the sea He made havens, and to rivers fords.

Ibid.

He loseth nothing that loseth not God.

Ibid.

God complains not, but doth what is fittin₁

Ibiₑ

God, and parents, and our master, can nevₑ be requited.

Ibiₑ

'Tis hard to find God, but to comprehenₐ Him, as He is, is labour without end.

Robert Herrick: *God Not to bₑ Comprehendeₐ*

God has His whips here to a twofold end.
The bad to punish, and the good t' amenₑ

Robert Herrick: *Noble Numberₑ*

God hath two wings, which He doth evₑ move,
The one is Mercy, and the next is Love:
Under the first the Sinners ever trust;
And with the last he still directs the Just.

Robert Herrick: *Mercy and Lovₑ*

Where God is merry, there write down thᵧ fears:
What He with laughter speaks, hear thoᵤ with tears.

Robert Herrick: *God's Mirth, Man'ₛ Mourningₑ*

God sends men cold according to their cloth₃ viz. afflictions according to their faith.

John Heywood: *Proverbs*

God is no botcher.

Ibid.

God is over all things, under all things; out-side all; within but not enclosed; without but not excluded; above but not raised up; below but not depressed; wholly above, pre-siding; wholly beneath, sustaining; wholly without, embracing; wholly within, filling.

Hildebert of Lavardin: *Epistles*

Why are you so anxious to see God with your eyes closed? See him with your eyes open—in the form of the poor, the starved, the illiterate and the afflicted.

Hindu to a Christian

Lord of the light unfading
From day to reborn day;
God of the worlds brocading
This planet's nightly way;
Master of Hope, and builder
Of life's immortal span,
Now, when the days bewilder,
Thunder again to man!

Leigh Mitchell Hodges: *Processional*, 1933

God loves an idle rainbow
No less than laboring seas.

Ralph Hodgson: *Reason Has Moons*

The great soul that sits on the throne of the
universe is not, never was, and never will be,
in a hurry.

Josiah Gilbert Holland: *Gold-Foil:
Patience*

One unquestioned text we read,
All doubt beyond, all fear above;
Nor crackling pile nor cursing creed
Can burn or blot it: GOD IS LOVE.

Oliver Wendell Holmes, Sr.: *What We
All Think*

Spontaneously to God should turn the soul
Like the magnetic needle to the pole.

Thomas Hood: *A Poem Addressed to
Rae Wilson*

Dangerous it were for the feeble brain of
man to wade far into the things of the Most
High. . . . Our soundest knowledge is to
know that we know him not as indeed he
is, neither can know him; and our safest
eloquence concerning him is our silence,
when we confess without confession that his
glory is inexplicable, his greatness above our
capacity and reach.

Richard Hooker: *Ecclesiastical Polity*,
Bk. I, ch. 2, sec. 3

The world is charged with the grandeur of
God.

Gerard Manley Hopkins: *God's Grandeur*

The essence of religion is a belief in a
relation to God involving duties superior
to those arising out of any human relation.
One cannot speak of religious liberty with

a proper appreciation of its essential and
historic significance without assuming the
existence of a belief in a supreme allegiance
to the will of God.

Charles Evans Hughes (Merlo J. Pusey:
Charles Evans Hughes [New York &
London: Columbia University
Press, 1963])

In this stupendous manner, at which Reason
stands aghast, and Faith herself is half con-
founded, was the grace of God to man at
length manifested.

Richard Hurd: *Sermons*, Vol. II, p. 287

Call on God, but row away from the rocks.

Indian Proverb

I have never understood why it should be
considered derogatory to the Creator to suppose that He has a sense of humour.

William R. Inge: in Marchant's *Wit and
Wisdom of Dean Inge*, Longmans
Green & Co., Ltd.

Far better in its place the lowliest bird
Should sing aright to Him the lowliest
song,
Than that a seraph strayed should take the
word
And sing His glory wrong.

Jean Ingelow: *Honours*, Pt. II

An honest God is the noblest work of man.

Robert Green Ingersoll: *The Gods*,
Pt. I, p. 2

God never shuts one door but He opens
another.

Irish Proverb

He who leaves God out of his reasoning does
not know how to count.

Italian Proverb

What is there in man so worthy of honor
and reverence as this, that he is capable of
contemplating something higher than his
own reason, more sublime than the whole
universe—that Spirit which alone is self-
subsistent, from which all truth proceeds,
without which is no truth?

Johann Georg Jacobi

175

The God of many men is little more than their court of appeal against the damnatory judgment passed on their failures by the opinion of the world.

William James: *Varieties of Religious Experience,* p. 138

God governs the world, and we have only to do our duty wisely, and leave the issue to him.

John Jay

All men . . . are endowed by their Creator with certain unalienable Rights . . . among these are Life, Liberty, and the pursuit of Happiness.

Thomas Jefferson

Resistance to tyrants is obedience to God.

Thomas Jefferson

Don't bargain with God.

Jewish Proverb

From thee, great God, we spring, to thee we tend,
Path, motive, guide, original, and end.

Samuel Johnson: *Motto for the Rambler,* no. 7

Our Father dwells in tents as well as in the temples, but His favourite abiding-place is in the hearts of mankind.

J. Fred Jones

God, to be God, must transcend what is. He must be the maker of what ought to be.

Rufus Matthew Jones, in Newton: *My Idea of God*

We know God easily, if we do not constrain ourselves to define him.

Joseph Joubert

The sun and every vassal star,
    All space, beyond the soar of angel's wings
Wait on His word; and yet He stays His car
For every sigh a contrite suppliant brings.

John Keble: *The Christian Year,* *Ascension Day*

If the blind put their hand in God's, they find their way more surely than those who see but have not faith or purpose.

Helen Keller, Doubleday & Company, Inc.

Who thou art I know not,
But this much I know:
Thou hast set the Pleiades
In a silver row.

Harry Kemp: *God, the Architect*

O God, I am thinking Thy thoughts after Thee.

Johannes Kepler (when studying astronomy)

Take comfort, and recollect however little you and I may know, God knows; He knows Himself and you and me and all things; and His mercy is over all His works.

Charles Kingsley

All but God is changing day by day.

Charles Kingsley: *The Saint's Tragedy,* *Prometheus*

There is no God but God.

The Koran, ch. 3

God is the best deviser of stratagems.

Ibid.

History is the revelation of providence.

Lajos Kossuth

The very impossibility in which I find myself to prove that God is not, discloses to me His existence.

Jean de La Bruyère: *Les Caractères,* sec. 16

Help yourself and Heaven will help you.

Jean de La Fontaine: *Fables,* Bk. VI, 18

The world appears very little to a soul that contemplates the greatness of God. My business is to remain in the presence of God.

Brother Lawrence

God is a sun, which, though, but one, is
sufficient to enlighten and vivify a whole
world.

Michael Le Faucheur

For God rewards good deeds done here
below—rewards them here.

Gotthold Ephraim Lessing: *Nathan der
Weise*, I, 2

There are two kinds of people: those who
say to God, "Thy will be done," and those
to whom God says, "All right, then, have it
your way."

C. S. Lewis: *The Great Divorce*

"How do you know," a Bedouin asked, "that
there is a God?" "In the same way," he replied, "that I know, on looking at the sand,
when a man or beast has crossed the desert—
by His footprints in the world around me."

Henry Parry Liddon

Sir, my concern is not whether God is on
our side; my great concern is to be on God's
side, for God is always right.

Abraham Lincoln: Reply to a deputation
of Southerners

I do not know how the loving father will
bring out light at last, but he knows and he
will do it.

David Livingstone

All is of God. If He but wave His hand,
  The mists collect, the rain falls thick and
    loud
Till, with a smile of light on sea and land,
  Lo, He looks back from the departing
    cloud.

Henry Wadsworth Longfellow

Man is unjust, but God is just; and finally
justice triumphs.

Henry Wadsworth Longfellow

Let nothing disturb thee,
Let nothing affright thee,
All things are passing,
God changeth never.

Henry Wadsworth Longfellow: *Santa
Teresa's Bookmark*

Though the mills of God grind slowly
  Yet they grind exceeding small;
Though with patience He stands waiting,
  With exactness grinds He all.

Henry Wadsworth Longfellow: *Retribu-
tion* (also tr. of Friedrich von Logan)

God has sifted three kingdoms to find the
wheat for this planting.

Henry Wadsworth Longfellow: *The
Courtship of Miles Standish*, IV

Behind the dim unknown,
Standeth God within the shadow, keeping
  watch above his own.

James Russell Lowell: *The Present Crisis*

God'll send the bill to you.

James Russell Lowell: *The Biglow Papers*

An' you've gut to git up airly
Ef you want to take in God.

Ibid.

Whom the heart of man shuts out,
Sometimes the heart of God takes in.

James Russell Lowell: *The Forlorn*

Darkness is strong, and so is Sin,
But surely God endures forever!

James Russell Lowell: *Villa Franca*,
Conclusion

'Tis heaven alone that is given away;
'Tis only God may be had for the asking.

James Russell Lowell: *The Vision of
Sir Launfal*

We do nothing without the leave of God.

Lucan: *De Bello Civili*, Bk. IX

Has God any dwelling-place save earth and
sea, the air of heaven and virtuous hearts?

177

Why seek the Deity further? Whatever we see is God, and wherever we go.

Lucan: *De Bello Civili*, Bk. IX

From God derived, to God by nature joined,
We act the dictates of His mighty mind;
And tho' the priests are mute, and temples still,
God never wants a voice to speak His will.

Ibid.

Is there any other seat of the Divinity than the earth, sea, air, the heavens, and virtuous minds? Why do we seek God elsewhere? He is whatever you see; he is wherever you move.

Lucan: *Pharsalia*, IX, 578

God doesn't always smooth the path, but sometimes he puts springs in the wagon.

Marshall Lucas

A mighty fortress is our God,
A bulwark never failing;
Our helper he amid the flood
Of mortal ills prevailing.

Martin Luther: *Ein Feste Burg*

When God contemplates some great work, He begins it by the hand of some poor, weak, human creature, to whom He afterwards gives aid, so that the enemies who seek to obstruct it are overcome.

Martin Luther: *Table Talk*

Though God have iron hands which when they strike pay home, yet hath he leaden feet which are as slow to overtake a sinner.

John Lyly: *Euphues*, p. 172

Trust in God and do something.

Mary Lyon

I fear no foe with thee at hand to bless;
Ills have no weight, and tears no bitterness.

Henry Francis Lyte: *Eventide*

God's thoughts, his will, his love, his judgments are all man's home. To think his thoughts, to choose his will, to love his loves, to judge his judgments, and thus to know that he is in us, is to be at home.

George Macdonald

How often we look upon God as our last and feeblest resource! We go to him because we have nowhere else to go. And then we learn that the storms of life have driven us, not upon the rocks, but into the desired haven.

George Macdonald

A voice in the wind I do not know;
A meaning on the face of the high hills
Whose utterance I cannot comprehend.
A something is behind them: that is God.

George Macdonald: *Within and Without*, Pt. I

All growth that is not towards God
Is growing to decay.

Ibid.

Who can know heaven except by its gifts? and who can find out God, unless the man who is himself an emanation from God?

Marcus Manilius: *Astronomica*

Everyone is in a small way the image of God.

Ibid.

Live near to God, and so all things will appear to you little in comparison with eternal realities.

Robert M. McCheyne

When a man comes to God, it is as if he looked from the other side of the sky, seeking the same things from another standpoint.

W. M. McGregor

The man who has lost contact with God lives on the same dead-end street as the man who denies him.

Milton A. Marcy

God should be the object of all our desires, the end of all our actions, the principle of all our affections, and the governing power of our whole souls.

Jean Baptiste Massillon

Amid all the war and contest and variety of human opinion, you will find one consenting conviction in every land, that there is one God, the king and father of all.

Maximus Tyrius

I have read up many queer religions; and there is nothing like the old thing, after all, I have looked into the most philosophical systems, and have found none that will work without a God.

James Clerk Maxwell

One sole God; One sole ruler,—his Law; One sole interpreter of that law—Humanity.

Giuseppe Mazzini: *Young Europe: General Principles*, no. 1

Each of us may be sure that if God sends us on stony paths, He will provide us with strong shoes. He will not send us out on any journey for which he does not equip us well.

Megiddo Message

I live and love in God's peculiar light.

Michelangelo

God, I can push the grass apart And lay my finger on Thy heart!

Edna St. Vincent Millay: "Renascence," from *Collected Poems*, Harper & Row, Publishers, Inc., copyright 1912–1940 by Edna St. Vincent Millay, used by permission of Norma Millay

Belief of God is acceptance of the basic principle that the universe makes sense, that there is behind it an ultimate purpose.

Carl Wallace Miller

To the reverent scientist . . . the simplest features of the world about us are in themselves so awe-inspiring that there seems no need to seek new and greater miracles of God's care.

Carl Wallace Miller

Just are the ways of God,
And justifiable to men;
Unless there be who think not God at all.

John Milton: *Samson Agonistes*, l. 293

Either man's work or his own gifts: who best
Bear his mild yoke, they serve him best; his state
Is kingly. Thousands at his bidding speed
And post o'er land and ocean without rest:
They also serve who only stand and wait.

John Milton: *On His Blindness*

O unexampl'd love!
Love nowhere to be found less than Divine!

John Milton: *Paradise Lost*, Bk. III, l. 410

Spin carefully, spin prayerfully, but leave the thread to God.

Missionary Tidings

Hope writes the poetry of the boy, but memory that of the man. Man looks forward with smiles, but backward with sighs. Such is the wise providence of God. The cup of life is sweetest at the brim, the flavor is impaired as we drink deeper, and the dregs are made bitter that we may not struggle when it is taken from our lips.

Adolphe Monod

If God would concede me His omnipotence for 24 hours, you would see how many changes I would make in the world. But if He gave me His wisdom too, I would leave things as they are.

J. M. L. Monsabre

God is a great expense but government would be impossible without Him.

George Moore: *Confessions of a Young Man*

I had a thousand questions to ask God; but when I met him they all fled and didn't seem to matter.

"I had a thousand questions . . ." from *Inward Ho!* by Christopher Morley, copyright 1923, 1950 by Christopher Morley, published by J. B. Lippincott

The Will of God—
Nothing More, Nothing Less.

Motto in G. Campbell Morgan's Study

How great a God we need; and how much
greater is our God than our greatest need.

Motto in a Business Office

Hammer away ye hostile hands!
Your hammers break;
God's anvil stands.

Motto on the seal of a Waldensian church

God has breathed and they are dispersed.

Motto on medal celebrating the victory
over the Spanish Armada

All things proclaim the existence of God.

Napoleon Bonaparte

God is always on the side of the big
battalions.

Napoleon Bonaparte (Tacitus, Voltaire,
de Bussy . . .)

Our Father which art in heaven.

New Testament: Matthew 6: 9

Fear not them which kill the body, but are
not able to kill the soul: but rather fear him
which is able to destroy both soul and body
in hell.

New Testament: Matthew 10: 28

What therefore God hath joined together,
let not man put asunder.

New Testament: Mark 10: 9

Render therefore unto Caesar the things
that are Caesar's, and unto God the things
that are God's.

New Testament: Mark 12: 17

There is one God; and there is none other
than he.

New Testament: Mark 12: 32

With God nothing shall be impossible.

New Testament: Luke 1: 37

Ye cannot serve God and mammon.

New Testament: Luke 16: 1

No man hath seen God at any time.

New Testament: John 1: 1

Behold the Lamb of God, which taketh awa
the sin of the world.

New Testament: John 1: 2

We have one Father, even God.

New Testament: John 8: 4

The Father is in me, and I in him.

New Testament: John 10: 3

If this counsel or this work be of men, it wil
come to nought: But if it be of God, y
cannot overthrow it.

New Testament: Acts 5: 38, 3

God is no respecter of persons.

New Testament: Acts 10: 3

I found an altar with this inscription, To the
Unknown God.

New Testament: Acts 17: 2]

For in him we live, and move, and have our
being; as certain also of your own poets have
said, For we are also his offspring.

New Testament: Acts 17: 28

Let God be true, but every man a liar.

New Testament: Romans 3: 4

There is no fear of God before their eyes.

New Testament: Romans 3: 18

God forbid.

New Testament: Romans 3: 31

We know that all things work together for
good to them that love God.

New Testament: Romans 8: 28

If God be for us, who can be against us?

New Testament: Romans 8: 31

God hath chosen the foolish things of the world to confound the wise; and God hath chosen the weak things of the world to confound the things which are mighty.

New Testament: I Corinthians 1: 27

Eye hath not seen, nor ear heard, neither have entered into the heart of man, the things which God hath prepared for them that love him.

New Testament: I Corinthians 2: 9

I have planted, Apollos watered; but God gave the increase.

New Testament: I Corinthians 3: 6

Be not deceived; God is not mocked . . .

New Testament: Galatians 6: 7

It is a fearful thing to fall into the hands of the living God.

New Testament: Hebrews 10: 31

Our God is a consuming fire.

New Testament: Hebrews 12: 29

For that ye ought to say, If the Lord will, we shall live, and do this, or that.

New Testament: James 4: 15 (Hence, "If the Lord will" came to be known as the St. James's reservation, and "Sub reservatione Jacobaeo" became a Latin proverb.)

God is love; and he that dwelleth in love dwelleth in God, and God in him.

New Testament: I John 4: 16

I am Alpha and Omega, the beginning and the end, the first and the last.

New Testament: Revelation 22: 13

It is the dominion of a spiritual being which constitutes a God: a true, supreme, or imaginary dominion makes a true, supreme or imaginary God. And from his true dominion it follows that the true God is a living, intelligent, and powerful Being; and from his other perfections, that he is supreme, or most perfect.

Sir Isaac Newton: *Principia*

Only God is permanently interesting. Other things we may fathom, but he out-tops our thought and can neither be demonstrated nor argued down.

Joseph Fort Newton: *My Idea of God*, p. 5

God acts the part of a Geometrician . . . His government of the world is no less exact than His creation of it.

John Norris: *Practical Discourses,* Vol. II, p. 228

A God-intoxicated man.

Novalis

Trumpeter, rally us, up to the heights of it! Sound for the City of God.

Alfred Noyes: "Trumpet Call," from *Collected Poems,* Vol. III. Copyright 1915, 1943 by Alfred Noyes, published by J. B. Lippincott Company

Shall not the Judge of all the earth do right?

Old Testament: Genesis 18: 25

God will provide.

Old Testament: Genesis 22: 8

God said unto Moses, I am that I am.

Old Testament: Exodus 3: 14

Thou shalt have no other gods before me.

Old Testament: Exodus 20: 3

The Lord God, merciful and gracious, long-suffering, and abundant in goodness and truth.

Old Testament: Exodus: 34: 6

Know therefore that the Lord thy God, he is God, the faithful God, which keepeth covenant and mercy with them that love him and keep his commandments to a thousand generations.

Old Testament: Deuteronomy 7: 9

The Lord your God is a God of gods, a Lord of lords, a great God, a mighty, and a terrible.

Old Testament: Deuteronomy 10: 17

The eternal God is thy refuge, and underneath are the everlasting arms.
Old Testament: Deuteronomy 33: 27

Be strong and of a good courage; be not afraid, neither be thou dismayed: for the Lord thy God is with thee, whithersoever thou goest.
Old Testament: Joshua 1: 9

Canst thou by searching find out God?
Old Testament: Job 11: 7

The fool hath said in his heart, There is no God.
Old Testament: Psalms 14: 1

The heavens declare the glory of God; and the firmament sheweth his handywork.
Old Testament: Psalms 19: 1

In thee, O Lord, do I put my trust.
Old Testament: Psalms 31: 1

I will say of the Lord, He is my refuge and my fortress: my God; in him will I trust.
Old Testament: Psalms 91: 2

For the Lord is a great God, and a great King above all gods.
Old Testament: Psalms 95: 3

The Lord reigneth; let the earth rejoice.
Old Testament: Psalms 97: 1

Give thanks unto him, and bless his name. For Jehovah is good; his lovingkindness endureth for ever, And his faithfulness unto all generations.
Old Testament: Psalms 100: 4, 5 (R.V.)

Who crowneth thee with lovingkindness and tender mercies.
Old Testament: Psalms 103: 4

The mercy of the Lord is from everlasting to everlasting upon them that fear him.
Old Testament: Psalms 103: 17

Who coverest thyself with light as with a garment: who stretchest out the heavens like a curtain: Who layeth the beams of his chambers in the waters: who maketh the clouds his chariot: who walketh upon the wings of the wind: Who maketh his angels spirits; his ministers a flaming fire.
Old Testament: Psalms 104: 2–4

O Lord, how manifold are thy works! in wisdom hast thou made them all: the earth is full of thy riches.
Old Testament: Psalms 104: 24

Though the Lord be high, yet hath he respect unto the lowly.
Old Testament: Psalms 138: 6

The fear of the Lord is the beginning of knowledge.
Old Testament: Proverbs 1: 7

Whom the Lord loveth he correcteth.
Old Testament: Proverbs 3: 12

A man's heart deviseth his way: but the Lord directeth his steps.
Old Testament: Proverbs 16: 9

Trust ye in the Lord for ever: for in the Lord Jehovah is everlasting strength.
Old Testament: Isaiah 26: 4

I am God, and there is none else.
Old Testament: Isaiah 45: 22

God must not be thought of as a physical being, or as having any kind of body. He is pure mind. He moves and acts without needing any corporeal space, or size, or form, or color, or any other property of matter.
Origen: De principiis, I

There is a God within us, and we glow when He stirs us.
Ovid: Fasti, VI, 5

If God be my friend, I cannot be wretched.
Ovid: Tristia, I, C. 10

Nothing is so lofty or so far above danger that it is not below and in the power of God.

Ovid: *Tristia*

As God is propitiated by the blood of a hundred bulls, so also is he by the smallest offering of incense.

Ibid.

Belief in a cruel God makes a cruel man.

Thomas Paine

It is wrong to say that God made rich and poor; He made only male and female, and He gave them the whole earth for their inheritance.

Thomas Paine

Suppose I had found a watch upon the ground . . . The mechanism being observed, . . the inference we think is inevitable that the watch must have a maker; that there must have existed, at some time, and at some place or other, an artificer or artificers, who formed it for the purpose which we find it actually to answer; who comprehended its construction, and designed its use.

William Paley: *Natural Theology*, ch. 1

The world we inhabit must have had an origin; that origin must have consisted in a cause; that cause must have been intelligent; that intelligence must have been supreme; and that supreme, which always was and is supreme, we know by the name of God.

Nikita Ivanovich Panin

Have no fear for the unsettlement or the disturbance of the Kingdom of heaven. It began in eternity, it will go on through everlasting; there is no panic in the divine personality. God is peace, God gives peace, God gives rest.

Joseph Parker

If a man is not made for God, why is he happy only in God? If man is made for God, why is he opposed to God?

Blaise Pascal: *Pensées*

The eternal Being is forever if he is at all.

Ibid.

We understand nothing of the works of God, if we do not assume that He has willed to blind some and enlighten others.

Ibid.

God's might to direct me,
God's power to protect me,
God's wisdom for learning,
God's eye for discerning,
God's ear for my hearing,
God's word for my clearing.

Attributed to St. Patrick (Sigerson, tr.)

You cannot serve God without Mammon.

Hesketh Pearson: *Biography of George Bernard Shaw*, Harper & Row Publishers, Inc.

God is not in the slightest degree baffled or bewildered by what baffles and bewilders us . . . He is either a present help or He is not much help at all.

J.B. Phillips: *New Testament Christianity*, The Macmillan Co., New York, and Hodder and Stoughton Ltd., London

One on God's side is a majority.

Wendell Phillips

The issue is in God's hands.

Pindar: *Olympian Odes*

If any man hopes, in whatever he does, to escape the eye of God, he is grievously wrong.

Ibid.

God is truth and light his shadow.

Plato

The world is God's epistle to mankind—his thoughts are flashing upon us from every direction.

Plato

To escape from evil we must be made, as far as possible, like God; and this resemblance consists in becoming just, and holy, and wise.

Plato

God is a geometrician.

Plato

All men are by nature equal, made, all, of the same earth by the same Creator, and however we deceive ourselves, as dear to God is the poor peasant as the mighty prince.

Plato

He best keeps from anger who remembers that God is always looking upon him.

Plato

God if He be good, is not the author of all things, but of a few things only, and not of most things that occur to man.

Plato: *The Republic*

There is indeed a God that hears and sees whate'er we do.

Titus Maccius Plautus: *Captivi*, II, 2, 63

It is ridiculous to suppose that the great head of things, whatever it be, pays any regard to human affairs.

Pliny the Elder: *Natural History*

It were better to have no opinion of God at all than such an one as is unworthy of him; for the one is only unbelief—the other is contempt.

Plutarch

Slave to no sect, who takes no private road.
But looks through Nature up to Nature's
    God.

Alexander Pope

All are but parts of one stupendous whole,
Whose body Nature is, and God the soul.

Alexander Pope

The people's voice is odd,
It is, and it is not, the voice of God.

Alexander Pope: *To Augustu*

He from thick films shall purge the visua
    ray,
And on the sightless eyeball pour the day

Alexander Pope: *Messial*

Who sees with equal eye, as God of all,
A hero perish or a sparrow fall,
Atoms or systems into ruin hurled
And now a bubble burst, and now a world

Alexander Pope: *Essay on Man*, Epis.

To Him no high, no low, no great, no small
He fills, He bounds, connects and equals all

Ibid

Lo, the poor Indian; whose untutored min
Sees God in clouds, or hears him in the wind

Ibid

Nor God alone in the still calm we find,
He mounts the storm, and walks upon th
    wind.

Alexander Pope: *Essay on Man*, Epis. I

Thou Great First Cause, least understood
  Who all my sense confin'd
To know but this, that thou art good,
  And that myself am blind.

Alexander Pope: *The Universal Praye*

Father of all! in every age,
  In every clime adored,
By saint, by savage, and by sage,
  Jehovah, Jove, or Lord!

Ibid

Without God I am a mere cipher, but wit
Him by my side I become a figure and ca
add, subtract, multiply and divide for th
Kingdom's business.

Presbyterian Tribune (permission granted
    by *Presbyterian Outlook*

'A still small voice" comes through the wild,
Like a father consoling his fretful child,
Which banishes bitterness, wrath, and fear,
Saying—Man is distant, but God is near!

Thomas Pringle: *Afar in the Desert*

Man proposes, God disposes.

Proverb

Who hath God hath all; who hath Him not,
hath less than nothing.

Proverb

In all thine actions think that God sees thee,
and in all His actions labor to see Him.—
That will make thee fear Him, and this will
move thee to love Him.—The fear of God is
the beginning of knowledge, and the knowledge of God is the perfection of love.

Francis Quarles

God is a light that is never darkened; an
unwearied life that cannot die; a fountain
always flowing; a garden of life; a seminary
of wisdom; a radical beginning of all goodness.

Francis Quarles: *Emblems*, Bk. I

Without Thy presence, wealth are bags of
cares;
Wisdom, but folly; joy, disquiet, sadness:
Friendship is treason, and delights are
snares;
Pleasure's but pain, and mirth but pleasing
madness.

Francis Quarles: *Emblems*, Bk. V

God is *alpha* and *omega* in the great world:
endeavour to make Him so in the little
world; make Him thy evening epilogue and
thy morning prologue . . . so shall thy rest
be peaceful, thy labours prosperous, thy life
pious, and thy death glorious.

Francis Quarles: *Enchiridion*, Cent. II,
no. 28

God moderates all at His pleasure.

François Rabelais: *Works*, Bk. II

He who bridles the fury of the billows, knows
also to put a stop to the secret plans of the
wicked.—Submitting to His holy will, I fear
God; I have no other fear.

Jean Baptiste Racine: *Athalie*, III

Man doth what he can, and God what he
will.

John Ray: *English Proverbs*, XCVII

Every conjecture we can form with regard to
the works of God has as little probability as
the conjectures of a child with regard to the
works of a man.

Thomas Reid: *Intellectual Powers*, Vol. I

God is an utterable sigh, planted in the
depths of the soul.

Jean Paul Richter

There are times when God asks nothing of
his children except silence, patience, and
tears.

Charles Seymour Robinson

God could have kept Daniel out of the lion's
den . . . He could have kept Paul and Silas
out of jail—He could have kept the three
Hebrew children out of the fiery furnace
. . . But God has never promised to keep us
out of hard places . . . What he has promised is to go with us through every hard
place, and to bring us through victoriously.

Merv Rosell

Give us a God—a living God,
One to wake the sleeping soul,
One to cleanse the tainted blood
Whose pulses in our bosoms roll.

C. G. Rosenberg: *The Winged Horn*, st. 7

If there wasn't a God we would have to
invent one to keep people sane.

Jean Jacques Rousseau (see also Voltaire)

God often visits us, but most of the time we
are not at home.

Joseph Roux: *Meditations of a Parish
Priest: God*, no. 65

We cannot break God's laws—but we can break ourselves against them.

A. Maude Royden

Anything that makes religion a second object makes it no object.—He who offers to God a second place offers Him no place.

John Ruskin

How can man understand God, since he does not yet understand his own mind, with which he endeavours to understand Him?

John Ruskin

When God shuts a door, He opens a window.

John Ruskin

With God, go over the sea—without Him, not over the threshold.

Russian Proverb

I fear God, and next to God I chiefly fear him who fears him not.

Saadi

In wonder—workings, or some bush aflame,
Men look for God and fancy Him concealed;
But in earth's common things He stands revealed
While grass and flowers and stars spell out His name.

Minot J. Savage: *In Common Things*

There is a God to punish and avenge.

Johann Christoph Friedrich von Schiller:
Wilhelm Tell, IV, 3, 37

We often praise the evening clouds,
And tints so gay and bold,
But seldom think upon our God,
Who tinged these clouds with gold.

Sir Walter Scott: *On The Setting Sun*

Nothing is void of God; He Himself fills His work.

Seneca: *De Beneficiis*

God never repents his first decision.

Ibid.

There's a divinity that shapes our ends,
rough-hew them how we will.

William Shakespeare: *Hamlet*
Act V, sc. 2, l. 10

God save the mark!

William Shakespeare: *Henry IV, Part I*
Act I, sc. 3, l. 56

We are in God's hand, brother, not in theirs

William Shakespeare: *Henry V*
Act III, sc. 6, l. 178

God is our fortress, in whose conquering name
Let us resolve to scale their flinty bulwarks

William Shakespeare: *Henry VI, Part I*
Act II, sc. 1, l. 26

God shall be my hope,
My stay, my guide and lantern to my feet

William Shakespeare: *Henry VI, Part II*
Act II, sc. 3, l. 24

Well, God's a good man.

William Shakespeare: *Much Ado About Nothing*, Act III, sc. 5, l. 39

The spirit of the worm beneath the sod
In love and worship, blends itself with God

Percy Bysshe Shelley

God helps those who help themselves.

Algernon Sidney: *Discourses Concerning Government*, ch. 2

Many millions search for God and find Him in their hearts.

Sikh Proverb

Tell them, I AM, Jehovah said
To Moses; while earth heard in dread,
And, smitten to the heart,
At once above, beneath, around,
All Nature, without voice or sound,
Replied, O LORD THOU ART.

Christopher Smart: *Song to David*

Our ground of hope is that God does not weary of mankind.

Ralph W. Sockman

In the days of my youth I remembered my
God!
And He hath not forgotten my age.

Robert Southey: *The Old Man's
Comforts, and How He
Gained Them*

Take what you want and pay for it.

Spanish Proverb

I take a totally different view of God and
Nature from that which the later Christians
usually entertain, for I hold that God is the
immanent, and not the extraneous, cause of
all things, I say, All is in God; all lives and
moves in God.

Benedict (Baruch) de Spinoza: *Epistle 21*

I looked at God and He looked at me, and
we were one forever.

Charles Haddon Spurgeon

As sure as ever God puts His children in the
furnace, He will be in the furnace with them.

Charles Haddon Spurgeon: *Privileges of
Trial*

When God had finished the creation of the
world He examined it and found it good.
Since then there has been no opinion expressed by Him.

K. K. Steincke

God tempers the wind to the shorn lamb.

Laurence Sterne

We had needs invent heaven if it had not
been revealed to us.

Robert Louis Stevenson: *St. Ives*

In all ranks of life the human heart yearns
for the beautiful; and the beautiful things
that God makes are his gift to all alike.

Harriet Beecher Stowe

He paints the lily of the field,
Perfumes each lily bell;
If he so loves the little flowers,
I know he loves me well.

Maria Straus

We do not resign ourselves to the will of
God; we relate ourselves to His will.

The Survey Bulletin

We are, because God is.

Emanuel Swedenborg: *Divine Providence,*
sec. 46

If we look closely at this world, where God
seems so utterly forgotten, we shall find that
it is he, who, after all, commands the most
fidelity and the most love.

Madam Anne Soymanov Swetchine

No man doth well but God hath part in him.

Algernon Charles Swinburne: *Atlanta in
Calydon: Chorus*

It is more religious and more reverent to
believe in the works of the Deity than to
comprehend them.

Tacitus: *Germania*

God, the ruler of all.

Ibid.

Under whose feet (subjected to His grace),
Sit nature, fortune, motion, time and place.

Torquato Tasso: *Gerusalemme*, IX, 56

I used to ask God to help me. Then I asked
if I might help him. I ended up by asking
him to do his work through me.

Hudson Taylor

It is a great mistake to suppose that God
is only, or even chiefly, concerned with
religion.

William Temple, Archbishop of
Canterbury

The old order changeth, yielding place to
new,
And God fulfils himself in many ways,
Lest one good custom should corrupt the
world.

Alfred, Lord Tennyson: *The Passing of
Arthur*

At last I heard a voice upon the slope
Cry to the summit, "Is there any hope?"
To which an answer pealed from that high
 land,
But in a tongue no man could understand;
And on the glimmering limit far withdrawn,
God made himself an awful rose of dawn.

Alfred, Lord Tennyson: *Vision of Sin*, V

Speak to Him, thou, for He hears, and Spirit
 with Spirit can meet—
Closer is He than breathing, and nearer than
 hands and feet.

Alfred, Lord Tennyson: *The Higher
Pantheism*, I, 2

Cast all your cares on God; that anchor
 holds.

Alfred, Lord Tennyson: *Enoch Arden*

I found Him in the shining of the stars,
I mark'd Him in the flowering of His fields,
But in His ways with men I find Him not.

Alfred, Lord Tennyson: *Idylls of the King*

There is an enmity between what is of God
and what is of man.

Tertullian: *The Christian's Defence*

I fled Him down the nights and down the
 days;
I fled Him, down the arches of the years;
I fled Him, down the labyrinthine ways
Of my own mind; and in the midst of
 tears
I hid from Him, and under running
 laughter.

Francis Thompson: *The Hound of
Heaven*

But with unhurrying chase,
And unperturbèd pace,
Deliberate speed, majestic instancy,
They beat—and a Voice beat
More instant than the Feet—
"All things betray Thee, who betrayest Me."

Ibid.

But I lose
Myself in Him, in Light ineffable!
Come, then, expressive Silence, muse Hi
 praise.
These, as they change, Almighty Father
 these
Are but the varied God. The rolling Year
Is full of Thee.

Ibic

What, but God?
Inspiring God! who bound less Spirit all,
And on emitting Energy, pervades,
Adjusts, sustains, and agitates the whole.

James Thomson: *The Seasons, Spring*
l. 84

Whate'er we leave to God, God does
And blesses us.

Henry David Thoreau: *Inspiratio*

If God were not a necessary being of himself
he might also seem to be made for the us
and benefit of men.

John Tillotson: *Works*, Sermon 9

God is he without whom one cannot live.

Leo Tolsto

There is one evident, indubitable manifesta
tion of the Divinity, and that is the laws o
right which are made known to the world
through Revelation.

Leo Tolstoy: *Anna Karenina*, Pt. VIII
ch. 1

Rock of Ages, cleft for me,
Let me hide myself in Thee!

Augustus Montague Toplady: *Rock o
Ages* (Hymn

He who serves God hath a good master.

Torriano: *Piazza Universale*, LXIX

When God is to be served, the cost we weig
In anxious balance, grudging the expense

Richard Chenevix Trench: *Sonne*

Time does not contain Him, nor space hol
Him. No intelligence can grasp Him no

imagination figure Him, nothing is like Him. But still He hears and sees all things.

Abdallah Ibn Tumart: *Tauhid, or Confession of Faith*

Reason refuseth its homage to a God who can be fully understood.

Martin Farquhar Tupper: *Proverbial Philosophy: Of a Trinity*

There is a beauty in the name appropriated by the Saxon nations to the Deity, unequalled except by the most venerated Hebrew appellation. They called Him "God" which is literally "The Good." The same word thus signifying the Deity and His most endearing quality. .

Charles Tennyson Turner

If you ask me how I believe in God, how God creates himself in me, and reveals himself to me, my answer may perhaps provoke your smiles or laughter, and even scandalize you. I believe in God as I believe in my friends, because I feel the breath of his affection, feel his invisible and tangible hand drawing me, leading me, grasping me.

Miguel de Unamuno: *Prosa Diversa,* Selection by J. L. Gili, 1939, Oxford University Press

God is no fault-finder, always looking for things to condemn in us. He estimates us at our best, not our worst.

The Upper Room

He is rich indeed whom God loves.

J. de la Veprie: *Les Proverbs Communs*

Reach up as far as you can, and God will reach down all the way.

John H. Vincent

If ye despise the human race, and mortal arms, yet remember that there is a God who is mindful of right and wrong.

Virgil: *Æneid,* Bk. I, l. 542

Where God and hard fortune call us, let us follow.

Virgil: *Æneid,* Bk. XII, l. 677

If God is not in us, He never existed.

Voltaire: *La Loi Naturelle: Exordium*

If there were no God, it would be necessary to invent Him.

Voltaire: *Letter to the author of the New Book of the Trinity*

God has made thee to love Him, and not to understand Him.

Voltaire: *La Henriade*

The world embarrasses me, and I cannot think
That this watch exists and has no Watchmaker.

Voltaire: *Epigram*

All things change, creeds and philosophies and outward systems—but God remains.

Mary Augusta Ward: *Robert Elsmere*

It is impossible to govern the world without God. He must be worse than an infidel that lacks faith, and more than wicked that has not gratitude enough to acknowledge his obligation.

George Washington

The most important thought I ever had was that of my individual responsibility to God.

Daniel Webster

Religion is the first thing and the last thing, and until a man has found God, and been found by God, he begins at no beginning and works to no end.

H. G. Wells

There are three things that only God knows: the beginning of things, the cause of things, and the end of things.

Welsh Proverb

In the faces of men and women I see God, and in my own face in the glass,
I find letters from God drop't in the street, and every one is signed by God's name,
And I leave them where they are, for I know that wheresoe'er I go,

Others will punctually come for ever and
ever.

Walt Whitman: *Song of Myself*

Yet, in the maddening maze of things,
And tossed by storm and flood,
To one fixed trust my spirit clings;
I know that God is good! . . .

I know not where His islands lift
Their fronded palms in air;
I only know I cannot drift
Beyond His love and care.

John Greenleaf Whittier: *The Eternal
Goodness*

Who fathoms the Eternal Thought?
Who talks of scheme and plan?
The Lord is God! He needeth not
The poor device of man.

Ibid.

And man is hate, but God is love!

John Greenleaf Whittier: *The Chapel
of the Hermits,* st. 75

Passive to His Holy will,
Trust I in my Master still,
Even though He slay me.

John Greenleaf Whittier: *Barclay of
Ury,* st. 7

God is, and all is well.

John Greenleaf Whittier: *My Birthday*

This I know is God's own truth, that pain
and troubles and trials and sorrows and
disappointments are either one thing or
another. To all who love God they are love
tokens from him. To all who do not love
God and do not want to love him they are
merely a nuisance. Every single pain that
we feel is known to God because it is the
most loving touch of his hand.

Edward Adrian Wilson, who died with
Scott in the Antarctic

He who sincerely praises God will soon discover within his soul an inclination to praise
goodness in his fellow man.

Oliver G. Wilson

God for His service needeth not proud work
of human skill.

William Wordsworth: *Poet's Dream,* I, 65
See 1473: 14

God is not the name of God, but an opinion
about Him.

Pope Xystus I: *The Ring*

When you speak of God, you are being
judged by God.

Ibid.

Thou, my all!
My theme! my inspiration! and my crown!
My strength in age—my rise in low estate!
My soul's ambition, pleasure, wealth!—my
world!
My light in darkness! and my life in death!
My boast through time! bliss through
eternity!
Eternity, too short to speak thy praise!
Or fathom thy profound of love to man!

Edward Young: *Night Thoughts,
Night IV*

By night an atheist half believes in God.

Edward Young: *Night Thoughts,
Night V*

A Deity believed, is joy begun;
A Deity adored, is joy advanced;
A Deity beloved, is joy matured.
Each branch of piety delight inspires.

Edward Young: *Night Thoughts,
Night VIII*

A God alone can comprehend a God.

Edward Young: *Night Thoughts,
Night IX*

Who worship God, shall find him. Humble
love,
And not proud reason, keeps the door of
heaven;
Love finds admission, where proud science
fails.

Ibid.

GOLDEN RULE

A God all mercy, is a God unjust.

Israel Zangwill: *Night*

GOLDEN RULE

Do unto others as they would do unto you
if they had a chance.

Anonymous

The Golden Rule is not a religion; it is
merely the expression of religion.

Charles L. Allen: *God's Psychiatry*

Confucianism: Surely it is the maxim of
loving-kindness: Do not unto others that
you would not have them do unto you.

Analects, XV, 23

Whatever the Christians do not wish to be
done to them, they do not to another.

St. Aristides: *Apology for the Christian
Faith,* XV

We should behave to friends as we would
wish friends to behave to us.

Aristotle

He has observed the golden rule
Till he's become the golden fool.

William Blake: *Epigram*

My duty towards my neighbor is to love him
as myself, and to do all men as I would they
should do unto me.

Book of Common Prayer: Catechism

Do as you would be done by is the surest way
that I know of pleasing.

Philip Dormer Stanhope, Lord Chesterfield: *Letters to His Son*

Zoroastrianism: That nature alone is good
which refrains from doing unto another
whatsoever is not good for itself.

Dadistan-i-dinik, 94: 5

GOLDEN RULE

Do other men, for they would do you.

Charles Dickens: *Martin Chuzzlewit,* ch. 11

All things whatsoever that thou wouldst not
wish to be done to thee, do thou also not to
another.

The Didache, or *Teachings of the Twelve
Apostles*

The Golden Rule works like gravitation.

Charles Fletcher Dole: *Cleveland Address*

Every man takes care that his neighbor does
not cheat him. But a day comes when he
begins to care that he do not cheat his
neighbor. Then all goes well.

Ralph Waldo Emerson: *Conduct of Life:
Worship*

Do as you would be done by.

English Proverb

What thou avoidest suffering thyself seek
not to impose on others.

Epictetus: *Encheiridion*

The rule of three, or golden rule, as it is
called in sacred algebray.

Daniel Featley: *Clavis Mystica,* p. 279

Do as ye wald be done to.

David Fergusson: *Scottish Proverbs*

Sometime when you have a few spare
moments, try to think of some other basic
principle that would cure all the world's
ills faster than the Golden Rule put into
practice.

Friendly Adventurer

Whatsoever you require that others should
do to you, that do ye to them.

Thomas Hobbes: *Leviathan,* I

Do not do to others what would anger you
if done to you by others.

Isocrates

191

I must always act in such a way that I can at the same time will that the maxim by which I act should become a universal law.

Immanuel Kant: *Grundlegung zur Metaphysik der Sitten*

The era of Christianity—peace, brotherhood, the Golden Rule as applied to governmental matters—is yet to come, and when it comes, then and then only, will the future of nations be sure.

Lajos Kossuth

Do unto others as you would have others do unto you in like case.

Pëtr Alekseivich Kropotkin: *La Morale Anarchiste*

The question was once put to Aristotle how we ought to behave to our friends, and his answer was, "As we should wish them to behave to us."

Diogenes Laertius: *Lives of the Philosophers*

Should that most unshaken rule of morality, and foundation of all social virtue, "that one should do as he would be done unto," be proposed to one who had never heard of it before, but yet is of capacity to understand its meaning, might he not without any absurdity ask a reason why?

John Locke: "Essay Concerning Human Understanding"

Skilful alike with tongue and pen,
He preached to all men everywhere
The Gospel of the Golden Rule,
The New Commandment given to men,
Thinking the deed, and not the creed,
Would help us in our utmost need.

Henry Wadsworth Longfellow: Prelude to *Tales of a Wayside Inn*, l. 217

This is the sum of all true righteousness: deal with others as thou wouldst thyself be dealt by. Do nothing to thy neighbor which thou wouldst not have him do to thee hereafter.

The Mahabharata

Brahamanism: This is the sum of duty: Do naught unto others which would cause you pain if done to you.

Ibid.

To do as one would be done by, and to love one's neighbor as one's self, constitute the ideal perfection of utilitarian morality.

John Stuart Mill: *Utilitarianism*

Three ideas stand out above all others in the influence they have exerted upon and are destined to exert upon the development of the human race: The idea of the Golden Rule, the idea of natural law, the idea of age-long growth, or evolution.

Robert Andrews Millikan: *Forbes Magazine*

The evil which you do not wish done to you, you ought to refrain from doing to another, so far as may be done without injury to a third person.

Henry More: *Encheiridion Ethicum*, IV

If you want a golden rule that will fit everybody, it is this: Have nothing in your houses that you do not know to be useful, or believe to be beautiful.

William Morris: *The Beauty of Life*

Deal with another as you'd have
Another deal with you;
What you're unwilling to receive,
Be sure you never do.

The New England Primer

Christianity: All things whatsoever ye would that men should do to you, do ye even so to them: for this is the law and the prophets.

New Testament: Matthew 7: 12

As ye would that men should do to you, do ye also to them likewise.

New Testament: Luke 6: 31

When we and ours have it in our power to do for you and yours what you and yours have done for us and ours, then we and ours will do for you and yours what you and yours have done for us and ours.

Old English Toast

The duty of man . . . is plain and simple, and consists of but two points: his duty to God, which every man must feel, and with respect to his neighbor, to do as he would be done by.

Thomas Paine: *The Rights of Man*

The Golden Rule would reconcile capital and labor, all political contention and uproar, all selfishness and greed.

Joseph Parker

Our conscience teaches us it is right, our reason teaches us it is useful, that men should live according to the Golden Rule.

W. Winwood Reade: *The Martyrdom of Man*, III

We ought to act that part towards another which we would judge to be right in him to act toward us, if we were in his circumstances and he in ours.

Thomas Reid: *Essays on the Active Powers*

Treat your inferiors as you would be treated by your betters.

Seneca: *Epistolae ad Lucilium*, Epis. XLVII, 11

Be just and gracious unto me,
As I am confident and kind to thee.

William Shakespeare: *Titus Andronicus*, Act I, sc. 1, l. 60

Reason shows me that if my happiness is desirable and a good, the equal happiness of any other person must be equally desirable.

Henry Sidgwick: *The Methods of Ethics*, III

If it be a duty to respect other men's claims, so also is it a duty to maintain our own.

Herbert Spencer: *Social Statics*, Pt. III, ch. 21, sec. 8

Desire nothing for yourself which you do not desire for others.

Benedict (Baruch) de Spinoza: *Ethica*, IV

Islam: No one of you is a believer until he desires for his brother that which he desires for himself.

Sunnah

Taoism: Regard your neighbor's gain as your own gain, and your neighbor's loss as your own loss.

T'ai Shang Kan Ying P'ien

Judaism: What is hateful to you, do not to your fellowmen. That is the entire Law; all the rest is commentary.

The Talmud, Shabbat, 31a

Which feature is most prominent in the human character, doing as we would be done by or doing as we are done by?

Nathaniel W. Taylor

The golden rule is moderation in all things.

Terence: *Andrea*

Absolutely speaking, *Do unto others as you would that they should do unto you* is by no means a golden rule, but the best of current silver. An honest man would have but little occasion for it.

Henry David Thoreau

Buddhism: Hurt not others in ways that you yourself would find hurtful.

Udana-Varga: 5, 18

Be you to others kind and true,
As you'd have others be to you;
And neither do nor say to men
Whate'er you would not take again.

Isaac Watts: *Divine Songs for Children*

Do unto the other feller the way he'd like to do unto you, an' do it fust.

Edward Noyes Westcott: *David Harum*

No man doth think others will be better to him than he is to them.

Benjamin Whichcote: *Moral and Religious Aphorisms*

His statecraft was the Golden Rule,
His right to vote a sacred trust;
Clear, over threat and ridicule,
All heard his challenge: "Is it just?"

John Greenleaf Whittier: *Sumner*

If a man any ways doubts whether what he is going to do to another man is agreeable to the law of nature, then let him suppose himself to be in that other man's room.

John Wise: *A Vindication of the Government of New England Churches*

As ye will that men do to you, and do ye to them in like manner.

John Wycliffe: Tr. of *Luke 6: 31*

GOOD AND EVIL

There is so much good in the worst of us,
And so much bad in the best of us,
That it ill behooves any of us
To find fault with the rest of us.

Anonymous

Do good, and evil shall not find you.

Apocrypha: Tobit 12: 7

Wicked men obey from fear; good men, from love.

Aristotle

It is characteristic of man that he alone has any sense of good and evil, or just and unjust, and the like, and the association of living things who have this sense makes a family and a state.

Aristotle: *Politics*, I

It is not every bad man that will ever be good, but there will no good man who was not at some time bad.

St. Augustine: *The City of God*, XV

God judged it better to bring good out of evil than to suffer no evil to exist.

St. Augustine: *Enchiridion*, XXVII, 421

Evil and good are God's right hand and left.

Philip James Bailey: *Festus, Proem*

There shall never be one lost good! What was shall live as before;
The evil is null, is nought, is silence implying sound;
What was good shall be good, with, for evil, so much good more;
On the earth the broken arcs; in the heaven a perfect round.

Robert Browning: *Abt Vogler*, st. 9

One that confounds good and evil is an enemy to good.

Edmund Burke: *Impeachment of Warren Hastings*

If you cannot hate evil, you cannot love good.

Struthers Burt: *Saturday Review*

It is as hard for the good to suspect evil, as it is for the bad to suspect good.

Cicero

Inability to tell good from evil is the greatest worry of man's life.

Cicero: *De Finibus*, Bk. I, ch. 13, sec. 43

What we all love is good touched up with evil—
Religion's self must have a spice of devil.

Arthur Hugh Clough: *Dipsychus*, Pt. I, sc. 3

Good and evil do not befall men without reason. Heaven sends them happiness or misery according to their conduct.

Confucius: *The Book of History*, IV

Socrates said that there was one only good, namely, knowledge; and one only evil, namely, ignorance.

Diogenes Laertius

If there is one thing that mankind should have learned from the agonies of the last four decades it is that it's never safe to do evil that good may come of it. The good gets lost and the evil goes on.

John Dos Passos: *The Theme is Freedom*

The first lesson of history, is, that evil is good.

Ralph Waldo Emerson

Good and evil are chiefly in the imagination.

Thomas Fuller: *Gnomologia*

Ah me! we believe in evil,
Where once we believed in good;
The world, the flesh, and the devil
Are easily understood.

Adam Lindsay Gordon: *Wormwood and Nightshade*, st. 8

There is no evil in human affairs that has not some good mingled with it.

Francesco Guicciardini: *Storia d' Italia*

He who does evil that good may come, pays a toll to the devil to let him into heaven.

Augustus William and Julius Charles Hare: *Guesses at Truth*, p. 444

Good and ill are one . . . To God all things are fair and good and right, but men hold some things wrong and some right.

Heraclitus

Evil no nature hath; the loss of good
Is that which gives to sin a livelihood.

Robert Herrick: *Evil*

Two urns by Jove's high throne have ever stood,
The source of evil, one, and one of good.

Homer, *Iliad*, Bk. XXIV, l. 663

As it is said of the greatest liar that he tells more truth than falsehoods, so it may be said of the worst man that he does more good than evil.

Samuel Johnson

The two great movers of the human mind are the desire of good, and the fear of evil.

Samuel Johnson

Evil is only good perverted.

Henry Wadsworth Longfellow: *The Golden Legend*, Pt. II

Once to every man and nation comes the moment to decide,
In the strife of Truth with Falsehood, for the good or evil side.

James Russell Lowell: *The Present Crisis*, st. 5

Good and evil, we know, in the field of this world grow up together almost inseparably.

John Milton: *Areopagitica*

Good has but one enemy, the evil; but the evil has two enemies, the good and itself.

Johannes von Müller

For the good that I would I do not; but the evil which I would not, that I do.

New Testament: Romans 7: 19

Abhor that which is evil; cleave to that which is good.

New Testament: Romans 12: 9

Be not overcome of evil, but overcome evil with good.

New Testament: Romans 12: 21

Someone has called evil: "the devil's quicksand." It has no real power of its own; its power comes when man strives to strike back, and, overcome by its force, gives in. Trying to get even spreads evil. We might say that in this respect evil is like poison ivy; the more you scratch, the more it itches, and the more it spreads.

A. Nicholas, in *Good Business*

Your eyes shall be opened, and ye shall be as gods, knowing good and evil.

Old Testament: Genesis 3: 5

Woe unto them that call evil good, and good evil.

Old Testament: Isaiah 5: 20

Out of the mouth of the most High proceedeth not evil and good?

Old Testament: Lamentations 3: 38

The power of choosing good and evil is within the reach of all.

Origen: *De Principiis,* Proem. 5

To a good man nothing that happens is evil.

Plato: *Apology of Socrates,* ch. 33, sec. 41

While time lasts there will always be a future, and that future will hold both good and evil, since the world is made to that mingled pattern.

Dorothy L. Sayers: *Begin Here,* Harper & Row, Publishers, Inc.

The evil that men do lives after them;
The good is oft interred with their bones.

William Shakespeare: *Julius Caesar,* Act III, sc. 2, l. 81

Evil minds change good to their own nature.

Percy Bysshe Shelley: *Prometheus Unbound,* Act I, l. 380

As surely as God is good, so surely there is no such thing as necessary evil.

Robert Southey

We too often forget that not only is there "a soul of goodness in things evil," but very generally also, a soul of truth in things erroneous.

Herbert Spencer: *First Principles,* Pt. I, ch. 1, sec. 1

So far as any one shuns evils, so far he does good.

Emanuel Swedenborg: *Doctrine of Life,* sec. 21

Man, as man, is averse to what is evil and wicked, for evil is unnatural and good is connatural to man.

Benjamin Whichcote: *Moral and Religious Aphorisms*

Some things must be good in themselves, else there could be no measure whereby to lay out good and evil.

Ibid.

Roaming in thought over the Universe, I saw the little that is
Good steadily hastening toward immortality
And the vast all that is called Evil I saw hastening to merge itself and become lost and dead.

Walt Whitman: *Roaming in Thought*

Perish with him the folly that seeks through evil good.

John Greenleaf Whittier: *Brown of Ossawatomie,* st. 6

GOODNESS

I expect to pass through this world but once; any good thing, therefore, that I can do, or any kindness that I can show to my fellow-creatures, let me do it now; let me not defer or neglect it, for I shall not pass this way again.

Anonymous

Good has two meanings: it means both that which is good absolutely and that which is good for somebody.

Aristotle: *The Nicomachean Ethics,* VII

Of all virtues and dignities of the mind, goodness is the greatest, being the character of the Deity; and without it, man is a busy, mischievous, wretched thing.

Sir Francis Bacon

Your actions in passing, pass not away, for every good work is a grain of seed for eternal life.

St. Bernard of Clairvaux

Good critics who have stamped out poet's hope,
Good statesmen who pulled ruin on the state,
Good patriots who for a theory risked a cause,

Good kings who disembowelled for a tax,
Good popes who brought all good to
jeopardy,
Good Christians who sat still in easy chairs
And damned the general world for stand-
ing up.—
Now may the good God pardon all good
men!

Elizabeth Barrett Browning: *Aurora
Leigh*, Bk. IV, l. 499

There's a further good conceivable
Beyond the utmost earth can realize.

Robert Browning: *Prince Hohenstiel-
Schwangau*

God does not intend people, and does not
like people, to be too good. He likes them
neither too good nor too bad, but a little
too bad is more venial with him than a little
too good.

Samuel Butler

Goodness consists not in the outward things
we do, but in the inward thing we are.—To
be good is the great thing.

Edwin Hubbell Chapin

In nothing do men approach so nearly to
the gods as in doing good to men.

Cicero

Be good and leave the rest to Heaven.

William Combe: *Dr. Syntax in Search of
the Picturesque*, Canto VII

True goodness springs from a man's own
heart. All men are born good.

Confucius: *Analects*

The Infinite Goodness has such wide arms
that it takes whatever turns to it.

Alighieri Dante

Who soweth good seed shall surely reap;
The year grows rich as it groweth old,
And life's latest sands are its sands of gold!

Julia Caroline Ripley Dorr: *To The
"Bouquet Club"*

The first condition of human goodness is
something to love; the second something to
reverence.

George Eliot: *Janet's Repentance*

When good men die their goodness does not
perish,
But lives though they are gone.

Euripides: *Temenidae,* frag. 734

I will speak ill of no man, and speak all the
good I know of everybody.

Benjamin Franklin

The ground that a good man treads is
hallowed.

Johann Wolfgang von Goethe: *Torquato
Tasso,* I

Goodness is love in action, love with its hand
to the plow, love with the burden on its
back, love following his footsteps who went
about continually doing good.

James Hamilton

In the heraldry of heaven goodness precedes
greatness, and so on earth it is more powerful.—The lowly and lovely may often do
more good in their limited sphere than the
gifted.

George Horne

God whose gifts in gracious flood
Unto all who seek are sent,
Only asks you to be good
And is content.

Victor Hugo: *God Whose Gifts in
Gracious Flood*

The greatest pleasure I know is to do a good
action by stealth, and to have it found out
by accident.

Charles Lamb

We must first be made good, before we can
do good; we must first be made just, before
our works can please God.—for when we are
justified by faith in Christ, then come good
works.

Hugh Latimer

197

The soul is stronger that trusts in goodness.

Philip Massinger

Goodness thinks no ill where no ill seems.

John Milton

There is no man so good, who, were he to submit all his thoughts and actions to the law, would not deserve hanging ten times in his life.

Michel Eyquem de Montaigne

Let your light so shine before men, that they may see your good works, and glorify your Father which is in heaven.

New Testament: Matthew 5: 16

Do good to them that hate you.

New Testament: Matthew 5: 44

All things work together for good to them that love God.

New Testament: Romans 8: 28

Prove all things; hold fast that which is good.

New Testament: I Thessalonians 5: 21

Goodness, armed with power, is corrupted; and pure love without power is destroyed.

Reinhold Niebuhr: *Beyond Tragedy,*
Charles Scribner's Sons

There is none that doeth good, no, not one.

Old Testament: Psalms 14: 3

Thou crownest the year with thy goodness.

Old Testament: Psalms 65: 11

No amount of good deeds can make us good persons. We must be good before we can do good.

Chester A. Pennington

The good must merit God's peculiar care;
But who but God can tell us who they are?

Alexander Pope: *Essay on Man,* Epis. IV,
l. 135

And this our life exempt from public haunt
Finds tongues in trees, books in the running brooks,
Sermons in stones and good in every thing.

William Shakespeare: *As You Like It,*
Act II, sc. 1, l. 15

The web of our life is of a mingled yarn, good and ill together.

William Shakespeare: *All's Well That Ends Well,* Act IV, sc. 3, l. 83

Men are made good by spirit and not by law. There is no goose-stepping goodness. Unless we live up to the spirit of the good life, we shall live down to the level of mental slavery and moral mediocrity.

Ralph W. Sockman

It is only great souls that know how much glory there is in being good.

Sophocles

He that is a good man, is three quarters of his way toward the being a good Christian, wheresoever he lives, or whatsoever he is called.

Robert South

Good is no good, but if it be spend;
God giveth good for none other end.

Edmund Spenser: *The Shepheardes Calender:* Maye, l. 71

The heart of a good man is the sanctuary of God.

Madame Anne Germaine de Staël

I thank the goodness and the grace
Which on my birth have smiled,
And made me, in these Christian days,
A happy Christian child.

Ann and Jane Taylor: *Hymns for Infant Minds. A Child's Hymn of Praise,* st. 1

Howe'er it be, it seems to me,
'Tis only noble to be good—

Kind hearts are more than coronets,
And simple faith than Norman blood.

Alfred, Lord Tennyson: *Lady Clara
Vere de Vere*

Be not merely good; be good for something.

Henry David Thoreau

Goodness is the only investment that never fails.

Henry David Thoreau: *Walden XI,
Higher Laws*

Real goodness does not attach itself merely to this life—it points to another world. Political or professional reputation cannot last forever, but a conscience void of offence before God and man is an inheritance for eternity.

Daniel Webster

Do all the good you can,
By all the means you can,
In all the ways you can,
In all the places you can,
At all the times you can,
To all the people you can,
As long as ever you can.

John Wesley: *John Wesley's Rule*

GOSPEL

The Gospel does not consist of what we can do for ourselves, but of what God stands ready to do for us.

Arkansas Methodist

There is not a book on earth so favorable to all the kind and to all the sublime affections, or so unfriendly to hatred, persecution, tyranny, injustice, and every sort of malevolence as the gospel.—It breathes, throughout, only mercy, benevolence, and peace.

James Beattie

The shifting systems of false religion are continually changing their places; but the gospel of Christ is the same forever. While other

false lights are extinguished, this true light ever shineth.

Theodore Ledyard Cuyler

The gospel in all its doctrines and duties appears infinitely superior to any human composition.—It has no mark of human ignorance, imperfection, or sinfulness, but bears the signature of divine wisdom, authority, and importance, and is most worthy of the supreme attention and regard of all intelligent creatures.

Nathanael Emmons

Talk about the questions of the day; there is but one question, and that is the gospel. It can and will correct everything needing correction.

William Ewart Gladstone

His word was Gospel.

Nicholas de Guildford: *The Owl and the
Nightingale*

It was a common saying among the Puritans, "Brown bread and the Gospel is good fare."

Matthew Henry: *Commentaries.
Isaiah XXX*

All is not Gospell that thou doest speake.

John Heywood: *Proverbes*, Pt. II, ch. 11

God writes the gospel not in the Bible alone, but on trees, and flowers, and clouds, and stars.

Martin Luther

The gospel belongs to the poor and sorrowful, and not to princes and courtiers who live in continual joy and delight, in security, void of all tribulation.

Martin Luther: *Table Talk*

The gospel is the fulfillment of all hopes, the perfection of all philosophy, the interpreter of all revelations, and a key to all the seeming contradictions of truth in the physical and moral world.

Hugh Miller

I search in vain in history to find the similar to Jesus Christ, or anything which can approach the gospel.

Napoleon Bonaparte

Go ye into all the world, and preach the gospel to every creature.

New Testament: Mark 16: 15

It is a strange and sickly world into which the gospel leads us—a world apparently out of a Russian novel.

Friederich Wilhelm Nietzsche: *The Antichrist,* **XXXI**

It is possible to be an athiest, it is possible not to know whether God exists, or why, and yet believe . . . that history as we know it now began with Christ and that Christ's gospel is its foundation.

Boris Pasternak: *Doctor Zhivago* (Copyright, Pantheon Books, 1958), Random House

We can learn nothing of the gospel except by feeling its truths. There are some sciences that may be learned by the head, but the science of Christ crucified can only be learned by the heart.

Charles Haddon Spurgeon

Did you ever notice that while the gospel sets before us a higher and more blessed heaven than any other religion, its hell is also deeper and darker than any other?

Samuel Warren

My heart has always assured and reassured me that the gospel of Christ must be a Divine reality.

Daniel Webster

GRACE

Grace comes into the soul, as the morning sun into the world; first a dawning; then a light; and at last the sun in his full and excellent brightness.

Thomas Adams

In the Bible there are three distinctive meanings of grace; it means the mercy and active love of God; it means the winsome attractiveness of God; it means the strength of God to overcome.

Charles L. Allen

What is grace? I know until you ask me; when you ask me, I do not know.

St. Augustine

The law detects, grace alone conquers sin.

St. Augustine: *Of Continence*

Grace groweth after governance.

Thomas Becon: *Early Works,* p. 395

God appoints our graces to be nurses to other men's weaknesses.

Henry Ward Beecher

An outward and visible sign of an inward and spiritual grace.

Book of Common Prayer: Catechism

There is no such way to attain to greater measure of grace as for a man to live up to the little grace he has.

Phillips Brooks

As heat is opposed to cold, and light to darkness, so grace is opposed to sin.—Fire and water may as well agree in the same vessel, as grace and sin in the same heart.

Thomas Benton Brooks

It is the very nature of grace to make a man strive to be most eminent in that particular grace which is most opposed to his bosom sin.

Thomas Benton Brooks

If you haven't grace, the Lord can give it to you. If you haven't learning, I'll help you to get it. But if you haven't common sense, neither I nor the Lord can give it to you.

John Brown of Haddington to his students.

Of all the thoughts of God that are
Borne inward into souls afar,

Along the Psalmist's music deep,
Now tell me if that any is,
For gift of grace, surpassing this:
"He giveth his beloved—sleep."

Elizabeth Barrett Browning: *Sleep*,
st. 1

Nor can a man with grace his soul inspire,
More than the candles set themselves on fire.

John Bunyan: *A Book for Boys and Girls*

Grace is given of God, but knowledge is bought in the market.

Arthur Hugh Clough: *The Bothie of Toberna-Vuolich*

Thus all below is strength, and all above is grace.

John Dryden: *Epistle to Congreve*, l. 19

By "riches of grace" the apostle means all the spiritual resources that are at the disposal of Christians through the redeeming work of Christ and the gracious presence of his Holy Spirit.

Henry W. DuBose

Grace is but glory begun, and glory is but grace perfected.

Jonathan Edwards

As grace is first from God, so it is continually from him, as much as light is all day long from the sun, as well as at first dawn or at sun-rising.

Jonathan Edwards

His grace is great enough to meet the great
things—
  The crashing waves that overwhelm the
  soul,
The roaring winds that leave us stunned
  and breathless,
  The sudden storms beyond our life's
  control.
His grace is great enough to meet the small
things—
  The little pin-prick troubles that annoy,

The insect worries, buzzing and persistent,
  The squeaking wheels that grate upon our
  joy.

Annie Johnson Flint

The glorious gospel of the grace of God is the profound heritage of the church and ministry for a lost world.

William E. Gilroy

Divine grace was never slow.

George Herbert: *Outlandish Proverbs*

Grace binds you with far stronger cords than the cords of duty or obligation can bind you. Grace is free, but when once you take it you are bound forever to the Giver, and bound to catch the spirit of the Giver. Like produces like. Grace makes you gracious, the Giver makes you give.

E. Stanley Jones: *The Way*, p. 196,
Abingdon Press

The custom of saying grace at meals had, probably, its origin in the early times of the world, and the hunter-state of man, when dinners were precarious things, and a full meal was something more than a common blessing; when a bellyful was a windfall, and looked like a special providence.

Charles Lamb: *Grace Before Meat*

Whatever man is able to do in order to experience the effects of divine grace is merely owing to the action of the Holy Spirit which draws us towards God.

August Lang

So grace is a gift of God and kind wit a chance.

William Langland: *Piers Plowman*,
Passus XV, l. 33

By the grace of God (Dei gratia).

Latin Phrase

The being of grace must go before the increase of it; for there is no growth without life, and no building without a foundation.

George Lavington

I want . . . to borrow from the language of the saints . . . to live "in grace" as much of the time as possible. By "grace" I mean an inner harmony, essentially spiritual, which can be translated into outward harmony. I would like to achieve a state of inner spiritual grace from which I could function and give as I was meant to in the eye of God.

> Anne Morrow Lindbergh: *Gift From the Sea,* Random House and Chatto & Windus, Ltd.

I need Thy presence every passing hour:
What but Thy grace can foil the tempter's power?

> Henry Francis Lyte: *Abide With Me*

God does not refuse grace to one who does what he can.

> Medieval Latin Proverb

In proportion as we "grow in grace and in the knowledge of Christ," we shall grow in the desire that the Redeemer's sovereignty may be more widely and visibly extended.

> Henry Melville

Prevenient grace descending had remov'd
The stony from their hearts.

> John Milton: *Paradise Lost*, Bk. XI, l. 3

Where sin abounded, grace did much more abound.

> *New Testament: Romans 5: 20*

Shall we continue in sin, that grace may abound? God forbid.

> *New Testament: Romans 6: 1-2*

If by grace, then it is no more of works; otherwise grace is no more grace. But if it be of works, then it is no more grace: otherwise work is no more work.

> *New Testament: Romans 11: 6*

Abundant grace.

> *New Testament: II Corinthians 4: 15*

God is able to make all grace abound toward you.

> *New Testament: II Corinthians 9: 8*

My grace is sufficient for thee: for my strength is made perfect in weakness.

> *New Testament: II Corinthians 12: 9*

The grace of the Lord Jesus Christ, and the love of God, and the communion of the Holy Ghost, be with you all.

> *New Testament: II Corinthians 13: 14*

Ye are fallen from grace.

> *New Testament: Galatians 5: 4*

By grace are ye saved through faith—and that not of yourselves—It is the gift of God, not of works, lest any man should boast.

> *New Testament: Ephesians 2: 8-9*

Unto every one of us is given grace according to the measure of the gift of Christ.

> *New Testament: Ephesians 4: 7*

Amazing grace! how sweet the sound,
  That saved a wretch like me;
I once was lost, but now I'm found;
  Was blind, but now I see.
'Twas grace that taught my heart to fear,
  And grace my fear relieved;
How precious did that grace appear
  The hour I first believed.
Through many dangers, toils and snares
  I have already come,
'Tis grace that brought me safe thus far,
  And grace will lead me home.

> John Newton

He giveth grace unto the lowly.

> *Old Testament: Proverbs 3: 34*

The growth of grace is like the polishing of metals. There is first an opaque surface; by and by you see a spark darting out, then a strong light; till at length it sends back a perfect image of the sun that shines upon it.

> Edward Payson

The breeze of divine grace is blowing upon us all. But one needs to set the sail to feel this breeze of grace.

> Ramakrishna

That word "grace"
In an ungracious mouth is but profane.
William Shakespeare: *Richard II,*
Act I, sc. 4, l. 89

Angels and ministers of grace defend us!
William Shakespeare: *Hamlet,* Act I,
sc. 4, l. 39

Hail to thee, lady! and the grace of heaven,
Before, behind thee and on every hand,
Enwheel thee round!
William Shakespeare: *Othello,* Act II,
sc. 1, l. 85

As dew never falls on a stormy night, so the
dews of His grace never come to the restless
soul.
A. B. Simpson: *The Alliance Witness*

There is nothing but God's grace. We walk
upon it; we breathe it; we live and die by it;
it makes the nails and axles of the universe;
and a puppy in pajamas prefers self-conceit.
Robert Louis Stevenson

Give us grace and strength to forbear and
to persevere. Give us courage and gaiety and
the quiet mind, spare to us our friends, soften
to us our enemies.
Robert Louis Stevenson: *Prayer*

I have never found anyone, however religious and devout who did not sometimes
experience withdrawal of grace, or feel a
lessening of devotion.
Thomas à Kempis

As the earth can produce nothing unless it is
fertilized by the sun, so we can do nothing
without the grace of God.
Vianney

Plenteous grace with Thee is found,
  Grace to cover all my sin;
Let the healing streams abound;
  Make and keep me pure within.
Charles Wesley: *Refuge*

Sanctification is the work of God's free grace,
whereby we are renewed in the whole man
after the image of God, and are enabled

more and more to die unto sin and live unto
righteousness.
Westminster Catechism

GRATITUDE

If a man carries his cross beautifully and
makes it radiant with glory of a meek and
gentle spirit, the time will come when the
things that now disturb will be the events
for which he will most of all give gratitude
to God.
Anonymous

Some people complain because God put
thorns on roses, while others praise Him for
putting roses among thorns.
Anonymous

Gratitude is the heart's memory.
Anonymous

But whether we have less or more,
Always thank we God therefore.
Anonymous: attributed to *Fabliau of
St. Cleves*

Gratitude is the sign of noble souls.
Aesop: *Androcles*

If gratitude is due from children to their
earthly parent, how much more is the gratitude of the great family of men due to our
father in heaven.
Hosea Ballou

Thou hast given so much to me . . . Give one
thing more—a grateful heart.
George Herbert

I am glad that he thanks God for anything.
Samuel Johnson

Gratitude is from the same root word as
"grace," which signifies the free and boundless mercy of God. Thanksgiving is from the
same root word as "think," so that to think
is to thank.
Willis P. King: *Pulpit Preaching*

Thank God every morning when you get up that you have something to do that day which must be done, whether you like it or not. Being forced to work, and forced to do your best, will breed in you temperance and self control, diligence and strength of will, cheerfulness and content, and a hundred virtues which the idle never know.

Charles Kingsley

A grateful thought toward heaven is of itself a prayer.

Gotthold Ephraim Lessing

Gratitude to God makes even a temporal blessing a taste of heaven.

William Romaine

He that urges gratitude pleads the cause both of God and men, for without it we can neither be sociable nor religious.

Seneca

O, Lord that lends me life,
Lend me a heart replete with thankfulness!

William Shakespeare: *Henry VI, Part II,*
Act I, sc. 1, l. 19

Let never day nor night unhallow'd pass,
But still remember what the Lord hath done.

William Shakespeare: *Henry VI, Part II,*
Act II, sc. 1, l. 85

Within this wall of flesh
There is a soul counts thee her creditor.

William Shakespeare: *King John,*
Act III, sc. 3, l. 20

Gratitude to God should be as habitual as the reception of mercies is constant, as ardent as the number of them is great, as devout as the riches of divine grace and goodness is incomprehensible.

Charles Simmons

From David learn to give thanks for everything.—Every furrow in the Book of Psalms is sown with the seeds of thanksgiving.

Jeremy Taylor

God is pleased with no music below so much as with the thanksgiving songs of relieved widows and supported orphans; of rejoicing, comforted, and thankful persons.

Jeremy Taylor

And then be thankful; O admire his ways,
Who fills the world's unempty'd granaries!
A thankless feeder is a thief, his feast
A very robbery, and himself no guest.

Henry Vaughan

Gratitude is not only the memory but the homage of the heart—rendered to God for his goodness.

Nathaniel Parker Willis

May silent thanks at least to God be given
with a full heart;
Our thoughts are heard in heaven.

William Wordsworth

GREATNESS

A contemplation of God's works, a generous concern for the good of mankind, and the unfeigned exercise of humility—these only, denominate men great and glorious.

Joseph Addison

The study of God's word, for the purpose of discovering God's will, is the secret discipline which has formed the greatest characters.

James W. Alexander

Great souls care only for what is great.

Henri Frédéric Amiel: *Journal*

Greatness is a spiritual condition worthy to excite love, interest, and admiration; and the outward proof of possessing greatness is, that we excite love, interest, and admiration.

Matthew Arnold: *Culture and Anarchy:
Sweetness and Light*

No man has come to true greatness who has not felt in some degree that his life belongs to his race, and that what God gives him he gives him for mankind.

Phillips Brooks

And I smiled to think God's greatness
flowed around our incompleteness,—
Round our restlessness, His rest.

Elizabeth Barrett Browning: *Rhyme of
the Duchess May,* Conclusion, st. 11

Man's Unhappiness, as I construe, comes of
his Greatness; it is because there is an Infinite
in him, which with all his cunning he cannot
quite bury under the Finite.

Thomas Carlyle: *Sartor Resartus,*
Bk. II, ch. 9

The greatest man is he who chooses the right
with invincible resolution, who resists the
sorest temptations from within and without,
who bears the heaviest burdens cheerfully,
who is calmest in storms and most fearless
under menace and frowns, whose reliance on
truth, virtue, on God, is most unfaltering;
and is this a greatness which is apt to make
a show, or which is most likely to abound in
conspicuous station?

William Ellery Channing: *Self-Culture*

Greatness and goodness are not means, but
ends!
Hath he not always treasures, always friends,
The good great man? three treasures, Love,
and Light,
And Calm Thoughts, regular as infant's
breath;
And three firm friends, more sure than day
and night.
Himself, his Maker, and the Angel Death!

Samuel Taylor Coleridge: *The Good
Great Man*

The truly great consider first, how they may
gain the approbation of God; and secondly,
that of their own conscience; having done
this, they would then willingly conciliate the
good opinion of their fellowmen.

Charles Caleb Colton

Some must be great. Great offices will have
great talents. And God gives to every man
the virtue, temper, understanding, taste that
lifts him into life and lets him fall just in
the niche he was ordained to fall.

William Cowper

A great man may be the personification and
type of the epoch for which God destines
him, but he is never its creator.

Jean Henri Merle D'Aubigné

Great men are they who see that spiritual
is stronger than any material force; that
thoughts rule the world.

Ralph Waldo Emerson

When divine souls appear, men are compelled by their own self-respect to distinguish
them.

Ralph Waldo Emerson: *Journals*

No horse gets anywhere until he is harnessed.
No steam or gas ever drives anything until
it is confined. No Niagara is ever turned into
light and power until it is tunneled. No life
ever grows great until it is focused, dedicated,
disciplined.

Harry Emerson Fosdick: *Living Under
Tension*

It is a grand mistake to think of being great
without goodness; and I pronounce it as
certain that there was never yet a truly great
man that was not at the same time truly
virtuous.

Benjamin Franklin: *The Busy-Body*

Great men are the gifts of kind Heaven to
our poor world; instruments by which the
Highest One works out his designs; light-
radiators to give guidance and blessing to
the travelers of time.

Moses Harvey: *Columbus*

Nothing can make a man truly great but
being truly good, and partaking of God's
holiness.

Matthew Henry

As the marsh-hen secretly builds on the
watery sod,
Behold I will build me a nest on the greatness of God:
I will fly in the greatness of God as the marsh-
hen flies

In the freedom that fills all the space 'twixt
the marsh and the skies.

Sidney Lanier: *The Marshes of Glynn*,
IV, 7

Great souls are not those which have less
passion and more virtue than common souls,
but only those which have greater designs.

François de La Rochefoucauld

No saint, no hero, no discoverer, no prophet,
no leader ever did his work cheaply and
easily, comfortably and painlessly, and no
people was ever great which did not pass
through the valley of the shadow of death
on its way to greatness.

Walter Lippmann

Great men stand like solitary towers in the
city of God.

Henry Wadsworth Longfellow:
Kavanagh, ch. 1

The wisest man could ask no more of Fate
Than to be simple, modest, manly, true,
Safe from the Many, honored by the Few;
To count as naught in the World, or Church
or State,
But inwardly in secret to be great.

James Russell Lowell

Goodness is not tied to greatness, but greatness to goodness.

Thomas Moffett: *Healths Improvement*,
CLXI

Whosoever will be chief among you, let him
be your servant.

New Testament: Matthew 20: 27

He that is least among you all, the same shall
be great.

New Testament: Luke 9: 48

Eleven out of twelve great men of history
were only agents of a great cause.

Friedrich Wilhelm Nietzsche

Thine, O Lord, is the greatness and the
power, and the glory, and the victory, and

the majesty: for all that is in the heaven and
in the earth is thine; thine is the kingdom,
O Lord, and thou art exalted as head above
all.

Old Testament: I Chronicles 29: 11

And seekest thou great things for thyself?
seek them not.

Old Testament: Jeremiah 45: 5

Why, then, is a wise man great? Because he
has a great soul.

Seneca: *Epistolae ad Lucilium*,
Epis. LXXXVII, sec. 18

But be not afraid of greatness: some are born
great, some achieve greatness, and some have
greatness thrust upon 'em.

William Shakespeare: *Twelfth Night*,
Act II, sc. 5, l. 156

In me there dwells
No greatness, save it be some far-off touch
Of greatness to know well I am not great.

Alfred, Lord Tennyson: *Idylls of the King*,
Lancelot and Elaine, l. 447

Greatness is not mortal. The qualities which
the great have to give, they give perpetually.
Their gifts are taken into the pattern of life,
and they appear thereafter in the fabric of
the lives of nations, renewing themselves as
the leaves of the trees are renewed by the
seasons.

Robert Trout: in a radio tribute to
Franklin D. Roosevelt

A solemn and religious regard to spiritual
and eternal things is an indispensable element of all true greatness.

Daniel Webster

GUILT

God hath yoked to guilt
Her pale tormentor, misery.

William Cullen Bryant: *Inscription for
the Entrance to a Wood*

Thank God, guilt was never a rational thing.

Edmund Burke: *Impeachment of Warren Hastings*

Father of Light! great God of Heaven!
Hear'st thou the accents of despair?
Can guilt like man's be e'er forgiven?
Can vice atone for crimes by prayer?

George Gordon, Lord Byron: *Prayer of Nature*

Guilt and sin are only a fear of the past.

Charles P. Curtis: *A Commonplace Book*, p. 191

There smiles no Paradise on earth so fair
But guilt will raise avenging phantoms there.

Felicia D. Hemans: *The Abencerrage*, Canto I, l. 133

The gods
Grow angry with your patience. 'Tis their care
And must be yours, that guilty men escape not.

Ben Jonson: *Catiline*, Act III, sc. 5

We have no choice but to be guilty.
God is unthinkable if we are innocent.

Archibald MacLeish: *J. B.*, Houghton Mifflin Co.

Whosoever shall keep the whole law, and yet offend in one point, he is guilty of all.

New Testament: James 2: 10

H

HAPPINESS

The person who has a firm trust in the Supreme Being is powerful in his power, wise by his wisdom, happy by his happiness.

Joseph Addison

No one praises happiness as one praises justice, but we call it "a blessing" deeming it something higher and more divine than things we praise.

Aristotle: *Nicomachean Ethics*, Bk. I, ch. 12, sec. 4

Where your pleasure is, there is your treasure: where your treasure, there your heart; where your heart, there your happiness.

St. Augustine

Happiness is not the end of life; character is.

Henry Ward Beecher

The strength and the happiness of a man consists in finding out the way in which God is going, and going in that way too.

Henry Ward Beecher

To enjoy true happiness we must travel into a very far country, and even out of ourselves.

Sir Thomas Browne: *Christian Morals*

How soon a smile of God can change the world!
How we are made for happiness—how work
Grows play, adversity a winning fight!

Robert Browning: *In a Balcony*

Little deeds of kindness, little words of love,
Help to make earth happy like the heaven above.

Julia A. Fletcher Carney: *Little Things*

The hand that in life grips with a miser's clutch, and the ear that refuses to heed the pleading voice of humanity forfeit the most precious of all gifts of earth and of heaven —the happiness that comes of doing good to others.

Amos G. Carter

There are briers besetting every path,
  Which call for patient care;
There is a cross in every lot,
  And an earnest need for prayer;
But a lowly heart that leans on Thee
  Is happy anywhere.

Alice Cary

The happiest heart that ever beat
Was in some quiet breast
That found the common daylight sweet,
And left to Heaven the rest.

John Vance Cheney: *The Happiest Heart*

The rich man is not one who is in possession of much, but one who gives much.

St. John Chrysostom: *Homilies*

What happiness is, the Bible alone shows clearly and certainly, and points out the way that leads to the attainment of it.—"In Cicero and Plato, and other such writers," says Augustine, "I meet with many things acutely said, and things that excite a certain warmth of emotions, but in none of them do I find these words, 'Come unto me, all ye

hat labor, and are heavy laden, and I will
;ive you rest.' "

Samuel Taylor Coleridge

Ne hold these truths to be self-evident: that
ıll men are created equal; that they are
ındowed by their Creator with certain in-
ılienable Rights; that among these are Life,
Liberty and the pursuit of Happiness.

The Declaration of Independence

Resigned to Heaven, we may with joy
To any state submit,
And in the world of miseries
Have happiness complete.

Daniel Defoe: *A Review of the Affairs of
France and of all Europe*, VIII

There is but one way to tranquillity of mind
and happiness, and that is to account no external things thine own, but to commit all
to God.

Epictetus

To attain happiness in another world we
need only to believe something, while to
secure it in this world we must needs do
something.

Charlotte Perkins Gilman

The happy man is he that knows the world
and cares not for it.

Joseph Hall

Happiness is the legitimate fruitage of love
and service. Set happiness before you as an
end, no matter in what guise of wealth, or
fame, or oblivion even, and you will not
attain it.—But renounce it and seek the
pleasure of God, and that instant is the birth
of your own.

Arthur S. Hardy

Happiness is the legal tender of the soul.

Robert Green Ingersoll: *Liberty of Man,
Woman and Child*

Do you wish never to be sad? Live rightly!

Isidorus of Aegae: *Scriptura*, XIII, 223

God does not love the man who is always
happy.

Jugo-Slavic Proverb

If an Arab in the desert were suddenly to
discover a spring in his tent, and so would
always be able to have water in abundance,
how fortunate he would consider himself—
so too, when a man, who has a physical being
is always turned toward the outside, thinking that his happiness lies outside him,
finally turns inward and discovers that the
source is within him, not to mention his
discovery that the source is his relation to
God.

Sören Kierkegaard

There may be love without happiness, but
there is never happiness without love.

La Femme et la Vie, Paris (*Quote*
Translation)

We wish to go to heaven because it is a place
of supreme happiness. We avoid hell because
it is a place of misery.

J. Gilchrist Lawson

We are happy now because God wills it.

James Russell Lowell: *The Vision of
Sir Launfal: Prelude*

Three things make us happy and content:
the seeing eye, the hearing ear, the responsive
heart.

Missionary Digest

Happy is the man whom God correcteth:
therefore despise not thou the chastening
of the Almighty.

Old Testament: Job 5: 17

The hope of the righteous shall be gladness.

Old Testament: Proverbs 10: 28

He that keepeth the law, happy is he.

Old Testament: Proverbs 29: 18

Wherefore are all they happy that deal very
treacherously?

Old Testament: Jeremiah 12: 1

HAPPINESS

Happiness lies in the absorption in some
vocation which satisfies the soul.

Sir William Osler

I believe in one God and no more, and I hope
for happiness beyond this life.

Thomas Paine: *The Age of Reason*, Pt. I

Happiness is neither within us only, or without us; it is the union of ourselves with God.

Blaise Pascal

It is interesting to note that even Jefferson
never proposed happiness as an inalienable
right. Our constitution talks of a right only
for the *pursuit* of happiness. Ours for the
seeking and the winning! Not free. Happiness is the result, the product, of endeavor.
Never God-given. Happiness is only God-
permitted.

Permanized Paper Quarterly

Human happiness has no perfect security but
freedom; freedom none but virtue; virtue
none but knowledge; and neither freedom,
virtue, nor knowledge has any vigor or immortal hope, except in the principles of the
Christian faith, and in the sanctions of the
Christian religion.

Josiah Quincy

Brethren, happiness is *not* our being's end
and aim. The Christian's aim is perfection,
not happiness; and every one of the sons
of God must have something of that spirit
which marked his Master.

Frederick William Robertson

Happiness is the sense that one matters. Happiness is an abiding enthusiasm. Happiness
is single-mindedness. Happiness is whole-
heartedness. Happiness is a by-product. Happiness is faith.

Samuel M. Shoemaker: *How You Can
Find Happiness*

If you want to have a good day, take a shave,
a good month, slay a pig, a good year, marry;
but if you want all your days to be good, become a priest.

Spanish Proverb

It is not how much we have, but how much
we enjoy, that makes happiness.

Charles Haddon Spurgeon

Have your heart right with Christ, and He
will visit you often, and so turn weekdays
into Sundays, meals into sacraments, homes
into temples and earth into heaven.

Charles Haddon Spurgeon

If I have faltered more or less
In my great task of happiness;
If I have moved among my race
And shown no glorious morning face; . . .
Lord, thy most pointed pleasure take,
And stab my spirit broad awake;
Or, Lord, if too obdurate I,
Choose thou, before that spirit die,
A piercing pain, a killing sin,
And to my dead heart run them in!

Robert Louis Stevenson: *The Celestial
Surgeon*

What right have we to decline to be happy,
until we shall have found a world full of
superlatives? God only is perfect, and He
alone can look for the blessedness that comes
from such spotless surroundings. Perfection
must be the goal of man; the aim of his soul
and mind, inward in thought and feeling,
and outward in acts and deeds, but his happiness must not wait for that divine end. The
same soul that longs for the absolutely beautiful must feed upon the common in the long
meanwhile.

David Swing

All the world is searching for joy and happiness, but these cannot be purchased for
any price in any market place, because they
are virtues that come from within, and like
rare jewels must be polished, for they shine
brightest in the light of faith, and in the
services of brotherly love.

Lucille R. Taylor: *Relief Society
Magazine*

Happy is the soul that has something to look
backward to with pride, and something to
look forward to with hope.

Oliver G. Wilson: "Life's Increasing Test,"
Wesleyan Methodist, February 11, 1959

hen we have the right sort of religion, and
ough to it, our lives will become lyric and
ic; we shall burst into songs which even
e angels will stop to hear.

Zion's Herald

EALTH, HEALING

onour a physician with the honour due
nto him for the uses which ye may have of
im: for the Lord hath created him. For of
e most High cometh healing, and he shall
ceive honour of the king. The skill of the
hysician shall lift up his head: and in the
ght of great men he shall be in admiration.

Apocrypha: Ecclesiasticus, 38: 1–3

e who has health has hope, and he who has
ope has everything.

Arab Proverb

alf the spiritual difficulties that men and
omen suffer arise from a morbid state of
ealth.

Henry Ward Beecher

o man propose this test: Thy body at its
best.
ow far can that project thy soul on its lone
way?

Robert Browning

have good health, good thoughts, and good
umour, thanks be to God Almighty.

William Byrd: *Diary*

etter to hunt in fields for health unbought,
han fee the doctor for a nauseous draught.
he wise, for cure, on exercise depend;
od never made his work for man to mend.

John Dryden: *To John Driden,* l. 92

he prayer that reforms the sinner and heals
e sick is an absolute faith that all things are
ossible to God,—a spiritual understanding
f Him, an unselfed love.

Mary Baker Eddy: *Science and Health
with Key to the Scriptures,* p. 1: 1–4

God heals, and the doctor takes the fee.

Benjamin Franklin

Miracles may be denied, but healings are not
. . . Christ produces a sound faith, and faith
has a therapeutic value.

John H. Gerstner: *The Theology of
the Major Sects*

A wise physician is a John Baptist, who
recognizes that his only mission is to prepare the way for a greater than himself.—
Nature.—

Arthur S. Hardy

Our prayers should be for a sound mind in
a healthy body.

Juvenal: *Satires,* Satire, X

God may forgive your sins, but your nervous
system won't.

Alfred Korzybski: *Healthways*

I wish above all things that thou mayest
prosper and be in health, even as thy soul
prospereth.

New Testament: III John 2

And the leaves of the tree were for the healing of the nations.

New Testament: Revelation 22: 2

O Lord, my God, I cried unto thee, and thou
hast healed me.

Old Testament: Psalm 30: 2

Who forgiveth all thine iniquities; who
healeth all thy diseases.

Old Testament: Psalm 103: 3

He healeth the broken in heart, and bindeth
up their wounds.

Old Testament: Psalm 147: 3

With his stripes are we healed.

Old Testament: Isaiah 53: 5

For I will restore health unto thee, and I will
heal thee of thy wounds, saith the Lord.

Old Testament: Jeremiah 30: 17

But unto you that fear my name shall the Sun of righteousness arise with healing in his wings.

Old Testament: Malachi 4: 2

The head of medical service in a great university hospital once said, "One should send for his minister (or priest or rabbi) as he sends for his doctor when he becomes ill." That is to say, God helps the sick in two ways, through the science of medicine and surgery and through the science of faith and prayer.

Norman Vincent Peale: *Today*

I feel no care of coin;
  Well-doing is my wealth;
My mind to me an empire is,
  While grace affordeth health.

Robert Southwell: *Content and Rich*

But what avail the largest gifts of Heaven,
  When drooping health and spirits go amiss?
How tasteless then whatever can be given!
Health is the vital principle of bliss.

James Thomson: *Castle of Indolence,*
Canto II, st. 57

Look to your health; and if you have it, praise God, and value it next to a good conscience; for health is the second blessing that we mortals are capable of; a blessing that money cannot buy.

Izaak Walton: *Compleat Angler,* Pt. I,
ch. 21

Say you are well, or all is well with you,
And God shall hear your words and make them true.

Ella Wheeler Wilcox: *Speech,* Rand
McNally & Co.

HEART

Culture of intellect, without religion in the heart, is only civilized barbarism and disguised animalism.

Christian Karl von Bunsen

The heart is like a viper, hissing, and spittin poison at God.

Jonathan Edwards: *The Freedom of th*
Wi

The Lord showed me, so that I did se clearly, that he did not dwell in these templ which men had commanded and set up, bu in people's hearts . . . his people were h temple, and he dwelt in them.

George Fox: *Journ*

One is nearer God's heart in a garden
Than anywhere else on earth.

Dorothy Frances Gurney: *God's Garde*

There is an awful warmth about my hea like a load of immortality.

John Keats: *Letter to J. H. Reynol*

Ye whose hearts are fresh and simple,
Who have faith in God and nature.

Henry Wadsworth Longfellow
Hiawatha: Introductio

Trust no future, howe'er pleasant!
Let the dead past bury its dead!
Act,—act in the living Present!
Heart within and God o'erhead.

Henry Wadsworth Longfellow
Psalm of Lif

The heart of a good man is the sanctuary o God in this world.

Madame Necke

Out of the abundance of the heart the mout speaketh.

New Testament: Matthew 12: 3
Luke 6: 4

Where your treasure is, there will your hear be also.

New Testament: Luke 12: 3

God . . . knoweth the secrets of the heart.

Old Testament: Psalm 44: 2

Create in me a clean heart, O God; and rene a right spirit within me.

Old Testament: Psalm 51: 1

HEART

Keep thy heart with all diligence; for out of it are the issues of life.

Old Testament: Proverbs 4: 23

He that is of a merry heart hath a continual feast.

Old Testament: Proverbs 15: 15

Two men please God—who serves Him with all his heart because he knows Him; who seeks Him with all his heart because he knows Him not.

Nikita Ivanovich Panin

Men may tire themselves in a labyrinth of search, and talk of God; but if we would know Him indeed, it must be from the impressions we receive of Him; and the softer our hearts are, the deeper and livelier those will be upon us.

William Penn

Give God thy broken heart, He whole will
   make it:
Give woman thy whole heart, and she will
   break it.

Edmund Prestwich: *The Broken Heart*

Many flowers open to the sun, but only one follows him constantly.—Heart, be thou the sunflower, not only open to receive God's blessing, but constant in looking to him.

Jean Paul Richter

The hearts of men, which fondly here admire
Fair seeming shows, and feed on vain delight,
Transported with celestial desire
Of those fair forms, may lift themselves up
   higher,
And learn to love, with zealous humble duty,
Th' Eternal Fountain of that heavenly
   beauty.

Edmund Spenser: *Hymn in Honour of
Beautie,* l. 16

Give God thy heart, thy service, and thy gold;
The day wears on, and the time is waxing old.

Sundial in the Cloister-garden of
Gloucester Cathedral

HEAVEN

Thou shalt rest sweetly if thy heart reprehend Thee not.

Thomas à Kempis: *Imitation of Christ,*
Pt. II, ch. 6

None but God can satisfy the longings of an immortal soul; that as the heart was made for Him, so He only can fill it.

Richard Chenevix Trench: *Notes on the
Parables. Prodigal Son*

God has two dwellings: one in heaven, and the other in a meek and thankful heart.

Izaak Walton

Is thy heart right, as my heart is with thine?
Dost thou love and serve God? It is enough.
I give thee the right hand of fellowship.

John Wesley

How else but through a broken heart
May Lord Christ enter in?

Oscar Wilde: *The Ballad of Reading Gaol*

HEAVEN

Planning is in the power of man, executing is in the hands of heaven.

Anonymous

Who spits against heaven, it falls in his face.

Anonymous

He who thinks most of heaven will do most for earth.

Anonymous

This world is but the vestibule of eternity. Every good thought or deed touches a chord that vibrates in heaven.

Anonymous

No coming to Heaven with dry eyes.

Thomas Adams: *Sermon*

Heaven is not to be looked upon only as the reward, but as the natural effect, of a religious life.

Joseph Addison

I'm gwine to Heaven on eagle's wing;
All don't see me, goin' to hear me sing.

American Negro Song

Love lent me wings; my path was like a stair;
A lamp unto my feet, that sun was given;
And death was safety and great joy to find;
But dying now, I shall not climb to
Heaven.

Michelangelo: *Sonnet LXIII, After
Sunset*

It is heaven upon earth to have a man's mind
move in charity, rest in providence, and turn
upon the poles of truth.

Sir Francis Bacon

Is heaven a place where pearly streams
Glide over silver sand?
Like childhood's rosy dazzling dreams
Of some far faery land?
Is heaven a clime where diamond dews
Glitter on fadeless flowers?
And mirth and music ring aloud
From amaranthine bowers?

Philip James Bailey: *Festus: Alcove and
Garden*

Where imperfection ceaseth, heaven begins.

Philip James Bailey: *Festus: Wood and
Water*

The gates of heaven are so easily found when
we are little, and they are always standing
open to let children wander in.

Sir James Matthew Barrie: *Sentimental
Tommy*, Charles Scribner's Sons

As high as Heaven, as deep as Hell.

Francis Beaumont and John Fletcher:
Honest Man's Fortune, Act IV, sc. 1

Heaven will be the endless portion of every
man who has heaven in his soul.

Henry Ward Beecher

If the way to heaven be narrow, it is not long;
and if the gate be straight, it opens into endless life.

William Beveridge

Heaven would hardly be heaven if we could
define it.

William E. Biederwolf

A robin redbreast in a cage
Puts all Heaven in a rage.

William Blake: *Poems: Auguries of
Innocence*, l. 5

We cannot go to Heaven on beds of down.

Richard Brathwaite: *The English
Gentlemen*

Earth's crammed with heaven.

Elizabeth Barrett Browning: *Aurora
Leigh*, Bk. VII, l. 820

God keeps a niche
In Heaven, to hold our idols; and albeit
He brake them to our faces, and denied
That our close kisses should impair their
white,—
I know we shall behold them raised, com-
plete,
The dust swept from their beauty, glorified,
New Memnons singing in the great God
light.

Elizabeth Barrett Browning: *Sonnet,
Futurity with the Departed*

Things learned on earth, we shall practise in
heaven.

Robert Browning: *Bells and Pome-
granates, Old Pictures in
Florence*, st. 17

Earth breaks up, time drops away,
In flows heaven, with its new day.

Robert Browning: *Christmas-Eve*, sec. 10

Ah, but a man's reach should exceed his
grasp,
Or what's a heaven for?

Robert Browning: *Men and Women,
Andrea del Sarto*

God's in His heaven—all's right with the
world!

Robert Browning: *Pippa Passes*

God said, "Be Light"—and light was on the grave!
No more alone to sage and hero given,
Ope for all life the impartial gates of Heaven!

> Edward George Bulwer-Lytton: *The New Timon*

All places are distant from heaven alike.

> Robert Burton: *Anatomy of Melancholy*, Pt. II, sec. 111, mem. 4

In hope to merit Heaven by making earth a Hell.

> George Gordon, Lord Byron: *Childe Harold*, Canto I, st. 20

Tis not where we lie, but whence we fell:
The loss of heaven's the greatest pain in hell.

> Pedro Calderon de la Barca: *Adventures of Five Hours, Act V*

To appreciate heaven well
Tis good for a man to have some fifteen minutes of hell.

> Will Carleton: *Farm Ballads. Gone with a Handsomer Man*

Heaven's help is better than early rising.

> Miguel de Cervantes: *Don Quixote,* Pt. II, Bk. IV, ch. 34, p. 674

Anyone can devise a plan by which good people may go to Heaven. Only God can devise a plan whereby sinners, who are His enemies, can go to Heaven.

> Lewis Sperry Chafer: *Moody Monthly*

Man says "So, so."
Heaven says, "No, no."

> Chinese Aphorism

The road to heaven lies as near by water as by land.

> Jeremy Collier: *Ecclesiastical History*

Heaven means to be one with God.

> Confucius

Whatever heaven ordains is best.

> Confucius

He on whom Heaven confers a sceptre knows not the weight till he bears it.

> Pierre Corneille

Do your duty, and leave the rest to heaven.

> Pierre Corneille: *Horace,* Act II, sc. 8

The sword of heaven is not in haste to smite,
Nor yet doth linger.

> Alighieri Dante: *Paradiso,* Canto XXII, l. 16

Which is the way to heaven? Take the first turn to the right and then straight ahead.

> *The Defender*

Who has not found the heaven below
Will fail of it above.
God's residence is next to mine,
His furniture is love.

> Emily Dickinson: *Poems*

Heav'n would no bargain for its blessings drive.

> John Dryden: *Astrea Redux,* l. 137

Too black for heaven, and yet too white for hell.

> John Dryden: *The Hind and the Panther,* Pt. I, l. 343

There is a heaven, for ever, day by day,
The upward longing of my soul doth tell me so.

> Paul Laurence Dunbar: *Theology*

Men do not go to Heaven laughing.

> Dutch Proverb

The way to Heaven is ascending; we must be content to travel up hill, though it be hard and tiresome, and contrary to the natural bias of our flesh.

> Jonathan Edwards: *The Christian Pilgrim*

May I reach
That purest heaven, be to other souls
The cup of strength in some great agony.

> George Eliot: *O May I Join the Choir Invisible*

A man may go to Heaven with half the pains it cost him to purchase Hell.

Henry Fielding: *Jonathan Wild*, IV

Beware, my lord! Beware lest stern Heaven hate you enough to hear your prayers!

Anatole France: *The Crime of Sylvestre Bonnard*, Pt. II, ch. 4

There is no going to Heaven in a sedan.

Thomas Fuller: *Gnomologia*

Heaven will make amends for all.

Ibid.

He will never get to Heaven who desire to go thither alone.

Ibid.

No man was ever scared into Heaven.

Ibid.

Better go to Heaven in rags than to Hell in embroidery.

Ibid.

Heaven is a cheap purchase, whatever it cost.

Ibid.

Where billows never break, nor tempests roar.

Sir Samuel Garth: *The Dispensary*, Canto III, l. 226

If God were not willing to forgive sin Heaven would be empty.

German Proverb

Heaven is the day of which grace is the dawn, the rich, ripe fruit of which grace is the lovely flower; the inner shrine of that most glorious temple to which grace forms the approach and outer court.

Thomas Guthrie

Heaven hath many tongues to talk of it, more eyes to behold it, but few hearts that rightly affect it.

Joseph Hall

Our heart is in heaven, our home is not here.

Reginald Heber: *Hymns: Fourth Sunday in Advent*

It is not talking but walking that will bring us to heaven.

Matthew Henry

All this, and Heaven too!

Philip Henry, in *Matthew Henry's Life of Philip Henry*, p. 70

Heaven is most fair, but fairer He
That made that fairest canopy.

Robert Herrick: *Heaven*

If a person does not enjoy the worship and services of the Lord, he no doubt would be out of place in heaven.

A. G. Hobbs, Jr.: *Christian Worker*

Heaven is not reached at a single bound;
But we build the ladder by which we rise
From the lowly earth to the vaulted skies,
And we mount to its summit round by round.

Josiah Gilbert Holland

Just are the ways of Heaven; from Heaven proceed
The woes of man; Heaven doom'd the Greeks to bleed.

Homer: *Odyssey*, Bk. VIII, l. 128 (Pope's trans.)

For mortal daring nothing is too high.
In our blind folly we storm heaven itself.

Horace: *Odes*, Bk. I, 3, l. 37

Heaven is a place prepared for those who are prepared for it.

Houston (Texas) *Times, All-Church Press*

Heaven protects children, sailors and drunken men.

Thomas Hughes: *Tom Brown at Oxford*, ch. 1

Good actions are the invisible hinges of the
doors of heaven.

Victor Hugo

Heaven is for those who think of it.

Joseph Joubert

We have created over you seven Heavens.

The Koran, II

The net of heaven has large meshes and yet
nothing escapes it.

Lao-tze: The Simple Way, no. 23

Struggle against it as thou wilt,
Yet Heaven's ways are Heaven's ways.

Gotthold Ephraim Lessing: Nathan der
Weise, Act III, sc. 1

When Christ ascended
Triumphantly, from star to star,
He left the gates of heaven ajar.

Henry Wadsworth Longfellow: The
Golden Legend, Pt. II, sc. 2

We see but dimly through the mists and
vapors;
Amid these earthly damps
What seem to us but sad, funereal tapers
May be heaven's distant lamps.

Henry Wadsworth Longfellow: Resignation. st. 4

For a cap and bells our lives we pay,
Bubbles we buy with a whole soul's task-
ing:
'Tis heaven alone that is given away,
'Tis only God may be had for the asking.

James Russell Lowell: The Vision of
Sir Launfal: Prelude

I would not give one moment of heaven for
all the joy and riches of the world, even if it
lasted for thousands and thousands of years.

Martin Luther

The joys of heaven are not the joys of passive
contemplation, of dreamy remembrance, of
perfect repose; but they are described thus,

"They rest not day or night." "His servants
serve him and see his face."

Alexander MacLaren

Paradise is to believe in it.

Catulle Mendès

I know not where lies Eden-land;
I only know 'tis like unto
God's kingdom, ever right at hand—
Ever right here in reach of you.

Joaquin Miller: With Love to You and
Yours, Pt. IV, sec. 12

Undaunted by the clouds of fear,
Undazzled by a happy day,
She made a Heaven about her here,
And took how much! with her away.

Richard Monckton Milnes: In Memoriam

Here we may reign secure; and in my choice
To reign is worth ambition, though in Hell:
Better to reign in Hell, than serve in Heav'n.

John Milton: Paradise Lost, Bk. I, l. 261

A Heaven on earth.

John Milton: Paradise Lost, Bk. IV, l. 208

Though in Heav'n the trees
Of life ambrosial fruitage bear, and vines
Yield nectar.

John Milton: Paradise Lost, Bk. V, l. 426

Be but the shadow of Heav'n and things
therein
Each to other like, more than on earth is
thought?

John Milton: Paradise Lost, Bk. V, l. 574

If God hath made this world so fair
Where sin and death abound,
How beautiful beyond compare
Will paradise be found.

James Montgomery

We talk about Heaven being so far away. It
is within speaking distance to those who
belong there.

Dwight L. Moody

No man can resolve himself into Heaven.

Dwight L. Moody: *Heaven*

Earth has no sorrow that Heaven cannot heal.

Sir Thomas Moore: *Come, Ye Disconsolate*

A Persian's Heaven is eas'ly made,
'Tis but black eyes and lemonade.

Sir Thomas Moore: *Intercepted Letters*

Joy, joy for ever!—my task is done—
The gates are pass'd, and Heaven is won!

Sir Thomas Moore *Lalla Rookh: Paradise
and the Peri*

Take all the pleasures of all the spheres,
And multiply each through endless years,—
One minute of Heaven is worth them all.

Ibid.

The Heaven of each is but what each desires.

Sir Thomas Moore: *Lalla Rookh: The
Veiled Prophet of Khorassan*

This world is all a fleeting show,
For man's illusion given;
The smiles of joy, the tears of woe,
Deceitful shine, deceitful flow,—
There's nothing true but Heaven!

Sir Thomas Moore: *This World is All a
Fleeting Show*

The way to Heaven out of all places is of like length and distance.

Sir Thomas More: *Utopia*

How vast is heaven? lo it will fit
In any space you give to it . . .
So broad—it takes in all things true;
So narrow—it can hold but you.

John Richard Moreland: *How Vast is
Heaven*

Blessed are they which are persecuted for righteousness' sake: for theirs is the kingdom of heaven.

New Testament: Matthew 5: 10

Rejoice, and be exceeding glad: for great is your reward in heaven: for so persecuted they the prophets which were before you.

New Testament: Matthew 5: 12

Lay up for yourselves treasures in heaven, where neither moth nor rust doth corrupt and where thieves do not break through nor steal.

New Testament: Matthew 6: 20

Not every one that saith unto me, Lord, Lord, shall enter into the kingdom of heaven; but he that doeth the will of my Father which is in heaven.

New Testament: Matthew 7: 21

I knew a man . . . caught up to the third heaven.

New Testament: II Corinthians 12: 2

Ye have in heaven a better and an enduring substance.

New Testament: Hebrews 10: 34

We, according to his promise, look for new heavens and a new earth, wherein dwelleth righteousness.

New Testament: II Peter 3: 13

If I ever reach heaven I expect to find three wonders there: first, to meet some I had not thought to see there; second, to miss some I had expected to see there; and third, the greatest wonder of all, to find myself there.

John Newton

O, human love, thou spirit given,
On Earth, of all we hope in Heaven!

Edgar Allan Poe: *Tamerlane*

Heaven is not always angry when he strikes,
But most chastises those whom most he likes.

John Pomfret: *Verses to His Friend under
Affliction*

Heaven is the presence of God.

Christina Georgina Rossetti: *Seek
and Find*

We are as near to heaven as we are far from
elf, and far from the love of a sinful world.

Samuel Rutherford

The hope of heaven under troubles is like
wind and sails to the soul.

Samuel Rutherford

Heaven knows its time; the bullet has its
billet.

Sir Walter Scott: *Count Robert of Paris,*
ch. 25

For love is heaven, and heaven is love.

Sir Walter Scott: *The Lay of the Last
Minstrel*

Socrates, being asked what countryman he
was, answered, "I am a citizen of the whole
world." But ask a Christian what countryman he is, and he will answer, "I am a citizen
of all heaven."

William Secker

The ascent from earth to heaven is not easy.

Seneca: *Hercules Furens,* CCCCXXXVII

The love of heaven makes one heavenly.

William Shakespeare

Our remedies oft in ourselves do lie,
Which we ascribe to heaven.

William Shakespeare: *All's Well that Ends
Well,* Act I, sc. 1, l. 231

Hark, hark! the lark at heaven's gate sings,
And Phoebus 'gins arise.

William Shakespeare: *Cymbeline,*
Act II, sc. 3, l. 22

Heaven . . . The treasury of everlasting joy.

William Shakespeare: *Henry VI, Part II,*
Act II, sc. 1, l. 17

There are more things in heaven and earth,
Horatio,
Than are dreamt of in your philosophy.

William Shakespeare: *Hamlet,*
Act I, sc. 5, l. 166

Heaven's face doth glow.

William Shakespeare: *Hamlet*
Act III, sc. 4, l. 48

My hopes in heaven do dwell.

William Shakespeare: *Henry VIII,*
Act III, sc. 2, l. 459

There's husbandry in heaven;
Their candles are all out.

William Shakespeare: *Macbeth,*
Act II, sc. 1, l. 4

Heaven still guards the right.

William Shakespeare: *Richard II,*
Act III, sc. 2, l. 62

Heaven's light forever shines, Earth's
shadows fly.

Percy Bysshe Shelley: *Adonais,* l. 11

Heaven's the perfection of all that can be
said or thought—riches, delight, harmony,
health, beauty; and all these not subject to
the waste of time, but in their height eternal.

James Shirley

The wisest judging of heaven is not to judge
of it at all.

Socrates

Heaven ne'er helps the men who will not act.

Sophocles: *Unknown Dramas,* frag. 288

What matter it *how* heaven we gain
If at the last we really get to heaven?

William Wetmore Story: *St. Peter's*

'Tis expectation makes a blessing dear,
Heaven were not heaven, if we knew what it
were.

Sir John Suckling: *Fragmenta Aurea:
Against Fruition,* st. 4

Better limp all the way to heaven than not
get there at all.

W. A. ("Billy") Sunday

Every man is received in heaven who receives heaven in himself while in the world, and he is excluded who does not.

Emanuel Swedenborg

One of the wonders of Heaven is that no one there is ever permitted to stand behind another and look at the back of his head.

Emanuel Swedenborg: *Heaven and Hell*

Heaven is such that all who have lived well, of whatever religion, have a place there.

Emanuel Swedenborg: *Divine Providence,* sec. 330

Far from mortal cares retreating,
Sordid hopes and vain desires,
Here, our willing footsteps meeting,
Every heart to heaven aspires.

Ann and Jane Taylor: *Hymn*

Heaven does not choose its elect from among the great and wealthy.

William Makepeace Thackeray: *The Virginians*, ch. 5

In heaven, to be even the least is a great thing, where all will be great; for all shall be called the children of God.

Thomas à Kempis

Short arm needs man to reach to Heaven,
So ready is Heaven to stoop to him.

Francis Thompson: *Grace of the Way*

Look for me in the nurseries of Heaven.

Francis Thompson: *To My Godchild*

Heaven may be defined as the place which men avoid.

Henry David Thoreau: *Excursions*

But I account it worth
All pangs of fair hopes crost—
All loves and honors lost—
To gain the heavens, at cost
Of losing earth.

Theodore Tilton: *Sir Marmaduke's Musings*

Who seeks for Heaven alone to save his soul
May keep the path, but will not reach the goal;
While he who walks in love may wander far,
Yet God will bring him where the blessed are.

Henry van Dyke: *Story of the Other Wise Man*, V, Harper & Row, Publishers, Inc.

God has two dwellings: one in heaven, and the other in a meek and thankful heart.

Izaak Walton

How do I pity those that dwell
Where ignorance and darkness reign!
They know no heaven—they fear no hell—
That endless joy—that endless pain.

Isaac Watts: *Praise for Birth in a Christian Land*

I have been there, and still would go;
'Tis like a little heaven below.

Isaac Watts: *Divine Songs*, XXVIII

Heaven-gates are not so highly arch'd
As princes' palaces; they that enter there
Must go on their knees.

John Webster: *The Duchess of Malfi*

If there were no Hell, no one would worry about Heaven.

Welsh Proverb

To get to heaven, turn right and keep straight.

Wesleyan Methodist

Entrance into Heaven is not at the hour of death, but at the moment of conversion.

Benjamin Whichcote: *Moral and Religious Aphorisms*

Changeless as heaven.

John Greenleaf Whittier

No man must go to heaven who hath not sent his hearth thither before.

Thomas Wilson: *Maxims of Piety*, LXV

As much of heaven is visible as we have eyes to see.

William Winter

Heaven lies about us in our infancy.

William Wordsworth: *Intimations of Immortality*, st. 5

Heaven wills our happiness, allows our doom.

Edward Young: *Night Thoughts*, Night VII, l. 1301

Taking the first footstep with a good thought, the second with a good word, and the third with a good deed, I entered Paradise.

Zoroaster

HELL

As greedy as the jaws of hell.

Anonymous

A guilty conscience is a hell on earth, and points to one beyond.

Anonymous

Hell is but the collected ruins of the moral world, and sin is the principle that has made them.

Anonymous

A single path leads to the house of Hades.

Aeschylus: *Telephus*, frag. 131

That the saints may enjoy their beatitude and the grace of God more abundantly they are permitted to see the punishment of the damned in hell.

St. Thomas Aquinas: *Summa theologiæ*

Hell is the wrath of God—His hate of sin.

Philip James Bailey: *Festus: Hell*, l. 194

Hell is more bearable than nothingness.

Philip James Bailey: *Festus: Heaven*

Hell is paved with infants' skulls.

Richard Baxter

Tell me not of the fire and the worm, and the blackness and darkness of hell. To my terrified conscience there is hell enough in this representation of it, that it is the common sewer of all that is abominable and abandoned and reckless as to principle, and depraved as to morals, the one common eddy where all things that are polluted and wretched and filthy are gathered together.

Joseph Beaumont

Hell is full of good intentions or desires.

St. Bernard of Clairvaux (Attributed also to Chrysostom, Francis de Sales, Samuel Johnson, Richard Baxter)

The road to Hell is easy to travel.

Bion

Hell is paved with great granite blocks hewn from the hearts of those who said, "I can do no other."

Heywood Broun: Syndicate Column, January 20, 1934

I have tried if I could reach that great resolution—to be honest without a thought of Heaven or Hell.

Sir Thomas Browne: *Religio Medici*

I thank God, and with joy I mention it, I was never afraid of Hell, nor never grew pale at the description of that place.

Ibid.

A vast, unbottom'd, boundless pit,
  Fill'd fou o' lowin brunstane,
Wha's ragin' flame an' scorchin' heat,
  Wad melt the hardest whunstane.

Robert Burns: *The Holy Fair*, st. 22

But quiet to quick bosoms is a hell,
And there hath been thy bane.

George Gordon, Lord Byron: *Childe Harold*, Canto III, st. 42

No ear can hear nor tongue can tell
The tortures of that inward hell!

George Gordon, Lord Byron: *The Giaour*,
l. 748

If there be a paradise for virtues, there must
be a hell for crimes.

Nicolas Caussin

In hell there is no retention.

Miguel de Cervantes: *Don Quixote*

Hell is paved with priests' skulls.

St. John Chrysostom

From all sides there is equally a way to the
lower world.

Cicero: *Tusc. Quaest*, Bk. I, 43, 104

From Hell, Hull and Halifax, good Lord
deliver us.

Anthony Copley: *Wits, Fits, etc.* CCII
(1594)

I found the original of my hell in the world
which we inhabit.

Alighieri Dante

Here sighs, pliants, and voices of the deepest
woe resounded through the starless sky.
Strange languages, horrid cries, accents of
grief and wrath, voices deep and hoarse, with
hands clenched in despair, made a commo-
tion which whirled forever through that air
of everlasting gloom, even as sand when
whirlwinds sweep the ground.

Alighieri Dante: *Inferno*

There is in hell a place stone-built through-
out,
Called Malebolge, of an iron hue,
Like to the wall that circles it about.

Ibid.

I had Ambition, by which sin
The angels fell;
I climbed, and, step by step, O Lord,
Ascended into Hell.

William Henry Davies: Quoted by Rae
Noel in *Classmate*

What is hell? I maintain that it is the suffering of being unable to love.

Feodor Dostoevski

Hot as hell-fire.

John Dryden

All hell is broken loose yonder!

Thomas D'Urfey: *Comical History of
Don Quixote*, Pt. II, Act II, sc. 1

The devil is waiting for them, hell is gaping
for them, the flames gather and flash about
them . . . When you come to be a firebrand
of hell . . . you will appear as you are, a
viper indeed . . . Then will you as a serpent
spit poison at God and vent your rage and
malice in fearful blasphemies.

Jonathan Edwards: *Men Naturally God's
Enemies* (Works, VII, 168)

Hell is truth seen too late—duty neglected
in its season.

Tryon Edwards

Hell is paved with the skulls of great scholars,
and paled in with the bones of great men.

Giles Firmin: *The Real Christian* (1670)

The pride of dying rich raises the loudest
laugh in hell.

John Foster

Hell and Chancery are always open.

Thomas Fuller: *Gnomologia*

Heaven for climate; Hell for society.

German Proverb

No hell will frighten men away from sin.

Thomas Haweis: *Speech in Season*, Bk. I,
Hell

Hell is full of good meanings and wishings.

George Herbert

There is nobody will go to hell for company.

George Herbert: *Jacula Prudentum*

Hell is no other but a soundless pit,
Where no one beam of comfort peeps in it.

Robert Herrick: *Noble Numbers, Hell*

Hell is paved with good intentions.

Samuel Johnson

Men might go to heaven with half the labor
they put forth to go to hell, if they would
but venture their industry in the right way.

Ben Jonson

They should say, and swear, hell were broken
loose, ere they went hence.

Ben Jonson: *Every Man in His Humour,*
Act IV, sc. 1

Hell is a circle about the unbelieving.

The Koran

The dreadful fear of hell, which disturbs the
life of man and renders it miserable, is to be
driven out.

Lucretius: *De Rerum Natura*, III, 37

Hell hath no limits, nor is circumscrib'd
In one self-place; for where we are is hell;
And where hell is, there must we ever be;
And to conclude, when all the world dis-
   solves,
And ever creature shall be purified,
All places shall be hell that are not heaven.

Christopher Marlowe: *Faustus*, I, 553

To be alone, completely alone, is hell.

Allen O. Miller

A dungeon horrible on all sides round
As one great furnace flam'd yet from those
   flames
No light, but rather darkness visible,
Serv'd only to discover sights of woe,
Regions of sorrow, doleful shades, where
   peace
And rest can never dwell, hope never comes
That comes to all, but torture without end.

John Milton: *Paradise Lost*, Bk. I, l. 61

Long is the way
And hard, that out of Hell leads up to Light.

John Milton: *Paradise Lost*, Bk. II, l. 432

All hell broke loose.

John Milton: *Paradise Lost*, Bk. IV, l. 918

When we preach on hell, we might at least
do it with tears in our eyes.

Dwight L. Moody

Wide is the gate, and broad is the way, that
leadeth to destruction, and many there be
which go in thereat: Because strait is the
gate, and narrow is the way, which leadeth
unto life, and few there be that find it.

New Testament: Matthew 7: 13, 14

Into hell, into the fire that never shall be
quenched: Where their worm dieth not.

New Testament: Mark 9: 43, 44

But he knoweth not that the dead are there;
and that her guests are in the depths of hell.

Old Testament: Proverbs 9: 18

Hell from beneath is moved for thee to meet
thee at thy coming.

Old Testament: Isaiah 14: 9

Heaven but the vision of fulfill'd Desire, and
Hell the Shadow from a Soul on fire.

Omar Khayyám: *Rubáiyát*

Hell is both sides of the tomb, and a devil
may be respectable and wear good clothes.

Charles Henry Parkhurst: *Sermons: The
Pharisee's Prayer*

Not even Hell can lay hands on the invincible.

Parmenio: Epitaph on Alexander

There is no redemption from hell.

Pope Paul III to Michelangelo

Hell is paved with good intentions and
roofed with lost opportunities.

Portuguese Proverb

The way to Hell's a seeming Heav'n.
Francis Quarles: *Emblems*, Bk. II, emb. 11

I see a brimstone sea of boiling fire,
And fiends, with knotted whips of flaming
wire,
Torturing poor souls, that gnash their teeth
in vain,
And gnaw their flame-tormented tongues for
pain.
Francis Quarles: *Emblems*, Bk. III, emb. 14

Hell is as ubiquitous as condemning conscience.
Frederick William Robertson

In the utmost solitudes of nature the existence of hell seems to me as legibly declared,
by a thousand spiritual utterances, as that
of heaven.
John Ruskin

If hell were nothing but eternal homesickness, it would still be hell.
Charles Reign Scoville, Evangelist

Divines and dying men may talk of hell, but
in my heart her several torments dwell.
William Shakespeare

The cunning livery of hell.
William Shakespeare: *Measure for
Measure*, Act III, sc. 1, l. 95

Black is the badge of hell,
The hue of dungeons and the suit of night.
William Shakespeare: *Love's Labour's
Lost*, Act IV, sc. 3, l. 254

Hell is empty,
And all the devils are here .
William Shakespeare: *Tempest*,
Act I, sc. 2, l. 214

If I owned Texas and Hell, I would rent out
Texas and live in Hell.
General Philip H. Sheridan

It has been more wittily than charitably said
that hell is paved with good intentions; they
have their place in heaven also.
Robert Southey: *Colloquies on Society*

When you speak of heaven let your face light
up . . . When you speak of hell—well, then
your everyday face will do.
Charles Haddon Spurgeon

It doesn't matter what they preach,
Of high or low degree;
The old Hell of the Bible
Is Hell enough for me.
Frank Lebby Stanton: *Hell*

The Lord casts no one down to hell, but the
spirit casts himself thither.
Emanuel Swedenborg

Self-love and the love of the world constitute
hell.
Emanuel Swedenborg: *Apocalypse
Explained*, par. 1144

The fire of Gehenna is sixty times as hot as
the fire of earth.
The Talmud: Berachoth

So, while their bodies moulder here,
Their souls with God himself shall dwell,—
But always recollect, my dear,
That wicked people go to hell.
Ann and Jane Taylor: *About Dying*

Hell itself may be contained within the compass of a spark.
Henry David Thoreau: *Journal*,
December 19, 1838

Smooth the descent and easy is the way;
(The Gates of Hell stand open night and
day):
But to return, and view the cheerful skies,
In this the task and mighty labour lies.
Virgil: *Æneid*, VI, 126 (Dryden tr.)

At Orcus' portal hold their lair
Wild Sorrow and avenging Care;

And pale Diseases cluster there,
And pleasureless Decay,
Dour Penury, and Fears that kill,
And Hunger, counsellor of ill.

> Virgil, *Æneid*, VI, 275 (Conington tr.)

In the deepest pits of 'Ell,
Where the worst defaulters dwell
(Charcoal devils used as fuel as you require
'em),
There's some lovely coloured rays,
Pyrotechnical displays,
But you can't expect the burning to admire
'em!

> Edgar Wallace: *Nature Fails: L'Envoi*

There is a dreadful hell,
And everlasting pains;
Where sinners must with devils dwell
In darkness, fire, and chains.

> Isaac Watts: *Heaven and Hell*

That's the greatest torture souls feel in hell:
In hell, that they must live, and cannot die.

> John Webster: *Duchess of Malfi*, Act IV,
> sc. 1, l. 84

Fierce and poisonous animals were created
for terrifying man, in order that he might be
made aware of the final judgment in hell.

> John Wesley

A man by persistent wrongdoing may create
within himself a quenchless inner hell. Its
fires will burn. Its lambent flames quietly
and slowly will eat him with pain and
despair. He is not only on his way to hell.
He carries it within his own bosom.

> *Western Christian Advocate*

What's the matter with Kansas? . . . We have
decided to send three or four harpies out
lecturing, telling the people that Kansas is
raising hell and letting the corn go to weeds.

> William Allen White: Editorial, *Emporia
> Gazette*, August 15, 1896

We are each our own devil, and we make this
world our hell.

> Oscar Wilde

Hell is given up *so* reluctantly by those who
don't expect to go there.

> Harry Leon Wilson: *The Spenders*, p. 241

For what, my small philosopher! is hell?
'Tis nothing but full knowledge of the truth,
When truth, resisted long is sworn our foe,
And calls eternity to do her right.

> Edward Young: *Night Thoughts*,
> Night IX, l. 2403

HERESY

From heresy, frenzy, and jealousy, good Lord
deliver me.

> Ludovico Ariosto: *Orlando Furioso* (tr. by
> Sir John Harington)

From all false doctrine, heresy, and schism,
Good Lord, deliver us.

> *Book of Common Prayer: The
> Litany*

Heresies perish not with their authors, but,
like the river Arethusa, though they lose
their currents in one place, they rise up again
in another.

> Sir Thomas Browne: *Religio Medici*, I

Ignorance is the mark of the heathen, knowledge of the true church, and conceit of the
heretics.

> Clement of Alexandria: *Stromateis*, I

It is surely harmful to souls to make it a
heresy to believe what is proved.

> Galileo Galilei: *The Authority of Scrip-
> ture in Philosophical Controversies.*
> (*Condemned by the Inquisition*)

Heresy is the school of pride.

> George Herbert: *Jacula Prudentum*

In the end it is worth to suppress dissent than
to run the risk of heresy.

> Oliver Wendell Holmes Lecture, Harvard,
> 1958, Harvard University Press

It is the customary fate of new truths to begin as heresies and to end as superstitions.

Thomas Henry Huxley: *The Coming of Age of "The Origin of Species"*

A man may be a heretic in the truth; and if he believes things only because his pastor says so, or the assembly so determines, without knowing other reason, though his belief be true, yet the very truth he holds becomes his heresy.

John Milton: *Areopagitica*

A man that is a heretick after the first and second admonition reject.

New Testament: Titus 3: 10

Damnable heresies.

New Testament: II Peter 2: 1

The heresy of the pious: to cut the arms off the cross and leave nothing but a pole, a vertical relationship with God with no outreach toward one's suffering fellow man.

Paul Calvin Payne

Blessed shall be he that doth revolt
From his allegiance to a heretic.

William Shakespeare: *King John,* Act III, sc. 1, l. 175

The law knows no heresy.

Decision of the Supreme Court of the United States in *Watson* vs. *Jones,* Dec. 1871

In our windy world
What's up is faith, what's down is heresy.

Alfred, Lord Tennyson: *Harold,* Act I, sc. 1

HOLINESS

It is a mistake to suppose that God does not want us to be holy until death, for that would mean that He wants us to be unholy until death. God does not want us to be unholy at any time.

Anonymous

To be holy and not happy is a contradiction.

Anonymous

God is not averse to deceit in a holy cause.

Aeschylus: *Frag. Incert.,* 11

Everything that lives is holy.

William Blake: *The Marriage of Heaven and Hell*

Where'er we tread 'tis haunted, holy ground.

George Gordon, Lord Byron: *Childe Harold*

The beauty of holiness has done more, and will do more, to regenerate the world and bring in everlasting righteousness than all the other agencies put together.—It has done more to spread religion in the world, than all that has ever been preached or written on the evidences of Christianity.

Thomas Chalmers

If it be the characteristic of a worldly man that he desecrates what is holy, it should be of the Christian to consecrate what is secular, and to recognize a present and presiding divinity in all things.

Thomas Chalmers

What Christianity most needs in her antagonism with every form of unbelief, is holy living.

Theodor Christlieb

Piety and holiness of life will propitiate the gods.

Cicero: *De Officiis,* II, 3

Things sacred should not only be untouched with the hands, but unviolated in thought.

Cicero: *In Verrem,* no. II, sec. 4

Being is holiness, harmony, immortality.

Mary Baker Eddy: *Science and Health With Key to the Scriptures,* p. 492: 7

Holiness appeared to me to be of a sweet, pleasant, charming, serene, calm nature;

which brought an inexpressible purity, brightness, peacefulness, and ravishment to the soul. In other words, that it made the soul like a field or garden of God, with all manner of pleasant flowers.

Jonathan Edwards: *Holiness*

He that sees the beauty of holiness, or true moral good, sees the greatest and most important thing in the world. . . . Unless this is seen nothing is seen that is worth seeing; for there is no other true excellence or beauty.

Jonathan Edwards: *Treatise of Religious Affections*

A holy life is not an ascetic, or gloomy, or solitary life, but a life regulated by divine truth and faithful in Christian duty.—It is living above the world while we are still in it.

Tryon Edwards

We believe that holiness confers a certain insight, because not by private, but by our public force can we share and know the nature of things.

Ralph Waldo Emerson: *Conduct of Life: Worship*

Real holiness has love for its essence, humility for its clothing, the good of others as its employment, and the honor of God as its end.

Nathanael Emmons

There is no true holiness without humility.

Thomas Fuller: *Gnomologia*

It is the great work of nature to transmute sunlight into life. So it is the great end of Christian living to transmute the light of truth into the fruits of holy living.

Adoniram J. Gordon

We do ourselves wrong, and too meanly estimate the holiness above us, when we deem that any act or enjoyment good in itself, is not good to do religiously.

Nathaniel Hawthorne: *Marble Faun*, Bk. II, ch. 7

Holiness is the symmetry of the soul.

Philip Henry

Holiness in us, is the copy or transcript of the holiness that is in Christ.—As the wax hath line for line from the seal, and the child feature for feature from the father, so is holiness in us from him.

Philip Henry

A holy habit cleanseth not a foul soul.

George Herbert: *Outlandish Proverbs*

Holiness is religious principle put into action.—It is faith gone to work. It is love coined into conduct; devotion helping human suffering, and going up in intercession to the great source of all good.

Frederic D. Huntington

Even the merest gesture is holy if it is filled with faith.

Franz Kafka

A holy life is a voice; it speaks when the tongue is silent, and is either a constant attraction or a perpetual reproof.

Robert Leighton

The essence of true holiness consists in conformity to the nature and will of God.

Samuel Lucas

Holiness consisteth not in a cowl or in a garment of gray.—When God purifies the heart by faith, the market is sacred as well as the sanctuary; neither remaineth there any work or place which is profane.

Martin Luther

There are two sorts of holiness, substantial and accidental. St. Francis was once substantially holy by his faith in Jesus Christ, but afterwards he became infatuated with the accidental holiness of the hood, an accessory wholly foreign to holiness.

Martin Luther: *Table Talk*

You may have living and habitual conversation in heaven, under the aspect of the most simple, ordinary life. Remember that holiness does not consist in doing uncommon things, but in doing every thing with purity of heart.

Cardinal Henry E. Manning

It is a great deal better to live a holy life than to talk about it. Lighthouses do not ring bells and fire cannon to call attention to their shining—they just shine.

Dwight L. Moody

Give not that which is holy unto the dogs, neither cast ye your pearls before swine, lest they trample them under their feet, and turn again and rend you.

New Testament: Matthew 7: 6

In the beauties of holiness.

Old Testament: Isaiah 6: 3

Holy, holy, holy, is the Lord of hosts: the whole earth is full of his glory.

Old Testament: Isaiah 6: 3

The serene, silent beauty of a holy life is the most powerful influence in the world, next to the might of the Spirit of God.

Blaise Pascal

Whoso lives the holiest life
Is fittest far to die.

Margaret J. Preston: *Ready*

He who the sword of heaven will bear
Should be as holy as severe.

William Shakespeare: *Measure for Measure*, Act III, sc. 2, l. 275

An evil soul producing holy witness
Is like a villain with a smiling cheek,
A goodly apple rotten at the heart:
O, what a goodly outside falsehood hath!

William Shakespeare: *Merchant of Venice*, Act I, sc. 3, l. 100

Holiness is the architectural plan upon which
God buildeth up His living temple.

Charles Haddon Spurgeon: *Holiness*

HOLY GHOST (SPIRIT)

The Holy Ghost is not of an inferior nature to the Father and the Son, but, so to say, cosubstantial and coeternal.

St. Augustine: *Of the Faith and of the Creed*

I should as soon attempt to raise flowers if there were no atmosphere, or produce fruits if there were neither light nor heat, as to regenerate men if I did not believe there was a Holy Ghost.

Henry Ward Beecher

When men surrender themselves to the Spirit of God, they will learn more concerning God and Christ and the Atonement and Immortality in a week, than they would learn in a lifetime, apart from the Spirit.

John Brown

We must not be content to be cleansed from sin; we must be filled with the Spirit.

John Fletcher

The word "Comforter" as applied to the Holy Spirit needs to be translated by some vigorous term. Literally, it means "with strength." Jesus promised His followers that "The Strengthener" would be with them forever. This promise is no lullaby for the faint-hearted. It is a blood transfusion for courageous living.

E. Paul Hovey

We have substituted relativity for reality, psychology for prayer, an inferiority complex for sin, social control for family worship, autosuggestion for conversion, reflex action for revelation, the spirit of the wheels for the power of the Spirit.

Hugh Thomson Kerr

Come, Holy Ghost, our souls inspire,
And lighten with celestial fire.

Rabanus Maurus (Archbishop of Mainz): *Veni Creator Spiritus*

The Spirit of God first imparts love; he next inspires hope, and then gives liberty; and that is about the last thing we have in many of our churches.

Dwight L. Moody

Whosoever speaketh against the Holy Ghost, it shall not be forgiven him, neither in this world, neither in the world to come.

New Testament: Matthew 12: 32

He said unto them, Have ye received the Holy Ghost since ye believed? And they said unto him, We have not so much as heard whether there be any Holy Ghost.

New Testament: Acts 19: 2

Every time we say, "I believe in the Holy Spirit," we mean that we believe that there is a living God able and willing to enter human personality and change it.

J. B. Phillips: *Plain Christianity*, p. 104, Copyright Epworth Press, 1957

Many are deceived in the end, who at first seemed to be led by the Holy Spirit.

Thomas à Kempis

HOME

The duties of home are discipline for the ministries of heaven.

Anonymous

What is home?
A world of strife shut out—a world of love shut in.
The only spot on earth where faults and failings of fallen humanity are hidden under the mantle of charity.
The father's kingdom, the children's paradise, the mother's world.
Where you are treated the best and grumble the most.

Anonymous

To be God's child, we must begin by proving ourselves faithful children of our earthly homes. That is the way our Lord took, and it remains the way of life for all who would follow him.

A. Ian Burnett: *Lord of All Life*

I've read in many a novel, that unless they've
    souls that grovel—
Folks prefer in fact a hovel to your dreary
    marble halls.

Charles Stuart Calverley: *In the Gloaming*

Whom God loves, his house is sweet to him.

Miguel de Cervantes: *Don Quixote*, Pt. II,
ch. 43

Home—the nursery of the infinite.

William Ellery Channing: *Note-Book:
Children*

Better do a good deed near at home than go far away to burn incense.

Chinese Proverb

Domestic Happiness, thou only bliss
Of Paradise that hast surviv'd the Fall!

William Cowper: *The Task*, Bk. III, l. 41

Good, honest, hardheaded character is a function of the home. If the proper seed is sown there and properly nourished for a few years, it will not be easy for that plant to be uprooted.

George A. Dorsey: *Why We Behave Like
Human Beings*, Harper & Row,
Publishers, Inc.

Strength of character may be acquired at work, but beauty of character is learned at home. There the affections are trained. There the gentle life reaches us, the true heaven life. In one word, the family circle is the supreme conductor of Christianity.

Henry Drummond

Every spirit makes its house, but afterwards the house confines the spirit.

Ralph Waldo Emerson: *Conduct of Life:
Fate*

The beauty of the house is order;
The blessing of the house is contentment;
The glory of the house is hospitality;
The crown of the house is godliness.

Fireplace motto

Charity and beating begin at home.

John Fletcher: *Wit Without Money,* V

Home as we now conceive it was the creation of the Puritan. Wife and child rose from being mere dependents on the will of husband or father, as husband or father saw in them saints like himself, souls hallowed by the touch of a divine Spirit, and called with a divine calling like his own.

John Richard Green: *A Short History of the English People,* VIII

Six things are requisite to create a "happy home." Integrity must be the architect, and tidiness the upholsterer. It must be warmed by affection, lighted up with cheerfulness; and industry must be the ventilator, renewing the atmosphere and bringing in fresh salubrity day by day; while over all, as a protecting canopy and glory, nothing will suffice except the blessing of God.

James Hamilton

To Adam paradise was home.—To the good among his descendants, home is paradise.

Augustus William and Julius Charles Hare

He that doth live at home, and learns to know God and himself, needeth no farther go.

Christopher Harvey: *Travels at Home*

Turn up the lights; I don't want to go home in the dark.

O. Henry: *Last Words* (quoted in biography by C. Alphonso Smith)

God oft hath a great share in a little house.

George Herbert: *Jacula Prudentum*

There is no synthetic replacement for a decent home life. Our high crime rate, particularly among juveniles, is directly traceable to a breakdown in moral fiber—to the disintegration of home and family life. Religion and home life are supplementary. Each strengthens the other. It is seldom that a solid and wholesome home life can be found in the absence of religious inspiration.

J. Edgar Hoover: *Christian Herald*

A palace without affection is a poor hovel, and the meanest hut with love in it is a palace for the soul.

Robert Green Ingersoll

The woman who creates and sustains a home, and under whose hands children grow up to be strong and pure men and women is a creator second only to God.

Helen Hunt Jackson

The happiness of the domestic fireside is the first boon of Heaven; and it is well it is so, since it is that which is the lot of the mass of mankind.

Thomas Jefferson: *Letter to John Armstrong*

The sober comfort, all the peace which springs
From the large aggregate of little things;
On these small cares of daughter, wife or friend,
The almost sacred joys of home depend.

Hannah More: *Sensibility*

Round the hearth-stone of home, in the land of our birth,
The holiest spot on the face of the earth.

George Pope Morris: *Land Ho!*

A man's foes shall be they of his own household.

New Testament: Matthew 10: 36

As for me and my house, we will serve the Lord.

Old Testament: Joshua 24: 15

As a bird that wandereth from her nest, so is a man that wandereth from his place.

Old Testament: Proverbs 28: 8

Home interprets heaven; Home is heaven for beginners.

Charles Henry Parkhurst: *Sermons: The Perfect Peace*

The only religion that is any good is home-made religion.

Paul Calvin Payne: *Presbyterian Life*

Our home joys are the most delightful earth affords, and the joy of parents in their children is the most holy joy of humanity. It makes their hearts pure and good, it lifts men up to their Father in heaven.

Johann Heinrich Pestalozzi

The home is a lighthouse which has the lamp of God on the table and the light of Christ in the window, to give guidance to those who wander in darkness.

Henry Rische: "The Windows of Home"

The voice of parents is the voice of gods, for to their children they are heaven's lieutenants.

William Shakespeare

Nor hell nor heaven shall that soul surprise,
    Who loves the rain,
    And loves his home,
And looks on life with quiet eyes.

Frances W. Shaw: *Who Loves the Rain*

When home is ruled according to God's word, angels might be asked to stay with us, and they would not find themselves out of their element.

Charles Haddon Spurgeon

A dining room table with children's eager, hungry faces around it, ceases to be a mere dining room table, and becomes an altar.

Simeon Strunsky: *No Mean City,*
E. P. Dutton Company

But such a tide as moving seems asleep,
    Too full for sound and foam,
When that which drew from out the boundless deep
    Turns again home.

Alfred, Lord Tennyson: *Crossing the Bar,*
st. 1

The hand that rocks the cradle
Is the hand that rules the world.

William Ross Wallace

O God, our help in ages past,
Our hope for years to come,

Our shelter from the stormy blast,
And our eternal home.

Isaac Watts: *Psalm XC,* st. 1

HOPE

Life with Christ is an endless hope, without Him a hopeless end.

Anonymous

There is more hope for a self-convicted sinner than there is for a self-conceited saint.

Anonymous

We are never beneath hope, while above hell; nor above hope, while beneath heaven.

Anonymous

Age is a quality of mind;
If you've left your
Dreams behind,
If hope is cold,
If you no longer look ahead,
If your ambitious fires
Are dead,
Then, you are old!

Anonymous

Today well-lived . . . makes every tomorrow a vision of Hope.

Anonymous

A religious hope does not only bear up the mind under her sufferings, but makes her rejoice in them.

Joseph Addison

Hopeful as the break of day.

Thomas Bailey Aldrich

When you say a situation or a person is hopeless, you are slamming the door in the face of God.

Charles L. Allen

Know then, whatever cheerful and serene
Supports the mind, supports the body too:
Hence, the most vital movement mortals feel
Is hope, the balm and lifeblood of the soul.

John Armstrong: *Art of Preserving Health,* Bk. IV, l. 318

Then, in such hour of need
Of your fainting, dispirited race,
Ye, like angels, appear,
Beacons of Hope ye appear!

    Matthew Arnold: *Rugby Chapel*, st. 13

What can be hoped for which is not believed?

    St. Augustine: *On Faith, Hope, and Charity*

Hope is the parent of faith.

    Cyrus Augustus Bartol: *Radical Problems: Hope*

That divinest hope, which none can know of
Who have not laid their dearest in the grave.

    Thomas Lovell Beddoes: *Death's Jest Book*

Land of Hope and Glory, Mother of the Free,
How shall we extol thee, who are born of thee?
Wider still and wider shall thy bounds be set;
God, who made thee mighty, make thee mightier yet.

    Arthur Christopher Benson: *Land of Hope and Glory, Chorus*

I live on hope and that I think do all
Who come into this world.

    Robert Bridges: *The Growth of Love*, sonnet 63

Our hope is ever livelier than despair, our joy
livelier and more abiding than our sorrows are.

    Robert Bridges: *The Testament of Beauty*

O little town of Bethlehem!
. . . . . .
The hopes and fears of all the years
Are met in thee tonight.

    Phillips Brooks: *O Little Town of Bethlehem*, st. 1

The praise of those who sleep in earth,
The pleasant memory of their worth,
The hope to meet when life is past,
Shall heal the tortured mind at last.

    William Cullen Bryant: *The Living Lost*, st. 3

Make no little plans. They have no magic to stir men's blood. Make big plans: aim high in hope and work.

    Daniel Hudson Burnham

I laugh, for hope hath happy place with me,
If my bark sinks, 'tis to another sea.

    William Ellery Channing: *A Poet's Hope*, st. 13

Abandon hope, all ye who enter here.

    Alighieri Dante: *Inferno III*, l. 9

If the cross is the measure of God's respect for man's freedom, then we can take new hope that freedom will survive all man's attempts to destroy it.

    D. R. Davies: *The Art of Dodging Repentance*

Long hope is the fainting of the soul.

    Thomas Draxe

All human wisdom is summed up in two words,—wait and hope.

    Alexandre Dumas the Elder: *The Count of Monte Cristo*, ch. 117

A sublime hope cheers ever the faithful heart, that elsewhere, in other regions of the universal powers, souls are now acting, enduring and daring, which can love us, and which we can love.

    Ralph Waldo Emerson

Hope writes the poetry of the boy, but memory that of the man. Man looks forward with smiles, but backward with sighs. Such is the wise providence of God. The cup of life

sweetness at the brim—the flavor is im-
aired as we drink deeper, and the dregs are
1ade bitter that we may not struggle when
is taken from our lips.

Ralph Waldo Emerson

Iope never spread her golden wings but in
.nfathomable seas.

Ralph Waldo Emerson

Vhile there is life there's hope, he cried.

John Gay: *Fables, Part 1. The Sick Man
and the Angel*

Iope is the second soul of the unhappy.

Johann Wolfgang von Goethe: *Sprüche
in Prosa*

Iope, like the gleaming taper's light
Adorns and cheers our way;
And still, as darker grows the night,
Emits a brighter ray.

Oliver Goldsmith: *The Captivity, An
Oratorio,* Act II

To the last moment of his breath,
On hope the wretch relies;
And even the pang preceding death
Bids expectation rise.

Ibid.

In all my wanderings round this world of
care,
In all my griefs—and God has given my
share—
I still had hopes my latest hours to crown,
Amidst these humble bowers to lay me down.

Oliver Goldsmith: *The Deserted Village,*
l. 81

Lord, dismiss us with thy blessing,
Hope, and comfort from above;
Let us each, thy peace possessing,
Triumph in redeeming love.

Robert Hawker: *Benediction*

Religion is the mother of dreams. Over the
gray world, ruined by deluge, and death, it
has sought ever, and found the arching rainbow of hope.

Albert Eustace Haydon, University of
Chicago Press

One leaf is for hope, and one is for faith,
And one is for love, you know,
And God put another in for luck.

Ella Higginson: *Four-Leaf Clover,* st. 2

The word which God has written on the
brow of every man is Hope.

Victor Hugo

Hope, child, tomorrow and tomorrow still,
And every tomorrow hope; trust while
you live.
Hope, each time the dawn doth heaven fill,
Be there to ask as God is there to give.

Victor Hugo

We, too, have our religion, and it is this:
Help for the living, hope for the dead.

Robert Green Ingersoll: *Address at a
Little Boy's Grave*

The man who lives only by hope will die
with despair.

Italian Proverb

Hope is the last thing that dies in man, and
although it be exceedingly deceitful, yet it
is of this good use to us, that while we are
traveling through life it conducts us in an
easier and more pleasant way to our journey's
end.

François de La Rochefoucauld

You cannot put a great hope into a small
soul.

Jenkin Lloyd-Jones

A hope beyond the shadow of a dream.

John Keats: *Endymion,* Bk. I, l. 857

So, when dark thoughts my boding spirit
shroud,
Sweet Hope! celestial influence round me
shed
Waving thy silver pinions o'er my head.

John Keats: *Hope,* st. 8

Hopers go to hell.

James Kelly: *Scottish Proverbs*

Around the child bend all the three
Sweet Graces—Faith, Hope, Charity.
Around the man bend other faces—
Pride, Envy, Malice, are his Graces.

Walter Savage Landor: *Around the Child*

The world dares say no more for its device,
than "while I live, I hope"; but the children
of God can add by virtue of a living hope,
"while I expire, I hope."

Robert Leighton

We shall nobly save or meanly lose the last,
best hope of earth.

Abraham Lincoln: *Second Annual
Message to Congress*

Tho' lost to sight, to memory dear
Thou ever wilt remain;
One only hope my heart can cheer,—
The hope to meet again.

George Linley: *Song*

Everything that is done in the world is done
by hope. No husbandman would sow one
grain of corn if he hoped not it would grow
up and become seed; no bachelor would
marry a wife if he hope not to have children;
no merchant or tradesman would set himself to work if he did not hope to reap benefit
thereby.

Martin Luther: *Table Talk*

Who bids me Hope, and in that charming
word
Has peace and transport to my soul restor'd.

George, Baron Lyttelton: *The Progress of
Love. Hope,* Eclogue II, l. 41

The resurrection of Jesus Christ is our hope
today. It is our assurance that we have a
living Saviour to help us live as we should
now, and that when, in the end, we set forth
on that last great journey, we shall not travel
an uncharted course, but rather we shall go
on a planned voyage—life to death to eternal
living.

Raymond MacKendree: *Queens' Gardens*

Hope proves man deathless. It is the struggle
of the soul, breaking loose from what is
perishable, and attesting her eternity.

Henry Melville

Yet I argue not
Against Thy hand or will, nor bate a jot
Of heart or hope, but still bear up and steer
Right onward.

John Milton

Hope against hope, and ask till ye receive

James Montgomery: *The World Before
the Flood,* Canto V, st. 10

The Gods are kind, and hope to men they
give.

William Morris: *The Earthly Paradise.
Bellerophon at Argos,* l. 1617

Eternity is the divine treasure house, and
hope is the window, by means of which mortals are permitted to see, as through a glass
darkly, the things which God is preparing.

William Mountford

Who against hope believed in hope.

New Testament: Romans 4: 18

Hope maketh not ashamed.

New Testament: Romans 5: 5

Now the God of hope fill you with all joy
and peace in believing, that ye may abound
in hope, through the power of the Holy
Ghost.

New Testament: Romans 15: 13

We have such hope, we use great plainness
of speech.

New Testament: II Corinthians 3: 12

Christ in you, the hope of glory.

New Testament: Colossians 1: 27

Putting on the breastplate of faith and love;
and for an helmet, the hope of salvation.

New Testament: I Thessalonians 5: 8

Our Lord Jesus Christ himself, and God, even our Father, which hath loved us, and hath given us everlasting consolation and good hope through grace.

New Testament: II Thessalonians 2: 16

Lay hold upon the hope set before us: which hope we have as an anchor of the soul, both sure and stedfast.

New Testament: Hebrews 6: 18b–19

Hope to the end.

New Testament: I Peter 1: 13

My days are swifter than a weaver's shuttle, and are spent without hope.

Old Testament: Job 7: 6

I will hope continually, and will yet praise thee more and more.

Old Testament: Psalm 71: 14

Hope deferred maketh the heart sick.

Old Testament: Proverbs 13: 12

Blessed is the man that trusteth in the Lord, and whose hope the Lord is.

Old Testament: Jeremiah 17: 7

Thou art my hope in the day of evil.

Old Testament: Jeremiah 17: 17

Prisoners of hope.

Old Testament: Zechariah 9: 12

The worldly Hope men set their Hearts upon
Turns ashes—or it prospers; and anon,
    Like Snow upon the Desert's dusty Face,
Lighting a little hour or two—is gone.

Omar Khayyám: Rubáiyát, st. 16

We need some imaginative stimulus, some not impossible ideal such as may shape vague hope, and transform it into effective desire, to carry us year after year, without disgust, through the routine-work which is so large a part of life.

Walter Pater: Marius the Epicurean,
ch. 25

What is hope? Hope is *wishing* for a thing to come true; faith is *believing* that it will come true. Hope is wanting something so eagerly that—in spite of all the evidence that you're not going to get it—you go right on wanting it. And the remarkable thing about it is that this very act of hoping produces a kind of strength of its own.

Norman Vincent Peale: Guideposts

Quick, open, open wide this gate of hell;
For I in truth can count it nothing less.
No one comes here who has not lost all hope
Of being good.

Titus Maccius Plautus: Bacchides, l. 368

Hope springs eternal in the human breast:
Man never is, but always to be, blest.

Alexander Pope: Essay on Man, Epis. I,
l. 95

Hope travels through, nor quits us when we die.

Alexander Pope: Essay on Man, Epis. II,
l. 273

For hope is but the dream of those that wake!

Matthew Prior: Solomon on the Vanity of
the World, Bk. 111, l. 102

Give me my scallop-shell of quiet,
    My staff of faith to walk upon,
My scrip of joy, immortal diet,
    My bottle of salvation,
My gown of glory, hope's true gage,
And thus I'll take my pilgrimage.

Sir Walter Raleigh: His Pilgrimage

Hope dead lives nevermore,
    No, not in heaven.

Christina Georgina Rosetti: Dead Hope

Hope is like a harebell trembling from its birth . . .

Christina Georgina Rossetti: Dead Hope
Like a Harebell

Who in Life's battle firm doth stand
Shall bear Hope's tender blossoms
Into the Silent Land.

Johann Gaudenz von Salis-Seewis: Ins
Stille Land

Thus grave these lessons on thy soul,—
Hope, faith, and love; and thou shalt find
Strength when life's surges rudest roll,
Light when thou else wert blind!

> Johann Christoph Friedrich von Schiller:
> *Hope, Faith, and Love*, st. 5

No affliction nor temptation, no guilt nor
power of sin, no wounded spirit nor terrified
conscience, should induce us to despair of
help and comfort from God.

> Thomas Scott

A high hope for a low heaven.

> William Shakespeare: *Love's Labour's
> Lost*, Act I, sc. 1, l. 194

The miserable have no other medicine
But only hope:
I've hope to live, and am prepar'd to die.

> William Shakespeare: *Measure for
> Measure*, Act III, sc. 1, l. 2

Past hope, past cure, past help!

> William Shakespeare: *Romeo and Juliet*,
> Act IV, sc. 1, l. 45

Through the sunset of hope,
Like the shapes of a dream,
What paradise islands of glory gleam!

> Percy Bysshe Shelley: *Hellas*, Semi-
> chorus I

But hope will make thee young, for Hope
and Youth
Are children of one mother, even Love.

> Percy Bysshe Shelley: *Revolt of Islam*,
> Canto VIII, st. 27

Take short views, hope for the best, and
trust in God.

> Sydney Smith, in Lady Holland's *Memoir*,
> Vol. I, ch. 6.

Fear cannot be without hope nor hope without fear.

> Benedict (Baruch) de Spinoza: *Ethics*,
> Part *III*, *Definition XIII*,
> *Explanation*

Gods fade; but God abides and in man's
heart

Speaks with the clear unconquerable cry
Of energies and hopes that can not die.

> John Addington Symonds: *Sonnet, On the
> Sacro Monte*

We need hope for living, far more than for
dying. Dying is easy work, compared to living.
Dying is a moment's transition; living, a
transaction of years. It is the length of the
rope that puts the sag in it. Hope tightens
the words and tunes up the heartstrings.

> *Telescope-Messenger*

And faintly trust the larger hope.

> Alfred, Lord Tennyson: *In Memoriam*,
> Pt. LV, st. 5

Sad soul, take comfort nor forget
The sunrise never failed us yet.

> Celia Laighton Thaxter

Hope and be happy that all's for the best!

> Martin Farquhar Tupper: *All's for the
> Best*, st. 3

Behind the cloud the starlight lurks,
Through showers the sunbeams fall;
For God, who loveth all His works,
Has left His hope for all.

> John Greenleaf Whittier

We did not dare to breathe a prayer
Or to give our anguish scope!
Something was dead in each of us,
And what was dead was Hope.

> Oscar Wilde: *The Ballad of Reading Gaol*,
> Pt. III, st. 31

Hope, the paramount duty that Heaven lays,
For its own honour, on man's suffering heart.

> William Wordsworth: *Poems Dedicated
> to National Independence*, Pt. II, No. 33

HUMILITY

When one asked a philosopher what the
great God was doing, he replied, "His whole
employment is to lift up the humble, and
to cast down the proud."

> Anonymous

The man who is to take a high place before his fellows must take a low place before his God.

Anonymous

It is the laden bough that hangs low, and the most fruitful Christian who is the most humble.

Anonymous

A mountain shames a molehill until they are both humbled by the stars.

Anonymous

Many would be scantily clad if clothed in their humility.

Anonymous

True humility is contentment.

Henri Frédéric Amiel: *Journal*

Do you wish to be great? Then begin by being. Do you desire to construct a vast and lofty fabric? Think first about the foundations of humility. The higher your structure is to be, the deeper must be its foundation.

St. Augustine

It was pride that changed angels into devils; it is humility that makes men as angels.

St. Augustine

Should you ask me: What is the first thing in religion? I should reply: The first, second, and third thing therein is humility.

St. Augustine

It is no great thing to be humble when you are brought low; but to be humble when you are praised is a great and rare attainment.

St. Bernard of Clairvaux

There is but one road to lead us to God—humility; all other ways would only lead astray, even were they fenced in with all virtues.

Nicolas Boileau-Despréaux

The true way to be humble is not to stoop until you are smaller than yourself, but to stand at your real height against some higher nature that will show you what the real smallness of your greatness is.

Phillips Brooks

Owe not thy humility unto humiliation from adversity, but look humbly down in that state when others look upwards upon thee.

Sir Thomas Browne: *Christian Morals*, Pt. I, sec. 14

Mountain gorses, do ye teach us . . .
That the wisest word man reaches
Is the humblest he can speak?

Elizabeth Barrett Browning: *Lessons from the Gorse*

He that is down, needs fear no fall;
He that is low, no pride;
He that is humble ever shall
Have God to be his guide.

John Bunyan

For it is a hard matter for a man to go down into the Valley of Humiliation, and to catch no slip by the way.

John Bunyan: *The Pilgrim's Progress*, Pt. I

The higher we are placed, the more humbly should we walk.

Cicero: *De Officiis*, ch. 26, sec. 90

Never be haughty to the humble; never be humble to the haughty.

Jefferson Davis: Speech in Richmond, July 22, 1861

'Umble we are, 'umble we have been, 'umble we shall ever be.

Charles Dickens: *David Copperfield*

I ate 'umble pie with an appetite.

Charles Dickens: *David Copperfield*

Nothing sets a person so much out of the devil's reach as humility.

Jonathan Edwards

True humility is not an abject, groveling, self-despising spirit; it is but a right estimate of ourselves as God sees us.

Tryon Edwards

None shall rule but the humble,
And none but Toil shall have.

Ralph Waldo Emerson: *Boston Hymn*

It is in vain to gather virtues without humility; for the spirit of God delights to dwell in the hearts of the humble.

Erasmus

They that know God will be humble; they that know themselves cannot be proud.

John Flavel

After crosses and losses men grow humbler and wiser.

Benjamin Franklin

My God, give me neither poverty nor riches, but whatsoever it may be thy will to give, give me, with it, a heart that knows humbly to acquiesce in what is thy will.

J. E. L. Gotthold

The Christian is like the ripening corn; the riper he grows the more lowly he bends his head.

Thomas Guthrie

Humble we must be, if to Heaven we go:
High is the roof there; but the gate is low:
When e'er thou speak'st, look with a lowly eye:
Grace is increased by humility.

Robert Herrick: *Noble Numbers*

Humility is the first of the virtues—for other people.

Oliver Wendell Holmes, Sr.

That very thing so many Christians want—Humility!

Thomas Hood: *Ode to Rae Wilson,* l. 218

Don't let us think that we need to be "stars in order to shine. It was by the ministry of a candle that the woman recovered her lost piece of silver.

John Henry Jowett

I have not the slightest feeling of humility towards the public, or to anything in existence but the Eternal Being, the principle of beauty, and the memory of great men.

John Keats: *Letter to J. H. Reynolds*

God hath sworn to lift on high
Who sinks himself by true humility.

John Keble: *Miscellaneous Poems: At Hooker's Tomb*

Humility is the genuine proof of Christian virtue.—Without it we keep all our defects, and they are only crusted over by pride which conceals them from others, and often from ourselves.

François de La Rochefoucauld

Humility is the altar upon which God wishes us to offer him sacrifices.

François de La Rochefoucauld: *Maximes Posthumes,* 537

Plenty of people want to be pious, but no one yearns to be humble.

François de La Rochefoucauld: *Maximes*

Humility and love are the essence of true religion; the humble formed to adore; the loving to associate with eternal love.

Johann Kaspar Lavater

None are more humble than Spirit-filled Christians. Self must be crucified before the Holy Spirit will dwell within.

J. Gilchrist Lawson

If thou wouldst find much favor and peace with God and man, be very low in thine own eyes. Forgive thyself little and others much.

Robert Leighton

Humility is the ability to act ashamed when you tell people how wonderful you are.

S. Lee Luchansky: *Look*

Humbleness is always grace; always dignity.

James Russell Lowell

True humility makes way for Christ, and throws the soul at his feet.

John Mason

The casting down of our spirits in true humility is but like throwing a ball to the ground, which makes it rebound the higher toward heaven.

John Mason

If we pull the blanket of self-righteousness too far up over our heads, it is possible to shut out the entire vista of religion which begins with humility.

Douglas Meador: Matador (Texas)
Tribune

No man will learn anything at all,
Unless he first will learn humility.

Owen Meredith: *Vanini*, l. 328

The truly godly are instinctively humble. There is no humility so deep and real as that which the knowledge of grace produces.

Andrew Miller

The saint that wears heaven's brightest crown in deepest adoration bends; the weight of glory bows him down the most when most his soul ascends; nearest the throne itself must be the footstool of humility.

James Montgomery

God has nothing to say to the self-righteous. Unless you humble yourself before him in the dust, and confess before him your iniquities and sins, the gate of heaven, which is open only for *sinners,* saved by *grace,* must be shut against you forever.

Dwight L. Moody

Humility, that low, sweet root,
From which all heavenly virtues shoot.

Thomas Moore: *Loves of the Angels:
Third Angel's Story*

It is from out of the depths of our humility that the height of our destiny looks grandest. Let me truly feel that in myself I am nothing, and at once, through every inlet of my soul, God comes in, and is everything in me.

William Mountford

Humility is perfect quietness of heart. It is to have no trouble. It is never to be fretted or irritated or sore or disappointed. It is to expect nothing, to wonder at nothing that is done to me. It is to be at rest when nobody praises me and when I am blamed or despised. It is to have a blessed home in the Lord, where I can go in and shut the door and kneel to my Father in secret, and am at peace as in the deep sea of calmness when all around and above is trouble.

Andrew Murray

Whosoever small smite thee on thy right cheek, turn to him the other also.

*New Testament: Matthew 5: 39;
Luke 6: 92*

Whosoever shall exalt himself shall be abased; and he that humbleth himself shall be exalted.

*New Testament: Matthew 32: 12;
Luke 14: 11*

God resisteth the proud, but giveth grace unto the humble.

New Testament: James 4: 6

Before honour is humility.

Old Testament: Proverbs 15: 33

Better is it to be of an humble spirit with the lowly than to divide the spoil with the proud.

Old Testament: Proverbs 16: 19

By humility, and the fear of the Lord are riches, and honour, and life.

Old Testament: Proverbs 22: 4

An able yet humble man is a jewel worth a kingdom.

William Penn

Sense shines with a double lustre when set in humility.

William Penn

No more lessen or dissemble thy merit, than overrate it; for though humility be a virtue, an affected one is not.

William Penn: *Fruits of Solitude*

Humility is the Christian's greatest honor; and the higher men climb, the further they are from heaven.

Jane Porter

If thou desire the love of God and man, be humble, for the proud heart, as it loves none but itself, is beloved of none but itself.— Humility enforces where neither virtue, nor strength, nor reason can prevail.

Francis Quarles

There is no humiliation for humility.

Joseph Roux: *Meditations of a Parish Priest,* Pt. IV, no. 5

The beloved of the Almighty are the rich who have the humility of the poor, and the poor who have the magnanimity of the rich.

Saadi

Humility is a virtue all men preach, none practise, and yet everybody is content to hear. The master thinks it good doctrine for his servants, the laity for the clergy, and the clergy for the laity.

John Selden: *Table Talk: Humility*

I thank my God for my humility.

William Shakespeare: *Richard III,*
Act II, sc. 1, l. 72

The proud man counts his newspaper clippings—the humble man his blessings.

Bishop Fulton J. Sheen

Humility is strong—not bold; quiet—not speechless; sure—not arrogant.

Estelle Smith: *Christian Woman*

True humility is intelligent self respect which keeps us from thinking too highly or too meanly of ourselves. It makes us mindful of the nobility God meant us to have. Yet it makes us modest by reminding us how far we have come short of what we can be.

Ralph W. Sockman: *Arkansas Methodist*

Humility is to make a right estimate of one's self. It is no humility for a man to think less of himself than he ought, though it might rather puzzle him to do that.

Charles Haddon Spurgeon: *Gleaning Among the Sheaves. Humility*

Do not consider yourself to have made any spiritual progress, unless you account yourself the least of all men.
God walks with the humble; he reveals himself to the lowly; he gives understanding to the little ones; he discloses his meaning to pure minds, but hides his grace from the curious and the proud.

Thomas à Kempis

Humble thyself in all things.

Thomas à Kempis: *Imitation of Christ*
Bk. III, ch. 24

Humility like darkness reveals the heavenly lights.

Henry David Thoreau: *Walden,*
Conclusion

HYPOCRISY

A hypocrite is a fellow who isn't himself on Sundays.

Anonymous

Some pious folk steal pigs, but give away the feet for God's sake.

Anonymous

Don't stay away from church because there are so many hypocrites. There's always room for one more.

Arthur R. Adams

Great hypocrites are the real atheists.

Sir Francis Bacon

An ill man is always ill, but he is worst of all when he pretends to be a saint.

Sir Francis Bacon: *Ornamenta Rationalia,*
no. 28

A man who hides behind the hypocrite is smaller than the hypocrite.

William E. Biederwolf

I saw about a peck of counterfeit dollars once. Did I go to the window and throw away all my good dollars? No! Yet you reject Christianity because there are hypocrites, or counterfeit Christians.

William E. Biederwolf

A saint abroad, and a devil at home.

John Bunyan: *The Pilgrim's Progress,*
Pt. I

Till Cant cease, nothing else can begin.

Thomas Carlyle: *The French Revolution,*
Pt. II, Bk. III

Built God a church, and laugh'd his word to scorn.

William Cowper: *Retirement,* l. 688

Better be a sinner than a hypocrite.

Danish Proverb

No rogue like to the godly rogue.

Thomas Fuller: *Gnomologia*

The world consists almost exclusively of people who are one sort and who behave like another sort.

Zona Gale

The only vice that cannot be forgiven is hypocrisy. The repentance of a hypocrite is itself hypocrisy.

William Hazlitt: *Characteristics,* no. 256

Hypocrites do the devil's drudgery in Christ's livery.

Matthew Henry

A man may cry Church! Church! at ev'ry word,
With no more piety than other people—
A daw's not reckoned a religious bird
Because it keeps a-cawing from a steeple.

Thomas Hood: *Ode to Rae Wilson,* l. 171

It is no fault of Christianity if a hypocrite falls into sin.

St. Jerome

Hypocrisy is the homage which vice renders to virtue.

François de La Rochefoucald: *Maximes*

For neither man nor angel can discern
Hypocrisy, the only evil that walks
Invisible, except to God alone.

John Milton: *Paradise Lost,* Bk. III, l. 682

When thou prayest, thou shalt not be as the hypocrites are: for they love to pray standing in the synagogues and in the corners of the streets, that they may be seen of men.

New Testament: Matthew 6: 5

Thou hypocrite, first cast out the beam out of thine own eye; and then shalt thou see clearly to cast out the mote out of thy brother's eye.

New Testament: Matthew 7: 5

Woe unto you, scribes and Pharisees, hypocrites! for ye are like unto whited sepulchres, which indeed appear beautiful outward, but are within full of dead men's bones, and of all uncleanness.

New Testament: Matthew 23: 27

He passed by on the other side.

New Testament: Luke 10: 31

The hypocrite was a man who stole the livery of the court of heaven to serve the devil in.

Channing Pollock

If the world despises hypocrites, what must be the estimate of them in heaven?

Madame Jeanne Manon Roland

The devil can cite Scripture for his purpose.
An evil soul producing holy witness
Is like a villain with a smiling cheek,
A goodly apple rotten at the heart:
O what a goodly outside falsehood hath!

William Shakespeare: *The Merchant of
Venice,* Act I, sc. 3, l. 99

Hypocrites in the Church? Yes, and in the
lodge, and at home. Don't hunt through the
Church for a hypocrite. Go home and look
in the glass. Hypocrites? Yes. See that you
make the number one less.

W. A. ("Billy") Sunday

The old-style hypocrite was a person who
tried to appear better than he actually was;
the new-style hypocrite tries to appear worse
than he or she is.

Charles Templeton

I

DOLS, IDOLATRY

There are four classes of idols which beset men's minds. To these for distinction's sake I have assigned names,—calling the first class *Idols of the Tribe*; the second, *Idols of the Cave*; the third, *Idols of the Market-Place*; the fourth, *Idols of the Theater*.

Sir Francis Bacon: *Novum Organum,*
Aphorism I

All worship whatsoever must proceed by symbols, by idols:—we may say, all idolatry is comparative, and the worst idolatry is only more idolatrous.

Thomas Carlyle: *Heroes and Hero-*
Worship, IV

We boast our emancipation from many superstitions; but if we have broken any idols, it is through a transfer of idolatry.

Ralph Waldo Emerson: *Character*

All men are idolaters, some of fame, others of self-interest, most of pleasure.

Baltasar Gracian y Morales: *The Art of*
Worldly Wisdom, XXVI

Mankind are an incorrigible race. Give them but bugbears and idols—it is all that they ask.

William Hazlitt: *Commonplaces,* no. 76

The heathen, in his blindness,
Bows down to wood and stone.

Reginald Heber: *From Greenland's Icy*
Mountains

We easily fall into idolatry, for we are inclined thereunto by nature, and coming to us by inheritance, it seems pleasant.

Martin Luther: *Table Talk*

Thou shalt not make unto thee any graven image, or any likeness of anything that is in heaven above, or that is in the earth beneath, or that is in the water under the earth.

Old Testament: Exodus 20: 4

For rebellion is as the sin of witchcraft, and stubbornness is as iniquity and idolatry.

Old Testament: I Samuel 15: 23

Men show no mercy and expect no mercy, when honor calls, or when they fight for their idols or their gods.

Johann Christoph Friedrich von Schiller:
The Maid of Orleans, l. 5

What art thou, thou idol ceremony?
What kind of god art thou, that suffer'st more
Of mortal griefs than do thy worshippers?

William Shakespeare: *Henry V,*
Act IV, sc. 1, l. 257

'Tis mad idolatry
To make the service greater than the god.

William Shakespeare: *Troilus and*
Cressida, Act II, sc. 2, l. 56

Ambition is our idol on whose wings
Great minds are carry'd only to extreme;
To be sublimely great, or to be nothing.

Thomas Southerne: *The Loyal Brother,*
Act I, sc. 1

IMMORTALITY

When John Wesley was asked what he would do if he knew he were to die that night, he said that he would eat his supper, preach at candlelight, say his prayers and go to bed.

Anonymous

243

Think of stepping on shore, and finding it
Heaven!
Of taking hold of a hand, and finding it
God's hand,
Of breathing new air, and finding it celestial
air,
Of feeling invigorated, and finding it
immortality,
Of passing from storm and tempest to an
unbroken calm,
Of waking up, and finding it Home!

Anonymous

Whence this pleasing hope, this fond desire,
This longing for immortality?
'Tis the divinity that stirs within us;
'Tis heaven itself that points out an here-
after,
And intimates eternity to man.

Joseph Addison

To look upon the soul as going on from
strength to strength, to consider that it is to
shine forever with new accessions of glory,
and brighten to all eternity; that it will be
still adding virtue to virtue, and knowledge
to knowledge—carries in it something wonderfully agreeable to that ambition which is
natural to the mind of men.

Joseph Addison

The stars shall fade away, the sun himself
Grow dim with age, and nature sink in years,
But thou shalt flourish in immortal youth,
Unhurt amidst the wars of elements,
The wrecks of matter, and the crush of
worlds.

Joseph Addison: *Cato,* Act V, sc. 1

The inn of a traveler on the way to Jerusalem.

Inscription on the grave of Dean Alford

Let us not lament too much the passing of
our friends. They are not dead, but simply
gone before us along the road which all must
travel.

Antiphanes: *Fragment*

God created man to be immortal, and made
him to be an image of his own eternity.

Apocrypha: Wisdom of Solomon 2: 23

Whatsoever that be within us that feels,
thinks, desires, and animates, is something
celestial and divine, and consequently it i
imperishable.

Aristotle

Immortality is the bravest gesture of our
humanity toward the unknown. It is alway
a faith, never a demonstration.

Glen Gaius Atkin

No man is prosperous whose immortality
is forfeited. No man is rich to whom the
grave brings eternal bankruptcy. No man i
happy upon whose path there rests but a
momentary glimmer of light, shining ou
between clouds that are closing over him in
darkness forever.

Henry Ward Beecher

Death? Translated into the heavenly tongue
that word means life!

Henry Ward Beecher

Immortality is a great affirmation of the sou
of man.

Hugh Black: *Greatest Thoughts or
Immortality,* p. 4

When we are dead, we are dead.

Napoleon Bonaparte: Remark to Gaspard
Gourgaud at St. Helena, 1818

Everything science has taught me—and con
tinues to teach me—strengthens my belief in
the continuity of our spiritual existence after
death.

Werner von Braun

As to immortality, my conviction stands
thus: If there be anything in me that is of
permanent worth and service to the universe,
the universe will know how to preserve it.
Whatsoever in me is not of permanent worth
and service, neither can nor should be preserved.

Horace James Bridges, in Newton:
My Idea of God

It is said that when a student in a moral
philosophy class of Mark Hopkins once asked

im who would go to heaven, Hopkins re-
lied that he did not know but that he was
ure no one would be there who did not feel
t home.

Margueritte Harmon Bro

We cherish the dream and it will not down.
We seek and find warrant for our hope that
sometime, somewhere we shall awake in His
likeness and be satisfied in that we too behold
he dead, small and great, standing before
God, conscious, aspiring, resolute, to be dealt
with in the ages to come by Him who is not
the God of the dead but of the living.

Charles R. Brown: *Living Again*, p. 57,
Harvard University Press

Christ turned a brilliant guess into a solid
certainty and endowed the hope of eternal
life with grace, reason, and majesty.

Hugh Elmer Brown

There is nothing strictly immortal, but immortality.

Sir Thomas Browne: *Hydriotaphia,* ch. 5,
sec. 12

No, at noonday in the bustle of man's work-
time
Greet the unseen with a cheer!
Bid him forward, breast and back as either
Should be,
"Strive and thrive!" cry, "Speed-fight on,
Fare ever
There as here!"

Robert Browning

You say, "Where goest thou?" I cannot tell,
And still go on. If but the way be straight
I cannot go amiss: but before me lies
Dawn and the day: the night behind me: that
Suffices me! I break the bounds: I see,
And nothing more; believe and nothing less.

Robert Browning

I go to prove my soul!
I see my way as birds their trackless way.
I shall arrive! what time, what circuit first,
I ask not; but unless God send his hail
Or blinding fireballs, sleet or stifling snow,
In some time, his good time, I shall arrive.

Robert Browning: *Paracelsus*, Pt. I

If I stoop
Into a dark tremendous sea of cloud,
It is but for a time; I press God's lamp
Close to my breast; its splendor soon or late
Will pierce the gloom; I shall emerge one
day.

Robert Browning: *Paracelsus,* last lines

Fool! All that is, at all,
Last ever, past recall;
Earth changes, but thy soul and God stand
sure:
What entered into thee,
That was, is, and shall be:
Time's wheel runs back or stops;
Potter and clay endure.

Robert Browning: *Rabbi Ben Ezra* st. 14

And I shall thereupon
Take rest, ere I be gone
Once more on my adventure brave and new.
Ibid.

If the Father deigns to touch with divine
power the cold and pulseless heart of the
buried acorn and to make it burst forth from
its prison walls, will He leave neglected in
the earth the soul of man made in the image
of his Creator?

William Jennings Bryan

On the imagination God sometimes paints,
by dream and symbol, the likeness of things
to come.—What the foolish-wise call fanaticism, belongs to the same part of us as hope.
—Each is the yearning of the soul for the
great "Beyond," which attests our immortality.

Edward George Bulwer-Lytton

We are born for a higher destiny than that
of earth. There is a realm where the rainbow
never fades, where the stars will be spread
before us like islands that slumber on the
ocean, where the beings that now pass over
before us like shadows will stay in our
presence forever.

Edward George Bulwer-Lytton

I have been dying for twenty years, now I am
going to live.

James Drummond Burns: *His Last Words*

Whitman once said to me that he would as soon hope to argue a man into good health as to argue him into a belief in immortality. He said he *knew* it was so without proof; but I never could ilght my candle at his great torch.

John Burroughs: *Life and Letters of John Burroughs*, Houghton Mifflin Co.

That which is the foundation of all our hopes and of all our fears; all our hopes and fears which are of any consideration: I mean a Future Life.

Joseph Butler: *Analogy of Religion*

Both free enterprize and the labor movement at their best believe in the worth of the individual. But such a faith is nonsense if men are cheap candles blown out at death, or drops of water absorbed into some vague ocean of being. Thus any real faith in personality rests on faith in the life everlasting.

George A. Buttrick: *So We Believe, So We Pray*, Abingdon Press

I feel my immortality o'ersweep all pains, all tears, all time, all fears, and like the eternal thunder of the deep, peal to my ears this truth: "Thou livest forever."

George Gordon, Lord Byron

A good man never dies.

Callimachus: *Epigrams*, X

Is this the end? I know it cannot be,
Our ships shall sail upon another sea;
New islands yet shall break upon our sight,
New continents of love and truth and might.

John White Chadwick

Immortality is the glorious discovery of Christianity.

William Ellery Channing

What a sublime doctrine it is, that goodness cherished now is eternal life already entered on!

William Ellery Channing

If I err in my belief that the souls of me* are immortal, I gladly err, nor do I wish thi* error, in which I find delight, to be wreste* from me.

Cicero: *De Senectut*

Whatever is that feels, and knows and wills and has the power of growth, is celestial an* divine, and for that reason must be immorta*

Cicero: *Tusculanarum Disputationum*

Without the hope of immortality no on* would ever face death for his country.

Ibid

When I go to sleep, it would be no pleasur* to think I might be awakened in the middl* of the night.

Georges Clemenceau

Though it is true that science presents nc weighty evidence for life eternal, it is only fair to point out also that science has found no cogent reason for supposing that what is of importance in a man can be buried in a grave. The truth is that science cannot supply a definite answer to this question. Immortality relates to an aspect of life which is not physical, that is, which cannot be detected and measured by any instrument, and to which the application of the laws of science can at best be only a well-considered guess.

Arthur H. Compton: *The Freedom of Man*, Yale University Press

Immortality
Alone could teach this mortal how to die.

Dinah Maria Mulock Craik: *Looking Death in the Face*, l. 77

Believing as I do that man in the distant future will be a far more perfect creature than he now is, it is an intolerable thought that he and all other sentient beings are doomed to complete annihilation after such long-continued slow progress. To those who fully admit the immortality of the human soul, the destruction of our world will not appear so dreadful.

Charles Darwin: *Life and Letters*

f course, I do not want to go—this is a
ighty interesting world, and I'm having a
ighty good time in it. But I am no more
raid of going than of going through the
oor of this study. For I know that I shall
en have a spiritual body to do with as I
ease, and I won't have to worry about the
hes and pains of this poor physical body.

Ozora S. Davis

or I never have seen, and never shall see,
at the cessation of the evidence of existence
 necessarily evidence of the cessation of
istence.

William Frend De Morgan: *Joseph Vance,*
ch. 40, Wm. Heinemann, Ltd., publisher

here is nothing innocent or good that dies
nd is forgotten: let us hold to that faith or
one.

Charles Dickens

he old, old fashion—death! Oh, thank
od, all who see it, for that older fashion
et—of immortality.

Charles Dickens

never saw a moor
 never saw the sea;
et know I how the heather looks,
nd what a wave must be.

never spoke with God,
Jor visited in heaven;
et certain am I of the spot
As if the chart were given.

Emily Dickinson

)ne short sleep past, we wake eternally,
And Death shall be no more: Death, thou
  shalt die.

John Donne: *Divine Poems: Holy Sonnets,*
no. 17

The thought of being nothing after death
s a burden insupportable to a virtuous man;
ve naturally aim at happiness and cannot
ear to have it confined to our present being.

John Dryden

Oh, may I join the choir invisible
Of those immortal dead who live again.

George Eliot: *The Choir Invisible*

Our dissatisfaction with any other solution
is the blazing evidence of immortality.

Ralph Waldo Emerson

We are much better believers in immortality
than we can give grounds for. The real evidence is too subtle or is higher than we can
write down in propositions.

Ralph Waldo Emerson

I have always thought that faith in immortality is proof of the sanity of a man's nature.

Ralph Waldo Emerson

We cannot resist the conviction that this
world is for us only the porch of another and
more magnificent temple of the Creator's
majesty.

Frederick William Faber

My mind can take no hold in the present
world nor rest in it a moment, but my whole
nature rushes onward with irresistible force
toward a future and a better state of being.

Immanuel Hermann von Fichte

The future is lighted for us with the radiant
colors of hope. Strife and sorrow shall disappear. Peace and love shall reign supreme.
The dream of poets, the lesson of priests and
prophet, the inspiration of the great musician
is confirmed in the light of modern knowledge.

John Fiske

When one strips himself of all convictions
about the future he stops living altogether.

Harry Emerson Fosdick

I believe in immortality fundamentally, not
because I vehemently crave it for myself as
an individual, but because its denial seems
to me to land the entire race in a hopeless
situation and to reduce philosophy to a
counsel of despair.

Harry Emerson Fosdick: *Greatest
Thoughts on Immortality,* p. 12

The Body of Benjamin Franklin, Printer,
(like the cover of an old book, its contents
torn out, and stript of its lettering and gild-
ing) lies here food for worms. Yet the work
itself shall not be lost; for it will (as he believed) appear once more in a new and more
beautiful edition, corrected and amended by
the Author.

Epitaph on Franklin's tombstone, written
by himself

Shall I doubt my Father's mercy?
Shall I think of death as doom,
Or the stepping o'er the threshold
To a bigger, brighter room?

Robert Freeman

Faith is positive, enriching life in the here
and now. Doubt is negative, robbing life of
glow and meaning. So though I do not understand immortality, I choose to believe.

Webb B. Garrison

Those who live in the Lord never see each
other for the last time.

German Motto

Those who hope for no other life are dead
even in this.

Johann Wolfgang von Goethe

The God about whose business I have tried
to be busy will not forget to look after mine
in any world to which I may go.

William Rainey Harper

Yet spirit immortal, the tomb cannot bind
thee,
But like thine own eagle that soars to the
sun,
Thou springest from bondage and leavest
behind thee
A name which before thee no mortal hath
won.

Attributed to Lyman Heath: The Grave
of Bonaparte

Work for immortality if you will; then wait
for it.

Josiah Gilbert Holland: Gold-Foil:
Patience

Immortality—twin sister of Eternity.

Josiah Gilbert Holland: Gold-Foil: T▮
Way to Grow O▮

As Darwin and his confreres found evol▮
tion, so man finds immortality. The thoug▮
of immortality is as well founded as any oth▮
well-authenticated postulate of the huma▮
reason.

John Haynes Holm▮

'Tis true; 'tis certain; man though dea▮
retains
Part of himself; the immortal mind remain▮

Homer: Iliad, Bk. XXIII, l. 122 (Pope▮
Trans▮

I shall not wholly die; large residue
Shall 'scape the queen of death.

Horace: Odes, Bk. III, ode 30, l.

Winter is on my head, but eternal spring ▮
in my heart. The nearer I approach the en▮
the plainer I hear around me the immort▮
symphonies which invite me.

Victor Hug▮

When I go down to the grave I can say, lik▮
so many others, I have finished my work▮
but I cannot say that I have finished my lif▮
My day's work will begin the next mornin▮
My tomb is not a blind alley. It is a thoroug▮
fare. It closes with the twilight to open wit▮
the dawn.

Victor Hug▮

I feel in me the assurance that the grave ca▮
not keep me. Worms may destroy what ▮
perishable in me, but the power to think
something in my ears, eyes and lips whic▮
we call "life," no power on earth can destro▮
Gentlemen of Science, let us live in the visibl▮
world, but also in the invisible. The grav▮
is a door which never opens again for th▮
world, but it opens for another.

Victor Hugo, to a meeting of Atheist▮

I am looking with an eager interest into th▮
"undiscovered country" and leaving thi▮
earth with no regret, except that I have no▮
accomplished more work. But I don't doub▮
we shall keep on working.

Helen Hun▮

neither deny nor affirm the immortality of
man. I see no reason for believing in it but,
on the other hand, I have no means of dis-
proving it.

Thomas Henry Huxley: *Letter to Charles
Kingsley*

know as much about the after-life as you—
nothing. I don't even know if there is one
. . I have no vision of "heaven" or a "wel-
coming God." I do not know what I shall
and. I must wait and see.

William R. Inge: from "Death of the
Dean," *Time*, March 8, 1954

Life is a narrow vale between the cold and
barren peaks of two eternities. We strive in
vain to look beyond the heights. We cry
aloud—and the only murmur is the echo of
our wailing cry. From the voiceless lips of
the unreplying dead there comes no word.
But in the night of Death, Hope sees a star,
and listening Love can hear the rustle of a
wing.

Robert Green Ingersoll in an address
delivered at the funeral of his brother

The idea of immortality . . . will continue
to ebb and flow beneath the mists and clouds
of doubt and darkness as long as love kisses
the lips of death. It is the rainbow—Hope,
shining upon the tears of grief.

Robert Green Ingersoll: *The Ghosts*

The saddest of all failures is that of a soul,
with its capabilities and possibilities, failing
f life everlasting and entering on that night
f death upon which no morning ever dawns.

Herrick Johnson

How gloomy would be the mansions of the
dead to him who did not know that he should
never die; that what now acts, shall continue
its agency, and what now thinks, shall think
on forever!

Samuel Johnson

After death the soul possesses self-consciousness, otherwise it would be the subject of
spiritual death, which has already been
disproved. With this self-consciousness neces-

sarily remains personality and the consciousness of personal identity.

Immanuel Kant

No, no, I'm sure,
My restless spirit never could endure
To brood so long upon one luxury,
Unless it did, though fearfully, espy
A hope beyond the shadow of a dream.

John Keats: *Endymion*, Bk. I

He ne'er is crowned
With immortality, who fears to follow
Where airy voices lead.

John Keats: *Endymion*, Bk. II

It is a great thing to know that if the eternal
doors swing wide open the other way for
you, you have a Friend on the other side
waiting to receive you.

Howard Kelly

Then to the grave I turned me to see what
therein lay;
'Twas the garment of the Christian, worn out
and thrown away.

Friedrich Adolf Krummacher: *Death and
the Christian*

Belief in the future life is the appetite of
reason.

Walter Savage Landor: *Imaginary Conversations: Marcus Tullius and
Quinctus Cicero*

Men are immortal till their work is done.

David Livingstone: *Letter*

Dust thou art, to dust returnest,
Was not spoken of the soul.

Henry Wadsworth Longfellow

The grave itself is but a covered bridge
leading from light to light through a brief
darkness.

Henry Wadsworth Longfellow

And in the wreck of noble lives
Something immortal still survives.

Henry Wadsworth Longfellow: *The
Building of the Ship*, l. 375

Immortality is not something to be improvised at death. Rather it is the slow accumulation of the years. It is the product of a life lived after the pattern of Jesus Christ.

Harold L. Lunger

In our sad condition, our only consolation is the expectancy of another life. Here below all is incomprehensible.

Martin Luther: *Table Talk*

The seed dies into a new life, and so does man.

George Macdonald

I came from God, and I'm going back to God, and I won't have any gaps of death in the middle of my life.

George Macdonald: *Mary Marston*, ch. 57

The thought of eternity consoles for the shortness of life.

Chrétien Guillaume de Malesherbes

The few little years we spend on earth are only the first scene in a Divine Drama that extends on into Eternity.

Edwin Markham: *Address*, at the funeral of Adam Willis Wagnalls. (Reprinted by permission of Virgil Markham)

To my reason immortality is the only possible solution to the mystery of life.

Alfred W. Martin

We do not believe in immortality because we have proved it, but we forever try to prove it because we believe it.

James Martineau

What no eyes have seen, what no ears have heard—that is the eternal happiness which I expect when I have laid aside my human body.

Karl F. P. von Martius

The spirit of man, which God inspired, cannot together perish with this corporeal clod.

John Milton

For who would lose,
Though full of pain, this intellectual being
Those thoughts that wander through
    eternity,
To perish rather, swallow'd up and lost
In the wide womb of uncreated night,
Devoid of sense and motion?

John Milton: *Paradise Lost*, Bk. II, l. 14

Beyond this vale of tears,
    There is a life above,
Unmeasured by the flight of years;
    And all that life is love.

James Montgomer

Without a belief in personal immortalit religion is surely like an arch resting on on pillar, like a bridge ending in an abyss.

Max Müll

The universe is a stairway leading nowher unless man is immortal.

Edgar Young Mullins, in Newton: *M
    Idea of God*, p. 19

I've got a home out yonder;
    Few days, few days;
I've got a home out yonder;
    I am going home.

The Negro Singer's Own Book, 184

Fear not that your life shall come to an en but rather that it shall never have a begi ning.

Cardinal John Henry Newma

I am the resurrection, and the life: He tha believeth in me, though he were dead, ye shall he live.

New Testament: John 11: 2

They do it to obtain a corruptible crow but we an incorruptible.

New Testament: I Corinthians 9: 2

In a moment, in the twinkling of an eye, a the last trump: for the trumpet shall soun and the dead shall be raised incorruptibl and we shall be changed.

New Testament: I Corinthians 15: 5

For this corruptible must put on incorruption, and this mortal must put on immortality.

New Testament: I Corinthians 15: 53

He that raised up Christ from the dead shall also quicken your mortal bodies by his Spirit that dwelleth in you.

New Testament: Romans 8: 11

Our Saviour Jesus Christ, who hath abolished death, and hath brought life and immortality to light through the gospel.

New Testament: II Timothy 1: 10

This is the promise that He hath promised us, even eternal life.

New Testament: I John 2: 25

My doctrine is live that thou mayest desire to live again—that is thy duty—for in any case thou wilt live again.

Friedrich Wilhelm Nietzsche: *Eternal Recurrence*

I shall take flight as a bird wings
Into the infinite blue—
What if my song comes ringing
Down through the stars and the dew?

Charles Leo O'Donnell: *Immortality* (Courtesy of Longmans Green, N.Y. and David McKay Co., Inc.)

If a man die, shall he live again? all the days of my appointed time will I wait, till my change come.

Old Testament: Job 14: 14

For I know that my redeemer liveth, and that he shall stand at the latter day upon the earth: And though after my skin worms destroy this body, yet in my flesh shall I see God.

Old Testament: Job 19: 25–26

As for me, I will behold thy face in righteousness: I shall be satisfied, when I awake, with thy likeness.

Old Testament: Psalms 17: 15

Or ever the silver cord be loosed, or the golden bowl be broken, or the pitcher be broken at the fountain, or the wheel broken at the cistern. Then shall the dust return to the earth as it was: and the spirit shall return unto God who gave it.

Old Testament: Ecclesiastes 12: 6–7

In the presence of so many mysteries which have been unveiled, in the presence of so many yet unsolved, the scientific student cannot be dogmatic and deny the possibility of a future state . . . of the things that are unseen science knows nothing, and at present has no means of knowing anything.

Sir William Osler

In my better part I shall be raised to immortality above the lofty stars.

Ovid: *Metamorphoses,* Bk. XV, 1

There is no death.
    They only truly live
Who pass into the life beyond, and see
    This earth is but a school preparative
For higher ministry.

John Oxenham: *The Vision Splendid*

I trouble not myself about the manner of future existence. I content myself with believing, even to positive conviction, that the power that gave me existence is able to continue it, in any form and manner he pleases, either with or without this body; and it appears more probable to me that I shall continue to exist hereafter than that I should have had existence, as I now have, before that existence began.

Thomas Paine: *The Age of Reason,* ch. 1

The dust goes to its place, and man to his own.—It is then I feel my immortality.—I look through the grave into heaven.—I ask no miracle, no proof, no reasoning, for me. —I ask no risen dust to teach me immortality. —I am conscious of eternal life.

Theodore Parker

What reason have atheists for saying that we cannot rise again? Which is the more difficult —to be born, or to rise again? That what has never been, should be, or that what has been, should be again? Is it more difficult to come into being than to return to it?

Blaise Pascal: *Pensées*

I know only scientifically determined truth, but I am going to believe what I wish to believe, what I cannot help but believe—I expect to meet this dear child in another world.

Louis Pasteur at the bedside of his dying daughter

We are like deep sea divers moving slowly and clumsily in the dim twilight of the depths, and we have our work to do. But this is not our element, and the relief of the diver in coming back to fresh air and sunlight and the sight of familiar faces is but a poor picture of the unspeakable delight with which we shall emerge from our necessary imprisonment into the loveliness and satisfaction of our true home.

J. B. Phillips: *Making Men Whole*

There is yet something remaining for the dead, and some far better thing for the good than for the evil.

Plato: *Phaedo*

His last day places man in the same state as before he was born; not after death has the body or soul any more feeling than they had before birth.

Pliny the Elder: *Naturalis Historia*

To me, my son didn't die—he's more alive than ever. Each of us has to keep a rendezvous with death . . . but I believe that life is the childhood of immortality.

Daniel A. Poling

Mortal though I be, yea, ephemeral, of but
    a moment
I gaze up to the night's starry domain of
    heaven,
Then no longer on earth I stand; I touch the
    Creator,
And my lively spirit drinketh immortality.

Ptolemy

We are no more responsible for the idea of immortality in the heart than for the eye of physical vision in the head.

Karl Reiland

I delight in the feeling that I am in eternity, that I can serve God now fully and effectively, that the next piece of road will come in sight when I am ready to walk in it.

Forbes Robinson

This life is but the passage of a day,
This life is but a pang and all is over;
But in the life to come which fades not away
Every love shall abide and every lover.

Christina Georgina Rossetti: *Saints and Angels*

Not all the subtilties of metaphysics can make me doubt for a moment of the immortality of the soul, and of a beneficent providence. I feel it. I believe it. I desire it. I hope for it. And I will defend it to my last breath.

Jean Jacques Rousseau

Had I no proof of the immortality of the soul than the oppression of the just and the triumph of the wicked in this world, this alone would prevent my having the least doubt of it. So shocking a discord amidst a general harmony of things would make me naturally look for a cause; I should say to myself, we do not cease to exist with this life; everything resumes its order after death.

Jean Jacques Rousseau

Here is the great discovery that awaits us: life is all of a piece. "We are not someday going to be, we already are immortal spirits."

A. Maude Royden

Death is not a journeying into an unknown land; it is a voyage home. We are going not to a strange country, but to our Father's house, and among our kith and kin.

John Ruskin

The certainty that He who went through death, who restored the connection between nature and the spiritual world, changes death to win a triumph, a triumph that is awaiting us like the warrior who is going toward a certain victory. Although I want to live and labor as long as God lets me, I consider the moment of my death as the most precious of my life.

Friedrich Wilhelm Joseph von Schelling

The mind is never right but when it is at peace within itself. The soul is in heaven even while it is in the flesh, if it be purged of its natural corruption and taken up with divine thoughts and contemplation.

Seneca

This life is only a prelude to eternity. For that which we call death is but a pause, in truth a progress into life.

Seneca

As the mother's womb holds us for ten months, making us ready, not for the womb itself, but for life, just so, through our lives, we are making ourselves ready for another birth . . . Therefore look forward without fear to that appointed hour—the last hour of the body, but not of the soul . . . That day, which you fear as being the end of all things, is the birthday of your eternity.

Seneca: *Epistolae ad Lucilium*, Epis. CII sec. 23

All that lives must die,
Passing through nature to eternity.

William Shakespeare: *Hamlet*, Act I, sc. 2, l. 72

We have passed Age's icy caves,
And Manhood's dark and tossing waves,
And Youth's smooth ocean, smiling to betray:
Beyond the glassy gulfs we flee
Of shadow-peopled Infancy,
Through Death and Birth to a diviner day.

Percy Bysshe Shelley: *Prometheus Unbound*, Act II, sc. 5, l. 98

It is simple dogmatism that would deny immortality; on scientific grounds at any rate, we have not the knowledge to take up such an attitude.

Sir James Young Simpson

The biggest fact about Joseph's tomb was that it wasn't a tomb at all—it was a room for a transient. Jesus stopped there a night or two on his way back to glory.

Herbert Booth Smith

It should be more difficult to believe that life will go on than to understand how it began.

Roy L. Smith: *The Methodist Story*

Christianity is a religion of the open tomb.

Ibid.

All men's souls are immortal, but the souls of the righteous are both immortal and divine.

Socrates

Our restlessness in this world seems to indicate that we are intended for a better. We have all of us a longing after happiness; and surely the Creator will gratify all the natural desires He has implanted in us.

Robert Southey

The Creator made us to be the image of His own eternity, and in the desire for immortality we feel we have sure proof of our capacity for it.

Robert Southey

What a world were this,
How unendurable its weight, if they
Whom Death hath sundered did not meet
again!

Robert Southey: *Inscription XVII: Epitaph*

If we accept, as we must, the theory of the indestructability of matter, no less must we accept the indestructability of the spirit with which matter is informed. Having known something of the brightness with which that spirit can burn within its corporeal envelope, I cannot believe that it is lost and utterly cast away.

Howard Spring: *And Another Thing*, Harper & Row, Publishers, Inc.

Divine wisdom, intending to detain us some time on earth, has done well to cover with a veil the prospect of the life to come; for if our sight could clearly distinguish the opposite bank, who would remain on this tempestuous coast of time?

Madame Anne Germaine de Staël

After the sun is down, and the west faded, the heavens begin to fill with stars.

Robert Louis Stevenson

The belief in the resurrection of Jesus is an act of faith; yes, it is, a faith in the justice, the reasonableness, the goodness, the square-ness of the moral universe.

George Craig Stewart

There is no death—the thing that we call death
Is but another, sadder name for life,
Which is itself an insufficient name,
Faint recognition of that unknown Life—
That Power whose shadow is the Universe.

Richard Henry Stoddard

Thou wilt not leave us in the dust:
Thou madest man, he knows not why,
He thinks he was not made to die;
And thou hast made him: thou art·just.

Alfred, Lord Tennyson

Thou canst not prove thou art immortal—no,
Nor yet that thou art mortal.

Alfred, Lord Tennyson: *The Ancient Sage*, l. 62

My own dim life should teach me this,
That life shall live for evermore.

Alfred, Lord Tennyson: *In Memoriam,*
Pt. XXXIV, st. 1

It may be we shall touch the Happy Isles,
And see the great Achilles, whom we knew.

Alfred, Lord Tennyson: *Ulysses*, l. 65

Time is but a stream I go a-fishing in. I drink at it. But while I drink, I see the sandy bottom and detect how shallow it is. Its thin current slips by, and eternity remains.

Henry David Thoreau

But felt through all this fleshy dress
Bright shoots of everlastingness.

Henry Vaughan: *The Retreat*

We see in the risen Christ the end for which man was made, and the assurance that the end is within our reach.

Brooke Foss Westcott

Joy, shipmate, joy!
(Pleased to my soul at death I cry)
Our life is closed, our life begins,
The long, long anchorage we leave,
The ship is clear at last, she leaps!
She swiftly courses from the shore,
Joy, shipmate, joy!

Walt Whitman

I do not think seventy years is the time of a man or woman . . .
Nor that years will ever stop the existence of me, or any one else.

Walt Whitman: *Who Learns My Lesson Complete*

I swear I think now that everything without exception has an eternal soul!
The trees have, rooted in the ground! the weeds of the sea have! the animals!

Walt Whitman: *To Think of Time*

Alas for him who never sees
The stars shine through his cypress-trees!
Who, hopeless, lays his dead away,
Nor looks to see the breaking day
Across the mournful marbles play!
Who hath not learned, in hours of faith,
The truth to flesh and sense unknown,
That Life is ever Lord of Death,
And Love can never lose its own!

John Greenleaf Whittier: *Snow-Bound,*
l. 203

Happy he whose inward ear
Angel comfortings can hear,
O'er the rabble's laughter;

And while Hatred's fagots burn,
Glimpses through the smoke discern
  Of the good hereafter.
    John Greenleaf Whittier: *Barclay of Ury,*
                                    st. 19

Is it reasonable to suppose that the "accident
of death" means an end to the nobler
powers? It is far easier for me to believe than
not believe in immortality.
                                    Mary Wooley

Hence in a season of calm weather
  Though inland far we be,
Our Souls have sight of that immortal sea
  Which brought us hither,
  Can in a moment travel thither,
And see the Children sport upon the shore,
And hear the mighty waters rolling ever-
    more.
                        William Wordsworth

  We see by the glad light
And breathe the sweet air of futurity;
And so we live, or else we have no life.
    William Wordsworth: *The Excursion,*
                                Bk. IX, l. 24

O joy! that in our embers
Is something that doth live.
    William Wordsworth: *Intimations of
                        Immortality,* l. 133

Seems it strange that thou shouldst live forever? Is it less strange that thou shouldst live
at all? This is a miracle; and that no more.
                                Edward Young

He sins against this life, who slights the next.
    Edward Young: *Night Thoughts,*
                            Night III, l. 399

Immortal! ages past, yet nothing gone!
Morn without eve! a race without a goal!
Unshorten'd by progression infinite!
Futurity for ever future! Life
Beginning still, where computation ends!
'Tis the description of a Deity!
    Edward Young: *Night Thoughts,*
                            Night VI, l. 542

'Tis immortality, 'tis that alone,
Amid life's pains, abasements, emptiness,
The soul can comfort, elevate, and fill.
That only, and that amply this performs.
    Edward Young: *Night Thoughts,*
                            Night VI, l. 573

But if man loses all, when life is lost,
He lives a coward, or a fool expires.
    Edward Young: *Night Thoughts,*
                            Night VII, l. 199

INCARNATION, THE

The one thoroughly laid down and safe way
to avoid all going wide of the truth is the
doctrine of the Incarnation—that one and
the same person is God and man; as God,
the end of our going; as man, the way we
are to go.
    St. Augustine: *The City of God,* XI

It is always safe to follow the religious belief
that our mother taught us; there never was
a mother yet who taught her child to be an
infidel.
                                Josh Billings

The doctrine of the incarnation is no un-
related speculation. It is the truth by which
we find God, and are found by God, both in
the common times and in times of crises. It
says to us that the glory of God can be revealed in the little place and in the everyday
event, as it was in the earthly life of Jesus;
and it makes us trust that the divine redeeming purpose cannot be killed by the evil
which may crucify it, and that in the love of
Christ the power of God stands by us even
when the world is dark.
    W. Russell Bowie: *The Chaplain,*
                            December, 1960

The incarnation is the supreme assertion
that only through the highest medium,
which is humanity, can the highest messages
be given to mankind.
                            Phillips Brooks

The wonder of the incarnation is not that God got himself embodied, but that he got himself expressed—expressed in the wonderful life and character of Christ.

William Newton Clarke

God clothed himself in man's vile flesh that so he might be weak enough to suffer woe.

John Donne: *Holy Sonnets,* XI

Only the Word made flesh can give any sort of hope in a world as grim and ugly and hard and sordid as ours.

Lynn Harold Hough

The Word of God, Jesus Christ, on account of his great love for mankind, became what we are in order to make us what he is himself.

St. Irenaeus: *Adversus haereses,* V

The mystery of the humanity of Christ, that He sunk Himself into our flesh, is beyond all human understanding.

Martin Luther: *Table Talk*

God is in our midst; he is now here. In him we live and move and have our being. Our very bodies become his temples, and our lives must be daily fashioned after the pattern of his presence.

J. C. Massee

The Word became flesh that he might become enfleshed in all men, thus crowning the created universe in the redemption of new-created souls.

F. F. Shannon

If we made God a little more real than otherwise he would be to any single human being, we have not wasted our little lives in a large world or lived in vain.

William Learoyd Sperry: *Strangers and Pilgrims*

And so the Word had flesh and wrought
With human hands the creed of creeds,
In loveliness of perfect deeds
More strong than all poetic thought.

Alfred, Lord Tennyson

INFIDELS, INFIDELITY

The great pillars and supporters of infidelity are either a vanity of appearing wiser than the rest of mankind, or an ostentation of courage in despising the terrors of another world.

Joseph Addison: *The Spectator*

Infidelity, indeed, is the root of all sin; for did man heartily believe the promises to obedience, and the threats to disobedience, they could hardly be so unreasonable as to forfeit the one or incur the other.

Isaac Barrow

The nurse of infidelity is sensuality.

Richard Cecil

Infidelity is one of the false coinages—a mass of base money that will not pass current with any heart that loves truly, or any head that thinks correctly.—It is a fearful blindness of the soul.

Thomas Chalmers

Infidelity and Faith look both through the same perspective-glass, but at contrary ends. Infidelity looks through the wrong end of the glass; and therefore, sees those objects near which are afar off, and makes great things little, diminishing the greatest spiritual blessings, and removing far from us threatened evils. Faith looks at the right end, and brings the blessings that are far off close to our eye, and multiplies God's mercies, which, in the distance, lost their greatness.

Joseph Hall

I do not know, sir, that the fellow is an infidel; but if he be an infidel, he is an infidel as a dog is an infidel; that is to say, he has never thought upon the subject.

Samuel Johnson

A sin so fearful that for the committing it both land and people must be destroyed, as it went with Jerusalem, with Rome, Greece, and other kingdoms.

Martin Luther: *Table Talk*

There is one single fact which we may oppose to all the wit and argument of infidelity, namely, that no man ever repented of being a Christian on his death-bed.

Hannah More

It is necessary to the happiness of man that he be mentally faithful to himself. Infidelity does not consist in believing or disbelieving; it consists in professing to believe what one does not believe.

Thomas Paine: *Age of Reason,* Pt. I

Infidelity reproves nothing that is bad. It only ridicules and denounces all that is good. It tears down, but never builds up; destroys, but never imparts life; attacks religion, but offers no adequate substitute.

Joseph R. Paxton

Faith in God hallows and confirms the union between parents and children, and subjects and rulers.—Infidelity relaxes every band, and nullifies every blessing.

Johann Heinrich Pestalozzi

Infidelity is seated in the heart; its origin is not in the head.—It is the wish that Christianity might not be true, that leads to an argument to prove it.

Charles Simmons

Infidelity has emanated chiefly from the learned.

Emanuel Swedenborg: *Heaven and Hell*

And a mouse is miracle enough to stagger sextillions of infidels.

Walt Whitman: *Leaves of Grass: Song of Myself,* 31

The wonder is, always and always, how there can be a mean man or an infidel.

Walt Whitman

J

JOY

Gladness of the heart is the life of man, and the joyfulness of a man prolongeth his days.

Apocrypha: Ecclesiasticus 30: 22

The Christian life that is joyless is a discredit to God and a disgrace to itself.

Maltbie D. Babcock

Joy is more divine than sorrow, for joy is bread and sorrow is medicine.

Henry Ward Beecher

O God, may I live to have one day of unsullied joy!

Ludwig von Beethoven: *The Testament of Heiligenstadt*

I have found that there is a tremendous joy in giving. It is a very important part of the joy of living.

William Black

Capacity for joy
Admits temptation.

Elizabeth Barrett Browning: *Aurora Leigh*, Bk. I, l. 703

Desire joy and thank God for it. Renounce it, if need be, for other's sake. That's joy beyond joy.

Robert Browning

All seek joy, but it is not found on earth.

St. John Chrysostom: *Homilies*, XVIII

All human joys are swift of wing,
For heaven doth so allot it;
That when you get an easy thing,
You find you haven't got it.

Eugene Field: *Ways of Life*

Joy is distinctly a Christian word and a Christian thing. It is the reverse of happiness. Happiness is the result of what happens of an agreeable sort. Joy has its springs deep down inside. And that spring never runs dry, no matter what happens. Only Jesus gives that joy. He had joy, singing its music within, even under the shadow of the cross. It is an unknown word and thing except as He has sway within.

Samuel Dickey Gordon

Real joy comes not from ease or riches or from the praise of men, but from doing something worth while.

Sir Wilfred Grenfell

It is a comely fashion to be glad,—
Joy is the grace we say to God.

Jean Ingelow: *Dominion*

To pursue joy is to lose it. The only way to get it is to follow steadily the path of duty, without thinking of joy, and then, like sheep, it comes most surely, unsought, and we "being in the way" the angel of God, bright-haired Joy, is sure to meet us.

Alexander MacLaren

There is joy in heaven when a tear of sorrow is shed in the presence of a truly understanding heart. And heaven will never weary of that joy.

Charles Malik: *YWCA Magazine*

Joy is the echo of God's life within us.

Joseph Marmion: *Orthodoxy*

Great joys, like griefs, are silent.

Shackerley Marmion: *Holland's Leaguer*, V

JOY

How fading are the joys we dote upon!
Like apparitions seen and gone;
But those which soonest take their flight
Are the most exquisite and strong;
Like Angel's visits short and bright,
Mortality's too weak to bear them long.

John Norris: *The Parting*, st. 4

Weeping may endure for a night, but joy cometh in the morning.

Old Testament: Psalms 30: 5

In the day of prosperity be joyful, but in the day of adversity consider.

Old Testament: Ecclesiastes 7: 14

Beauty for ashes, the oil of joy for mourning.

Old Testament: Isaiah 61: 3

The word "joy" is too great and grand to be confused with the superficial things we call happiness. It was joy and peace which Jesus said he left men in his will.

Kirby Page: *Living Joyously*, Holt, Rinehart & Winston, Inc.

The joy of heaven will begin as soon as we attain the character of heaven, and do its duties.

Theodore Parker

It is heaven's will for sorrow to follow joy.

Titus Maccius Plautus: *Amphitruo*, Act II, sc. 2, l. 635

For, when the power of imparting joy
Is equal to the will, the human soul
Requires no other Heaven.

Percy Bysshe Shelley: *Queen Mab*, Canto III, l. 11

If you have no joy in your religion, there's a leak in your Christianity somewhere.

W. A. ("Billy") Sunday

Joy to the world! the Lord is come;
Let earth receive her King.

Isaac Watts: *Psalm XCVIII*, st. 1

JUDGMENT, JUDGMENT DAY

A Last Judgment is not for the purpose of making Bad Men better, but for the Purpose of hindering them from oppressing the Good with Poverty & Pain . . .

William Blake: From Blake's MS Book concerning his picture of The Last Judgment

So, I think, God hides some souls away.
Sweetly to surprise us, the last day.

Mary Bolles Branch: *The Petrified Fern*

Foolish men imagine that because judgment for an evil thing is delayed, there is no justice, but only accident here below. Judgment for an evil thing is many times delayed some day or two, some century or two, but it is sure as life, it is sure as death!

Thomas Carlyle

You may juggle human laws, you may fool with human courts, but there is a judgment to come, and from it there is no appeal.

Orin Philip Gifford

Fools measure actions after they are done, by the event; wise men beforehand, by the rules of reason and right. The former look to the end to judge of the act. Let me look to the act, and leave the end to God.

Richard Hill

He has sounded forth the trumpet that shall never call retreat
He is sifting out the hearts of men before His Judgment Seat.

Julia Ward Howe: *Battle Hymn of the Republic*

God himself, sir, does not propose to judge man until the end of his days.

Samuel Johnson

The deeds we do, the words we say,
Into still air they seem to fleet,
We count them ever past;
But they shall last,—

In the dread judgment they
And we shall meet.

John Keble: *The Effect of Example*

Are you ready? Are you ready?
Ready for the Judgment Day?
  When the saints and the sinners
Shall be parted right and left—
Are you ready for the Judgment Day?

Methodist Hymn

In men whom men condemn as ill
I find so much of goodness still,
In men whom men pronounce divine
I find so much of sin and blot,
I do not dare to draw a line
Between the two, where God has not.

Joaquin Miller: *Byron*

The aged earth aghast
With terror of that blast
  Shall from the surface to the center shake,
When, at the world's last session,
The dreadful Judge in middle air shall
    spread
His throne.

John Milton: *On the Morning of Christ's
Nativity*

Flee from the wrath to come.

New Testament: Matthew 3: 7

Judge not, that ye be not judged.

New Testament: Matthew 7: 1

And why beholdest thou the mote that is in
thy brother's eye, but considereth not the
beam that is in thine own eye? Or how wilt
thou say to thy brother, Let me pull out the
mote out of thine eye; and, behold, a beam
is in thine own eye? Thou hypocrite, first cast
out the beam out of thine own eye; and then
shalt thou see clearly to cast out the mote
out of thy brother's eye.

New Testament: Matthew 7: 3–5

Therefore be ye also ready: for in such an
hour as ye think not the Son of man cometh.

New Testament: Matthew 24: 44

Judge not, and ye shall not be judged: condemn not, and ye shall not be condemned:
forgive, and ye shall be forgiven.

New Testament: Luke 6: 37

Out of thine own mouth will I judge thee.

New Testament: Luke 19: 22

The judgments of the Lord are true and
righteous altogether. More to be desired are
they than gold, yea, than much fine gold:
sweeter also than honey and the honeycomb.

Old Testament: Psalms 19: 9–10

Thou are weighed in the balances, and art
found wanting.

Old Testament: Daniel 5: 27

A thousand pounds and a bottle of hay
Is all one thing at Doomsday.

John Ray: *English Proverbs*

For every event is a judgment of God.

Johann Christoph Friedrich von Schiller:
Wallenstein's Death, I, 7, 32

Commonly we say a Judgment falls upon a
Man for something in him we cannot abide.

John Selden: *Table Talk: Judgments*

We shall be judged, not by what we might
have been, but what we have been.

William Sewell: *Passing Thoughts on
Religion: Sympathy in Gladness*

He that of greatest works is finisher
Oft does them by the weakest minister:
So holy writ in babes hath judgment shown,
When judges have been babes.

William Shakespeare: *All's Well That
Ends Well*, Act II, sc. 1, l. 139

Why, all the souls that were, were forfeit
    once;
And He that might the vantage best have
    took
Found out the remedy. How would you be,
If He, which is the top of judgement, should
But judge you as you are?

William Shakespeare: *Measure for
Measure*, Act II, sc. 2, l. 73

God judges a man not by the point he has reached, but by the way he is facing; not by distance, but by direction.

James S. Stewart

Till the sun grows cold,
And the stars are old,
And the leaves of the judgment Book unfold.

Bayard Taylor: *Bedouin Song*

If after death, love, comes a waking,
And in their camp so dark and still
The men of dust hear bugles, breaking
Their halt upon the hill.

To me the slow and silver pealing
That then the last high trumpet pours
Shall softer than the dawn come stealing,
For, with its call, comes yours!

Frederic Herbert Trench: *I Heard
a Soldier*

I dimly guess from blessings known
Of greater out of sight,
And, with the chastened Psalmist, own
His judgments too are right.

John Greenleaf Whittier: *The Eternal
Goodness*

Man judges from a partial view.
None ever yet his brother knew;
The Eternal Eye that sees the whole
May better read the darkened soul,
And find, to outward sense denied,
The flower upon its inmost side!

John Greenleaf Whittier: *The Pressed
Gentian*

JUSTICE

To be perfectly just is an attribute of the divine nature: to be so to the utmost of our abilities is the glory of man.

Joseph Addison

There is no virtue so truly great and godlike as justice.

Joseph Addison: *The Guardian*, no. 99

One hour of justice is worth a hundred of prayer.

Arab Proverb

Justice is that virtue of the soul which is distributive according to desert.

Aristotle: *Metaphysics: On the Virtues
and Vices, Justice*

The four pillars of government . . . religion, justice, counsel and treasure.

Sir Francis Bacon

It is due to Justice that man is a God to man and not a wolf.

Sir Francis Bacon: *De Augmentis
Scientiarum: Justitia*

The place of justice is a hallowed place.

Sir Francis Bacon: *Essays: Of Judicature*

For it is written by the finger of the Almighty in the ever-lasting tablets of the Universe that no nation can endure and prosper into and through whose life does not run the golden thread of equal, exact and universal Justice.

David Josiah Brewer

God's justice, tardy though it prove perchance
Rests never on the track until it reach Delinquency.

Robert Browning: *Cenciaja*

Those eternal laws of justice, which are our rule and our birthright.

Edmund Burke: *Impeachment of Warren
Hastings*

Heaven gives long life to the just and the intelligent.

Confucius: *The Book of History*

God aims at satisfying justice in the eternal damnation of sinners.

Jonathan Edwards: *God's Chief End in
Creation*

Who shall put his finger on the work of justice, and say, "It is there?" Justice is like the kingdom of God: it is not without us as a fact; it is within us as a great yearning.

George Eliot: *Romola*, Bk. III, ch. 7

Whoever fights, whoever falls,
Justice conquers, evermore. . . .
And he who battles on her side,
God, though he were ten times slain,
Crowns him victor glorified,
Victor over death and pain.

Ralph Waldo Emerson: *Voluntaries*,
Pt. IV

God's justice is a bed where we
Our anxious hearts may lay
And, weary with ourselves, may sleep
Our discontent away.
For right is right, since God is God;
And right the day must win;
To doubt would be disloyalty,
To falter would be sin.

Frederick William Faber

We evaluate our friends with a Godlike justice, but we want them to evaluate us with a Godlike compassion.

Sydney J. Harris: Chicago *Daily News*

Justice is vengeance dressed up in Sunday clothes.

Stephen Hequet

And Heav'n, that ev'ry virtue bears in mind,
Ev'n to the ashes of the just is kind.

Homer: *Iliad*, XXIV, 523

Impersonal as the justice of God.

Victor Hugo

Justice is truth in action.

Joseph Joubert: *Pensées*

Man is unjust, but God is just; and finally justice triumphs.

Henry Wadsworth Longfellow:
Evangeline, Pt. I, sec. 3, l. 34

But the sunshine aye shall light the sky,
As round and round we run;
And the Truth shall ever come uppermost,
And Justice shall be done.

Charles Mackay: *Eternal Justice*, st. 4

When twenty-six lynchers were turned loose in Greenville, South Carolina, Peter Marshall, chaplain of the United States Senate, told a congregation packed with Southerners, "Yes, Justice wears a blindfold, but that does not hold her tears."

Frank S. Mead: *Christian Herald*

Just are the ways of God,
And justifiable to men;
Unless there be who think not God at all.

John Milton: *Samson Agonistes*, l. 293

When a federal judge in Texas instructed a jury to return a verdict of innocent in a car theft case, the jury foreman dutifully announced: "We find the boy that stole the car not guilty, your honor."

Minneapolis *Tribune*

He that ruleth over men must be just.

Old Testament: II Samuel 23: 3

The path of the just is as the shining light, that shineth more and more unto the perfect day.

Old Testament: Proverbs 4: 18

None calleth for justice, nor any pleadeth for truth: they trust in vanity, and speak lies; they conceive mischief, and bring forth iniquity.

Old Testament: Isaiah 59: 4

Justice is the idea of God; the ideal of men; the rule of conduct writ in the nature of mankind.

Theodore Parker

God gives manhood but one clue to success, utter and exact justice; that, He guarantees, shall be always expediency.

Wendell Phillips

When Infinite Wisdom established the rule of the right and honesty, He saw to it that justice should be always in the highest expediency.

Wendell Phillips

And earthly power doth then show likest God's
When mercy seasons justice.

William Shakespeare: *The Merchant of Venice*, Act IV, sc. 1, l. 196

Truth is justice's handmaid, freedom is its child, peace is its companion, safety walks in its steps, victory follows in its train; it is the brightest emanation from the gospel; it is the attribute of God.

Sydney Smith, in Lady Holland's *Memoir*, Vol. I, p. 29

Of moral justice if thou scorn the rod, believe and tremble, thou art judged of God.

Milo Sweetman

It seems clear to me that God designed us to live in society—just as He has given the bees the honey; and as our social system could not subsist without the sense of justice and injustice, He has given us the power to acquire that sense.

Voltaire: *Letter to Frederick the Great*

The memory of the just survives in Heaven.

William Wordsworth: *The Excursion*, Bk. VII, l. 388

K

KINDNESS

The ministry of kindness is a ministry which may be achieved by all men, rich and poor, learned and illiterate. Brilliance of mind and capacity for deep thinking have rendered great service to humanity, but by themselves they are impotent to dry a tear or mend a broken heart.

Anonymous

Paradise is open to all kind hearts.

Pierre Jean de Béranger

If you treat your friend shabbily while he lives, you have no right to try to even up matters by whining over him when he is dead.

Joseph F. Berry

'Twas a thief said the last kind word to Christ:
Christ took the kindness and forgave the theft.

Robert Browning: *The Ring and the Book*, Pt. VI, l. 869

The heart benevolent and kind
The most resembles God.

Robert Burns: *A Winter Night*

Have you had a kindness shown?
Pass it on;
'Twas not given for thee alone,
Pass it on;
Let it travel down the years,
Let it wipe another's tears,
'Till in Heaven the deed appears—
Pass it on.

Henry Burton: *Pass It On*

Heaven in sunshine will requite the kind.

George Gordon, Lord Byron

The early Church unleashed a flood of kindness in a world of racial strife; the modern Church has too often unleashed a flood of resolutions.

Editorial: *Christianity Today*

Father and mother are kind, but God is kinder.

Danish Proverb

Better to do a kindness near at home than walk a thousand miles to burn incense.

The Defender

The greatest thing a man can do for his heavenly Father is to be kind to some of His other children.

Henry Drummond

Kindness has converted more sinners than zeal, eloquence or learning.

Frederick William Faber

Kind words are the music of the world. They have a power which seems to be beyond natural causes, as if they were some angel's song which had lost its way and come on earth. It seems as if they could almost do what in reality God alone can do—soften the hard and angry hearts of men. No one was ever corrected by a sarcasm—crushed, perhaps, if the sarcasm was clever enough, but drawn nearer to God, never.

Frederick William Faber

It was said of Henry Ward Beecher that no one ever felt the full force of his kindness until he did Beecher an injury.

Harry Emerson Fosdick: *Manhood of the Master*

KINDNESS

Make a rule, and pray to God to help you to keep it, never, if possible, to lie down at night without being able to say: "I have made one human being at least a little wiser, or a little happier, or at least a little better this day."

Charles Kingsley

Neither genius, fame, nor love show the greatness of the soul. Only kindness can do that.

Jean Baptiste Henri Lacordaire

Requite injury with kindness.

Lao-tze

The kindest are those who forgive and forget.

Megiddo Message

Jesus and Socrates, out of very different backgrounds, are saying the same thing. Intelligence is kindness. Kindness is intelligence. The fundamental, which the two terms suggest in different ways . . . is the same quality on which all human civilization is built.

Alexander Meiklejohn: W. L. Sperry,
*Religion and Education—Religion
in the Post-War World, Vol. IV,*
Harvard, 1945

God is merciful to those who are kind.

Moroccan Proverb

In her tongue is the law of kindness.

Old Testament: Proverbs 31: 26

Whoever gives a small coin to a poor man has six blessings bestowed upon him, but he who speaks a kind word to him obtains eleven blessings.

The Talmud

So many gods, so many creeds,
    So many paths that wind and wind,
    While just the art of being kind
Is all the sad world needs.

Ella Wheeler Wilcox: *The World's Need,*
Rand McNally & Co.

KINGDOM OF GOD

That best portion of a good man's life,
His little, nameless, unremembered acts
Of kindness and of love.

William Wordsworth: *Tintern Abbey*

KINGDOM OF GOD

His kingdom is coming; Oh, tell me the story!
    God's banner exalted shall be;
The earth shall be filled with His wonder
        and glory,
    As waters that cover the sea.

Anonymous

The kingdom of God will not come in a day; it will not be left with the morning milk.

S. Parkes Cadman

The kingdom of God is not realm but reign; not domain but dominion.

William Newton Clarke

The kingdom of God is a kingdom of love; and love is never a stagnant pool.

Henry W. DuBose

Wherever God rules over the human heart as King, there is the kingdom of God established.

Paul W. Harrison

The kingdom of God does not exist because of your effort or mine. It exists because God reigns. Our part is to enter this kingdom and bring our life under his sovereign will.

T. Z. Koo

We can have a world of peace, justice, happiness, the kingdom of God, as soon as we want it. Every new scientific discovery can bend to aid humanity if people will love Christ and one another. But we must pay a price.

Frank C. Laubach

It is easier for a camel to go through the eye of a needle, than for a rich man to enter into the kingdom of God.

New Testament: Matthew 19: 24

Suffer the little children to come unto me, and forbid them not: for of such is the kingdom of God

New Testament: Mark 10: 14

Blessed be ye poor: for yours is the kingdom of God.

New Testament: Luke 6: 20

Communism is the devil's latest substitute for the Christian concept of the Kingdom of God.

Frederick H. Olert

If you do not wish God's kingdom, don't pray for it. But if you do, you must do more than pray for it; you must work for it.

John Ruskin

If you want to work for the kingdom of God, and to bring it, and enter into it, there is just one condition to be first accepted. You must enter into it as children, or not at all.

John Ruskin

There is no structural organization of society which can bring about the coming of the Kingdom of God on earth, since all systems can be perverted by the selfishness of man.

William Temple, Archbishop of Canterbury: *The Malvern Manifesto*

L

LIFE

Man cannot live by bread alone,
  This has been proven o'er and o'er—
Yet still men try to satisfy
  The inner life with earthly store.

Anonymous

Our lives are a manifestation of what we
think about God.

Anonymous

There may be a Heaven;
  There must be a Hell;
Meanwhile, we have our life here—
  Well?

Anonymous

This is what Christianity is for—to teach
men the art of Life. And its whole curriculum lies in one word, "Learn of me."

Anonymous

Every man's life is a fairy tale, written by
God's fingers.

Hans Christian Andersen

This Being of mine, whatever it really is,
consists of a little flesh, a little breath, and
the ruling reason.

Marcus Aurelius: *Meditations*, Bk. II,
sec. 2

We live in deeds, not years; in thought, not
  breath;
In feelings, not in figures on a dial.
We should count time by heart-throbs. He
  most lives
Who thinks most, feels the noblest, acts the
  best.
Life's but a means unto an end; that end

Beginning, mean, and end of all things—
  God.

Philip James Bailey: *Festus: A Country
Town*

God asks no man whether he will accept life.
That is not the choice. You *must* take it.
The only choice is *how.*

Henry Ward Beecher: *Life Thoughts*

He liveth long who liveth well!
  All other life is short and vain;
He liveth longest who can tell
  Of living most for heavenly gain.

Horatius Bonar: *He Liveth Long Who
Liveth Well*

From fibers of pain and hope and trouble
  And toil and happiness,—one by one,—
Twisted together, or single or double,
  The varying thread of our life is spun.
Hope shall cheer though the chain be galling;
Light shall come though the gloom be falling;
Faith will list for the Master calling
  Our hearts to his rest,—when the day is
  done.

Alonzo B. Bragdon: *When the Day is Done*

There is not one life which the Life-giver
ever loses out of His sight: not one which
sins so that He casts it away; not one which
is not so near to Him that whatever touches
it touches Him with sorrow or with joy.

Phillips Brooks

Be such a man, and live such a life,
That if every man were such as you,
And every life a life like yours,
This earth would be God's Paradise.

Phillips Brooks

There is an eternity behind and an eternity before, and this little speck in the center, however long, is comparatively but a minute.

John Brown, after his arrest at Harper's Ferry

Life is a pure flame, and we live by an invisible sun within us.

Sir Thomas Browne: *Urn Burial*

I have lived,
And seen God's hand thro a life time,
And all was for best.

Robert Browning

A man can have but one life, and one death,
One heaven, one hell.

Robert Browning: *In a Balcony*

I count life just a stuff
To try the soul's strength on.

Ibid.

Life is probation, and the earth no goal
But starting-point of man.

Robert Browning: *The Ring and The Book*, Pt. X, l. 1436

So live that when thy summons comes to join
The innumerable caravan which moves
To that mysterious realm where each shall take
His chamber in the silent halls of death,
Thou goest not, like the quarry-slave at night,
Scourged to his dungeon, but sustained and soothed
By an unfaltering trust, approach thy grave
Like one that wraps the drapery of his couch
About him, and lies down to pleasant dreams.

William Cullen Bryant

Archbishop Leighton used often to say that if he were to choose a place to die in, it should be an inn; it looking like a pilgrim's going home, to whom this world was all as an inn, and who was weary with the noise and confusion in it . . . And he obtained what he desired, for he died at the Bell Inn in Warwick Lane.

Gilbert Burnet: *History of My Own Times*

Mankind a future life must have to balance life's unequal lot.

Sir Richard Francis Burton: *The Kasida of Haji Abdu El-Yazd*

Life is a ladder infinite-stepped, that hide its rungs from human eyes;
Planted its foot in chaos gloom, its head soars high above the skies.

Ibid

Every man's life is a plan of God.

Horace Bushnell

Live as with God; and whatever be your calling, pray for the gift that will perfectly qualify you in it.

Horace Bushnell

Thy life is no idle dream, but a solemn reality; it is thine own, and it is all thou hast to front eternity with.

Thomas Carlyle

The poorest day that passes over us is the conflux of two Eternities; it is made up of currents that issue from the remotest Past and flow onwards into the remotest Future.

Thomas Carlyle: *Essays: Signs of the Times*

One life;—a little gleam of Time between two Eternities.

Thomas Carlyle: *Heroes and Hero-Worship*, Lect. V

He who lives well is the best preacher.

Miguel de Cervantes: *Don Quixote*, VI, 19

Life is a fragment, a moment between two eternities; influenced by all that has preceded, and to influence all that follows. The only way to illumine it is by extent of view.

William Ellery Channing: *Note-book: Life*

The creed of the true saint is to make the most of life, and to make the best of it.

Edwin Hubbell Chapin

The rule that governs my life is this: Anything that dims my vision of Christ, or takes away my taste for Bible study, or cramps my prayer life, or makes Christian work difficult, is wrong for me, and I must, as a Christian, turn away from it.

J. Wilbur Chapman

Why should a man certain of immortality think of his life at all?

Joseph Conrad: *Under Western Eyes*, Pt. II, l. 4, J. M. Dent & Sons, Ltd.

No man is living at his best who is not living at his best spiritually.

W. Marshall Craig

Perfect conformity to the will of God is the sole sovereign and complete liberty.

Jean Henri Merle D'Aubigné

One should never think of death. One should think of life. That is real piety.

Benjamin Disraeli: *Endymion*, ch. 27

"Live, while you live," the epicure would say,
"And seize the pleasures of the present day,"
"Live, while you live," the sacred *preacher* cries,
"And give to God each moment as it flies,"
"Lord, in my views let both united be;
"I live in *pleasure*, when I live to *Thee*."

Philip Doddridge: Lines written under Motto of his Family Album

But I believe that God is overhead;
And as life is to the living, so death is to the dead.

Mary Mapes Dodge: *The Two Mysteries*, st. 5

I count all that part of my life lost which I spent not in communion with God, or in doing good.

John Donne

A man's ingress into the world is naked and bare,
His progress through the world is trouble and care;

And lastly, his egress out of the world, is nobody knows where.
If we do well here, we shall do well there;
I can tell you no more if I preach a whole year.

John Edwin: *The Eccentricities of John Edwin*, Vol. I, p. 74

Little self-denials, little honesties, little passing words of sympathy, little nameless acts of kindness, little silent victories over favorite temptations—these are the silent threads of gold which, when woven together, gleam out so brightly in the pattern of life that God approves.

Frederic William Farrar

Life is like a library owned by an author. In it are a few books which he wrote himself, but most of them were written for him.

Harry Emerson Fosdick

The facts of existence are like so much loose type which can be set up into many meanings. One man leaves these facts in chaotic disarrangement, or sets them up into cynical affirmations, and he exists. But another man takes the same facts and by spiritual insight makes them mean glorious things and he lives indeed.

Harry Emerson Fosdick

He lives long that lives well; and time misspent is not lived, but lost. God is better than his promise if he takes from him a long lease, and gives him a freehold of a better value.

Thomas Fuller

We are in this life as it were in another man's house . . . In heaven is our home, in the world is our Inn: do not so entertain thyself in the Inn of this world for a day as to have thy mind withdrawn from longing after thy heavenly home.

Paul Gerhardt: *Meditations*, XXXVIII

A useless life is only an early death.

Johann Wolfgang von Goethe

There are nine requisites for contented living: health enough to make work a pleasure;

wealth enough to support your needs; strength to battle with difficulties and overcome them; grace enough to confess your sins and forsake them; patience enough to toil until some good is accomplished; charity enough to see some good in your neighbor; love enough to move you to be useful and helpful to others; faith enough to make real the things of God; hope enough to remove all anxious fears concerning the future.

Johann Wolfgang von Goethe

Life is the childhood of our immortality.

Johann Wolfgang von Goethe

In the morning of life, work, in the midday give counsel, in the evening pray.

Hesiod: *Harpocration*

Life seems to me like a Japanese picture which our imagination does not allow to end with the margin.

Justice Oliver Wendell Holmes, Jr.: *Message to the Federal Bar Association, 1932,* Harvard University Press

Life, as we call it, is nothing but the edge of the boundless ocean of existence where it comes on soundings.

Oliver Wendell Holmes, Sr.: *The Professor at the Breakfast-Table,* V

Live blameless; God is near.

Inscription over door of the House of Linnaeus, Sweden

The great use of life is to spend it for something that outlasts it.

William James (permission to reprint granted by Paul R. Reynolds & Son)

Teach me to live that I may dread
The grave as little as my bed.

Thomas Ken: *Evening Hymn*

If we are to survive the atomic age, we must have something to live by, to live on, and to live for. We must stand aside from the world's conspiracy of fear and hate and grasp once more the great monosyllables of life;

faith, hope and love. Men must live by these if they live at all under the crushing weight of history.

O. P. Kretzmann, D.D.: *Illinois Medical Journal*

And in the wreck of noble lives
Something immortal still survives.

Henry Wadsworth Longfellow: *Building of the Ship,* l. 375

Life is real! Life is earnest!
And the grave is not its goal.

Henry Wadsworth Longfellow: *A Psalm of Life*

Oh thou child of many prayers!
Life hath quicksands,—life hath snares!

Henry Wadsworth Longfellow: *Maidenhood*

Someone has said that all living is just learning the meaning of words. That does not mean the long ten syllable words we have to look up in the dictionary. The really great words to master are short ones—work, love, hope, joy, pain, home, child, life, death.

Halford E. Luccock: *Christian Herald*

Religion is fitted to make us better in every situation in life.

Mary Lyon

Only those are fit to live who are not afraid to die.

General Douglas MacArthur to Filipino Air Force, 1941

Make sure the thing you're living for is worth dying for.

Charles Mayes: *World Vision Magazine*

Life is a mission. Every other definition of life is false, and leads all who accept it astray. Religion, science, philosophy, though still at variance upon many points, all agree in this, that every existence is an aim.

Giuseppe Mazzini: *Life and Writings,* ch. 5

The final test of our lives will not be how much we have lived but *how* we have lived, not how tempestuous our lives have been, but how much bigger, better and stronger these trials have left us. Not how much money, fame or fortune we have laid up here on earth, but how many treasures we have laid up in heaven!

Megiddo Message

Life's a voyage that's homeward bound.

Herman Melville

Mohammed's truth lay in a holy Book, Christ's in a sacred Life.

Richard Monckton Milnes:
Mohammedanism

Nor love thy life, nor hate; but what thou liv'st
Live well; how long or short permit to Heav'n.

John Milton: *Paradise Lost,* Bk. XI, l. 553

Life is vain; a little love, a little hate, and then—Good-day! Life is short; a little hoping, a little dreaming, and then—Good-night! Life is whatever God wills it; and, such as it is, it's enough!

Léon van Montenaeken: *Peu de Chose et Presque Trop*

So live that after the minister has ended his remarks, those present will not think they have attended the wrong funeral.

The Mortarboard

Strait is the gate, and narrow is the way, which leadeth unto life.

New Testament: Matthew 7: 14

He that findeth his life shall lose it: and he that loseth his life for my sake shall find it.

New Testament: Matthew 10: 39

In him was life; and the life was the light of men.

New Testament: John 1: 4

I am the bread of life.

New Testament: John 6: 35

I am come that they might have life, and that they might have it more abundantly.

New Testament: John 10: 10b

I am the way, the truth, and the life: no man cometh unto the Father, but by me.

New Testament: John 14: 6

The gift of God is eternal life.

New Testament: Romans 6: 23

To live is Christ, and to die is gain.

New Testament: Philippians 1: 21

What is your life? It is even a vapour, that appeareth for a little time, and then vanisheth away.

New Testament: James 4: 14

Be thou faithful unto death, and I will give thee a crown of life.

New Testament: Revelation 2: 10

I would not live alway: let me alone; for my days are vanity.

Old Testament: Job 7: 16

Lord, make me to know mine end, and the measure of my days, what it is; that I may know how frail I am.

Old Testament: Psalms 39: 4

But helpless Pieces of the Game He plays
Upon this Checker-board of Nights and Days;
Hither and thither moves, and checks, and slays,
And one by one back in the Closet lays.

Omar Khayyám: *Rubáiyát,* LXIX

This also, that I live, I consider a gift of God.

Ovid: *Tristia,* Bk. I, eleg. 1, l. 20

Love to his soul gave eyes; he knew things are not as they seem.
The dream is his real life: the world around him is the dream.

Francis Turner Palgrave: *Dream of Maxim Wledig*

The truest end of life is to know the life that never ends.

William Penn

Live every day as if it were your last. Do every job as if you were the boss. Drive as if all other vehicles were police cars. Treat everybody else as if he were you.

Phoenix Flame

The boundaries which divide Life from Death are at best shadowy and vague. Who shall say where the one ends, and where the other begins?

Edgar Allan Poe: The Premature Burial

Make no doubt of it, to have had an unhappy life is to have failed in life. It is the one consummate error, and around the death-bed of such a one the very angels weep.

Llewelyn Powys: Impassioned Clay, p. 98

My soul, sit thou a patient looker-on;
Judge not the play before the play is done:
Her plot hath many changes; every day
Speaks a new scene; the last act crowns the play.

Francis Quarles: Respice Finem

And up from the pits when these shiver, and
  up from the heights when those shine,
Twin voices and shadows swim starward, and
  the essence of life is divine.

Richard Realf: Indirection

Life, like the waters of the seas, freshens only when it ascends toward heaven.

Jean Paul Richter

Many think themselves to be truly God-fearing when they call this world a valley of tears. But I believe they would be more so, if they called it a happy valley. God is more pleased with those who think everything right in the world, than with those who think nothing right. With so many thousand joys, is it not black ingratitude to call the world a place of sorrow and torment?

Jean Paul Richter

The purpose of life is not to be happy—but to matter, to be productive, to be useful, to have it make some difference that you lived at all.

Leo Rosten: Library Journal, June 1, 1962

I believe that the true purpose of education is not only to fill man's mind with knowledge and his belly with food, but to deepen his spiritual insights.

David Sarnoff: Teacher's College Record October, 1960

Our todays make our tomorrows, and our present lives determine the bridge on which we must enter the next life.

Minot J. Savage

By having reverence for life, we enter into a spiritual relation with the world.

Albert Schweitzer: Atlantic Monthly

Life is neither a good nor an evil; it is simply the place where good and evil exist.

Seneca: Epistolae ad Lucilium, Epis. XCIX, 12

Life . . . is a tale
Told by an idiot, full of sound and fury,
Signifying nothing.

William Shakespeare: Macbeth, Act V, sc. 5, l. 26

Peace, peace! he is not dead, he doth not sleep—
He hath awakened from the dream of life.

Percy Bysshe Shelley: Adonais

The One remains, the many change and pass;
Heaven's light forever shines, Earth's shadows fly;
Life, like a dome of many-coloured glass,
Stains the white radiance of Eternity.

Ibid.

We have two lives;
The soul of man is like the rolling world,
One half in day, the other dipt in night;

'he one has music and the flying cloud,
'he other, silence and the wakeful stars.
> Alexander Smith: *Horton*, l. 76

The end of life is to be like God, and the
oul following God will be like him.
> Socrates

Man is an organ of life, and God alone is
life.
> Emanuel Swedenborg: *True Christian
> Religion*, par. 504

But this thing is God, to be man with thy
> might,
To grow straight in the strength of thy spirit,
> and live out thy life as the light.
> Algernon Charles Swinburne: *Hertha*,
> st. 15

Our life is scarce the twinkle of a star
In God's eternal day.
> Bayard Taylor: *Autumnal Vespers*

Life is the gift of God but it is capital that
must be spent or it dissipates.
> Charles Templeton: *Life Looks Up*,
> Harper & Row, Publishers, Inc.

My life is like a stroll upon the beach.
> Henry David Thoreau: *A Week on the
> Concord and Merrimack Rivers*

The only significance of life consists in helping to establish the kingdom of God; and this
can be done only by means of the acknowledgment and profession of the truth by each
one of us.
> Leo Tolstoy: *The Kingdom of God*, ch. 12

I desire to have both heaven and hell ever in
my eye, while I stand on this isthmus of life,
between two boundless oceans.
> John Wesley: *Letter to Charles Wesley*

Some laugh, while others mourn;
> Some toil, while others pray;
One dies, and one is born:
> So runs the world away.
> Samuel Wesley: *The Way of the World*

We are immortal till our work is done.
> George Whitefield

Take care of your life; and the Lord will take
care of your death.
> George Whitefield

Our lives are albums written through
With good or ill, with false or true;
And as the blessed angels turn
> The pages of our years,
God grant they read the good with smiles,
And blot the ill with tears!
> John Greenleaf Whittier: *Written in a
> Lady's Album*

Our lives are songs; God writes the words
And we set them to music at pleasure;
And the song grows glad, or sweet or sad,
As we choose to fashion the measure.
> Ella Wheeler Wilcox: *Our Lives*, st. 102,
> Rand McNally & Co.

Ah! somehow life is bigger after all
Than any painted Angel could we see
The God that is within us!
> Oscar Wilde: *Humanitad*, st. 60

THE LORD'S PRAYER

I think it is the most fearful prayer to pray
in the world.
> Henry Ward Beecher

The prayer "Thy Kingdom come," if we
only knew, is asking God to conduct a major
operation.
> George A. Buttrick: *So We Believe, So We
> Pray*, Abingdon Press

I desire no other proof of Christianity than
the Lord's Prayer.
> Madame Anne Germaine de Staël

The Lord's Prayer is the prayer above all
prayers. It is a prayer which the most high
Master taught us, wherein are comprehended
all spiritual and temporal blessings, and the

strongest comforts in all trials, temptations and troubles, even in the hour of death.

Martin Luther: *Table Talk*

The Lord's Prayer is not, as some fancy, the easiest, the most natural of all devout utterances. It may be committed to memory quickly, but it is slowly learned by heart.

John F. D. Maurice

Do you wish to find out the really sublime? Repeat the Lord's Prayer.

Napoleon Bonaparte: *Sayings of Napoleon*

Begin the day with Christ and His prayer— you need no other. Creedless, with it you have religion; creed-stuffed, it will leaven any theological dough in which you stick.

Sir William Osler

The Lord's Prayer, for a succession of solemn thought, for fixing the attention upon a few great points, for suitableness to every condition, for sufficiency, for conciseness without obscurity, for the weight and real importance of its petition, is without equal or rivalry.

William Paley

I believe I should have been swept away by the flood of French infidelity, if it had not been for one thing, the remembrance of the time when my sainted mother used to make me kneel by her side, taking my little hands in hers, and caused me to repeat the Lord's Prayer.

John Randolph

The Lord's Prayer is short and mysterious, and like the treasures of the Spirit, full of wisdom and latent senses: it is not improper to draw forth these excellencies which are intended and signified by every petition, that by so excellent an authority we may know what it is lawful to beg of God.

Jeremy Taylor

The Lord's Prayer contains the sum total of religion and morals.

Arthur Wellesley, Duke of Wellington

LOVE

If you have to tell your children that yo love them, then you certainly do not.

Anonymou

The Holiness of God excuses no sin, but th love of God forgives all sin through Chris

Anonymou

Absence sharpens love, presence strengthen it.

Anonymou

Like hash, love can be enjoyed only by on who has confidence in it.

Anonymou

Love is more than a characteristic of God it is His character.

Anonymou

Love is the doorway through which th human soul passes from selfishness to servic and from solitude to kinship with all man kind.

Anonymou

Love is the fire of life; it either consumes o purifies.

Anonymous

Love is the key to the universe which unlocks all doors.

Anonymous

Love is the only service that power cannot command and money cannot buy.

Anonymous

Love makes people look at the bright side of things. They do see the bad things, but they make a great effort to see the good, so they do see the good.

Anonymous

Love seeks not limits but outlets.

Anonymous

The heart that loves is always young.

Anonymous

The love that kept us through the passing
   night
Will guide and keep us still.

Anonymous

To love abundantly is to live abundantly,
and to love forever is to live forever.

Anonymous

We should love those who point out our
faults, but we seldom do.

Anonymous

Love rules without a sword,
Love binds without a cord.

Anonymous

There is a Law that man should love his
neighbor as himself. In a few hundred years
it should be as natural to mankind as breathing or the upright gait; but if he does not
learn it he must perish.

Alfred Adler: *Social Interest*

By the law of love, above every other law,
men ought to live. It provides the constraining dynamic for spiritual and moral achieve-
ment. God gave the law and to live by it
is to live on the highest level of human
experience.

Clifton J. Allen: *Points for Emphasis*,
Broadman Press

To love anyone is nothing else than to wish
that person good.

St. Thomas Aquinas

No one loves the man whom he fears.

Aristotle

It is love that asks, that seeks, that knocks,
that finds, and that is faithful to what it finds.

St. Augustine

Love, and do what you like.

St. Augustine

To be loved, love.

Decimus Magnus Ausonius: *Epigrams*

Respect is what we owe; love, what we give.

Philip James Bailey

Ask not of me, love, what is love?
Ask what is good of God above—
Ask of the great sun what is light—
Ask what is darkness of the night—
Ask sin of what may be forgiven—
Ask what is happiness of Heaven—
Ask what is folly of the crowd—
Ask what is fashion of the shroud—
Ask what is sweetness of thy kiss—
Ask of thyself what beauty is.

Philip James Bailey: *Festus: A Large
Party and Entertainment*

Love spends his all, and still hath store.

Ibid.

Love is to the moral nature exactly what the
sun is to the earth.

Honoré de Balzac

I never knew a night so black
   Light failed to follow in its track.
I never knew a storm so gray
   It failed to have its clearing day.
I never knew such bleak despair
   That there was not a rift somewhere.
I never knew an hour so drear
   Love could not fill it full of cheer.

John Kendrick Bangs

Wisdom has nothing to do with love.

Philip Barry: *You and I*, Act III

A "bit of love" is the only bit that will
bridle the tongue.

Fred Beck

It is one of the severest tests of friendship to
tell your friend his faults. So to love a man
that you cannot bear to see a stain upon him,
and to speak painful truth through loving
words, that is friendship.

Henry Ward Beecher

Love is not a possession but a growth. The
heart is a lamp with just oil enough to burn
for an hour, and if there be no oil to put in

again its light will go out. God's grace is the oil that fills the lamp of love.

Henry Ward Beecher

Love is ownership. We own whom we love. The universe is God's because he loves.

Henry Ward Beecher

Love is the medicine of all moral evil. By it the world is to be cured of sin.

Henry Ward Beecher

Of all earthly music that which reaches farthest into heaven is the beating of a truly loving heart.

Henry Ward Beecher

We never know how much one loves till we know how much he is willing to endure and suffer for us; and it is the suffering element that measures love. The characters that are great must, of necessity, be characters that shall be willing, patient and strong to endure for others. To hold our nature in the willing service of another, is the divine idea of manhood, of the human character.

Henry Ward Beecher

Love demands all, and has a right to all.

Ludwig von Beethoven: Letter to the Countess Guicciordi

One hour of downright love is worth an hour of dully living on.

Aphra Behn: *The Rover*

It is only the souls that do not love that go empty in this world.

Robert Hugh Benson: *The History of Richard Raynal Solitary*

What we love we shall grow to resemble.

St. Bernard of Clairvaux

The true measure of loving God is to love him without measure.

St. Bernard of Clairvaux

Love looks through a telescope; envy, through a microscope.

Josh Billings

Love is that orbit of the restless soul
Whose circle grazes the confines of space,
Bounding within the limits of its race
Utmost extremes.

George Henry Boker: *Sonnet: Love*

Any old woman can love God better than a doctor of theology can.

St. Bonaventure

The mind has a thousand eyes,
The heart but one;
Yet the light of a whole life dies
When love is done.

Francis William Bourdillon: *The Night Has a Thousand Eyes*

It is ever the invisible that is the object of our profoundest worship. With the lover it is not the seen but the unseen that he muses upon.

Christian Nestell Bovee

The difference between "duty" and "love" is that the first represents Sinai and the second represents Calvary.

Richard Braunstein

Where love is, there's no lack.

Richard Brome: *A Jovial Crew*, Act III

Now God be thanked Who has matched us with His hour,
And caught our youth, and wakened us from sleeping . . .
And all the little emptiness of love!

Rupert Brooke: "Peace," *The Collected Poems of Rupert Brooke,* reprinted by permission of Dodd, Mead & Company, Sidgwick & Jackson, Ltd. and McClelland and Stewart, Ltd.

Love is a tender plant; when properly nourished, it becomes sturdy and enduring, but neglected it will soon wither and die.

Hugh B. Brown

Whoever lives true life will love true love.

Elizabeth Barrett Browning: *Aurora Leigh*, I

Whoso loves believes the impossible.

Elizabeth Barrett Browning: *Aurora Leigh*, V

I think, am sure, a brother's love exceeds All the world's loves in its unworldliness.

Robert Browning: *A Blot on the 'Scutcheon*, Act II, sc. 1

Love is not a levelling; love meets everyone as the person he is and takes him seriously in his particular being. To confront the representatives of political power with the intention of giving them their due, is an outworking of love.

Emil Brunner: *The Letter to the Romans* (tr. by H. A. Kennedy). Copyright, 1959, Lutterworth Press. Used by permission

Faith has to do with the basis, the ground on which we stand. Hope is reaching out for something to come. Love is just being there and acting.

Emil Brunner: *Faith, Hope and Love*, Copyright, 1956, W. L. Jenkins. The Westminster Press. Used by permission

Love does not die easily. It is a living thing. It thrives in the face of all life's hazards, save one—neglect.

James D. Bryden: *Presbyterian Life*

It is astonishing how little one feels poverty when one loves.

John Bulwer

And this is that Homer's golden chain, which reacheth down from heaven to earth, by which every creature is annexed, and depends on his Creator.

Robert Burton: *Anatomy of Melancholy*, Pt. III, sec. 1, mem. 1, subsec. 7

To love God is to have good health, good looks, good sense, experience, a kindly nature, and a fair balance of cash in hand. We know that all things work together for good to them that love God.

Samuel Butler

Yes, Love indeed is light from heaven;
A spark of that immortal fire
With angels shared, by Allah given,
To lift from earth our low desire.

George Gordon, Lord Byron: *The Giaour*, l. 1131

Devotion wafts the mind above,
But Heaven itself descends in love;
A feeling from the Godhead caught,
To wean from self each sordid thought;
A Ray of him who form'd the whole;
A Glory circling round the soul!

George Gordon, Lord Byron: *The Giaour*, l. 1135

Soon or late love is his own avenger.

George Gordon, Lord Byron: *Don Juan*, IV

Love! the surviving gift of Heaven,
The choicest sweet of Paradise,
In life's else bitter cup distilled.

Thomas Campbell: *Ode to the Memory of Burns*, l. 16

Love isn't like a reservoir. You'll never drain it dry. It's much more like a natural spring. The longer and the farther it flows, the stronger and the deeper and the clearer it becomes.

Eddie Cantor: *The Way I See It* (Prentice-Hall)

Love is ever the beginning of knowledge, as fire is of light.

Thomas Carlyle

There is nothing so loyal as love.

Alice Cary

These Christians love each other even before they are acquainted.

St. Celsus

We ought to love our Maker for His own sake, without either hope of good or fear of pain.

Miguel de Cervantes

The cure for all the ills and wrongs, the cares, the sorrows, and the crimes of humanity, all lie in that one word "love." It is the divine vitality that everywhere produces and restores life. To each and every one of us, it gives the power of working miracles if we will.

Lydia Maria Child

He prayeth best, who loveth best,
All things both great and small;
For the dear God who loveth us,
He made and loveth all.

Samuel Taylor Coleridge

Love Laughs at Locksmiths.

George Colman the Younger (Title of Comedy)

Can there be a love which does not make demands on its object?

Confucius: Analects

Love, like a spring rain, is pretty hard to be in the middle of without getting some on you.

Reprinted from The Country Parson by Frank A. Clark, by permission of The Register and Tribune Syndicate

Lukewarmness I account a sin,
As great in love as in religion.

Abraham Cowley: The Request

Life bears Love's cross, death brings Love's crown.

Dinah Maria Mulock Craik: Lettice

You must love the poor very much, or they will hate you for giving them bread.

St. Vincent de Paul

Love is a symbol of eternity. It wipes out all sense of time, destroying all memory of a beginning and all fear of an end.

Madame Anne Germaine de Staël: Corinne

Love: A season's pass on the shuttle betwee heaven and hell.

Don Dickerma

We are all born for love; it is the principl of existence and its only end.

Benjamin Disraeli: Sybi

Life is given to the peaceful, and death i given to the guilty, the peaceful being "h who does what is loved," and the guilty, "h who does what is hated."

Document of 3500 B.C

Instead of allowing yourself to be so un happy, just let your love grow as God want it to grow; seek goodness in others, love mor persons more; love them more impersonally more unselfishly, without thought of return The return, never fear, will take care of itself

Henry Drummonc

The pains of love be sweeter far
Than all other pleasures are.

John Dryder

Love is love's reward.

John Dryden: Palamon and Arcite

Most men need more love than they deserve.

Marie von Ebner-Eschenbach

To infinite, ever-present Love, all is Love, and there is no error, no sin, sickness, nor death.

Mary Baker Eddy: Science and Health, p. 567: 7–8

Love, which is the essence of God, is not for levity, but for the total worth of man.

Ralph Waldo Emerson: Essays, First Series: Friendship

The solid, solid universe
Is pervious to Love;
With bandaged eyes he never errs,
Around, below, above,
His binding light
He flingeth white

On God's and Satan's brood,
  And reconciles
  By mystic wiles
The evil and the good.
  Ralph Waldo Emerson: *Cupido*

Love makes the world go round.
  English Proverb

Love will find a way.
  English Proverb

Love knows no mean or measure.
  Phineas Fletcher: *Piscatory Eclogues*

If you would be loved, love and be lovable.
  Benjamin Franklin: *Poor Richard's Almanac*

Love is wont rather to ascend than descend.
  Thomas Fuller: *Gnomologia*

There is more Pleasure in loving, than in being beloved.
  Ibid.

Thou canst not pray to God without praying to Love, but mayest pray to Love without praying to God.
  Richard Garnett: *De Flagello Myrteo,* XIII

Perfect love casteth out prudery together with fear.
  Richard Garnett: *De Flagello Myrteo,* LIX

We are shaped and fashioned by what we love.
  Johann Wolfgang von Goethe

The best way to know God is to love many things.
  Vincent van Gogh

Love: Love is not blind—it sees more, not less. But because it sees more, it is willing to see less.
  Rabbi Julius Gordon

There is no heaven like mutual love.
  George Granville: *Peleus and Thetis*

Love and hatred are natural exaggerators.
  Hebrew Proverb

If you would be loved, love.
  Hecato: *Fragments*

The deepest truth blooms only from the deepest love.
  Heinrich Heine

Love, like the opening of the heavens to the saints, shows for a moment, even to the dullest man, the possibilities of the human race. He has faith, hope, and charity for another being, perhaps but the creation of his imagination; still it is a great advance for a man to be profoundly loving, even in his imagination.
  Sir Arthur Helps

Love makes all hard hearts gentle.
  George Herbert: *Outlandish Proverbs*

Love rules his kingdom without a sword.
  Ibid.

No man at one time can be wise and love.
  Robert Herrick

Love is a circle, that doth restless move
In the same sweet eternity of love.
  Robert Herrick: *Love, What It Is*

Love is a thing most nice; and must be fed
To such a height; but never surfeited.
  Robert Herrick: *Hesperides*

Divine love is a sacred flower, which in its early bud is happiness, and in its full bloom is heaven.
  Eleanor Louisa Hervey

Who says pull never gets you anywhere? If love tugs at your heartstrings, you're sitting on top of the world.
  Burton Hillis: *Better Homes and Gardens,* Meredith Publishing Co.

In all the crowded universe
There is but one stupendous word: Love.
There is no tree that rears its crest,
No fern or flower that cleaves the sod
Nor bird that sings above its nest,
But tries to speak this word of God.

Josiah Gilbert Holland

As love is never perfect, a cockney prefixing
an "h" to his "eight" seems to say truly,
"Even in 'I love you,' there are hate letters."

John Andrew Holmes: *Telescope
Messenger*

Love is the greatest constraining power in
the world. Tell me what you love, and I will
tell you what you are. The man who loves
needs no law to impel him to action. This
works on both sides of the moral line. The
man who loves right and righteousness will
do right, law or no law, while the man who
loves wrong will do wrong in spite of all law.

Home Missions

Love is the thing that enables a woman to
sing while she mops up the floor after her
husband has walked across it in his barn
boots.

Hoosier Farmer

While faith makes all things possible, it is
love that makes all things easy.

Evan H. Hopkins: *Wesleyan Methodist*

In love there are two evils: war and peace.

Horace: *Satires,* II

Tell me whom you love, and I will tell you
what you are.

Arsène Houssaye

The love of wealth makes bitter men; the
love of God, better men.

W. L. Hudson

The greatest happiness of life is the conviction that we are loved—loved for ourselves,
or rather, loved in spite of ourselves.

Victor Hugo

If we are to make a mature adjustment to
life, we must be able to give and receive love.

Anna Trego Hunter

That divine swoon.

Robert Green Ingersoll: *Orthodoxy.
Works,* Vol. II, p. 420

Who loves, fears.

Italian Proverb

Nobody will know what you mean by saying
that "God is love" unless you act it as well.

Lawrence Pearsall Jacks

It is a beautiful necessity of our nature to
love something.

Douglas Jerrold

Love is the wisdom of the fool and the folly
of the wise.

Samuel Johnson

If we spend our lives in loving, we have no
leisure to complain, or to feel unhappiness.

Joseph Joubert

Love is never without jealousy.

James Kelly: *Complete Collection of
Scottish Proverbs*

Give even to those who revile you and persecute you and say all manner of evil against
you—that is the supreme test of Christian
love as Christ taught it.

Timothy Kendall

If the tender, profound, and sympathizing
love, practised and recommended by Jesus,
were paramount in every heart, the loftiest
and most glorious idea of human society
would be realized, and little be wanting to
make this world a kingdom of heaven.

Friedrich Adolf Krummacher

Man, while he loves, is never quite depraved.

Charles Lamb

The heart of him who truly loves is a paradise on earth; he has God in himself, for God is love.

Abbé Félicité Robert de Lamennais

Love is the leech of life, next to our Lord,
It is the graft of peace, the nearest road to heaven.

William Langland: *Piers Plowman*

By the accident of fortune a man may rule the world for a time, but by virtue of love he may rule the world forever.

Lao-tze: *The Simple Way*

It is with true love as with ghosts. Everyone talks of it, but few have ever seen it.

François de La Rochefoucauld: *Maximes*

There is only one kind of love, but there are a thousand imitations.

Ibid.

We are nearer loving those who hate us than those who love us more than we like.

Ibid.

As every lord giveth a certain livery to his servants, love is the very livery of Christ. Our Savior who is the Lord above all lords, would have his servants known by their badge, which is love.

Hugh Latimer

A man is not where he lives, but where he loves.

Latin Proverb

Love cannot be commanded.

Latin Proverb

There can be no peace on earth until we have learned to respect the dignity of man and are willing to build on the foundation of human love the kind of world that the great teachers of mankind have portrayed to us from the time of the Ten Commandments and the Sermon on the Mount. These are the true lessons of mortal life.

David Lawrence: "Wisdom In a Troubled World," *U. S. News and World Report,* February 8, 1960

If Satan knew how to love he would cease being bad.

Le Digeste Français, Montreal

Without love, life is pointless and dangerous. Man is on his way to Venus, but he still hasn't learned to live with his wife. Man has succeeded in increasing his life span, yet he exterminates his brothers six million at a whack. Man now has the power to destroy himself and his planet; depend upon it, he will—should he cease to love.

Harper Lee: "Love—In Other Words," *Vogue,* April 15, 1961

How shall I do to love? Believe. How shall I do to believe? Love.

Robert Leighton

God hears no sweeter music than the cracked chimes of the courageous human spirit ringing in imperfect acknowledgment of His perfect love.

Joshua Loth Liebman: *Peace of Mind,* Simon & Schuster

Like Dian's kiss, unask'd, unsought,
Love gives itself, but is not bought.

Henry Wadsworth Longfellow: *Endymion,* st. 4

That love for one from which there doth not spring
Wide love for all is but a worthless thing.

James Russell Lowell

Faith, like light, should always be simple and unbending; while love, like warmth, should beam forth on every side, and bend to every necessity of our brethren.

Martin Luther

Love is an image of God, and not a lifeless image, but the living essence of the divine nature which beams full of all goodness.

Martin Luther

Whatever a man loves, that is his god. For he carries it in his heart; he goes about with it night and day; he sleeps and wakes with it, be it what it may—wealth or self, pleasure or renown.

Martin Luther

Love can hope where reason would despair.

George, Baron Lyttelton

The rock of the divine love is deeper down than the human buildings that have been reared upon it.

Alexander MacLaren

Love of humanity tends readily to become abstract, to exist in fancy rather than in reality. Love needs to be concentrated on specific objects. One cannot love all men equally. We choose, and we ought to choose the objects of our love. Love, humanity, must be positive. People often take the hatred of another nation to be the love of one's own. It is far higher to feel no hatred, but to love positively.

Thomas G. Masaryk

Love that seeks to do men good is cowardice when it refuses to prevent them from doing wrong.

Shailer Mathews

The tragedy of love is indifference.

William Somerset Maugham: *The Trembling of a Leaf*, Doubleday & Co., Inc. and A. P. Watt's & Son

There's only one thing in this world that's worth having. Love. L-o-v-e. You love somebody, somebody loves you. That's all there is to it. But if you don't get that, you've got nothing. So you take the next best thing. You take power or money or fame or whatever little morsel you can pick up for yourself as second best.

Charles Mergendahl: *The Next Best Thing*

Whatever of outward service or obedience we render to God or man, if love is withheld, the law is not fulfilled.

Frederick B. Meyer

As God's my judge, I do cry holy, holy, Upon the name of love, however brief.

Edna St. Vincent Millay: "Sonnet CXXIX" from *Collected Poems*, Harper & Row, Publishers, copyright 1939 by Edna St. Vincent Millay, used by permission of Norma Millay

It is not the most lovable individuals who stand more in need of love, but the most unlovable.

Ashley Montagu

The measure of a man's humanity is the extent and intensity of his love for mankind.

Ashley Montagu: *On Being Human*

Where there is love there is no sin.

Montenegrin Proverb

If you haven't love in your heart, you should throw your hope to the four winds and go and get a better one.

Dwight L. Moody

"Tell me, what's Love?" said Youth, one day,
To drooping Age, who crost his way.—
"It is a sunny hour of play,
For which repentance dear doth pay,
  Repentance! Repentance!
And this is Love, as wise men say."

Thomas Moore: *Youth and Age*

The difference between Loyalty and Disloyalty is not D-I-S but L-O-V-E.

Paul Morrison

Two souls with but a single thought,
Two hearts that beat as one.

Franz Joseph von Münch-Bellinghausen: *Ingomar the Barbarian*

Love your enemies.

New Testament: Matthew 5: 44, Luke 6: 27

These things I command you, that ye love one another.

New Testament: John 15: 17

Love is the fulfilling of the law.

New Testament: Romans 13: 10

And now abideth faith, hope, love, these three; but the greatest of these is love.

New Testament: I Corinthians 13: 13
(R.S.V.)

All the law is fulfilled in one word, even in this; Thou shalt love thy neighbour as thyself.

New Testament: Galatians 5: 14

Whom the Lord loveth he chasteneth.

New Testament: Hebrews 12: 6

Love covereth a multitude of sins.

New Testament: I Peter 4: 8

Beloved, let us love one another: for love is of God; and every one that loveth is born of God, and knoweth God.

New Testament: I John 4: 7

He that loveth not knoweth not God; for God is love.

New Testament: I John 4: 8

If we love one another, God dwelleth in us, and his love is perfected in us.

New Testament: I John 4: 12

Perfect love casteth out fear.

New Testament: I John 4: 18

I have somewhat against thee, because thou hast left thy first love.

New Testament: Revelation 2: 4

Until I truly loved, I was alone.

Caroline Norton: The Lady of La Garaye,
Pt. II, l. 381

Thy love to me was wonderful, passing the love of women.

Old Testament: II Samuel 1: 26

He brought me to the banqueting house, and his banner over me was love.

Old Testament: Song of Solomon 2: 4

I am sick of love.

Old Testament: Song of Solomon 2: 5

Love is strong as death.

Old Testament: Song of Solomon 8: 6

Many waters cannot quench love, neither can the floods drown it.

Old Testament: Song of Solomon 8: 7

To assail the changes that have unmoored us from the past is futile, and, in a deep sense, I think it is wicked. . . . This cannot be an easy life. We shall have a rough time of it to keep our minds open, and to keep them deep . . . in a great, open, windy world; but this is, as I see it, the condition of man; and in this condition we can help, because we can love one another.

J. Robert Oppenheimer

Lovers remember all things.

Ovid: Heroides

Love is not blind. Lust is blind. If love is blind, God is blind.

Gordon Palmer

Human things must be known to be loved: but Divine things must be loved to be known.

Blaise Pascal

The knowledge of God is very far from the love of Him.

Blaise Pascal

Force may subdue, but love gains, and he who forgives first wins the laurel.

William Penn

Love is indeed heaven upon earth; since heaven above would not be heaven without it; for where there is not love, there is fear; but, "Perfect love casteth out fear." And yet we naturally fear most to offend what we most love.

William Penn

Love is the hardest lesson in Christianity; but, for that reason, it should be most our care to learn it.

William Penn

Love is the crowning grace of humanity, the holiest right of the soul, the golden link which binds us to duty and truth, the redeeming principle that chiefly reconciles the heart of life, and is prophetic of eternal good.

Petrarch

God's love is not a conditional love; it is an open-hearted, generous self-giving which God offers to men. Those who would carefully limit the operation of God's love . . . have missed the point.

J. B. Phillips in *New Testament Christianity*, Hodder & Stoughton Ltd., London, and The Macmillan Co., New York

Those who love deeply never grow old; they may die of old age, but they die young.

Sir Arthur Wing Pinero

All loves should be simply stepping-stones to the love of God. So it was with me; and blessed be his name for his great goodness and mercy.

Plato

Hate cannot destroy hate, but love can and does. Not the soft and negative thing that has carried the name and misrepresented the emotion, but love that suffers all things and is kind, love that accepts responsibility, love that marches, love that suffers, love that bleeds and dies for a great cause—but to rise again.

Daniel A. Poling

Look round our world; behold the chain of love
Combining all below and all above.

Alexander Pope: *Essay on Man*, Epis. III, l. 7

Love finds an altar for forbidden fires.

Alexander Pope: *Eloise to Abelard*, l. 182

Love must be learned again and again; there is no end to it. Hate needs no instruction, but waits only to be provoked.

Katherine Anne Porter: *The Days Before*

If thou neglectest thy love to thy neighbor, in vain thou professest thy love to God; for by thy love to God, the love to thy neighbor is begotten, and by the love to thy neighbor, thy love to God is nourished.

Francis Quarles

Man has here two and a half minutes—one to smile, one to sigh, and a half to love; for in the midst of this minute he dies.

Jean Paul Richter

Suffering is the true cement of love.

Paul Sabatier

Love is a little blind; when we love someone dearly we unconsciously overlook many faults.

Beatrice Saunders: *Portraits of Genius*

Mortals, while through the world you go,
Hope may succor and faith befriend,
Yet happy your hearts if you can but know,
Love awaits at the journey's end!

Clinton Scollard: *The Journey's End: Envoy*, Houghton Mifflin Co.

The rose is sweetest wash'd with morning dew,
And Love is loveliest when embalm'd in tears.

Sir Walter Scott: *Lady of the Lake*, Canto IV, st. 1

In peace, Love tunes the shepherd's reed;
In war, he mounts the warrior's steed;
In halls, in gay attire is seen;
In hamlets, dances on the green.
Love rules the court, the camp, the grove,
And men below, and saints above;
For love is heaven, and heaven is love.

Sir Walter Scott: *The Lay of the Last Minstrel*

True Love's the gift which God has given
To man alone beneath the heaven:
 It is not fantasy's hot fire,
 Whose wishes soon as granted fly;
 It liveth not in fierce desire,
 With dead desire it doth not die;
It is the secret sympathy
The silver link, the silken tie,
Which heart to heart and mind to mind
In body and in soul can bind.
 Sir Walter Scott: *Lay of the Last Minstrel*

A pennyweight o' love is worth a pound o'
law.
 Scottish Proverb

Better to have loved and lost, than not to
have loved at all.
 Seneca: *Epistles*, 99 (See also Tennyson)

Let me not to the marriage of true minds
 Admit impediments: love is not love
Which alters when it alteration finds.
 William Shakespeare: *Sonnet CXVI*

Men have died from time to time and worms
have eaten them, but not for love.
 William Shakespeare: *As You Like It*,
 Act IV, sc. 1, l. 108

Then, must you speak of one that loved not
wisely but too well; of one not easily jealous,
but being wrought perplex'd in the extreme.
 William Shakespeare: *Othello*,
 Act V, sc. 2, l. 343

Ay me! for aught that I could ever read,
Could ever hear by tale or history,
The course of true love never did run
 smooth.
 William Shakespeare: *A Midsummer-
 Night's Dream*, Act I, sc. 1, l. 132

There's beggary in the love that can be
reckon'd.
 William Shakespeare: *Antony and
 Cleopatra*, Act I, sc. 1, l. 15

And when Love speaks, the voice of all the
 gods
Make heaven drowsy with the harmony.
 William Shakespeare: *Love's Labour's
 Lost*, Act IV, sc. 3, l. 344

Love sought is good, but given unsought is
better.
 William Shakespeare: *Twelfth Night*,
 Act III, sc. 1, l. 168

In the triangle of love between ourselves,
God and other people, is found the secret of
existence, and the best foretaste, I suspect,
that we can have on earth of what heaven
will probably be like.
 Samuel M. Shoemaker

All's fair in love and war.
 Francis Edward Smedley: *Frank Fairlegh*,
 ch. 50

The love of God is the ultimate reality, the
deepest and strongest force in the universe;
and it is revealed to the man who resolutely
girds himself to the conflict.
 David Smith

O love, resistless in thy might, thou triumph-
est even over gold!
 Sophocles: *Antigone*

 Love is indestructible;
Its holy flame forever burneth;
From heaven it came, to heaven returneth.
 Robert Southey

Not where I breathe, but where I love, I live.
 Robert Southwell

They are the true disciples of Christ, not who
know most, but who love most.
 Frederich Spanheim the Elder

He who finds not love finds nothing.
 Spanish Proverb

He who loves God cannot endeavor to bring
it about that God should love him in return.
 Benedict de Spinoza

285

Love is the livery of Christ.

Charles Haddon Spurgeon

There is no permanent love but that which has duty for its eldest brother; so that if one sleeps the other watches, and honor is safe.

P. J. Stahl

To love as Christ loves is to let our love be a practical and not a sentimental thing.

Sir Charles Villiers Stanford

"God is Light." "God is Love." That which professes to be light yet lacks love, is not of God; while that which calls itself love, but is not according to light is equally not of God.

J. Charleton Steen

So long as we love, we serve. So long as we are loved by others, I would almost say we are indispensable; and no man is useless while he has a friend.

Robert Louis Stevenson

Love is the life of man.

Emanuel Swedenborg

If love were what the rose is,
    And I were like the leaf,
Our lives would grow together
In sad or singing weather,
Blown fields or flowerful closes,
    Green pleasure or gray grief.

Algernon Charles Swinburne: *A Match*

Our way lies where God knows
    And Love knows where:
We are in Love's hand today.

Algernon Charles Swinburne: *Love at Sea*

For love's humility is Love's true pride.

Bayard Taylor: *Poet's Journal, Third Evening, The Mother*

Love is the greatest thing that God can give us, for himself is love; and it is the greatest thing we can give to God, for it will also give ourselves, and carry with it all that is ours. The apostle calls it the bond of perfection;

it is the old, the new, and the great commandment, and all the commandments, for it is the fulfilling of the law. It does the work of all the other graces without any instrument, but its own immediate virtue.

Jeremy Taylor

More and more clearly every day out of biology, anthropology, sociology, history economic analysis, psychological insight plain human decency, and common sense the necessary mandate of survival that we show love of our neighbors as we do ourselves, is being confirmed and reaffirmed.

Ordway Tead: *Illinois Medical Journal*

But friend to me
He is all fault who hath no fault at all.
For who loves me must have a touch of earth.

Alfred, Lord Tennyson

I hold it true, whate'er befall,
    I feel it, when I sorrow most;
'Tis better to have loved and lost
Than never to have loved at all.

Alfred, Lord Tennyson: *In Memoriam*

Let Love clasp Grief lest both be drown'd.

Ibid.

Wheresoever a man seeketh his own, there he falleth from love.

Thomas à Kempis: *Imitation of Christ*

It is strange that men will talk of miracles, revelations, inspiration, and the like, as things past, while love remains.

Henry David Thoreau

There is no remedy for love but to love more.

Henry David Thoreau

You must get your living by loving.

Henry David Thoreau: *Journal*

There is no love which does not become help.

Paul Tillich

Where love is, there is God also.

Leo Tolstoy

You are as prone to love as the sun is to shine; it being the most delightful and natural employment of the Soul of Man: without which you are dark and miserable. For certainly he that delights not in Love makes vain the universe, and is of necessity to himself the greatest burden.

Thomas Traherne: *Centuries of Meditations*

The man is happy, Lord, who love like this doth owe:
Loves thee, his friend in thee, and for thy sake, his foe.

Richard Chenevix Trench

God, from a beautiful necessity, is Love.

Martin Farquhar Tupper

Love is the weapon which Omnipotence reserved to conquer rebel man when all the rest had failed. Reason he parries; fear he answers blow for blow; future interest he meets with present pleasure; but love is that sun against whose melting beams the winter cannot stand. There is not one human being in a million, nor a thousand men in all earth's huge quintillion whose clay heart is hardened against love.

Martin Farquhar Tupper

Money will buy a fine dog, but only love will make him wag his tail.

Ulster (Northern Ireland) *Post*

Love conquers all.

Virgil: *Eclogues*, X

To love is to believe, to hope, to know;
'Tis an essay, a taste of Heaven below!
Edmund Waller: *Divine Love*, Canto III, l. 17

It is easy for them who have never been loved to sneer at love.

Welsh Proverb

And I know that the hand of God is the promise of my own,

And I know that the spirit of God is the brother of my own,
And that all the men ever born are also my brothers, and the women my sisters and lovers,
And that a kelson of the creation is love.

Walt Whitman: *Song of Myself*, sec. 5

I know not where His islands lift
Their fronded palms in air;
I only know I cannot drift
Beyond His love and care.

John Greenleaf Whittier: *The Eternal Goodness*

Life is ever lord of Death
And love can never lose its own.

John Greenleaf Whittier: *Snow-Bound*

O Brother Man, fold to thy heart thy brother;
Where pity dwells, the peace of God is there;
To worship rightly is to love each other,
Each smile a hymn, each kindly deed a prayer.

John Greenleaf Whittier

When we climb to Heaven, 'tis on the rounds of love to men.

John Greenleaf Whittier

Love can canonize people. The saints are those who have been most loved.

Oscar Wilde

There is a land of the living and a land of the dead, and the bridge is love.

Thornton Wilder: *The Bridge of San Luis Rey*

There is a comfort and a strength in love;
'Twill make a thing endurable, which else
Would overset the brain, or break the heart.

William Wordsworth

Humble love, and not proud science, keeps the door of heaven.

Owen D. Young

M

MAN

Do you know what makes man the most suffering of all creatures? It is that he has one foot in the finite and the other in the infinite, and that he is torn between two worlds.

Anonymous

God sleeps in the tree, dreams in the animal, and wakes in the man.

Anonymous

Man is an able creature, but he has made 32,600,000 laws and hasn't yet improved on the Ten Commandments.

Anonymous

Man, woman, and devil, are the three degrees of comparison.

Anonymous

We need not worry so much about what man descends from—it's what he descends to that shames the human race.

Anonymous

I realize with intensity that man in all he does that is great and noble is only the organ of something or someone higher than himself.

Henri Frédéric Amiel

The test of every religious, political, or educational system is the man that it forms.

Henri Frédéric Amiel

Man is either a beast or a god.

Aristotle: *Politics*, Bk. I, ch. 1

Be neither saint nor sophist led, but be a man.

Matthew Arnold: *Empedocles on Etna*

An earthly animal, but worthy of Heaven.

St. Augustine: *The City of God*, XXII

God made man to be somebody—not just to have things.

Brotherhood Journal

After all our wanderings through the labyrinths of science, religion is the haven and Sabbath of man's contemplation.

Sir Francis Bacon

Let each man think himself an act of God, His mind a thought, his life a breath of God.

Philip James Bailey: *Festus: Proëm*, l. 163

Man is the nobler growth our realms supply And souls are ripened in our northern sky.

Anna Letitia Barbauld: *The Invitation*

God in making man intended by him to reduce all His Works back again to Himself.

Matthew Barker: *Natural Theology*, p. 85

Man is his own star; and the soul that can Render an honest and a perfect man, Commands all light, all influence, all fate; Nothing to him falls early or too late.

Francis Beaumont and John Fletcher: *The Honest Man's Fortune: Epilogue*

Man is God's creation. Everything else is the nursery and nurse of man.

Henry Ward Beecher

Man is nothing else than . . . a sack of dung, the food of worms.

St. Bernard of Clairvaux: *Meditationes piissimae*

All sorts and conditions of men.

> Book of Common Prayer: Prayer for all
> Conditions of Men

Indisputably a great good, handsome man is the first of created things.

> Charlotte Brontë

Nature tells me I am the image of God, as well as Scripture. He that understands not thus much hath not his introduction or first lesson, and is yet to begin the alphabet of man.

> Sir Thomas Browne: Religio Medici

Bad as you please,
You've felt they were God's men and women still.

> Robert Browning: A Blot on the
> 'Scutcheon, Act II

The not-incurious in God's handiwork
(This man's-flesh he hath admirably made,
Blown like a bubble, kneaded like a paste,
To coop up and keep down on earth a space
That puff of vapour from his mouth, man's soul).

> Robert Browning: An Epistle: Karshish,
> l. 2

Men are not angels, neither are they brutes.

> Robert Browning: Bishop Blougram's
> Apology

Strike from mankind the principle of faith, and men would have no more history than a flock of sheep.

> John Bulwer

From God he's a backslider;
Of ways, he loves the wider;
With wickedness a' sider;
More venom than a spider;
In sin he's a confider;
A make-bate and divider;
Blind reason is' his guider;
The Devil is his rider.

> John Bunyan: A Book for Boys and Girls

Good Lord, what is man? for as simple as he looks,

Do but try to develop his hooks and his crooks!
With his depths and his shallows, his good and his evil:
All in all he's a problem must puzzle the devil.

> Robert Burns: Inscribed to the Hon.
> C. J. Fox

Are we a piece of machinery that, like the Aeolian harp, passive, takes the impression of the passing accident? Or do these workings argue something within us above the trodden clod.

> Robert Burns: Letter to Mrs. Dunlop

And Man, whose heav'n-erected face
    The smiles of love adorn—
Man's inhumanity to man
    Makes countless thousands mourn.

> Robert Burns: Man Was Made to Mourn,
> st. 7

Do what thy manhood bids thee do, from none but self expect applause; he noblest lives and noblest dies who makes and keeps his self-made laws. All other Life is living Death, a world where none but Phantoms dwell, a breath, a wind, a sound, a voice, a tinkling of the camel-bell.

> Sir Richard Francis Burton

A man alone is either a saint or a devil.

> Robert Burton: The Anatomy of
> Melancholy, I

We are an inferior part of the creation of God. There are natural appearances of our being in a state of degradation.

> Joseph Butler: The Analogy of Religion

Man is God's highest present development,
He is the latest thing in God.

> Samuel Butler

Lord of himself;—that heritage of woe!

> George Gordon, Lord Byron: Lara,
> Canto I, st. 2

Half dust, half deity, alike unfit to sink or soar.

George Gordon, Lord Byron: *Manfred,* I

He is of the earth, but his thoughts are with the stars. Mean and petty his wants and desires; yet they serve a soul exalted with grand, glorious aims,—with immortal longings,—with thoughts which sweep the heavens, and wander through eternity. A pigmy standing on the outward crest of this small planet, his far-reaching spirit stretches outward to the infinite, and there alone finds rest.

Thomas Carlyle

The older I grow, and I now stand on the bring of eternity—the more comes back to me that sentence in the Catechism I learned when a child, and the fuller and deeper its meaning becomes: "What is the chief end of man? To glorify God and enjoy him forever."

Thomas Carlyle

There are depths in man that go to the lowest hell, and heights that reach the highest heaven, for are not both heaven and hell made out of him, ever-lasting miracle and mystery that he is.

Thomas Carlyle

We are the miracles, the great inscrutable mystery of God.

Thomas Carlyle

Every man is as God made him, ay, and often worse.

Miguel de Cervantes: *Don Quixote,* Pt. II, ch. 4

The old Latin saw "I am a man, and nothing human is alien to me," may be applied to God himself: "I am God, and nothing—no field of man's interest, no area of his study —is alien to me."

The Christian Century

A self-made man? Yes—and worships his creator.

Henry Clapp. Said also by John Bright of Disraeli

Men are not angels.

John Clarke: *Paraemiologia Anglo-Latina*

Dark fluxion, all unfixable by thought,
A phantom dim of past and future wrought,
Vain sister of the worm—life, death, soul, clod—
Ignore thyself, and strive to know thy God!

Samuel Taylor Coleridge: *Self-Knowledge*

If a man is not rising upwards to be an angel, depend upon it, he is sinking downward to be a devil. He cannot stop at the beast. The most savage of men are not beasts; they are worse, a great deal worse.

Samuel Taylor Coleridge: *Table-Talk*

To have known one good old man—one man who, through the chances and mischances of a long life, has carried his heart in his hand, like a palm branch, waving all discords into peace—helps our faith in God, in ourselves, and in each other, more than many sermons.

George William Curtis

O mortal men, be wary how ye judge.

Alighieri Dante

There is a saying in Russia that man used to be a body and soul; Communists abolished the soul, and man now consists of a body and passport.

Elmer Davis: *Harper's Bazaar*

A sacred spark created by his breath,
  The immortal mind of man his image bears;
A spirit living 'midst the forms of death,
  Oppressed, but not subdued, by mortal cares.

Sir Humphry Davy: *Written After Recovery from a Dangerous Illness*

There is practically nothing that men do not prefer to God. A tiresome detail of business, an occupation utterly pernicious to health, the employment of time in ways one does not dare to mention. Anything rather than God.

François de Salignac de La Mothe Fénelon

If God is lacking, nothing a man does is of more consequence than the acts of a mouse.

José Luis Martin Descalzo: *God's Frontier*

'Twas much, that man was made like God before,
But, that God should be made like man, much more.

John Donne: *Holy Sonnets*, no. 15

His tribe were God Almighty's gentlemen.

John Dryden: *Absalom and Achitophel,*
Pt. I, l. 645

Surely, if all the world was made for man, then man was made for more than the world.

Pierre Alexandre Duplessis

Man is not matter; he is not made up of brain, blood, bones, and other material elements. The Scriptures inform us that man is made in the image and likeness of God. Matter is not that likeness.

Mary Baker Eddy: *Science and Health,
with Key to the Scriptures,* p. 475: 6–10

A little, wretched, despicable creature; a worm, a mere nothing, and less than nothing; a vile insect that has risen up in contempt against the majesty of Heaven and earth.

Jonathan Edwards: *The Justice of God in
the Damnation of Sinners*

Every man is a divinity in disguise, a god playing the fool.

Ralph Waldo Emerson

God defend me from ever looking at a man as an animal.

Ralph Waldo Emerson

Man is a god in ruins.

Ralph Waldo Emerson: *Nature*

Man is a little soul carrying around a corpse.

Epictetus: *Fragments*

The history of the world suggests that without a love of God there is a little likelihood of a love for man that does not become

corrupt. For it is only in ways one does not dare to mention. Anything rather than God.

François de Salignac de La Mothe
Fénelon

The birth of every new baby is God's vote of confidence in the future of man.

Imogene Fey

Man is his own star, and the soul that can Render an honest and a perfect man, Commands all light.

John Fletcher: *Upon an Honest Man's
Fortune,* l. 33

The man down in nature occupies himself in guarding, in feeding, in warming and multiplying his body, and as long as he knows no more, we justify him; but presently a mystic change is wrought, a new perception opens, and he is made a citizen of the world of souls; he feels what is called duty; he is aware that he owes a higher allegiance to do and live as a good member of this universe.

James Anthony Froude

Man is Creation's masterpiece. But who says so? Man!

Gavarni: *Apothegms*

Man is an animal; but he is an animal plus something else. He is a mythic earth-tree, whose roots are in the ground, but whose topmost branches may blossom in the heavens.

Henry George

Man is greater than a world—than systems of worlds; there is more mystery in the union of soul with body than in the creation of a universe.

Henry Giles

God send us men whose aim will be
Not to defend some ancient creed,
But to live out the laws of Right
In every thought, and word and deed.

F. J. Gillman

Man himself is the crowning wonder of creation; the study of his nature the noblest study the world affords.

William Ewart Gladstone

Man is sin.

Robert Greene: *The Penitent Palmer's Ode*

An evil man is clay to God, and wax to the devil; a good man is God's wax, and Satan's clay.

Joseph Hall

The proud man hath no God; the envious man hath no neighbor; the angry man hath not himself. What good then, in being a man, if one has neither himself nor a neighbor nor God.

Joseph Hall

Though every prospect pleases,
And only man is vile.

Reginald Heber: *From Greenland's Icy Mountains*

Whoever considers the study of anatomy, I believe will never be an atheist; the frame of man's body, and coherence of his parts, being so strange and paradoxical, that I hold it to be the greatest miracle of nature.

Edward Herbert, Lord of Cherbury

Man is God's image; but a poor man is Christ's stamp to boot.

George Herbert: *The Church-Porch*, st. 64

God give us men. A time like this demands
Strong minds, great hearts, true faith and
ready hands!
Men whom the lust of office does not kill,
Men whom the spoils of office cannot buy,
Men who possess opinions and a will,
Men who love honor, men who cannot lie.

Josiah Gilbert Holland: *Wanted*

The sense of being lost does not make a man a Christian. It only proves he is a man.

From *Christian Roots of Democracy* by Arthur E. Holt. Missionary Education Movement, N. Y. Used by permission. Now out of print

We all know that man had advanced to a very creditable stage from a low beginning, but to hear sentimentalists talk, one would

think man began as an angel and ended up as a savage.

Edgar Watson Howe

When God measures a man, He puts the tape around the heart instead of the head.

Indiana *Freemason*

I can make a lord, but only the Almighty can make a gentleman.

James I

Man is dearer to the gods than he is to himself.

Juvenal: *Satires*, Sat. X, l. 350

Let us try to follow the Savior's steps; let us remember all day long what it is to be *men*; that it is to have everyone whom we meet for our brother in the sight of God; that it is this, never to meet any one, however bad he may be, for whom we cannot say, "Christ died for that man, and Christ cares for him still. He is precious in God's eyes, and he shall be precious in mine also."

Charles Kingsley

Bounded in his nature, infinite in his desires, man is a fallen god a recollection of heaven.

Alphonse de Lamartine: *Nouvelles Meditations Poetique*

We believe in men not merely as production units, but as the children of God. We believe that the purpose of our society is not primarily to assure the "safety of the State" but to safeguard human dignity and the freedom of the individual.

David E. Lilienthal

We are, after all, like lumps of clay.
There are brittle pieces, hard pieces.
We have little shape or beauty.
But we need not despair.
If we are clay, let us remember there is a Potter, and His wheel.

Peter Marshall: *Mr. Jones, Meet the Master*

A spirit, zealous, as he seem'd, to know
More of th' Almighty's works, and chiefly
Man,
God's latest image.

John Milton: *Paradise Lost*, Bk. IV, l. 565

Man sees himself lodged here in the mud and filth of the world, nailed and fastened to the most lifeless and stagnant part of the universe, in the lowest story of the house, at the furthest distance from the vault of Heaven, with the vilest animals; and yet in his imagination, he places himself above the circle of the moon, and brings Heaven under his feet.

Michel Eyquem de Montaigne: *Essays II*

A pilgrim panting for the rest to come;
An exile, anxious for his native home;
A drop dissevered from the boundless sea;
A moment parted from eternity.

Hannah More: *Reflections of King Hezekiah*

O man, strange composite of Heaven and earth!
Majesty dwarf'd to baseness! fragrant flower
Running to poisonous seed! and seeming worth
Cloaking corruption! weakness mastering power!

Cardinal John Henry Newman: *The Dream of Gerontius*

The last state of that man is worse than the first.

New Testament: *Matthew 12: 45*

What manner of man is this?

New Testament: *Luke 4: 41*

I am made all things to all men.

New Testament: *I Corinthians 9: 22*

The man is not of the woman; but the woman of the man. Neither was the man created for the woman; but the woman for the man.

New Testament: *I Corinthians 11: 89*

The first man is of the earth, earthy.

New Testament: *I Corinthians 15: 47*

Whatsoever a man soweth, that shall he also reap.

New Testament: *Galatians 6: 7*

So God created man in his own image, in the image of God created he him; male and female created he them.

Old Testament: *Genesis 1: 27*

The Lord God formed man of the dust of the ground, and breathed into his nostrils the breath of life; and man became a living soul.

Old Testament: *Genesis 2: 7*

Man doth not live by bread only.

Old Testament: *Deuteronomy 8: 3*

A man after his own heart.

Old Testament: *I Samuel 13: 14*

And Nathan said to David, Thou art the man.

Old Testament: *II Samuel 12: 7*

Shall a man be more pure than his maker?

Old Testament: *Job 4: 17*

Man that is born of a woman is of few days, and full of trouble. He cometh forth like a flower, and is cut down: he fleeth also as a shadow and continueth not.

Old Testament: *Job 14: 1, 2*

What is man, that thou art mindful of him?

Psalms 8: 4

Thou hast made him a little lower than the angels.

Old Testament: *Psalms 8: 5*

Man being in honor abideth not: he is like the beasts that perish.

Old Testament: *Psalms 49: 12, 20*

As for man, his days are as grass: as a flower of the field, so he flourisheth.

Old Testament: *Psalms 103: 15*

I am fearfully and wonderfully made.

Old Testament: *Psalms 139: 14*

Seest thou a man wise in his own conceit? there is more hope of a fool than of him.

Old Testament: *Proverbs 26: 12*

God hath made man upright; but they have sought out many inventions.

Old Testament: Ecclesiastes 7: 29

We are the clay, and thou [Lord] our potter.

Old Testament: Isaiah 64: 8

Thus saith the Lord; Cursed be the man that trusteth in man.

Old Testament: Jeremiah 17: 5

We are none other than a moving row
of magic Shadow-Shapes that come and go
Round with the Sun-Illuminated Lantern held
In midnight by the Master of the Show.

Omar Khayyám: Rubáiyát

God gave man an upright countenance to survey the heavens, and to look upward to the stars.

Ovid: Metamorphoses, l. 85

Man is a microcosm, or a little world, because he is an extract from all the stars and planets of the whole firmament, from the earth and the elements; and so he is their quintessence.

Paracelsus: Archidoxies, I

What a chimera is man! what a confused chaos! what a subject of contradiction! A professed judge of all things, and yet a feeble worm of the earth! the great depositary and guardian of truth, and yet a mere huddle of uncertainty! the glory and the scandal of the universe!

Blaise Pascal

Man was made by the Gods for them to toy and play withal.

Plato

Man only,—rash, refined, presumptuous Man—
Starts from his rank, and mars Creation's plan!
Born the free heir of nature's wide domain,
To art's strict limits bounds his narrow'd reign;

Resigns his native rights for meaner things,
For Faith and Fetters, Laws and Priests and Kings.

Poetry of the Anti-Jacobin, The Progress of Man, l. 55

Laugh where we must, be candid where we can,
But vindicate the ways of God to man.

Alexander Pope: Essay on Man, Epis. I

Great lord of all things, yet a prey to all;
Sole judge of truth, in endless error hurled;
The glory, jest and riddle of the world!

Alexander Pope: Essay on Man, Epis. II

An honest man's the noblest work of God.

Alexander Pope: Essay on Man, Epis. IV

Man has been placed in the world in order that he may develop and expand his talents and capacities to their fullest extent. If he is to do so, he needs four things—knowledge, art, technical skill, morality and religion; for truth must be known, beauty fashioned, good practiced and God feared and loved.

Ottokar Prohaszka: Meditations on the Gospels

Man is Heaven's masterpiece.

Francis Quarles: Emblems, Bk. II, emb. 6

Man is man's A, B, C. There's none that can Read God aright, unless he first spell man.

Francis Quarles: Hieroglyphics of the Life of Man

In these two things the greatness of man consists, to have God so dwelling in us as to impart his character to us, and to have him dwelling in us, that we recognize his presence, and know that we are his, and he is ours.—The one is salvation; the other, the assurance of it.

Frederick William Robertson

God made man a little lower than the angels, and he has been getting a little lower ever since.

Will Rogers

I never could believe that Providence had sent a few men into the world, ready booted and spurred to ride, and millions ready saddled and bridled to be ridden.

Richard Rumbold

What a piece of work is man! How noble in reason! How infinite in faculty! In form and moving
   How express and admirable! In action how like an angel! In apprehension how like a god!

William Shakespeare: *Hamlet,*
Act II, sc. 2, l. 323

God made him, and therefore let him pass for a man.

William Shakespeare: *The Merchant of Venice,* Act I, sc. 2, l. 60

We are such stuff
As dreams are made on.

William Shakespeare: *The Tempest,*
Act IV, sc. 1, l. 156

A man without God is not like a cake without raisins; he is like the cake without the flour and milk; he lacks the essential ingredients of happiness.

Bishop Fulton J. Sheen

Nature gives man corn but he must grind it; God gives man a will, but he must make the right choices.

Bishop Fulton J. Sheen

Man is of soul and body, formed for deeds Of high resolve; on fancy's boldest wing.

Percy Bysshe Shelley: *Queen Mab,*
Canto IV, l. 160

God made man to be somebody—not just to have things.

Brotherhood Journal

A Christian is the gentlest of men; but then *he is a man.*

Charles Haddon Spurgeon

Before the beginning of years,
   There came to the making of man
Time, with a gift of tears;
Grief, with a glass that ran;
Pleasure, with pain for leaven;
   Summer, with flowers that fell;
Remembrance fallen from Heaven,
   And madness risen from Hell;
Strength without hands to smite;
   Love that endures for a breath;
Night, the shadow of light,
And life, the shadow of death.

Algernon Charles Swinburne: *Atalanta in Calydon*

Man is born with his hands clenched, but his hands are open in death, because on entering the world he desires to grasp everything, but on leaving, he takes nothing away.

The Talmud

For a man is not as God,
But then most Godlike being most a man.

Alfred, Lord Tennyson: *Love and Duty,*
l. 30

Not for this
Was common clay ta'en from the common earth.
Moulded by God, and temper'd with the tears
Of angels to the perfect shape of man.

Alfred, Lord Tennyson: *The Palace of Art: Introduction*

God never deceives; but man is deceived whenever he puts too much trust in himself. Man proposes, but God disposes.

Thomas à Kempis

The noble man is only God's image.

Ludwig Tieck: *Genoveva*

What a dreadful thing it is for such a wicked little creature as man to have absolute power.

Horace Walpole

Silver is the king's stamp; man God's stamp, and a woman is man's stamp; we are not current till we pass from one man to another.

John Webster: *Northward Hoe,* l. 186

Part mortal clay, and part etheral fire,
Too proud to creep, too humble to aspire.

Richard West: *Ad Amicos*

In thy lone and long night-watches, sky
    above and sea below,
Thou didst learn a higher wisdom than the
    babbling schoolmen know;
God's stars and silence taught thee, as His
    angels only can,
That the one sole sacred thing beneath the
    cope of Heaven is Man!

John Greenleaf Whittier: *The Branded
Hand*, st. 9

When faith is lost, when honor dies,
    The man is dead!

John Greenleaf Whittier: *Ichabod*, st. 8

I sometimes think that God in creating man
somewhat overestimated his ability.

Oscar Wilde

Man is the favorite animal on earth.

John Wise: *A Vindication of the Government of New England Churches*, II

Man is too noble to serve anyone but God.

Cardinal Wyszynski

Man is more precious in the sight of God
than the angels.

Pope Xystus I: *The Ring*

Though man sits still and takes his ease,
    God is at work on man;
No means, no method unemploy'd
    To bless him, if he can.

Edward Young: *Resignation*, Pt. I, st. 119

How poor, how rich, how abject, how august
how complicate, how wonderful is man!
distinguished link in being's endless chain!
midway from nothing to the Deity! dim
miniature of greatness absolute! an heir of
glory! a frail child of dust! helpless immortal!
insect infinite! a worm! a God!

Edward Young

MARRIAGE

If a child of God marries a child of the devil,
said child of God is sure to have some trouble
with his father-in-law.

Anonymous

He that hath a wife and children hath given
hostages to fortune; for they are impediments to great enterprises, either of virtue
or mischief.

Sir Francis Bacon: *Essays: Of Marriage
and Single Life*

One should believe in marriage as in the immortality of the soul.

Honoré de Balzac

The Christian religion, by confining marriage to pairs, and rendering the relation
indissoluble, has by these two things done
more toward the peace, happiness, settlement, and civilization of the world, than by
any other part in this whole scheme of divine
wisdom.

Edmund Burke

Marriage and hanging go by destiny; matches
are made in heaven.

Robert Burton: *Anatomy of Melancholy*

The ever-living Christ is here to bless you.
The nearer you keep him, the nearer you
will be to one another.

Geoffrey Francis Fisher, Archbishop of
Canterbury, at the wedding of
Princess Elizabeth

Marriages may be made in heaven, but man
is responsible for the maintenance work.

Changing Times: from "Notes on these
changing times"

Thus grief still treads upon the heels of
    pleasure,
Marry'd in haste, we may repent at leisure.

William Congreve: *The Old Bachelor*,
Act V, sc. 1

Where there is strife betwixt a man and wife,
'tis hell,
And mutual love may be compar'd to heaven.

Joshua Cooke: *How a Man May Choose a Good Wife*, Act I, sc. 1

When two people, in a dramatic service of divine worship, extend open and defenseless hands and clasp them together, they are showing to God and to the world their readiness to learn from each other the mysterious penetration of real love.

Robert C. Dodds: *Two Together.* Copyright © 1959, 1962 by Thomas Y. Crowell Company, N.Y., publishers

Some people believe in a decree, viz, that God has determined in all cases that particular men and women should be married to each other, and that it is impossible they should marry any other person. But I say, hush! for if that be the case, then God appoints all matches: but I believe the Devil appoints a great many.

Lorenzo Dow: *Reflections on Matrimony*

Where there's marriage without love, there will be love without marriage.

Benjamin Franklin: *Poor Richard*

Remember the nightingales which sing only some months in the spring, but commonly are silent when they have hatched their eggs, as if their mirth were turned into care for their young ones. Yet all the molestations of Marriage are abundantly recompensed with other comforts which God bestoweth on them who make a wise choice of a wife.

Thomas Fuller: *The Holy State*

The sanctity of marriage and the family relation make the corner-stone of our American society and civilization.

James Abram Garfield

Marriage is Heaven and Hell.

German Proverb

Matrimony is always a vice, all that can be done is to excuse it and to sanctify it; therefore it was made a religious sacrament.

St. Jerome: *The Virgin's Confession*

Marriage has many pains, but celibacy has no pleasures.

Samuel Johnson: *Works*, XI, 74

A good marriage is not a contract between two persons but a sacred covenant between three. Too often Christ is never invited to the wedding and finds no room in the home. Why? Is it because we have misrepresented Him and forgotten His joyful outlook on life?

Donald T. Kauffman: *Gist of the Lesson*

The voice that breathed o'er Eden,
That earliest wedding-day,
The primal marriage blessing,
It hath not passed away.

John Keble: *Holy Matrimony*

Even if marriages are made in heaven, man has to be responsible for the maintenance.

Kroehler News

We've got to combine church with home. Then maybe we'll stop worshipping electric iceboxes and we'll have a resurgence of faith and religion.

Samuel S. Leibowitz

God has set the type of marriage everywhere throughout the creation.—Every creature seeks its perfection in another.—The very heavens and earth picture it to us.

Martin Luther

The state of matrimony is the chief in the world after religion; but people shun it because of its inconveniences, like one who, running out of the rain, falls into the river.

Martin Luther: *Table Talk*

On what pretense can man have interdicted marriage, which is a law of nature? 'Tis as though we were forbidden to eat, to drink, to sleep.

Ibid.

Let nothing break our bond but Death,
For in the world above
'Tis the breaker Death that soldereth
Our ring of Wedded Love.

Gerald Massey: *On a Wedding Day*, st. 2

Marriage, to tell the truth, is an evil, but a necessary evil.

Menander: *Fragment*

Hail wedded love, mysterious law, true source of human offspring, sole propriety in Paradise of all things common else. By thee adulterous lust was driven from men among the bestial herds to range; by thee founded in reason, loyal, just, and pure, relations dear, and all the charities of father, son, and brother first were known.

John Milton

Therefore God's universal law
Gave to the man despotic power
Over his female in due awe,
Not from that right to part an hour,
Smile she or lour.

John Milton: *Samson Agonistes*, l. 1053

What therefore God hath joined together, let not man put asunder.

New Testament: Matthew 19: 6

When they shall rise from the dead, they neither marry, nor are given in marriage; but are as the angels which are in heaven.

New Testament: Mark 12: 25

It is better to marry than to burn.

New Testament: I Corinthians 7: 9

He that is married careth for the things that are of the world, how he may please his wife.

New Testament: I Corinthians 7: 33

She that is married careth for the things of he world, how she may please her husband.

New Testament: I Corinthians 7: 34

For this cause shall a man leave his father and mother, and shall be joined unto his wife, and they two shall be one flesh.

New Testament: Ephesians 5: 31

It is not good that the man should be alone.

Old Testament: Genesis 2: 18

A prudent wife is from the Lord.

Old Testament: Proverbs 19: 14

True it is that marriages be done in heaven and performed on earth.

William Painter: *Palace of Pleasure,*
III, 24

Marriage is love personified.

Phoenix Flame

Marriage with peace is this world's Paradise;
With strife, this life's Purgatory.

Politeuphuia, p. 277

Good Heav'n, no doubt, the nuptial state approves,
Since it chastises still what best it loves.

Alexander Pope: *January and May*, I

The sacred academy of man's life,
Is holy wedlock in a happy wife.

Francis Quarles: *History of Queen Esther,*
Sec. III, med. 3

There are two rocks, in this world of ours, on which the soul must either anchor or be wrecked—the one is God, and the other is the sex opposite.

Frederick William Robertson

God, the best maker of all marriages,
Combine your hearts in one.

William Shakespeare: *Henry V,*
Act V, sc. 2, l. 387

A world-without-end bargain.

William Shakespeare: *Love's Labour's
Lost*, Act V, sc. 2, l. 799

The ancient saying is no heresy,
Hanging and wiving goes by destiny.

William Shakespeare: *The Merchant of
Venice*, Act II, sc. 9, l. 82

God help the man who won't marry until he finds the perfect woman, and God help him still more if he finds her.

Benjamin Tillett

Now I do hate those words, "an excellent marriage." In them is contained more of wicked worldliness than any other words one ever hears spoken.

Anthony Trollope: *The Small House at Allington*, ch. 39

Marriage was instituted by God himself for the purpose of preventing promiscuous intercourse of the sexes, for promoting domestic felicity, and for securing the maintenance and security of children.

Noah Webster: *An American Dictionary of the English Language*, 1828

Marriages are made in heaven, but they are lived on earth.

George P. Weiss: *The Link*

Why do not words, and kiss, and solemn pledge,
And nature that is kind in woman's breast,
And reason that is in man is wise and good,
And fear of Him who is a righteous Judge,—
Why do not these prevail for human life,
To keep two hearts together, that began
Their spring-time with one love.

William Wordsworth: *Excursion*, Bk. VI

MARTYRS

For a tear is an intellectual thing,
And a sigh is the sword of an angel king,
And the bitter groan of a martyr's woe
Is an arrow from the Almighty's bow.

William Blake: *Jerusalem*, ch. 11, sec. 52

The noble army of Martyrs.

Book of Common Prayer

The prophet and the martyr do not see the hooting throng. Their eyes are fixed on the eternities.

Benjamin N. Cardozo: *Law and Literature*

Christianity has made martyrdom sublime, and sorrow triumphant.

Edwin Hubbell Chapin

To know how to say what other people only think, is what makes men poets and sages; and to dare to say what others only dare to think, makes men martyrs or reformers.

Elizabeth Rundle Charles: *Chronicles of the Schonberg-Cotta Family*, XIV

The ashes of martyrs drive away demons.

St. John Chrysostom: *Homilies*, VIII

Two things are necessary to a modern martyr,—some to pity, and some to persecute, some to regret, and some to roast him. If martyrdom is now on the decline, it is not because martyrs are less zealous, but because martyr-mongers are more wise.

Charles Caleb Colton

He that dies a martyr proves that he was not a knave, but by no means that he was not a fool; since the most absurd doctrines are not without such evidence as martyrdom can produce. A martyr, therefore, by the mere act of suffering, can prove nothing but his own faith.

Charles Caleb Colton

For some not to be martyred is a martyrdom.

John Donne

Men reject their prophets and slay them, but they love their martyrs and honour those whom they have slain.

Feodor Dostoyevsky: *The Brothers Karamazov*, Pt. XI, Bk. VI, ch. 3

All have not the gift of martyrdom.

John Dryden: *The Hind and the Panther*, Pt. XI, l. 59

The martyr cannot be dishonoured. Every lash inflicted is a tongue of fame; every prison a more illustrious abode; every burned book or house enlightens the world; every suppressed or expunged word reverberates through the earth from side to side. Hours of sanity and consideration are always arriving to communities, as to individuals, when the truth is seen and the martyrs are justified.

Ralph Waldo Emerson: *Compensation*

The torments of martyrdoms are probably most keenly felt by the bystanders. The torments are illusory. The first suffering is the last suffering, the later hurts being lost on insensibility.

Ralph Waldo Emerson: *Courage*

It is not the suffering but the cause which makes a martyr.

English Proverb

As for me, I have no inclination to risk my life for the truth. . . . Popes and emperors must settle the creeds. If they settle them well, so much the better; if ill, I shall keep on the safe side.

Desiderius Erasmus: *Letter to Archbishop Warham of Canterbury*

There's no religion so irrational but can boast its martyrs.

Joseph Glanvill: *The Vanity of Dogmatizing*, XIV

A little bread and wine in a dungeon sufficed for the liturgy of the martyrs.

Philip Gilbert Hamerton: *Modern Frenchmen: Henri Perreyre*

Perhaps there is no happiness in life so perfect as the martyr's.

O. Henry

The only method by which religious truth can be established is by martyrdom.

Samuel Johnson

He who risks his life and hands it over to God will share in the life of the world to come, whether martyrdom is his lot or not; but cowardice is certain death for the soul.

Sherman E. Johnson

It is more difficult, and calls for higher energies of soul, to live a martyr than to die one.

Horace Mann

Martyrs! who left for our reaping,
Truths you have sown in your blood!

Thomas Moore: *Where Is Your Dwelling*

When we read, we fancy we could be martyrs, when we come to act, we cannot bear a provoking word.

Hannah More

The disciples of a martyr suffer much more than the martyr.

Friedrich Wilhelm Nietzsche: *Human All-too-Human*, I

Every step of progress the world has made has been from scaffold to scaffold, and from stake to stake.

Wendell Phillips: *Woman's Rights*

Who perisheth in needless danger is the devil's martyr.

John Ray: *English Proverbs*

Like a pale martyr in his shirt of fire.

Alexander Smith: *A Life Drama*, sc. 2

And martyrs, when the joyful crown is given,
Forget the pain by which they purchased heaven.

George Stepney: *To King James II*

Even in this world they will have their judgment-day; and their names, which went down in the dust like a gallant banner trodden in the mire, shall rise again all glorious in the sight of nations.

Harriet Beecher Stowe

The blood of the martyrs is the seed of the Church.

Tertullian: *Apologeticus*

The more ye mow us down, the more quickly we grow; the blood of Christians is fresh seed.

Ibid.

These Christs that die upon the barricades,
God knows it I am with them, in some things.

Oscar Wilde: *Sonnet to Liberty*

The world would use us just as it did the martyrs, if we loved God as they did.

Thomas Wilson: *Maxims of Piety,* XC

MERCY

For mercy shall soon pardon the meanest: but mighty men shall be mightily tormented.

Apocrypha: Wisdom of Solomon 6: 6

The mercy of God (may be found) between the bridge and the stream.

St. Augustine: *Confessions.* Said of a man falling into a river

Society, like the Roman youth at the circus, never shows mercy to the fallen gladiator.

Honoré de Balzac

The greatest attribute of heaven is mercy.

Francis Beaumont and John Fletcher

Mercy is for the merciful.

George Gordon, Lord Byron: *Lines on Hearing Lady Byron Was Ill*

Among the attributes of God, although they are all equal, mercy shines with even more brilliancy than justice.

Miguel de Cervantes

Mercy among the virtues is like the moon among the stars,—not so sparkling and vivid as many, but dispensing a calm radiance that hallows the whole. It is the bow that rests upon the bosom of the cloud when the storm is past. It is the light that hovers above the judgment-seat.

Edwin Hubbell Chapin

Mercy passeth right.

Geoffrey Chaucer: *Troylus and Cryseyde*

Mercy imitates God, and disappoints Satan.

St. John Chrysostom: *Homilies,* XXI

Mercifulness makes us equal to the gods.

Claudian

Man may dismiss compassion from his heart, But God will never.

William Cowper

We hand folks over to God's mercy, and show none ourselves.

George Eliot: *Adam Bede,* ch. 42

There is a mercy which is weakness, and even treason against the common good.

George Eliot: *Romola,* Bk. III, ch. 59

There's a wideness in God's mercy
Like the wideness of the sea;
There's a kindness in His justice
Which is more than liberty.

Frederick William Faber

The greatest attribute of heaven is mercy;
And 'tis the crown of justice, and the glory,
Where it may kill with right, to save with pity.

John Fletcher: *Lover's Progress,* Act III, sc. 3

Mercy the wise Athenians held to be
Not an affection, but a Deity.

Robert Herrick: *Mercy*

I say that we are wound
With mercy round and round
As if with air.

Gerard Manley Hopkins: *Mary Mother of Divine Grace*

Being all fashioned of the self-same dust, Let us be merciful as well as just.

Henry Wadsworth Longfellow: *Tales of a Wayside Inn,* Pt. III

Yet I shall temper so
Justice with mercy, as may illustrate most
Them fully satisfied, and thee appease.

John Milton: *Paradise Lost,* Bk. X, l. 77

Blessed are the merciful: for they shall obtain mercy.

New Testament: Matthew 5: 7

Surely goodness and mercy shall follow me all the days of my life: and I will dwell in the house of the Lord for ever.

Old Testament: Psalms 23: 6

The wicked borroweth, and payeth not again: but the righteous sheweth mercy, and giveth.

Old Testament: Psalms 37: 21

He is ever merciful, and lendeth; and his seed is blessed.

Old Testament: Psalms 37: 26

Have mercy upon me, O God, according to thy lovingkindness: according unto the multitude of thy tender mercies.

Old Testament: Psalms 51: 1

The mercy of the Lord is from everlasting to everlasting upon them that fear him.

Old Testament: Psalms 103: 17

Let not mercy and truth forsake thee: bind them about thy neck; write them upon the table of thine heart.

Old Testament: Proverbs 3: 3

The merciful man doeth good to his own soul.

Old Testament: Proverbs 11: 17

He that hath mercy on the poor, happy is he.

Old Testament: Proverbs 14: 21

What doth the Lord require of thee, but to do justly, and to love mercy, and to walk humbly with thy God?

Old Testament: Micah 6: 8

Teach me to feel another's woe,
To hide the fault I see;
That mercy I to others show,
That mercy show to me.

Alexander Pope: *Universal Prayer*

The quality of mercy is not strain'd,
It droppeth as the gentle rain from heaven
Upon the place beneath: it is twice blest,
It blesseth him that gives and him that takes:
'Tis mightiest in the mightiest: it becomes

The throned monarch better than his crown . . .
It is enthroned in the hearts of kings,
It is an attribute of God himself . . .

William Shakespeare: *The Merchant of Venice*, Act IV, sc. 1, l. 184

We do pray for mercy;
And that same prayer doth teach us all to render
The deeds of mercy.

William Shakespeare: *The Merchant of Venice*, Act IV, sc. 1, l. 200

Who will not mercy unto others show, how can he mercy ever hope to have.

Herbert Spencer

Hate shuts her soul when dove-eyed Mercy pleads.

Charles Sprague

We may imitate the Deity in all his moral attributes, but mercy is the only one in which we can pretend to equal him.—We cannot, indeed, give like God, but surely we may forgive like him.

Laurence Sterne

Mercy is like the rainbow, which God hath set in the clouds; it never shines after it is night.—If we refuse mercy here, we shall have justice in eternity.

Jeremy Taylor

Mercy is not for them that sin and fear not, but for them that fear and sin not.

Thomas Watson

Hark! the herald angels sing,
"Glory to the new-born King;
Peace on earth, and mercy mild,
God and sinners reconciled!"

Charles Wesley: *Christmas Hymn*

Sweet Mercy! to the gates of Heaven
This Minstrel lead, his sins forgiven;
The rueful conflict, the heart riven
With vain endeavour,

And memory of earth's bitter leaven
Effaced forever.

> William Wordsworth: *Thoughts Suggested on the Banks of the Nith*

A God all mercy is a God unjust.

> Edward Young: *Night Thoughts*, Night IV, l. 234

MIND

Man is a soul formed by divine ideas, and bodying forth their image. His mind is the unit and measure of things visible and invisible.

> Amos Bronson Alcott: *Tablets*, II

I had rather believe all the fables in the Legends and the Talmud and the Alcoran, than that this universal frame is without a mind.

> Sir Francis Bacon: *Essays: Of Atheism*

All the choir of Heaven and furniture of earth . . . have not any substance without a mind.

> George Berkeley: *The Principles of Human Knowledge*

There is one Mind. It is absolutely omnipresent, giving mentality to all things.

> Giordano Bruno: *De monade numero et figura*

As for my feeble mind, that I will leave behind me, for that I have no need of that in the place whither I go; nor is it worth bestowing upon the poorest pilgrim; wherefore, when I am gone, I desire that you would bury it in a dunghill.

> John Bunyan: *Pilgrim's Progress*, II

The more accurately we search into the human mind, the stronger traces we everywhere find of the wisdom of Him who made it.

> Edmund Burke

The Kingdom of Heaven is not a place, but a state of mind.

> John Burroughs: *The Light of Day*

A perfectly just and sound mind is a rare and invaluable gift. But it is still more unusual to see such a mind unbiased in all its actings. God has given this soundness of mind but to few: and a very small number of these few escape the bias of some predilection perhaps habitually operating; and none are at all times perfectly free. An exquisite watch went irregularly, though no defect could be discovered in it. At last it was found that the balance wheel had been near a magnet; and here was all the mischief. If the soundest mind be magnetized by any predilection, it must act irregularly.

> Richard Cecil

A mind enlighted is like heaven; a mind in darkness is like hell.

> Chinese Proverb

The cultivation of the mind is a kind of food supplied for the soul of man.

> Cicero: *De Finibus Bonorum et Malorum*, V, 19

My mind to me a kingdom is
Such perfect joy therein I find
As far exceeds all earthly bliss
That God or nature hath assigned.

> Sir Edward Dyer: *My Mind to Me a Kingdom Is*

Mortal mind and body are one. Neither exists without the other, and both must be destroyed by immortal Mind.

> Mary Baker Eddy: *Science and Health with Key to the Scriptures*, p. 177: 8–9

God is Mind, and God is infinite; hence all is Mind.

> Mary Baker Eddy: *Science and Health, with Key to the Scriptures*, p. 492:25–26

Nothing is at last sacred but the integrity of your own mind.

> Ralph Waldo Emerson: *Essays, First Series: Self-Reliance*

Every individual is a king in the castle of his own mind. As king of his thoughts he can think those thoughts which will make him an unhappy and fearful monarch, or he can make his reign joyous and harmonious by listening to the Father within himself before making decisions.

Lowell Fillmore: "Things to be Remembered," *Weekly Unity*, January 2, 1955

Our brains are seventy-year clocks. The Angel of Life winds them up once for all, then closes the case, and gives the key into the hand of the Angel of the Resurrection.

Oliver Wendell Holmes, Sr.: *The Autocrat of the Breakfast Table*, ch. 8

The stream of knowledge is heading towards a non-mechanical reality. Mind no longer appears as an accidental intruder into the realm of matter. The universe begins to look more like a great thought than a great machine.

Sir James H. Jeans: *The Mysterious Universe*, Cambridge University Press

The mind is the atmosphere of the soul.

Joseph Joubert: *Pensées*

What is mind? No matter. What is matter? Never mind.

Thomas Hewitt Key

No barriers, no masses of matter however enormous, can withstand the powers of the mind; the remotest corners yield to them; all things succumb; the very Heaven itself is laid open.

Marcus Manilius: *Astronomica*, I

The mind may be compared to a garden, which it is as necessary to cultivate as any plot of earth, if order and beauty are to be manifested through it . . . Ideas, as well as flowers, in order to attain their full beauty, must be kept free from encumbering influences, whatever tends to weaken or degrade or detract from planned perfection . . . The riotous bramble is not to be compared to the perfect rose. The bramble may manifest a certain freedom and vigor, but it is the

rose which, petal by petal, shows forth the Great Artist's shaping hand.

Joyce Mayhew: *Argonaut*

O Nature, and O soul of man! how far beyond all utterance are your linked analogies! no the smallest atom stirs or lives in matter, bu has its cunning duplicate in mind.

Herman Melville

Our mind is God.

Menander

The intellect in everyone of us is God.

Menander: *Fragments*

The mind is its own place, and in itself
Can make a heaven of Hell, a hell of Heaven.

John Milton: *Paradise Lost*, I

In his right mind.

New Testament: Mark 5: 15

I delight in the law of God after the inward man: But I see another law in my members, warring against the law of my mind, and bringing me into captivity to the law of sin.

New Testament: Romans 7: 22–23

Let every man be fully persuaded in his own mind.

New Testament: Romans 14: 5

For God hath not given us the spirit of fear; but of power, and of love, and of a sound mind.

New Testament: II Timothy 1: 7

It is the mind that makes the man, and our vigour is in our immortal soul.

Ovid: *Metamorphoses*, XIII

The modern intelligent mind, which has had its horizons widened in dozens of different ways, has got to be shocked afresh by the audacious central fact that as a sober matter of history, God became one of us.

J. B. Phillips: *New Testament Christianity*

great, a good, and a right mind is a kind
f divinity lodged in flesh, and may be the
lessing of a slave, as well as of a prince.—
t came from heaven, and to heaven it must
eturn; and it is a kind of heavenly felicity
which a pure and virtuous mind enjoys, in
ome degree, even on earth.

Seneca

ove looks not with the eyes, but with the
mind;
and therefore is wing'd Cupid painted
blind.

William Shakespeare: *A Midsummer-
Night's Dream,* Act I, sc. 1, l. 234

There seems to be a fresh need to examine
he career of the human self in the modern
world, with his religious development espe-
ially in mind.

Lewis Joseph Sherrill: *The Struggle of the
Soul*

My mind is unChristian, for it keeps no day
of rest.

Esaias Tegner: *Letter to F. M. Franzen*

Our minds are finite, and yet even in these
circumstances of finitude we are surrounded
by possibilities that are infinite, and the purpose of human life is to grasp as much as we
can out of that infinitude.

Alfred North Whitehead: *Dialogues of
Alfred North Whitehead,* p. 163

MINISTERS

An upright minister asks, *what* recommends
a man; a corrupt minister, *who*.

Charles Caleb Colton: *Lacon: Reflections,*
no. 9

To show the world that now and then
Great ministers are mortal men.

John Dryden: *Epistles: To Sir G.
Etheredge,* l. 43

The Lord opened unto me that being bred
at Oxford or Cambridge was not enough to
fit and qualify men to be ministers of Christ.

George Fox: *Journal*

The life of a pious minister is visible
rhetoric.

Herman Hooker

It is Lucifer,
The son of mystery;
And since God suffers him to be,
He, too, is God's minister,
And labors for some good
By us not understood.

Henry Wadsworth Longfellow: *The
Golden Legend: Epilogue*

The minister lives behind a "stained glass
curtain." The layman has opportunities for
evangelism which a minister will never have.

James McCord

One of the tragedies of our time is that
the minister is both overworked and unemployed; overworked in a multitude of tasks
that do not have the slightest connection
with religion, and unemployed in the serious
concerns and exacting labors of maintaining
a disciplined spiritual life among mature
men and women.

Samuel H. Miller

The preacher is not an artist but a prophet.
It is possible to sacrifice the prophet for the
artist. Not how beautiful but how essential
is the quality of the ministry.

G. Campbell Morgan

The Christian ministry is the worst of all
trades, but the best of all professions.

John Newton

Canst thou not minister to a mind diseased,
Pluck from the memory a rooted sorrow,
Raze out the written troubles of the brain
And with some sweet oblivious antidote
Cleanse the suff'd bosom of that perilous
matter
Which weighs upon the heart?

William Shakespeare: *Macbeth,*
Act V, sc. 3, l. 40

"Three things," says Luther, "make a Divine
—prayer, meditation, and trials." These

make a Christian; but a Christian minister needs three more, talent, application, and acquirements.

Charles Simmons

If there were not a minister in every parish, you would quickly find cause to increase the number of constables; and if churches were not employed as places to hear God's law, there would be need of them to be prisons for lawbreakers.

Robert South

MIRACLES

It is almost impossible to exaggerate the proneness of the human mind to take miracles as evidence, and to seek for miracles as evidence.

Matthew Arnold: *Literature and Dogma*, V

Why, they ask, do not those miracles, which you preach of as past events, happen nowadays? I might reply that they were necessary before the world believed, to bring the world to believe; but whoever is still looking for prodigies to make him believe is himself a great prodigy for refusing to believe where the world believes.

St. Augustine: *The City of God*, XXII, 427

There was never miracle wrought by God to convert an atheist, because the light of nature might have led him to confess a God: but miracles have been wrought to convert idolaters and the superstitious, because no light of nature extendeth to declare the will and true worship of God.

Sir Francis Bacon: *The Advancement of Learning*, II

Every believer is God's miracle.

Philip James Bailey: *Festus: Home*

One miracle is just as easy to believe as another.

William Jennings Bryan: At Scopes Trial, July 21, 1925

The Age of Miracles is forever here!

Thomas Carlyle: *Heroes and Hero Worship: The Hero as a Pries*

Miracles are not the proofs, but the necessary results, of revelation.

Samuel Taylor Coleridge: *Omniana*

Miracle seems vastly more reasonable, to all but one mind out of 100,000, than any rationalistic material explanation whatsoever.

Michael J. Dee: *Conclusions*, IV

When asked, "Why do you believe in miracles?" Henry Drummond replied: "Because I see them everyday in the changed lives of men and women who are saved and lifted through faith in the power of the living Christ."

Henry Drummond

We must not sit down, and look for miracles. Up, and be doing, and the Lord will be with thee. Prayer and pains, through faith in Christ Jesus, will do anything.

John Eliot: *Indian Grammar Begun: Postscript*

However skilfully the modern ingenuity of semi-belief may have tampered with supernatural interpositions, it is clear to every honest and unsophisticated mind that, if miracles be incredible, Christianity is false.

Frederic William Farrar: *The Witness of History to Christ*

Miracles are the swaddling-clothes of infant churches.

Thomas Fuller: *Church History*, Vol. II, p. 239

Your messages I hear, but faith has not been given;
The dearest child of Faith is Miracle.

Johann Wolfgang von Goethe: *Faust*

Man is the miracle in nature. God is the One Miracle to man.

Jean Ingelow: *Story of Doom*, Bk. VII, l. 271

MIRACLES

A miracle I take to be a sensible operation, which being above the comprehension of the spectator, and in his opinion contrary to the established course of nature, is taken by him to be divine.

John Locke

Miracles arise from our ignorance of nature, not from nature itself.

Michel Eyquem de Montaigne

I have never seen a greater monster or miracle in the world than myself.

Michel Eyquem de Montaigne: *Essays,* Bk. III, ch. 2

Every moment of this strange and lovely life from dawn to dusk, is a miracle. Somewhere, always, a rose is opening its petals to the dawn. Somewhere, always, a flower is fading in the dusk. The incense that rises with the sun, and the scents that die in the dark, are all gathered, sooner or later, into the solitary fragrance that is God. Faintly, elusively, that fragrance lingers over all of us.

From *The Fool Hath Said* by Beverley Nichols. Copyright 1935, 1936 by Beverley Nichols. Reprinted by permission of Doubleday & Company, Inc. and Jonathan Cape, Ltd.

The story of the whale swallowing Jonah, though a whale is large enough to do it, borders greatly on the marvellous: but it would have approached nearer to the idea of miracle if Jonah had swallowed the whale.

Thomas Paine: *The Age of Reason,* I

The incredulous are the most credulous. They believe the miracles of Vespasian that they may not believe those of Moses.

Blaise Pascal: *Pensées*

Had it not been for the miracles, there would have been no sin in not believing in Jesus Christ.

Ibid.

Miracles and truth are necessary, because it is necessary to convince the entire man, in body and soul.

Ibid.

I should not be a Christian but for the miracles.

Ibid.

To the true disciple a miracle only manifests the power and love which are silently at work everywhere as divinely in the gift of daily bread as in the miraculous multiplication of the loaves.

Frederick William Robertson

The water owns a power Divine,
And conscious blushes into wine;
Its very nature changed displays
The power Divine that it obeys.

Sedulius: *Scotus Hybernicus*

A miracle is a work exceeding the power of any created agent, consequently being an effect of the divine omnipotence.

Robert South

What is easy to understand we despise; we need prodigies and miracles.

Synesius: *Egyptian Tales*

There are too many people who expect God to work by miracle what God expects people to work by muscle.

W. Galloway Tyson

To me every hour of the light and dark is a miracle,
Every cubic inch of space is a miracle.

Walt Whitman: *Miracles,* l. 17

Seems it strange that thou shouldst live forever? Is it less strange that thou shouldst live at all?—This is a miracle; and that no more.

Edward Young

MISSIONS, MISSIONARIES

You have the Gospel because missionaries came your way.

Anonymous

The measure of the Church's successful missionary effort reveals the moral biography of her individual membership.

Anonymous

The reason some folks don't believe in missions is that the brand of religion they have isn't worth propagating.

Anonymous

Your love has a broken wing if it cannot fly across the sea.

Maltbie D. Babcock

We are the children of the converts of foreign missionaries; and fairness means that I must do to others as men once did to me.

Maltbie D. Babcock

It is the pagan heart that needs the redeeming message of Christ whether the person who has the heart lives in Shanghai or New York.

John W. Decker

Our task is a world task. It cannot longer be divided into the artificial and geographical compartments of home and foreign.

John W. Decker

Things are saturated with moral law . . . Every cause in Nature is nothing but a disguised missionary.

Ralph Waldo Emerson: *Lectures: Perpetual Forces*

A church without missions is a church without a mission.

The Friendly Messenger

If God calls you to be a missionary, don't stoop to be a king.

Jordan Grooms

For every one dollar contributed to religious organizations, crime costs the citizens of our nation nine.

J. Edgar Hoover

Our missionary giving is more like a thermostat than a thermometer. A thermometer merely reflects the temperature in a room, whereas a thermostat determines it.

Ralph M. Johnson: *Missions*

We want Jesus Christ to take out his first and second naturalization papers in Japan.

Toyohiko Kagawa: *New Life Through God*, Harper & Row, Publishers, Inc.

The spirit of missions is the spirit of our Master; the very genius of His religion. A diffusive philanthropy of Christianity itself. It requires perpetual propagation to attest its genuineness.

David Livingstone

If missions fail, the rest of us will have to shut up shop.

David Lloyd-George

The Spirit of Christ is the spirit of missions, and the nearer we get to Him the more intensely missionary we must become.

Henry Martyn

I have but one candle of life to burn, and would rather burn it out where people are dying in darkness than in a land which is flooded with lights.

A missionary

Everything vital to the missionary enterprise hinges upon prayer.

John Raleigh Mott

They are the messengers of the churches, and the glory of Christ.

New Testament: II Corinthians 8: 23

The world has many religions; it has but one Gospel.

George Owen

Very few of us would be Christians today if there had not been missionaries yesterday.

Roy L. Smith: *The Methodist Story*

The foreign missionary undertaking is the expression of the essential nature of the Christian faith.

Robert E. Speer

Those who deblaterate against missions, have only one thing to do, to come and see them on the spot.

Robert Louis Stevenson

God sifted a whole nation that he might send choice grain over into this wilderness.

William Stoughton: *Election Sermon.* Boston, April 29, 1669

I look upon foreign missionaries as the scaffolding around a rising building. The sooner it can be dispensed with, the better; or rather, the sooner it can be transferred to other places, to serve the same temporary use, the better.

Hudson Taylor: *World Vision Magazine*

The benefit conferred upon this people by the missionaries is so prominent, so palpable, and so unquestioned, that the frankest compliment I can pay them, and the best, is simply to point to the condition of the Sandwich Islands in Captain Cook's time, and their condition today. The work speaks for itself.

Mark Twain

For God so loved the world, not just a few,
The wise and great, the noble and the true,
Or those of favoured class or race or hue.
God loved the world. Do you?

Grace E. Uhler

MONEY

Money is an article which may be used as a universal passport to everywhere except heaven, and as a universal provider of everything except happiness.

Anonymous

Dug from the mountainside, washed from the glen,
Servant am I or master of men.
Steal me, I curse you;
Earn me, I bless you;
Grasp me and hoard me, a fiend shall possess you;
Live for me, die for me,
Covet me, take me,
Angel or devil, I am what you make me.

Anonymous

Mammon holds the one outpost Christianity has not been able to conquer.

Anonymous

You can't take it with you.

Anonymous

I have no time to make money. I am searching for truth.

Jean Louis Agassiz

The deepest depth of vulgarism is that of setting up money as the ark of the covenant.

Thomas Carlyle

There are no pockets in a shroud.

Church bulletin board

Let us despise money.

St. John Chrysostom: *The Weak Things of God*

Stamps God's own name upon a lie just made,
To turn a penny in the way of trade.

William Cowper: *Table-Talk,* l. 421

The Americans have little faith. They rely on the power of the dollar.

Ralph Waldo Emerson: *Nature, Addresses and Lectures*

The love of money, if unjustly gained, is impious, and, if justly, shameful; for it is unseemly to be merely parsimonious even with justice on one's side.

Epicurus: *Fragments, Vatican Collection,* XLIII

The body is well but the purse is sick.

Desiderius Erasmus: *Familiar Colloquies*

Money never made a man happy yet, nor will it. There is nothing in its nature to produce happiness. The more a man has, the more he wants. Instead of its filling a vacuum, it makes one. If it satisfies one want, it doubles and trebles that want another way. That was a true proverb of the wise man, rely upon it: "Better is little with the fear of the Lord, than great treasure, and trouble therewith."

Benjamin Franklin

It is my opinion that a man's soul may be buried and perish under a dungheap, or in a furrow of the field, just as well as under a pile of money.

Nathaniel Hawthorne

Money is the god of our time, and Rothschild is his prophet.

Heinrich Heine: *Wit, Wisdom and Pathos: Lutetia*

Money spent on myself may be a millstone about my neck; money spent on others may give me wings like the angels.

Roswell Dwight Hitchcock

Put not your trust in money, but put your money in trust.

Oliver Wendell Holmes, Sr.

All our money has a moral stamp. It is coined over again in an inward mint. The uses we put it to, the spirit in which we spend it, give it a character which is plainly perceptible to the eye of God.

Thomas Starr King

He that serves God for money will serve the Devil for better wages.

Sir Roger L'Estrange: *Tr. of Aesop: Fables*

It's good to have money and the things that money can buy, but it's good, too, to check up once in a while and make sure that you haven't lost the things that money can't buy.

George Horace Lorimer

Make to yourselves friends of the mammon of unrighteousness.

New Testament: Luke 16: 9

Thy money perish with thee.

New Testament: Acts 8: 20

The love of money is the root of all evil.

New Testament: I Timothy 6: 10

Teaching things which they ought not, for filthy lucre's sake.

New Testament: Titus 1: 11

Money answereth all things.

Old Testament: Ecclesiastes 10: 19

Without money and without price.

Old Testament: Isaiah 55: 1

God makes, and apparel shapes, but it's money that finishes the man.

John Ray: *English Proverbs*

When money speaks the truth is silent.

Russian Proverb

By doing good with his money, a man, as it were, stamps the image of God upon it, and makes it pass current for the merchandise of heaven.

John Rutledge

Mammon is the largest slave-holder in the world.

Frederick Saunders

No man is really consecrated until his money is dedicated.

Roy L. Smith: *The Methodist Story*

Mammon has enriched his thousands, and has damned his ten thousands.

Robert South

Money is an amoral instrument, and like science serves good and evil alike. There's no such thing as dirty money; the stain is only on the hand that holds it as giver or taker.

A. M. Sullivan: *Dun's Review*

Nothing that is God's is obtainable by money.

Tertullian: *The Christian's Defence*

The lack of money is the root of all evil.

Mark Twain

Make all you can, save all you can, give all you can.

John Wesley

When I have any money I get rid of it as quickly as possible, lest it find a way into my heart.

John Wesley

Money buys everything except love, personality, freedom, immortality.

Wisdom

MORALITY

Morals without religion will wither and die, like seed sown upon stony ground or among thorns.

Anonymous

The people of our nation and the people of the whole world need to be gripped by the moral imperatives which grow out of the nature of God, by a sense of right, by principles of truth, and by ideals of decency. Nothing is more needed by this sinful world than a revival of simple goodness and genuine uprightness.

Clifton J. Allen: *Points for Emphasis,*
Broadman Press

There is no true and abiding morality that is not founded in religion.

Henry Ward Beecher

The moral life of any people rises or falls with the vitality or decay of its religious life.

John Sutherland Bonnell

No mere man since the Fall, is able in this life perfectly to keep the Commandments.

*Book of Common Prayer: Shorter
Catechism*

The divorcement of morals and piety is characteristic of all pagan religions.

David J. Burrell

Morality, taken as a part from religion, is but another name for decency in sin.

Horace Bushnell

Morality is the vestibule of religion.

Edwin Hubbell Chapin

Morality, said Jesus, is kindness to the weak; morality, said Nietzsche, is the bravery of the strong; morality, said Plato, is the effective harmony of the whole. Probably all three doctrines must be combined to find a perfect ethic; but can we doubt which of the elements is fundamental?

Will Durant: *The Story of Philosophy,*
Simon & Schuster, Inc.

Piety and morality are but the same spirit differently manifested.—Piety is religion with its face toward God; morality is religion with its face toward the world.

Tryon Edwards

Men talk of "mere Morality," which is much as if one should say "Poor God, with nobody to help him."

Ralph Waldo Emerson: *Conduct of Life:
Worship*

It is not guided missiles but guided morals that is our great need today.

George L. Ford: *Wesleyan Methodist*

To become Love, Friendship needs what Morality needs to become Religion—the fire of emotion.

Richard Garnett: *De Flagello Myrteo,* IV

Atheistic morality is not impossible, but it will never answer our purpose.

Roswell Dwight Hitchcock

All moral obligation resolves itself into the obligation of conformity to the will of God.

Charles Hodge

Religion without morality is a superstition and a curse, and morality without religion is impossible.—The only salvation for man is in the union of the two as Christianity unites them.

Mark Hopkins

The Christian religion is the only one that puts morality on its proper and right basis: the fear and love of God.

Samuel Johnson

It is God's will, not merely that we should *be* happy, but that we should *make* ourselves happy. This is the true morality.

Immanuel Kant: Lecture at Königsberg

To give a man full knowledge of true morality, I would send him to no other book than the New Testament.

John Locke

Morality without religion is only a kind of dead-reckoning—an endeavor to find our place on a cloudy sea by measuring the distance we have run, but without any observation of the heavenly bodies.

Henry Wadsworth Longfellow

Men are not made religious by performing certain actions which are externally good, but they must first have righteous principles, and then they will not fail to perform virtuous actions.

Martin Luther

Christian morality assumes to itself no merit —it sets up no arrogant claim to God's favor —it pretends not to "open the gates of heaven"; it is only the handmaid in conducting the Christian believer in his road toward them.

Richard Mant

The morality of the gospel is the noblest gift ever bestowed on man by God.

Charles Louis de Secondat Montesquieu

Religion, blushing, veils her sacred fires,
And unawares Morality expires.

Alexander Pope: *The Dunciad*, Bk. IV, l. 649

The highest morality, if not inspired and vitalized by religion, is but as the marble statue, or the silent corpse, to the living and perfect man.

Samuel I. Prime

There are many religions, but there is only one morality.

John Ruskin: *Lectures on Art*, lec. 2, sec. 37

The only morality that is clear in its course, pure in its precepts, and efficacious in its influence, is the morality of the gospel. All else, at last, is but idolatry—the worship of something of man's own creation, and that, imperfect and feeble like himself, and wholly insufficient to give him support and strength.

John Sargeant

Only he who knows God is truly moral.

Friedrich Wilhelm Joseph von Schelling

Morality without religion is a tree without roots; a stream without any spring to feed it; a house built on the sand; a pleasant place to live in till the heavens grow dark, and the storm begins to beat.

James Boylan Shaw

The great secret of morals is love.

Percy Bysshe Shelley: *The Defence of Poetry*

All sects are different, because they come from men; morality is everywhere the same, because it comes from God.

Voltaire

Morality is religion in practice; religion is morality in principle.

Ralph Wardlaw

Reason and experience both forbid us to expect that national morality can prevail in exclusion of religious principle.

George Washington

Morality does not make a Christian, yet no man can be a Christian without it.

Daniel Wilson

Morality was made for man, not man for morality.

Israel Zangwill: *Children of the Ghetto*

MOTHER

God pardons like a mother who kisses the offense into everlasting forgetfulness.

Henry Ward Beecher

A mother's love is indeed the golden link that binds youth to age; and he is still but a child, however time may have furrowed his cheek, or silvered his brow, who can yet recall, with a softened heart, the fond devotion, or the gentle chidings, of the best friend that God ever gives us.

Christian Nestell Bovee

The sweetest sounds to mortals given
Are heard in Mother, Home and Heaven.

William Goldsmith Brown: *Mother, Home, Heaven*

A mother is a mother still,
The holiest thing alive.

Samuel Taylor Coleridge: *The Three Graves*

I think it must somewhere be written that the virtues of mothers shall be visited on their children, as well as the sins of their fathers.

Charles Dickens

What are Raphael's Madonnas but the shadow of a mother's love, fixed in permanent outline forever?

Thomas Wentworth Higginson

Maternal love: a miraculous substance which God multiplies as He divides it.

Victor Hugo

God could not be everywhere, so He made mothers.

Jewish Proverb

Maids must be wives and mothers, to fulfil
Th' entire and holiest end of woman's being.

Frances Anne Kemble: *Woman's Heart*

The instruction received at the mother's knee, and the paternal lessons, together with the pious and sweet souvenirs of the fireside, are never effaced entirely from the soul.

Abbé Félicité Robert de Lamennais

No man is poor who has had a Godly mother.

Abraham Lincoln

Even He that died for us upon the cross, in the last hour, in the unutterable agony of death, was mindful of His mother, as if to teach us that this holy love should be our last worldly thought,—the last point of earth from which the soul should take its flight for heaven.

Henry Wadsworth Longfellow

When Eve was brought unto Adam, he became filled with the Holy Spirit, and gave her the most sanctified, the most glorious of appelations. He called her Eva, that is to say, the Mother of All. He did not style her wife, but simply mother,—mother of all living creatures. In this consists the glory and the most precious ornament of woman.

Martin Luther

Honour thy father and mother; which is the first commandment with promise.

New Testament: Ephesians 6: 2

The mother in her office holds the key of the soul; and she it is who stamps the coin of character and makes the being who would be a savage, but for her gentle cares, a Christian man! Then crown her the queen of the world.

Old Play

And Adam called his wife's name Eve; because she was the mother of all living.

Old Testament: Genesis 3: 20

Honour thy father and thy mother: that thy days may be long upon the land which the Lord thy God giveth thee.

Old Testament: Exodus 20: 12

A mother in Israel.

Old Testament: Judges 5: 7

My son, hear the instruction of thy father, and forsake not the law of thy mother.

Old Testament: Proverbs 1: 8

Despise not thy mother when she is old.

Old Testament: Proverbs 23: 22

Her children arise up, and call her blessed.

Old Testament: Proverbs 31: 28

As is the mother, so is her daughter.

Old Testament: Ezekiel 16: 44

The angels . . . singing unto one another,
Can find among their burning terms of love,
None so devotional as that of "mother."

Edgar Allan Poe: *To My Mother*

The mother love is like God's love; He loves us not because we are lovable, but because it is His nature to love, and because we are His children.

Earl Riney: *Church Management*

And say to mothers what a holy charge
Is theirs—with what a kingly power their love
Might rule the fountains of the new-born mind.

Lydia Huntley Sigourney: *The Mother o, Washington*, l. 35

An ounce of mother is worth a ton of priest.

Spanish Proverb

Who is best taught? He who has first learned from his mother.

The Talmud

For God, who lives above the skies,
Would look with vengeance in His eyes,
If I should ever dare despise
    My mother.

Ann and Jane Taylor: *Original Poems for Infant Minds*

Mother is the name for God in the lips and hearts of little children.

William Makepeace Thackeray: *Vanity Fair*, Vol. II, ch. 12

Thou, while thy babies around thee cling,
Shalt show us how divine a thing
A woman may be made.

William Wordsworth: *To a Young Lady*

N

never trod a rock so bare,
  Unblessed by verdure-brightened sod,
But some small flower, half-hidden there,
  Exhaled the fragrant breath of God.
                              Anonymous

The little cares that fretted me,
  I lost them yesterday,
Among the fields above the sea,
  Among the winds at play, . . .
Among the hushing of the corn,
  Where drowsy poppies nod,
Where ill thoughts die and good are born—
  Out in the fields of God.
          Anonymous: *Out in the Fields*

This is my Father's world—His own design
But in His goodness He has made it mine!
                              Faye Carr Adams

If there's a power above us (and that there
    is all nature cries aloud
Through all her works) he must delight in
    virtue.
    Joseph Addison: *Cato*, Act V, sc. 1

The study of Nature is intercourse with the
Highest Mind. You should never trifle with
Nature.

  Jean Louis Agassiz: *Agassiz at Penikese*

God made the beauties of nature like a child
playing in the sand.
        Ascribed to Apollonius of Tyana

God Almighty first planted a garden.
        Sir Francis Bacon: *Of Gardens*

Art is man's nature: nature is God's art.
                    Philip James Bailey

Flowers are the sweetest things God ever
made and forgot to put a soul into.
              Henry Ward Beecher

Nature is God's tongue. He speaks by
summer and by winter. He can manifest himself by the wind, by the storm, by the calm.
Whatever is sublime and potent, whatever is
sweet and gentle, whatever is fear-inspiring,
whatever is soothing, whatever is beautiful
to the eye or repugnant to the taste, God
may employ. The heavens above, and the
procession of the seasons as they month by
month walk among the stars, are various
manifestations of God.

              Henry Ward Beecher

What unnumbered cathedrals has He reared
in the forest shades, vast and grand, full of
curious carvings, and haunted evermore by
tremulous music; and in the heavens above,
how do stars seem to have flown out of His
hand faster than sparks out of a mighty forge!
              Henry Ward Beecher

Now nature is not a variance with art, nor
art with nature, they being both servants
of his providence; art is the perfection of
nature; were the world now as it was the
sixth day, there were yet a chaos; nature hath
made one world, and art another. In brief,
all things are artificial; for nature is the art
of God.
  Sir Thomas Browne: *Religio Medici*,
                              Pt. XVI

  God is seen God
In the star, in the stone, in the flesh, in the
  soul and the clod.
        Robert Browning: *Saul*, st. 17

I trust in Nature for the stable laws
Of beauty and utility. Spring shall plant
And Autumn garner to the end of time,
I trust in God—the right shall be the right
And other than the wrong, while he endures;
I trust in my own soul, that can perceive
The outward and the inward, Nature's good
And God's.

> Robert Browning: *A Soul's Tragedy*

Nature, which is the time-vesture of God and
reveals Him to the wise, hides Him from the
foolish.

> Thomas Carlyle: *Sartor Resartus*, III

It is truly a most Christian exercise to extract
a sentiment of piety from the works and
appearances of nature. Our Saviour expatiates on a flower, and draws from it the
delightful argument of confidence in God.
He gives us to see that taste may be combined
with piety, and that the same heart may be
occupied with all that is serious in the con-
templations of religion, and be, at the same
time, alive to the charms and loveliness of
nature.

> Thomas Chalmers

Nature, the vicar of th' almighty Lord.

> Geoffrey Chaucer: *The Parlement of
> Foules*, l. 379

The man who can really, in living union
of the mind and heart, converse with God
through nature, finds in the material forms
around him, a source of power and happiness
inexhaustible, and like the life of angels.—
The highest life and glory of man is to be
alive unto God; and when this grandeur of
sensibility to him, and this power of communion with him is carried, as the habit of
the soul, into the forms of nature, then the
walls of our world are as the gates of heaven.

> George B. Cheever

At home with Nature, and at one with God!

> Florence Earle Coates: *The Angelus*

All Nature ministers to Hope.

> Hartley Coleridge: *Sonnets*, no. 35

God made the country, and man made the
town.

> William Cowper

Nature is but a name for an effect whose
cause is God.

> William Cowper

What man has written man may read;
But God fills every root and seed
With cryptic words, too strangely set
For mortals to decipher yet.

> Charles Dalmon: *Document*

Nature is the art of God Eternal.

> Alighieri Dante: *De monarchia*

Love all God's creation, the whole and every
grain of sand in it. Love every leaf, every ray
of God's light. Love the animals, love the
plants, love everything. If you love everything, you will perceive the divine mystery
in things. Once you perceive it, you will begin to comprehend it better every day. And
you will come at last to love the whole world
with an all-embracing love.

> Feodor Dostoevski: *The Brothers
> Karamazov*

Nature and revelation are alike God's books;
each may have mysteries, but in each there
are plain practical lessons for everyday duty.

> Tryon Edwards

Nature is too thin a screen; the glory of the
omnipresent God bursts through everywhere.

> Ralph Waldo Emerson

I do not count the hours I spend
In wandering by the sea;
The forest is my loyal friend,
Like God it useth me.

> Ralph Waldo Emerson: *Waldeinsamkeit*

Nature is the living, visible garment of God.

> Johann Wolfgang von Goethe

Sympathy with nature is part of the good
man's religion.

> Frederic Henry Hedge

From Thy hand
The worlds were cast; yet every leaflet claims
From that same hand its little shining sphere
Of star-lit dew.

Oliver Wendell Holmes, Sr.

Look at Nature. She never wearies of saying
over her floral pater-noster. In the crevices
of Cyclopean walls,—on the mounds that
bury huge cities, in the dust where men lie,
dust also,—still that same sweet prayer and
benediction. The amen of Nature is always
a flower.

Oliver Wendell Holmes, Sr.

Nature, the Handmaid of God Almighty.

James Howell: *Familiar Letters: To
Dr. T. P.*, Bk. II

Natural objects themselves, even when they
make no claim to beauty, excite the feelings,
and occupy the imagination. Nature pleases,
attracts, delights, merely because it is nature.
We recognize in it an Infinite Power.

Karl Wilhelm von Humboldt

As a countenance is made beautiful by the
soul's shining through it, so the world is
beautiful by the shining through it of God.

Johann Georg Jacobi

Study nature as the countenance of God.

Charles Kingsley

And Nature, the old nurse, took
The child upon her knee,
Saying, "Here is a story-book
Thy Father has written for thee."

"Come, wander with me," she said,
"Into regions yet untrod;
And read what is still unread
In the manuscripts of God."

Henry Wadsworth Longfellow: *Fiftieth
Birthday of Agassiz*

I hold that we have a very imperfect knowledge of the works of nature till we view
them as the works of God,—not only as
works of mechanism, but works of intelligence, not only as under laws, but under a
Lawgiver, wise and good.

James McCosh

God makes the glow worm as well as the star;
the light in both is divine.

George Macdonald

A voice is in the wind I do not know;
A meaning on the face of the high hills
Whose utterance I cannot comprehend.
A something is behind them: that is God.

George Macdonald: *Within and Without,*
Pt. I, sc. 1

Behold! the Holy Grail is found,
Found in each poppy's cup of gold;
And God walks with us as of old.
Behold! the burning bush still burns
For man, whichever way he turns;
And all God's earth is holy ground.

Joaquin Miller: *Dawn at San Diego*

Every formula which expresses a law of
nature is a hymn of praise to God.

Maria Mitchell

And not from Nature up to Nature's God,
But down from Nature's God look Nature
through.

Robert Montgomery: *Luther: A Landscape of Domestic Life*

There is a signature of wisdom and power
impressed on the works of God, which evidently distinguishes them from the feeble
imitations of men,—Not only the splendor
of the sun, but the glimmering light of the
glowworm, proclaims his glory.

John Newton

The heavens declare the glory of God; and
the firmament sheweth his handywork.

Old Testament: Psalms 19: 1

Laws of Nature are God's thoughts thinking
themselves out in the orbits and the tides.

Charles Henry Parkhurst: *Sermons:
Pattern in Mount*

Nature has some perfections, to show that
she is the image of God; and some defects, to
show that she is only His image.

Blaise Pascal: *Pensées*, XXIV

All are but parts of one stupendous whole,
Whose body Nature is, and God the soul.

Alexander Pope: *Essay on Man*, Ep. I,
l. 267

Slave to no sect, who takes no private road,
But looks through Nature up to Nature's
God.

Alexander Pope: *Essay on Man*, Ep. IV
l. 331

"Look at us," said the violets blooming at
her feet. "All last winter we slept in the seeming death, as your mother is sleeping now;
but at the right time God awakened us, and
here we are to comfort you."

Edward Payson Roe

And this our life exempt from public haunt
Finds tongues in trees, books in the running
brooks,
Sermons in stones and good in every thing.

William Shakespeare: *As You Like It*,
Act II, sc. 1, l. 15

Go thou and seek the House of Prayer!
I to the woodlands wend, and there,
In lovely Nature see the God of Love.

Robert Southey: *Written on Sunday
Morning*

Blessed are they who never read a newspaper,
for they shall see Nature, and through her,
God.

Henry David Thoreau: *Essays and Other
Writings*

Talk not of temples, there is one
  Built without hands, to mankind given;
Its lamps are the meridian sun
  And all the stars of heaven,
Its walls are the cerulean sky,
  Its floor the earth so green and fair,
The dome its vast immensity
  All Nature worships there!

David Vedder: *The Temple of Nature*

Grant me, O God, the power to see
In every rose, eternity.
In every bud, the coming day;
In every snow, the promised May.
In every storm the legacy
Of rainbows smiling down at me!

Virginia Wuerfel

The course of nature governs all!
The course of nature is the heart of God.

Edward Young: *Night Thoughts*,
Night IX, l. 1280

NEIGHBORS

We can never be the better for our religion
if our neighbor is the worse for it.

Anonymous

Hast thou heard a word against thy neighbor? Let it die within thee, trusting that it
will not burst thee.

Apocrypha: Ecclesiasticus 19: 10

Most people repent of their sins by thanking
God they ain't so wicked as their neighbor.

Josh Billings

To God be humble, to thy friend be kind,
And with thy neighbors gladly lend and
  borrow.
His chance to-night, it may be thine tomorrow.

William Dunbar: *No Treasure Without
Gladness*

Nor knowest thou what argument
Thy life to thy neighbor's creed has lent,
All are needed by each one;
Nothing is fair or good alone.

Ralph Waldo Emerson: *Each and All*

Love your neighbor, but be careful of your
neighborhood.

John Hay

He who prays for his neighbor will be heard
for himself.

Hebrew Proverb

He who wins honors through his neighbor's shame will never reach Paradise.

Hebrew Proverb

Love your neighbor, yet pull not down your hedge.

George Herbert: *Jacula Prudentum*

All is well with him who is beloved of his neighbors.

Ibid.

If you want your neighbor to know what Christ will do for him, let the neighbor see what Christ has done for you.

Houston (Texas) *Times, All-Church Press*

There is more pleasure in being shocked by the sin of one's neighbor or one's neighbor's wife than in eating cream buns.

Robert Lynd

You've got to save your own soul first, and then the souls of your neighbors if they will let you; and for that reason you must cultivate, not a spirit of criticism, but the talents that attract people to the hearing of the Word.

George Macdonald: *The Marquis of Lossie*, ch. 27

Love thy neighbour as thyself.

New Testament: Matthew 19: 19

Thou shalt not bear false witness against thy neighbour.

Old Testament: Exodus 20: 16

He that is void of wisdom despiseth his neighbour: but a man of understanding holdeth his peace.

Old Testament: Proverbs 11: 12

Debate thy cause with thy neighbour himself; and discover not a secret to another.

Old Testament: Proverbs 25: 9

Withdraw thy foot from thy neighbour's house; lest he be weary of thee, and so hate thee.

Old Testament: Proverbs 25: 17

Better is a neighbour that is near than a brother far off.

Old Testament: Proverbs 27: 10

The most pious may not live in peace, if it does not please his wicked neighbor.

Johann Christoph Friedrich von Schiller:
Wilhelm Tell, IV, 3, 124

Your neighbor's right is God's right.

Turkish Proverb

Looking through the wrong end of a telescope is an injustice to the astronomer, to the telescope, and to the stars; likewise, looking at our neighbor's faults instead of the attributes gives us an incorrect conception of ourselves, our neighbor, and our God.

William A. Ward: Tulsa *Herald, All-Church Press*

O

OBEDIENCE

The distinguishing mark of religion is not so much liberty as obedience, and its value is measured by the sacrifices which it can extract from the individual.

Henri Frédéric Amiel

Wicked men obey from fear, good men, from love.

Aristotle

He who is false to present duty breaks a thread in the loom, and will find the flaw when he may have forgotten its cause.

Henry Ward Beecher

Thirty years of our Lord's life are hidden in these words of the gospel: "He was subject unto them."

Jacques Bénigne Bossuet

Obedience must be the struggle and desire of our life. Obedience, not hard and forced, but ready, loving and spontaneous; the doing of duty, not merely that the duty may be done, but that the soul in doing it may become capable of receiving and uttering God.

Phillips Brooks

I'll go where you want me to go, dear Lord,
  O'er mountain or plain or sea;
I'll say what you want me to say, dear Lord,
  I'll be what you want me to be.

Mary Brown: Hymn: I'll Go Where You Want Me To Go

The fear of some divine and supreme powers keep men in obedience.

Robert Burton: Anatomy of Melancholy, Pt. III, sc. 4, mem. 1, subs. 2

As long as we work on God's line, He will aid us. When we attempt to work on our own lines, He rebukes us with failure.

Theodore Ledyard Cuyler

How will you find good? It is not a thing of choices; it is a river that flows from the foot of the invisible throne, and flows by the path of obedience.

George Eliot

It is vain thought to flee from the work that God appoints us, for the sake of finding a greater blessing, instead of seeking it where alone it is to be found—in loving obedience.

George Eliot

Obedience to God is the most infallible evidence of sincere and supreme love to him.

Nathanael Emmons

No principle is more noble, as there is none more holy, than that of a true obedience.

Henry Giles

There is one proposition in which the whole matter, as it is relevant to human duty, may be summed up; that all our works, alike inward and outward, great and small, ought to be done in obedience to God.

William Ewart Gladstone

A dying Christian father bade farewell to his family and then turning to his wife said, "My dear, see that you bring the children up to honor and obey you, for if they don't obey you when they are young, they won't obey God when they are older."

Harry A. Ironside: Houston (Texas) Times, All-Church Press

Nothing is really lost by a life of sacrifice; everything is lost by failure to obey God's call.

Henry Parry Liddon

I find the doing of the will of God, leaves me no time for disputing about His plans.

George Macdonald: *Marquis of Lossie,*
ch. 72

That is best which God sends;
It was His will; it is mine.

Owen Meredith

That thou art happy, owe to God;
That thou continuest such, owe to thyself,
That is, to thy obedience.

John Milton: *Paradise Lost,* Bk. V, l. 520

Ascend, I follow thee, safe guide, the path
Thou lead'st me, and to the hand of heav'n submit.

John Milton: *Paradise Lost,* Bk. XI, l. 371

Henceforth I learn that to obey is best,
And love with fear the only God.

John Milton: *Paradise Lost,* Bk. XII, l. 561

The first law that ever God gave to man was a law of obedience; it was a commandment pure and simple, wherein man had nothing to inquire after or to dispute, for as much as to obey is the proper office of a rational soul acknowledging a heavenly superior and benefactor. From obedience and submission spring all other virtues, as all sin does from self-opinion and self-will.

Michel Eyquem de Montaigne

Rebellion to tyrants is obedience to God.

Motto on Thomas Jefferson's Seal

If ye love me, keep my commandments.

New Testament: John 14: 15

We ought to obey God rather than men.

New Testament: Acts 5: 29

When thou art in tribulation, and all these things are come upon thee, even in the latter days, if thou turn to the Lord thy God, and shalt be obedient unto his voice; (For the Lord thy God is a merciful God;) he will not forsake thee, neither destroy thee, nor forget the covenant of thy fathers which he sware unto them.

Old Testament: Deuteronomy 4: 30–31

To obey is better than sacrifice, and to hearken than the fat of rams.

Old Testament: I Samuel 15: 22

If ye be willing and obedient, ye shall eat the good of the land.

Old Testament: Isaiah 1: 19

Let the ground of all religious actions be obedience; examine not why it is commanded, but observe it because it is commanded. True obedience neither procrastinates nor questions.

Francis Quarles

It has been well remarked, it is not said that *after* keeping God's commandments, but *in* keeping them there is great reward. God has linked these two things together, and no man can separate them—obedience and peace.

Frederick William Robertson

Obedience decks the Christian most.

Johann Christoph Friedrich von Schiller:
Fight With the Dragon

We are born subjects, and to obey God is perfect liberty. He that does this shall be free, safe, and happy.

Seneca

To obey God in some things and not in others shows an unsound heart. Childlike obedience moves toward every command of God, as the needle points where the loadstone draws.

Thomas Watson

OBEDIENCE

In simple trust like theirs who heard
  Beside the Syrian sea
The gracious calling of the Lord,
Let us, like them, without a word
  Rise up and follow Thee.

John Greenleaf Whittier

OBEDIENCE

God is too great to be withstood, too just to do wrong, too good to delight in any one's misery. We ought, therefore, quietly to submit to His dispensations as the very best.

Daniel Wilson

God does not listen to the prayer of him who does not obey his parents.

Pope Xystus I: *The Ring*

P

PAIN

The greatest pain is physical pain.

St. Augustine: *Soliloquies*, I

Pain is in itself an evil, and indeed without exception, the only evil.

Jeremy Bentham: *Principles of Morals and Legislation*, X

He preaches patience that never knew pain.

Henry George Bohn: *Handbook of Proverbs*

Pain is the outcome of sin.

Gautama Buddha

No man can be brave who thinks pain the greatest evil; nor temperate, who considers pleasure the highest good.

Cicero: *De Officiis*, Bk. I, ch. 2, sec. 5

Resolved. When I feel pain, to think of the pains of martyrdom, and of Hell.

Jonathan Edwards: *Resolutions*

He has seen but half the universe who never has been shewn the house of Pain.

Ralph Waldo Emerson: *Natural History of Intellect: The Tragic*

Pain is the price that God putteth upon all things.

James Howell: *Proverbs*, p. 19

Pain is no evil, Unless it conquer us.

Charles Kingsley: *St. Maura*

This life of ours is a wild aeolian harp
of many a joyous strain,

But under them all there runs a loud perpetual wail, as of souls in pain.

Henry Wadsworth Longfellow: *Christus. The Golden Legend*, Pt. IV, st. 2

There is purpose in pain,
Otherwise it were devilish.

Owen Meredith: *Lucile*, Pt. II, Canto V, st. 8

Although today He prunes my twigs with pain,
Yet doth His blood nourish and warm my root:
Tomorrow I shall put forth buds again
And clothe myself with fruit.

Christina Georgina Rossetti: *From House to House*

The scourge of life, and death's extreme disgrace,
The smoke of hell,—that monster called Paine.

Sir Philip Sidney: *Sidera Paine*

Pain is the correlative of some species of wrong—some kind of divergence from that course of action which perfectly fills our requirements.

Herbert Spencer: *The Data of Ethics*, XV

Pain and pleasure, like light and darkness, succeed each other; and he only who knows how to accommodate himself to their returns, and can wisely extract the good from the evil, knows how to live.

Laurence Sterne

When pain can't bless, heaven quits us in despair.

Edward Young: *Night Thoughts*, Night IX, l. 500

323

PATRIOTISM

These gentry are invariably saying all they can in dispraise of their native land; and it is my opinion, grounded upon experience, that an individual who is capable of such baseness would not hesitate at the perpetration of any villainy, for next to the love of God, the love of country is the best preventive of crime.

George Borrow: *The Bible in Spain*, ch. 4

Patriotism consists not in waving the flag, but in striving that our country shall be righteous as well as strong.

James Bryce

Standing as I do in view of God and eternity, I realize that patriotism is not enough, I must have no hatred or bitterness towards anyone. They have all been very kind to me here.

Edith Cavell. To the English chaplain at Brussels the night before her execution

Who loves his country cannot hate mankind.

Charles Churchill

Sincere Christianity and true patriotism have much in common. Our finest patriotic hymn, "My Country 'Tis of Thee," was written in 1832 by a Baptist clergyman, Samuel Francis Smith; and the pledge of allegiance to the flag was written in 1892 by another Baptist minister, Francis Bellamy.

Ernest K. Emurian

My country is the world; my countrymen are mankind.

William Lloyd Garrison

Strike—for your altars and your fires;
Strike—for the green graves of your sires;
God—and your native land!

Fitz-Greene Halleck: *Marco Bozzaris*

Indeed, I tremble for my country when I reflect that God is just.

Thomas Jefferson: *Notes on Virginia;
Manners*

And how can men die better
Than facing fearful odds,
For the ashes of his fathers
And the temples of his gods?

Thomas Babington Macaulay: *Horatius*,
st. 27

Patriotism is a kind of religion; it is the egg from which wars are hatched.

Guy de Maupassant: *My Uncle Sosthenes*

Brave men and worthy patriots, dear to God, and famous to all ages.

John Milton: *Tractate of Education*

Blessed is the nation whose God is the Lord.

Old Testament: Psalms 33: 12

Righteousness exalteth a nation.

Old Testament: Proverbs 14: 34

My country is the world, and my religion is to do good.

Thomas Paine: *Rights of Man*, ch. 5

I do love
My country's good with a respect more
tender,
More holy and profound, than my own life.

William Shakespeare: *Coriolanus*,
Act III, sc. 3, l. 112

Be just and fear not:
Let all the ends thou aim'st at be thy
country's,
Thy God's and truth's.

William Shakespeare: *Henry VIII*,
Act III, sc. 2, l. 446

After what I owe to God, nothing should be more dear or more sacred to me than the love and respect I owe to my country.

Jacques Auguste de Thou

Whatever makes men good Christians makes them good citizens.

Daniel Webster

America is the crucible of God. It is the melting pot where all races are fusing and reforming . . . these are the fires of God you've come to . . . into the crucible with you all. God is making the American.

Israel Zangwill: *The Melting Pot*

PEACE

Peace—good will effectively asserted against greed.

Anonymous

With every recurring Christmas morning the prospects of the world's peace grow brighter, and the practice of universal brotherhood comes a little nearer to the door.

Anonymous

Thou hast touched me and I have been translated into thy peace.

St. Augustine: *Confessions*, Bk. X, ch. 27

Peace is our final good.

St. Augustine: *The City of God*, XV

That peace which the world cannot give.

Book of Common Prayer: Evening Prayer

The pessimist's darkest suspicion is that the human race, deep down in its heart, hates peace.

Reprinted by special permission of *The* (Boston) *Globe*

If there is righteousness in the heart there will be beauty in the character. If there be beauty in the character, there is harmony in the home, there will be order in the nation. When there is order in the nation, there will be peace in the world.

Chinese Proverb

I prefer the most unfair peace to the most righteous war.

Cicero: *Epistola ad Atticum*

Peace is liberty in tranquility.

Cicero: *Philippics*

Nor is heaven always at peace.

Claudian: *De Bello Gothico*, l. 62

Peace is the evening star of the soul, as virtue is its sun; and the two are never far apart.

Charles Caleb Colton

Those Christians best deserve the name
Who studiously make peace their aim;
Peace, both the duty and the prize
Of him that creeps and him that flies.

William Cowper: *The Nightingale and Glow-Worm*

If we will have Peace without a worm in it, lay we the foundations of Justice and Righteousness.

Oliver Cromwell: *Speech*, January 23, 1656 (*Letters and Speeches*, IV, 13)

In his will is our peace.

Alighieri Dante: *Paradiso*, Bk. III, l. 85

The world will never have lasting peace so long as men reserve for war the finest human qualities. Peace, no less than war, requires idealism and self-sacrifice and a righteous and dynamic faith.

John Foster Dulles

I could not live in peace if I put the shadow of a wilful sin between myself and God.

George Eliot

With peace in his soul a man can face the most terrifying experiences. But without peace in his soul he cannot manage even as simple a task as writing a letter.

An English psychiatrist

With God in charge of our defenses, there will be peace within.

T. T. Faichney

Speak, move, act in peace, as if you were in prayer. In truth, this is prayer.

François de Salignac de La Mothe Fénelon

Peace doth not dwell in outward things, but within the soul; we may preserve it in the midst of the bitterest pain, if our will remain firm and submissive. Peace in this life springs from acquiescence, not in an exemption from suffering.

François de Salignac de La Mothe
Fénelon

Peace, like every other rare and precious thing, doesn't come to you. You have to go and get it.

Faith Forsyte: *Tit-Bits*

Peace is such a precious jewel that I would give anything for it but truth.

Matthew Henry

Where there is peace, God is.

George Herbert: *Jacula Prudentum,*
no. 729

We've got to recognize that we are not working (primarily) for a peaceful world. Peace will be a by-product of something else. We are working for a world of justice and rightness. Peace is a by-product of justice and mercy.

Stanley High: *The Evangel*

Depart in peace, ye messengers of peace.

Jewish Prayer for the Eve of Sabbath

If we have not peace within ourselves, it is in vain to seek it from outward sources.

François de La Rochefoucauld

God will keep no nation in supreme peace that will not do supreme duty.

William McKinley

The world will be safe and secure in its peace only when nations adopt the principles of Christ and play fair with them.

William Pierson Merrill

Peace hath her victories
No less renown'd than war.

John Milton

Blessed are the peacemakers.

New Testament: *Matthew 5: 9*

Think not that I am come to send peace on earth: I came not to send peace, but a sword.

New Testament: *Matthew 10: 34*

Glory to God in the highest, and on earth peace, good will toward men.

New Testament: *Luke 2: 14*

Peace be to this house.

New Testament: *Luke 10: 5*

Peace I leave with you, my peace I give unto you.

New Testament: *John 14: 27*

To be spiritually minded is life and peace.

New Testament: *Romans 8: 6*

If it be possible, as much as lieth in you, live peaceably with all men.

New Testament: *Romans 12: 18*

The peace of God, which passeth all understanding.

New Testament: *Philippians 4: 7*

The Lord will bless his people with peace.

Old Testament: *Psalms 29: 11*

Mark the perfect man, and behold the upright: for the end of that man is peace.

Old Testament: *Psalms 37: 37*

Great peace have they which love thy law: and nothing shall offend them.

Old Testament: *Psalms 119: 165*

Peace be within thy walls, and prosperity within thy palaces.

Old Testament: *Psalms 122: 7*

Her ways are ways of pleasantness, and all her paths are peace.

Old Testament: *Proverbs 3: 17*

When a man's ways please the Lord, he maketh even his enemies to be at peace with him.

Old Testament: Proverbs 16: 7

His name shall be called . . . The Prince of Peace.

Old Testament: Isaiah 9: 6

Thou wilt keep him in perfect peace, whose mind is stayed on thee: because he trusteth in thee.

Old Testament: Isaiah 26: 3

How beautiful upon the mountains are the feet of him that bringeth good tidings, that publisheth peace.

Old Testament: Isaiah 52: 7

They have healed also the hurt of the daughter of my people slightly, saying, Peace, peace, when there is no peace.

Old Testament: Jeremiah 6: 14

Fair peace is becoming to men; fierce anger belongs to beasts.

Ovid: *Ars Amatoria*

Five great enemies of peace inhabit with us —avarice, ambition, envy, anger, and pride; if these were to be banished, we should infallibly enjoy perpetual peace.

Petrarch

An effective organization for world peace will be established not through political diplomats around a peace table, but through Christian teachers in all lands, teaching citizens in Sunday School and public school the sacredness of human life.

J. M. Price

No peace was ever won from fate by subterfuge or agreement; no peace is ever in store for any of us, but that which we shall win by victory over shame or sin,—victory over the sin that oppresses, as well as over that which corrupts.

John Ruskin

People are always expecting to get peace in heaven: but you know whatever peace they get there will be ready-made. Whatever

making of peace *they* can be blest for, must be on the earth here.

John Ruskin: *The Eagle's Nest,* Lecture IX

You may either win your peace or buy it: win it, by resistance to evil; buy it, by compromise with evil.

John Ruskin: *The Two Paths,* Lecture V

In peace there's nothing so becomes a man As modest stillness and humility.

William Shakespeare: *Henry V,* Act III, sc. 1, l. 3

Peace is not absence of war, it is a virtue, a state of mind, a disposition for benevolence, confidence, justice.

Benedict de Spinoza

Peace is not the absence of conflict from life, but the ability to cope with it.

Sun Dial

Like one who leaves the trampled street
For some cathedral, cool and dim,
Where he can hear in music beat
The heart of prayer, that beats for him;
Restored and comforted, I go
To grapple with my tasks again;
Through silent worship taught to know
The blessed peace that follows pain.

Bayard Taylor

All men desire peace, but very few desire those things that make for peace.

Thomas à Kempis

From his cradle to his grave a man never does a single thing which has any first and foremost object save one—to secure peace of mind, spiritual comfort, for himself.

Mark Twain

The Bible teaches us that there is no foundation for enduring peace on earth, except in righteousness; that it is our duty to suffer for that cause if need be; that we are bound to fight for it if we have the power; and that if God gives us the victory we must use it for the perpetuation of righteous peace.

Henry van Dyke: *What Peace Means*

Drop thy still dews of quietness till all our
striving cease;
Take from our souls the strain and stress,
And let our ordered lives confess
The beauty of thy Peace.

John Greenleaf Whittier

As on the Sea of Galilee
The Christ is whispering "Peace."

John Greenleaf Whittier: *Tent on the
Beach: Kallundborg Church*

When earth as if on evil dreams
Looks back upon her wars,
And the white light of Christ outstreams
From the red disc of Mars,
His fame, who led the stormy van
Of battle, well may cease;
But never that which crowns the man
Whose victory was peace.

John Greenleaf Whittier: *William Francis
Bartlett*

There is no kind of peace which can be purchased on the bargain counter.

Carey Williams: *Forbes*

Open covenants of peace, openly arrived at.

Woodrow Wilson: Address to Congress,
January 8, 1918

PERFECTION

Perfection consists not in doing extraordinary things, but in doing ordinary things
extraordinarily well. Neglect nothing; the
most trivial action may be performed to
God.

Angélique Arnauld

The pursuit of perfection, then, is the pursuit of sweetness and light . . . He who works
for sweetness and light united, works to make
reason and the will of God prevail.

Matthew Arnold: *Culture and Anarchy.
Preface*

We want an aim that can never grow vile
and which cannot disappoint our hope.
There is but one such on earth, and it is
that of being like God. He who strives after
union with perfect love must grow out of
selfishness, and his success is secured in the
omnipotent holiness of God.

Seth Brooks

The body of all true religion consists, to be
sure, in obedience to the will of the Sovereign
of the world, in a confidence in His declara-
tions, and in imitation of His perfections.

Edmund Burke: *Reflections on the
Revolution in France*

Pray to be perfect, though material leaven
Forbid the spirit so on earth to be;
But if for any wish thou darest not pray,
Then pray to God to cast that wish away.

Hartley Coleridge: *Poems (Posthumous):
Prayer*

He who stops being better stops being good.

Oliver Cromwell

God made thee perfect, not immutable.

John Milton: *Paradise Lost,* Bk. V, l. 524

Be ye therefore perfect, even as your Father
which is in heaven is perfect.

New Testament: Matthew 5: 48

He that seeks perfection on earth leaves
nothing new for the saints to find in heaven;
as long as men teach, there will be mistakes
in divinity; and as long as they govern, errors
in state.

Francis Osborne

If we pretend to have reached either perfection or satisfaction, we have degraded ourselves and our work. God's work only may
express that, but ours may never have that
sentence written upon it, "Behold it was very
good."

John Ruskin

Human excellence, apart from God, is like
the fabled flower which, according to the

Rabbis, Eve plucked when passing out of Paradise. Severed from its native root, it is only the touching memorial of a lost Eden —sad while charming and beautiful, but dead.

Sir Charles Villiers Stanford

The divine nature is perfection; and to be nearest to the divine nature is to be nearest to perfection.

Xenophon

PIETY

Piety is the opposite of spiritual pauperism.

Anonymous

If your neighbor has made one pilgrimage to Mecca, watch him; if two, avoid him; if three, move to another street.

Arab Proverb

One day lived after the perfect rule of piety, is to be preferred before sinning immortality.

Sir Thomas Browne: *To a Friend*, sec. 29

Religious persecution may shield itself under the guise of a mistaken and over-zealous piety.

Edmund Burke: *Impeachment of Warren Hastings*

Piety is a silver chain uniting heaven and earth, temporal and spiritual, God and man together.

Nicolas Caussin

Piety is the foundation of all virtues.

Cicero: *Pro Cnaeo Plancio*, sec. 12

Every thought which genius and piety throw into the world, alters the world.

Ralph Waldo Emerson: *Essays: Of Politics*

All is vanity which is not honest, and there is no solid wisdom but in true piety.

John Evelyn

True piety hath in it nothing weak, nothing sad, nothing constrained. It enlarges the heart; it is simple, free, and attractive.

François de Salignac de La Mothe Fénelon

I do not doubt but that genuine piety is the spring of peace of mind; it enables us to bear the sorrows of life, and lessens the pangs of death; the same cannot be said of irreligion.

Jean de La Bruyère

Piety requires us to renounce no ways of life where we can act reasonably, and offer what we do to the glory of God.

William Law: *A Serious Call to a Devout and Holy Life*, XI

True piety is this: to look on all things with a master eye, and mind at peace.

Lucretius: *De Rerum Natura*, Bk. V

Young Obadias,
David, Josias,
All were pious.

The New England Primer

Let them learn first to shew piety at home.

New Testament: I Timothy 5: 4

The Moving Finger writes; and, having writ,
Moves on: nor all your Piety nor Wit
Shall lure it back to cancel half a Line,
Nor all your Tears wash out a Word of it.

Omar Khayyám: *The Rubáiyát*

Experience makes us see an enormous difference between piety and goodness.

Blaise Pascal

There is no piety but amongst the poor.

Thomas Randolph: *On the Content He Enjoys in the Muses*

From Piety, whose soul sincere
Fears God, and knows no other fear.

William Smyth: Ode for the Installation of the Duke of Gloucester as Chancellor of Cambridge

Be happy, but be happy through piety.
> Madame Anne Germaine de Staël:
> *Corinne*, Bk. XX, ch. 3

The Child is father of the Man;
And I could wish my days to be
Bound each to each by natural piety.
> William Wordsworth: *My Heart Leaps
> Up When I Behold*

Continence is the foundation of genuine piety.

> Pope Xystus I: *The Ring*

PITY

Piety and pity were originally the same. The "e" of piety is simply dropped in pity.

> Anonymous

Him who pitieth suffering men
Zeus pitieth, and his ways are sweet on earth.
> Aeschylus: *The Eumenides*

Compassion will cure more sins than condemnation.
> Henry Ward Beecher: *Proverbs from
> Plymouth Pulpit*

Pity is best taught by fellowship in woe.
> Samuel Taylor Coleridge

What humanity needs is not the promise of scientific immortality, but compassionate pity in this life and infinite mercy on the Day of Judgment.
> Joseph Conrad: *Notes on Life and Letters*,
> J. M. Dent & Sons, Ltd.

Pity is love when grown into excess.
> Sir Robert Howard: *The Vestal Virgin*

Love's pale sister, Pity.
> Sir William Jones: *Hymn to Darga*

Heaven arms with pity those whom it would not see destroyed.
> Lao-tze

To pity distress is but human; to relieve it is Godlike.
> Horace Mann: *Lectures on Education*,
> Lecture VI

Be ye all of one mind, having compassion one of another.
> New Testament: *I Peter 3: 8*

Shutteth up his bowels of compassion.
> New Testament: *I John 3: 17*

I have no longing for things great and fair,
Beauty and strength and grace of word or deed;
For all sweet things my soul has ceased to care;
Infinite pity—that is all its need.
> J. B. B. Nichols: *During Music*

It is of the Lord's mercies that we are not consumed, because his compassions fail not.
> Old Testament: *Lamentations 3: 22*

I warn you beforehand so to have pity on others that others may not have to take pity on you.
> Titus Maccius Plautus: *Trinummus*,
> Act II, sc. 2, l. 61

O God, show compassion on the wicked. The virtuous have already been blessed by Thee in being virtuous.
> Prayer of a Persian Dervish

We pity in others only those evils that we have ourselves experienced.
> Jean Jacques Rousseau

Compassion is the basis of all morality.
> Arthur Schopenhauer: *Basis of Morality*

Nothing but infinite pity is sufficient for the infinite pathos of human life.
> Joseph Henry Shorthouse

Pity's akin to love; and every thought
Of that soft kind is welcome to my soul.
> Thomas Southerne: *Oroonoko*, Act II,
> sc. 2, l. 64

All say, "How hard it is to die"—a strange complaint from people who have had to live. Pity is for the living, envy for the dead.

Mark Twain: *Pudd'nhead Wilson's Calendar*

Oh, brother man, fold to thy heart thy brother; where pity dwells, the peace of God is there.

John Greenleaf Whittier: *Worship*

POSSESSIONS

That man does not possess his estate; his estate possesses him.

Anonymous

To him that hath, we are told,
Shall be given. Yes, by the Cross!
To the rich man fate sends gold,
To the poor man loss on loss.

Thomas Bailey Aldrich: *From the Spanish*

Man should not consider his outward possessions as his own, but as common to all, so as to share them without hesitation when others are in need.

St. Thomas Aquinas

The wise man carries his possessions within him.

Bias of Priene

Most of the happiness in this world consists in possessing what others can't get.

Josh Billings

The rich are indeed rather possessed by their money than possessors.

Robert Burton: *Anatomy of Melancholy*, Pt. I, sec. 2, mem. 3, subsect. 12

We are Goddes stewardes all, nought of our owne we bare.

Thomas Chatterton: *Excelente Balade of Charitie*

The pleasure of possessing
Surpasses all expressing;
But 'tis too short a blessing,
And love too long a pain.

John Dryden: *Farewell, Ungrateful Traitor*

Possess your soul with patience.

John Dryden: *The Hind and the Panther*, Pt. III, l. 839

Mankind, by the perverse depravity of their nature, esteem that which they have most desired as of no value the moment it is possessed, and torment themselves with fruitless wishes for that which is beyond their reach.

François de Salignac de La Mothe Fénelon: *Télémaque*, Bk. XVIII

What we call real estate—the solid ground to build a house on—is the broad foundation on which nearly all the guilt of this world rests.

Nathaniel Hawthorne: *The House of the Seven Gables*

You will not rightly call him a happy man who possesses much; he more rightly earns the name of happy who is skilled in wisely using the gifts of the gods, and in suffering hard poverty, and who fears disgrace as worse than death.

Horace: *Carmina*, IX, Bk. IV, 9, 45

Use everything as if it belongs to God. It does. You are His steward.

Houston (Texas) *Times, All-Church Press*

I am happy in having learned to distinguish between ownership and possession. Books, pictures, and all the beauty of the world belong to those who love and understand them —not usually to those who possess them. All of these things that I am entitled to have I have—I own by divine right. So I care not a bit who possesses them.

James Howard Kehler: Houston (Texas) *Times, All-Church Press*

Possession's beef and ale—
Soft bed, fair wife, gay horse, good steel.—
Are they naught?
Possession means to sit astride of the world,
Instead of having it astride of you.

Charles Kingsley: *The Saint's Tragedy*, I

Enjoy thy possessions as if about to die, and use them sparingly, as if about to live. That man is wise who understands both these commandments, and hath applied a measure both to thrift and unthrift.

Lucian: *Greek Anthology*, Bk. X, epig. 26

Happily for our blessedness, the joy of possession soon palls.

George Macdonald

All the possessions of mortals are mortal.

Metrodorus: *Fragments*, frag. 35

Is it not lawful for me to do what I will with mine own?

New Testament: Matthew 20: 15

Unto every one that hath shall be given, and he shall have abundance: but from him that hath not shall be taken away even that which he hath.

New Testament: Matthew 25: 29

As having nothing, and yet possessing all things.

New Testament: II Corinthians 6: 10

What is thine is mine, and all mine is thine.

Titus Maccius Plautus: *Trinummus*,
Act II, sc. 2

For peace, with justice and honor, is the fairest and most profitable of possessions, but with disgrace and shameful cowardice it is the most infamous and harmful of all.

Polybius: *Histories*, IV, 31

The goods we spend we keep; and what we save
We lose: and only what we lose we have.

Francis Quarles: *Divine Fancies*, Bk. IV,
art. 70

Let the moment come when nothing is left but life, and you will find that you do not hesitate over the fate of material possessions.

Eddie Rickenbacker

I believe that every right implies a responsibility; every opportunity, an obligation; every possession, a duty.

John D. Rockefeller, Jr.: Address at Fisk
University, May 3, 1941

Much is required of them to whom much is given.

Sam Slick: *Wise Saws*, ch. 3

I am amused to see from my window here how busily man has divided and staked off his domain. God must smile at his puny fences running hither and thither everywhere over the land.

Henry David Thoreau: *Journal*

The Present, the Present, is all thou hast
For thy sure possessing;
Like the patriarch's angel hold it fast
Till it gives its blessing.

John Greenleaf Whittier: *My Soul and I*,
st. 34

POVERTY

There are God's poor and the Devil's poor.

Thomas Adams: *Sermons*, XI

The life of the poor is the curse of the heart.

Apocrypha: Ecclesiasticus 38: 19

In one important respect a man is fortunate in being poor. His responsibility to God is so much the less.

Christian Nestell Bovee

God only, who made us rich, can make us poor.

Elizabeth Barrett Browning: *Sonnets from
the Portuguese*, XXIV

overty is the wicked man's tempter, the
ood man's perdition, the proud man's curse,
he melancholy man's halter.

Edward George Bulwer-Lytton

)f all God's creatures, man
lone is poor.

Jane Welsh Carlyle: *To a Swallow
Building Under Our Eaves*

wise man poor is like a sacred book that's
ever read; to himself he lives and to all else
eems dead.

Thomas Dekker

Vhat the poor are to the poor, is little
nown, excepting to themselves and God.

Charles Dickens

'Tis as hard f'r a rich man to enther th' king-
lom iv Hiven as it is f'r a poor man to get
ut iv Purgatory.

Finley Peter Dunne: *Mr. Dooley's
Philosophy. Casual Observations*

The greatest man in history was the poorest.

Ralph Waldo Emerson: *Domestic Life*

As poor as a church mouse.

English Phrase

Poverty has this defect: it prompts a man to
evil deeds.

Euripides: *Electra*

Poverty is not a sin, but it is better to hide it.

French Proverb

As poor as Job.

John Gower: *Confessio Amantis*, V

I have now disposed of all my property to
my family; there is one thing more I wish
I could give them, and that is the Christian
religion. If they had this, and I had not given
them one shilling, they would be rich; but
if they had not that, and I have given them
all the world, they would be poor.

The will of Patrick Henry

Poverty is no sin.

George Herbert: *Outlandish Proverbs*

God could have made all rich, or all men
poor;
But why He did not, let me tell wherefore:
Had all been rich, where then had Patience
been?
Had all been poor, who had His Bounty
seen?

Robert Herrick: *Riches and Poverty*

Poor men have no souls.

John Heywood: *Proverbs*

Yes, child of suffering, thou may'st well be
sure
He who ordained the Sabbath loves the poor.

Oliver Wendell Holmes, Sr.: *Urania; or,
A Rhymed Lesson*, l. 325

My soul . . . will not own a notion so unholy,
As thinking that the rich by easy trips
May go to heav'n, whereas the poor and
lowly
Must work their passage, as they do in ships.

Thomas Hood: *Ode to Rae Wilson*, l. 129

O God! that bread should be so dear,
And flesh and blood so cheap!

Thomas Hood: *The Song of the Shirt*

There's none poor but such as God hates.

James Howell: *Proverbs*

Poverty is a blessing hated by all men.

Italian Proverb

The poor too often turn away, unheard,
From hearts that shut against them with a
snap
That will be heard in heaven.

Henry Wadsworth Longfellow

Lord God, I thank thee that thou hast been
pleased to make me a poor and indigent man
upon earth. I have neither house nor land
nor money to leave behind me.

Martin Luther

God has always been hard on the poor, and
He always will be.

Jean Paul Marat: *Letter to Camille
Desmoulins*

Poverty of possessions may easily be cured, but poverty of soul never.

Michel Eyquem de Montaigne: *Essays,*
Bk. III, ch. 10

Blessed are the poor in spirit: for theirs is the kingdom of heaven.

New Testament: Matthew 5: 3

The poor always ye have with you.

New Testament: John 12: 8

The needy shall not always be forgotten: the expectation of the poor shall not perish for ever.

Old Testament: Psalms 9: 18

Blessed is he that considereth the poor: the Lord will deliver him in time of trouble.

Old Testament: Psalms 41: 1

So shall thy poverty come as one that traveleth, and thy want as an armed man.

Old Testament: Proverbs 6: 11

The destruction of the poor is their poverty.

Old Testament: Proverbs 10: 15

There is that maketh himself rich, yet hath nothing: there is that maketh himself poor, yet hath great riches.

Old Testament: Proverbs 13: 7

Whoso mocketh the poor reproacheth his Maker.

Old Testament: Proverbs 17: 5

He that hath pity upon the poor lendeth unto the Lord.

Old Testament: Proverbs 19: 17

Give me neither poverty nor riches.

Old Testament: Proverbs 30: 8

What mean ye that ye beat my people to pieces, and grind the faces of the poor? saith the Lord God of Hosts.

Old Testament: Isaiah 3: 15

They sold the righteous for silver, and th poor for a pair of shoes.

Old Testament: Amos 2:

And the mistake of the best men throug generation after generation, has been th great one of thinking to help the poor b almsgiving, and by preaching of patience o of hope, and by every other means, emollien or consolatory, except the one thing whic God orders for them, justice.

John Ruski

Poverty comes from God, but not dirt.

The Talmu

POWER

A well known philosopher has written "Every man would like to be God if it were possible; some few find it difficult to admit the impossibility."

Anonymous

Energy is Eternal Delight.

William Blake: *Proverbs of Hell*

The great need of the world today is the spiritual power necessary for the overthrow of evil, for the establishment of righteousness, and for the ushering in of the era of perpetual peace; and that spiritual power begins in the surrender of the individual to God. It commences with obedience to the first commandment.

William Jennings Bryan

I know of nothing sublime which is not some modification of power.

Edmund Burke

We readily admit that Jesus and all the genuine saints throughout history had spiritual power and that they had a deep prayer life. We believe that there must be some connection between their power and their life of prayer.

Sherwood Eddy

Taught by that Power that pities me,
I learn to pity them.
Oliver Goldsmith: *Hermit*, st. 6

God of the present age and hour,
Thrill us anew with holy power!
William Stewart Gordon

The boast of heraldry, the pomp of power,
And all that beauty, all that wealth e'er
gave,
Await alike the inevitable hour,
The paths of glory lead but to the grave.
Thomas Gray: *Elegy in a Country
Churchyard*

I know
My God commands, whose power no power
resists.
Robert Greene: *Looking-Glass for
London and England*

There is more power in the open hand than
in the clenched fist.
Hardware News

The love of liberty is the love of others; the
love of power is the love of ourselves.
William Hazlitt: *The Rotarian*

Forget youth! but know, the Power above
With ease can save each object of his love;
Wide as his will, extends his boundless grace.
Homer: *Odyssey*, Bk. III, l. 285 (Pope's
trans.)

Praise the Power that hath made and pre-
served us a nation!
Then conquer we must when our cause it is
just,
And this be our motto, "In God is our trust!"
Francis Scott Key: *Star-Spangled Banner*

All our natural powers can be used mightily
by God, but only when we think nothing of
them and surrender ourselves to be simply
the vehicles of divine power, letting God use
us as He wills, content to be even despised
by men if He be glorified.
G. H. Knight

All public power proceeds from God.
Pope Leo XIII: *Immortale Dei*

That Power Which erring men call Chance.
John Milton: *Comus*, I

All power is given unto me in heaven and in
earth.
New Testament: Matthew 28: 18

The powers that be are ordained of God.
New Testament: Romans 13: 1

But we have this treasure in earthen vessels,
that the excellency of the power may be of
God, and not of us.
New Testament: II Corinthians 4: 7

Now unto him that is able to do exceeding
abundantly above all that we ask or think,
according to the power that worketh in us.
Unto him be glory in the church by Christ
Jesus.
New Testament: Ephesians 3: 20–21

The basic difference between physical and
spiritual power is that men use physical
power but spiritual power uses men.
Justin Wroe Nixon: *Advance*
(Congregational)

Not by might, nor by power, but by my
spirit, saith the Lord of hosts.
Old Testament: Zechariah 4: 6

Divine power plays with human affairs.
Ovid: *Epistulae ex Ponto*, Bk. IV,
Epis. III, l. 49

Nothing is so high and above all danger
that is not below and in the power of God.
Ovid: *Tristia*, IV, 8, 47

Give me the power to live for mankind;
Make me the mouth for such as cannot
speak.
Theodore Parker

A greater power than we can contradict
Hath thwarted our intents.
William Shakespeare: *Romeo and Juliet*,
Act V, sc. 3, l. 153

Confidence should arise from beneath, and
power descend from above.

> Emmanuel Joseph Sieyès, in Thiers:
> *Consulate and Empire*, Vol. I, p. 44

Power is a dangerous thing to handle, even
in religion.

> Joseph R. Sizoo: *Preaching Unashamed*,
> Abingdon Press

The power of kings (if rightly understood)
Is but a grant from Heaven of doing good.

> William Somerville: *Fables*, no. 12

Once more the Heavenly Power
    Makes all things new,
And domes the red-plough'd hills
    With loving blue;
The blackbirds have their wills,
    The throstles too.

> Alfred, Lord Tennyson: *Early Spring*, st. 1

He never sold the truth to serve the hour,
Nor paltered with Eternal God for power.

> Alfred, Lord Tennyson: *Ode on the Death
> of the Duke of Wellington*

To whatever side you turn, you are forced
to acknowledge your own ignorance and the
boundless power of the Creator.

> Voltaire

There is nothing so powerful as truth; and
often nothing so strange.

> Daniel Webster: *Arguments on the
> Murder of Captain White*,
> Vol. VI, p. 68

Right and truth are greater than any power,
and all power is limited by right.

> Benjamin Whichcote: *Moral and
> Religious Aphorisms*

PRAYER

The wings of prayer carry high and far.

> Anonymous

If Christians spent as much time praying a.
they do grumbling, they would soon have
nothing to grumble about.

> Anonymou

Prayer and provender hinder no man's
journey.

> Anonymous

Away in foreign fields they wondered how
    Their simple words had power—
At home the Christians, two or three had met
    To pray an hour.
Yes, we are always wondering, wondering
        how—
    Because we do not see
Someone—perhaps unknown and far away—
    On bended knee.

> Anonymous

In the morning, prayer is the key that opens
to us the treasures of God's mercies and blessings; in the evening, it is the key that shuts
us up under His protection and safeguard.

> Anonymous

Doubt not but God who sits on high,
    Thy secret prayers can hear;
When a dead wall thus cunningly
    Conveys soft whispers to the ear.

> Anonymous

Long tarries destiny, but comes to those who
pray.

> Aeschylus: *Chaephorae*, l. 464

I sit beside my lonely fire
    And pray for wisdom yet:
For calmness to remember
    Or courage to forget.

> Charles Hamilton Äidé: *Remember or
> Forget*

The only prayer which a well-meaning man
can pray is, O ye gods, give me whatever is
fitting unto me!

> Apollonius of Tyana

Prayer is the pillow of religion.

> Arab Proverb

know that thou art freed from all desires when thou hast reached such a point that thou prayest to God for nothing except what thou canst pray for openly.

Athenodorus: *Fragment: De Superstitione*

Grant us grace, Almighty Father, so to pray as to deserve to be heard.

Jane Austen

Our prayers must mean something to us if they are to mean anything to God.

Maltbie D. Babcock

Prayer is the spirit speaking truth to Truth.

Philip James Bailey: *Festus: Elsewhere*

'Oh, God, if I were sure I were to die tonight I would repent at once." It is the commonest prayer in all languages.

Sir James Matthew Barrie: *Sentimental Tommy*, p. 98, Charles Scribner's Sons

Seven days without prayer makes one weak.

Allen E. Bartlett

The man who says his prayers in the evening is a captain posting his sentries. After that, he can sleep.

Charles Baudelaire

If you are swept off your feet, it's time to get on your knees.

Fred Beck: *Evangelical Beacon*

I pray on the principle that wine knocks the cork out of a bottle. There is an inward fermentation, and there must be a vent.

Henry Ward Beecher

Prayer covers the whole of a man's life. There is no thought, feeling, yearning, or desire, however low, trifling, or vulgar we may deem it, which, if it affects our real interest or happiness, we may not lay before God and be sure of sympathy. His nature is such that our often coming does not tire him. The whole burden of the whole life of every man

may be rolled on to God and not weary him, though it has wearied the man.

Henry Ward Beecher

It is not well for man to pray cream, and live skim milk.

Henry Ward Beecher

To labor is to pray.

Motto of the Benedictine Order

He who ceases to pray ceases to prosper.

Sir William Gurney Benham: *Proverbs,* p. 783

Pray devoutly, but hammer stoutly.

Sir William Gurney Benham: *Proverbs,* p. 827

Do you know what is wrong with the world today? There's too much theologian and not enough kneeologian.

Dallas F. Billington: *Akron Baptist Journal*

Prayers plough not! Praises reap not!

William Blake: *Proverbs of Hell*

Prayer is not conquering God's reluctance, but taking hold of God's willingness.

Phillips Brooks

Prayer, in its simplest definition, is merely a wish turned God-ward.

Phillips Brooks

O, do not pray for easy lives. Pray to be stronger men. Do not pray for tasks equal to your powers. Pray for powers equal to your tasks.

Phillips Brooks: *Going Up to Jerusalem*

Prayer crowns God with the honor and glory due to His name, and God crowns prayer with assurance and comfort. The most praying souls are the most assured souls.

Thomas Benton Brooks

God hears no more than the heart speaks; and if the heart be dumb, God will certainly be deaf.

Thomas Benton Brooks

If you would have God hear you when you pray, you must hear Him when He speaks.

Thomas Benton Brooks

Every wish
Is like a prayer—with God.

Elizabeth Barrett Browning: *Aurora Leigh*

God answers sharp and sudden on some prayers.
And thrusts the thing we have prayed for in our face,
A gauntlet with a gift in't.

Ibid.

The greatest prayer is patience.

Gautama Buddha

He who runs from God in the morning will scarcely find Him the rest of the day.

John Bunyan

Prayer is a sincere, sensible, affectionate pouring out of the soul to God, through Christ in the strength and assistance of the Spirit, for such things as God has promised.

John Bunyan

The best prayers have often more groans than words.

John Bunyan

When thou prayest, rather let thy heart be without words than thy words without heart.

John Bunyan

They never sought in vain that sought the Lord aright!

Robert Burns: *The Cotter's Saturday Night*, st. 6

Ave Maria! 'tis the hour of prayer!

George Gordon, Lord Byron: *Don Juan,* Canto III, st. 103

Prayer is and remains always a native and deepest impulse of the soul of man.

Thomas Carlyle: *Letter to George A. Duncan*

Prayer is the most powerful form of energy one can generate. The influence of prayer on the human mind and body is as demonstrable as that of the secreting glands. Prayer is a force as real as terrestrial gravity. It supplies us with a flow of sustaining power in our daily lives.

Alexis Carrel: *Prayer*

God's way of answering the Christian's prayer for more patience, experience, hope and love often is to put him into the furnace of affliction.

Richard Cecil

Whoso will pray, he must fast and be clean, And fat his soul, and make his body lean.

Geoffrey Chaucer: *Canterbury Tales: Summoner's Tale*

I used to pray that God would do this or that. Now I pray that God will make His will known to me.

Mme. Chiang Kai-shek

Prayers are little messages sent up to God at night to get a cheaper rate.

A Child's Definition

Now, boys, remember one thing: do not make long prayers: always remember that the Lord knows something.

Ascribed by Joseph H. Choate to a speaker addressing a graduating class at a theological seminary in Tennessee

Prayer requires more of the heart than of the tongue.

Adam Clarke

Prayer is conversation with God.

Clement of Alexandria: *Stromateis*, VII

Prayer . . . the very highest energy of which the mind is capable.

Samuel Taylor Coleridge

But maybe prayer is a road to rise,
A mountain path leading toward the skies
To assist the spirit who truly tries,
But it isn't a shibboleth, creed nor code,

It isn't a pack-horse to carry your load,
It isn't a wagon, it's *only* a road.
And perhaps the reward of the spirit who
    tries
Is not the goal, but the exercise.

Edmund Vance Cooke: *Prayer. The
Uncommon Commoner*

This is that incense of the heart,
Whose fragrance smells to Heaven.

Nathaniel Cotton: *The Fireside,* st. 11

A man ought to know when to pray—it's
pretty late to pray for oars when the boat's
on the brink of the falls.

The Country Parson: Register-Tribune
Syndicate

Two went to pray? Oh, rather say
One went to brag, the other to pray;
One stands up close and treads on high
Where the other dares not send his eye;
One nearer to God's altar trod,
The other to the altar's God.

Richard Crashaw

Prayer is the spiritual gymnasium in which
we exercise and practice Godliness.

V. L. Crawford: *Christian Herald*

Let the Divine Mind flow through your own
mind, and you will be happier. I have found
the greatest power in the world in the power
of prayer. There is no shadow of doubt of
that. I speak from my own experience.

Cecil B. De Mille

To get nations back on their feet, we must
get down on our knees first.

Letter to Editor: Des Moines *Register*

I ask not a life for the dear ones,
    All radiant, as others have done,
But that life may have just enough shadow
    To temper the glare of the sun;
I would pray God to guard them from evil,
    But my prayer would bound back to my-
    self:
Ah! a seraph may pray for a sinner,
    But a sinner must pray for himself.

Charles M. Dickinson: *The Children*

Prayer is the little implement
Through which men reach
Where presence is denied them.

Emily Dickinson: *Poems,* Pt. J, no. 80

Every time you pray, if your prayer is sincere,
there will be new feeling and new meaning
in it which will give you fresh courage, and
you will understand that prayer is an education.

Feodor Dostoevski: *The Brothers
Karamazov,* Bk. VI, ch. 3

Our vows are heard betimes! and Heaven
    takes care
To grant, before we can conclude the pray'r:
Preventing angels met it half the way,
And sent us back to praise, who came to
    pray.

John Dryden: *Britania Rediviva,* I, 1

There can be prayers without words just as
well as songs, I suppose.

George Busson DuMaurier: *Trilby,*
Pt. VIII

The highest prayer is not one of faith merely;
it is demonstration. Such prayer heals sickness, and must destroy sin and death.

Mary Baker Eddy: *Science and Health
with Key to the Scriptures,* p. 16: 2–5

Pray, and then start answering your prayer.

Deane Edwards

What we seek we shall find; what we flee
from flees from us; as Goethe said, "What we
wish for in youth, comes in heaps on us in
old age," too often cursed with the granting
of our prayer; and hence the high caution,
that, since we are sure of having what we
wish, we beware to ask only for high things.

Ralph Waldo Emerson: *Conduct of Life:
Fate*

Prayer that craves a particular commodity,
anything less than all good, is vicious . . .
Prayer as a means to a private end is meanness and theft.

Ralph Waldo Emerson: *Essays, First
Series: Self-Reliance*

The prayer of the farmer kneeling in his field to weed it, the prayer of the rower kneeling with the stroke of his oar, are true prayers heard throughout nature.

Ralph Waldo Emerson: *Essays, First Series: Self-Reliance*

No man ever prayed heartily without learning something.

Ralph Waldo Emerson: *Miscellanies: Nature*

Though I am weak, yet God, when prayed, Cannot withhold his conquering aid.

Ralph Waldo Emerson: *The Nun's Aspiration*

Prayer is the contemplation of the facts of life from the highest point of view. It is the soliloquy of a beholding and jubilant soul. It is the Spirit of God pronouncing his works good.

Ralph Waldo Emerson

To pray . . . is to desire; but it is to desire what God would have us desire. He who desires not from the bottom of his heart, offers a deceitful prayer.

François de Salignac de La Mothe Fénelon: *Advice Concerning Prayer*

He who prays without confidence cannot hope that his prayers will be granted.

François de Salignac de La Mothe Fénelon: *Maximes: On Prayer*

Prayer is the soul getting into contact with the God in whom it believes.

Harry Emerson Fosdick

God is not a cosmic bell-boy for whom we can press a button to get things.

Harry Emerson Fosdick: *Prayer*

He prays well who is so absorbed with God that he does not know he is praying.

St. Francis de Sales

Work as if you were to live 100 years; pray as if you were to die tomorrow.

Benjamin Franklin: *Poor Richard's Almanac*

Serving God is doing good to man, but praying is thought an easier service and therefore more generally chosen.

Benjamin Franklin

Prayer is a cry of hope.

French Proverb

A good prayer, though often used, is still fresh and fair in the ears and eyes of Heaven.

Thomas Fuller: *Good Thoughts in Bad Times*

Ejaculations are short prayers darted up to God on emergent occasions.

Ibid.

Prayer should be the key of the day and the lock of the night.

Thomas Fuller: *Gnomologia*

None can pray well but he that lives well.

Ibid.

Pray as though no work would help, and work as though no prayer would help.

German Proverb

When you cannot pray as you would, pray as you can.

Dean Edward M. Goulburn

Good prayers never come creeping home. I am sure I shall receive either what I ask, or what I should ask.

Joseph Hall

Prayer serves as an edge and border to preserve the web of life from unraveling.

Robert Hall

Prayer is like the turning on of an electric switch. It does not create the current; it simply provides a channel through which the electric current may flow.

Max Handel: *Rosicrucian Fellowship Magazine*

The person who asks the gods for special protection is a racketeer by nature.

Henry S. Haskins

Prayer . . . is the recovery of the soul's breathing.

Gerald Heard: *The Christian Century*

God does not listen to the prayers of the proud.

Hebrew Proverb

It is good for us to keep some account of our prayers, that we may not unsay them in our practice.

Matthew Henry

Who goes to bed, and doth not pray,
Maketh two nights to every day!

George Herbert: *Charms and Knots*

Prayers and provender hinder no journey.

George Herbert: *Jacula Prudentum*, no. 273

Resort to sermons, but to prayers most:
Praying's the end of preaching.

George Herbert: *The Temple*

God, who's in Heav'n, will hear from thence,
If not to th' sound, yet to the sense.

Robert Herrick: *God Hears Us*

Prayers and Praises are those spotless two
Lambs, by the Law, which God requires as due.

Robert Herrick: *God's Part*

In prayer the lips ne'er act the winning part
Without the sweet concurrence of the heart.

Robert Herrick: *The Heart*

Good when he gives, supremely good,
Nor less when he denies,
E'en crosses from his sovereign hand
Are blessings in disguise.

James Hervey: *Hymn*

Pray for yourself, I am not sick.

John Heywood: *Proverb*, Pt. II, ch. 7

I know not by what methods rare,
But this I know: God answers prayer.
I know not if the blessing sought
Will come in just the guise I thought.
I leave my prayer to Him alone
Whose will is wiser than my own.

Eliza M. Hickok

Who hearkens to the gods, the gods give ear.

Homer: *Iliad*, Bk. I, l. 280

The spectacle of a nation praying is more awe-inspiring than the explosion of an atomic bomb. The force of prayer is greater than any possible combination of man-controlled powers, because prayer is man's greatest means of trapping the infinite resources of God.

J. Edgar Hoover

Our prayer and God's mercy are like two buckets in a well; while the one ascends the other descends.

Mark Hopkins

Certain thoughts are prayers. There are moments when, whatever be the attitude of the body, the soul is on its knees.

Victor Hugo

Those who always pray are necessary to those who never pray.

Victor Hugo

I have lived to thank God that all of my prayers have not been answered.

Jean Ingelow

Is there never a chink in the world above
Where they listen for words from below?

Jean Ingelow: *Supper at the Mill*

Father, I scarcely dare to pray,
So clear I see, now it is done,
How I have wasted half my day,
And left my work but just begun.

Helen Hunt Jackson: *A Last Prayer*, st. 1

Energy which but for prayer would be bound is by prayer set free and operates.

William James (permission to reprint granted by Paul R. Reynolds & Son)

To saints their very slumber is a prayer.

St. Jerome

Every man wants to pray the day before he dies. As he does not know when his time will come, he must pray every day in order to be safe.

Jewish Proverb

I know of no good prayers but those in the Book of Common Prayer.

Samuel Johnson

You should pray for a sound mind in a sound body; for a stout heart that has no fear of death.

Juvenal: *Satires*

And help us, this and every day,
To live more nearly as we pray.

John Keble: *The Christian Year: Morning*

Prayer is exhaling the spirit of man and inhaling the spirit of God.

Edwin Keith

I kneel not now to pray that thou
    Make white one single sin,—
I only kneel to thank thee, Lord,
    For what I have not been.

Harry Kemp: *A Prayer*

Prayer does not change God, but changes him who prays.

Sören Kierkegaard

There is an "Archimedian" point outside the world which is the little chamber where a true suppliant prays in all sincerity, where he lifts the world off its hinges.

Sören Kierkegaard

Woe be unto those who pray, and who are negligent at their prayer: who play the hypocrites, and deny necessaries to the needy.

The Koran, ch. 107

I ask and wish not to appear
    More beauteous, rich or gay:

Lord, make me wiser every year,
    And better every day.

Charles Lamb: *A Birthday Thought*

Prayer at its highest is a two-way conversation—and for me the most important part is listening to God's replies.

Frank C. Laubach

We ought to act with God in the greatest simplicity, speaking to Him frankly and plainly, and imploring His assistance in our affairs, just as they happen.

Brother Lawrence

I have been driven many times to my knees by the overwhelming conviction that I had nowhere else to go.

Abraham Lincoln

We, on our side, are praying to Him to give us victory, because we believe we are right; but those on the other side pray Him, too, for victory, believing they are right. What must He think of us?

Abraham Lincoln

You know I say
Just what I think, and nothing more or less,
And, when I pray, my heart is in my prayer.
I cannot say one thing and mean another:
If I can't pray, I will not make believe.

Henry Wadsworth Longfellow: *Christus,*
Pt. III

Let one unceasing, earnest prayer
Be, too, for light,—for strength to bear
Our portion of the weight of care,
    That crushes into dumb despair.
One half the human race.

Henry Wadsworth Longfellow: *The
Goblet of Life*, st. 10

The fewer words the better prayer.

Martin Luther

Prayer is a strong wall and fortress of the church; it is a goodly Christian weapon.

Martin Luther: *Table Talk: Of Prayer*

To pray well is the better half of study.

Martin Luther: *Table Talk: Of Prayer*

Prayer is love raised to its greatest power; and the prayer of intercession is the noblest and most Christian kind of prayer because in it love—and imagination—reach their highest and widest range.

Robert J. McCracken: "What Happens When We Pray for Others?" *The Reader's Digest,* October, 1956

He who fashions sacred images of gold or marble does not make them gods, he makes them such who prays to them.

Martial: *Epigrams,* Bk. VIII, ep. 24, l. 5

Religion is no more possible without prayer than poetry without language or music without atmosphere.

James Martineau

All seeking is not in vain because it does not achieve its purpose as quickly as our impatience for God demands.

Philip Mauro

Prayer has marked the trees across the wilderness of a skeptical world to direct the traveller in distress and all paths lead to a single light.

Douglas Meador: Matador (Texas) *Tribune*

Lord, help me live from day to day
In such a self-forgetful way,
That even when I kneel to pray,
My prayer shall be for—*others.*

Charles Delucena Meigs: *Others*

Trouble and perplexity drive me to prayer, and prayer drives away perplexity and trouble.

Philip Melanchthon

He offered a prayer so deeply devout that he seemed kneeling and praying at the bottom of the sea.

Herman Melville: *Moby Dick*

Let not that happen which I wish, but that which is right.

Menander: *Fragment*

Do not lose the habit of praying to the unseen Divinity. Prayer for worldly goods is worse than fruitless, but prayer for strength of soul is that passion of the soul which catches the gift it seeks.

George Meredith

Who rises from prayer a better man, his prayer is answered.

George Meredith: *The Ordeal of Richard Feverel,* ch. 12

Not what we wish, but what we want,
Oh! let thy grace supply,
The good unask'd, in mercy grant;
The ill, though ask'd, deny.

James Merrick: *Hymn*

This is the secret of delayed prayer. Prayer is educative. The man who prays grows; and the muscles of the soul swell from this whipcord to iron bands.

Frederick B. Meyer

They who have steeped their souls in prayer
Can every anguish calmly bear.

Richard Monckton Milnes: *The Sayings of Rabia*

If by prayer
Incessant I could hope to change the will
Of him who all things can, I would not cease
To weary him with my assiduous cries.

John Milton: *Paradise Lost,* Bk. XI, l. 307

Rewards for prayers said by people assembled together are twice those said at home.

Mohammed

There are few men who dare publish to the world the prayers they make to Almighty God.

Michel Eyquem de Montaigne

Prayer moves the arm which moves the world,
And brings salvation down.

James Montgomery: *Prayer*

343

Prayer is the soul's sincere desire,
Uttered or unexpressed,
The motion of a hidden fire
That trembles in the breast.

Prayer is the burden of a sigh,
The falling of a tear,
The upward glancing of an eye
When none but God is near.

James Montgomery: *What Is Prayer?*

Spread out your petition before God, and
then say, "Thy will, not mine, be done."
The sweetest lesson I have learned in God's
school is to let the Lord choose for me.

Dwight L. Moody

Prayer is not eloquence, but earnestness; not
the definition of helplessness, but the feeling
of it; not figures of speech, but earnestness of
soul.

Hannah More

O sad estate
Of human wretchedness; so weak is man,
So ignorant and blind, that did not God
Sometimes withhold in mercy what we ask,
We should be ruined at our own request.

Hannah More: *Moses in the Bulrushes,*
Pt. I

Prayer is not artful monologue
Of voice uplifted from the sod;
It is Love's tender dialogue
Between the soul and God.

John Richard Moreland

Come to prayer! Come to prayer!
For prayer is better than sleep!

Call of the Moslem muezzin at the five
daily hours of prayer

Prayer is not merely an occasional impulse
to which we respond when we are in trouble:
prayer is a life attitude.

Walter A. Mueller: *The ABC's of Prayer:
United Church Herald*

Prayer is not monologue, but dialogue;
God's voice in response to mine is its most

essential part. Listening to God's voice is the
secret of the assurance that He will listen to
mine.

Andrew Murray

Beware in your prayer, above everything, of
limiting God, not only by unbelief, but by
fancying that you know what He can do.

Andrew Murray: Houston (Texas) *Times,
All-Church Press*

Now I lay me down to sleep,
I pray thee, Lord, my soul to keep;
If I should die before I wake,
I pray thee, Lord, my soul to take.

New England Primer

When thou prayest, thou shalt not be as the
hypocrites are: for they love to pray standing
in the synagogues and in the corners of the
streets, that they may be seen of men. . . .
But thou, when thou prayest, enter into thy
closet, and when thou hast shut thy door,
pray to thy Father which is in secret; and
thy Father which seeth in secret shall reward
thee openly.

New Testament: Matthew 6: 5–6

Your Father knoweth what things ye have
need of, before ye ask him.

New Testament: Matthew 6: 8

Ask, and it shall be given you; seek, and ye
shall find; knock, and it shall be opened
unto you.

New Testament: Matthew 7: 7

Every one that asketh receiveth; and he that
seeketh findeth.

New Testament: Matthew 7: 8

My house shall be called the house of prayer;
but ye have made it a den of thieves.

New Testament: Matthew 21: 13

What things soever ye desire, when ye pray,
believe that ye receive them, and ye shall
receive them.

New Testament: Mark 11: 24

Lord, teach us to pray.

New Testament: Luke 11: 1

Men ought always to pray, and not to faint.

New Testament: Luke 18: 1

If ye abide in me, and my words abide in you, ye shall ask what ye will, and it shall be done unto you.

New Testament: John 15: 7

Pray without ceasing.

New Testament: I Thessalonians 5: 17

Pray for us.

New Testament: II Thessalonians 3: 1

The prayer of faith shall save the sick.

New Testament: James 5: 15

The effectual fervent prayer of a righteous man availeth much.

New Testament: James 5: 16

Thou art coming to a King,
Large petitions with thee bring
For His grace and power are such
None can ever ask too much.

John Newton

Prayer is not only "the practice of the presence of God," it is the realization of His presence.

Joseph Fort Newton

God grant me the serenity to accept things I cannot change, courage to change things I can, and wisdom to know the difference.

Reinhold Niebuhr

The most important thing in any prayer is not what we say to God, but what God says to us. We are apt to pray and then hurry away without giving God a chance to answer.

North Carolina *Christian Advocate*

Prayer is the chief agency and activity whereby men align themselves with God's purpose. Prayer does not consist in battering the walls of heaven for personal benefits or the success of our plans. Rather it is the committing of ourselves for the carrying out of His pur-

poses. It is a telephone call to headquarters for orders. It is not bending God's will to ours, but our will to God's. In prayer, we tap vast reservoirs of spiritual power whereby God can find fuller entrance into the hearts of men.

G. Ashton Oldham

He who prays as he ought, will endeavor to live as he prays.

John Owen

Prayer opens our eyes that we may see ourselves and others as God sees us.

Clara Palmer, in *Weekly Unity*

"Prayer, like radium," scientist Alexis Carrel once said, "is a luminous and self-generating form of energy."

Norman Vincent Peale: *Pageant*

Sometimes . . . God answers our prayers in the way our parents do, who reply to the pleas of their children with "Not just now" or "I'll have to think about that for a little while."

Roy M. Pearson: *United Church Herald*

Prayer is not a lazy substitute for work. It is not a short cut to skill or knowledge. And sometimes God delays the answer to our prayer in final form until we have time to build up the strength, accumulate the knowledge, or fashion the character that would make it possible for Him to say "yes" to what we ask.

Ibid.

I pray God to keep me from being proud.

Samuel Pepys: *Diary*

Prayers travel more strongly when said in unison.

Petronius: *Fragments*, no. 92

Pray for peace and grace and spiritual food,
For wisdom and guidance, for all these are good,
But don't forget the potatoes.

John Tyler Pettee: *Prayer and Potatoes*

From every place below the skies
The grateful song, the fervent prayer,—
The incense of the heart,—may rise
To heaven, and find acceptance there.
John Pierpont: *Every Place a Temple*

God answers prayers; sometimes, when
hearts are weak,
He gives the very gifts believers seek.
But often faith must learn a deeper rest,
And trust God's silence, when He does not
speak;
For He whose name is Love will send the
best:
Stars may burn out nor mountain walls
endure
But God is true; His promises are sure
To those who seek.
M. G. Plantz

The world is full of faces, black with anger,
green with envy and red with shame, which
could be made radiantly white with holiness
and spirituality aglow by the transfiguring
power of prayer.
Samuel Henry Price

Heaven is never deaf but when man's heart
is dumb.
Francis Quarles

Prayer changes things? No! Prayer changes
people, and people change things.
Quote

The monkey's paternoster.
François Rabelais: *Works*, Bk. I, ch. 11

The deepest wishes of the heart find expression in secret prayer.
George E. Rees

Let prayer be the key of the day and the bolt
of the night.
Jean Paul Richter

Were half the breath that's vainly spent,
To heaven in supplication sent,
Our cheerful song would oftener be,
"Hear what the Lord has done for me."
Garnet Rolling

Prayers, the sweet ambassadors to God,
The heralds to prepare a better life.
Francis Rous: *Thule*

Faithful prayer always implies correlative
exertion. No man can ask, honestly and
hopefully to be delivered from temptation
unless he has honestly and firmly determined
to do the best he can to keep out of it.
John Ruskin

Pray to God, but row for the shore.
Russian Proverb

I pray the prayer the Easterners do,
May the peace of Allah abide with you;
Wherever you stay, wherever you go,
May the beautiful palms of Allah grow;
Through days of labor, and nights of rest,
The love of Good Allah make you blest;
So I touch my heart—as the Easterners do,
May the peace of Allah abide with you.
Salaam Alaikum (Peace be with you).
Author Unknown

Fear drives the wretched to prayer.
Seneca: *Agamemnon*, l. 510

Nothing costs so much as what is bought by
prayers.
Seneca: *De Beneficiis*, Bk. II, sec. 1

Pray for a sound mind and for good health,
first of soul and then of body . . . Call boldly
upon God; for you will not be asking him
for that which belongs to another.
Seneca: *Epistolue ad Lucilium*

Live among men as if God beheld you; speak
with God as if men were listening.
Ibid.

Don't ask for what you'll wish you hadn't
got.
Ibid.

We, ignorant of ourselves,
Beg often our own harms, which the wise
powers

Deny us for our good; so find we profit
By losing of our prayers.

William Shakespeare: *Antony and
Cleopatra,* Act II, sc. 1, l. 7

My words fly up, my thoughts remain below:
Words without thoughts never to heaven go.

William Shakespeare: *Hamlet,*
Act III, sc. 3, l. 97

Nay, that's past praying for.

William Shakespeare: *Henry IV, Part I,*
Act II, sc. 4, l. 211

Watch to-night, pray to-morrow.

William Shakespeare: *Henry IV, Part I,*
Act II, sc. 4, l. 306

Now I am past all comforts here, but prayers.

William Shakespeare: *Henry VIII,*
Act IV, sc. 2, l. 123

Pray you now, forget and forgive.

William Shakespeare: *King Lear,*
Act IV, sc. 7, l. 84

When I pray and think, I think and pray
To several subjects; Heaven hath my empty
words.

William Shakespeare: *Measure for
Measure,* Act II, sc. 4, l. 1

Prayer or no prayer, you can't eat out of an
empty bowl.

Slovak Proverb

The first purpose of the prayer is to move
the pray-er.

Roy L. Smith: *The Methodist Story*

Our prayers should be for blessings in general, for God knows best what is good for us.

Socrates

I know no blessing so small as to be reasonably expected without prayer, nor any so
great but may be attained by it.

Robert South

Four things which are not in thy treasury,
I lay before thee, Lord, with this petition:—
My nothingness, my wants,
My sins, and my contrition.

Robert Southey: *Occasional Pieces,* no. 19

Prayers are heard in heaven very much in
proportion to our faith. Little faith will
get very great mercies, but great faith still
greater.

Charles Haddon Spurgeon: *Gleanings
Among the Sheaves: Believing Prayer*

To pray together, in whatever tongue or
ritual, is the most tender brotherhood of
hope and sympathy that man can contract
in this life.

Madame Anne Germaine de Staël:
Corinne, Bk. X, ch. 5

A generous prayer is never presented in vain.

Robert Louis Stevenson: *The Merry Men*

Time spent on the knees in prayer will do
more to remedy heart strain and nerve worry
than anything else.

George David Stewart: *Lecture*

Prayer is a means of adding power to the
strength we already possess. Sometimes we
know what is right, but we lack the will
power to do it.

Harry Thomas Stock, from *Today,* June,
1943. Copyright 1943, The Westminster Press. Used by permission

Don't expect a thousand-dollar answer to a
ten cent prayer.

Sunshine Magazine

Praying is dangerous business. Results do
come.

G. Christie Swain

Truth is what prays in man, and a man is
continually at prayer when he lives according to truth.

Emanuel Swedenborg: *Apocalypse
Explained,* p. 493

Wishing isn't prayer. Neither is mere resignation to what you believe to be God's will.

Prayer is a definite act of the mind—a gesture by which the human spirit seeks out the spirit of the universe. In prayer you call upon the Infinite to help. Prayer is far less a thing "asked for" than it is a thing "done" —a reaching forth to link oneself to the sources of celestial power.

William C. Taggart: "Your Prayers Are Answered," *American Magazine*

Prayers for rain should not be offered just before the season for rain.

The Talmud

In prayer a man should always unite himself with the community.

Ibid.

Whatsoever we beg of God, let us also work for it.

Jeremy Taylor

Prayer is the peace of our spirit, the stillness of our thoughts, the evenness of our recollection, the sea of our meditation, the rest of our cares, and the calm of our tempest.

Jeremy Taylor

Her eyes are homes of silent prayer.

Alfred, Lord Tennyson

Speak to Him thou for He hears, and spirit with spirit can meet—
Closer is He than breathing, and nearer than hands and feet.

Alfred, Lord Tennyson: *Higher Pantheism*

More things are wrought by prayer
Than this world dreams of. Wherefore, let thy voice
Rise like a fountain for me night and day.
For what are men better than sheep or goats
That nourish a blind life within the brain,
If, knowing God, they lift not hands of prayer
Both for themselves and those who call them friends?
For so the whole round earth is every way
Bound by gold chains about the feet of God.

Alfred, Lord Tennyson: *Morte d'Arthur*

348

Battering the gates of heaven with storms of prayer.

Alfred, Lord Tennyson: *St. Simeon Stylites*, l. 7

A man of settled views, whose thoughts are few and hardened like his bones, is truly mortal, and his only resource is to say his prayers.

Henry David Thoreau

The only prayer for a brave man is to be a-doing.

Henry David Thoreau: *Autumn*

There are two main pitfalls on the road to mastery of the art of prayer. If a person gets what he asks for, his humility is in danger. If he fails to get what he asks for, he is apt to lose confidence. Indeed, no matter whether prayer seems to be succeeding or failing humility and confidence are two virtues which are absolutely essential.

A Trappist Monk

Prayer is not overcoming God's reluctance; it is laying hold of His highest willingness.

Richard Chenevix Trench

Lord, what a change within us one short hour
Spent in Thy presence will avail to make!
What heavy burdens from our bosoms take
What parched grounds refresh as with a shower!

Richard Chenevix Trench: *Prayer*

Whatever a man prays for, he prays for a miracle. Every prayer reduces itself to this "God grant that twice two be not four."

Ivan Sergeyevich Turgenev: *Prayer*

I don't know of a single foreign product that enters this country untaxed except the answer to prayer.

Mark Twain

It is best to read the weather forecasts before we pray for rain.

Mark Twain

PRAYER

It is not my habit of mind to think otherwise than solemnly of the feeling which prompts prayer. It is a power which I should like to see guided, not extinguished—devoted to practical objects instead of wasted upon air.

> John Tyndall: *Title of Treatise Fragments of Science:* Vol. II, *Prayer as a Form of Physical Energy*

Prayer is The world in tune,
 A spirit-voice, And vocal joys,
Whose echo is heaven's bliss.

> Henry Vaughan: *The Morning Watch*

Cease to think that the decrees of the gods can be turned aside by prayers.

> Virgil: *Æneid*, Bk. VI, l. 376

I have never made but one prayer to God, a very short one: "O Lord, make my enemies ridiculous." And God granted it.

> Voltaire: *Letter to M. Damiliville*

Prayer moves the Hand which moves the world.

> John Aikman Wallace: *There Is an Eye That Never Sleeps*, l. 19

Prayer is the golden key that opens heaven.

> Thomas Watson

The simple heart that freely asks in love, obtains.

> John Greenleaf Whittier

Every chain that spirits wear
Crumbles in the breath of prayer.

> John Greenleaf Whittier

I am groping for the keys
Of the heavenly harmonies.

> John Greenleaf Whittier: *Andrew Rykman's Prayer*

I prayed the prayer of Plato old;
 God make thee beautiful within,
And let thine eyes the good behold
 In everything save sin!

> John Greenleaf Whittier: *My Namesake*

PREACHERS, PREACHING

Making their lives a prayer.

> John Greenleaf Whittier: *To A. K. on Receiving a Basket of Sea Mosses*

Prayer is a rising up and a drawing near to God in mind, and in heart, and in spirit.

> Alexander Whyte

Though smooth be the heartless prayer, no ear in heaven will mind it;
And the finest phrase falls dead, if there is no feeling behind it.

> Ella Wheeler Wilcox: *Art and Heart*, Rand McNally & Co.

When the gods wish to punish us they answer our prayers.

> Oscar Wilde: *An Ideal Husband*, Act II

Prayer, man's rational prerogative.

> William Wordsworth: *Ecclesiastical Sonnets*, Pt. II, no. 23

The sure relief of prayer.

> William Wordsworth: *Miscellaneous Sonnets*, Pt. II, no. 15

The imperfect offices of prayer and praise.

> William Wordsworth: *The Excursion*, Bk. I, l. 216

Pray to God at the beginning of all thy works that thou mayest bring them all to a good ending.

> Xenophon

God does not listen to the prayer of the lazy.

> Pope Xystus I: *The Ring*

Pray to God only for those things which you cannot obtain from man.

> *Ibid.*

PREACHERS, PREACHING

A popular preacher once said of his pulpit efforts, "I always roar when I have nothing to say."

> Anonymous

It is in vain for the preacher to hope to please all alike. Let a man stand with his face in what direction he will, he must necessarily turn his back on one-half of the world.

Anonymous

Once have a priest for an enemy, good-bye to peace.

Sarah Flower Adams: *Viva Perpetua,*
Act III, sc. 2

I met a preacher there I knew, and said,
"Ill and o'erworked, how fare you in this scene?"
"Bravely?" said he, "for I of late have been
Much cheer'd with thoughts of Christ, the living bread."

Matthew Arnold: *East London*

A preacher should live perfectly and do as he teaches truly.

John Awdelay: *Poems,* p. 31

I preached as never sure to preach again,
And as a dying man to dying men.

Richard Baxter: *Love Breathing Thanks
and Praise*

Actors speak of things imaginary as if they were real, while you preachers too often speak of things real as if they were imaginary.

Thomas Betterton

As the caterpillar chooses the fairest leaves to lay her eggs on, so the priest lays his curse on the fairest joys.

William Blake: *Proverbs of Hell*

They said this mystery never shall cease:
The priest promotes war, and the soldier peace.

William Blake: *Gnomic Verses,* no. 3

The world is dying for want, not of good preaching, but of good hearing.

George Dana Boardman

Let us, even to the wearing of our tongues to the stumps, preach and pray.

John Bradford: *Sermon on Repentance*

Preaching is truth through personality.

Phillips Brooks

For the preacher's merit or demerit,
It were to be wished the flaws were fewer
In the earthen vessel, holding treasure
Which lies as safe in a golden ewer;
But the main thing is, does it hold good measure?
Heaven soon sets right all other matters!

Robert Browning: *Christmas Eve,*
Pt. XXII

Vows can't change nature; priests are only men.

Robert Browning: *The Ring and the
Book,* Pt. I, l. 1057

Hear how he clears the points o' Faith
Wi' rattlin' an' thumpin'!
Now meekly calm, now wild in wrath,
He's stampin', an' he's jumpin'!

Robert Burns: *The Holy Fair,* st. 13

To love to preach is one thing—to love those to whom we preach, quite another.

Richard Cecil

The world looks at ministers out of the pulpit to know what they mean when in it.

Richard Cecil

He preaches well that lives well, quoth Sancho, that's all the divinity I understand.

Miguel de Cervantes: *Don Quixote,* Pt. II,
Bk. III, ch. 20, p. 575

Priests are extremely like other men, and neither the better or worse for wearing a gown or a surplice.

Philip Dormer Stanhope, Lord
Chesterfield: *Letters*

The priesthood is the profession of a gentleman.

Jeremy Collier: *The Immorality and
Profaneness of the English Stage*

The Christian messenger cannot think too highly of his Prince, or too humbly of himself.

Charles Caleb Colton

PREACHERS, PREACHING

There goes the parson, oh, illustrious spark!
And there, scarce less illustrious, goes the
clerk.

William Cowper: *On Observing Some
Names of Little Note*

I venerate the man whose heart is warm,
Whose hands are pure, whose doctine and
whose life,
Coincident, exhibit lucid proof
That he is honest in the sacred cause.

William Cowper: *Task,* Bk. II, l. 372

Would I describe a preacher, . . .
I would express him simple, grave, sincere;
In doctrine uncorrupt; in language plain,
And plain in manner; decent, solemn, chaste,
And natural in gesture; much impress'd
Himself, as conscious of his awful charge,
And anxious mainly that the flock he feeds
May feel it too, affectionate in look,
And tender in address, as well becomes
A messenger of grace to guilty men.

William Cowper: *The Task,* Bk. II, l. 394

He that negotiates between God and man,
As God's ambassador, the grand concerns
Of judgment and mercy, should beware
Of lightness in his speech.

William Cowper: *The Task,* Bk. II, l. 463

All pastors are alike
To wand'ring sheep, resolv'd to follow none.

William Cowper: *The Task,* Bk. VI, l. 890

The parson knows enough who knows a
Duke.

William Cowper: *Tirocinium,* l. 403

I preach forever, but I preach in vain.

George Crabbe: *The Parish Register*

I repeat, you cannot have a live church with
a clergyman who is devoid of humor or
dramatics.

George W. Crane

Go forth and preach impostures to the world,
But give them truth to build on.

Alighieri Dante: *Vision of Paradise,*
Canto XXIX, l. 116

PREACHERS, PREACHING

And of all plagues with which mankind are
curst,
Ecclesiastic tyranny's the worst.

Daniel Defoe: *The True-Born Englishman,* Pt. II, l. 299

Keeping our hearts warm and our heads cool,
we clergy need do nothing emphatically.

Charles Dickens: *Mystery of Edwin
Drood,* ch. 16

When want of learning kept the laymen low,
And none but priests were authoriz'd to
know;
When what small knowledge was, in them
did dwell;
And he a god, who could but read or spell.

John Dryden: *Religio Laici,* l. 372

From the point of view of morals, life seems
to be divided into two periods. In the first,
we indulge; in the second, we preach.

Will Durant: *The Story of Philosophy,*
Simon & Schuster, Inc.

Alas for the unhappy man that is called to
stand in the pulpit, and *not* give the bread
of life.

Ralph Waldo Emerson: Address to the
Senior Class in Divinity College,
Cambridge, July 15, 1838

When we preach unworthily it is not always
quite in vain. There is poetic truth concealed in all the commonplaces of prayer and
of sermons, and though foolishly spoken,
they may be wisely heard.

Ralph Waldo Emerson: Address at the
Divinity College, Cambridge, Mass.

I like the silent church before the service
begins, better than any preaching.

Ralph Waldo Emerson: *Essays, First
Series: Self-Reliance*

Taylor, the Shakespeare of divines.
His words are music in my ear,
I see his cowled portrait dear;
And yet, for all his faith and see,
I would not the good bishop be.

Ralph Waldo Emerson: *The Problem*

351

Whoever would preach Christ in these times must say nothing about him.

Ralph Waldo Emerson

There is not in the universe a more ridiculous nor a more contemptible animal than a proud clergyman.

Henry Fielding: *Amelia*, Bk. X, ch. 10

Preaching is personal counseling on a group scale.

Harry Emerson Fosdick

It is no use walking anywhere to preach unless we preach as we walk.

St. Francis of Assisi

The test of a preacher is that his congregation goes away saying, not what a lovely sermon, but, I will do something!

St. Francis de Sales: *Introduction to the Devout Life*

None preaches better than the ant, and she says nothing.

Benjamin Franklin: *Poor Richard*

When knaves fall out, honest men get their goods; when priests dispute, we come at the truth.

Ibid.

Bad priests bring the devil into the church.

Thomas Fuller: *Gnomologia*, no. 835

The unruliest students make the most pious preachers.

German Proverb

To a philosophic eye the vices of the clergy are far less dangerous than their virtues.

Edward Gibbon: *Decline and Fall of the Roman Empire*, ch. 49

Paul's preaching usually ended in a riot or in a revival.

Orin Philip Gifford

At church, with meek and unaffected grace,
His looks adorn'd the venerable place;
Truth from his lips prevail'd with double sway,

And fools, who came to scoff, remain'd to pray.

Oliver Goldsmith: *The Deserted Village*

Send your audience away with a desire for, and an impulse toward spiritual improvement, or your preaching will be a failure.

Dean Edward M. Goulburn

A strong and faithful pulpit is no mean safeguard of a nation's life.

John Hall

Judge not the preacher; for he is thy Judge:
If thou mislike him, thou conceiv'st him not.
God calleth preaching folly. Do not grudge
To pick our treasures from an earthen pot.
The worst speak something good: If all want sense,
God takes a text, and preacheth patience.

George Herbert: *The Church-Porch*, st. 72

The parson exceeds not an hour in preaching, because all ages have thought that a competency.

George Herbert: *A Priest of the Temple*, ch. 7

I don't like those mighty fine preachers who round off their sentences so beautifully that they are sure to roll off the sinner's conscience.

Rowland Hill

For years I have attended the ministrations of the house of God on the Sabbath, and though my pursuits are literary, I tell you I have received, through all these years, more intellectual nourishment and stimulus from the pulpit, than from all other sources combined.

Josiah Gilbert Holland

Even ministers of good things are like torches, a light to others, waste and destruction to themselves.

Richard Hooker

The life of a pious minister is visible rhetoric.

Richard Hooker

In every country and in every age, the priest has been hostile to liberty. He is always in alliance with the despot, abetting his abuses in return for protection to his own.

Thomas Jefferson: *Writings*, Vol. XIV, p. 119

Avoid, as you would the plague, a clergyman who is also a man of business.

St. Jerome

A man who is good enough to go to Heaven is good enough to be a clergyman.

Samuel Johnson

A man who preaches in the stocks will always have hearers enough.

Samuel Johnson

Sir, a woman preaching is like a dog's walking on his hind legs. It is not done well: but you are surprised to find it done at all.

Samuel Johnson

The preacher for this day must have the heart of a lion, the skin of a hippopotamus, the agility of a greyhound, the patience of a donkey, the wisdom of an elephant, the industry of an ant, and as many lives as a cat.

Edgar DeWitt Jones: Address at Transylvania College, Lexington, Ky.

Without Benefit of Clergy.

Rudyard Kipling: Title of short story. (Kipling used the phrase in the sense of unmarried.) By permission of Mrs. George Bambridge

Many chaplains are chaste, but charity is wanting;
There are none harder nor hungrier than men of holy church.

William Langland: *Piers Plowman*, Passus II, l. 187

The preaching of the word of God unto the people . . . the Scripture calleth meat; not strawberries, that come but once a year, and

tarry not long, but are soon gone; but it is meat, it is no dainties.

Hugh Latimer: *Sermon of the Ploughers*

We must practise what we preach.

Sir Roger L'Estrange: *Seneca's Morals*, ch. 2

I don't like to hear cut-and-dried sermons. When I hear a man preach I like to see him act as if he were fighting bees.

Abraham Lincoln

A preacher should have the skill to teach the unlearned simply, roundly, and plainly; for teaching is of more importance than exhorting.

Martin Luther

When I preach I regard neither doctors nor magistrates, of whom I have above forty in the congregation; I have all my eyes on the servant maids and on the children. And if the learned men are not well pleased with what they hear, well, the door is open.

Martin Luther

A preacher must be both soldier and shepherd. He must nourish, defend, and teach; he must have teeth in his mouth, and be able to bite and fight.

Martin Luther: *Table Talk*

An upright, godly and true preacher should direct his preaching to the poor, simple sort of people, like a mother that stills her child, dandles and plays with it, presenting it with milk from her own breast, and needing neither malmsey nor muscadin for it.

Ibid.

The minister may be a dud at his business, but his business is not a dud.

Alvin E. Magary: *Your Life*

Improve your style, monsieur! You have disgusted me with the joys of heaven.

Francois de Malherbe

I never see my preacher's eyes
Tho' they with light may shine—
For when he prays he closes his,
And when he preaches, mine!

Complaint of a "Man in the Pew"

An ounce of mother-wit is worth a pound of clergy.

Andrew Marvell: *Growth of Popery*

Theological preaching is deservedly unpopular if all it does is settle a lot of problems people never heard of, and ask a lot of questions nobody ever asks. . . .

Robert J. McCracken: *The Making of the Sermon*, Harper & Row, Publishers, Inc.

Every Christian occupies some kind of pulpit and preaches some kind of sermon every day.

The Methodist Story

New Presbyter is but Old Priest writ large.

John Milton: *On the New Forces of Conscience*

The best way to revive a church is to build a fire in the pulpit.

Dwight L. Moody

Whatever mood may characterize other man, it is demanded of the minister that he be a man of hope, of daring expectancy, of deep-grounded optimism.

Charles Clayton Morrison

It pleased God by the foolishness of preaching to save them that believe.

New Testament: I Corinthians 1: 21

For we preach not ourselves, but Christ Jesus the Lord.

New Testament: II Corinthians 4: 5

Preach the word; be instant in season, out of season; reprove, rebuke, exhort with all long-suffering and doctrine.

New Testament: II Timothy 4: 2

My grand point in preaching is to break the hard heart, and to heal the broken one.

John Newton

Of all vocations the Christian ministry is the most sacred, the most exacting, the most humbling.

Sir William Robertson Nicoll

Like people, like priest.

Old Testament: Hosea 4: 9

Genius is not essential to good preaching, but a live man is.

Austin Phelps

Dulness is sacred in a sound divine.

Alexander Pope: *The Dunciad*, Bk. II, l. 352

A minister, but still a man.

Alexander Pope: *Epistle to James Craggs*

He was a shrewd and sound divine,
Of loud Dissent the mortal terror;
And when, by dint of page and line,
He 'stablished Truth, or started Error,
The Baptist found him far too deep,
The Deist sighed with saving sorrow,
And the lean Levite went to sleep,
And dreamed of eating pork to-morrow.

Winthrop Mackworth Praed: *The Vicar*

An ounce of practice is worth a pound of preaching.

John Ray: *English Proverbs*

Something near a century ago the advice was given to young preachers: "When you go to the city to preach, take your best coat; when you go to the country, take your best sermon."

Religious Telescope

The lilies say: Behold how we
Preach without words of purity.

Christina Georgina Rossetti: *Consider the Lilies of the Field*

No sermon is of any value, or likely to be useful, which has not the three R's in it;

ruin by the fall, redemption by Christ and regeneration by the Holy Spirit. My aim in every sermon, is loudly to call Sinners, to quicken saints, and to be made a blessing to all.

John C. Ryland

It is our duty to bark in the house of the Lord.

Saying of medieval preachers

Preachers say, Do as I say, not as I do.

John Selden: *Table Talk: Preaching*

"I have heard many great orators," said Louis XIV to Massilon, "and have been highly pleased with them; but whenever I hear you, I go away displeased with myself." This is the highest encomium that could be bestowed on a preacher.

Charles Simmons

That we should practise what we preach is generally admitted; but anyone who preaches what he and his hearers practise must incur the gravest moral disapprobation.

Logan Pearsall Smith

A Curate—there is something which excites compassion in the very name of a Curate!

Sydney Smith: *Persecuting Bishops*

What bishops like best in their clergy is a dropping-down-deadness of manner.

Sydney Smith: *First Letter to Archdeacon Singleton*

As the French say, there are three sexes,— men, women, and clergymen.

Sydney Smith, in Lady Holland's *Memoirs*

Preaching has become a by-word for long and dull conversation of any kind; and whoever wishes to imply, in any piece of writing, the absence of everything agreeable and inviting, calls it a sermon.

Ibid.

The object of preaching is, constantly to remind mankind of what they are constantly forgetting; not to supply the defects of human intelligence, but to fortify the feebleness of human resolutions; to recall mankind from the bypaths where they turn into that broad path of salvation which all know, but few tread.

Sydney Smith: *Six Sermons*

He taught them how to live and how to die.

William Somerville: *In the Memory of the Rev. Mr. Moore*

They admire the Vicar of Bray, whose principle was to be Vicar of Bray, whether the church was Protestant or Popish.

Charles Haddon Spurgeon: *John Ploughman*, ch. 18

Don't go out for popularity. Preach nothing down but the devil, nothing up but the Christ.

Charles Haddon Spurgeon

A pastor needs the tact of a diplomat, the strength of Samson, the patience of Job, the wisdom of Solomon—and a cast-iron stomach.

James Street: *The Gauntlet*, p. 70, Doubleday, Doran & Co. Inc.

I never saw, heard, nor read that the clergy were beloved in any nation where Christianity was the religion of the country. Nothing can render them popular but some degree of persecution.

Jonathan Swift: *Thoughts on Religion*

Now hear an allusion:—A mitre, you know, Is divided above, but united below. If this you consider, our emblem is right; The bishops divide, but the clergy unite.

Jonathan Swift: *On the Irish Bishops*

A genius in a reverend gown Must ever keep its owner down; 'Tis an unnatural conjunction, And spoils the credit of the function.

Jonathan Swift: *To Dr. Delany*

The preaching of divines helps to preserve well-inclined men in the course of virtue, but seldom or never reclaims the vicious.

Jonathan Swift: *Thoughts on Various Subjects*

For their tender minds he served up half a Christ.

Algernon Charles Swinburne

A pleasing preacher is too often an appeasing preacher.

Universalist Leader

What village parson would not like to be pope?

Voltaire: *Letters on the English*, no. 5

A dying preacher I have been,
To dying hearers such as you.
Though dead, a preacher still I am
To such as come my grave to view.
Let this to you a warning be
That quickly you must follow me.

Epitaph for Elder Samuel Waldo, South Dover (Wingdale) Cemetery, Dutchess County, New York

A Scotch woman said to her minister, "I love to hear you preach. You get so many things out of your text that aren't really there."

Watchman-Examiner

Though we live in a reading age and in a reading community, yet the preaching of the Gospel is the form in which human agency has been and still is most efficaciously employed for the spiritual improvement of men.

Daniel Webster

Many a meandering discourse one hears, in which the preacher aims at nothing, and— hits it.

Richard Whately

Preach not because you have to say something, but because you have something to say.

Richard Whately: *Apothegms*

To preach more than half an hour, a man should be an angel himself or have angels for hearers.

George Whitefield

God's true priest is always free;
Free, the needed truth to speak,
Right the wronged, and raise the weak.

John Greenleaf Whittier: *The Curse of the Charter-Breakers*

PREJUDICE

Christ wanted men to see, to see far and to see truly. To get that kind of vision requires avoidance of hypocrisies and group prejudice which distort the vision and make men imagine they see what is not really there.

John Foster Dulles

He that is possessed with a prejudice is possessed with a devil, and one of the worst kind of devils, for it shuts out the truth, and often leads to ruinous error.

Tryon Edwards

Race prejudice is as thorough a denial of the Christian God as atheism, and a far more common form of apostasy.

Harry Emerson Fosdick: *Missions*

Prejudice is generally incorrect. History shows that prejudices against certain individuals and movements were wrong. The word Quaker was a reproach hurled at the followers of George Fox. Today the word Quaker is a badge of honor . . . The word Christian was a sneer addressed to the followers of Jesus. Today we bless God to be numbered among them.

Archie H. Hook: *The Congregational Way*

Thoughtful men, once escaped from the blinding influences of traditional prejudice, will find in the lowly stock whence man has sprung the best evidence of the splendor of his capacities, and will discern in his long progress through the past, a reasonable ground of faith in his attainment of a noble future.

Thomas Henry Huxley: *Cardiff, What Great Men Think of Religion*

Shake off all the fears of servile prejudices, under which weak minds are servilely crouched. Fix reason firmly in her seat, and call on her tribunal for every fact, every opinion. Question with boldness even the existence of a God; because, if there be one, he must more approve of the homage of reason than that of blindfolded fear.

Thomas Jefferson: To Peter Carr (nephew)

Most people are akin to the old theologian who said he was entirely open to conviction, but would like to see anybody who could convince him.

The Link

Prejudice is the conjuror of imaginary wrongs, strangling truth, over-powering reason, making strong men weak, and weak men weaker. God gave us the large-hearted charity which "beareth all things, believeth all things, hopeth all things, endureth all things," which "thinketh no evil!"

John Macduff

All prejudices may be traced to the intestines. A sedentary life is the real sin against the Holy Ghost.

Friedrich Wilhelm Nietzsche: *Ecce Homo*

No person is strong enough to carry a cross and a prejudice at the same time.

William A. Ward: Houston (Texas) *Times, All-Church Press*

PRIDE

Pride is hateful before God and man.

Apocrypha: Ecclesiasticus 10: 7

Pride is the beginning of sin.

Apocrypha: Ecclesiasticus 10: 13

As proud as Lucifer.

Philip James Bailey: *Festus. Sc. A Country Town*

The pride of the peacock is the glory of God.

William Blake

From pride, vain-glory, and hypocrisy; from envy, hatred, and malice, and all uncharitableness, good Lord, deliver us.

Book of Common Prayer: The Litany

I thank God, amongst those millions of vices I do inherit and hold from Adam, I have escaped one, and that a mortal enemy to charity,—the first and father sin, not only of man, but of the Devil,—pride.

Sir Thomas Browne: *Religio Medici*

Pride is the master sin of the devil.

Edwin Hubbell Chapin

He was so proud that should he meet
The Twelve Apostles in the street
He'd turn his nose up at them all
And shove his Saviour from the wall.

Charles Churchill: *Independence*. (The reference is to William Warburton, Bishop of Gloucester)

And the Devil did grin, for his darling sin
Is pride that apes humility.

Samuel Taylor Coleridge: *The Devil's Thoughts*

Of all marvellous things, perhaps there is nothing that angels behold with such supreme astonishment as a proud man.

Charles Caleb Colton

There is no greater pride than in seeking to humiliate ourselves beyond measure! and sometimes there is no truer humility than to attempt great works for God.

Abbé de Saint-Cyran

The first peer and president of Hell.

Daniel Defoe: *The True-Born Englishman*, I

Pride ruined the angels.

Ralph Waldo Emerson: *The Sphinx*

The pride of dying rich raises the loudest laugh in hell.

John Foster

But of all prides, since Lucifer's attaint,
The proudest swells a self-elected saint.

Thomas Hood: *Blanca's Dream*

Pride and grace dwelt never in one place.

James Kelly: *Complete Collection of
Scottish Proverbs*

A man may be poor in purse, yet proud in spirit.

John Mason: *McGuffey's Third Reader,*
p. 110

One may be humble out of pride.

Michel Eyquem de Montaigne: *Of
Presumption,* Bk. XI, ch. 17

I loved the garish day, and, spite of fears,
Pride ruled my will: remember not past years.

Cardinal John Henry Newman: *The
Pillar of the Cloud*

God resisteth the proud, and giveth grace to the humble.

New Testament: I Peter 5: 5

When pride cometh, then cometh shame.

Old Testament: Proverbs 11: 2

The Lord will destroy the house of the proud.

Old Testament: Proverbs 15: 25

Pride goeth before destruction, and an haughty spirit before a fall.

Old Testament: Proverbs 16: 18

A man's pride shall bring him low: but honour shall uphold the humble in spirit.

Old Testament: Proverbs 29: 23

Pride brake the angels in heaven, and spoils all the heads we find cracked here.

Francis Osborne

In pride, in reas'ning pride, our error lies;
All quit their sphere and rush into the skies.
Pride still is aiming at the bless'd abodes,
Men would be angels, angels would be gods.

Alexander Pope: *Essay on Man,* Epis. I,
l. 124

Though the Bible urges us on to perfection it gives no encouragement to suppose that perfection is achieved. . . . *A man who thinks he is righteous is not righteous—* . . . for the reason, primarily, that he is full of spiritual pride, the most deadly form that sin can take.

D. Elton Trueblood

God hates the proud.

Turkish Proverb

A proud man hath no God.

Benjamin Whichcote: *Moral and
Religious Aphorisms*

PROPHET, PROPHECY

Divinations, and soothsayings, and dreams are vain.

Apocrypha: Ecclesiasticus 34: 5

Don't ever prophesy; for if you prophesy wrong, nobody will forget it: and if you prophesy right, nobody will remember it.

Josh Billings

When the prophet beats the ass,
The angel intercedes.

Elizabeth Barrett Browning: *Aurora
Leigh,* Bk. VIII, l. 795

The best of prophets of the future is the past.

George Gordon, Lord Byron: *Journal*

Father! no prophet's laws I seek,—
Thy laws in Nature's works appear,—

I own myself corrupt and weak,
Yet will I pray, for thou wilt hear.
George Gordon, Lord Byron: *Prayer of
Nature*

Farther than the arrow, higher than wings,
fly poet's song and prophet's word.
Roscoe Conkling: *Inscription for a door
of the Library*

I like the church, I like a cowl,
I love a prophet of the soul;
And on my heart monastic aisles
Fall like sweet strains or pensive smiles;
Yet not for all his faith can see,
Would I that cowlèd churchman be.
Ralph Waldo Emerson: *The Problem*

God had granted to every people a prophet
in its own tongue.
The Koran

Experience is the only prophecy of wise men.
Alphonse de Lamartine: *Speech, at Mâcon*

Don't never prophesy—onless ye know.
James Russell Lowell: *The Biglow Papers,*
Series XI, "The Courtin'," st. 21, no. 2

Beware of false prophets, which come to you
in sheep's clothing, but inwardly they are
ravening wolves.
New Testament: Matthew 7: 15

A prophet is not without honour, but in his
own country, and among his own kin, and
in his own house.
New Testament: Mark 6: 4

We know in part, and we prophesy in part.
New Testament: I Corinthians 13: 9

Touch not mine anointed, and do my
prophets no harm.
Old Testament: I Chronicles 16: 22

If the prophet be deceived when he hath
spoken a thing, I the Lord have deceived
that prophet, and I will stretch out my hand
upon him, and will destroy him.
Old Testament: Ezekiel 14: 9

Your sons and your daughters shall prophesy,
your old men shall dream dreams, your
young men shall see visions.
Old Testament: Joel 2: 28

Your fathers, where are they? and the prophets, do they live forever?
Old Testament: Zechariah 1: 5

The revelations of devout and learn'd
Who rose before us, and as prophets burn'd,
Are all but stories, which, awoke from
sleep
They told their comrades, and to sleep
return'd.
Omar Khayyám: *Rubáiyát*

To see clearly is poetry, prophecy, and re-
ligion, all in one.
John Ruskin: *Modern Painters,* Vol. III,
Pt. IV, ch. 16, sec. 28

For lo! the days are hastening on,
By prophet-bards foretold,
When with the ever-circling years,
Comes round the age of gold.
Edmund Hamilton Sears: *The Angel's
Song*

Jesters do oft prove prophets.
William Shakespeare: *King Lear,*
Act V, sc. 3, l. 71

I am about to die, and that is the hour in
which men are gifted with prophetic power.
Socrates

Prognostics do not always prove prophecies,
—at least the wisest prophets make sure of
the event first.
Horace Walpole: *Letter to Thomas
Walpole*

PROVIDENCE

We are all of us apt to play Providence in
our private minds and to be very cross when
our little decrees don't come off.
Anonymous

359

The rich man in his castle,
The poor man at his gate,
God made them, high or lowly,
And ordered their estate.

Cecil Frances Alexander: *All Things
Bright*

Confide ye aye in Providence,
For Providence is kind:
An' bear ye a' life's changes
Wi' a calm an' tranquil mind.
Tho' pressed and hemmed on every side,
Ha'e faith, an' ye'll win through;
For ilka blade o' grass,
Keeps its ain drap o' dew.

James Ballantine: *Its Ain Drap O' Dew*

I am not one to fly in the face of Providence.

Sabine Baring-Gould: *The Queen of Love*

Some one has said that in war Providence is
on the side of the strongest regiments. And
I have noticed that Providence is on the side
of clear heads and honest hearts; and wherever a man walks faithfully in the ways that
God has marked out for him, Providence, as
the Christian says,—luck as the heathen says,
—will be on that man's side. In the long run
you will find that God's providence is in
favor of those that keep His laws, and against
those that break them.

Henry Ward Beecher

Providence cares for every hungry mouth.

Robert Browning: *Ferishtah's Fancies:
The Eagle*

Providence labors with quaint instruments,
dilapidating Troy by means of a wooden
rocking-horse, and loosing sin into the universe through a half-eaten apple.

James Branch Cabell: *Cream of the Jest,*
p. 87

Providence is a greater mystery than revelation. The state of the world is more humi-
liating to our reason than the doctrines of
the Gospel. A reflecting Christian sees more
to excite his astonishment, and to exercise
his faith, in the state of things between

Temple Bar and St. Paul's, than in what he
reads from Genesis to Revelations.

Richard Cecil

Chance is a nickname for Providence.

Sebastien R. N. Chamfort: *Maxims and
Thoughts*, LXII

Behind a frowning providence
He hides a shining face.

William Cowper: *Olney Hymns: Light
Shining Out of Darkness*

The longer I live, the more faith I have in
Providence, and the less faith in my interpretation of Providence.

Jeremiah Day

Providence has a wild, rough, incalculable
road to its end, and it is of no use to try to
whitewash its huge, mixed instrumentalities,
or to dress up that terrific benefactor in a
clean shirt and white neckcloth of a student
in divinity.

Ralph Waldo Emerson: *Conduct of Life:
Fate*

What is the operation we call Providence?
There lies the unspoken thing, present,
omnipresent. Every time we converse we
translate it into speech.

Ralph Waldo Emerson: *Essays, Second
Series: New England Reformers*

Any one thing in the creation is sufficient to
demonstrate a Providence to an humble and
grateful mind.

Epictetus: *Discourses*, ch. 16

Sometimes providences, like Hebrew letters,
must be read backward.

John Flavel

Providence is like a curious piece of arras,
made up of thousands of shreds, which single
we know not what to make of, but put together they present us with a beautiful
history.

John Flavel

God governs in the affairs of man; and if a sparrow cannot fall to the ground without His notice, is it probable that an empire can rise without His aid?

Benjamin Franklin

If you leap into a Well, Providence is not bound to fetch you out.

Thomas Fuller: *Gnomologia*, no. 2795

To doubt the providence of God is presently to wax impatient with his commands.

Edward Garrett

Shall ignorance of good and ill
Dare to direct the eternal will?
Seek virtue, and, of that possest,
To Providence resign the rest.

John Gay: *Fables: The Father and Jupiter*

We sometimes had those little rubs which Providence sends to enhance the value of its favours.

Oliver Goldsmith: *The Vicar of Wakefield*, ch. 1

We ought to feel deep cheerfulness, as I may say, that a happy Providence kept it from being any worse.

Thomas Hardy: *Far from the Madding Crowd*, ch. 8

Providence seldom vouchsafes to mortals any more than just that degree of encouragement which suffices to keep them at a reasonably full exertion of their powers.

Nathaniel Hawthorne: *The House of the Seven Gables*, ch. 3

Providence knows what we need better than we ourselves.

Jean de La Fontaine: *Fables*, Bk. VI, no. 4

By going a few minutes sooner or later, by stopping to speak with a friend on the corner, by meeting this man or that, or by turning down this street instead of the other, we may let slip some impending evil, by which the whole current of our lives would have been changed. There is no possible solution in the dark enigma but the one word, "Providence."

Henry Wadsworth Longfellow

A marciful Providunce fashioned to holler
O' purpose thet we might our principles swaller.

James Russell Lowell: *The Biglow Papers*, Series I, no. 4, st. 2

Behind the dim unknown,
Standeth God within the shadow,
keeping watch above his own.

James Russell Lowell: *The Present Crisis*

What in me is dark
Illumine, what is low raise and support;
That to the height of this great argument
I may assert eternal Providence,
And justify the ways of God to men.

John Milton: *Paradise Lost*, Bk. I, l. 22

God of our fathers, what is man!
That thou towards him with hand so various,
(Or might I say contrarious?)
Temper'st thy providence through his short course.

John Milton: *Samson Agonistes*, l. 667

Providence is always on the side of the last reserve.

Attributed to Napoleon

He putteth down one and setteth up another.

Old Testament: Psalms 75: 7

Who finds not Providence all good and wise,
Alike in what he gives and what he denies?

Alexander Pope

What is chance but the rude stone which receives its life from the sculptor's hand? Providence gives us chance—and man must mould it to his own designs.

Johann Christoph Friedrich von Schiller: *Don Carlos*, Act III, sc. 9, l. 13

Call it Nature, Fate, Fortune; all these are names of the one and selfsame God.

Seneca: *De Beneficiis*, Bk. IV, sec. 8

361

PROVIDENCE

We must follow, not force providence.

William Shakespeare

There's a special providence in the fall of a sparrow.

William Shakespeare: *Hamlet,*
Act V, sc. 2, l. 232

Arming myself with patience,
To stay the providence of some high powers
That govern us below.

William Shakespeare: *Julius Caesar,*
Act V, sc. 1, l. 106

Providence requires three things of us before it will help us—a stout heart, a strong arm, and a stiff upper lip.

Sam Slick: *Wise Saws,* ch. 13

To make our reliance upon providence both pious and rational, we should prepare all things with the same care, diligence, and activity, as if there were no such thing as providence for us to depend upon; and then, when we have done all this, we should as wholly and humbly rely upon it, as if we had made no preparation at all.

Robert South

God tempers the wind to the shorn lamb.

Laurence Sterne

I once asked a hermit in Italy how he could venture to live alone, in a single cottage, on the top of a mountain, a mile from any habitation? He replied, that Providence was his next-door neighbor.

Laurence Sterne

Providence has at all times been my only dependence, for all other resources seem to have failed us.

George Washington

So, darkness in the pathway of Man's life
Is but the shadow of God's providence,
By the great Sun of Wisdom cast thereon;
And what is dark below is light in Heaven.

John Greenleaf Whittier: *Tauler,* l. 79

362

PURITY

The great events with which old story rings
Seem vain and hollow; I find nothing great;
Nothing is left which I can venerate:
So that a doubt almost within me springs
Of Providence, such emptiness at length
Seems at the heart of all things.

William Wordsworth: *Poems Dedicated to National Independence,* Pt. I, no. 22

PURITY

Purity of soul cannot be lost without consent.

St. Augustine: *On Lying*

The pure soul
Shall mount on native wings, disdaining little sport,
And cut a path into the heaven of glory,
Leaving a track of light for men to wonder at.

William Blake: *King Edward the Third*

Meek and lowly, pure and holy,
Chief among the "blessed three."

Charles Jeffreys: *Charity*

Still to the lowly soul
He doth Himself impart,
And for His cradle and His throne
Chooseth the pure in heart.

John Keble: *The Christian Year: The Purification*

For in heaven there's a lodge, and St. Peter keeps the door,
And none can enter in but those that are pure.

The Masonic Hymn

Blessed are the pure in heart: for they shall see God.

New Testament: Matthew 5: 8

Whatsoever things are pure . . . think on these things.

New Testament: Philippians 4: 8

Unto the pure all things are pure.

New Testament: Titus 1: 15

And every man that hath this hope in him purifieth himself, even as he is pure.

New Testament: I John 3: 3

With the pure thou wilt show thyself pure.

Old Testament: II Samuel 22: 27

Shall a man be more pure than his maker?

Old Testament: Job 4: 17

He that loveth pureness of heart, for the grace of his lips the king shall be his friend.

Old Testament: Proverbs 22: 11

Pour the full tide of eloquence along,
Serenely pure, and yet divinely strong.

Alexander Pope: *Imitations of Horace: Epistles*, Bk. II, Epis. II, l. 171

A purer soul and one more like yourselves.
Ne'er entered at the golden gates of bliss.

Dante Gabriel Rossetti: *Lady Jane Grey,* Act I, sc. 1

There fled the purest soul that ever dwelt
In mortal clay.

Tobias Smollett: *The Regicide,* Act V, sc. 8

I pray thee, O God, that I may be beautiful within.

Socrates

A true man, pure as faith's own vow,
Whose honour knows not rust.

Algernon Charles Swinburne: *The Tale of Balen*, Pt. I, st. 1

Simplicity reaches out after God; purity discovers and enjoys him.

Thomas à Kempis

Make my breast transparent as pure crystal, that the world, jealous of me, may see the foulest thought my heart does hold.

George Villiers, Duke of Buckingham

The body is the soul's image; therefore keep it pure.

Pope Xystus I: *The Ring*

R

RELIGION

Nobody is anything except as he joins himself to something. You cannot be a whole unless you join a whole. This, I believe, is religion.

Anonymous

If we make religion our business, God will make it our blessedness.

H. G. J. Adam

The appearance of religion only on Sunday proves that it is only an appearance.

John Adams

Men can be attracted but not forced to the faith. You may drive people to baptism, you won't move them one step further to religion.

Alcuin: *To Charlemagne*

Religion—that voice of the deepest human experience.

Matthew Arnold

Children of men! the unseen Power, whose eye
Forever doth accompany mankind,
Hath look'd on no religion scornfully
That men did ever find.

Matthew Arnold: *Progress*, st. 10

Business is religion, and religion is business. The man who does not make a business of his religion has a religious life of no force, and the man who does not make a religion of his business has a business life of no character.

Maltbie D. Babcock

When I was a boy I was taught that a person ought to put something into religion. Today the idea is to get something out of it.

Marcus Bach

The greatest vicissitude of things amongst men, is the vicissitude of sects and religions.

Sir Francis Bacon: *Essays: Of Vicissitude of Things*

The true religion is built upon the rock; the rest are tossed upon the waves of time.

Ibid.

A religion that is jealous of the variety of learning, discourse, opinions, and sects, as misdoubting it may shake the foundations, or that cherisheth devotion upon simplicity and ignorance, as ascribing ordinary effects to the immediate working of God, is adverse to knowledge.

Sir Francis Bacon: *Of the Interpretation of Nature*, ch. 25

The whole history of civilization is strewn with creeds and institutions which were invaluable at first, and deadly afterwards.

Walter Bagehot

Some people want a religion that will make them feel respectable, but not require that they be.

Banking

Even if God did not exist, religion would still be holy and divine.

Charles Baudelaire

Many would like religion as a sort of lightning rod to their houses, to ward off, by and by, the bolts of divine wrath.

Henry Ward Beecher

I should like to see Christian leaders disregard their timid followers and, like Francis of Assisi or John Wesley, go out of the church buildings, shake the dust of denominationalism from impatient feet, and appeal to the folks generally. Americans will listen to religion if and when it claims to have relationship to real life. Let the churches recognize that their job is not to nurture the pious nearly so much as it is to rouse, convict of sin, convert, a pagan nation.

Bernard Iddings Bell: *Argosy*

Religion is to mysticism what popularization is to science.

Henri Bergson: *Creative Evolution*, p. 227

Religion brought forth riches, and the daughter devoured the mother.

St. Bernard of Clairvaux

Impiety—your irreverence toward my deity.

Ambrose Bierce: *The Devil's Dictionary*

No mere man since the Fall, is able in this life perfectly to keep the commandments.

Book of Common Prayer: Shorter Catechism

When someone tells me that he has never had a moment of probing religious doubt I find myself wondering whether he had ever known a moment of vital religious conviction.

Harold A. Bosley

I could not be interested in any man's religion if his knowledge of God did not bring him more joy, did not brighten his life, did not make him want to carry this joy into every dark corner of the world. I have no understanding of a longfaced Christian. If God is anything, He must be joy.

Joe E. Brown: *Laughter Is a Wonderful Thing*

Persecution is a bad and indirect way to plant religion.

Sir Thomas Browne: *Religio Medici*

Methinks there be not impossibilities enough in religion for an active faith.

Ibid.

The religion of one seems madness unto another.

Sir Thomas Browne: *Hydriotaphia, or Urne-Buriall*

The writers against religion, whilst they oppose every system, are wisely careful never to set up any of their own.

Edmund Burke: *A Vindication of Natural Society*, Preface, Vol. I, p. 7

Nothing is so fatal to religion as indifference, which is at least, half infidelity.

Edmund Burke: *Letter to William Smith*

Man is by his constitution a religious animal.

Edmund Burke: *Reflections on the Revolution in France*

People differ in their discourse and profession about these matters, but men of sense are really but of one religion. . . . "What religion?" . . . the Earl said, "Men of sense never tell it."

Gilbert Burnet: *History of his Own Times*, Vol. I, Bk. I, sec. 96

One religion is as true as another.

Robert Burton: *Anatomy of Melancholy*, Bk. III, sec. 4, mem. 2, subsec. 1

It is only religion, the great bond of love and duty to God, that makes any existence valuable or even tolerable.

Horace Bushnell

As if Religion were intended
For nothing else but to be mended.

Samuel Butler: *Hudibras*, Pt. I, Canto I, l. 205

My altars are the mountains and the ocean,
Earth, air, stars,—all that springs from the great Whole,

Who hath produced and will receive the soul.

George Gordon, Lord Byron: *Don Juan*, Canto III, st. 104

His religion, at best, is an anxious wish:— like that of Rabelais, "a Great Perhaps."

Thomas Carlyle

Everywhere the human soul stands between a hemisphere of light and another of darkness; on the confines of two everlasting hostile empires, Necessity and Freewill.

Thomas Carlyle: *Essays: Goethe's Works*

On the whole we must repeat the often repeated saying, that it is unworthy a religious man to view an irreligious one either with alarm or aversion; or with any other feeling than regret, and hope, and brotherly commiseration.

Thomas Carlyle: *Essays on Voltaire*

It is well said, in every sense, that a man's religion is the chief fact with regard to him. . . . By religion I do not mean here the church-creed which he professes. . . . This is not what I call religion . . . but the thing a man does practically believe; the thing a man does practically lay to heart, and know for certain, concerning his vital relations to this mysterious Universe, and his duty and destiny there, . . . that is his religion.

Thomas Carlyle: *Heroes and Hero-Worship: The Hero as Divinity*

A man's "religion" consists not of the many things he is in doubt of and tries to believe, but of the few he is assured of, and has no need of effort for believing.

Thomas Carlyle: *Latter-Day Pamphlets*, no. 8

(Religion) brings to man an inner strength, spiritual light, ineffable peace.

Alexis Carrel

A man who puts aside his religion because he is going into society is like one taking off his shoes because he is about to walk on thorns.

Richard Cecil

Never trust anybody not of sound religion, for he that is false to God can never be true to man.

William Cecil, Lord Burghley

It is no good reason for a man's religion that he was born and brought up in it; for then a Turk would have as much reason to be a Turk as a Christian a Christian.

William Chillingworth

Things sacred should not only be untouched with the hands, but unviolated in thought.

Cicero: *Orationes in Verrem*, II, 4, 45

Religion is life, philosophy is thought; religion looks up, friendship looks in. We need both thought and life, and we need that the two shall be in harmony.

James Freeman Clarke: *Ten Great Religions*, Pt. I, ch. 7, sec. 9

You may depend upon it, religion is, in its essence, the most gentlemanly thing in the world. It will alone gentilize, if unmixed with cant; and I know nothing else that will, alone.

Samuel Taylor Coleridge

Men will wrangle for religion; write for it; fight for it; die for it; anything but—live for it.

Charles Caleb Colton: *Lacon*, Vol. I, 25

. . . In their essence there can be no conflict between science and religion. Science is a reliable method of finding truth. Religion is the search for a satisfying basis for life. . . . If our religious leaders are to bring to the present day the vital, living spirit of their faith, they must take science seriously . . . a world that has science needs, as never before, the inspiration that religion has to offer. . . . Beyond the nature taught by science is the spirit that gives meaning to life.

Arthur H. Compton: "Science and the Supernatural," *Scientific Monthly*, December, 1946

God is for men, and religion for women.

Joseph Conrad: *Nostromo*, J. M. Dent & Sons, Ltd.

Men of sense are really all of one religion.
But men of sense never tell what it is.

Anthony Ashley Cooper

Religion, if in heav'nly truths attir'd,
Needs only to be seen to be admir'd.

William Cowper: *Expostulation*, l. 492

Religion does not censure or exclude
Unnumbered pleasures, harmlessly pursued.

William Cowper: *Retirement*, l. 782

Sacred religion! Mother of Form and Fear!

Samuel Daniel: *Musophilus*, st. 47

I have never been an atheist in the sense of
denying the existence of a God. I think that
generally (more & more so as I grow older)
but not always, that an agnostic would be
the most correct description of my state of
mind.

Charles Darwin: Letter to Reverend J.
Fordyce

The mystery of the beginning of all things
is insoluble to us; and I for one must be content to remain an agnostic.

Charles Darwin: *Life and Letters*

"As for that," said Waldenshare, "sensible
men are all of the same religion." "Pray,
what is that?" inquired the Prince. "Sensible
men never tell."

Benjamin Disraeli: *Endymion*,
ch. 81. (Also credited to the
Earl of Shaftesbury)

Religion should be the rule of life, not a
casual incident of it.

Benjamin Disraeli: *Lothair*, ch. 17

I would no more quarrel with a man because
of his religion than I would because of his
art.

Mary Baker Eddy: *The First Church of
Christ, Scientist and Miscellany*,
p. 270: 28–9

True religion extends alike to the intellect
and the heart. Intellect is in vain if it lead
not to emotion, and emotion is vain if it is
not enlightened by intellect; and both are
vain if not guided by truth and leading to
duty.

Tryon Edwards

What we need in religion is not new light,
but new sight; not new paths, but new
strength to walk in the old ones; not new
duties, but new strength from on high to
fulfill those that are plain to us.

Tryon Edwards

Religion, in its purity, is not so much a
pursuit as a temper; or rather it is a temper, leading to the pursuit of all that is
high and holy. Its foundation is faith; its
action, works; its temper, holiness; its aim,
obedience to God in improvement of self
and benevolence to men.

Tryon Edwards

Science without religion is lame, religion
without science is blind.

Albert Einstein: *The World As I See It*

Religion is the sum of the expansive impulses of a being.

Havelock Ellis

I do not find that the age or country makes
the least difference; no, nor the language the
actors spoke, nor the religion which they
professed, whether Arab in the desert or
Frenchmen in the Academy, I see that sensible men and conscientious men all over
the world were of one religion.

Ralph Waldo Emerson: *Lectures and
Biographical Sketches: The
Preacher*

We measure all religions by their civilizing
power.

Ralph Waldo Emerson: *Uncollected
Lectures: Natural Religion*

God builds his temple in the heart on the
ruins of churches and religions.

Ralph Waldo Emerson: *Conduct of Life:
Worship*

Religion must always be a crab fruit; it cannot be grafted and keep its wild beauty.

Ralph Waldo Emerson: *Conduct of Life:*
Worship

Unless we place our religion and our treasure in the same thing, religion will always be sacrificed.

Epictetus

There is no age which religion does not become.

Desiderius Erasmus

The youth cannot have a sound development of character nor a fair American chance in life without religion.

Justice Lewis L. Fawcett

It is right to be religious, but one should shun religiosity.

Publius Nigidius Figulus: *Commentariorum Grammaticorum*, Bk. XI

Religion is something you do, not something you wait for.

Charles G. Finney

Religious contention is the devil's harvest.

Charles Fontaine

Religion, like music, is not in need of defense, but rendition.

Harry Emerson Fosdick

Religion is the appreciation of life's spiritual values and the interpretation of life, its origin, its purpose, and its destiny, in terms of them.

Harry Emerson Fosdick

Science and religion no more contradict each other than light and electricity.

William Hiram Foulkes

If men are so wicked with religion, what would they be without it?

Benjamin Franklin

When a religion is good, I conceive it will support itself; and when it does not support itself, and God does not take care to support it so that its professors are obliged to call for help of the civil power, 'tis a sign, I apprehend, of its being a bad one.

Benjamin Franklin: *Works*, Vol. XIII,
p. 506

There are at bottom but two possible religions—that which rises in the moral nature of man, and which takes shape in moral commandments, and that which grows out of the observation of the material energies which operate in the external universe.

James Anthony Froude: *Short Studies on*
Great Subjects: Calvinism

But our captain counts the image of God, nevertheless, his image—cut in ebony as if done in ivory; and in the blackest Moors he sees the representation of the King of heaven.

Thomas Fuller: *Holy and Profane States.*
The Good Sea-Captain, Maxim V

No man's Religion ever survives his Morals.

Thomas Fuller

Religion is the best armour in the world, but the worst cloak.

Thomas Fuller: *Gnomologia*, no. 4011

There can be no good government without law and order; nor that, without authority; nor that, without justice; nor that, without God.

Edward Gibbon

To have a positive religion is not necessary. To be in harmony with yourself and the universe is what counts, and this is possible without positive and specific formulation in words.

Johann Wolfgang von Goethe

There is no common denominator in the world today except religion; the world has become a neighborhood without brotherhood.

Billy Graham

Religion believes optimistically and hopefully in man. Man has progressed; he must
progress. We do not say all's right with the
world. But neither do we say all's riot with
the world.

Rabbi David Graubart

If a man's religion doesn't make him happy
here, what chance has it in the hereafter?

Grit

To avoid the risk of losing their religion,
many people do not take it with them into
their places of business.

Grit

A religion without its mysteries is a temple
without a God.

Robert Hall

Man, without religion, is the creature of circumstances.

Augustus William and Julius Charles
Hare: Guesses at Truth, Bk. I

Men despise religion; they hate it, and fear
it is true.

James Harrington

Every man, either to his terror or consolation, has some sense of religion.

James Harrington: Oceana, p. 484

Those solemn souls who object to humor in
religion forget that the Christian Church
was founded on a pun—"Peter" and "rock"
being the same word in Greek.

Sydney J. Harris: Chicago Daily News

The atheist who seriously studies religion in
order to attack it is closer to the spirit of
God than the bovine believer who supports
religion because it is comfortable, respectable, and offers consolation without thought.

Ibid.

The crown (or Paris) is well worth a mass.

Attributed to Henry IV

I would give nothing for that man's religion
whose very dog and cat are not better for it.

Rowland Hill

Religion is not a dogma, nor an emotion, but
a service.

Roswell Dwight Hitchcock: Eternal
Atonement

Religion is of two kinds—deeds and creeds.

Hobo News

No religion is a true religion that does not
make men tingle to their finger tips with a
sense of infinite hazard.

William Ernest Hocking

We require a world-religion just because we
do not require a world-state.

William Ernest Hocking: The Meaning of
God in Human Experience

To know a person's religion, we need not
listen to his profession of faith but must find
his brand of intolerance.

Eric Hoffer: The Passionate State of Mind,
Harper & Row, Publishers, Inc.

Each cloud-capped mountain is a holy altar;
An organ breathes in every grove;
And the full heart's a Psalter,
Rich in deep hymns of gratitude and love.

Thomas Hood: Ode to Rae Wilson, l. 385

Religion reveals the place of man in the
scheme of things—and the reason many do
not want anything to do with religion is
because they do not want to face what they
really are.

Houston (Texas) Times, All-Church Press

Religion is not an intelligence test, but a
faith.

Edgar Watson Howe

Should all the banks of Europe crash,
The bank of England smash,
Bring all your notes to Zion's bank,
You're sure to get your cash.

Henry Hoyt: Zion's Bank, or Bible
Promises Secured to all Believers

We are for religion, against the religions.

Victor Hugo

369

Look for a people entirely destitute of religion, and if you find them at all, be assured they are but a few degrees removed from brutes.

David Hume

My creed is this:
Happiness is the only good.
The place to be happy is here.
The time to be happy is now.
The way to be happy is to help make others so.

Robert Green Ingersoll

Many people think they have religion when they are troubled with dyspepsia.

Robert Green Ingersoll

I belong to the Great Church which holds the world within its starlit aisles; that claims the great and good of every race and clime; that finds with joy the grain of gold in every creed, and floods with light and love the germs of good in every soul.

Robert Green Ingersoll: Declaration in Discussion with Rev. Henry M. Field on *Faith and Agnosticism* (Farrell's *Life*, Vol. VI)

Religion is always a dull habit or an acute fever.

William James (permission to reprint granted by Paul R. Reynolds & Son)

Religion is a man's total reaction upon life.

Ibid.

Religion is a monumental chapter in the history of human egotism.

William James: *The Varieties of Religious Experience* (permission to reprint granted by Paul R. Reynolds & Son)

I never told my own religion, nor scrutinized that of another. I never attempted to make a convert, nor wished to change another's creed. I have ever judged of others' religion

by their lives . . . for it is from our lives and not from our words, that our religion must be read.

Thomas Jefferson: Letter to John Adams
Works, Vol. XV

Religion's in the heart, not in the knee.

Douglas Jerrold: *The Devil's Duca*

A man who has never had religion before no more grows religion when he is sick, than a man who has never learnt figures can count when he has need of calculation.

Samuel Johnson

A life that will bear the inspection of men and of God, is the only certificate of true religion.

Samuel Johnson

To one man religion is his literature and his science; to another, his delight and his duty.

Joseph Joubert: *Pensées*, no. 26

There is only one true religion, but there may be many forms of belief.

Immanuel Kant

Religion is the individual's attitude toward God and man as expressed in faith, in worship, in life and in service.

Charles Foster Kent

Any religion that professes to be concerned with the souls of men and is not concerned with the slums that damn them, the economic conditions that strangle them, and the social conditions that cripple them, is a dry-as-dust religion.

Martin Luther King

What I want is, not to possess religion but to have a religion that shall possess me.

Charles Kingsley

Every child is born into the religion of nature; its parents make it a Jew, a Christian, or a Magian.

The Koran

Things are coming to a pretty pass when religion is allowed to invade private life.

William Lamb, Lord Melbourne

Every sect is a moral check on its neighbor. Competition is as wholesome in religion as in commerce.

Walter Savage Landor

Religion is the elder sister of Philosophy.

Walter Savage Landor: *Imaginary Conversations: David Hume and John Home*

The broad-minded see the truth in different religions; the narrow-minded see only their differences.

Lao-tze

I have lived long enough to know what I did not at one time believe—that no society can be upheld in happiness and honor without the sentiment of religion.

Pierre Simon de Laplace

A man without religion is like a beast without a bridle.

Latin Proverb

All belief that does not render us more happy, more free, more loving, more active, more calm, is, I fear, an erroneous and superstitious belief.

Johann Kaspar Lavater

The only assurance of our nation's safety is to lay our foundations in morality and religion.

Abraham Lincoln

How many evils has religion caused!

Lucretius: *De Rerum Natura*, l. 102

The heart of religion lies in its personal pronouns.

Martin Luther

Religion is the sigh of the oppressed creature, the feeling of a heartless world, just as it is

the spirit of unspiritual conditions. It is the opium of the people.

Karl Marx: *Introduction, Critique of the Hegelian Philosophy of Right, Deutsch-Franzoesische Yahrbuecher*, 1844

It will cost something to be religious: it will cost more to be not so.

John Mason

Religion would not have any enemies if it were not an enemy to their vices.

Jean Baptiste Massillon

The service of the Christian religion and my own faith in essential Christianity would not be diminished one iota if it should in some way be discovered that no such individual as Jesus existed.

Robert Andrews Millikan, Yale University Press

I conceive the essential task of religion to be "to develop the consciences, the ideals, and the aspirations of mankind."

Ibid.

Nobody can deny but religion is a comfort to the distressed, a cordial to the sick, and sometimes a restraint on the wicked; therefore, whoever would laugh or argue it out of the world, without giving some equivalent for it, ought to be treated as a common enemy.

Mary Wortley Montagu: *Letter to the Countess of Bute*

The pious man and the atheist always talk of religion; the one of what he loves, and the other of what he fears.

Charles Louis de Secondat Montesquieu

The friend of him who has no friend— Religion.

James Montgomery: *The Pillow*, l. 152

Genius without religion is only a lamp on the outer gate of a palace; it may serve to cast a gleam of light on those that are without, while the inhabitant is in darkness.

Hannah More: Quoted in *New Outlook*

All religions have been made by men.

Napoleon Bonaparte

Religion is the dominion of the soul. It is the hope of life, the anchor of safety, the deliverance of the soul.

Napoleon Bonaparte

Religion is the vaccine of the imagination; she preserves it from all dangerous and absurd beliefs.

Napoleon Bonaparte

A nation must have a religion, and that religion must be under the control of the government.

Napoleon Bonaparte: *To Count Thibaubeau*

If any man among you seem to be religious, and bridleth not his tongue, but deceiveth his own heart, this man's religion is vain. Pure religion and undefiled before God and the Father is this: To visit the fatherless and widows in their affliction, and to keep himself unspotted from the world.

New Testament: James 1: 26–27

Religion is the best armor in the world, but the worst cloak.

John Newton

Men who fight about religion have no religion to fight about, since they do in the name of religion the thing which religion itself forbids.

Joseph Fort Newton

True religion is a profound uneasiness about our highest social values.

Reinhold Niebuhr: *Beyond Tragedy*

They that wait upon the Lord, shall renew their strength; they shall mount up with wings as eagles; they shall run, and not be weary; and they shall walk, and not faint.

Old Testament: Isaiah 40: 31

Religion without joy is no religion.

Joseph Parker

To have Religion upon Authority, and not upon Conviction, is like a Finger Watch, to be set forwards or backwards, as he pleases that has it in keeping.

William Penn

Religion is the fear and love of God; its demonstration is good works; and faith is the root of both, for without faith we cannot please God; nor can we fear and love what we do not believe.

William Penn

No pain, no palm; no thorns, no throne; no gall, no glory; no cross, no crown.

William Penn: *No Cross, No Crown*

To be furious in religion is to be irreligiously religious.

William Penn: *Fruits of Solitude*

Religion is nothing else but love of God and man.

Ibid.

If you are not right toward God, you can never be so toward man; and this is forever true, whether wits and rakes allow it or not.

William Pitt, Lord Chatham

A city may as well be built in the air, as a commonwealth or kingdom be either constituted or preserved without the support of religion.

Plutarch

Religion, blushing, veils her sacred fires,
And unawares Morality expires.

Alexander Pope: *The Dunciad*, Bk. IV, l. 649

Some people can be exposed to religion all their lives without ever catching it, just as some people can get a doctor's degree in philosophy without being educated.

Harry G. Post: *Household Magazine*

Common men talk bagfuls of religion but act not a grain of it, while the wise man speaks little, but his whole life is a religion acted out.

Ramakrishna

We cannot meet needs by repeating creeds.

Religious Telescope

I do not know how philosophers may ultimately define religion; but from Micah to James it has been defined as service to one's fellow men rendered by following the great rule of justice and mercy, of wisdom and righteousness.

Theodore Roosevelt: *The Americanism of Theodore Roosevelt,* compiled by Herman Hagedorn, p. 87

All false religion is in conflict with nature.

Jean Jacques Rousseau

I believe all that I can understand of religion, and I respect the rest without rejecting it.

Jean Jacques Rousseau: *Julie,* Pt. V, Letter 3

Religion is not an escape from life; it is life. It is not an abstraction; it is a career.

S. A. C. Sidelights

Most men's anger about religion is as if two men should quarrel for a lady they neither of them care for.

Sir George Savile, Lord Halifax: *Works,* p. 221

Religion is a soul with its allegiance fixed, moving about the common streets with the stamp and seal of *forever* on it. It is bolted down to eternity as an engine is bolted down to a cement floor, lest it shake itself to pieces in ten minutes.

Paul E. Scherer: *The Pastor*

Religion is the metaphysics of the people.

Arthur Schopenhauer

A good religion is an attitude toward some Supreme Power other than self which results in progressive realization of truth, goodness, and beauty in life. This is a definition which holds for all the great religions of the world, regardless of their creeds, historical background, civilization, theologies or philosophies.

Carl Emil Seashore: "One World, One Religion," *School and Society,* September 7, 1946

We look after religion as the butcher did after his knife, when he had it in his mouth.

John Selden

Religion is like the fashion: one man wears his doublet slashed, another laced, another plain; but every man has a doublet. So every man has his religion. We differ about trimming.

John Selden: *Table Talk: Religion*

Religion is regarded by the common people as true, by the wise as false, and by the rulers as useful.

Seneca

Religion which is merely ritual and ceremonial can never satisfy. Neither can we be satisfied by a religion which is merely humanitarian or serviceable to mankind. Man's craving is for the spiritual.

Samuel M. Shoemaker

The luxury of false religion is to be unhappy.

Sydney Smith: *Letter to Francis Horner*

The test of religion is whether it fits us to meet emergencies. A man has no more character than he can command in time of crisis.

Ralph W. Sockman

No man's religion ever survives his morals.

Robert South

By its enemies religion has been called a drug. It is a drug, and furthermore, the only drug that can counteract the virus of hatred now flowing in the blood of men and nations.

Francis, Cardinal Spellman: *Action This Day*

I would not give much for your religion unless it can be seen. Lamps do not talk, but they do shine.

Charles Haddon Spurgeon

A religious life is a struggle and not a hymn.

Madame Anne Germaine de Staël:
Corinne, Bk. X, ch. 5

Religion has nothing more to fear than not being sufficiently understood.

Stanislas I (King of Poland): Maxims, no. 36

Religion consists not so much in joyous feelings as in constant devotedness to God, and laying ourselves out for the good of others.

George E. Stewart, Jr.

Going to church doesn't make you a Christian any more than going to a garage makes you an automobile.

W. A. ("Billy") Sunday

Religion is not a way of looking at certain things, but a certain way of looking at all things.

Sunshine Magazine

We have enough religion to make us hate, but not enough to make us love one another.

Jonathan Swift: Thoughts on Various Subjects

It is a mistake to assume that God is interested only, or even chiefly, in religion.

William Temple, Archbishop of Canterbury

What is religion? That which is never spoken.

Henry David Thoreau

No religion is irrelevant if it helps people to see the hidden glory of the common things they do.

D. Elton Trueblood

Religion hath no landmarks.

Martin Farquhar Tupper: Of Estimating Character

Religious feeling is as much a verity as any other part of human consciousness; and against it, on the subjective side, the waves of science beat in vain.

John Tyndall

A great teacher once said: "The only way to save religion is to allow religion to save you."

The Upper Room

We are anxious to win our friends to our political beliefs or new diet fads, but our religion we keep strictly to ourselves.

Ibid.

Religion is the reaching out of one's whole being—mind, body, spirit, emotions, intuitions, will—for completion, for inner unity, for true relation with those about us, for right relation to the universe in which we live. Religion is life, a certain kind of life, life as it could and should be, a life of harmony within and true adjustment without —life, therefore, in harmony with the life of God Himself.

Henry Pitt Van Dusen: Life's Meaning

Religion is the law that binds man to his Creator.

Lew Wallace

Orthodoxy is my doxy; heterodoxy is another man's doxy.

William Warburton

Truth has never been, can never be, contained in any one creed.

Mary Augusta Ward

Religion is as necessary to reason as reason is to religion. The one cannot exist without the other.

George Washington

While just government protects all in their religious rites, true religion affords government its surest support.

George Washington

The Soviet Commissar of Education once said: "I find that religion is like a nail: the harder you hit it, the deeper you drive it in."

Watchman-Examiner

Amusements will help you forget things; religion will help you surmount things.

Weekly Unity

Educate children without religion and you make a race of clever devils out of them.

Arthur Wellesley, Duke of Wellington

Some people have just enough religion to make them uncomfortable.

John Wesley

Opinion is not religion, not even right opinion.

John Wesley

If our religion is not true, we are bound to change it; if it is true, we are bound to propagate it.

Richard Whately

If a man has any religion he must either give it away—or give it up.

Richard Whately

Religion is not a hearsay, a presumption, a supposition; is not a customary pretension and profession; is not an affectation of any mode; is not a piety of particular fancy, consisting of some pathetic devotions, vehement expressions, bodily severities, affected anomalies, and aversion from the innocent usages of others; but consisteth in a profound humility, and a universal charity.

Benjamin Whichcote: *Sermons*

Religion is tending to degenerate into a decent formula wherewith to embellish a comfortable life.

Alfred North Whitehead: *Science and the Modern World,* Cambridge University Press

I say the whole earth and all the stars in the sky are for religion's sake.

Walt Whitman

Religion is the history of man's mistrust, his fear, and his unbelief, all dramatically overcome. It is the record and the saga of man's longest unbroken quest in history. . . .

Albert N. Williams: "Our Petrified Prophets," *Saturday Review,* April 10, 1954

I would rather think of my religion as a gamble than to think of it as an insurance premium.

Stephen S. Wise: *Religion*

Religion's all. Descending from the skies
To wretched man, the goddess in her left
Holds out this world, and, in her right, the next.

Edward Young: *Night Thoughts,* Night IV, l. 550

REPENTANCE

To repent is to alter one's way of looking at life; it is to take God's point of view instead of one's own.

Anonymous

True repentance is to cease from sin.

St. Ambrose

God hath promised pardon to him that repenteth, but he hath not promised repentance to him that sinneth.

St. Anselm

Repent one day before thy death.

Apocrypha Ecclesiasticus

There is one case of death-bed repentance recorded, that of the penitent thief, that none should despair; and only one that none should presume.

St. Augustine

Before God can deliver us we must undeceive ourselves.

St. Augustine

Repentance may begin instantly, but reformation often requires a sphere of years.

Henry Ward Beecher

Whoever . . . prefers the service of princes before his duty to his Creator, will be sure, early or late, to repent in vain.

Bidpai: *The Prince and His Minister,* ch. 3, fab. 3

Repentance does not mean *remorse*. Repentance means giving up sin.

W. E. Biederwolf

The hardest sinner in the whole lot to convert is the one who spends half of his time in sinning and the other half in repentance.

Josh Billings

And he who seeks repentance for the Past Should woo the Angel Virtue in the future!

Edward George Bulwer-Lytton: *The Lady of Lyons*, Act V, sc. 2

Of all acts of man, repentance is the most divine. The greatest of all faults is to be conscious of none.

Thomas Carlyle

Repentance, to be of any avail, must work a change of heart and conduct.

Theodore Ledyard Cuyler

No power can the impenitent absolve.

Alighieri Dante: *Inferno*, Canto XXVII, l. 118

Repentance, without amendment, is like continually pumping without mending the leak.

Lewis W. Dillwyn

Death-bed repentance is burning the candle of life in the service of the devil, then blowing the snuff in the face of heaven.

Lorenzo Dow

When prodigals return great things are done.

A. A. Dowty: *The Siliad*

Anger and folly walk cheek by jole; repentance treads on both their heels.

Benjamin Franklin: *Poor Richard*

You cannot repent too soon, because you do not know how soon it may be too late.

Thomas Fuller

When all is gone, repentance comes too late.

Thomas Fuller: *Gnomologia*, no. 5545

When the soul has laid down its faults at the feet of God, it feels as though it had wings.

Eugénie de Guérin

If only one man repents for his sins, the whole world is pardoned.

Hebrew Proverb

Restore to God His due in tithe and time; A tithe purloin'd cankers the whole estate.

George Herbert: *The Church-Porch*, st. 65

Who after his transgression doth repent, Is half, or altogether innocent.

Robert Herrick: *Penitence*

A noble mind disdains not to repent.

Homer: *Iliad*, Bk. XV, l. 227

The best repentance is to get up and act for righteousness, and forget that you ever had relations with sin.

William James (permission to reprint granted by Paul R. Reynolds & Son)

A death-bed repentance seldom reaches to restitution.

Junius: *Letters: Dedication*

Our repentance is not so much regret for the ill we have done as fear of the ill that may happen to us in consequence.

François de La Rochefoucauld: *Maximes*, no. 180

He well repents that will not sin, yet can; But Death-bed sorrow rarely shews the man.

Nathaniel Lee: *Princess of Cleve*, Act IV, sc. 3

Repentance is a heart sorrow for our past misdeeds, and a sincere resolution and an endeavor to the utmost of our power, to conform all our actions to the law of God. It does not consist in one single act of sorrow, but in doing works meet for repentance; in a sincere obedience to the law of Christ for the remainder of our lives.

John Locke

To do it no more is the truest repentance.

Martin Luther: *Of Repentance*

Harm done, too late followeth repentance.

John Lydgate: *Fall of Princes*, Bk. III, l. 915

Repentance is not only grief on account of this or that particular act; it is a deep-seated sorrow on account of the discrepancy between the outward acts of the will and that ideal which is presented to the conscience in the new Adam—the typical—the Christian man.

Hans L. Martensen

All things, save silence only bring repentance.

Menander: *Fragments*, no. 1105

The golden key that opens the palace of eternity.

John Milton

There are two kinds of repentance: one is that of Judas, the other that of Peter; the one is ice broken, the other ice melted. Repentance unto life will be repentance in the life.

William Nevins

Repent ye: for the kingdom of heaven is at hand.

New Testament: *Matthew 3: 2*

I am not come to call the righteous but sinners to repentance.

New Testament: *Matthew 9: 13*

Except ye repent ye shall all likewise perish.

New Testament: *Luke 13: 3*

Joy shall be in heaven over one sinner that repenteth, more than over ninety and nine just persons, which need no repentance.

New Testament: *Luke 15: 7*

Repent ye, therefore, and be converted that your sins may be blotted out.

New Testament: *Acts 3: 19*

Ye sorrowed to repentance.

New Testament: *II Corinthians 7: 9*

Godly sorrow worketh repentance.

New Testament: *II Corinthians 7: 10*

I abhor myself, and repent in dust and ashes.

Old Testament: *Job 42: 6*

Come, fill the Cup, and in the fire of Spring,
Your Winter-garment of Repentance fling:
The Bird of Time has but a little way
To flutter—and the Bird is on the Wing.

Omar Khayyám: *The Rubáiyát* (First Edition), st. 7

There is a greater depravity in not repenting of sin when it has been committed, than in committing it at first. To deny, as Peter did, is bad; but not to weep bitterly, as he did, when we have denied, is worse.

Edward Payson

I view my crime, but kindle at the view,
Repent old pleasures, and solicit new.

Alexander Pope: *Eloisa to Abelard*

It is never too late to repent.

John Ray: *English Proverbs*

The dream is short, repentance long.

Johann Christoph Friedrich von Schiller: *Lied von der Glocke*

He who repents his sins is well-nigh innocent.

Seneca: *Agamemnon*, l. 243

God never repents of what He has first resolved upon.

Seneca: *De Beneficiis*

A true repentance shuns the evil itself
More than the external suffering or the shame.

William Shakespeare

Repentance is the heart's sorrow, and a clear life ensuing.

William Shakespeare

REPENTANCE

Confess yourself to heaven;
Repent what's past; avoid what is to come.
William Shakespeare: *Hamlet,*
Act III, sc. 4, l. 149

I never did repent for doing good,
Nor shall not now.
William Shakespeare: *The Merchant of
Venice,* Act III, sc. 4, l. 10

Repentance hath a purifying power and
every tear is of the cleansing virtue; but
these penitential clouds must be still kept
dropping; one shower will not suffice; for
repentance is not one single action but a
course.

Robert South

It is one thing to mourn for sin because it
exposes us to hell, and another to mourn
for it because it is an infinite evil; one thing
to mourn for it because it is injurious to ourselves, and another thing to mourn for it
because it is wrong and offensive to God. It
is one thing to be terrified; another, to be
humbled.

Gardiner Spring

Whatever stress some may lay upon it, a
death-bed repentance is but a weak and
slender plank to trust our all upon.

Laurence Sterne

True repentance hates the sin, and not
merely the penalty; and it hates the sin most
of all because it has discovered and felt God's
love.

William Mackergo Taylor

The repentance consists in the heart being
broken for sin and broken from sin. Some
often repent, yet never reform; they resemble
a man travelling in a dangerous path, who
frequently starts and stops, but never turns
back.

Bonnell Thornton

RESURRECTION

Repentance for past crimes is just and easy;
But Sin-no-more's a task too hard for mortals.
Sir John Vanbrugh: *The Relapse,* Act V,
sc. 4

Mere sorrow, which weeps and sits still, is
not repentance. Repentance is sorrow converted into action; into a movement toward
a new and better life.

Marvin Richardson Vincent

Repentance must be something more than
mere remorse for sins: it comprehends a
change of nature befitting heaven.
Lew Wallace: *Ben Hur,* Bk. VI, ch. 2

There's no repentance in the grave.
Isaac Watts: *Solemn Thoughts*

He that repents is angry with himself; I need
not be angry with him.
Benjamin Whichcote: *Moral and
Religious Aphorisms*

The vain regret that steals above the wreck
of squandered hours.
John Greenleaf Whittier

RESURRECTION

Christianity begins where religion ends . . .
with the Resurrection.

Anonymous

Spring in the world!
And all things are made new.
Spring in the heart!
And a bird-note in the blue!
And we are somehow sure
By this dumb turmoil in the soul of man
Of an impending Resurrection.

Anonymous

Immortal Hope dispels the gloom!
An angel sits beside the tomb.
Sarah Flower Adams: *The Mourners
Came at Break of Day*

We could not call it resurrection unless the soul returned to the same body, for resurrection means a second rising.

St. Thomas Aquinas: *Summa theologica*, III

Earth to earth, ashes to ashes, dust to dust, in sure and certain hope of the resurrection.

Book of Common Prayer: Burial of the Dead

This mortal does not put on immortality, this corruption does not put on incorruption, until after the coming of Christ . . . The resurrection is not yet.

Book of Mormon (Alma XL, 2–3)

I believe that our estranged and divided ashes shall unite again; that our separated dust, after so many pilgrimages and transformations into the parts of minerals, plants, animals, elements, shall, at the voice of God, return to their primitive shapes, and join again to make up their primary and predestinate forms.

Sir Thomas Browne: *Religio Medici*, I

The resurrection is a true sunrising, the inbursting of a cloudless sky on all the righteous dead.

Horace Bushnell

Yet at the resurrection we shall see
A fair edition, and of matchless worth,
Free from erratas, new in heaven set forth.

Joseph Capen: *Lines upon Mr. John Foster*

I do believe, that die I must,
And be return'd from out my dust:
I do believe, that when I rise,
Christ I shall see, with these same eyes.

Robert Herrick: *Noble Numbers*

I shall not wholly die; large residue
Shall 'scape the queen of death.

Horace: *Odes*, Bk. III, ode 30, l. 6

Wherever ye be, God will bring you all back at the resurrection.

The Koran

Easter is not a passport to another world; it is a quality of perception for this one.

W. P. Lemon

The resurrection cannot be tamed or tethered by any utilitarian test. It is a vast watershed in history, or it is nothing. It cannot be tested for truth; it is the test of lesser truths. No light can be thrown on it; its own light blinds the investigator. It does not compel belief; it resists it. But once accepted as fact, it tells more about the universe, about history, and about man's state and fate than all the mountains of other facts in the human accumulation.

Editorial in *Life*. © 1956, Time, Inc.

Our Lord has written the promise of the resurrection not in books alone, but in every leaf in springtime.

Martin Luther

Faith cannot long keep death in view. Resurrection is that which fills the vision of faith; and in the power thereof, it can rise up from the dead.

Charles Mackintosh

The trumpet! the trumpet! the dead have all heard:
Lo, the depths of the stone-cover'd charnels are stirr'd:
From the sea, from the land, from the south and the north,
The vast generations of man are come forth.

Henry Hart Milman: *Hymns for Church Service*, Second Sunday in Advent, st. 3

The hour is coming, in the which all that are in the graves shall hear his voice, and shall come forth; they that have done good, unto the resurrection of life; and they that have done evil, unto the resurrection of damnation.

New Testament: John 5: 28-29

My flesh shall rest in hope.

New Testament: Acts 2: 26

379

Why should it be thought a thing incredible with you, that God should raise the dead?

New Testament: Acts 26: 8

For since by man came death, by man came also the resurrection of the dead.

New Testament: I Corinthians 15: 21

For as in Adam all die, even so in Christ shall all be made alive.

New Testament: I Corinthians 15: 22

Many of them that sleep in the dust of the earth shall awake, some to everlasting life, and some to shame and everlasting contempt.

Old Testament: Daniel 12: 2

In my part I shall be raised to immortality above the lofty stars.

Ovid: Metamorphoses, Bk. XV, l. 875

What reason have atheists for saying that we cannot rise again? Which is the more difficult, to be born, or to rise again? That what has never been, should be, or that what has been, should be again? Is it more difficult to come into being than to return to it?

Blaise Pascal: Pensées, XXIV

Every parting gives a foretaste of death; every coming together again a foretaste of the resurrection.

Arthur Schopenhauer: Studies in Pessimism. Psychological Observations

It was inevitable that Jesus Christ should be crucified; it was also inevitable that he should rise again.

H. R. L. Sheppard

The biggest fact about Joseph's tomb was that it wasn't a tomb at all—it was a room for a transient. Jesus just stopped there a night or two on his way back to glory.

Herbert Booth Smith

Our life's a flying shadow, God's the pole,
The index pointing at Him is our soul;
Death the horizon, when our sun is set,

Which will through Christ a resurrection get.

Sun Dial inscription once on the South wall of Glasgow Cathedral

Too vital to be lost in the mists of antiquity, too vital to be subjected to permanent misrepresentation, (Jesus) is, apparently too vital to die.

Ernest Fremont Tittle: Jesus After Nineteen Centuries, Abingdon Press

REVELATION

The vast bulk of the population believe that morality depends entirely on revelation; and if a doubt could be raised among them that the Ten Commandments were given by God from Mount Sinai, men would think they were at liberty to steal, women consider themselves absolved from the restraints of chastity.

John Campbell: Argument for the prosecution in Rex vs. H. Hetherington

Lochiel, Lochiel! beware of the day;
For, dark and despairing, my sight I may seal
But man cannot cover what God would reveal.

Thomas Campbell: Lochiel's Warning

'Tis revelation satisfies all doubts,
Explains all mysteries except her own,
And so illuminates the path of life,
That fools discover it, and stray no more.

William Cowper: The Task, Bk. II, l. 527

A revelation is not made for the purpose of showing to indolent men that which, by faculties already given to them, they may show to themselves; no: but for the purpose of showing that which the moral darkness of man will not, without supernatural light, allow him to perceive.

Thomas De Quincey: The True Relations of the Bible to Merely Human Science

Belshazzar had a letter,—
He never had but one;
Belshazzar's correspondence
Concluded and begun
In that immortal copy
The conscience of us all
Can read without its glasses
On revelation's wall.

Emily Dickinson: *Poems*, XXV:
Belshazzar Had a Letter

Nature is a revelation of God;
Art a revelation of man.

Henry Wadsworth Longfellow: *Hyperion,*
Bk. III, ch. 5

God hides nothing. His very work from the beginning is *revelation*—a casting aside of veil after veil, a showing unto men of truth after truth. On and on from fact divine he advances, until at length in his son Jesus he unveils his very face.

George Macdonald

We may scavenge the dross of the nation,
we may shudder past bloody sod,
But we thrill to the new revelation that
we are parts of God.

Robert Haven Schauffler: *New Gods for
Old*

If God has spoken, why is the universe not convinced?

Percy Bysshe Shelley: *Queen Mab*

The simplicity and delicacy of Christ's revelation of God are the surest proofs of his diety. Some day we shall come to see that the simplicity of Christ's revelation accentuates its quality.

Walter H. Smith

REVERENCE

Reverence is one of the signs of strength; irreverence one of the surest indications of weakness. No man will rise high who jeers at sacred things. The fine loyalties of life must be reverenced or they will be foresworn in the day of trial.

Anonymous

"Honour thy father and thy mother" stands written among the three laws of most revered righteousness.

Aeschylus: *Suppliants,* l. 707

Reverence is an ennobling sentiment; it is felt to be degrading only by the vulgar mind, which would escape the sense of its own littleness by elevating itself into an antagonist of what is above it. He that has no pleasure in looking up is not fit so much as to look down.

Washington Allston

The generality of men are naturally apt to be swayed by fear rather than by reverence, and to refrain from evil rather because of the punishment that it brings, than because of its own foulness.

Aristotle: *Nicomachean Ethics,* X

Cleanness of body was ever deemed to proceed from a due reverence to God.

Sir Francis Bacon: *Advancement of
Learning,* Bk. II

When Newton and Bossuet uncovered their heads in all simplicity, pronouncing the name of God, they were, perhaps, more truly worthy of admiration than when the first was weighing those worlds, the dust of which the latter taught men to despise.

François René de Chateaubriand

Always and in everything let there be reverence.

Confucius: *The Book of Rites,* I

A man who bows down to nothing, can never bear the burden of himself.

Feodor Dostoevski: *A Raw Youth*

Henceforth the Majesty of God revere;
Fear him and you have nothing else to fear.

James Fordyce: *Answer to a Gentleman
who Apologized to the Author for
Swearing*

The soul of the Christian religion is reverence.

Johann Wolfgang von Goethe

REVERENCE

Let thy speeches be seriously reverent when thou speakest of God or His attributes; for to jest or utter thyself lightly in matters divine is an unhappy impiety, provoking Heaven to justice, and urging all men to suspect thy belief.

Francis Hawkins: *Youth's Behavior,* VII

I have in my heart a small, shy plant called reverence; I cultivate that on Sunday mornings.

Oliver Wendell Holmes, Sr.

Ye shall keep my sabbaths, and reverence my sanctuary: I am the Lord.

Old Testament: Leviticus 19: 30

God is greatly to be feared in the assembly of the saints, and to be had in reverence of all them that are about him.

Old Testament: Psalms 89: 7

We treat God with irreverence by banishing him from our thoughts, not by referring to his will on slight occasions.

John Ruskin

Rather let my head
Stoop to the block than these knees bow to any
Save to the God of Heaven.

William Shakespeare: *Henry VI, Part II,*
Act IV, sc. 1, l. 124

Reverence is the very first element of religion; it cannot but be felt by every one who has right views of the divine greatness and holiness, and of his own character in the sight of God.

Charles Simmons

Let knowledge grow from more to more,
But more of reverence in us dwell;
That mind and soul, according well,
May make one music as before.

Alfred, Lord Tennyson: *In Memoriam,*
Prologue, st. 7

Dear Lord and Father of mankind,
Forgive our foolish ways!
Reclothe us in our rightful mind,

RICHES, WEALTH

In purer lives Thy service find,
In deeper reverence, praise.

John Greenleaf Whittier: *The Brewing of Soma*

RICHES, WEALTH

No man can tell whether he is rich or poor by turning to his ledger. It is the heart that makes a man rich. He is rich according to what he is, not according to what he has.

Henry Ward Beecher

Riches are not an end of life, but an instrument of life.

Henry Ward Beecher

A man's true wealth is the good he does in this world.

Bendixline

Since all the riches of this world
May be gifts from the devil and earthly kings,
I should suspect that I worshipped the devil
If I thanked my God for worldly things.

William Blake: *Riches*

Lay not up for yourselves treasure upon earth; where the rust and moth doth corrupt.

Book of Common Prayer: The Communion

But I have learned a thing or two; I know as sure as fate,
When we lock up our lives for wealth, the gold key comes too late.

Will Carleton: *The Ancient Miner's Story*

The wealth of a man is the number of things which he loves and blesses, and which he is loved and blessed by.

Thomas Carlyle

Midas-eared Mammonism, double-barrelled Dilettantism, and their thousand adjuncts and corollaries, are *not* the Law by which God Almighty has appointed this His universe to go.

Thomas Carlyle: *Past and Present,* ch. 6

The fundamental idea of the gospel of wealth is that surplus wealth should be considered as a sacred trust to be administered by those into whose hands it falls, during their lives, for the good of the community.

Andrew Carnegie: *The Gospel of Wealth,* p. 55, Harvard University Press

The gospel of wealth advocates leaving free the operation of laws of accumulation.

Andrew Carnegie: "The Advantages of Poverty" in *The Gospel of Wealth,* p. 71, Harvard University Press

Riches are not forbidden, but the pride of them is.

St. John Chrysostom: *Homilies,* II

Wealth is like a viper, which is harmless if a man knows how to take hold of it; but if he does not, it will twine round his hand and bite him.

St. Clement

Wealth consists not in having great possessions but in having few wants.

Epicurus

If your riches are yours, why don't you take them with you to t'other world?

Benjamin Franklin: *Poor Richard's Almanac*

Who is rich? He that is content. Who is that? Nobody.

Ibid.

Ahab sold himself for a vineyard, Judas, a bag of silver, Achan, a wedge and a garment, Gehazi, silver and raiment. Are you for sale?

Orin Philip Gifford

Ill fares the land, to hastening ills a prey, Where wealth accumulates, and men decay.

Oliver Goldsmith: *The Deserted Village*

Rich people should consider that they are only trustees for what they possess, and should show their wealth to be more in doing good than merely in having it.—They should not reserve their benevolence for pur-

poses after they are dead, for those who give not of their property till they die show that they would not then if they could keep it any longer.

Joseph Hall

There is a burden of care in getting riches; fear in keeping them; temptation in using them; guilt in abusing them; sorrow in losing them; and a burden of account at last to be given concerning them.

Matthew Henry

Wealth is not of necessity a curse, nor poverty a blessing.

Roswell Dwight Hitchcock

Know from the bounteous heavens all riches flow;
And what man gives, the gods by man bestow.

Homer: *Odyssey,* Bk. XVIII, l. 26

All things, divine and human,—virtue, fame, honor—are slaves to the beauty of riches.

Horace: *Satires,* Bk. II, sat. 3, l. 94

Riches are the pettiest and least worthy gifts which God can give a man. What are they to God's Word, to bodily gifts, such as beauty and health; or to the gifts of the mind, such as understanding, skill, wisdom! Yet men toil for them day and night, and take no rest. Therefore God commonly gives riches to foolish people to whom he gives nothing else.

Martin Luther

Mammon lead them on—
Mammon, the least erected Spirit that fell
From Heaven: for even in Heaven his looks and thoughts
Were always downward bent, admiring more
The riches of Heaven's pavement, trodden gold,
Than aught divine or holy else enjoyed
In vision beatific.

John Milton: *Paradise Lost,* Bk. I, l. 678

Riches are not from an abundance of worldly goods, but from a contented mind.

Sunnah: Sayings of Mohammed

Lay not up for yourselves treasures upon earth, where moth and rust doth corrupt, and where thieves break through and steal.

New Testament: Matthew 6: 19

It is easier for a camel to go through the eye of a needle, than for a rich man to enter into the kingdom of God.

New Testament: Matthew 19: 24

Rich in good works.

New Testament: I Timothy 6: 18

But thou shalt remember the Lord thy God: for it is he that giveth thee power to get wealth.

Old Testament: Deuteronomy 8: 18

He heapeth up riches, and knoweth not who shall gather them.

Old Testament: Psalms 39: 6

A good name is rather to be chosen than great riches.

Old Testament: Proverbs 22: 1

Riches certainly make themselves wings; they fly away as an eagle toward heaven.

Old Testament: Proverbs 23: 5

He that maketh haste to be rich shall not be innocent.

Old Testament: Proverbs 28: 20

Riches, the incentives to evil, are dug out of the earth.

Ovid: *Metamorphoses,* Bk. I, l. 40

Some have much, and some have more,
Some are rich, and some are poor,
Some have little, some have less,
Some have not a cent to bless
Their empty pockets, yet possess
True riches in true happiness.

John Oxenham: *True Happiness*

A man's wealth does not depend so much on what he has as on what he can do without.

Earl Riney: *Church Management*

A man who possesses wealth, possesses power, but it is a power to do evil as well as good.

Azel Stevens Roe

For often evil men are rich, and good men poor;
But we will not exchange with them
Our virtue for their wealth, since one abides alway,
While riches change their owners every day.

Solon: *Fragments,* frag. 15

There are not a few who believe in no God but Mammon, no devil but the absence of gold, no damnation but being poor, and no hell but an empty purse; and not a few of their descendants are living still.

Robert South

To value riches is not to be covetous. They are the gift of God, and, like every gift of his, good in themselves, and capable of a good use. But to overvalue riches, to give them a place in the heart which God did not design them to fill, this is covetousness.

Herman Lincoln Wayland

I saw that a humble man, with the blessing of the Lord, might live on a little; and that where the heart was set on greatness, success in business did not satisfy the craving; but that commonly, with an increase of wealth, the desire of wealth increased.

John Woolman: *Journal,* II

The wealthiest man among us is the best.

William Wordsworth: *Poems Dedicated to National Independence,* Pt. I, no. 13

RIGHTEOUSNESS

Unclean in the sight of God is everyone who is unrighteous: clean therefore is everyone who is righteous; if not in the sight of men, yet in the sight of God, who judges without error.

St. Augustine: *On Lying*

What is all righteousness that men devise?
What—but a sordid bargain for the skies?
> William Cowper: *Truth*, l. 75

The company of just and righteous men is better than wealth and a rich estate.
> Euripides: *Aegeus*, frag. 7

Righteousness as exemplified by Christ is not merely the absence of vice or the presence of virtue. It is a consuming passion for God which sends you forth in His name to establish His kingdom.
> Irving Peake Johnson

Blessed are they which do hunger and thirst after righteousness: for they shall be filled.
> *New Testament: Matthew 5: 6*

I have been young and now am old; yet have I not seen the righteous forsaken, nor his seed begging bread.
> *Old Testament: Psalms 37: 25*

Verily there is a reward for the righteous.
> *Old Testament: Psalms 58: 11*

Mercy and truth are met together; righteousness and peace have kissed each other.
> *Old Testament: Psalms 85: 10*

The righteous shall flourish like the palm-tree: he shall grow like a cedar in Lebanon.
> *Old Testament: Psalms 92: 12*

The wicked flee when no man pursueth: but the righteous are bold as a lion.
> *Old Testament: Proverbs 28: 1*

Be not righteous over much; neither make thyself over wise.
> *Old Testament: Ecclesiastes 7: 16*

The righteous perisheth, and no man layeth it to heart.
> *Old Testament: Isaiah 57: 1*

He put on righteousness as a breastplate.
> *Old Testament: Isaiah 59: 17*

All our righteousnesses are as filthy rags.
> *Old Testament: Isaiah 64: 6*

The quest for righteousness is Oriental, the quest for knowledge, Occidental.
> Sir William Osler: *Life of Sir William Osler*, by Harvey Cushing, Vol. II, ch. 34

"The wicked flee when no man pursueth." But they make better time when the righteous go after them.
> Charles Henry Parkhurst: *Ethical Outlook*, published by American Ethical Union

Righteousness is just rightness. Sometimes we make it too theological as a Biblical word. Rightness is not easy of definition, but everybody knows what it is. We are conscious of rightness even if we cannot adequately define it.
> Harry Lathrop Reed

Obedience insures greatness, whilst disobedience leads to repulse. Whosoever possesseth the qualities of righteousness placeth his head on the threshold of obedience.
> Saadi

O Fortune, that enviest the brave, what unequal rewards thou bestowest on the righteous!
> Seneca: *Hercules Furens*, 524

Ay me, how many perils do enfold
The righteous man to make him daily fall!
> Edmund Spenser: *Faerie Queene*, Bk. I, Canto VIII, st. 1

Clothe yourself with the silk of piety, with the satin of sanctity, with the purple of modesty, so shall God Himself be your suitor.
> Tertullian

S

SABBATH, SUNDAY

The law of the Sabbath is the key stone of
the arch of public morals; take it away and
the whole structure falls.

Anonymous

Monday's child is fair of face,
Tuesday's child is full of grace,
Wednesday's child is full of woe,
Thursday's child has far to go,
Friday's child is loving and giving,
Saturday's child has to work for its living,
But a child that's born on the Sabbath day
Is fair and wise and good and gay.

Anonymous

Sunday clears away the rust of the whole
week.

Joseph Addison: *The Spectator*, no. 112

I sing the sabbath of eternal rest.

Sir William Alexander: *Doomsday: The
First Hour*, st. 1

God's altar stands from Sunday to Sunday,
and the seventh day is no more for religion
than any other—it is for rest.—The whole
seven are for religion, and one of them for
rest, for instruction, for social worship, for
gaining strength for the other six.

Henry Ward Beecher

Through the week we go down into the
valleys of care and shadow. Our Sabbaths
should be hills of light and joy in God's
presence; and so as time rolls by we shall
go on from mountain top to mountain top,
till at last we catch the glory of the gate, and
enter in to go no more out forever.

Henry Ward Beecher

To that in men which is secular and animal,
Sunday says, "Rest"; to that which is intellectual, moral, and social, "Grow."

Henry Ward Beecher

Too many persons try to make Sunday a
sponge with which to wipe out sins of the
week.

Henry Ward Beecher

The one great poem of New England is her
Sunday.

Henry Ward Beecher: *Proverbs from
Plymouth Pulpit*

Two generations ago, Dr. Haegler, of Switzerland, discovered that more oxygen was lost
in a day's toil than was recovered by a night's
rest; but the Sabbath rest made good the
cumulative losses of the week. Since then
many similar tests have confirmed Dr. Haegler's findings.

Robert M. Blackford: *Moody Monthly*

A corruption of morals usually follows a
profanation of the Sabbath.

Sir William Blackstone

The keeping of one day in seven holy, as a
time of relaxation and refreshment as well
as public worship is of inestimable benefit
to a state, considered merely as a civil institution.

Sir William Blackstone

The Sabbath is God's present to the working
man, and one of its chief objects is to prolong
his life, and preserve efficient his working
tone. The savings bank of human existence
is the weekly Sabbath.

William G. Blaikie

A man's Sunday self and his weekday self are like two halves of a round-trip ticket: not good if detached.

Lee H. Bristol, Jr.

The streams of religion run deeper or shallower, as the banks of the Sabbath are kept up or neglected. A preacher in Holland called the Sabbath "God's dyke, shutting out an ocean of evils."

Lady Maria Callcott

I feel as if God had, by giving the Sabbath, given fifty-two springs in every year.

Samuel Taylor Coleridge

I am no fanatic, I hope, as to Sunday; but as I look abroad over the map of popular freedom in the world, it does not seem to me accidental that Switzerland, Scotland, England, and the United States—the countries which best observe Sunday—constitute almost the entire map of safe popular government.

Joseph Cook

We doctors, in the treatment of nervous diseases, are now constantly compelled to prescribe periods of rest. Some periods are, I think, only Sundays in arrears.

Sir James Crichton-Browne

The Lord's Day is a firm foundation on which to build a six-story week.

The Defender

There is a Sunday conscience as well as a Sunday coat; and those who make religion a secondary concern put the coat and conscience carefully by to put on only once a week.

Charles Dickens

Some keep the Sabbath going to church;
I keep it staying at home,
With a bobolink for a chorister,
And an orchard for a dome.

Emily Dickinson: Part II, *Nature*, LVII, st. 1

Hail hallowed day, that binds a yoke on vice, gives rest to toil, proclaims God's holy truth, blesses the family, secures the state, prospers communities, nations exalts, pours life and light on earth and points the way to heaven.

Tryon Edwards

Sunday is the core of our civilization, dedicated to thought and reverence. It invites to the noblest solitude and to the noblest society.

Ralph Waldo Emerson

'Tis a strange thing, Sam, that among us people can't agree the whole week because they go different ways upon Sundays.

George Farquhar: *Letter from Leyden*

A child born on Sunday never dies of the plague.

French Proverb

It would be as difficult to take an inventory of the benefits the world receives from the sunshine as to enumerate the blessings we derive from the Christian Sabbath.

Hervey Doddridge Ganse

I believe that the institution of the Sabbath is one of the greatest benefits the human race ever had. I believe in the strict enforcement of the law that prevents servile labour being carried on on the seventh day.

Henry George

From a moral, social and physical point of view, the observance of Sunday is a duty of absolute consequence.

William Ewart Gladstone

Hail Sabbath! thee I hail, the poor man's day.

James Grahame: *The Sabbath*

A Sabbath well spent brings a week of content,
And health for the toils of the morrow;
But a Sabbath profan'd,
Whatso'er may be gain'd,
Is a certain forerunner of sorrow.

Sir Matthew Hale: *Golden Maxim*

387

A holiday Sabbath is the ally of despotism.

Arthur Henry Hallam

Gently on tiptoe Sunday creeps,
Cheerfully from the stars he peeps,
Mortals all are asleep below,
None in the village hears him go;
Even chanticleer keeps very still,
For Sunday whispered, 'twas his will.

John Peter Hebel: *Sunday Morning*

Sundays observe: think when the bells do chime
'Tis angels' music.

George Herbert: *The Church-Porch*, st. 65

Oh, day most calm, most bright!
The fruit of this, the next world's bud,
Th' indorsement of supreme delight,
Writ by a Friend, and with His blood;
The couch of Time; Care's balm and bay;
The week were dark, but for thy light:
Thy torch doth show the way.

George Herbert: *Sunday*, l. 1

The other days and thou
Make up one man; whose face thou art,
Knocking at heaven with thy brow;
The worky-days are the back-part;
The burden of the week lies there.

George Herbert: *Sunday*, l. 8

On Sunday heaven's gate stands ope;
Blessings are plentiful and rife,
More plentiful than hope.

George Herbert: *Sunday*, l. 29

I think the world of today would go mad, just frenzied with strain and pressure, but for the blessed institution of Sunday.

Brooke Herford

This solemn pause, the breathing-space of man,
The halt of toil's exhausted caravan,—
Comes sweet with music to thy wearied ear;
Rise with its anthems to a holier sphere!

Oliver Wendell Holmes, Sr.

Who backs his rigid Sabbath, so to speak,
Against the wicked remnant of the week.

Thomas Hood: *Ode to Rae Wilson*, l. 183

Sunday does not belong to business. It does not belong to the merchants. It does not belong to industry. It does not belong to government . . . It belongs to God.

Samuel A. Jeanes: *Free Methodist*

Sunday should be different from another day. People may walk, but not throw stones at birds.

Samuel Johnson

If the Sabbath goes, everything else goes with it.

Marion Lawrence

Golf may be played on Sunday, not being a game within view of the law, but being a form of moral effort.

Stephen Butler Leacock: "Why I Refuse to Play Golf," from *Wet Wit and Dry Humor*, Dodd, Mead & Co.

One of the miseries of war is that there is no Sabbath, and the current of work and strife has no cessation. How can we be pardoned for all our offenses?

Robert E. Lee: Letter to his daughter Annie

Everything has its weekday side and its Sunday side.

Georg Christoph Lichtenberg

As we keep or break the Sabbath, we nobly save or meanly lose the last best hope by which man rises.

Abraham Lincoln

Behold congenial Autumn comes,
The Sabbath of the year!

John Logan: *Ode Written on a Visit to the Country in Autumn*

Sunday is like a stile between the fields of toil, where we can kneel and pray, sit and meditate.

Henry Wadsworth Longfellow

Sunday is the golden clasp that binds together the volume of the weeks.

Henry Wadsworth Longfellow

Day of the Lord, as all our days should be!

Henry Wadsworth Longfellow: *John Endicott*, Act II, sc. 2

Take the Sunday with you through the week,
And sweeten with it all the other days.

Henry Wadsworth Longfellow: *Michael Angelo*, Pt. I, st. 5

Man needs a day of rest from the cares, toils and trials of the six days of work in the material realm. He needs to reflect, meditate, contemplate, and to turn his eyes inward, as it were, rather than outward. This has always been true, but surely it is truer now in this strenuous age of the world than ever before.

The Lookout

He who ordained the Sabbath loves the poor.

James Russell Lowell

Sunday, that day so tedious to the triflers of earth, so full of beautiful repose, of calmness and strength for the earnest and heavenly-minded.

Maria McIntosh

The Church as a visible force and power could not exist without the Sabbath.

Donald McLeod

If Sunday had not been observed as a day of rest during the last three centuries, I have not the slightest doubt that we should have been at this moment a poorer people and less civilized.

Thomas Babington Macaulay

Where there is no Christian Sabbath, there is no Christian morality, and without these our free institutions cannot long be sustained.

John MacLean, of the United States Supreme Court

Without a Sabbath, no worship; without worship, no religion; and without religion, no permanent freedom.

Charles Forbes Montalembert

You show me a nation that has given up the Sabbath, and I will show you a nation that has got the seed of decay.

Dwight L. Moody

And he said unto them, The sabbath was made for man, and not man for the sabbath.

New Testament: Mark 2: 27

Day of all the week the best,
Emblem of eternal rest.

John Newton: *Saturday Evening*

God blessed the seventh day, and sanctified it: because that in it he had rested from all his work which God created and made.

Old Testament: Genesis 2: 3

Remember the sabbath day, to keep it holy. Six days shalt thou labour, and do all thy work: but the seventh day is the sabbath of the Lord thy God.

Old Testament: Exodus 20: 8–10

Six years thou shalt sow thy field, and six years thou shalt prune thy vineyard, and gather in the fruit thereof; but in the seventh year shall be a sabbath of rest unto the land, a sabbath for the Lord: thou shalt neither sow thy field, nor prune thy vineyard.

Old Testament: Leviticus 25: 3–4

This is the day which the Lord hath made; we will rejoice and be glad in it.

Old Testament: Psalms 118: 24

I never knew a man escape failures in either mind or body, who worked seven days a week.

Sir Robert Peel

The green oasis, the little grassy meadow in the wilderness; where, after the weekday's journey, the pilgrim halts for refreshment and repose.

Charles Reade

Come day, go day, God send Sunday.
> Scottish Proverb

Give the world one-half of Sunday and you will soon find that religion has no strong hold on the other half.
> Sir Walter Scott

The Lord's Day is the shadow of Christ on the hot highway of time.
> Robert E. Speer

I always like to begin a journey on Sundays, because I shall have the prayers of the Church to preserve all that travel by land or by water.
> Jonathan Swift: *Polite Conversation,*
> Dialogue XI

When Christians dare God's Sabbath to abuse
They make themselves a scorn to Turks and Jews.
> John Taylor: *Observations and Travel*
> *from London to Hamburg*

The Sabbaths of Eternity.
One Sabbath deep and wide.
> Alfred, Lord Tennyson: *St. Agnes' Eve,*
> st. 3

I do wish that all tired people did but know the infinite rest there is in fencing off the six days from the seventh—in anchoring the business ships of our daily life as the Saturday draws to its close, leaving them to ride peacefully upon the flow or the ebb until Monday morning comes again.
> Anna Bartlett Warner

Break down Sunday, close the churches, open the bars and theatres on that day, and where would values be? What was the real estate worth in Sodom?
> Herman Lincoln Wayland

Sunday is nature's law as well as God's. No individual or nation habitually disregarding it has failed to fall upon disaster and grief.
> Daniel Webster

The longer I live the more highly do I estimate the Christian Sabbath, and the more grateful do I feel to those who impress its importance on the community.
> Daniel Webster

What a child is taught on Sunday it will remember on Monday.
> Welsh Proverb

O what a blessing is Sunday, interposed between the waves of worldly business like the divine path of the Israelites through the sea.
> Samuel Wilberforce

SACRAMENTS

No barrier of race or creed or nation
Can break that sacramental comradeship of bread and wine
As long as mankind prays,
"Our Father, who art in heaven!"
> Anonymous

The spiritual virtue of a sacrament is like light: although it passes among the impure, it is not polluted.
> St. Augustine: *Tract on St. John,* ch. 5, 15

As bells answer bells and strike with sweet collision in the air, so may heart answer heart, and joy answer joy, when those who are affianced to God are openly united to him in Holy Communion.
> Henry Ward Beecher

If there be any who hunger and thirst, come: here is bread, and here is wine. "But I am not a member of any church." That makes no difference. Christ calls not the righteous but sinners.
> Henry Ward Beecher

I oft had seen the dawnlight run
As red wine through the hills, and break
Through many a mist's inurning;
But, here, no earth profaned the sun;
Heaven, ocean, did alone partake
The sacrament of morning.
> Elizabeth Barrett Browning: *A Sabbath*
> *Morning at Sea*

The sacraments are efficacious because by means of them Christ, through the Holy Spirit, effects His grace in the soul.

Continuation Committee (Lausanne)

In all sacramental doctrine and practice the original and ultimate authority is Christ Himself.

Edinburgh Conference

Coming by faith, and thus truly partaking of the bread and the wine, we receive anew the assurance that we are pardoned sinners.

M. Patterson

In every sacrament the principal inward reality (*res sacramenti*) is a divine act.

Oliver Chase Quick

Embodied acts, such as the sacramental act, are beneath acts purely mental and spiritual, such as prayer is.

Benjamin Whichcote: *Moral and Religious Aphorisms*

SACRIFICE

That which we should value in ourselves and in one another is the dignity of God's image and the great price at which we were bought.

Anonymous

Self-preservation is the first law of nature; self-sacrifice the highest rule of grace.

Anonymous

In this world it is not what we take up, but what we give up, that makes us rich.

Henry Ward Beecher

When bad men combine, the good must associate; else they will fall, one by one, an unpitied sacrifice in a contemptible struggle.

Edmund Burke: *Thoughts on the Cause of the Present Discontent*

The altar of sacrifice is the touchstone of character.

O. P. Clifford

Good manners are made up of petty sacrifices.

Ralph Waldo Emerson

Reckon the days in which you have not been angry. I used to be angry every day; now every other day; then every third and fourth day; and if you miss it as long as thirty days, offer a sacrifice of thanksgiving to God.

Epictetus

Every Christian truth, gracious and comfortable, has a corresponding obligation, searching and sacrificial.

Harry Emerson Fosdick

To love is to know the sacrifices which eternity exacts from life.

John Oliver Hobbes: *School for Saints,* ch. 25

I never made a sacrifice. We ought not to talk of "sacrifice" when we remember the great sacrifice which He made who left His Father's throne on high to give Himself for us.

David Livingstone

It is not possible that the blood of bulls and of goats should take away sins.

New Testament: Hebrews 10: 4

To obey is better than sacrifice, and to hearken than the fat of rams.

Old Testament: I Samuel 15: 22

Neither will I offer burnt offerings unto the Lord my God of that which doth cost me nothing.

Old Testament: II Samuel 24: 24

The sacrifices of God are a broken spirit: a broken and contrite heart, O God, thou wilt not despise.

Old Testament: Psalms 51: 17

There is but one virtue—the eternal sacrifice of self.

George Sand

God is not to be worshipped with sacrifices and blood; for what pleasure can He have in the slaughter of the innocent? but with a pure mind, a good and honest purpose. Temples are not to be built for Him with stones piled on high; God is to be consecrated in the breast of each.

Seneca: *Fragment*, V, 204

Go with me, like good angels, to my end;
And, as the long divorce of steel falls on me,
Make of your prayers one sweet sacrifice,
And lift my soul to heaven.

William Shakespeare: *Henry VIII*,
Act II, sc. 1, l. 75

Cast not the clouded gem away,
Quench not the dim but living ray,—
My brother man, Beware!
With that deep voice which from the skies
Forbade the Patriarch's sacrifice,
God's angel, cries, Forbear!

John Greenleaf Whittier: *Human
Sacrifice*, Pt. VII

SAINTS

The seeds of godlike power are in us still:
Gods we are, Bards, Saints, Heroes, if we will.

Matthew Arnold: *Sonnet 4* (Written in
Emerson's Essays)

To be a great man and a saint for oneself, that is the one important thing.

Charles Baudelaire: *Mon Coeur Mis à
Nu*, LII

I hope those old water-logged saints that died soaking in damp stone cells were taken to Heaven. They had Hell enough on earth.

Henry Ward Beecher: *Royal Truths*

The saint who works no miracles has few pilgrims.

Sir William Gurney Benham: *Proverbs*,
p. 850

Saint: a dead sinner revised and edited.

Ambrose Bierce: *The Devil's Dictionary*

Saints, to do us good,
Must be in heaven.

Robert Browning: *The Ring and the
Book*, Pt. VI, l. 176

The soberest saints are more stiff-necked
Than th' hottest-headed of the wicked.

Samuel Butler: *Miscellaneous Thoughts,* I

The saints will aid if men will call:
For the blue sky bends over all.

Samuel Taylor Coleridge: *Christabel*,
Conclusion to Part I

Some reputed saints that have been canonized ought to have been cannonaded.

Charles Caleb Colton: *Lacon*

Poet and Saint! to thee alone are given
The two most sacred names of earth and heaven.

Abraham Cowley: *On the Death of
Mr Crashaw*

And Satan trembles when he sees
The weakest saint upon his knees.

William Cowper and John Newton:
Olney Hymns

Be it resolved: The earth is the Lord's and the fullness thereof. Be it resolved: That the fullness thereof belongs to the saints. Be it resolved: That we are the saints!

Document found in old New England
Church

Every saint, as every man, comes one day to be superfluous.

Ralph Waldo Emerson: *Journals*

A saint is a sceptic once in every twenty-four hours.

Ibid.

The greater the saint, the sweeter the incense.

French Proverb

To every saint his own candle.

Thomas Fuller: *Gnomologia*

Holy, Holy, Holy! all the saints adore Thee,
Casting down their golden crowns around
the glassy sea.

Reginald Heber: *Hymn*

The saints are God's jewels, highly esteemed
by and dear to him; they are a royal diadem
in his hand.

Matthew Henry

Those Saints, which God loves best,
The Devil tempts not least.

Robert Herrick: *Temptation*

The tears of Saints more sweet by far
Than all the songs of sinners are.

Robert Herrick: *Tears*

A saint is one who makes goodness attractive.

Laurence Housman

The way of this world is to praise dead saints
and persecute living ones.

Nathaniel Howe: *Sermon*

It is possible in these days of Christian
civilization to live a moral life without
Christ, but we ought to be too proud to draw
thus upon the bank of the saints.

Sheila Kaye-Smith

A lure more strong, a wish more faint,
Makes one a monster, one a saint.

Walter Learned: *On the Flyleaf of
"Manon Lescaut"*

Saints in stone have done more in the world
than living ones.

Georg Christoph Lichtenberg: *Reflections*

A man can be as truly a saint in a factory as
in a monastery, and there is as much need
of him in the one as in the other.

Robert J. McCracken

The Lord . . . forsaketh not his saints.

Old Testament: *Psalms 37: 28*

Precious in the sight of the Lord is the death
of his saints.

Old Testament: *Psalms 116: 15*

To make a man a saint, it must indeed be
by grace; and whoever doubts this does not
know what a saint is, or a man.

Blaise Pascal: *Pensées, XXIV*

All are not saints that go to church.

Poor Robin's Almanac

The worst of madmen is a saint run mad.

Alexander Pope: *The First Epistle of the
First Book of Horace,* l. 26

A sad saint is a poor saint.

H. D. Ranns

Saints are persons who make it easier for
others to believe in God.

Nathan Söderblom

A saint is a sinner who keeps on trying.

The Upper Room

Some rivers, historians tell us, pass through
others without mingling with them; just so
should a saint pass through this world.

Ralph Venning

A true saint is a divine landscape or picture,
where all the rare beauties of Christ are lively
portrayed and drawn forth. He hath the same
spirit, the same judgment, the same will with
Christ.

Thomas Watson

A saint is a man of convictions, who has been
dead a hundred years, canonized now, but
cannonaded while living.

Herman Lincoln Wayland

The only difference between the saint and
the sinner is that every saint has a past and
every sinner a future.

Oscar Wilde: *A Woman of No Importance,*
Act III

SALVATION

Salvation is free for you because someone else paid.

Anonymous

If a man born among infidels and barbarians does what lies in his power God will reveal to him what is necessary for salvation, either by inward inspiration or by sending him a preacher of the faith.

St. Thomas Aquinas: *Summa theologica,* II

Three things are necessary for the salvation of man: to know what he ought to believe; to know what he ought to desire; and to know what he ought to do.

St. Thomas Aquinas: *Two Precepts of Charity*

Outside of the Catholic church everything may be had except salvation.

St. Augustine: *Works,* Vol. IX, p. 122

Despair of ever being saved, "except thou be born again," or of seeing God "without holiness," or of having part in Christ except thou "love Him above father, mother, or thy own life." This kind of despair is one of the first steps to Heaven.

Richard Baxter: *The Saint's Everlasting Rest,* VI

You are not saved by Christ if your blood does not boil at the gross injustice and injury to mankind of the slums, or of unemployment, or of war, or of maldistribution of the means of life.

Albert David Belden

The fearless man is his own salvation.

Robert Bridges: *The First Seven Divisions*

Salvation's free, we tell! we tell!
Shouted the Methodist bell.

George W. Bungay: *The Creeds of the Bells,* st. 6

With crosses, relics, crucifixes,
Beads, pictures, rosaries, and pixes,—

The tools of working our salvation
By mere mechanic operation.

Samuel Butler: *Hudibras,* Pt. III, Canto I, l. 1495

For *my* salvation must its doom receive,
Not from what *others,* but what *I* believe.

John Dryden: *Religio Laici,* l. 303

Souls are not saved in bundles.

Ralph Waldo Emerson: *Conduct of Life: Worship*

The knowledge of sin is the beginning of salvation.

Epicurus: *Fragments,* frag. 522

"But what can mortal man do to secure his own salvation?" Mortal man can do just what God bids him do. He can repent and believe. He can arise and follow Christ as Matthew did.

Washington Gladden

Belief unto salvation is first of all a terrible sincerity, probing into every pus pocket of individual and social inconsistency.

Samuel Harkness

All that is necessary to salvation is contained in two virtues: faith in Christ, and obedience to laws.

Thomas Hobbes: *Leviathan,* XLIII

The quickest way to the goal of the world's unity is the longest way round; it is the conversion of men's hearts to the loving will of God.

Douglas Horton

A publishing concern ran the following advertisement: "You can save $2.00 on The Life of the Lord Jesus Christ." Which leads one to question what we mean when we use the words "save" and "salvation."

E. Paul Hovey

No man has the right to abandon the care of his salvation to another.

Thomas Jefferson: *Notes on Religion*

Salvation comes from God alone.
Latin Phrase

We are saved by someone doing for us what we cannot do for ourselves.
Donald Lester

We do not know the man wise enough to have saved the world from its present sufferings; and we do not know the man wise enough to deliver it now.
Madras Conference

The way to be saved is not to delay, but to come and take.
Dwight L. Moody

The love of God is no mere sentimental feeling; it is redemptive power.
Charles Clayton Morrison

In no single act or passion can salvation stand; far hence, beyond Orion and Andromeda, the cosmic process works and shall work forever through unbegotten souls.
Frederic William Henry Myers: *Human Personality*, ch. 10

Salvation is of the Jews.
New Testament: John 4: 22

I am the door: by me if any man enter in, he shall be saved.
New Testament: John 10: 9

What must I do to be saved?
New Testament: Acts 16: 30

Behold, now is the accepted time; behold, now is the day of salvation.
New Testament: II Corinthians 6: 2

Work out your own salvation.
New Testament: Philippians 2: 12

And for a helmet, the hope of salvation.
New Testament: I Thessalonians 5: 8

The Lord is my strength and song, and he is become my salvation.
Old Testament: Exodus 15: 2

The Lord is my light and my salvation; whom shall I fear? the Lord is the strength of my life; of whom shall I be afraid?
Old Testament: Psalms 27: 1

He only is my rock and my salvation: he is my defence; I shall not be moved.
Old Testament: Psalms 62: 6

Salvation is not something that is done for you but something that happens within you. It is not the clearing of a court record, but the transformation of a life attitude.
Albert W. Palmer

There is hope of salvation where shame reproaches a man.
Publilius Syrus: *Sententiae*, no. 633

Outside the church there is no salvation.
Roman Catholic Church, Maxim

The will to be saved means a great deal.
Seneca: *Epistolae ad Lucilium*, Epis. III, sec. 3

Therefore, Jew,
Though justice by thy plea, consider this,
That in the course of justice none of us
Should see salvation.
William Shakespeare: *The Merchant of Venice*, Act IV, sc. 1, l. 197

No one can be redeemed by another. No God and no saint is able to shield a man from the consequences of his evil doings. Every one of us must become his own redeemer.
Subhadra Bhikshu: *A Buddhist Catechism*

A man may be damned for despairing to be saved.
Jeremy Taylor: *Holy Living*, p. 259

'Twas to save thee, child, from dying,
Save my dear from burning flame,
Bitter groans and endless crying,
That thy blest Redeemer came.
Isaac Watts: *Divine Songs for Children*

395

SELF

Beware of no man more than thyself.

Anonymous

If my religion's not all
That it ought to be,
The trouble's not with God,
The trouble's with me.

Anonymous

God lends a helping hand to the man who tries hard.

Aeschylus: *The Persians*

Would'st thou have thy flesh obey thy spirit? Then let thy spirit obey thy God. Thou must be governed, that thou may'st govern.

St. Augustine

The reverence of a man's self is, next to religion, the chiefest bridle of all vices.

Sir Francis Bacon: *New Atlantis*

No man can quench his thirst with sand, or with water from the Dead Sea; so no man can find rest from his own character, however good, or from his own acts, however religious.

Horatius Bonar

Deliver me, O Lord, from that evil man, myself.

Thomas Benton Brooks

In the play *Green Pastures,* Noah says to the Lord, "I ain't very much, but I'se all I got."

Marc Connelly: *Green Pastures*, De Lisle, Ltd.

So long as we are full of self we are shocked at the faults of others. Let us think often of our own sin, and we shall be lenient to the sins of others.

François de Salignac de La Mothe Fénelon

Let us pray God that he would root out of our hearts everything of our own planting and set out there, with his own hand, the tree of life bearing all manner of fruits.

Ibid.

God helps those that help themselves.

Benjamin Franklin

Help thyself, and God will help thee.

George Herbert

He who reigns himself and rules his passions, desires and fears is more than a king.

John Milton

I have had more trouble with myself than with any other man.

Dwight L. Moody

We are very apt to be full of ourselves, instead of Him, that made what we so much value, and but for whom we have no reason to value ourselves. For we have nothing that we can call our own, no, not ourselves; for we are all but tenants, and at will too, of the great Lord of ourselves, and of this great farm, the world we live upon.

William Penn

It's fun to believe in yourself, but don't be too easily convinced.

T. Harry Thompson: *Sales Management*

Great God, I ask thee for no meaner pelf
Than that I may not disappoint myself.

Henry David Thoreau: *My Prayer*

Let not soft slumber close your eyes,
Before you've collected thrice
The train of action through the day!
Where have my feet chose out their way?
What have I learnt, where'er I've been,
From all I've heard, from all I've seen?
What have I more that's worth the knowing?
What have I done that's worth the doing?
What have I sought that I should shun?
What duty have I left undone,
Or into what new follies run?
These self-inquiries are the road
That leads to virtue and to God.

Isaac Watts: *Self Examination*

SELF-CONTROL

Those who wish to transform the world must be able to transform themselves.

Konrad Heiden

But I will write of him who fights
  And vanquishes his sins,
Who struggles on through weary years
  Against himself and wins.

Caroline Bigelow Le Row: *True Heroism*

If you would learn self-mastery, begin by
yielding yourself to the One Great Master.

Johann Friedrich Lobstein

Let not any one say that he cannot govern
his passions, nor hinder them from breaking
out and carrying him to action; for what he
can do before a prince or a great man, he
can do alone, or in the presence of God if he
will.

John Locke

He that is slow to anger is better than the
mighty; and he that ruleth his spirit than he
that taketh a city.

Old Testament: Proverbs 16: 32

Self-control is promoted by humility. Pride
is a fruitful source of uneasiness.

Lydia Huntley Sigourney

More dear in the sight of God and His angels
than any other conquest is the conquest of
self.

Arthur P. Stanley

Self-reverence, self-knowledge, self-control,
These three alone lead life to sovereign
  power.

Alfred, Lord Tennyson

SELF-DENIAL

Inwardness, mildness, and self-renounce-
ment do make for man's happiness.

Matthew Arnold: *Literature and Dogma,*
ch. 3

It is more necessary to be self-denying to be
a Christian, than it is to be an artist, or an
honest man, or a man at all in distinction
from a brute.

Henry Ward Beecher

Self-denial is a kind of holy association with
God; and by making him your partner
interests him in all your happiness.

Robert Boyle

As a man goes down in self, he goes up in
God.

George B. Cheever

Heroism, magnanimity, and self-denial, in
all instances in which they do not spring
from a principle of religion, are but splendid
altars on which we sacrifice one kind of self-
love to another.

Charles Caleb Colton

Self-sacrifice is the real miracle out of which
all the reported miracles grew.

Ralph Waldo Emerson: *Society and*
Solitude: Courage

Whoever will labor to get rid of self, to
deny himself according to the instructions
of Christ, strikes at once at the root of every
evil, and finds the germ of every good.

François de Salignac de La Mothe
Fénelon

The very act of faith by which we receive
Christ is an act of utter renunciation of self
and all its works, as a ground of salvation.

Mark Hopkins

The more a man denies himself, so much the
more will he receive from the gods.

Horace: *Odes*, Bk. III, ode 16, l. 21

One single act performed with true self-
denial, in renunciation of the world, is
infinitely more of a revival and more of
Christianity than 1,000 or 10,000 or 100,000
or 1,000,000 persons, so long as they keep it
ambiguous.

Sören Kierkegaard

All along the Christian course, there must
be set up altars to God on which you sacrifice
yourself, or you will never advance a step.

Alexander MacLaren

They that deny themselves for Christ, shall
enjoy themselves in Christ.

John Mason

397

SELF-DENIAL

One secret act of self-denial, one sacrifice of inclination to duty, is worth all the mere good thoughts, warm feelings, passionate prayers in which idle people indulge themselves.

Cardinal John Henry Newman

If any man will come after me, let him deny himself, and take up his cross, and follow me.

New Testament: Matthew 16: 24

Greater love hath no man than this, that a man lay down his life for his friends.

New Testament: John 15: 13

Present your bodies a living sacrifice, holy, acceptable unto God.

New Testament: Romans 12: 1

Self-denial is indispensable to a strong character, and the loftiest kind thereof comes only of a religious stock—from consciousness of obligation and dependence on God.

Theodore Parker

Sacrifice alone, bare and unrelieved, is ghastly, unnatural, and dead; but self-sacrifice, illuminated by love, is warmth, and life; it is the death of Christ, the life of God, and the blessedness and only proper life of man.

Frederick William Robertson

'Tis much the doctrine of the times, that men should not please themselves, but deny themselves everything they take delight in; not look upon beauty, wear no good clothes, eat no good meat, etc. which seems the greatest accusation that can be upon the maker of all good things. If they be not to be used, why did God make them?

John Selden

Self-denial is the result of a calm, deliberate, invincible attachment to the highest good, flowing forth in the voluntary renunciation of everything inconsistent with the glory of God or the good of our fellow-men.

Gardiner Spring

SELFISHNESS

You cannot be your brother's keeper if you are caged by selfishness.

Anonymous

"ME" is always at the bottom of all sin. One little word M-E. It may spell drink, lust, pride, covetousness, self-will; but it is some form of "me."

Anonymous

One can be a miser or a savage and be selfish, but not a Christian.

Anonymous

Self-preservation is the first law of nature, but self-sacrifice is the highest rule of grace.

Anonymous

A man is quickly convinced of the truth of religion who finds it not against his interest that it should be true.

Joseph Addison: *The Spectator*

Self-interest is but the survival of the animal in us. Humanity only begins for a man with self-surrender.

Henri Frédéric Amiel

The world has been controlled by two parties: those who have governed by "love of self to the point of contempt of God" and those who have governed by "love of God to the point of contempt of self."

St. Augustine: *The City of God*

I think we have one foot in heaven and the other on the banana peel of self-interest.

Lawrence W. Bash: Minneapolis *Tribune*

It is part of our human nature but there is that within us which always wants to make self the center of its own universe and, in that selfish way, wants to tear God from His throne and deny his brother and advance his own ambition.

Robert R. Brown

The very heart and root of sin is an independent spirit.—We erect the idol self, and not only wish others to worship, but worship it ourselves.

Richard Cecil

If you wish to travel far and fast, travel light. Take off all your envies, jealousies, unforgiveness, selfishness and fears.

Glenn Clark

Milton has carefully marked in his Satan, the intense selfishness which would rather reign in hell than serve in heaven.

Samuel Taylor Coleridge

We men are all thieves who have stolen the self which was meant as a part of God and tried to keep it for ourselves alone.

Joy Davidman: *Joy on the Mountain*, c/r 1953-4, Joy Davidman, The Westminster Press

Every personal consideration that we allow, costs us heavenly state. We sell the thrones of angels for a short and turbulent pleasure.

Ralph Waldo Emerson

Selfishness is the root and source of all natural and moral evils.

Nathanael Emmons

Every man for himself, and the Devil take the hindmost.

English Proverb

Most men are so possessed by themselves that they have no vacuum into which God's deep water may rise.

Thomas Erskine

That household god, a man's own self.

John Flavel

Selfishness is the greatest curse of the human race.

William Ewart Gladstone

Every man for himself and God for us all.

John Heywood: *Proverbs*, Pt. II, ch. 9

Selfishness, Love's cousin.

John Keats: *Isabella*, st. 31

Usually he is most empty who is most full of himself.

A. G. Lawson

No one is happy or free who lives only for himself. Joy in living comes from immersion in something one recognizes to be bigger, better, worthier, more enduring than he himself is. True happiness and true freedom come from squandering one's self for a purpose.

Carl W. McGeehon: "How Free Are We?"
Link

Our error is in making ourselves our own centre and thinking more of our claims on others than of our obligations to them. Christ teaches us that these are one.

Alexander MacLaren

That which of all things unfits man for the reception of Christ as a Saviour, is not gross profligacy and outward, vehement transgression, but it is self-complacency, fatal self-righteousness and self-sufficiency.

Alexander MacLaren

Every man brings an egg and every one wants an omelette—but without breaking his own egg. That poses a most difficult situation.

Frank Mar

The world remains selfish enough, but it will not accept a selfish religion.

Sir William Robertson Nicoll

We are too much haunted by ourselves, projecting the central shadow of self on everything around us.—And then comes the Gospel to rescue us from this selfishness.—Redemption is this, to forget self in God.

Frederick William Robertson

To set up self is to deny Christ; to exalt Christ is to reject self.

Henry Sandham

SELF-KNOWLEDGE

The wretch concentred all in self,
Living, shall forfeit fair renown,
And, doubly dying, shall go down
To the vile dust from whence he sprung,
Unwept, unhonor'd and unsung.

Sir Walter Scott: *The Lay of the Last*
Minstrel, VI

Twin-sister of Religion, Selfishness!

Percy Bysshe Shelley: *Queen Mab*, Pt. V,
l. 22

Selfishness is the great unknown sin. No selfish person ever thought himself selfish.

Southern Churchman

Mere tax-paying is not a substitute for the springs of human brotherhood. Collective self-indulgence cannot take the place of self-sacrifice.

Robert E. Speer

He who lives only to benefit himself confers on the world a benefit when he dies.

Tertullian

Everybody thinks of changing humanity and nobody thinks of changing himself.

Leo Tolstoy

The selfishness of man goes contrary to the spirit of nature and brings about all the evils for which men blame others rather than themselves.

Arnold J. Toynbee

The most difficult thing the good Lord has to deal with in the man of today is his sense of self-sufficiency. He is too prone to think he can get along pretty well without God.

Western Christian Advocate

SELF-KNOWLEDGE

The first step to improvement, whether mental, moral, or religious, is to know ourselves—our weaknesses, errors, deficiencies, and sins, that, by divine grace, we may overcome and turn from them all.

Tryon Edwards

SELF-RIGHTEOUSNESS

Do not shelter the mirror which reflects your soul's lack of beauty; rather welcome the truth, and believe that next to the knowledge of God nothing is so precious as the knowledge of self.

Jean Nicolas Grou: *Alliance Weekly*

Only by knowledge of that which is not thyself, shall thyself be learned.

Owen Meredith: *Know Thyself*

The kingdom of heaven is within you: and whosoever knoweth himself shall find it.

New Sayings of Jesus (Greek Papyrus
discovered in 1903)

Know then thyself, presume not God to scan;
The proper of study of mankind is Man.

Alexander Pope: *Essay on Man*
Epis. II, l. 1

To know one's self is the true; to strive with one's self is the good; to conquer one's self is the beautiful.

Joseph Roux: *Meditations of a Parish*
Priest, Pt. X, no. 60

Know thyself.

Thales

An humble knowledge of thyself is a surer way to God than a deep search after learning.

Thomas à Kempis

SELF-RIGHTEOUSNESS

Self-righteousness is the devil's masterpiece to make us think well of ourselves.

Thomas Adams

Regret not that which is past; and trust not to thine own righteousness.

St. Anthony

God hates those who praise themselves.

St. Clement: *First Epistle to the Corinthians*

They are most deceived that trust the most in themselves.

Queen Elizabeth I

There are few people who are more often in the wrong than those who cannot endure to be thought so.

François de La Rochefoucauld

While a man rests on his own merits for acceptance with God, it is of little consequence whether he be a pagan idolator, or a proud, ignorant Pharisee.—I know not which of the two is most distant from the kingdom of God.

James Milner

You can always tell when a man is a great way from God—when he is always talking about himself, how good he is.

Dwight L. Moody

O God, help me to hold a high opinion of myself.

Old Edinburgh Weaver

SERMONS, SERMON ON THE MOUNT

Of 318 persons asked, "Of all the speeches ever made, which two would you like to have heard in person?" 88 per cent listed either the Sermon on the Mount or Lincoln's Gettysburg Address.

Anonymous

The ten commandments and the sermon on the mount contain my religion.

John Adams: *To Jefferson*

It takes only fifteen minutes to read the greatest sermon ever preached—and when you have finished it, you will have read a complete summary of all that Jesus taught.

Charles L. Allen

"Great Sermons" ninety-nine times in a hundred are nuisances. They are like steeples without any bells in them; things stuck up high in the air, serving for ornament, attracting observation, but sheltering nobody, warming nobody, helping nobody.

Henry Ward Beecher

A sermon is not like a Chinese firecracker to be fired off for the noise which it makes. It is the hunter's gun, and at every discharge he should look to see his game fall.

Henry Ward Beecher

The sermon has dimensions—height, depth, and breadth. The people who do the listening are sometimes painfully aware of a fourth dimension—length.

Charles R. Brown

That is not the best sermon which makes the hearers go away talking to one another, and praising the speaker, but which makes them go away thoughtful and serious, and hastening to be alone.

Gilbert Burnet

Nature teaches more than she preaches. There are no sermons in stones. It is easier to get a spark out of a stone than a moral.

John Burroughs: *Time and Change: The Gospel of Nature*

Every attempt in a sermon to cause emotion, except as the consequence of an impression made on the reason, or the understanding, or the will, I will hold to be fanatical and sectarian.

Samuel Taylor Coleridge: *Table-Talk*

The sermon will be better if you listen as a Christian rather than as a critic.

Construction Digest

401

Let your sermon grow out of your text, and aim only to develop and impress its thought. —Of a discourse that did not do this it was once wittily said, "If the text had the small-pox, the sermon would never catch it."

Tryon Edwards

Great sermons lead the people to praise the preacher. Good preaching leads the people to praise the Saviour.

Charles G. Finney: *Autobiography*, p. 72

If you were to take the sum total of all the authoritative articles ever written by the most qualified of psychologists and psychiatrists on the subject of mental hygiene—if you were to combine them, and refine them, and cleave out the excess verbiage—if you were to take the whole of the meat and none of the parsley, and if you were to have these unadulterated bits of pure scientific knowledge concisely expressed by the most capable of living poets. you would have an awkward and incomplete summation of the Sermon on the Mount.

From *A Few Buttons Missing* by James T. Fisher and Lowell S. Hawley. Copyright 1951 by J. B. Lippincott Company, published by J. B. Lippincott Company

The belly hates a long sermon.

Thomas Fuller: *Gnomologia*

A good example is the best sermon.

Thomas Fuller: *Gnomologia* (also Benjamin Franklin: *Poor Richard*)

A good sermon helps people in a couple of ways. Some rise from it greatly strengthened. Others wake from it refreshed.

Grit

I'd rather see a sermon than hear one any day;
I'd rather one should walk with me than merely tell the way.

Edgar A. Guest: *Sermons We See*

Calling all sermons contrabands,
In that great Temple that's not made with hands.

Thomas Hood: *Ode to Rae Wilson, I*

The priests have so disfigured the simple religion of Jesus that no one who reads the sophistications they have engrafted on it, with the jargon of Plato, or Aristotle, and other mystics, would conceive these could have been fathered on the sublime preacher of the Sermon on the Mount.

Thomas Jefferson

The average man's idea of a good sermon is one that goes over his head—and hits one of his neighbors.

Journeyman Barber

The sermon, it seems to me, has a double function—to instruct the mind and to stir the emotions; but the modern sermon is a mere tickling of the ears.

Sheila Kaye-Smith

A friend told us of his grandfather's formula for a successful sermon: "Begin low, go slow, rise higher, take fire, and sit down in the storm."

KVP Philosopher

The bells themselves are the best of preachers,
Their brazen lips are learned teachers,
From their pulpits of stone, in the upper air,
Sounding aloft, without crack or flaw,
Shriller than trumpets under the Law.
Now a sermon and now a prayer.

Henry Wadsworth Longfellow: *Christus. The Golden Legend*, Pt. III

Some plague the people with too long sermons; for the faculty of listening is a tender thing, and soon becomes weary and satiated.

Martin Luther

He that has but one word of God before him, and out of that word cannot make a sermon, can never be a preacher.

Martin Luther: *Table Talk*

The sermon is one thing, the preacher nother.

Michel Eyquem de Montaigne: *Essays*,
Bk. II, ch. 10

The American people are so tense that it is impossible even to put them to sleep with a ermon.

Norman Vincent Peale

A good, honest, and painful sermon.

Samuel Pepys: *Diary*

His sermon never said or showed
    That Earth is foul, that Heaven is gracious,
Without refreshment on the road
    From Jerome, or from Athanasius;
And sure a righeous zeal inspired,
    The hand and head that penned and
        planned them,
For all who understood, admired—
    And some who did not understand them.

Winthrop Mackworth Praed: *The Vicar*

The sight of a drunkard is a better sermon against that vice than the best that was ever preached on that subject.

Sir George Savile, Lord Halifax

A sermon without St. Augustine is a stew without bacon.

Spanish Proverb

Few sinners are saved after the first twenty minutes of a sermon.

Mark Twain

The silent colossal National Lie that is the support and confederate of all the tyrannies and shams and inequalities and unfairness that afflict the peoples—that is the one to throw bricks and sermons at.

Mark Twain: *My First Lie*, Harper &
Row, Publishers, Inc.

A man must have very little to do at church that can give an account of the sermon.

Sir John Vanbrugh: *The Relapse*, Act I

The Sermon edifies, the example destroys.
Practice what you preach.

Abbé de Villiers: From a story in *L'Arte
de Prêcher*

I find more profit in sermons on either good tempers or good works than in what are vulgarly called gospel sermons. The term has now become a mere cant word: I wish none of our society would use it. It has no determinate meaning. Let but a pert, self-sufficient animal, that has neither sense nor grace, bawl out something about Christ, or his blood, or justification by faith, and his hearers cry out, "What a fine gospel sermon!"

John Wesley

Once in seven years I burn all my sermons; for it is a shame if I cannot write better sermons now than I did seven years ago.

John Wesley: *Journal*

It is a poor sermon that gives no offense; that neither makes the hearer displeased with himself nor with the preacher.

George Whitefield

If a man can write a better book, preach a better sermon, or make a better mouse-trap than his neighbor, though he builds his house in the woods the world will make a beaten path to his door.

Attributed to Emerson by Sarah S. B. Yule
and Mary S. Keene: *Borrowing*

SERVANTS, SERVICE

Life is like a game of tennis; the player who serves well seldom loses.

Anonymous

No service in itself is small,
    None great though earth it fill;
But that is small that seeks it sown,
    And great that seeks God's will.

Anonymous

Service is the rent we pay for the space we occupy.

Anonymous

Go, labour on; spend and be spent—
Thy joy to do the Father's will;
It is the way the Master went;
Should not the servant tread it still?

Horatius Bonar

All service ranks the same with God:
With God, whose puppets, best and worst,
Are we, there is no last nor first.

Robert Browning: *Pippa Passes,* Pt. IV

There never was a bad man that had ability
for good service.

Edmund Burke: *Speech in Opening the
Impeachment of Warren Hastings*

The most acceptable service of God is doing
good to man.

Benjamin Franklin: *Autobiography,* ch. 1

The highest of distinctions is the service of
others.

King George VI in his Coronation broadcast of May 12, 1937

None are so well served as by religious
servants.

George Herbert: *A Priest to the Temple,* I

God likes help when helping people.

Irish Proverb

It is a great gift of God to have a good
servant.

Hugh Latimer: *Sermons on the Lord's
Prayer,* VI

A Christian man is the most free lord of all,
and subject to none; a Christian man is the
most dutiful servant of all, and subject to
everyone.

Martin Luther

The church is a workshop, not a dormitory;
and every Christian man and woman is
bound to help in the common cause.

Alexander MacLaren

The world cannot always understand one's
profession of faith, but it can understand
service.

Ian Maclaren

Ye cannot serve God and mammon.

New Testament: Matthew 6: 24

He that is greatest among you shall be your
servant.

New Testament: Matthew 23: 11

Well done, thou good and faithful servant,
thou hast been faithful over a few things, I
will make thee ruler over many things.

New Testament: Matthew 25: 21

Lord, now lettest thou thy servant depart in
peace.

New Testament: Luke 2: 29

We are unprofitable servants: we have done
that which was our duty to do.

New Testament: Luke 17: 10

They serve God well, Who serve his creatures.

Caroline Norton: *The Lady of La Garaye.
Conclusion,* l. 9

Speak Lord; for thy servant heareth.

Old Testament: I Samuel 3: 9

Serve the Lord with fear, and rejoice with
trembling.

Old Testament: Psalms 2: 11

Accuse not a servant unto his master.

Old Testament: Proverbs 30: 10

What we have done for ourselves alone dies
with us. What we have done for others and
the world remains and is immortal.

Albert Pine

God's servants making a snug living
By guiding Mammon in smug giving.

Keith Preston: *Professional Welfare
Workers*

It is not the possession of extraordinary gifts that makes extraordinary usefulness, but the dedication of what we have to the service of God.

Frederick William Robertson

Had I but serv'd my God with half the zeal
I serv'd my king, he would not in mine age
Have left me naked to mine enemies.
William Shakespeare: *Henry VIII,*
Act III, sc. 2, l. 456

O servant of God's holiest charge,
The minister of praise at large.
Christopher Smart: *A Song to David,* st. 3

Doctrine divides but service unites.
Nathan Söderblom

If but the least and frailest, let me be
Evermore numbered with the truly free
Who find Thy service perfect liberty!
John Greenleaf Whittier: *What of the
Day?* l. 13

SIN

Sin is man's declaration of independence of God.
Anonymous

He sins as much who holds the bag as he who puts into it.
Anonymous

Sin. Rub out the first and last letters, and you have I—or carnal self—the root of sin.
Anonymous

Your sins are like your corns—you should get rid of them if they are continually being stepped on.
Akron *Baptist Journal*

There is no Bible authority for believing there is any such thing as a little sin.
Ibid.

Sin we have explain'd away;
Unluckily, the sinners stay.
William Allingham: *Blackberries*

The way of sinners is made plain with stones but at the end thereof is the pit of hell.
Apocrypha: Ecclesiasticus 21: 10

All sin is a kind of lying.
St. Augustine

Sin is energy in the wrong channel.
St. Augustine

To abstain from sin when a man cannot sin is to be forsaken by sin, not to forsake it.
St. Augustine: *Sermons: De Paenitentibus*

There is often a sin of omission as well as of commission.
Marcus Aurelius: *Meditations,* Bk. IX,
sec. 5

There is no death without sin.
Babylonian Talmud: Shabbath, fo. 55a

There is no sinner like a young saint.
Aphra Behn: *The Rover,* Pt. I, Act I, sc. 2

The sin is not in the sinning, but in the being found out.
Sir William Gurney Benham: *Proverbs,*
p. 851

Our sense of sin is in proportion to our nearness to God.
Thomas D. Bernard

It is much easier to repent of sins that we have committed than to repent of those we intend to commit.
Josh Billings

One leak will sink a ship; and one sin will destroy a sinner.
John Bunyan: *The Pilgrim's Progress,*
Pt. II

Respectable sin is, in principle, the mother of all basest crime.—Follow it to the bitter end, and there is ignominy as well as guilt eternal.
Horace Bushnell

The deadliest sins were the consciousness of no sin.

Thomas Carlyle

The greatest security against sin is to be shocked at its presence.

Thomas Carlyle

Sin is twisting and distorting out of its proper shape a human personality which God designed to be a thing of beauty and a joy forever.

Walter L. Carson: *Interpretation*

Who sins and mends commends himself to God.

Miguel de Cervantes: *Don Quixote*, Pt. II, ch. 28

Take away the motive, and the sin is taken away.

Miguel de Cervantes: *Don Quixote*, Pt. II, ch. 67

The worst effect of sin is within, and is manifest not in poverty, and pain, and bodily defacement, but in the discrowned faculties, the unworthy love, the low ideal, the brutalized and enslaved spirit.

Edwin Hubbell Chapin

For to sin, indeed is human: but to persevere in sin is not human but altogether satanic.

St. John Chrysostom: *Adhortatio at Theodorum Lapsum*

It is lawful for no one to sin.

Cicero: *Tusculanarum Disputationum*, Bk. V, ch. 19, sec. 55

He who sins against Heaven has nowhere left for prayer.

Confucius

Every sin is the result of a collaboration.

Stephen Crane

We claim a certain indulgence for that apparent necessity of nature which we call our besetting sin.

Henry Drummond: *Natural Law in the Spiritual World*

Sin makes its own hell, and goodness its own heaven.

Mary Baker Eddy: *Science and Health with Key to the Scriptures, p. 196: 18–19*

Sin brought death, and death will disappear with the disappearance of sin.

Mary Baker Eddy: *Science and Health with Key to the Scriptures, p. 426: 28–29*

Little sins make room for great, and one brings in all.

Thomas Edwards: *Gangrene of Heresy*

That which we call sin in others is experiment for us.

Ralph Waldo Emerson: *Essays: Second Series: Experience*

The gods visit the sins of the fathers upon the children.

Euripides: *Fragments*, no. 970

Every man carries the bundle of his sins
Upon his own back.

John Fletcher: *Rule a Wife and Have a Wife*, Act IV

No sins afflict society whose central residence is not in ourselves.

Harry Emerson Fosdick

Sin is not hurtful because it is forbidden, but it is forbidden because it is hurtful. Nor is a duty beneficial because it is commanded, but it is commanded because it is beneficial.

Benjamin Franklin: *Poor Richard*

Sin is to be overcome, not so much by direct opposition to it as by cultivating opposite principles. Would you kill the weeds in your garden, plant it with good seed; if the ground

be well occupied there will be less need of
the hoe.

Abraham Fuller

He that falls into sin is a man; that grieves
at it, is a saint; that boasteth of it, is a devil.

Thomas Fuller: *The Holy and the
Profane State: Of Self-Praising*

Sin writes histories, goodness is silent.

Johann Wolfgang von Goethe

If I were God, this world of sin and suffering
would break my heart.

Johann Wolfgang von Goethe

Sins are like circles in the water when a stone
is thrown into it; one produces another.—
When anger was in Cain's heart, murder was
not far off.

Philip Henry

God pardons those who do through frailty
sin,
But never those that persevere therein.

Robert Herrick: *Pardon*

What is human sin but the abuse of human
appetites, of human passions, of human
faculties, in themselves all innocent?

Roswell Dwight Hitchcock

Sin is strong and fleet of foot outrunning
everything.

Homer: *Iliad,* IX, 505

Sin has four characteristics: self-sufficiency
instead of faith, self-will instead of submission, self-seeking instead of benevolence,
self-righteousness instead of humility.

E. Paul Hovey

Naught that delights is sin.

Ben Jonson: *Explorata*

The mere wish to sin entails the penalty, for
he who meditates a crime within his breast
has all the guilt of the deed.

Juvenal: *Satires,* Sat. XIII, l. 208

He that plots secret crime his soul within
Is straightway guilty of the actual sin.

Juvenal

It would be better to eschew sin than to flee
death.

Thomas à Kempis: *Imitation of Christ,*
Bk. I, ch. 23, sec. 5

The sin ye do by two and two ye must pay
for one by one!

Rudyard Kipling: *Tomlinson,* l. 62. Permission of Mrs. George Bambridge

The recognition of sin is the beginning of
salvation.

Martin Luther

Sin is, essentially a departure from God.

Martin Luther

Be a sinner and sin mightily, but more
mightily believe and rejoice in Christ.

Martin Luther: *Letter to Melanchthon*

Every sin is a mistake, as well as a wrong;
and the epitaph for the sinner is, "Thou
fool!"

Alexander MacLaren

Palliation of a sin is the hunted creature's
refuge and final temptation. Our battle is
ever between spirit and flesh. Spirit must
brand the flesh, that it may live.

George Meredith: *Diana of the Crossways,*
ch. 1

Sin and her shadow Death, and Misery
Death's harbinger.

John Milton: *Paradise Lost,* Bk. IX, l. 10

How immense appear to us the sins that we
have not committed.

Madame Necker

In *Adam's* fall—
We sinned all.

New England Primer

God be merciful to me a sinner.

New Testament: Luke 18: 13

407

He that is without sin among you, let him first cast a stone.

New Testament: John 8: 7

The wages of sin is death.

New Testament: Romans 6: 23

All human sin seems so much worse in its consequences than in its intentions.

Reinhold Niebuhr: Leaves from the Notebook of a Tamed Cynic

Fixed as a habit or some darling sin.

John Oldham: A Letter from the Country

Be sure your sin will find you out.

Old Testament: Numbers 32: 23

Fools make a mock at sin.

Old Testament: Proverbs 14: 9

Though your sins be as scarlet, they shall be white as snow.

Old Testament: Isaiah 1: 18

Woe unto them that draw iniquity with cords of vanity, and sin as it were with a cart rope.

Old Testament: Isaiah 5: 18

Who's free to sin, sins less: the very power Robs evildoing of its choicest flower.

Ovid: Amores, III, 4, 9 (King tr.)

If Jupiter hurls his thunderbolts as often as men sinned, he would soon be out of thunderbolts.

Ovid: Tristia

My sin is the black spot which my bad act makes, seen against the disk of the Sun of Righteousness.

Charles Henry Parkhurst: Sermons: Pattern in the Mount

There are only two kinds of men: the righteous who believe themselves sinners; the rest, sinners, who believe themselves righteous.

Blaise Pascal

How shall I lose the sin yet keep the sense, And love th' offender, yet detest the offence?

Alexander Pope: Eloise to Abelard, l. 191

Our outward act is prompted from within, And from the sinner's mind proceeds the sin.

Matthew Prior: Henry and Emma, l. 481

A sin confessed is half forgiven.

John Ray: English Proverbs

I hate the sin, but I love the sinner.

Thomas Buchanan Read: What a Word May Do

It is as supreme folly to talk of a little sin as it would be to talk of a small decalogue that forbids it, or a diminutive God that hates it, or a shallow hell that will punish it.

Charles Seymour Robinson

I conclude also that "sin," except in the sense of conduct toward which the agent, or the community, feels an element of disapproval, is a mistaken concept, calculated to promote needless cruelty and vindictiveness when it is others that are thought to sin, and a morbid self-abasement when it is ourselves whom we condemn.

Bertrand Russell: Human Society in Ethics and Politics, Simon & Schuster, Inc., 1952

A sinful heart makes feeble hand.

Sir Walter Scott: Marmion, Canto VI, st. 31

Other men's sins are before our eyes; our own behind our backs.

Seneca: De Ira, Bk. II, sec. 28

We are all sinful. Therefore whatever we blame in another we shall find in our own bosoms.

Seneca: De Ira, Bk. III, sec. 26

More men abstain from forbidden actions because they are ashamed of sinning, than because their inclinations are good.

Seneca: Epistolae ad Lucilium, Epis. 83, 20

Sin can be well-guarded, but free from
anxiety it cannot be.
> Seneca: *Epistolae ad Lucilium,* Epis. 97, 13

He who does not forbid sin when he can,
encourages it.
> Seneca: *Troades,* l. 291

Some have sinned with safety, but none with
peace of soul.
> Seneca: *Hippolytus*

Sin is a state of mind, not an outward act.
> William Sewell: *Passing Thoughts on
> Religion: Wilful Sin*

Our compell'd sins
Stand more for number than for accompt.
> William Shakespeare: *Measure for
> Measure,* Act II, sc. 4, l. 58

I am a man
More sinn'd against than sinning.
> William Shakespeare: *King Lear,*
> Act III, sc. 2, l. 59

Forbear to judge, for we are sinners all.
> William Shakespeare: *Henry VI, Part II,*
> Act III, sc. 3, l. 31

Sin is a sovereign till sovereign grace de-
thrones it.
> Charles Haddon Spurgeon

Our sins, like our shadows when day is in
its glory, scarce appear; toward evening, how
great and monstrous they are!
> Sir John Suckling

Mankind is still in need of a Savior, for sin
is still sin though we call it by many new
psychological names.
> F. M. Swaffield

Sin may open bright as the morning, but it
will end dark as night.
> Thomas De Witt Talmage

Commit a sin twice and it will not seem to
thee a crime.
> *The Talmud*

No sin is small. No grain of sand is small in
the mechanism of a watch.
> Jeremy Taylor

Sin is too dull to see beyond himself.
> Alfred, Lord Tennyson: *Queen Mary,*
> Act V, sc. 2

My soul is like a mirror in which the glory
of God is reflected, but sin, however insigni-
ficant, covers the mirror with smoke.
> St. Theresa

Sin is first a simple suggestion, then a strong
imagination, then delight, then assent.
> Thomas à Kempis

We cannot well do without our sins; they
are the highway of our virtue.
> Henry David Thoreau: *Journal*

Sin may be clasped so close we cannot see its
face.
> Richard Chenevix Trench

Sins of the mind have less infamy than those
of the body, but not less malignity.
> Benjamin Whichcote

Sin, every day, takes out a new patent for
some new invention.
> Edwin Percy Whipple: *Essays: Romance
> of Rascality*

Sin and dandelions are a whole lot alike—
they're a lifetime fight that you never quite
win.
> William Allen White: quoted in *Better
> Homes and Gardens,* c/r Meredith
> Publishing Co.

But he who never sins can little boast
Compared to him who goes and sins no
more!
The "sinful Mary" walks more white in
heaven
Than some who never "sinn'd and were
forgiven!"
> Nathaniel Parker Willis: *The Lady Jane,*
> Canto II, st. 44

SINCERITY

The other fellow's sins, like the other fellow's car lights, always seem more glaring than our own.

Wisconsin Dells *Events*

SINCERITY

It it often said it is no matter what a man believes if he is only sincere. But let a man sincerely believe that seed planted without ploughing is good as with; that January is as favorable for seed-sowing as April; and that cockle seed will produce as good a harvest as wheat, and is it so?

Henry Ward Beecher

Loss of sincerity is loss of vital power.

Christian Nestell Bovee: *Summaries of Thought: Sincerity*

The only guide to a man is his conscience; the only shield to his memory is the rectitude and sincerity of his actions.

Sir Winston Churchill: *Tribute to Neville Chamberlain*, Houghton Mifflin Company

Sincerity and truth are the basis of every virtue.

Confucius

Sincerity is the face of the soul, as dissimulation is the mask.

S. Dubay

Every sincere man is right.

Ralph Waldo Emerson: *Essays: Natural History of Intellect*

Of all the evil spirits abroad at this hour in the world, insincerity is the most dangerous.

James Anthony Froude: *Short Studies on Great Subjects: Education*

No man can produce great things who is not thoroughly sincere in dealing with himself.

James Russell Lowell

SOLITUDE

Then grow as God hath planted, grow
A lordly oak or daisy low,
As He hath set His garden, be
Just what thou art, or grass or tree.

Joaquin Miller: *With Love to You and Yours*, Pt. II, sec. 8

This I pray . . . That ye may approve things that are excellent; that ye may be sincere and without offence till the day of Christ.

New Testament: Philippians 1: 9, 10

Fear the Lord, and serve him in sincerity and in truth.

Old Testament: Joshua 24: 14

We are not sent into this world to do anything into which we cannot put our hearts.

John Ruskin

SOLITUDE

At cool of day, with God I walk
My garden's grateful shade;
I hear His voice among the trees
And I am not afraid.

Anonymous

If chosen men had never been alone
In deepest silence open-doored to God,
No greatness ever had been dreamed or done

Anonymous

In every heart He wishes to be first:
He therefore keeps the secret key Himself
To open all its chambers, and to bless
With perfect sympathy, and holy peace,
Each solitary soul which comes to Him.

Anonymous

An old Danish peasant on his death bed asked of his son only one promise: that he should sit *alone* for a half-hour each day in the best room in the house. The son did this and became a model for the whole district

Anonymous

Converse with men makes sharp the glitter-
ing wit,
But God to man doth speak in solitude.
John Stuart Blackie: *Highland Solitude*

Indeed, though in a wilderness, a man is
never alone, not only because he is with himself and his own thoughts, but because he
is with the Devil, who ever consorts with our
solitude . . . There is no such thing as solitude, nor anything that can be said to be
alone and by itself, but God.
Sir Thomas Browne: *Religio Medici*,
Pt. II, sec. 2

If from society we learn to live, it is solitude
should teach us how to die.
George Gordon, Lord Byron

'Tis solitude should teach us how to die;
It hath no flatterers; vanity can give
No hollow aid; alone—man with his God
must strive.
George Gordon, Lord Byron: *Childe
Harold*, Canto IV, st. 33

Thrice happy he, who by some shady grove,
Far from the clamorous world, doth live
his own;
Though solitary, who is not alone,
But doth converse with that eternal love.
William Drummond: *Urania*

When you have closed your doors and darkened your room, remember never to say that
you are alone, for you are not alone; God is
within, and your genius is within—and what
need have they of light to see what you are
doing?
Epictetus: *Discourses*, Bk. I, ch. 14

Solitude is intolerable, even in Paradise.
Italian Proverb

Why should we faint and fear to live alone,
Since all alone, so Heaven has willed, we die,
Nor even the tenderest heart and next our
own

Knows half the reasons why we smile and
sigh.
John Keble: *Christian Year: Twenty-
Fourth Sunday after Trinity*

A solitude is the audience-chamber of God.
Walter Savage Landor: *Imaginary Con-
versations: Lord Brooke and Sir Philip
Sydney*

Two paradises 'twere in one,
To live in Paradise alone.
Andrew Marvell: *The Garden*

Now the New Year reviving old Desires,
The thoughtful Soul to Solitude retires.
Omar Khayyám: *Rubáiyát*, st. 4

Whosoever is delighted in solitude, is either
a wild beast or a god.
Plato: *Protag*, l. 337

There are some solitary wretches who seem
to have left the rest of mankind only as Eve
left Adam, to meet the devil in private.
Alexander Pope: *Thoughts on Various
Subjects*

One can acquire everything in solitude—
except character.
Stendhal: *Fragments*, I

The person who has not learned to be happy
and content while completely alone for an
hour a day, or a week has missed life's greatest serenity.
H. Clay Tate: *Building a Better Home
Town*, Harper & Row,
Publishers, Inc.

Consider what Saint Augustine said,—that
he sought God within himself. Settle yourself in solitude, and you will come upon Him
in yourself.
St. Theresa

Why should I feel lonely? is not our planet
in the Milky Way?
Henry David Thoreau: *Walden: Solitude*

411

SORROW

SORROW

Not until each loom is silent
And the shuttles cease to fly,
Will God unroll the pattern
And explain the reason why
The dark threads are as needful
In the Weaver's skilful hand
As the threads of gold and silver
For the pattern which He planned.

Anonymous

Blessed to us is the night, for it reveals the stars.

Anonymous

Nine times out of ten it is over the Bridge of Sighs that we pass the narrow gulf between youth to manhood.

Anonymous

My life is but the weaving
  Between my God and me.
I only choose the colors
  He weaveth steadily.
Sometimes He weaveth sorrow
  And I in foolish pride,
Forget He sees the upper
  And I the under side.

Anonymous

Night brings out stars as sorrow shows us truths.

Philip James Bailey: *Festus, Sc. Water and Wood, Midnight*

Suffering well borne is better than suffering removed.

Henry Ward Beecher

Sorrows are often like clouds, which though black when they are passing over us, when they are past become as if they were the garments of God thrown off in purple and gold along the sky.

Henry Ward Beecher

We are never ripe till we have been made so by suffering.

Henry Ward Beecher

Wherever souls are being tried and ripened, in whatever commonplace and homely way, there God is hewing out the pillars for His temple.

Phillips Brooks

There are nettles everywhere
But smooth green grasses are more common still;
The blue of heaven is larger than the cloud.

Elizabeth Barrett Browning

Grief should be the instructor of the wise; sorrow is knowledge; they who know the most must mourn the deepest o'er the fatal truth.

George Gordon, Lord Byron

Out of suffering have emerged the strongest souls; the most massive characters are seamed with scars; martyrs have put on their coronation robes glittering with fire, and through their tears have the sorrowful first seen the gates of heaven.

Edwin Hubbell Chapin

The soul would have no rainbow had the eye no tears.

John Vance Cheney

You cannot prevent the birds of sorrow from flying over your head, but you can prevent them from building nests in your hair.

Chinese Proverb

Sorrow is given us on purpose to cure us of sin.

St. John Chrysostom: *Homilies, V*

God send you joy, for sorrow will come fast enough.

John Clarke: *Paraemiologia Anglo-Latina*

The path of sorrow, and that path alone, leads to the land where sorrow is unknown; no traveller ever reached that blessed abode who found not thorns and briers in his road.

William Cowper

God sometimes washes the eyes of His children with tears, in order that they may read aright His providence and His commandments.

Theodore Ledyard Cuyler

Thou shalt sorrow enough in hell.

Gesta Romanorum

Sorrow is only one of the lower notes in the oratorio of our blessedness.

Adoniram J. Gordon

I walked a mile with Sorrow
And ne'er a word said she;
But, oh, the things I learned from her
When Sorrow walked with me.

Robert Browning Hamilton: *Along the Road*

Sorrow is a fruit: God does not make it grow on limbs too weak to bear it.

Victor Hugo

Sorrow is our John the Baptist, clad in grim garments, with rough arms, a son of the wilderness, baptizing us with bitter tears, preaching repentance; and behind him comes the gracious, affectionate, healing Lord, speaking peace and joy to the soul.

Frederic D. Huntington

Often the clouds of sorrow reveal the sunshine of His face.

Hilys Jasper

There is no wisdom in useless and hopeless sorrow, but there is something in it so like virtue that he who is wholly without it cannot be loved.

Samuel Johnson

Sorrow is a kind of rust of the soul, which every new idea contributes in its passage to scour away.

Samuel Johnson: *The Rambler*

Alas by some degree of woe
We every bliss must gain;

The heart can ne'er a transport know
That never feels a pain.

George, Baron Lyttelton

Afflictions are but the shadow of God's wings.

George Macdonald

Despise not thy school of sorrow, O my Soul; it will give thee a unique part in the universal song.

George Matheson

Sorrows humanize our race; tears are the showers that fertilize the world.

Owen Meredith

A grace within his soul hath reigned
Which nothing else can bring;
Thank God for all that I have gained
By that high sorrowing.

Richard Monckton Milnes: *Sorrow*

Earth has no sorrow that Heaven cannot heal.

Thomas Moore: *Come, Ye Disconsolate*

Then sorrow, touch'd by Thee, grows bright
With more than rapture's ray;
As darkness shows us worlds of light
We never saw by day.

Thomas Moore: *Oh, Thou Who Dry'st the Mourner's Tear*

There's nae sorrow there, John,
There's neither cauld nor care, John,
The day is aye fair,
In the land o' the leal.

Carolina Nairne: *The Land o' the Leal*

Blessed are they that mourn: for they shall be comforted.

New Testament: Matthew 5: 4

By sorrow of the heart the spirit is broken.

Old Testament: Proverbs 15: 13

Sorrow is better than laughter: for by the sadness of the countenance the heart is made better.

Old Testament: Ecclesiastes 7: 3

Sorrow and sighing shall flee away.

Old Testament: Isaiah 35: 10

A man of sorrows, and acquainted with grief.

Old Testament: Isaiah 53: 3

Is it nothing to you, all ye that pass by?
behold, and see if there be any sorrow like
unto my sorrow.

Old Testament: Lamentations 1: 12

Sorrows remembered sweeten present joy.

Robert Pollok: *Course of Time*, Bk. I,
l. 464

Do not cheat thy Heart and tell her,
  "Grief will pass away,
Hope for fairer times in future,
  And forget to-day."
Tell her, if you will, that sorrow
  Need not come in vain;
Tell her that the lesson taught her
  Far outweighs the pain.

Adelaide Ann Procter: *Friend Sorrow*

He that hath pity on another man's sorrows
shall be free from it himself; and he that
delighteth in and scorneth the misery of
another shall one time or other fall into it
himself.

Sir Walter Raleigh

Joys are our wings, sorrows our spurs.

Jean Paul Richter

Sorrows gather around great souls as storms
do around mountains; but like them, they
break the storm and purify the air of the
plain beneath them.

Jean Paul Richter

  This sorrow's heavenly,
It strikes where it doth love.

William Shakespeare: *Othello*,
Act V, sc. 2, l. 21

  Each time we love,
We turn a nearer and a broader mark
To that keen archer, Sorrow, and he strikes.

Alexander Smith: *City Poems: A Boy's
Dream*

All pains are nothing in respect of this
All sorrows short that gain eternal bliss.

Edmund Spenser: *Amoretti*, Sonnet LXIII

The Lord gets his best soldiers out of the
highlights of affliction.

Charles Haddon Spurgeon

Sorrow is divine. Sorrow is reigning on all
the thrones of the universe, and the crown
of all crowns has been one of thorns. There
have been many books that treat of the sympathy of sorrow, but only one that bids us
glory in tribulation, and count it all joy
when we fall into divers afflictions, that so
we may be associated with that great fellowship of suffering of which the incarnate Son
of God is the head, and through which He is
carrying a redemptive conflict to a glorious
victory over evil. If we suffer with Him, we
shall also reign with Him.

Harriet Beecher Stowe

Short is the glory that is given and taken by
men; and sorrow followeth ever the glory of
the world.

Thomas à Kempis: *Imitation of Christ*,
Pt. II, ch. 6

Sorrow is held the eldest child of sin.

John Webster: *Duchess of Malfi*, Act V,
Sc. 5

Where there is sorrow, there is holy ground.

Oscar Wilde: *De Profundus*

SOUL

An honest confession is good for the soul,
but bad for the reputation.

Anonymous

What sculpture is to a block of marble, education is to the soul.

Joseph Addison: *Spectator*, no. 215

Gratitude is the sign of noble souls.

Aesop: *Androcles*

Life's greatest tragedy is the man with a 10 by 12 intellect and a 2 by 4 soul.

L. R. Akers: *Eighth Fear and other Sermons*, Abingdon Press

The wealth of a soul is measured by how much it can feel; its poverty by how little.

William Rounseville Alger

Heaven-born, the soul a heavenward course must hold; beyond the world she soars; the wise man, I affirm, can find no rest in that which perishes, nor will he lend his heart to aught that doth on time depend.

Michelangelo

A man's soul is sometimes wont to bring him tidings, more than seven watchmen that sit on high on a watchtower.

Apocrypha: Ecclesiasticus 37: 14

The souls of the righteous are in the hand of God, and there shall be no torment touch them. In the sight of the unwise they seemed to die: and their departure is taken for misery, and their going from us to be utter destruction: but they are in peace.

Apocrypha: Wisdom of Solomon 3: 1–3

As sight is in the body, so is reason in the soul.

Aristotle: *Nicomachean Ethics*

And see all sights from pole to pole,
  And glance, and nod, and bustle by,
And never once possess our soul
  Before we die.

Matthew Arnold: *A Southern Night*, st. 18

Calm Soul of all things! make it mine
  To feel, amid the city's jar,
That there abides a peace of thine,
  Man did not make, and can not mar.

Matthew Arnold: *Lines Written in Kensington Gardens*, st. 10

Fate gave, what Chance shall not control,
His sad lucidity of soul.

Matthew Arnold: *Resignation*

Strong is the Soul, and wise, and beautiful:
The seeds of godlike power are in us still:
Gods are we, Bards, Saints, Heroes, if we will.

Matthew Arnold: *Sonnet 4* (Written in Emerson's Essays)

The soul, which is spirit, can not dwell in dust; it is carried along to dwell in the blood.

St. Augustine: *Decretum*, IX, 32, 2

The life whereby we are joined unto the body is called the soul.

St. Augustine: *Of the Faith and of the Creed*

A soul as white as Heaven.

Francis Beaumont and John Fletcher: *The Maid's Tragedy*, Act IV, sc. 1

My soul still flies above me for the quarry it shall find.

William Rose Benét: *The Falconer of God*

John Brown's body lies a mould-ring in the grave,
His soul goes marching on.

Thomas Brigham Bishop: *John Brown's Body*

The iron entered into his soul.

Book of Common Prayer: *The Psalter: Psalms 105: 18*

No coward soul is mine,
  No trembler in the world's storm-troubled sphere:
I see Heaven's glories shine,
  And faith shines equal, arming me from fear.

Emily Brontë: *Last Lines*, st. 1

I should not dare to call my soul my own.

Elizabeth Barrett Browning: *Aurora Leigh*, Bk. II, l. 786

'Tis an awkward thing to play with souls,
And matter enough to save one's own.

Robert Browning: *A Light Woman*

I trust in my own soul, that can perceive
The outward and the inward, Nature's good
And God's.
Robert Browning: *A Soul's Tragedy*, Act I

I go to prove my soul!
I see my way as birds their trackless way.
I shall arrive!
Robert Browning: *Paracelsus*, Pt. I

So, let him wait God's instant men call years;
Meantime hold hard by truth and his great soul,
Do out the duty! Through such souls alone
God stooping shows sufficient of his light
For us i' the dark to rise by.
Robert Browning: *The Ring and the Book*, VII, *Pompilia*

If this invisible germ of life in the grain of wheat can thus pass unimpaired through three thousand resurrections, I shall not doubt that my soul has power to clothe itself with a new body, suited to its new existence, when this earthly frame has crumbled into dust.
William Jennings Bryan: *The Prince of Peace*

It seems to me as if not only the form but the soul of man was made to walk erect and look upon the stars.
John Bulwer

The first string that the musician usually touches is the bass, when he intends to put all in tune. God also plays upon this string first, when he sets the soul in tune for himself.
John Bunyan: *Pilgrim's Progress*, Pt. II

Faith is the pencil of the soul that pictures heavenly things.
Thomas Burbridge

And he that makes his soul his surety,
I think, does give the best security.
Samuel Butler: *Hudibras*, Pt. III, Canto I, l. 203

For the sword outwears its sheath,
And the soul wears out the breast.
George Gordon, Lord Byron: *So We'll Go No More a Roving*

Soul is the Man.
Thomas Campion: *Are You What Your Fair Looks Express?*

Everywhere the human soul stands between a hemisphere of light and another of darkness; on the confines of two everlasting hostile empires, Necessity and Freewill.
Thomas Carlyle: *Essays: Goethe's Works*

Sensuality is the grave of the soul.
William Ellery Channing

Everything here, but the soul of man, is a passing shadow.—The only enduring substance is within.—When shall we awake to the sublime greatness, the perils, the accountableness, and the glorious destinies of the immortal soul?
William Ellery Channing

The countenance is the portrait of the soul, and the eyes mark its intentions.
Cicero: *De Oratore*, III, 59

From the looks—not the lips, is the soul reflected.
McDonald Clarke: *The Rejected Lover*

Faith is the ear of the soul.
Clement of Alexandria

The soul of man is larger than the sky,
Deeper than ocean, or abysmal dark
Of the unfathomed centre.
Hartley Coleridge: *Poems: To Shakespeare*

Either we have an immortal soul, or we have not. If we have not, we are beasts; the first and wisest of beasts it may be; but still beasts. We only differ in degree and not in kind; just as the elephant differs from the slug. But by the concession of the materialists, we are not of the same kind as beasts; and this also we say from our own consciousness. Therefore, methinks, it must be the possession of a soul within us that makes the difference.

Samuel Taylor Coleridge

I take it, no fool ever made a bargain for his soul with the devil: the fool is too much of a fool, or the devil too much of a devil—I don't know which.

Joseph Conrad, J. M. Dent & Sons, Ltd.

A soul,—a spark of the never-dying flame that separates man from all the other beings on earth.

James Fenimore Cooper: *Afloat and Ashore*, ch. 12

Thought is deeper than all speech,
  Feeling deeper than all thought;
Souls to souls can never teach
  What unto themselves was taught.

Christopher Pearse Cranch: *Thought (Gnosis)*, st. 1

The body, that is but dust; the soul, it is a bud of eternity.

Nathaniel Culverwel

The soul selects her own society,
Then shuts the door.

Emily Dickinson: *Part 1, Life*, XIII, st. 1

Hope is the thing with feathers
That perches in the soul,
And sings the tune without the words,
And never stops at all.

Emily Dickinson: *Part 1, Life*, XXXII, st. 1

The soul unto itself
Is an imperial friend,—
Or the most agonizing spy
An enemy could send.

Emily Dickinson: *Part 1, Life*, XLI, st. 1

The human soul is like a republic. The legislative power is the intellect, the judicial power is the conscience and the executive power is the will. Each of these in the soul of a child demands training.

E. M. Donnell

Our souls sit close and silently within,
And their own web from their own entrails
  spin;
And when eyes meet far off, our sense is such,
That, spider-like, we feel the tenderest
  touch.

John Dryden: *Marriage-à-la-Mode*, Act II, sc. 1

Jealousy, the jaundice of the soul.

John Dryden: *The Hind and the Panther*, Pt. III, l. 73

I have a soul that, like an ample shield,
Can take in all, and verge enough for more.

John Dryden: *Sebastian*, Act I, sc. 1

Immortality will come to such as are fit for it; and he who would be a great soul in the future must be a great soul now.

Ralph Waldo Emerson

The problem of restoring to the world original and eternal beauty is solved by the redemption of the soul.

Ralph Waldo Emerson

The Supreme Critic on the errors of the past and the present, and the only prophet of that which must be, is that great nature in which we rest as the earth lies in the soft arms of the atmosphere; that Unity, that Over-Soul, within which every man's particular being is contained and made one with all other.

Ralph Waldo Emerson: *Essays, First Series: The Over-Soul*

The one thing in the world, of value, is the active soul.

Ralph Waldo Emerson: *Nature, Addresses, and Lectures: The American Scholar*

The passive Master lent his hand
To the vast soul that o'er him planned.

Ralph Waldo Emerson: *Poems: The Problem*, st. 3

Though a sound body cannot restore an unsound mind, yet a good soul can, by its virtue, render the body the best possible.

Ralph Waldo Emerson: *Representative Men: Plato*

I believe that man will not merely endure; he will prevail. He is immortal, not because he alone among creatures has an inexhaustible voice, but because he has a soul, a spirit capable of compassion and sacrifice and endurance.

William Faulkner: Nobel Prize acceptance speech, Stockholm, December, 1950

In a real dark night of the soul it is always three o'clock in the morning.

From *The Crack-up* by F. Scott Fitzgerald, copyright 1945 by New Directions. Reprinted by permission of New Directions

Gravity is the ballast of the soul, which keeps the mind steady.

Thomas Fuller: *Holy and Profane States. Gravity*

I am fully convinced that the soul is indestructible, and that its activity will continue through eternity. It is like the sun, which, to our eyes, seems to set in night; but it has in reality only gone to diffuse its light elsewhere.

Johann Wolfgang von Goethe

Out of the night that covers me,
  Black as the pit from pole to pole,
I thank whatever gods may be
  For my unconquerable soul.
It matters not how strait the gate,
  How charged with punishment the scroll,
I am the master of my fate:
  I am the captain of my soul.

William Ernest Henley

Salute thyself; see what thy soul doth wear.

George Herbert: *The Church-Porch*

The sublimest song to be heard on earth is the lisping of the human soul on the lips of children.

Victor Hugo: *Ninety-Three*, Pt. III, Bk. III, ch. 1

Nothing is so like a soul as a bee. It goes from flower to flower as a soul from star to star, and it gathers honey as a soul gathers light.

Victor Hugo: *Ninety-Three*, Pt. III, Bk. III, ch. 3

The production of souls is the secret of unfathomable depth.

Victor Hugo: *Shakespeare*, Bk. V, ch. 1

Man does not *have* a soul; he *is* one.

Harold Bruce Hunting

No thought which I have ever had has satisfied my soul.

Richard Jefferies: *The Story of My Heart*, ch. 6

Awake, my Soul, and with the Sun,
Thy daily stage of Duty run;
Shake off dull Sloth, and early rise,
To pay thy Morning Sacrifice.

Thomas Ken: *Morning Hymn*

Why put a soul on trial and then rule out its own testimony?

Willis P. King: *Pulpit Preaching*

The soul is the mirror of an indestructible universe.

Gottfried Wilhelm von Leibnitz: *The Monadology*, LXXVII

The intellect of man sits visibly enthroned upon his forehead and in his eye, and the heart of man is written upon his countenance. But the soul reveals itself in the voice only, as God revealed Himself to the prophet of old in the still small voice, and in the voice from the burning bush.

Henry Wadsworth Longfellow

Ah, the souls of those that die
Are but sunbeams lifted higher.

> Henry Wadsworth Longfellow: *The
> Golden Legend*, Pt. IV: *The
> Cloisters*, l. 19

Hands of invisible spirits touch the strings
Of that mysterious instrument, the soul,
And play the prelude of our fate. We hear
The voice prophetic, and are not alone.

> Henry Wadsworth Longfellow: *The
> Spanish Student*, Act I, sc. 3, l. 111

All thoughts that mould the age begin
Deep down within the primitive soul.

> James Russell Lowell: *An Incident in a
> Railroad Car*, st. 13

The nurse of full-grown souls is solitude.

> James Russell Lowell: *Columbus*

Great Truths are portions of the soul of
man;
Great Souls are portions of Eternity.

> James Russell Lowell: *Sonnet VI*

The shell disdained a soul had gained,
The lyre had been discovered.

> James Russell Lowell: *The Finding of the
> Lyre*, st. 4

Not only around our infancy
Doth heaven with all its splendors lie;
Daily, with souls that cringe and plot,
We Sinais climb and know it not.

> James Russell Lowell: *The Vision of Sir
> Launfal*, Pt. I, Prelude, st. 2

For it is unknown what is the real nature of
the soul, whether it be born with the bodily
frame or be infused at the moment of birth,
whether it perishes along with us, when
death separates the soul and body, or whether
it visits the shades of Pluto and bottomless
pits, or enters by divine appointment into
other animals.

> Lucretius: *De Rerum Natura*, l. 113

Every soul is a melody which needs to be
readjusted.

> Stéphane Mallarmé: *Verse and Prose*

The dust's for crawling, heaven's for flying,
Wherefore, O Soul, whose wings are grown,
Soar upward to the sun!

> Edgar Lee Masters: *The Spoon River
> Anthology: Julian Scott*

You cannot hide the soul.

> Herman Melville: *Moby Dick*

And if I drink oblivion of a day,
So shorten I the stature of my soul.

> George Meredith: *Modern Love*, st. 12

Ah what a dusty answer gets the soul
When hot for certainties in this our life!

> George Meredith: *Modern Love*, st. 50

The world stands out on either side
No wider than the heart is wide;
Above the world is stretched the sky,—
No higher than the soul is high.
The heart can push the sea and land
Farther away on either hand;
The soul can split the sky in two,
And let the face of God shine through.

> Edna St. Vincent Millay: "Renascence,"
> from *Collected Poems*, Harper & Row,
> Publishers, copyright 1912, 1940, by
> Edna St. Vincent Millay, used by
> permission of Norma Millay

The soul that feeds on books alone—
I count that soul exceding small
That lives alone by book and creed,—
A soul that has not learned to read.

> Joaquin Miller: *The Larger College*, st. 10

The worth of the soul consists not in going
loftily, but orderly. Its greatness is not put
to the proof in greatness, but in mediocrity.

> Michel Eyquem de Montaigne

The souls of emperors and cobblers are cast
in the same mould.

> Michel Eyquem de Montaigne: *Apology
> for Raimond Sebond*

The soul, of origin divine, God's glorious
image, freed from clay, in heaven's eternal
sphere shall shine, a star of day!—The sun

is but a spark of fire, a transient meteor in the sky; the soul immortal as its sire, shall never die.

Robert Montgomery

The soul, aspiring, pants its source to mount, As streams meander level with their fount.

Robert Montgomery: *Omnipresence of the Deity*, Pt. I

The soul on earth is an immortal guest, compelled to starve at an unreal feast; a pilgrim panting for the rest to come; an exile, anxious for his native home.

Hannah More: *Reflections of King Hezekiah*, l. 125

For what is a man profited, if he shall gain the whole world, and lose his own soul? or what shall a man give in exchange for his soul?

New Testament: Matthew 16: 26

My soul doth magnify the Lord.

New Testament: Luke 1: 46

Soul, thou hast much goods laid up for many years; take thine ease, eat, drink, and be merry.

New Testament: Luke 12: 19

Thou fool, this night thy soul shall be required of thee.

New Testament: Luke 12: 20

In your patience possess ye your souls.

New Testament: Luke 21: 19

Abstain from fleshly lusts, which war against the soul.

New Testament: 1 Peter 2: 11

And the Lord God formed man of the dust of the ground, and breathed into his nostrils the breath of life; and man became a living soul.

Old Testament: Genesis 2: 7

He restoreth my soul: he leadeth me in the paths of righteousness for his name's sake.

Old Testament: Psalms 23: 3

As the hart panteth after the water-brooks, so panteth my soul after thee.

Old Testament: Psalms 42: 1

Why art thou cast down, O my soul? and why art thou disquieted in me?

Old Testament: Psalms 42: 5

My soul is continually in my hand.

Old Testament: Psalms 119: 109

Our soul is escaped as a bird out of the snare of the fowlers.

Old Testament: Psalms 124: 7

I shall go softly all my years in the bitterness of my soul.

Old Testament: Isaiah 38: 15

I sent my Soul through the Invisible,
Some letter of the after-life to spell,
　And by and by my Soul returned to me,
And answered, "I Myself am Heav'n and
　Hell."

Omar Khayyám: *Rubáiyát*

There is a divinity within our breast.

Ovid: *Epistolae ex Ponto*, Bk. III, Epis. IV, l. 93

To every man there openeth
A Way, and Ways, and a Way,
The High Soul climbs the High Way,
The Low Soul gropes the Low,
And in between, on the misty flats,
The rest drift to and fro.

John Oxenham: *The Ways*

Suspicion is the companion of mean souls, and the bane of all good society.

Thomas Paine: *Common Sense*

These are the times that try men's souls.

Thomas Paine: *The American Crisis*, no. 1

Given the hardest terms, supposing our days are indeed but a shadow, even so, we may well adorn and beautify, in scrupulous self-respect, our souls, and whatever our souls touch upon.

> Walter Pater: *Marius, the Epicurean,*
> ch. 8

The soul is immortal, and is clothed successively in many bodies.

> Plato

Thinking is the talking of the soul with itself.

> Plato

Of all things which a man has, next to the gods, his soul is the most divine and most truly his own.

> Plato: *Laws,* Bk. IV, sec. 252

The soul of man is immortal and imperishable.

> Plato: *The Republic,* Bk. X, 601–D

The soul has in itself a capacity for affection, and loves just as naturally as it perceives, understands, and remembers.

> Plutarch: *Lives: Solon,* sec. 7

All are but parts of one stupendous whole, Whose body Nature is, and God the soul.

> Alexander Pope: *Essay on Man*

The soul, uneasy and confin'd from home, Rests and expatiates in a life to come.

> *Ibid.*

Script to the naked soul.

> Alexander Pope: *Lines to Mrs. Grace
> Butler*

Speech is a mirror of the soul: as a man speaks, so is he.

> Publilius Syrus: *Maxim*

Yet stab at thee that will, No stab the soul can kill!

> Sir Walter Raleigh: *The Lie*

And though thy soul sail leagues and leagues beyond,— Still, leagues beyond those leagues, there is more sea.

> Dante Gabriel Rossetti: *The House of
> Life: The Choice,* III

The soul is the captain and ruler of the life of mortals.

> Sallust: *Jugurtha,* ch. 1

The human soul is like a bird that is born in a cage. Nothing can deprive it of its natural longings, or obliterate the mysterious remembrance of its heritage.

> Epes Sargent

The soul alone renders us noble.

> Seneca: *Epistolae ad Lucilium,* Epis. 44, 5

Do you ask where the Supreme Good dwells? In the soul. And unless the soul be pure and holy, there is no room in it for God.

> Seneca: *Epistolae ad Lucilium,* Epis 87, 21

The soul is our king.

> Seneca: *Epistolae ad Lucilium,*
> Epis. 114, 24

The soul has this proof of its divinity: that divine things delight it.

> Seneca: *Naturales Questiones,* Bk. I,
> *Praefatio*

God be prais'd, that to believing souls Gives light in darkness, comfort in despair!

> William Shakespeare: *Henry VI,*
> Pt. II, Act II, sc. 1, l. 66

Heaven take my soul, and England keep my bones!

> William Shakespeare: *King John,*
> Act IV, sc. 3, l. 10

Now my soul hath elbow-room.

> William Shakespeare: *King John,*
> Act V, sc. 7, l. 28

Well, God's above all; and there be souls must be saved, and there be souls must not be saved.

William Shakespeare: *Othello,*
Act II, sc. 3, l. 106

Throughout this varied and eternal world Soul is the only element.

Percy Bysshe Shelley: *Queen Mab,* III

The man who in this world can keep the whiteness of his soul, is not likely to lose it in any other.

Alexander Smith: *Dreamthorp,* ch. 1

The soul of man is like the rolling world, One half in day, the other dipt in night; The one has music and the flying cloud, The other, silence and the wakeful stars.

Alexander Smith: *Horton*

If you are losing your leisure, look out; you may be losing your soul.

Logan Pearsall Smith

Most people sell their souls, and live with a good conscience on the proceeds.

Logan Pearsall Smith

The soul takes nothing with her to the other world but her education and culture; and these, it is said, are of the greatest service or of the greatest injury to the dead man, at the very beginning of his journey thither.

Socrates: *Dialogues of Plato: Phaedo,* 107

Whate'er of earth is form'd, to earth returns,
*   *   *   The soul
Of man alone, that particle divine,
Escapes the wreck of worlds, when all things fail.

William Somerville: *The Chase,*
Bk. IV, l. 1

For of the soule the bodie forme doth take:
For soule is forme, and doth the bodie make.

Edmund Spenser: *An Hymne in Honour of Beautie,* l. 132

The soul is a fire that darts its rays through all the senses; it is in this fire that existence consists; all the observations and all the efforts of philosophers ought to turn toward this ME, the centre and moving power of our sentiments and our ideas.

Madame Anne Germaine de Staël:
Germany, Pt. III, ch. 11

There is no evil in the atom; only in men's souls.

Adlai Stevenson: Speech, Hartford, Connecticut, September 18, 1952

Before ever land was,
  Before ever the sea,
Or soft hair of the grass,
  Or fair limbs of the tree,
Or the flesh-coloured fruit of my branches,
  I was, and thy soul was in me.

Algernon Charles Swinburne: *Hertha,*
st. 1

I am that which began;
  Out of me the years roll;
Out of me God and man;
  I am equal and whole;
God changes, and man, and the form of them bodily; I am the soul.

Ibid.

No seed shall perish which the soul hath sown.

John Addington Symonds: *Sonnet: A Belief*

My soul is a dark ploughed field
  In the cold rain;
My soul is a broken field
  Ploughed by pain.

Sara Teasdale: *The Broken Field*

Star to star vibrates light; may soul to soul Strike thro' a finer element of her own?

Alfred, Lord Tennyson: *Aylmer's Field,*
l. 578

What profits now to understand
  The merits of a spotless shirt—
A dapper boot—a little hand—
  If half the little soul is dirt.

Alfred, Lord Tennyson: *The New Timon and the Poets*

Life is the soul's nursery—its training place for the destinies of eternity.
William Makepeace Thackeray

The human soul is a silent harp in God's quire, whose strings need only to be swept by the divine breath to chime in with the harmonies of creation.
Henry David Thoreau: *Journal*, August 10, 1838

Be careless in your dress if you must, but keep a tidy soul.
Mark Twain: *Pudd'nhead Wilson's Calendar*

Liberty of thought is the life of the soul.
Voltaire: *Essay on Epic Poetry* (written in English)

The soul's dark cottage, batter'd and decay'd, Lets in new light through chinks that Time has made.
Edmund Waller: *On the Divine Poems*

Were I so tall to reach the pole,
Or grasp the ocean with my span,
I must be measured by my soul:
The mind's the standard of the man.
Isaac Watts: *Horae Lyricae*, Bk. II, *False Greatness*

Every impulse of generosity, when carried to fruition, gives a diastole to the soul which lifts it one step closer to the gates of heaven.
Kendall Weisiger: *The Rotarian*

My soul is all an aching void.
A charge to keep I have,
A God to glorify:
A never-dying soul to save,
And fit it for the sky.
Charles Wesley: *Hymn*

Jesus, lover of my soul,
Let me to Thy bosom fly,
While the nearer waters roll,
While the tempest still is high;

Hide me, O my Saviour, hide,
Till the storm of life is past;
Safe into the haven glide,
O receive my soul at last.
Charles Wesley: *Jesus, Lover of My Soul*

If thou of fortune be bereft
And in thy store there be but left
Two loaves, sell one and with the dole
Buy hyacinths to feed thy soul.
James Terry White: *Not By Bread Alone*

What do you suppose will satisfy the soul, except to walk free and own no superior?
Walt Whitman: *Leaves of Grass: Laws for Creations*, III

I loafe and invite my soul.
Walt Whitman: *Leaves of Grass: Song of Myself*, I

O we can wait no longer,
We too take ship O soul,
Joyous we too launch out on trackless seas,
Fearless for unknown shores.
Walt Whitman: *Leaves of Grass: Passage to India*, 8

The windows of my soul I throw
Wide open to the sun.
John Greenleaf Whittier: *My Psalm*, st. 2

And God, who studies each commonplace soul,
Out of commonplace things makes His beautiful whole.
Sarah Chauncey Woolsey (Susan Coolidge): *Commonplace*

For the Gods approve
The depth, and not the tumult, of the soul.
William Wordsworth: *Loadamia*

Our birth is but a sleep and a forgetting:
The soul that rises with us, our life's star,
Hath had elsewhere its setting,
And cometh from afar: . . .
William Wordsworth: *Ode: Intimations of Immortality*, st. 5

Though inland far we be,
Our souls have sight of that immortal sea
Which brought us hither.

William Wordsworth: *Ode: Intimations of Immortality*, st. 9

SPIRIT

A contented spirit is the sweetness of existence.

Anonymous

There's naught, no doubt, so much the spirit calms as rum and true religion.

George Gordon, Lord Byron: *Don Juan*, Canto II, st. 34

I envy no mortal, though ever so great,
Nor scorn I a wretch for his lowly estate;
But what I abhor and esteem as a curse
Is poorness of Spirit, not poorness of Purse.

Henry Carey: *General Reply to the Libelling Gentry*

Who can resist the conclusion that, under the matter must be something superior which our languages doing the best they can, call spirit?

Abbé Ernest Dimnet: *What We Live By*, Copyright 1932, Simon & Schuster

Spirit is immortal Truth; matter is mortal error.

Mary Baker Eddy: *Science and Health with Key to the Scriptures*, p. 468: 11–12

Oh, why should the spirit of mortal be proud?
Like a swift-flitting meteor, a fast-flying cloud,
A flash of the lightning, a break of the wave,
He passeth from life to his rest in the grave.

William Knox: *Oh, Why Should the Spirit of Mortal Be Proud?*

When my spirit soars, my body falls on its knees.

Georg Christoph Lichtenberg

Radar may make possible the avoidance of unseen dangers for plane, ship and car. Radar of the spirit may enable man, in time, to avoid war, forms of disease, and sins of selfishness, arrogance and pride. Radar of the spirit may tap resources of spiritual power long dreamed of, but never made widely available to man. Such power may send man over the mountains of racial antagonism, social and economic barriers, and denominational differences.

Arthur L. Miller: *Christian Herald*

In this world there are two forces: the sword and the spirit. The spirit has always conquered the sword.

Napoleon Bonaparte

The spirit indeed is willing, but the flesh is weak.

New Testament: Matthew 26: 41

Into thy hands I commend my spirit.

New Testament: Luke 23: 46

It is the spirit that quickeneth.

New Testament: John 6: 63

Not of the letter, but of the spirit: for the letter killeth, but the spirit giveth life.

New Testament: II Corinthians 3: 6

The spirits of just men made perfect.

New Testament: Hebrews 12: 23

The ornament of a meek and quiet spirit, which is in the sight of God of great price.

New Testament: I Peter 3: 4

The spirit of a man will sustain his infirmity; but a wounded spirit who can bear?

Old Testament: Proverbs 18: 14

The spirit of man is the candle of the Lord.

Old Testament: Proverbs 20: 27

He that hath no rule over his own spirit is like a city that is broken down, and without walls.

Old Testament: Proverbs 25: 28

A new heart also will I give you, and a new spirit will I put within you.

Old Testament: Ezekiel 36: 26

Because I have confidence in the power of truth and of the spirit, I believe in the future of mankind.

From *Out of My Life and Thought* by Albert Schweitzer. Copyright 1933, 1949 by Holt, Rinehart & Winston. Reprinted by permission of Holt, Rinehart & Winston Inc. and George Allen & Unwin, Ltd.

Joy is an elation of spirit—of a spirit which trusts in goodness and truth of its own possessions.

Seneca

All spirits are enslaved which serve things evil.

Percy Bysshe Shelley: *Prometheus Unbound*, Act II, sc. 4

Body and spirit are twins: God only knows which is which.

Algernon Charles Swinburne: *The Higher Pantheism in a Nutshell*, st. 7

We have allowed our metaphysical and mystical powers to become stupefied. For this reason, we are no longer the children of God, but victims of the mechanical powers and functions of the economic cycle. Because the spirit has deserted us, we are nothing more than consumers and consumed. Because there no longer exists for us any absolute value, we are worth only so much as we pay and are paid.

Franz Werfel: *Harper's Bazaar*

STARS, THE

Jean Bon St. André, the French revolutionist and atheist, said to a lowly farmer, "I will have all your steeples pulled down, so that you may no longer have any object by which you may be reminded of your old superstitions." "Ah," said the farmer, "but you can't help leaving us the stars."

Anonymous

After hearing a westerner describe the wonders of the telescope, an Arab shiek replied, "You foreigners see millions of stars, but nothing beyond. We Arabs see only a few stars—and God."

Anonymous

Though my soul may set in darkness, it will rise in perfect light;
I have loved the stars too fondly to be fearful of the night.

Anonymous: *An Old Astronomer to His Pupil*

The Spacious Firmament on high,
With all the blue Ethereal sky,
And spangled Heav'ns, a shining Frame,
Their great Original proclaim.

Joseph Addison: *Ode*

What are ye orbs?
The words of God? the Scriptures of the skies?

Philip James Bailey: *Festus: Everywhere*

When the stars threw down their spears,
And water'd heaven with their tears,
Did he smile his work to see?
Did he who made the lamb make thee?

William Blake: *Songs of Experience: The Tiger*, st. 5

The pale populace of Heaven.

Robert Browning: *Balaustion's Adventure*, l. 205

Ah! the lamps numberless,
The mystical jewels of God,
The luminous, wonderful,
Beautiful lights of the Veil!

Robert Williams Buchanan: *Book of Orm: First Song*

Ye stars, that are the poetry of heaven!

George Gordon, Lord Byron

Look up, and behold the eternal fields of light that lie round about the throne of God. Had no star ever appeared in the heavens, to man there would have been no heavens; and he would have laid himself down to his last sleep, in a spirit of anguish, as upon a gloomy earth vaulted over by a material arch —solid and impervious.

Thomas Carlyle

Religion cannot pass away. The burning of a little straw may hide the stars of the sky, but the stars are there, and will reappear.

Thomas Carlyle

The stars rule men but God rules the stars.

Christoph Cellarius: *Harmonica Macro-cosmica: Preface*

If the stars should appear one night in a thousand years, how men would believe and adore and preserve for many generations the remembrance of the city of God which had been shown.

Ralph Waldo Emerson

There's no rood has not a star above it.

Ralph Waldo Emerson: *Poems: Musketaquid*

Who falls for love of God shall rise a star.

Ben Jonson: *Underwoods—32: To a Friend*

Two things fill the mind with ever new and increasing wonder and awe—the starry heavens above me and the moral law within me.

Immanuel Kant: *Critique of Pure Reason: Conclusion*

Silently, one by one, in the infinite meadows of Heaven,
Blossomed the lovely stars, the forget-me-nots of the angels.

Henry Wadsworth Longfellow: *Evangeline, I*

Then stars arise, and the night is holy.

Henry Wadsworth Longfellow: *Hyperion, Bk. I, ch. 1*

The starry cope of Heav'n.

John Milton: *Paradise Lost, Bk. IV, l. 992*

The bright and morning star.

New Testament: Revelation 22: 16

Let there be lights in the firmament of the heaven to divide the day from the night.

Old Testament: Genesis 1: 14

The stars in their courses fought against Sisera.

Old Testament: Judges 5: 20

When the morning stars sang together, and all the sons of God shouted for joy.

Old Testament: Job 38: 7

Canst thou bind the sweet influences of Pleiades, or loose the bands of Orion?

Old Testament: Job 38: 31

Canst thou guide Arcturus with his sons?

Old Testament: Job 38: 32

He telleth the number of the stars; he calleth them all by their names.

Old Testament: Psalms 147: 4

O powers illimitable! it is but the outer hem of God's great mantle, our poor stars do gem.

John Ruskin

Men at some time are masters of their fates:
The fault, dear Brutus, is not in our stars,
But in ourselves, that we are underlings.

William Shakespeare: *Julius Caesar, Act I, sc. 2, l. 138*

There's not the smallest orb which thou behold'st
But in his motion like an angel sings.

William Shakespeare: *The Merchant of Venice, Act V, sc. 1, l. 60*

There they stand, the innumerable stars, shining in order like a living hymn, written in light.

Nathaniel Parker Willis

But He is risen, a later star of dawn.

William Wordsworth: *A Morning Exercise*

STEWARDSHIP

Christian Stewardship is the matching of gift for matchless gift: our life and its whole substance for the gift of perfect love. And though God's Son and His precious death are matchless—in the strange economy of God our gift returned is made sufficient. My all for His all. Stewardship is your commitment; the asking of God to take you back unto Himself —all that you have and all that you are.

Lawrence L. Durgin: *Mission Today*

Stewardship is what a man does after he says, "I believe."

W. H. Greever

Our children, relations, friends, honors, houses, lands, and endowments, the goods of nature and fortune, nay, even of grace itself, are only lent. It is our misfortune, and our sin to fancy they are given. We start, therefore, and are angry when the loan is called in. We think ourselves masters, when we are only stewards, and forget that to each of us it will one day be said, "Give an account of thy stewardship."

Thomas H. Horne

Stewardship is the acceptance from God of personal responsibility for all of life and life's affairs.

Roswell C. Long

There is no portion of our time that is our time, and the rest God's; there is no portion of money that is our money, and the rest God's money. It is all His; He made it all, gives it all, and He has simply trusted it to us for His service. A servant has two purses, the master's and his own, but we have only one.

Adolphe Monod

It is required in stewards, that a man be found faithful.

New Testament: I Corinthians 4: 2

As to all that we have and are, we are but stewards of the Most High God.—On all our possessions, on our time, and talents, and influence, and property, he has written, "Occupy for me, and till I shall come."—To obey his instructions and serve him faithfully, is the true test of obedience and discipleship.

Charles Simmons

God has never had on His side a majority of men and women. He does not need a majority to work wonders in history, but He does need a minority fully committed to Him and His purpose. In the world today Christian stewardship is a necessity.

Ernest Fremont Tittle

STRENGTH

Your weakness is no excuse: "He giveth power to the faint."

Anonymous

For the victory of battle standeth not in the multitude of an host; but strength cometh from heaven.

Apocrypha: I Maccabees 3: 18, 19

No, no! The energy of life may be
Kept on after the grave, but not begun;
And he who flagg'd not in the earthly strife,
From strength to strength advancing—only he
His soul well-knit, and all his battles won,
Mounts, and that hardly, to eternal life.

Matthew Arnold: *Sonnet: Immortality*

I count life just a stuff
To try the soul's strength on.

Robert Browning: *In a Balcony*

The strength of a country is the strength of its religious convictions.

Calvin Coolidge

The past is littered with the wreckage of nations which tried to meet the crises of their times by physical means alone.

Raymond B. Fosdick: *World Affairs Interpreter*

Nothing is so strong as gentleness: nothing so gentle as real strength.

St. Francis de Sales

These three things deplete man's strength: fear, travel, and sin.

Hebrew Proverb

There is no merit where there is no trial; and till experience stamps the mark of strength, cowards may pass for heroes, and faith for falsehood.

Aaron Hill

A strong and faithful pulpit is no mean safeguard of a nation's life.

John of Salisbury

In every pang that rends the heart,
The man of Sorrows has a part.

John Henry Jowett

There is no strength in unbelief. Even the unbelief of what is false is no source of might. It is the truth shining from behind that gives the strength to disbelieve.

George Macdonald: *The Marquis of Lossie*, ch. 42

My strength is made perfect in weakness.

New Testament: II Corinthians 12: 9

As thy days, so shall thy strength be.

Old Testament: Deuteronomy 33: 25

Out of the mouths of babes and sucklings hast thou ordained strength.

Old Testament: Psalms 8: 2

The Lord is my light and my salvation; whom shall I fear? the Lord is the strength of my life; of whom shall I be afraid?

Old Testament: Psalms 27: 1

God is our refuge and strength, a very present help in trouble.

Old Testament: Psalms 46: 1

Thy God hath commanded thy strength.

Old Testament: Psalms 68: 28

Blessed is the man whose strength is in thee.

Old Testament: Psalms 84: 5

The days of our years are threescore years and ten; and if by reason of strength they be fourscore years, yet is their strength labour and sorrow; for it is soon cut off, and we fly away.

Old Testament: Psalms 90: 10

A wise man is strong; yea, a man of knowledge increaseth strength.

Old Testament: Proverbs 24: 5

But they that wait upon the Lord shall renew their strength; they shall mount up with wings as eagles; they shall run, and not be weary; they shall walk, and not faint.

Old Testament: Isaiah 40: 31

Spiritual power is a hidden power, locked in the silence of the soul. We cannot force it to come at command of will. But when in extremity our strength is as water, our will as the sighing of the wind, when we yield all physical being and lean hard on the spiritual strength within us, the soul's strength rises to assure us as the sun rises over the rim of night.

This spiritual strength is man's inheritance, the eternal power granted him at the Creation. It is God's breath within him. On that strength we can go forward; we can take whatever comes and know it is well with us always.

Angelo Patri: *Redbook*

The gods always favor the strong.

Tacitus: *Annals*, IV

My strength is as the strength of ten,
Because my heart is pure.
> Alfred, Lord Tennyson: *Sir Galahad*, st. 1

Eternal Father! strong to save,
Whose arm hath bound the restless wave,
Who bidd'st the mighty ocean deep
Its own appointed limits keep:
O, hear us when we cry to Thee
For those in peril on the sea!
> William Whiting: *Eternal Father, Strong
> to Save*, st. 1

So let it be in God's own might
We gird us for the coming fight,
And, strong in Him whose cause is ours
In conflict with unholy powers,
We grasp the weapons He has given,—
The Light and Truth, and Love of Heaven.
> John Greenleaf Whittier: *The Moral
> Warfare*

SUCCESS

To have grown wise and kind is real success.
> Anonymous

If you wish to succeed in life, make perseverance your bosom friend, experience your wise counselor, caution your elder brother, and hope your guardian genius.
> Joseph Addison

'Tis not in mortals to command success,
But we'll do more . . . we'll deserve it.
> Joseph Addison

Success in men's eyes is God and more than God.
> Aeschylus: *Chaephoroi*, l. 59

There's no defeat, in truth, save from within;
Unless you're beaten there, you're bound
to win.
> Henry Austin

I once heard a very great man say that any deed worth doing or any institution worthy

of survival must have a compound of three ingredients: A plan, a power and a prayer.
> Joseph A. Batchelor: *Indiana Freemason*

To find his place and fill it is success for a man.
> Phillips Brooks

God will estimate Success one day.
> Robert Browning: *Prince Hohenstiel-
> Schwangau*

Better have failed in the high aim, as I,
Than vulgarly in the low aim succeed
As, God be thanked! I do not.
> Robert Browning: *The Inn Album*, IV

They never fail who die in a great cause.
> George Gordon, Lord Byron: *Marino
> Faliero*

Hast thou not learn'd what thou art often told,
A truth still sacred, and believed of old,
That no success attends on spears and swords
Unblest, and that the battle is the Lord's?
> William Cowper: *Expostulation*, l. 350

Try not to become a man of success but rather try to become a man of value.
> Albert Einstein: Personal memoir of
> William Miller

I look on that man as happy, who, when there is question of success, looks into his work for a reply.
> Ralph Waldo Emerson: *Conduct of Life:
> Worship*

An open mind, humility, determination, enthusiasm, unselfishness, plus a love of action (inspired work) are the steps in a moving stairway to the stars.
> Melvin J. Evans: *It Works*

Everybody finds out, sooner or later, that all success worth having is founded on Christian rules of conduct.
> Henry Martyn Field

To a young man learning to perform on the flying trapeze a veteran circus performer once said: "Throw your heart over the bars and your body will follow." In every field of endeavor those who put their hearts in their work are the real leaders . . . Falling in love with one's job is the secret of success.

Frat

The Lord gave you two ends—one for sitting and one for thinking. Your success depends on which you use—heads you win, tails you lose.

Gas Flame

'Tis man's to fight, but Heaven's to give success.

Homer: *Iliad*, Bk. VI, l. 427

Success—"the bitch-goddess, Success," in William James's phrase—demands strange sacrifices from those who worship her.

Aldous Huxley: *Proper Studies*, p. 318,
Harper & Row Publishers, Inc.

Your success and happiness lie in you. External conditions are the accidents of life. The great enduring realities are love and service. Joy is the holy fire that keeps our purpose warm and our intelligence aglow. Resolve to keep happy, and your joy and you shall form an invincible host against difficulty.

Helen Keller

What do we mean by "success" anyway? Success by whose standards? The Bible teaches that God is the final Judge before whom we shall all stand one day. God will then proclaim us successful or unsuccessful.

Bill Krisher: *The Goal and the Glory*
(*America's Athletes Speak Their Faith*)

A man who is a success never has to prove it. The reason why spectacular spenders throw their money around so conspicuously is because they are trying to prove to others— and to themselves—that they are successful. What they are really demonstrating is their spiritual poverty. Success—the real, not the flashing kind—can never be measured by

bank balances; money measures only prosperity. Success is a matter of character.

The Little Gazette

To have faith where you cannot see; to be willing to work on in the dark; to be conscious of the fact that, so long as you strive for the best, there are better things on the way, this in itself is success.

Katherine Logan

Not in the clamor of the crowded street,
Not in the shouts and plaudits of the throng,
But in ourselves are triumph and defeat.

Henry Wadsworth Longfellow

The race is not to the swift, nor the battle to the strong, neither yet bread to the wise, nor yet riches to men of understanding, nor yet favour to men of skill; but time and chance happeneth to them all.

Old Testament: Ecclesiastes 9: 11

Have a sincere desire to serve God and mankind, and stop doubting, stop thinking negatively . . . Simply start living by faith, pray earnestly and humbly, and get into the habit of looking expectantly for the best . . . When you live on a faith basis, your desire will be only for that which you can ask in God's name . . . By success, of course, I do not mean that you may become rich, famous, or powerful . . . I mean the development of mature and constructive personality.

Norman Vincent Peale

Being *humble* involves the willingness to be reckoned a failure in everyone's sight but God's.

Roy M. Pearson: *Here's a Faith for You*,
Abingdon Press

Success is in the way you walk the paths of life each day; it's in the little things you do, and in the things you say. Success is not in getting rich, or rising high to fame. It's not alone in winning goals, which all men hope to claim.

Success is being big of heart, and clean and broad in mind; it's being faithful to your friends, and to the stranger, kind. It's in the hildren whom you love, and all they learn rom you; success depends on character, and verything you do.

Pepper Box, St. Louis Rotary Club

The success of the wicked entices many more.

Phaedrus: *Fables*, Bk. II, fab. 3, l. 7

Asked the secret of his power as a preacher, a Negro minister in Washington, D.C., declared: " It's simple. I read myself full. I think myself clear. I pray myself hot. And then I let go."

Pure Oil News

The true measure of success in life lies in production for use and the welfare of the community. And of all failings, the ugliest is the lust for personal success.

Dagobert D. Runes: *Letters to My Son*

It is surprising to observe how much more anybody may become by simply being always in His place.

Salina Watchman

He has achieved success who has lived well, laughed often and loved much.

Bessie Anderson Stanley: *Success* (prize winning definition in a contest conducted by the *Brown Book Magazine*, 1904)

Why should we be in such desperate haste to succeed, and in such desperate enterprises? If a man does not keep pace with his companions, perhaps it is because he hears a different drummer.

Henry David Thoreau: *Walden*

Success is to be measured not by wealth, power, or fame, but by the ratio between what a man is and what he might be.

H. G. Wells

SUFFERING

God washes the eyes by tears until they can behold the invisible land where tears shall come no more.

Henry Ward Beecher

In suffering one learns to pray best of all.

Harold A. Bosley: *On Final Ground*

Suffering is the sole origin of consciousness.

Feodor Dostoevski

We, by our suff'rings, learn to prize our bliss.

John Dryden: *Astraea Redux*, l. 210

It is only the strong who are strengthened by suffering; the weak are made weaker.

Lion Feuchtwanger: *Paris Gazette*

Our present joys are sweeter for past pain; To Love and Heaven by suffering we attain.

George Granville: *The British Enchanters*, Act V, sc. 2

Pain is the deepest thing we have in our nature, and union through pain and suffering has always seemed more real and holy than any other.

Arthur Henry Hallam

Happiness is not a reward—it is a consequence. Suffering is not a punishment—it is a result.

Robert Green Ingersoll: *The Christian Religion*

We need to suffer that we may learn to pity.

Letitia Elizabeth Landon

Know how sublime a thing it is To suffer and be strong.

Henry Wadsworth Longfellow: *The Reaper and the Flowers*

Our suffering is not worthy the name of suffering. When I consider my crosses, tribulations, and temptations, I shame myself almost to death, thinking what are they in comparison of the sufferings of my blessed Saviour Christ Jesus.

Martin Luther: *Table Talk*

It is suffering and then glory. Not to have the suffering means not to have the glory.

Robert C. McQuilkin

431

Suffering accepted and vanquished . . . will give you a serenity which may well prove the most exquisite fruit of your life.

Cardinal Mercier

Which way shall I fly
Infinite wrath and infinite despair?
Which way I fly is hell; myself am hell;
And in the lowest deep a lower deep,
Still threat'ning to devour me, opens wide,
To which the hell I suffer seems a heaven.

John Milton: *Paradise Lost*, Bk. IV, l. 73

It requires more courage to suffer than to die.

Napoleon Bonaparte, to Gaspard Gowgaud

For I reckon that the sufferings of this present time are not worthy to be compared with the glory which shall be revealed in us.

New Testament: Romans 8: 18

Weep not for him who departs from life, for there is no suffering beyond death.

Palladas

Great souls suffer in silence.

Johann Christoph Friedrich von Schiller: *Don Carlos*, I, 4, 52

Whoever is spared personal pain must feel himself called to help in diminishing the pain of others. We must all carry our share of the misery which lies upon the world.

Albert Schweitzer in *The World of Albert Schweitzer* by Erica Anderson, Harper & Row, Publishers, Inc.

O, I have suffer'd
With those that I saw suffer.

William Shakespeare: *The Tempest*, Act I, sc. 2, l. 5

To be born is to suffer; to grow old is to suffer; to die is to suffer; to lose what is loved is to suffer; to be tied to what is not loved is to suffer; to endure what is distasteful is to suffer. In short, all the results of individu-

ality, of separate self-hood, necessarily involve pain or suffering.

Subhadra Bhikshu

O, well for him whose will is strong!
He suffers, but he will not suffer long;
He suffers, but he cannot suffer wrong.

Alfred, Lord Tennyson: *Will*, l. 1

It is by those who have suffered that the world has been advanced.

Leo Tolstoy

A Christian! going, gone!
Who bids for God's own image?—for his grace,
Which that poor victim of the market-place
Hath in her suffering won?

John Greenleaf Whittier: *Voices of Freedom. The Christian Slave*

Is it so, O Christ in heaven, that the highest suffer most,
That the strongest wander farthest, and more hopelessly are lost,
That the mark of rank in nature is capacity for pain,
That the anguish of the singer makes the sweetness of the strain?

Sarah Williams: *Is It So, O Christ in Heaven?*

Yet tears to human suffering are due;
And mortal hopes defeated and o'erthrown
Are mourned by man, and not by man alone.

William Wordsworth: *Laodamia*, l. 164

SUPERSTITION

As it addeth deformity to an ape to be so like a man, so the similitude of superstition to religion makes it the more deformed.

Sir Francis Bacon

Freedom and not servitude is the cure of anarchy; as religion, and not atheism, is the true remedy for superstition.

Edmund Burke: *Second Speech on Conciliation with America: The Thirteen Resolutions*

Religion is not removed by removing superstition.

Cicero: *De Divinatione*, II, 72

Ignorance and superstition ever bear a close and even a mathematical, relation to each other.

James Fenimore Cooper: *Jack Tier*, ch. 13

Superstitions are, for the most part, but the shadows of great truths.

Tryon Edwards

Superstition renders a man a fool, and scepticism makes him mad.

Henry Fielding

The superstition of science scoffs at the superstition of faith.

James Anthony Froude: *The Lives of the Saints*

Superstition is godless religion, devout impiety.

Joseph Hall: *Of the Superstitious*

Superstition always inspires bitterness, religion, grandeur of mind.—The superstitious man raises beings inferior to himself to deities.

Johann Kaspar Lavater

Superstition, idolatry, and hypocrisy have ample wages, but truth goes a begging.

Martin Luther: *Table Talk*

Yet, if he would, man cannot live all to this world. If not religious, he will be superstitious. If he worship not the true God, he will have his idols.

Theodore Parker: *A Lesson for the Day*

To carry piety as far as superstition is to destroy it.

Blaise Pascal

Religion worships God, while superstition profanes that worship.

Seneca

Superstition is related to this life, religion to the next; superstition is allied to fatality, religion to virtue; it is only by the vivacity of earthly desires, that we become superstitious; it is, on the contrary, by the sacrifice of these desires that we become religious.

Madame Anne Germaine de Staël (See Abel Steven's *Life of Madame de Staël*, ch. 34)

Superstition may be defined as constructive religion which has grown incongruous with intelligence.

John Tyndall: *Fragments of Science*, Vol. I: *Science and Man*

Whatever you do, crush the infamous thing (superstition), and love those who love you.

Voltaire: *Letter to d'Alembert*

Superstition is not, as has been defined, an excess of religious feeling, but a misdirection of it, an exhausting of it on vanities of man's devising.

Richard Whately

SYMPATHY

How long, oh how long will it take us to learn that there are only two things in life that really count—one is character and the other is human sympathy.

Anonymous

A brother's suff'rings claim a brother's pity.

Joseph Addison: *Cato*, Act I, sc. 1

People may excite in themselves a glow of compassion, not by toasting their feet at the fire and saying, "Lord, teach me more compassion," but by going and seeking an object that requires compassion.

Henry Ward Beecher

The truest help we can render an afflicted man is not to take his burden from him, but to call out his best strength that he may be able to bear the burden.

Phillips Brooks

Next to love, sympathy is the divinest passion of the human heart.

Edmund Burke

For compassion a human heart suffices; but for full, adequate sympathy with joy, an angel's.

Samuel Taylor Coleridge: *Notebooks*

There is in souls a sympathy with sounds.

William Cowper: *The Task,* Bk. VI, l. 1

The secrets of life are not shown except to sympathy and likeness.

Ralph Waldo Emerson

Our modern industrialized society is a good deal like the subway—it throws men together in physical proximity without uniting them in spiritual sympathy.

Harry Emerson Fosdick

Sympathy without relief is like mustard without beef.

Richard Lawson Gales: *Vanished Country Folk,* p. 204

Our sympathy is cold to the relation of distant misery.

Edward Gibbon: *The Decline and Fall of the Roman Empire,* III

He watch'd and wept, he pray'd and felt for all.

Oliver Goldsmith: *The Deserted Village,* l. 166

The craving for sympathy is the common boundary-line between joy and sorrow.

Augustus William and Julius Charles Hare: *Guesses at Truth*

I am an agnostic with sympathies.

William Somerset Maugham, Copyright 1954 by The New York Times Company. Reprinted by permission

Rejoice with them that do rejoice, and weep with them that weep.

New Testament: Romans 12: 15

Teach me to feel another's woe,
To hide the fault I see:
That mercy I to others show,
That mercy show to me.

Alexander Pope: *The Universal Prayer*

There is much satisfaction in work well done; praise is sweet; but there can be no happiness equal to the joy of finding a heart that understands.

Victor Robinson

Bring thy soul and interchange with mine.

Johann Christoph Friedrich von Schiller: *Votive Tablets: Value and Worth*

For thou hast given me in this beauteous face
A world of earthly blessings to my soul,
If sympathy of love unite our thoughts.

William Shakespeare: *Henry VI, Part II,* Act I, sc. 1, l. 21

Sympathy is a thing to be encouraged apart from humane consideration, because it supplies us with the materials for wisdom.

Robert Louis Stevenson

It is remarkable with what Christian fortitude and resignation we can bear the suffering of other folks.

Jonathan Swift

And nothing, not God, is greater to one than one's self is,
And whoever walks a furlong without sympathy walks to his own funeral drest in his shroud.

Walt Whitman: *Song of Myself,* sec. 48

T

TEMPERANCE

Drink from the well!
In rapture rang the Temperance bell.
> George W. Bungay: *The Creeds of the Bells*, st. 11

Temperance is a bridle of gold, and he that can use it aright is liker a God than a man; for as it will transform a beast to a man again, so it will make a man a God.
> Richard E. Burton

Temperance is the moderating of one's desires in obedience to reason.
> Cicero: *De Finibus*

No man can be brave who thinks pain the greatest evil; nor temperate, who considers pleasure the highest good.
> Cicero: *De Officiis*, l. 2

Temp'rate in every place—abroad, at home,
Thence will applause, and hence will profit come;
And health from either—he in time prepares
For sickness, age, and their attendant cares.
> George Crabbe: *Borough*, Letter XVII, l. 198

I dare not drink for my own sake, I ought not to drink for my neighbor's sake.
> Theodore Ledyard Cuyler

Temperance is to the body what religion is to the soul—the foundation of health, strength and peace.
> Tryon Edwards

Temperance is the noblest gift of the gods.
> Euripides: *Medea*

Temperance puts wood on the fire, meal in the barrel, flour in the tub, money in the purse, credit in the country, contentment in the house, clothes on the children, vigor in the body, intelligence in the brain, and spirit in the whole constitution.
> Benjamin Franklin

Since the creation of the world there has been no tyrant like Intemperance and no slaves so cruelly treated as his.
> William Lloyd Garrison

Drink not the third glass, which thou canst not tame,
When once it is within thee; but before
Mayst rule it, as thou list: and pour the shame,
Which it would pour on thee, upon the floor.
It is most just to throw that on the ground,
Which would throw me there, if I keep the round.
> George Herbert: *The Temple*

First the man—takes the drink,
Next the drink—takes the drink,
Then the drink—takes the man.
> Japanese Proverb

The habit of intemperance by men in office has occasioned more injury to the public and more trouble to men than all other causes; and, were I to commence my administration again, the first question I would ask respecting a candidate for office would be, "Does he use ardent spirits?"
> Thomas Jefferson

435

Abstinence is as easy to me as temperance would be difficult.

Samuel Johnson: Hannah More's
Johnsoniana, 467

Drinking is the refuge of the weak; it is crutches for lame ducks.

E. Stanley Jones: *The Way,* p. 148,
Abingdon Press

We lead but one life here on earth. We must make that beautiful. And to do this, health and elasticity of mind are needful; and whatever endangers or impedes these must be avoided.

Henry Wadsworth Longfellow

Of my merit
On that pint you yourself may jedge:
All is, I never drink no sperit,
Nor I haint never signed no pledge.

James Russell Lowell: *Biglow Papers,*
First Series, No. 7, st. 9

Impostor do not charge most innocent Nature,
As if she would her children should be riotous
With her abundance; she, good cateress,
Means her provision only to the good
That live according to her sober laws,
And holy dictate of spare Temperance.

John Milton: *Comus,* l. 762

O madness to think use of strongest wines
And strongest drinks our chief support of health;
When God with these forbidden made choice to rear
His might champion, strong above compare,
Whose drink was only from the liquid brook.

John Milton: *Samson Agonistes,* l. 553

Temperate in all things.

New Testament: I Corinthians 9: 25

But the fruit of the Spirit is love, joy, peace, longsuffering, gentleness, goodness, faith, Meekness, temperance: against such there is no law.

New Testament: Galatians 5: 22, 23

Temperance is corporal piety; it is the preservation of divine order in the body.

Theodore Parker

Reason's whole pleasure, all the joys of sense,
Lie in three words—Health, Peace, and Competence.
But health consists with temperance alone,
And peace, O Virtue! peace is all thy own.

Alexander Pope: *Essay on Man,* Epis. IV,
l. 79

The sight of a drunkard is a better sermon against the vice than the best sermon that was ever preached on that subject.

Sarah E. Saville

Ask God for temperance; that's the appliance only
Which your disease requires.

William Shakespeare: *Henry VIII,*
Act I, Sc. 1, l. 124

Temperance is reason's girdle, and passion's bride, the strength of the soul, and the foundation of virtue.

Jeremy Taylor

Temperance, that virtue without pride, and fortune without envy, that gives vigor of frame and tranquility of mind; the best guardian of youth and support of old age, the precept of reason as well as religion, the physician of the soul as well as the body, the tutelar goddess of health, and universal medicine of life.

Sir William Temple

Temperance is moderation in the things that are good and total abstinence from the things that are foul.

Frances E. Willard

Temperance is the nurse of chastity.

William Wycherley: *Love in a Wood,*
Act III, sc. 3

TEMPTATION

Temptations that find us dwelling in God are to our faith like winds that more firmly root the tree.

Anonymous

There was never any one so good that he was exempt from trials and temptations.

Anonymous

Most people who fly from temptation usually leave a forwarding address.

Anonymous

Greater is he who is above temptation than he who being tempted overcomes.

Amos Bronson Alcott: *Orphic Sayings*

It is good to be without vices, but it is not good to be without temptation.

Walter Bagehot: *Biographical Studies,* p. 237

Temptation is the fire that brings up the scum of the heart.

Thomas Boston

Why comes temptation, but for man to meet
And master and make crouch beneath his foot,
And so be pedestaled in triumph?

Robert Browning: *The Ring and the Book: The Pope,* l. 1185

Temptation provokes me to look upward to God.

John Bunyan

Temptations, when we first meet them, are as the lion that roared upon Samson; but if we overcome them, the next time we see them we shall find a nest of honey within them.

John Bunyan

Temptation is the tempter looking through the keyhole into the room where you are living; sin is your drawing back the bolt and making it possible for him to enter.

J. Wilbur Chapman

Better shun the bait than struggle in the snare.

John Dryden

As the Sandwich Islander believes that the strength and valor of the enemy he kills passes into himself, so we gain the strength of the temptation we resist.

Ralph Waldo Emerson: *Essays, First Series: Compensation*

Every moment of resistance to temptation is a victory.

Frederick William Faber

Temptations are a file which rub off much of the rust of our self-confidence.

François de Salignac de La Mothe Fénelon

An open door may tempt a saint.

Thomas Fuller: *Gnomologia*

Many a dangerous temptation comes to us in fine gay colours, that are but skin-deep.

Matthew Henry: *Commentaries: Genesis,* III

When Eve upon the first of men
The apple pressed, with specious cant,
Oh! what a thousand pities then
That Adam was not Adamant!

Thomas Hood

Yield not to temptation,
For yielding is sin.

Hymn

Honest bread is very well—it's the butter that makes the temptation.

Douglas Jerrold: *The Catspaw*

In so far as you approach temptation to a man, you do him an injury; and if he is overcome, you share his guilt.

Samuel Johnson

Few can review the days of their youth without recollecting temptations which shame rather than virtue enabled them to resist.

Samuel Johnson: *The Rambler*

Do today's duty, fight today's temptation; and do not weaken and distract yourself by looking forward to things which you cannot see, and could not understand if you saw them.

Charles Kingsley

No man knows how bad he is until he has tried to be good. There is a silly idea about that good people don't know what temptation means.

C. S. Lewis: *The Screwtape Letters*

Temptations are like tramps. Treat them kindly and they return bringing others with them.

The Link

My temptations have been my masters in divinity.

Martin Luther

God chooses that men should be tried, but let a man beware of tempting his neighbor.

George Macdonald

Lead us not into temptation, but deliver us from evil.

New Testament: Matthew 6: 13

Watch and pray, that ye enter not into temptation.

New Testament: Matthew 26: 41

Blessed is the man that endureth temptation: for when he is tried, he shall receive the crown of life, which the Lord hath promised to them that love him.

New Testament: James 1: 12

God is better served in resisting a temptation to evil than in many formal prayers.

William Penn

Where there is no temptation, there can be little claim to virtue.

William Hickling Prescott: *The Conquest of Peru*, Bk. I, ch. 5

No one can ask honestly or happily to be delivered from temptation unless he has honestly and firmly determined to do the best he can to keep out of it.

John Ruskin

To pray against temptation, and yet to rush into occasion, is to thrust your fingers into the fire, and then pray they might not be burnt.

Thomas Secker

It is one thing to be tempted, another thing to fall.

William Shakespeare

Bell, book, and candle shall not drive me back
When gold and silver becks me to come on.

William Shakespeare: *King John,* Act III, sc. 3, l. 12

The tempter or the tempted, who sins most?

William Shakespeare: *Measure for Measure,* Act II, sc. 2, l. 163

Learn to say no; it will be of more use to you than to be able to read Latin.

Charles Haddon Spurgeon

Some temptations come to the industrious, but all temptations attack the idle.

Charles Haddon Spurgeon

Temptations from without have no power unless there be corresponding desire within.

Sunshine Magazine

Every temptation is great or small according as the man is.

Jeremy Taylor

Fire tries iron, and temptation tries a just man.

Thomas à Kempis: *Imitation of Christ,* Bk. I, ch. 13

There are several good protections against temptation, but the surest is cowardice.

Mark Twain

THANKSGIVING

It is easier to stay out than get out.

Mark Twain: *Pudd'nhead Wilson's New Calendar*

To attempt to resist temptation, abandon our bad habits, and to control our dominant passions in our own unaided strength, is like attempting to check by a spider's thread the progress of a ship borne along before wind and tide.

Benjamin Waugh

I can resist everything except temptation.

Oscar Wilde

No degree of temptation justifies any degree of sin.

Nathaniel Parker Willis

When a man resists sin on human motives only, he will not hold out long.

Daniel Wilson

THANKSGIVING, THANKFULNESS

I thank Thee for a daily task to do,
  For books that are my ships with golden wings,
For mighty gifts let others offer praise—
  Lord, I am thanking Thee for little things.

Anonymous

Without Thy sunshine and Thy rain
We could not have the golden grain;
Without Thy love we'd not be fed;
We thank Thee for our daily bread.

Anonymous

Pride slays thanksgiving, but an humble mind is the soil out of which thanks naturally grow.—A proud man is seldom a grateful man, for he never thinks he gets as much as he deserves.

Henry Ward Beecher

Some people always sigh in thanking God.

Elizabeth Barrett Browning: *Aurora Leigh*

THANKFULNESS

Some hae meat and canna eat,
And some wad eat that want it;
But we hae meat, and we can eat,
And sae the Lord be thankit.

Robert Burns: *The Selkirk Grace*

The people wait at the haven's gate to greet
  the men who win!
Thank God for peace! Thank God for peace,
  when the great gray ships come in!

Guy Wetmore Carryl: *When the Great Gray Ships Come In,* st. 4

A thankful heart is not only the greatest virtue, but the parent of all other virtues.

Cicero: *Oratio Pro Cnaeo Plancio,* XXXIII

John Henry Jowett said: "Gratitude is a vaccine, an antitoxin, and an antiseptic." This is a most searching and true diagnosis. Gratitude can be a vaccine that can prevent the invasion of a disgruntled attitude. As antitoxins prevent the disastrous effects of certain poisons and diseases, Thanksgiving destroys the poison of faultfinding and grumbling. When trouble has smitten us, a spirit of thanksgiving is a soothing antiseptic.

Clinton C. Cox: *The Upper Room Pulpit,* November, 1952, Vol. 10, no. 2

As we offer our small rejoicing
  For the love that surrounds our days,
All the wonderful works of Thy goodness
  Shall open before our gaze;
Through the gates of our narrow thanksgiving
  We shall enter Thy courts of praise.

Annie Johnson Flint

Many favors which God gives us ravel out for want of hemming through our unthankfulness; for, though prayer purchases blessings, giving praise keeps the quiet possession of them.

Thomas Fuller

The finest test of character is seen in the amount and the power of gratitude we have.

Milo H. Gates

439

Thanksgiving for a former, doth invite God to bestow a second benefit.

Robert Herrick: *Noble Numbers*

An easy thing, O Power Divine,
To thank Thee for these gifts of Thine,
For summer's sunshine, winter's snow,
For hearts that kindle, thoughts that glow;
But when shall I attain to this—
To thank Thee for the things I miss?

Thomas Wentworth Higginson: *The Things I Miss*

I don't think the Lord wants any pompous proclamation of thanks on one Thursday in November as much as He wants a little humble service from us every day in the year.

Burton Hillis: *Better Homes and Gardens,* © Meredith Publishing Company

Lord, for the erring thought
Not into evil wrought:
Lord, for the wicked will
Betrayed and baffled still:
For the heart from itself kept,
Our thanksgiving accept.

William Dean Howells: *Thanksgiving*

Rest and be thankful.

Inscription on stone seat in the Scottish Highlands; title of one of Wordsworth's poems

If you have good health, unimpaired eyesight, clear mental faculties and full use of all your limbs, you have the four greatest causes of thankfulness in this world. These are four great corner-stone blessings.

I. Q. M.

Gratitude is born in hearts that take time to count up past mercies.

Charles E. Jefferson

Life without thankfulness is devoid of love and passion. Hope without thankfulness is lacking in fine perception. Faith without thankfulness lacks strength and fortitude. Every virtue divorced from thankfulness is maimed and limps along the spiritual road.

John Henry Jowett

Thanksgiving was never meant to be shut up in a single day.

Robert Caspar Lintner

Thanksgiving is nothing if not a glad and reverent lifting of the heart to God in honour and praise for His goodness.

James R. Miller

In every thing give thanks.

New Testament: I Thessalonians 5: 18

Count your blessings,
Name them one by one;
Count your blessings,
See what God hath done.

J. Oatman, Jr.

It is a good thing to give thanks unto the Lord.

Old Testament: Psalms 92: 1

Enter into his gates with thanksgiving, and into his courts with praise.

Old Testament: Psalms 100: 4

O give thanks unto the Lord, for he is good: for his mercy endureth for ever.

Old Testament: Psalms 107: 1

The worship most acceptable to God comes from a thankful and cheerful heart.

Plutarch

"Before theology comes doxology." John Baillie thinks thankfulness is the germ of religious response. The very fact that a man is thankful implies Someone to be thankful to.

Eliot Porter. From *Forward,* 1937, copyright 1937, by the Presbyterian Board of Christian Education, U.S.A. Used by permission

Were there no God, we would be in this glorious world with grateful hearts: and no one to thank.

Christina Georgina Rossetti

Wouldst thou first pause to thank thy God
for every pleasure, for mourning over griefs
thou wouldst not find the leisure.

Friedrich Ruckert

O Lord, that lends me life, lend me a heart
replete with thankfulness.

William Shakespeare: *Henry VI, Part II,*
Act I, sc. 1, l. 20

Let never day nor night unhallow'd pass,
But still remember what the Lord hath done.

William Shakespeare: *Henry VI, Part II,*
Act II, sc. 1, l. 85

Shakespeare called thanks "the exchequer of
the poor." Let us thank God that He has
made it possible for us to give something
back to Him.

William C. Skeath: *Today,* copyright
1942, The Westminster Press

From too much love of living,
From hope and fear set free,
We thank with brief thanksgiving
Whatever gods may be
That no life lives forever;
That dead men rise up never;
That even the weariest river
Winds somewhere safe to sea.

Algernon Charles Swinburne: *The
Garden of Proserpine,* st. 11

The private and personal blessings we enjoy,
the blessings of immunity, safeguard, liberty,
and integrity, deserve the thanksgiving of a
whole life.

Jeremy Taylor

Be thankful for the least gift, so shalt thou
be meet to receive greater.

Thomas à Kempis

In thankfulness for present mercies nothing
so becomes us as losing sight of past ills.

Lew Wallace: *Ben Hur*

Now thank we all our God,
With heart and hand and voices
Who wondrous things hath done,
In whom His world rejoices.

Catherine Winkworth: Tr. of Johann
Crüger: *Nun danket alle Gott*

THEOLOGY

A blind man in a dark room searching for a
black cat which isn't there—and finding it.

Anonymous

All my theology is reduced to this narrow
compass, "Jesus Christ came into the world
to save sinners."

Archibald Alexander

Theology is but the science of mind applied
to God. As schools change, theology must
necessarily change. Truth is everlasting, but
our ideas of truth are not. Theology is but
our ideas of truth classified and arranged.

Henry Ward Beecher

The post-obits of theology.

George Gordon, Lord Byron: *Don Juan,* I

A theology at war with the laws of physical
nature would be a battle of no doubtful
issue. The laws of our spiritual nature give
still less chance of success to the system which
would thwart or stay them.

William Ellery Channing

None but a theology that came out of eternity
can carry you and me safely to and through
eternity.

Theodore Ledyard Cuyler

I have only a small flickering light to guide
me in the darkness of a thick forest. Up comes
a theologian and blows it out.

Denis Diderot

The broad ethics of Jesus were quickly nar-
rowed to village theologies.

Ralph Waldo Emerson: *Conduct of Life:
Fate*

The cure for false theology is mother-wit.

Ralph Waldo Emerson: *Conduct of Life:
Worship*

The theological problems of original sin,
origin of evil, predestination, and the like
are the soul's mumps, and measles, and
whooping-coughs.

Ralph Waldo Emerson: *Spiritual Laws*

Theology is anthropology.

Ludwig Andreas Feuerbach: *Das Wesen des Christenthums*

Sacrifice is the first element of religion, and resolves itself in theological language into the love of God.

James Anthony Froude: *Short Studies on Great Subjects: Sea Studies*

We can no more have exact religious thinking without theology, than exact mensuration and astronomy without mathematics, or exact iron-making without chemistry.

John Hall

The theological systems of men and schools are always determined by the character of their ideal of Christ, the great central fact of the Christian system.

Josiah Gilbert Holland

In theology we must consider the predominance of authority; in philosophy the predominance of reason.

Johannes Kepler: *Astronomia nova*

Theology should be empress, and philosophy and the other arts merely her servants.

Martin Luther: *Table Talk*

It is taught by demons, it teaches about demons, and it leads to demons.

Albertus Magnus

To be still searching what we know not by what we know still closing up truth to truth as we find it (for all her body is homogeneal and proportional), this is the golden rule in theology as well as in arithmetic, and makes up the best harmony in a church.

John Milton: *Areopagitica*

The best theology is rather a divine life than a divine knowledge.

Jeremy Taylor

We live in a time when theology has been able to attract so many virile minds that even those who have tried to ignore theology are beginning to find it difficult to maintain their pose.

D. Elton Trueblood

TIME

What time is it?
Time to do well,
Time to live better,
Give up that grudge,
Answer that letter,
Speak the kind word to sweeten a sorrow,
Do that kind deed you would leave 'till tomorrow.

Anonymous: *What Time Is It?*

Time is an education for eternity.

Anonymous

Take time to work—it is the price of success;
Take time to think—it is the source of power;
Take time to play—it is the secret of perpetual youth;
Take time to read—it is the foundation of wisdom;
Take time to worship—it is the highway to reverence;
Take time to be friendly—it is the road to happiness;
Take time to dream—it is hitching our wagon to a star;
Take time to love and be loved—it is the privilege of the gods.

Anonymous

Live full today, and let no pleasure pass untasted—
And no transient beauty scorn;
Fill well the storehouse of the soul's delight
With light of memory—
Who knows? Tomorrow may be—Night.

Anonymous

We have to live but one day at a time, but we are living for eternity in that one day.

Anonymous

I have only just a minute,
Only sixty seconds in it.
Forced upon me—can't refuse it.

But it's up to me to use it.
I must suffer if I lose it.
Give account if I abuse it.
Just a tiny little minute,
But eternity is in it.

Anonymous

Our time is a very shadow that passeth away.

Apocrypha: Wisdom of Solomon 2: 5

God is perpetually pouring his soul through time and space though but few know it. Not one man in a thousand ever understands a great nature in his own age. We see this on the human plane; and how much more should we expect to see it in the divine sphere!

Henry Ward Beecher

Eternity is in love with the productions of time.

William Blake

He said, "What's time? Leave Now for dogs and apes!
Man has Forever."

Robert Browning: *A Grammarian's Funeral*

Fool! All that is, at all,
Last ever, past recall;
Earth changes, but thy soul and God stand sure:
What entered into thee,
That was, is, and shall be:
Time's wheel runs back nor stops: Potter and clay endure.

Robert Browning: *Rabbi Ben Ezra*, st. 27

Time is the only purgatory.

Samuel Butler: *Note-Books*

Time is a great physician.

Benjamin Disraeli

Time goes, you say? Ah no!
Alas, Time stays, *we* go.

Henry Austin Dobson: "The Paradox of Time," from *The Complete Poetical Works of Austin Dobson*, Oxford University Press

All my possessions for a moment of time.

Last Words of Queen Elizabeth I

God had infinite time to give us; but how did He give it? In one immense tract of a lazy millenium? No, but He cut it up into a neat succession of new mornings, and, with each, therefore, a new idea, new inventions, and new applications.

Ralph Waldo Emerson

The surest method of arriving at a knowledge of God's eternal purposes about us is to be found in the right use of the present moment. Each hour comes with some little fagot of God's will fastened upon its back.

Frederick William Faber

God, who is liberal in all his other gifts, shows us, by the wise economy of his providence, how circumspect we ought to be in the management of our time, for he never gives us two moments together.

François de Salignac de La Mothe Fénelon

Time is the father of truth.

John Florio: *First Frutes*

Who hath time hath life.

Ibid.

The time God allots to each one of us is like a precious tissue which we embroider as we best know how.

Anatole France: *The Crime of Sylvestre Bonnard*

Time trieth truth in every doubt.

John Heywood: *Proverbs*, Pt. II, ch. 5

Time is a child of eternity, and resembles its parent as much as it can.

William R. Inge: in Marchant's *Wit and Wisdom of Dean Inge*, Longmans Green & Co., Ltd., London

God has commanded Time to console the unhappy.

Joseph Joubert

443

The great rule of moral conduct is, next to God, to respect time.

Johann Kaspar Lavater

Time worketh, let me work too;
Time undoeth; let me do;
Busy as time my work I'll ply
Till I rest in the rest of eternity.

Roland Leavell

Lives of great men all remind us
We can make our lives sublime,
And, departing, leave behind us
Footprints on the sands of time.

Henry Wadsworth Longfellow: *A Psalm of Life*

What is time? The shadow on the dial, the striking of the clock, the running of the sand, day and night, summer and winter, months, years, centuries—these are but arbitrary and outward signs, the measure of Time, not Time itself. Time is the Life of the soul.

Henry Wadsworth Longfellow: *Hyperion,* Bk. II, ch. 6

No man ever sank under the burden of the day. It is when tomorrow's burden is added to the burden of today that the weight is more than a man can bear. Never load yourself so. If you find yourself so loaded, at least remember this: it is your own doing, not God's. He begs you to leave the future to Him, and mind the present.

George Macdonald

Time is Eternity begun.

James Montgomery: *A Mother's Love,* st. 8

Let the year be given to God in its every moment! The year is made up of minutes: let these be watched as having been dedicated to God! It is in the sanctification of the small that hallowing of the large is secure.

G. Campbell Morgan

Go, sir, gallop, and don't forget that the world was made in six days. You can ask me for anything you like, except time.

Napoleon Bonaparte to an aide

Can ye not discern the signs of the times?

New Testament: Matthew 16: 3

A thousand years in thy sight are but as yesterday when it is past, and as a watch in the night.

Old Testament: Psalms 90: 4

To every thing there is a season, and a time to every purpose under the heaven.

Old Testament: Ecclesiastes 3: 1

There is . . . a time to be born, and a time to die; a time to plant, and a time to pluck up that which is planted; A time to kill, and a time to heal; a time to break down, and a time to build up; A time to weep, and a time to laugh; a time to mourn, and a time to dance. . . . A time to love, and a time to hate.

Old Testament: Ecclesiastes 3: 1–8

O Time! whose verdicts mock our own,
The only righteous judge art thou!

Thomas William Parsons: *On a Bust of Dante*

Time is the image of eternity.

Plato

See how time makes all grief decay.

Adelaide Ann Procter: *Life in Death*

Time is the soul of the world.

Pythagoras, in Plutarch: *Platonic Questions*, VIII, 4

There is a time to be born, and a time to die, says Solomon, and it is the memento of a truly wise man; but there is an interval between these two times of infinite importance.

Legh Richmond

God created time and gave it to us. It is his fundamental gift, for all other gifts are conditioned upon it. Why should we give it so grudgingly to his service? Why should we not lavish time upon the things that God knows and we know are the vital things?

E. A. Rountree: *Watchman-Examiner*

Time consecrates;
What is grey with age becomes religion.

Johann Christoph Friedrich von Schiller: *Die Piccolomini*, Act IV, sc. 4

Time is man's angel.

Johann Christoph Friedrich von Schiller: *Theklas Monolog*, V, 11

Time and tide wait for no man.

Sir Walter Scott: *Fortunes of Nigel*, ch. 26

Time discovers the truth.

Seneca: *De Ira*, XI

Old Time the clock-setter, that bald sexton Time.

William Shakespeare: *King John*, Act III, sc. 1, l. 324

Time is the nurse and breeder of all good.

William Shakespeare: *The Two Gentlemen of Verona*, Act III, sc. 1, l. 244

As fast as they are made, forgot as soon As done.

William Shakespeare: *Troilus and Cressida*, Act III, sc. 3, l. 149

Time is a gentle deity.

Sophocles: *Electra*, l. 179

The angels in Heaven do not know what time is, for in Heaven there are no days and years, but only changes of state.

Emanuel Swedenborg: *Arcana Coelestia*

No preacher is listened to but time, which gives us the same train and turn of thought that elder people have in vain tried to put into our heads before.

Jonathan Swift: *Thoughts on Various Subjects*

I dimly guess what Time in mists confounds;
Yet ever and anon a trumpet sounds
From the hid battlements of Eternity;
Those shaken mists a space unsettle, then
Round the half-glimpsed turrets slowly wash
    again.

Francis Thompson: *The Hound of Heaven*, l. 143

You cannot kill time without injuring eternity.

Henry David Thoreau

Time is our destiny. Time is our hope. Time is our despair. And time is the mirror in which we see eternity. Let me point to three of the many mysteries of time: its power to devour anything within its sphere; its power to receive eternity within itself; and its power to drive toward an ultimate end, a new creation.

Paul Tillich: *The Shaking of the Foundations*. Charles Scribner's Sons, 1948

Time is infinite movement without one moment of rest.

Leo Tolstoy: *War and Peace: Epilogue*, Pt. II, ch. 10

Wait, thou child of hope, for Time shall teach thee all things.

Martin Farquhar Tupper: *Of Good in Things Evil*

To the philosopher, time is one of the fundamental quantities. To the average man, time has something to do with dinner.

J. A. VanHorn: *Physics Today*

God's ways seem dark, but, soon or late,
    They touch the shining hills of day;
    The evil cannot brook delay,
The good can well afford to wait.
    Give ermined knaves their hour of crime;
    Yet have the future grand and great,
    The safe appeal of Truth to Time.

John Greenleaf Whittier: *For Righteousness' Sake*

445

TRINITY

Now the Catholic faith is this: that we worship one God in Trinity, and Trinity in Unity, neither confounding the Persons, nor dividing the substance, for there is one Person of the Father, another of the Son, and another of the Holy Ghost; but the godhead of the Father, of the Son, and of the Holy Ghost is one, the glory equal, the majesty co-eternal . . .

Athanasian Creed

The Trinity is one God, not so that the Father be the same Person, who is also the Son and the Holy Ghost; but that the Father be the Father, and the Son be the Son, and the Holy Ghost be the Holy Ghost, and this Trinity One God.

St. Augustine: *Of the Faith and of the Creed*

I believe in the Father, the Son, and the Holy Ghost, as three distinct Persons: but I believe that above our knowledge there is a point of coincidence and unity between them. What it is I do not know. That is the unrevealed part.

Henry Ward Beecher: *Royal Truths*

Snow is water, and ice is water, and water is water, these three are one.

Joseph Dare

Holy, Holy, Holy! Merciful and Mighty!
God in Three Persons, blessed Trinity!

Reginald Heber: *Holy, Holy, Holy*

The three persons in the Godhead are three in one sense and one in another. We cannot tell how—and that is the mystery.

Samuel Johnson, in *Boswell's Tour to the Hebrides*

The three Persons of the Blessed Trinity are one and the same God, having one and the same divine nature, or substance.

John McCaffrey: *A Catechism of Christian Doctrine for General Use*

There are three that bear record in heaven, the Father, the Word, and the Holy Ghost: and these three are one.

New Testament: I John 5: 7

Tell me how it is that in this room there are three candles and but one light, and I will explain to you the mode of the divine existence.

John Wesley

TROUBLE

A great many people are always ready to pray when the devil gets them into trouble; but when they get out of trouble they soon forget God.

Anonymous

The lions never get out of the road of the man who waits to see the way clear before he starts.

Anonymous

Whenever God gives us a cross to bear, it is a prophecy that He will also give us strength.

Anonymous

Nations and men are much alike. They seldom appeal to God unless they are getting licked.

Baltimore *Sun*

Troubles are often the tools by which God fashions us for better things.

Henry Ward Beecher

There are many troubles which you cannot cure by the Bible and the hymn book, but which you can cure by a good perspiration and a breath of fresh air.

Henry Ward Beecher

I see not a step before me as I tread on another year;
But I've left the Past in God's keeping,—the Future His mercy shall clear;
And what looks dark in the distance may brighten as I draw near.

Mary Gardiner Brainard: *Not Knowing*

The eternal stars shine out as soon as it is dark enough.

Thomas Carlyle

Deep is the plowing of grief! But often-times less would not suffice for the agriculture of God.

Thomas DeQuincey

It is a pity that our tears on account of our troubles should so blind our eyes that we should not see our mercies.

John Flavel

Life is mostly froth and bubble;
Two things stand like stone:
Kindness in another's trouble
Courage in our own.

Adam Lindsay Gordon: *Ye Weary Way-farer. Finis Exoptatus*

If the sun of God's countenance shine upon me, I may well be content to be wet with the rain of affliction.

Joseph Hall

Prosperity is a great teacher: adversity is a greater. Possession pampers the mind; privation trains and strengthens it.

William Hazlitt

When troubles come from God, then naught behoves like patience; but for troubles wrought of men, patience is hard—I tell you it is hard.

Jean Ingelow

The Christian under trouble doesn't break up—he breaks out.

E. Stanley Jones: *The Way*, p. 235, Abingdon Press

Sure the world is full of trouble, but as long as we have people undoing trouble we have a pretty good world.

Helen Keller

If trouble comes, it'll keep our religion from getting rusty. That's the great thing about persecution; it keeps you up to the mark. It's habit, not hatred, that is the real enemy of the church of God.

Charles T. Leber: *Is God There?*

The whole trouble is that we won't let God help us.

George Macdonald: *The Marquis of Lossie*, ch. 27

God's darkest threatenings are always accompanied with a revelation of the way of escape. The ark is always along with the flood. Zoar is pointed out when God foretells Sodom's ruin. The brazen serpent is ever reared where the venomous snakes bite and burn.

Alexander MacLaren

Nobody knows the trouble I've seen,
Nobody knows but Jesus.

Negro Spiritual

Let not your heart be troubled.

New Testament: John 14: 1

Man is born unto trouble, as the sparks fly upward.

Old Testament: Job 5: 7

Man that is born of a woman is of few days, and full of trouble.

Old Testament: Job 14: 1

Blessed is he that considereth the poor: the Lord will deliver him in time of trouble.

Old Testament: Psalms 41: 1

It is distrust of God, to be troubled about what is to come; impatience against God, to be troubled with what is present; and anger at God, to be troubled for what is past.

Simon Patrick

Of our troubles we must seek some other cause than God.

Plato: *The Republic*, Bk. II, sec. 19

Trouble knocked at the door, but hearing a laugh within hurried away.

Poor Richard, Jr.

Why should I tremble at the plough of my Lord, that maketh deep furrows on my soul? I know He is no idle husbandman, He purposeth a crop.

Samuel Rutherford

447

Now, God be prais'd, that to believing souls
Gives light in darkness, comfort in despair!
William Shakespeare: *Henry VI, Part II,*
Act II, sc. 1, l. 66

Trouble . . . Why do we fear it? Why do we
dread ordeal? Every good thing the human
race has experienced was trouble for somebody. Our birth was trouble for our mothers.
To support us was trouble for our fathers.
Books, paintings, music, great buildings,
good food, ideas, the nameless joys and ex-
citements which added up to what we call
"a good life" came out of the travail of countless hearts and minds.
Lillian Smith: *Now Is the Time*

If you tell your troubles to God, you put
them into the grave; they will never rise
again, when you have committed them to
Him. If you roll your burden anywhere else,
it will roll back again, like the stone of
Sisyphus.
Charles Haddon Spurgeon

Every time trouble comes, consider that
through it the Lord is giving you a needed
lesson.
Paramahansa Yogananda: *Self-*
Realization Magazine

TRUST

You may trust the Lord too little, but you
can never trust Him too much.
Anonymous

Beware of despairing about yourself: you are
commanded to put your trust in God, and
not in yourself.
St. Augustine

Trust begets truth.
Sir William Gurney Benham: *Proverbs,*
p. 748

We trust as we love, and where we love.—If
we love Christ much, surely we shall trust
Him much.
Thomas Benton Brooks

There is but one way to browbeat this world,
Dumb-founder doubt, and repay scorn in
kind,—
To go on trusting, namely, till faith move
Mountains.
Robert Browning: *The Ring and the*
Book

. . . . . sustained and soothed
By an unfaltering trust, approach thy grave,
Like one that wraps the drapery of his couch
About him, and lies down to pleasant
dreams.
William Cullen Bryant: *Thanatopsis*

Trust God for great things; with your five
loaves and two fishes, He will show you a
way to feed thousands.
Horace Bushnell

Build a little fence of trust
    Around to-day;
Fill the space with loving work,
    And therein stay;
Look not through the sheltering bars
    Upon to-morrow;
God will help thee bear what comes
    Of joy or sorrow.
Mary Frances Butts: *Trust*

Trust in God, and keep your powder dry.
Oliver Cromwell

A little trust that when we die
We reap our sowing, and so—Good-bye.
George Busson DuMaurier: *Trilby*

All I have seen teaches me to trust the
Creator for all I have not seen.
Ralph Waldo Emerson

God has delivered yourself to your care, and
says: "I had no fitter to trust than you."
Epictetus

To trust God when we have securities in our
iron chest is easy, but not thankworthy; but
to depend on Him for what we cannot see,
as it is more hard for man to do, so it is more
acceptable to God.
Owen Feltham

An undivided heart, which worships God alone, and trusts Him as it should, is raised above all anxiety for earthly wants.

John Cunningham Geikie

God provides for him that trusteth.

George Herbert: *Outlandish Proverbs*

Cast the spear and leave the rest to Jove.

Homer: *Iliad*, Bk. XVII, l. 622

From whom I trust may God defend me;
From whom I trust not, I defend myself.

Italian Proverb

Trusting in Him who can go with me and remain with you, and be everywhere for good, let us confidently hope that all will yet be well.

Abraham Lincoln

O holy trust! O endless sense of rest!
  Like the beloved John
To lay his head upon the Saviour's breast,
  And thus to journey on!

Henry Wadsworth Longfellow: *Hymn*, st. 5

Trust God where you cannot trace Him. Do not try to penetrate the cloud He brings over you; rather look to the bow that is on it. The mystery is God's; the promise is yours.

John Macduff

Courage, brother! do not stumble,
  Though thy path be dark as night;
There's a star to guide the humble;
  Trust in God and do the Right.

Norman Macleod: *Trust in God*, st. 1

The things which must be, must be for the best,
God helps us do our duty and not shrink,
And trust His mercy humbly for the rest.

Owen Meredith: *Imperfections*

Trust . . . in the living God.

New Testament: I Timothy 6: 17

Though he slay me, yet will I trust in him.

Old Testament: Job 13: 15

God is our refuge and strength, a very present help in trouble. Therefore will not we fear, though the earth be removed, and though the mountains be carried into the midst of the sea.

Old Testament: Psalms 46: 1, 2

In God have I put my trust: I will not be afraid what man can do unto me.

Old Testament: Psalms 56: 11

Trust in him at all times; ye people, pour out your heart before him: God is a refuge for us.

Old Testament: Psalms 62: 8

Put not your trust in princes.

Old Testament: Psalms 146: 3

Thou trustest in the staff of this broken reed.

Old Testament: Isaiah 36: 6

Trust, like the soul, never returns, once it is gone.

Publilius Syrus: *Sententiae*

Trust in God does not supersede the employment of prudent means on our part. To expect God's protection while we do nothing is not to honor but to tempt providence.

Pasquier Quesnel

How calmly may we commit ourselves to the hands of Him who bears up the world.

Jean Paul Richter

I have never committed the least matter to God, that I have not had reason for infinite praise.

Anna Shipton

When you have no helpers, see all your helpers in God. When you have many helpers, see God in all your helpers. When you have nothing but God, see all in God; when you have everything, see God in everything. Under all conditions, stay thy heart only on the Lord.

Charles Haddon Spurgeon

449

Behold, we know not anything;
  I can but trust that good shall fall
At last—far off—at last, to all,
And every winter change to spring.

Alfred, Lord Tennyson: *In Memoriam,*
LIV

Don't try to hold God's hand; let Him hold
yours. Let Him do the holding, and you the
trusting.

Hammer William Webb-Peploe

And I will trust that He who heeds
  The life that hides in mead and wold,
Who hangs yon alder's crimson beads,
  And stains these mosses green and gold,
Will still, as He hath done, incline
His gracious care to me and thine.

John Greenleaf Whittier: *Last Walk in*
Autumn, st. 26

TRUTH

What a shaking thing
The truth can be,
Especially when found
On the family tree.

Anonymous

Truth does not consist in minute accuracy of
detail, but in conveying a right impression;
and there are vague ways of speaking that are
truer than strict facts would be. When the
Psalmist said, "Rivers of water run down
mine eyes, because men keep not thy law,"
he did not state the fact, but he stated a truth
deeper than fact, and truer.

Henry Alford

To hate truth as truth . . . is the same as to
hate goodness for its own sake.

Ethan Allen: *Reason the Only Oracle of*
Man, I

Truth is the disciple of the ascetic, the quest
of the mystic, the faith of the simple, the
ransom of the weak, the standard of the
righteous, the doctrine of the meek, and the
challenge of Nature. Together, all these constitute the Law of the Universe.

John Hay Allison

Pilate asked, *Quid est veritas?* And then some
other matter took him in the head, and so
up he rose and went his way before he had
his answer.

Lancelot Andrewes: *Sermons: Of the*
Resurrection

Above all things truth beareth away the
victory.

Apocrypha: I Esdras 3: 12

Christianity knows no truth which is not the
child of love and the parent of duty.

Phillips Brooks

To hear truth and not accept it does not
nullify truth.

Brotherhood Journal

For truth is precious and divine—
Too rich a pearl for carnal swine.

Samuel Butler: *Hudibras,* Canto II, l. 257

No words suffice the secret soul to show,
For Truth denies all eloquence to Woe.

George Gordon, Lord Byron: *Corsair,*
Canto III, st. 22

Truth! though the Heavens crush me for
following her.

Thomas Carlyle: *Sartor Resartus,* II

Every man seeks for truth, but God only
knows who has found it.

Philip Dormer Stanhope, Lord
Chesterfield: *Letters*

We live in the present, we dream of the
future, but we learn eternal truths from the
past.

Madame Chiang Kai-shek

Truth is incontrovertible. Panic may resent
it; ignorance may deride it; malice may distort it; but there it is.

Sir Winston Churchill, quoted in
Information

It fortifies my soul to know
That, though I perish, Truth is so.

Arthur Hugh Clough: *With Whom Is No Variableness*

The greatest friend of truth is Time, her greatest enemy is Prejudice, and her constant companion is Humility.

Charles Caleb Colton: *Lacon*

God has revealed many truths which He has not explained. We will just have to be content to let Him know some things we do not and take Him at His word.

B. A. Copass

All truth is precious, if not all divine.

William Cowper: *Charity*, l. 331

But what is truth? 'Twas Pilate's question, put
To Truth itself, that deign'd him no reply.

William Cowper: *The Task*, Bk. III, l. 270

What we have in us of the image of God is the love of truth and justice.

Demosthenes

In religion the truth shines ahead as a beacon showing us the path; we do not ask to attain it, it is better far that we be permitted to seek.

Sir Arthur Stanley Eddington: *Science and the Unseen World*, Allen and Unwin, London

Much of the glory and sublimity of truth is connected with its mystery. To understand everything we must be as God.

Tryon Edwards

God offers to every mind its choice between truth and repose. Take which you please—you can never have both.

Ralph Waldo Emerson: *Intellect*

Hark! Hark! my soul, angelic songs are swelling
O'er earth's green fields, and ocean's wave-beat shore;

How sweet the truth those blessed strains are telling
Of that new life when sin shall be no more!

Frederick William Faber: *Pilgrims of the Night*

One of the deep guilts in our present civilization is the bad conscience so many people have about the truth.

James T. Farrell: *The Writer and His Conscience, Humanist*, Vol. XVIII, no. 3

Truth makes the Devil blush.

Thomas Fuller: *Gnomologia*

In proportion as we perceive and embrace the truth we do become just, heroic, magnanimous, divine.

William Lloyd Garrison: *Free Speech and Free Inquiry*

The grave of one who dies for the truth is holy ground.

German Proverb

And fierce though the fiends may fight, and long though the angels hide,
I know that truth and right have the universe on their side.

Washington Gladden: *Ultima Veritas*

The devil sometimes speaks the truth.

Henry Glapthorne: *Lady Mother*, Act I, sc. 3

If you tell the truth, you have infinite power supporting you; but if not, you have infinite power against you.

General Charles ("Chinese") Gordon

The name of God is Truth.

Hindu Proverb

Religious truth, touch what points of it you will, has always to do with the being and government of God, and is, of course, illimitable in its reach.

Roswell Dwight Hitchcock

No one truth is rightly held till it is clearly conceived and stated, and no single truth is adequately comprehended till it is viewed in harmonious relations to all the other truths of the system of which Christ is the centre.

Archibald Alexander Hodge

Wrong rules the land and waiting Justice sleeps.

Josiah Gilbert Holland: *Wanted*

If you find truth anywhere in the world, seize upon it, for real truth cannot contradict the Bible.

W. Douglas Hudgins

History warns us that it is the customary fate of new truths to begin as heresies and to end as superstitions.

Thomas Henry Huxley: *Science and Culture: Origin of Species*

The man who finds a truth lights a torch.

Robert Green Ingersoll: *The Truth*

Truth is man's proper good, and the only immortal thing was given to our immortality to use.

Ben Jonson: *Explorata: Veritas Proprium Hominis*

It takes few words to tell the truth.

Chief Joseph of the Nez Percé

Gradually I came to see that I could use the Bible, which had so baffled me, as an instrument for digging out precious truths, just as I could use my hindered, halting body for the high behests of my spirit.

Helen Keller

When all treasures are tried, Truth is the best . . .
For he who is True with his tongue, True with his hands
Working True works therewith, and wishing ill to none,
He is a god, the gospel says, in earth and heaven.

William Langland: *Piers Plowman*, Pt. II

But there are seven sisters ever serving Truth,
Porters of the Posterns; one called Abstinence,
Humility, Charity, Chastity be the chief maidens there;
Patience and Peace help many a one;
Lady Almsgiving lets in full many.

William Langland: *Piers Plowman*, Pt. VIII

Reason teaches that the truths of divine revelation and those of nature cannot really be opposed to one another, and that whatever is at variance with them must necessarily be false.

Pope Leo XIII: *Libertas praestantissimum*

If God should hold enclosed in his right hand all truth, and in his left hand only the ever-active impulse after truth, although with the condition that I must always and forever err, I would with humility turn to his left hand and say, "Father, give me this: pure truth is for thee alone."

Gotthold Ephraim Lessing: *Anti-Götze*

Who dares
To say that he alone has found the truth?

Henry Wadsworth Longfellow: *John Endicott*, Act II, sc. 3

Once to every man and nation comes the moment to decide
In the strife of Truth with Falsehood, for the good or evil side.

James Russell Lowell: *The Present Crisis*, st. 5

Truth forever on the scaffold, Wrong forever on the throne.

James Russell Lowell: *The Present Crisis*, st. 8

Then to side with Truth is noble when we share her wretched crust,
Ere her cause bring fame and profit, and 'tis prosperous to be just;
Then it is the brave man chooses, while the coward stand aside,

Doubting in his abject spirit, till his Lord
is crucified.

James Russell Lowell: *The Present Crisis,*
st. 11

They must upward still, and onward, who
would keep abreast of Truth.

James Russell Lowell: *The Present Crisis,*
st. 18

Peace if possible, but truth at any rate.

Martin Luther

Superstition, idolatry, and hypocrisy have
ample wages, but truth goes a begging.

Martin Luther: *Table Talk*

Truth is a divine word. Duty is a divine law.

Douglas Clyde Macintosh

Keep one thing forever in view—the truth;
and if you do this, though it may seem to
lead you away from the opinion of men, it
will assuredly conduct you to the throne of
God.

Horace Mann

A judicious silence is always better than
truth spoken without charity.

Philip Mann: *York Trade Compositor*

Truth is the capital that finances expeditions
into the lofty mountains of character and
across the river of eternity.

Douglas Meador: Matador (Texas)
Tribune

Servant of God, well done! well hast thou
fought
The better fight, who single hast maintain'd
Against revolted multitudes the cause
Of truth.

John Milton: *Paradise Lost,* Bk. VI, l. 29

We are born to inquire after truth; it belongs
to a greater power to possess it. It is not, as
Democritus said, hid in the bottom of the
deeps, but rather elevated to an infinite
height in the divine knowledge.

Michel Eyquem de Montaigne: *Essays,*
Bk. III, ch. 8, "Of the Art of
Conversation"

Ye shall know the truth, and the truth shall
make you free.

New Testament: John 8: 32

When he, the Spirit of truth, is come, he will
guide you into all truth.

New Testament: John 16: 13

Wherefore putting away lying, speak every
man truth with his neighbour.

New Testament: Ephesians 4: 25

I do not know what I may appear to the
world, but to myself I seem to have been
only like a boy playing on the seashore and
diverting myself in now and then finding
a smoother pebble or a prettier shell than
ordinary, whilst the great ocean of truth lay
all undiscovered before me.

Sir Isaac Newton

His truth shall be thy shield and buckler.

Old Testament: Psalms 91: 4

The lip of truth shall be established for ever:
but a lying tongue is but for a moment.

Old Testament: Proverbs 12: 19

Buy the truth, and sell it not.

Old Testament: Proverbs 23: 23

These are the things that ye shall do; Speak
ye every man the truth to his neighbour;
execute the judgment of truth and peace in
your gates.

Old Testament: Zechariah 8: 16

There are two peculiarities in the truths of
religion: a divine beauty which renders them
lovely, and a holy majesty which makes them
venerable. And there are two peculiarities in
errors: an impiety which renders them horrible, and an impertinence which renders
them ridiculous.

Blaise Pascal

Of all duties, the love of truth, with faith
and constancy in it, ranks first and highest.
To love God and to love truth are one and
the same.

Silvio Pellico

This coming to know Christ is what makes
Christian truth redemptive truth, the truth
that transforms, not just the truth that
informs. . . .

Harold Cooke Phillips

Christian truth, then is redemptive truth because it requires not simply knowledge about
something, but knowledge of someone. It is
personal.

Harold Cooke Phillips

Truth is one forever absolute, but opinion
is truth filtered through the moods, the
blood, the disposition of the spectator.

Wendell Phillips: *Idols*

God is truth and light his shadow.

Plato

Truth is the beginning of every good thing,
both in Heaven and on earth; and he who
would be blessed and happy should be from
the first a partaker of the truth, for then he
can be trusted.

Plato: *Laws*, IV

Truth is so great a perfection, that if God
would render himself visible to men, he
would choose light for his body and truth
for his soul.

Pythagoras

Speak the truth and shame the Devil.

François Rabelais: *Works*, Bk. V, Author's
Prologue

Truth is God's daughter.

John Ray: *English Proverbs*

Truth is given the eternal years of God because she needs them every one.

Thomas B. Reed: Speech at Bowdoin
College, Maine

Truth lies in character. Christ did not simply
speak the truth; he was Truth—Truth
through and through, for truth is a thing
not of words but a life and being.

Frederick William Robertson

It is not the number of books you read, nor
the variety of sermons you hear, nor the
amount of religious conversation in which
you mix, but it is the frequency and earnestness with which you meditate on these things
till the truth in them becomes your own and
part of your being, that ensures your growth.

Frederick William Robertson

It is the modest, not the presumptuous, in-
quirer who makes a real and safe progress
in the discovery of divine truths. One follows
Nature and Nature's God; that is, he follows
God in his works and in his word.

Henry St. John: *Letter to Mr. Pope*

The most emotionally mature person who
ever lived was Jesus, and all the great religions teach the same fundamental truths
which we psychiatrists try to drive home to
our patients—that life has meaning and
responsibilities, and that serving others is
as much a part of living as enjoying life's
good things.

Robert V. Seliger: "Why Don't I Ever Get
a Break?", *American Magazine*

To thine own self be true,
And it must follow, as the night the day,
Thou canst not then be false to any man.

William Shakespeare: *Hamlet*,
Act I, sc. 3, l. 78

What! can the devil speak true?

William Shakespeare: *Macbeth*,
Act I, sc. 3, l. 107

The truth is usually discreditable to all concerned, including God.

Spanish Proverb

A lie travels round the world while Truth
is putting on her boots.

Charles Haddon Spurgeon: *Truth and
Falsehood*

Truth in spirit, not truth to letter, is the true veracity.

Robert Louis Stevenson: *Truth of Intercourse*

So long as you believe in some truth you do not believe in yourself. You are a servant, a man of faith.

Max Stirner: *The Ego and His Own*

Truth without charity is often intolerant and even persecuting, as charity without truth is weak in concession and untrustworthy in judgment.—But charity, loyal to truth and rejoicing in it, has the wisdom of the serpent with the harmlessness of the dove.

Josua Swartz

When two truths seem to directly oppose each other, we must not question either, but remember there is a third—God—who reserves to himself the right to harmonize them.

Madam Anne Soymanov Swetchine

Truth is eternal, and the son of heaven.

Jonathan Swift: *Ode: Dr. Wm. Sancroft*

If the truth shall have made thee free, thou shalt not care for the vain words of men.

Thomas a Kempis: *Imitation of Christ,* Bk. III, ch. 4

The purpose of life is the quest for truth.

Daniel L. Thrapp: *The Choice of Truth*

For Truth makes holy Love's illusive dreams, And their best promise constantly redeems.

Henry Theodore Tuckerman: *Sonnets,* no. 22

Seize upon truth, wherever it is found, amongst your friends, amongst your foes, on Christian or on heathen ground; the flower's divine where'er it grows.

Isaac Watts

Everyone wishes to have truth on his side, but it is not everyone that sincerely wishes to be on the side of truth.

Richard Whately

But let the free-winged angel Truth their guarded passes scale,
To teach that right is more than might, and justice more than mail!

John Greenleaf Whittier: *Brown of Ossawatomie*

Falsehoods which we spurn to-day
Were the truths of long ago.

John Greenleaf Whittier: *Calef in Boston,* st. 4

God blesses still the generous thought, And still the fitting word He speeds, And Truth, at His requiring taught, He quickens into deeds.

John Greenleaf Whittier: *Channing,* st. 23

We search the world for truth. We cull
The good, the pure, the beautiful,
From graven stone and written scroll,
From all old flower-fields of the soul;
And, weary seekers of the best,
We come back laden from the quest,
To find that all the sages said
Is in the Book our mothers read.

John Greenleaf Whittier: *Miriam*

Truth is on the march and nothing can stop it.

Émile Zola: *J'Accuse*

U

UNBELIEF

They that deny a God destroy man's nobility; for certainly man is of kin to the beasts by his body; and if he be not of kin to God by his spirit, he is a base and ignoble creature.

Sir Francis Bacon: *Essays: Of Atheism*

Mock on, mock on, Voltaire, Rousseau;
Mock on, mock on; 'tis all in vain!
You throw the sand against the wind,
And the wind blows it back again.

William Blake: *Mock On*

In all unbelief there are these two things; a good opinion of one's self, and a bad opinion of God.

Horatius Bonar

All unbelief is the belief of a lie.

Horatius Bonar

Nobody talks so constantly about God as those who insist that there is no God.

Heywood Broun

"There is no God," the foolish saith,
But none, "There is no sorrow":
And nature oft the cry of faith
In bitter need will borrow.
Eyes, which the preacher could not school,
By wayside graves are raised;
And lips say, "God be pitiful,"
Who ne'er said, "God be praised."

Elizabeth Barrett Browning: *The Cry of
the Human*

All we have gained then by our unbelief
Is a life of doubt diversified by faith,
For one of faith diversified by doubt:

We called the chess-board white,—we call it black.

Robert Browning: *Bishop Blougram's
Apology*

Just when we're safest, there's a sunset-touch,
A fancy from a flower-bell, some one's death,
A chorus-ending from Euripides,—
And that's enough for fifty hopes and fears . . .
The grand Perhaps!

Ibid.

He who does not believe that God is above all is either a fool or has no experience of life.

Cæcilius Statius: *Fragments*, no. 15

There is but one thing without honor, smitten with eternal barrenness, inability to do or to be, and that is unbelief. He who believes nothing, who believes only the show of things, is not in relation with nature and fact at all.

Thomas Carlyle

The fearful Unbelief is unbelief in yourself.

Thomas Carlyle: *Sartor Resartus: The
Everlasting No*, Bk. II, ch. 7

There is no unbelief;
Whoever plants a seed beneath the sod
And waits to see it push away the clod,
He trusts in God.

There is no unbelief;
Whoever sees 'neath winter's field of snow
The silent harvest of the future grow—
God's power must know.

Lizzie York Case in Detroit *Free Press*

No man is an unbeliever, but because he will be so; and every man is not an unbeliever, because the grace of God conquers some, changes their wills, and binds them to Christ.

Stephen Charnock

Narrowness is the mother of unbelief. Obtain a broad outlook if you would agree with God in your philosophy and be able to transmit God's own thought into your life.

Joseph Cook

Blind unbelief is sure to err,
  And scan his work in vain;
God is his own interpreter,
  And he will make it plain.

William Cowper: *Light Shining Out of Darkness*

The wildest scorner of his Maker's laws
Finds in a sober moment time to pause.

William Cowper: *Tirocinium*, l. 55

Profound minds are the most likely to think lightly of the resources of human reason, and it is the superficial thinker who is generally strongest in every kind of unbelief.

Sir Humphrey Davy

Unbelief, in distinction from disbelief, is a confession of ignorance where honest inquiry might easily find the truth. "Agnostic" is but the Greek for "ignoramus."

Tryon Edwards

How deeply rooted must unbelief be in our hearts, when we are surprised to find our prayers answered, instead of feeling sure that they will be so, if they are only offered up in faith, and in accordance with the will of God!

Augustus William and Julius Charles Hare

The infidels of one age have been the aureoled saints of the next. The destroyers of the old are the creators of the new.

Robert Green Ingersoll: *The Great Infidels*

Fools! who fancy Christ mistaken;
  Man a tool to buy and sell;

Earth a failure, God-forsaken,
  Ante-room of Hell.

Charles Kingsley: *The World's Age*

Unbelief does nothing but darken and destroy. It makes the world a moral desert, where no divine footsteps are heard, where no angels ascend and descend, where no living hand adorns the fields, feeds the birds of heaven, or regulates events.

Friedrich Wilhelm Krummacher

If a man of sober habits, moderate, chaste, and just in all his dealings should assert there is no God, he would at least speak without interested motives; but such a man is not to be found.

Jean de La Bruyère: *Caractères*, XVI

In the blood of the martyrs to intolerance are the seeds of unbelief.

Walter Lippmann

God is not dumb, that He should speak no more;
If thou hast wanderings in the wilderness
And find'st not Sinai, 'tis thy soul is poor.

James Russell Lowell: *Bibliolatres*

Unbelief is criminal because it is a moral act, an act of the whole nature.—Belief or unbelief is a test of a man's whole spiritual condition, because it is the whole being, affections, will, conscience, as well as the understanding, which are concerned in it.

Alexander MacLaren

Unbelief is blind.

John Milton: *Comus*, l. 519

There are two things which I abhor: the learned in his infidelities, and the fool in his devotions.

Mohammed, in Emerson, *Conduct of Life: Worship*

You think you are too intelligent to believe in God.—I am not like you.—Not every one who wishes to be is an atheist.

Napoleon Bonaparte

Lord, I believe; help thou mine unbelief.

New Testament: Mark 9: 24

The fool hath said in his heart, There is no God.

Old Testament: Psalms 14: 1; 53: 1

Infidelity does not consist in believing or in disbelieving: it consists in professing to believe what one does not believe.

Thomas Paine: *Age of Reason,* Pt. I

Better that they had ne'er been born who read to doubt, or read to scorn.

Sir Walter Scott

No one is so thoroughly superstitious as the godless man. Life and death to him are haunted grounds, filled with goblin forms of vague and shadowy dread.

Harriet Beecher Stowe

What behaved well in the past or behaves well to-day is not such a wonder,
The wonder is always and always how there can be a mean man or an infidel.

Walt Whitman: *Song of Myself,* Pt. XXII, l. 28

UNDERSTANDING

I shall light a candle of understanding in thine heart, which shall not be put out.

Apocrypha: II Esdras 14: 25

Understanding is the reward of faith. Therefore seek not to understand that thou mayest believe, but believe that thou mayest understand.

St. Augustine: *On the Gospel of St. John*

Man is always inclined to be intolerant toward the thing, or person, he hasn't taken time adequately to understand, and consequently, you get quite inconceivable things cast into your teeth from people who don't understand.

Robert R. Brown

To understand everything is to forgive everything.

Gautama Buddha

The prayer that reforms the sinner and heals the sick is an absolute faith that all things are possible to God,—a spiritual understanding of Him, an unselfed love.

Mary Baker Eddy: *Science and Health with Key to the Scriptures,* p. 1: 1–4

Sometimes the church is unpopular because it understands our sin and righteousness too well, and because sometimes it points at us with the words, "Thou art the man."

Edward L. R. Elson: *America's Spiritual Recovery*

We adhere, as though to a raft, to those ideas which represent our understanding.

John Kenneth Galbraith: *The Affluent Society*

A doctrine that is understood is shorn of its strength.

Eric Hoffer

Let us have faith that right makes might; and in that faith let us to the end dare to do our duty as we understand it.

Abraham Lincoln

The ignorant man always adores what he cannot understand.

Cesare Lombroso: *The Man of Genius,* Part III, ch. 3

I do not understand; I pause; I examine.

Michel Eyquem de Montaigne: *Inscription for his Library*

When I was a child, I spake as a child, I understood as a child, I thought as a child: but when I became a man, I put away childish things.

New Testament: I Corinthians 13: 11

A wise and an understanding heart.

Old Testament: I Kings 3: 12

With the ancient is wisdom; and in length of days understanding.

Old Testament: Job 12: 12

I have more understanding than all my teachers: for thy testimonies are my meditation.

Old Testament: Psalms 119: 99

Thou First Great Cause, least understood.

Alexander Pope: Universal Prayer

If you would judge, understand.

Seneca: Medea

Great Spirit, help me never to judge another until I have walked two weeks in his moccasins.

Sioux Indian Prayer

I know of no evil so great as the abuse of the understanding and yet there is no one vice more common.

Sir Richard Steele

It is not the eye that sees the beauty of the heaven, nor the ear that hears the sweetness of music or the glad tidings of a prosperous occurrence, but the soul, that perceives all the relishes of sensual and intellectual perfections; and the more noble and excellent the soul is, the greater and more savory are its perceptions.

Jeremy Taylor

Flower in the crannied wall,
I pluck you out of the crannies,
I hold you here, root and all, in my hand,
Little flower—but if I could understand
What you are, root and all, and all in all,
I should know what God and man is.

Alfred, Lord Tennyson: Flower in the
Crannied Wall

Were the works of God readily understandable by human reason, they would be neither wonderful nor unspeakable.

Thomas à Kempis

UNIVERSE, THE

Ernest Haeckel, the great German philosopher, was asked what he thought was his most bothersome question. He said, "The question I would most like to have answered is, 'Is the universe friendly?'"

Anonymous

The universe is a single life comprising one substance and one soul.

Marcus Aurelius

One Universe made up of all things; and one God in it all, and one principle of Being, and one Law, one Reason, shared by all thinking creatures and one Truth.

Marcus Aurelius: Meditations, Bk. VII,
sec. 9

Of the "real" universe we know nothing, except that there exist as many versions of it as there are perceptive minds. Each man lives alone in his private universe.

Gerald Bullett: Dreaming

The whole universe is one commonwealth of which both gods and men are members.

Cicero: De Legibus, Bk. I, ch. 7, sec. 23

It is not impossible that to some infinitely superior being the whole universe may be as one plain, the distance between planet and planet being only as the pores in a grain of sand, and the spaces between system and system no greater than the intervals between one grain and the grain adjacent.

Samuel Taylor Coleridge: Omniana

There is no chance, and no anarchy, in the universe. All is system and gradation. Every god is there sitting in his sphere.

Ralph Waldo Emerson: The Conduct of
Life, IX

The whole creation is made of hooks and eyes, of bitumen, of sticking-plaster . . . it coheres in a perfect ball.

Ralph Waldo Emerson: The Conduct of
Life: Worship

The universe is not composed of newts only; it has its Newtons.

Harry Emerson Fosdick: Easter Sermon

The moral system of the universe is like a document written in alternate ciphers, which change from line to line.

James Anthony Froude: *Short Studies on Great Subjects: Calvinism*

Man is not born to solve the problems of the universe, but to find out where the problems begin, and then to take his stand within the limits of the intelligible.

Johann Wolfgang von Goethe

The greatest object in the universe, says a certain philosopher, is a good man struggling with adversity; yet there is a still greater, which is the good man that comes to relieve it.

Oliver Goldsmith

The universe is not hostile, nor yet is it friendly. It is simply indifferent.

John Haynes Holmes: *The Sensible Man's View of Religion,* Harper & Row, Publishers, Inc.

The chess-board is the world, the pieces are the phenomena of the universe, the rules of the game are what we call the laws of Nature, the players on the other side is hidden from us.

Thomas Henry Huxley: *Liberal Education: In Science and Education*

O God! Put back Thy universe and give me yesterday.

Henry Arthur Jones: *Silver King*

Space is the stature of God.

Joseph Joubert: *Pensées,* no. 183

There is nothing uncultivated, nothing sterile, nothing dead, in the universe; there is no chaos, no confusion, except in appearance.

Gottfried Wilhelm von Leibnitz: *The Monadology,* LXIX

The universe is fireproof, and it is quite safe to strike a match.

James Russell Lowell

Every mortal man of us holds stock in the only public debt that is absolutely sure of payment, and that is the debt of the Maker of this Universe to the Universe he has made.

James Russell Lowell: *On a Certain Condescension in Foreigners*

Thro' worlds unnumber'd tho' the God be known,
'Tis ours to trace him only in our own.

Alexander Pope: *Essay on Man,* Epis. I, l. 21

The universe is a thought of God.

Johann Christoph Friedrich von Schiller: *Essays: Aesthetical and Philosophical,* Letter IV

When I view the universe as a whole, I admit that it is a marvelous structure; and what is more, I insist that it is of what I may call an intelligent design . . . There is really very little difference between my own thoughts about the matter and the thoughts of a Fundamentalist.

William Francis Gray Swann: *The Architecture of the Universe*

The vastness of God's creation should ever keep us humble. The new telescope at Mt. Palomar enables man to photograph planets over one billion light years away. This distance as miles amounts to a total of 186,000 (miles per second) × 60 seconds × 60 minutes × 24 hours × 365 days × 1,000,000,000 (years). How many billions of planets there are, no one can guess. One astronomer, when asked how he could believe in a God, replied, "I keep enlarging my idea of God."

Obert C. Tanner: *Christ's Ideals for Living,* Deseret Sunday School Union Board

One God, one law, one element,
And one far-off divine event,
To which the whole creation moves.

Alfred, Lord Tennyson: *In Memoriam: Conclusion*

In Tune with the Infinite.
　　Ralph Waldo Trine—title of a book

The world, the race, the soul—in space and
　　time the universes,
All bound as is befitting each—all surely
　　going somewhere.
　　Walt Whitman: *Leaves of Grass: Going
　　　　　　　　　　Somewhere*

Prais'd be the fathomless universe.
　　Walt Whitman: *Leaves of Grass: When
　　　　Lilacs Last in the Door-yard
　　　　　　Bloom'd,* XIV

V

VIRGIN BIRTH, THE

The angel of the Lord declared unto Mary, and she conceived of the holy Ghost.

The Angelus

I believe . . . in Jesus Christ . . . Who was conceived by the Holy Ghost, Born of the Virgin Mary. . . .

The Apostles' Creed

I believe that Christ was born of a Virgin because I have read it in the Gospel.

St. Augustine: *On the Christian Conflict*

A Virgin conceived, a Virgin bore, and after the birth was a Virgin still.

St. Augustine: *On the Creed*

The Turks are of opinion that 'tis no uncommon thing for a virgin to bear a child. I would by no means introduce this belief into my family.

Martin Luther: *Table Talk*

This is the month, and this the happy morn,
Wherein the Son of Heav'n's eternal King,
Of wedded maid and virgin mother born,
Our great redemption from above did bring;
For so the holy sages once did sing,
That He our deadly forfeit should release,
And with His Father work us a perpetual peace.

John Milton: *On the Morning of Christ's Nativity*, st. 1, l. 1

Now all this was done, that it might be fulfilled which was spoken of the Lord by the prophet, saying, Behold, a virgin shall be with child, and shall bring forth a son, and

they shall call his name Emmanuel, which being interpreted is, God with us.

New Testament: Matthew 1: 22–23

Why cannot a virgin bear a child? Does not a hen lay eggs without a cock?

Blaise Pascal: *Pensées*

VIRTUE

Here will I hold. If there's a Power above
(And that there is all nature cries aloud
Through all her works), he must delight in virtue;
And that which he delights in must be happy.

Joseph Addison: *Cato*, Act V, sc. 1

Virtue consists in doing our duty in the various relations we sustain to ourselves, to our fellowmen, and to God, as it is made known by reason, revelation and Providence.

Archibald Alexander

Virtue is not to be considered in the light of mere innocence, or abstaining from harm; but as the exertion of our faculties in doing good.

Joseph Butler

Virtue is its own reward.

Cicero: *De finibus*, III

I dislike the frequent use of the word *virtue*, instead of *righteousness*, in the pulpit: in prayer or preaching before a Christian community it sounds too much like pagan philosophy.

Samuel Taylor Coleridge: *Aids to Reflection*

Virtue is uniform and fixed, because she looks for approbation only from Him who is the same yesterday, today and forever.

Charles Caleb Colton

Virtue is the Beauty of the Soul.

Thomas Fuller: *Gnomologia*

The virtue of Paganism was strength; the virtue of Christianity is obedience.

Augustus William and Julius Charles Hare

Purity lives and derives its life solely from the Spirit of God.

Augustus William and Julius Charles Hare

The moral virtues are habits, and habits are formed by acts.

Robert M. Hutchins: *Commonweal*

Virtue is the habitual sense of right, and the habitual courage to act up to the sense of right, combined with benevolent sympathies, and the charity which thinketh no evil. The union of the highest conscience and highest sympathy fulfils my notion of virtue.

Anna Brownell Jameson

His virtues walked their narrow round,
 Nor made a pause, nor left a void;
And sure th' Eternal Master found
 The single talent well employed.

Samuel Johnson: *On the Death of Mr. Robert Lovett*

Virtue is the health of the soul. It gives a flavor to the smallest leaves of life.

Joseph Joubert: *Pensées*, no. 131

To be discontented with the divine discontent, and to be ashamed with the noble shame, is the very germ of the first upgrowth of all virtue.

Charles Kingsley: *Health and Education: The Science of Health*

Virtue is to the soul what health is to the body.

François de La Rochefoucauld: *Maximes Posthumes*, no. 541

If mankind suddenly took to virtue, many thousands would inevitably be reduced to starvation.

Georg Christoph Lichtenberg

Prudence, justice, fortitude, and temperance, are the Four Cardinal Virtues.

John McCaffrey: *A Catechism of Christian Doctrine for General Use*

Virtue is an angel; but she is a blind one and must ask of knowledge to show her the path that leads to her goal.

Horace Mann: *A Few Thoughts for a Young Man*

It would not be easy, even for an unbeliever, to find a better translation of the rule of virtue from the abstract into the concrete, than to endeavor so to live that Christ would approve our life.

John Stuart Mill

Mortals, who would follow me,
Love virtue, she alone is free:
She can teach you how to climb
Higher than the sphery clime;
Or if virtue feeble were,
Heaven itself would stoop to her.

John Milton

God sure esteems the growth and completing of one virtuous person, more than the restraint of ten vicious.

John Milton: *Areopagitica*

Virtue is the doing good to mankind in obedience to the will of God, and for the sake of everlasting happiness.

William Paley: *The Principles of Moral and Political Philosophy*, I

For virtue only finds eternal Fame.

Petrarch: *The Triumph of Fame*, Pt. I, l. 183

Virtue is a kind of health, beauty and good habit of the soul.

Plato: *The Republic*, IV

Divinity has three elements of superiority, incorruption, power, and virtue, and the most reverend and divinest of these is virtue; for in fundamental justice nothing participates except through the exercise of intelligent reasoning powers.

Plutarch: *Lives: Aristides,* ch. 6, sec. 2

Know then this truth (enough for man to know):
Virtue alone is happiness below.

Alexander Pope: *An Essay on Man,* IV

Wealth is a weak anchor, and glory cannot support a man; this is the law of God, that virtue only is firm, and cannot be shaken by a tempest.

Pythagoras

What the world calls virtue, without Christ, is a name and a dream. The foundation of all human excellence must be laid deep in the blood of the Redeemer's cross and in the power of His resurrection.

Frederick William Robertson

There are Seven Deadly Virtues: Respectability, Childishness, Mental Timidity, Dullness, Sentimentality, Censoriousness, Depression of Spirits.

Dorothy L. Sayers: *Creed or Chaos?,* Harper & Row, Publishers, Inc.

Virtue is the dictate of reason, or the remains of the divine light, by which men are made beneficent and beneficial to each other. Religion proceeds from the same end, and the good of mankind so entirely depends upon these two, that no people ever enjoyed anything worth desiring that was not the product of them.

Algernon Sidney

The only impregnable citadel of virtue is religion; for there is no bulwark of more morality which some temptation may not overtop, or undermine and destroy.

Sir Philip Sidney

When men grow virtuous in old age they are merely making an offering to God of the devil's leavings.

Jonathan Swift

You are a man, not God; you are human, not an angel. How can you expect to remain always in a constant state of virtue, when this was not possible even for an angel of Heaven, nor for the first man in the Garden?

Thomas à Kempis

Give me simple laboring folk,
Who love their work,
Whose virtue is a song
To cheer God along.

Henry David Thoreau: *A Week on the Concord and Merrimack Rivers*

Virtue is its own reward, but it's very satisfactory when Providence throws in some little additional bonus.

Woman's Home Companion

VISION, VISIONS

A vision without a task is a dream;
A task without a vision is drudgery;
A vision and a task is the hope of the world.

Anonymous

Vision is the Aladdin's lamp of the soul. It is the divine spark that lights the lamp of progress. It is the hand that pushes aside the curtains of night to let the sunrise in. It is vision that guides a log-cabin boy to the presidency of our Republic. Vision gave wings to man, pulled atomic energy from the sun, subdued the forces of nature, making them the soulless and untiring slaves of those whom such powers held in bondage since time began.

American Way

Perfect blessedness, which consists in a vision of God.

St. Thomas Aquinas: *Summa theologica*

Open your eyes and the whole world is full of God.

Jakob Böhme

Golden hours of vision come to us in this present life when . . . our faculties work together in harmony.

Charles Fletcher Dole: *The Hope of Immortality*

The people's prayer, the glad diviner's theme!
The young men's vision, and the old men's dream.

John Dryden: *Absalom and Achitophel,*
Pt. I, l. 238

Poor eyes limit your sight; poor vision limits your deeds.

Franklin Field

Forward, on the same old journey, let us follow where she leads,
Let us chase the beckoning glory of the Vision that Recedes.

Sam Walter Foss: *The Vision that Recedes*

We read the past by the light of the present, and the forms vary as the shadows fall, or as the point of vision alters.

James Anthony Froude: *Short Studies on Great Subjects: Society in Italy in the Last Days of the Roman Republic*

Only he who can see the invisible can do the impossible.

Frank Gaines: *Forbes*

Visions of glory, spare my aching sight!

Thomas Gray: *The Bard,* l. 107

A blind man's world is bounded by the limits of his touch; an ignorant man's world by the limits of his knowledge; a great man's world by the limits of his vision.

E. Paul Hovey

A vision foretells what may be ours. It is an invitation to do something. With a great mental picture in mind we go from one accomplishment to another, using the materials about us only as steppingstones to that which is higher and better and more satisfying. We thus become possessors of the unseen values which are eternal.

Katherine Logan

Vision is of God. A vision comes in advance of any task well done.

Katherine Logan

The wicked and the weak, by some dark law,
Have a strange power to shut and rivet down
Their own horizons round us, to unwing
Our heaven-aspiring visions.

James Russell Lowell

An angel stood and met my gaze,
Through the low doorway of my tent;
The tent is struck, the vision stays;
I only know she came and went.

James Russell Lowell: *She Came and Went*

Give us clear vision that we may know where to stand and what to stand for, because unless we stand for something, we shall fall for anything.

Peter Marshall: *Mr. Jones, Meet the Master*

Whereupon, O King Agrippa, I was not disobedient unto the heavenly vision.

New Testament: Acts 26: 19

Where there is no vision, the people perish.

Old Testament: Proverbs 29: 18

I have multiplied visions, and used similitudes.

Old Testament: Hosea 12: 10

And it shall come to pass afterward, that I will pour out my spirit upon all flesh; and your sons and your daughters shall prophesy, your old men shall dream dreams, your young men shall see visions.

Old Testament: Joel 2: 28

Write the vision, and make it plain upon tables, that he may run that readeth it.

Old Testament: Habakkuk 2: 2

I simply dream dreams and see visions, and then I paint around those dreams and visions.

Raphael

Vision is the art of seeing things invisible.

Jonathan Swift: *Thoughts on Various Subjects*

Vision does not come by inspiration. It comes from knowledge, intelligently cultivated.

Robert A. Weaver

W

WAR

War, being a consequence of the disregard of God, is not inevitable if man will turn to him in repentance and obey his law. There is, then, no irresistible tide that is carrying man to destruction. Nothing is impossible with God.

Amsterdam Assembly

I am of the opinion that, unless you could bray Christianity in a mortar and mold it into a new paste, there is no possibility of a holy war.

Sir Francis Bacon

God is generally for the big squadrons against the little ones.

Roger de Bussy-Rabutin: *Letters*

War will never yield but to the principles of universal justice and love, and those have no sure roots but in the religion of Jesus Christ.

William Ellery Channing

Men will carry guns until they learn to carry the cross.

Employment Counselor

Praise the Lord and pass the ammunition.

Chaplain Howell M. Forgy: at Pearl Harbor, December 7, 1941

There never was a good war or a bad peace.

Benjamin Franklin: *Letter to Quincy*

Between Christ and war there is unalterable opposition; there cannot possibly be harmony.

Charles W. Gilkey

It is the business of the church to make my business impossible.

Sir Douglas Haig

A day of battle is a day of harvest for the devil.

William Hook: *Sermon*

The last great hope for the survival of mankind rests not in implements of war but in a strong and abiding faith in God.

H. S. Jackson: Indiana *Freemason*

There have been three historic scourges: famine, pestilence and war. The first two have been slain by science. The last one science cannot kill. War can be abolished only by love.

Charles E. Jefferson

If Christian nations were nations of Christians there would be no wars.

Soame Jenyns

The first casualty when war comes is truth.

Hiram Johnson: Speech, U.S. Senate

There is no such thing as an inevitable war. If war comes it will be from failure of human wisdom.

Andrew Bonar Law: Speech before World War I

O, God assist our side: at least, avoid assisting the enemy and leave the rest to me.

Prince Leopold of Anhalt-Dessau: according to Carlyle—*Life of Frederick the Great*, Bk. XV, ch. 14

Fondly do we hope, fervently do we pray, that this mighty scourge of war will speedily pass away.

Abraham Lincoln

467

Ez fer war, I call it murder,—
  Ther you hev it plain and flat;
I don't want to go no furder
  Than my Testyment fer that.

James Russell Lowell: *The Biglow Papers*

We kind o' thought Christ went agin war an'
pillage.

Ibid.

Cannons and fire-arms are cruel and damnable machines; I believe them to have been the direct suggestion of the Devil. If Adam had seen in a vision the horrible instruments his children were to invent, he would have died of grief.

Martin Luther: *Table Talk*

Wars and rumours of wars.

New Testament: Matthew 24: 6

Scatter thou the people that delight in war.

Old Testament: Psalms 68: 30

There is no discharge in that war.

Old Testament: Ecclesiastes 8: 8

Terrible as an army with banners.

Old Testament: Song of Solomon 6: 4

He shall judge among the nations, and shall rebuke many people: and they shall beat their swords into plowshares, and their spears into pruninghooks: nation shall not lift up sword against nation, neither shall they learn war any more.

Old Testament: Isaiah 2: 4

It is the province of kings to cause war, and of God to end it.

Cardinal Pole, to Henry VIII

He that preaches war is the devil's chaplain.

John Ray: *English Proverbs*, p. 27

O war! thou son of hell!

William Shakespeare: *Henry VI, Part II,*
Act V, sc. 2, l. 33

In disarming Peter, Christ disarmed every soldier.

Tertullian

What is human warfare but just this—an effort to make the laws of God and nature take sides with one party.

Henry David Thoreau

Men who have nice notions of religion have no business to be soldiers.

Arthur Wellesley, Duke of Wellington

Take my word for it, if you had seen but one day of war, you would pray to Almighty God, that you might never see such a thing again.

Arthur Wellesley, Duke of Wellington

WISDOM

The good Lord set definite limits on man's wisdom, but set no limits on his stupidity —and that's just not fair!

Konrad Adenauer: *The Churchman*

The greatest good is wisdom.

St. Augustine: *Soliloquies*, I

There are but two classes of the wise; the men who serve God because they have found him, and the men who seek him because they have found him not. All others may say, "Is there not a lie in my right hand?"

Richard Cecil

God never meant that man should scale the
  heavens
By strides of human wisdom.

William Cowper: *The Task*, Bk. III, l. 221

The intellect of the wise is like glass; it admits the light of heaven and reflects it.

Augustus William and Julius Charles
Hare

For never, never, wicked man was wise.

Homer: *Odyssey*, Bk. II, l. 320

Wisdom precedes, religion follows; for the knowledge of God comes first, His worship is the result of knowledge.

Lactantius: *Divine Institutes*

The wise man does not lay up treasure.

Lao-tze: *The Simple Way,* no. 81

Be ye therefore wise as serpents, and harmless as doves.

New Testament: Matthew 10: 16

Wisdom is justified of her children.

New Testament: Matthew 11: 19

The children of this world are in their generation wiser than the children of light.

New Testament: Luke 16: 8

The wisdom of this world is foolishness with God.

New Testament: I Corinthians 3: 19

The price of wisdom is above rubies.

Old Testament: Job 28: 18

Great men are not always wise.

Old Testament: Job 32: 9

So teach us to number our days, that we may apply our hearts unto wisdom.

Old Testament: Psalms 90: 12

Wisdom is the principle thing; therefore get wisdom: and with all thy getting get understanding.

Old Testament: Proverbs 4: 7

Wisdom is better than rubies.

Old Testament: Proverbs 8: 11

In much wisdom is much grief.

Old Testament: Ecclesiastes 1: 18

Wisdom giveth life to them that have it.

Old Testament: Ecclesiastes 7: 12

The words of the wise are as goads.

Old Testament: Ecclesiastes 12: 11

Well, God give them wisdom that have it; and those that are fools, let them use their talents.

William Shakespeare: *Twelfth Night,*
Act I, sc. 5, l. 14

The divine essence itself is love and wisdom.

Emanuel Swedenborg: *Divine Love and
Wisdom,* par. 28

To have a low opinion of our own merits and to think highly of others is an evidence of wisdom.

Thomas à Kempis

He who provides for this life, but takes no care for eternity, is wise for a moment, but a fool forever.

John Tillotson

Wisdom is not finally tested in the schools,
Wisdom cannot be passed from one having it to another not having it,
Wisdom is of the soul, is not susceptible of proof, is its own proof.

Walt Whitman: *Song of the Open Road,*
sec. 6

The chief aim of wisdom is to enable one to bear with the stupidity of the ignorant.

Pope Xystus I: *The Ring*

The wise man is also the just, the pious, the upright, the man who walks in the way of truth. The fear of the Lord, which is the beginning of wisdom, consists in a complete devotion to God.

Otto Zöckler

WOMAN

The weaker sex, to piety more prone.

Sir William Alexander: *Doomsday: The
Fifth Hour,* st. 55

Despise not yourselves, ye women: the Son of God was born of a woman.

St. Augustine: *On the Christian Conflict*

Not she with trait'rous kiss her Saviour
    stung,
Not she denied Him with unholy tongue;
She, while apostles shrank, could dangers
    brave,
Last at the cross and earliest at the grave.

    Eaton Stannard Barrett: *Woman,* Pt. I,
        l. 141

The man who strikes his wife or child lays
violent hands upon the holiest of holy
things.

    Marcus Porcius Cato the Elder

God, when he made the first woman . . . made
her not of the head of Adam, for she should
not climb to great lordship . . . also certes,
God made not woman of the foot of Adam,
for she should not be holden too low; for
she can not patiently suffer; but God made
woman of the rib of Adam, for woman
should be fellow unto man.

    Geoffrey Chaucer: *The Persones Tale,*
        sec. 79

Heav'n has no rage, like love to hatred
    turn'd,
Nor Hell a fury like a woman scorn'd.

    William Congreve: *The Mourning Bride,*
        Act III

Women are doormats and have been—the
years these mats applaud—they keep the
men from going in—with muddy feet to
God.

    Mary Carolyn Davies

I'm not denying the women are foolish: God
Almighty made 'em to match the men.

    George Eliot

There is no worse evil than a bad woman;
and nothing has ever been produced better
than a good one.

    Euripides: *Melanippe*

A man without religion is to be pitied, but
a Godless woman is a horror above all things.

    Augusta Jane Evans

I met with a sort of people that held women
have no souls, adding, in a light manner, no
more than a goose. But I reproved them, and
told them that was not right; for Mary said,
"My soul doth magnify the Lord, and my
spirit hath rejoiced in God my Saviour."

    George Fox: *Journal,* I (the quotation is
        from *Luke 1: 46–57*)

Woman's wishes are God's wishes.

    French Proverb

A woman has the form of an angel, the heart
of a serpent, and the mind of an ass.

    German Proverb

A woman without religion is as a flower
without scent.

    German Proverb

When toward the Devil's House we tread,
Woman's a thousand steps ahead.

    Johann Wolfgang von Goethe: *Faust,* Pt. I

A beautiful and chaste woman is the perfect
workmanship of God, and the true glory of
the angels, the rare miracle of earth, and the
sole wonder of the world.

    Georg Hermes

God in his harmony has equal ends
For cedar that resists and reed that bends;
For good it is a woman sometimes rules,
Holds in her hand the power, and manners,
    schools,
And laws, and mind; succeeding master
    proud,
With gentle voice and smiles she leads the
    crowd,
The somber human troop.

    Victor Hugo: *Evidarnus,* V

Christianity has lifted woman to a new place
in the world . . . And just in proportion as
Christianity has a way, will she rise to a
higher dignity in human life . . . What she
has now, and all she shall have of privilege
and true honor, she owes to that gospel
which took those qualities which had been
counted weak and unworthy and gave them
a divine glory in Christ.

    Herrick Johnson

God has placed the genius of women in their hearts; because the works of this genius are always works of love.

> Alfonse de Lamartine

The woman was not taken
  From Adam's head, we know,
To show she must not rule him—
  'Tis evidently so.
The woman she was taken
  From under Adam's arm,
So she must be protected
  From injuries and harm.

> Abraham Lincoln: *Adam and Eve's Wedding Song*

Earth's noblest thing, a Woman perfected.

> James Russell Lowell: *Irene*, l. 62

Earth has nothing more tender than a woman's heart when it is the abode of piety.

> Martin Luther

Too fair to worship, too divine to love.

> Henry Hart Milman: *Apollo Belvidere*

O fairest of creation! last and best
Of all God's works! creature in whom
  excell'd
Whatever can to sight or thought be form'd,
Holy, divine, good, amiable, or sweet!

> John Milton: *Paradise Lost*, Bk. IX, l. 896

God created woman. And boredom did indeed cease from that moment—but many other things ceased as well! Woman was God's *second* mistake.

> Friedrich Wilhelm Nietzsche: *The Antichrist*, Aphorism, XLVIII

It is better to dwell in a corner of the housetop, than with a brawling woman in a wide house.

> *Old Testament: Proverbs 21: 9*

O woman! lovely woman! Nature made thee
To temper man: we had been brutes without
  you;
Angels are painted fair, to look like you:
There's in you all that we believe of Heaven,
Amazing brightness, purity, and truth,
Eternal joy, and everlasting love.

> Thomas Otway: *Venice Preserved*, Act I, sc. 1

To chase the clouds of life's tempestuous
  hours,
To strew its short but weary way with flow'rs,
New hopes to raise, new feelings to impart,
And pour celestial balsam on the heart;
For this to man was lovely woman giv'n,
The last, best work, the noblest gift of
  Heav'n.

> Thomas Love Peacock: *The Visions of Love*

Woman, the last, the best reserv'd of God.

> Alexander Pope: *January and May*

The buckling on of a knight's armor by his lady's hand was not a mere caprice of romantic fashion. It is the type of an eternal truth that the soul's armor is never well set to the heart unless a woman's hand has braced it, and it is only when she braces it loosely that the honor of manhood fails.

> John Ruskin

O Woman! in our hours of ease
Uncertain, coy, and hard to please,
And variable as the shade
By the light quivering aspen made;
When pain and anguish wring the brow,
A ministering angel thou!

> Sir Walter Scott: *Marmion*, Canto VI, st. 30

In the beginning, said a Persian poet—Allah took a rose, a lily, a dove, a serpent, a little honey, a Dead Sea apple, and a handful of clay. When he looked at the amalgam—it was a woman.

> William Sharp: *Portfolio*

God save us all from wives who are angels in the street, saints in the church, and devils at home.

> Charles Haddon Spurgeon: *John Ploughman*, ch. 13

All virtuous women, like tortoises, carry their house on their heads, and their chappel in their heart, and their danger in their eye, and their souls in their hands, and God in all their actions.

Jeremy Taylor: *Life of Christ*, Pt. I, 2, 4

God made the woman for the use of man, And for the good and increase of the world.

Alfred, Lord Tennyson: *Edwin Morris*, l. 91

The judgment of God upon your sex endures even today; and with it inevitably endures your position of criminal at the bar of justice. You are the gateway of the Devil.

Tertullian: *Women's Dress*

Woman, God bless her by that name, for it is a far nobler name than lady.

Walter von der Vogelweide: *Woman and Lady*

Not from his head was woman took, As made her husband to o'erlook; Not from his feet, as one designed The footstool of the stronger kind; But fashioned for himself a bride; An equal, taken from his side.

Charles Wesley: *Short Hymns on Select Passages of the Holy Scriptures*

If the time should ever come when women are not Christians and houses are not homes, then we shall have lost the chief cornerstones on which civilization rests.

Andrew Dickson White

WORK

When God wanted sponges and oysters, He made them, and put one on a rock, and the other in the mud. When He made man, He did not make him to be a sponge, or an oyster; He made him with feet and hands, and head, and heart, and vital blood, and a place to use them, and said to him, "Go, work!"

Henry Ward Beecher: *Royal Truths*

He who labors as he prays lifts his heart to God with his hands.

St. Bernard of Clairvaux

I stood up straight and worked
My veritable work. And as the soul
Which grows within a child makes the child grow,
Or, as the fiery sap, the touch of God,
Careering through a tree, dilates the bark
And toughs with scale and knob, before it strikes
The summer foliage out in a green flame—
So life, in deepening with me, deepened all
The course I took, the work I did.

Elizabeth Barrett Browning

Free men freely work:
Whoever fears God, fears to sit at ease.

Elizabeth Barrett Browning: *Aurora Leigh*, Bk. VIII, l. 784

Man's work is to labour and leaven—
As best he may—earth here with heaven;
'Tis work for work's sake that he's needing.

Robert Browning: *Of Pacchiarotto*, st. 21

The *best* worship, however, is stout working.

Thomas Carlyle: *Letter to His Wife*

Genuine Work alone, what thou workest faithfully, that is eternal, as the Almighty Founder and World-Builder himself.

Thomas Carlyle: *Past and Present*, Bk. II, ch. 17

God sells us all things at the price of labor.

Leonardo da Vinci

Now I get me up to work,
I pray the Lord I may not shirk,
And if I die before tonight,
I pray my work will be all right.

Thomas Osborne Davis: President of Rotary, in acceptance speech

The gods sell us all good things for hard work.

Epicharmus

Work! God wills it. That, it seems to me, is clear.

Gustave Flaubert: *Letter to Louise Colet*

It is not doing the thing which we like to do, but liking to do the thing which we have to do, that makes life blessed.

Johann Wolfgang von Goethe

God gives every bird its food, but he does not throw it into the nest.

Josiah Gilbert Holland

Occupation was one of the pleasures of Paradise, and we cannot be happy without it.

Anna Brownell Jameson

Who first invented work, and bound the free
And holyday-rejoicing spirit down . . .
To that dry drudgery at the desk's dead
   wood? . . .
Sabbathless Satan!

Charles Lamb: *Work*

No man is born into the world whose work
Is not born with him; there is always work,
And tools to work withal, for those who will;
And blessed are the horny hands of toil!

James Russell Lowell: *A Glance Behind
the Curtain*

It is my belief that every man has the divine right to work.

Ernest Lundeen: Speech in the Senate,
April 8, 1939

God be thank'd that the dead have left still
   Good undone for the living to do—
Still some aim for the heart and the will
   And the soul of a man to pursue.

Owen Meredith: *Epilogue*

The labourer is worthy of his hire.

New Testament: Luke 10: 7

I must work the works of him that sent me, while it is day: the night cometh, when no man can work.

New Testament: John 9: 4

If any would not work, neither should he eat.

New Testament: II Thessalonians 3: 10

In the sweat of thy face shalt thou eat bread.

Old Testament: Genesis 3: 19

Six days shalt thou work, but on the seventh day thou shalt rest.

Old Testament: Exodus 34: 21

Establish thou the work of our hands upon us; yea, the work of our hands establish thou it.

Old Testament: Psalms 90: 17

Man goeth forth unto his work and to his labour until the evening.

Old Testament: Psalms 104: 23

All things are full of labour; man cannot utter it: the eye is not satisfied with seeing, nor the ear filled with hearing.

Old Testament: Ecclesiastes 1: 8

It is no man's business if he has genius or not. Work he must, whatever he is, but quietly and steadily; and the natural and enforced results of such work will always be the thing that God meant him to do, and will be his best.

John Ruskin

Men are naturally tempted by the devil, but an idle man positively tempts the devil.

Spanish Proverb

God never calls a lazy, disgruntled man to a job which requires the finer qualities of real manhood. Every worker may make the commonest job an immortal task.

Charles Stelzle

If a man love the labor of any trade, apart from any question of success or fame, the Gods have called him.

Robert Louis Stevenson

473

Greater even than the pious man is he who eats that which is the fruit of his own toil; for Scripture declares him twice-blessed.

The Talmud

Work as though work alone thine end could gain;
But pray to God as though all work were vain.

D'Arcy Wentworth Thompson: *Sales Attici*

Good for the body is the work of the body, good for the soul the work of the soul, and good for either the work of the other.

Henry David Thoreau: *Journal*

Let us be grateful to Adam our benefactor. He cut us out of the "blessing" of idleness and won for us the "curse" of labor.

Mark Twain

WORLD, THE

The ship's place is in the sea, but God pity the ship when the sea gets into it. The Christian's place is in the world, but God pity the Christian if the world gets the best of him.

Anonymous

We believe in a Christlike world. We can conceive of nothing better. We can be satisfied with nothing less.

Anonymous

What the soul is in a body, this the Christians are in the world . . . Christians hold the world together.

Anonymous

Hell is God's justice; heaven is His love; earth, His long-suffering.

Anonymous

God is the author, men are only the players. These grand pieces which are played upon earth have been composed in heaven.

Honoré de Balzac: *Socrate Chrétien*

The world is God's workshop for making men.

Henry Ward Beecher

The heavens and the earth alike speak of God, and the great natural world is but another Bible, which clasps and binds the written one; for nature and grace are one—grace the heart of the flower, and nature its surrounding petals.

Henry Ward Beecher

A brave world, sir, full of religion, knavery and change! We shall shortly see better days.

Aphra Behn: *The Roundheads*, I

The world, the flesh and the Devil.

Book of Common Prayer: The Litany

For the world I count it not an inn, but an hospital, and a place not to live, but to die in.

Sir Thomas Browne: *Religio Medici*, II

O world, as God has made it! All is beauty:
And knowing this, is love, and love is duty,
   What further may be sought for or declared?

Robert Browning: *The Guardian-Angel*

You've seen the world—
The beauty and the wonder and the power,
The shapes of things, their colors, lights and shades,
Changes, surprises—and God made it all.

Robert Browning: *Fra Lippo Lippi*

The year's at the Spring
And day's at the morn;
Morning's at seven;
The hillside's dew-pearled;
The lark's on the wing;
The snail's on the thorn:
God's in his Heaven—
All's right with the world!

Robert Browning: *Pippa Passes*

That one vast thought of God which we call the world.

Edward George Bulwer-Lytton

The true Sovereign of the world, who moulds the world like soft wax, according to his pleasure, is he who lovingly sees into the world.

Thomas Carlyle: *Essays: Death of Goethe*

The great soul of this world is just.

Thomas Carlyle: *Letter to Thomas Erskine*

God hath not taken all that pains in forming, framing, furnishing, and adorning this world, that they who were made by him to live in it, should despise it; it will be well enough if they do not love it so immoderately as to prefer it before him who made it.

Edward Hyde, Lord Clarendon

The world that is and the world to come are enemies . . . We cannot be the friends of both; but must bid farewell to this world to consort with that to come.

St. Clement: *Second Epistle to the Corinthians*

'Tis pleasant, through the loopholes of retreat,
To peep at such a world; to see the stir
Of the Great Babel, and not feel the crowd.

William Cowper: *Task*, Bk. IV, l. 88

Like pilgrims to th' appointed place we tend:
The world's an inn, and death the journey's end.

John Dryden: *Palamon and Arcite*, Bk. III, l. 887

Good-by, proud world! I'm going home;
Thou art not my friend, and I'm not thine.

Ralph Waldo Emerson: *Good-By*

The world is a divine dream, from which we may presently awake to the glories and certainties of day.

Ralph Waldo Emerson: *Nature, Addresses and Lectures: Spirit*

One is happy in the world only when one forgets the world.

Anatole France

The world in itself has no value, it is merely zero; but with Heaven before it, it means much.

Baltasar Gracian y Morales: *The Art of Worldly Wisdom*, CCXI

The world, as in the ark of Noah, rests,
Compos'd as then: few men and many beasts.

Edward Herbert, Lord of Cherbury: *The State of Progress of Ill*

The world's a theatre, the earth a stage
Which God and nature do with actors fill.

John Heywood: *The Author to His Book*

The early Christians not only moved the world; they turned it upside down.

George Jackson: *First Things Tell*

Buying, possessing, accumulating, this is not worldliness.—But doing this in the love of it, with no love to God paramount—doing it so that thoughts of God and eternity are an intrusion—doing it so that one's spirit is secularized in doing it—this is worldliness.

Herrick Johnson

It is not accident that wherever we point the telescope we see beauty, that wherever we look with the microscope there we find beauty. It beats in through every nook and cranny of the mighty world.

Rufus Matthew Jones: *The World Within*

What a glorious world Almighty God has given us! How thankless and ungrateful we are, and how we labor to mar His gifts.

Robert E. Lee: Letter to his Wife

Glorious indeed is the world of God around us, but more glorious the world of God within us. There lies the Land of Song; there lies the poet's native land.

Henry Wadsworth Longfellow: *Hyperion*, Bk. I, ch. 8

The world is nothing but a reversed Decalogue of the Ten Commandments backwards, a mask and picture of the Devil.

Martin Luther: *Table Talk*

While the Creator great His constellations set
And the well-balanc'd world on hinges hung.

John Milton: *On the Morning of Christ's Nativity*, l. 120

Open, ye heavens, your living doors; let in
The great Creator from His work return'd
Magnificent, His six days' work, a world!

John Milton: *Paradise Lost*, VII

The unrest of this weary world is its unvoiced cry after God.

Theodore T. Munger

Know ye not that the friendship of the world is enmity with God? whosoever therefore will be a friend of the world, is the enemy of God.

New Testament: James 4: 4

For all that is in the world, the lust of the flesh, and the lust of the eyes, and the pride of life, is not of the Father, but is of the world.

New Testament: I John 2: 16

The world passeth away, and the lust thereof.

New Testament: I John 2: 17

A soul disengaged from the world is a heavenly one; and then are we ready for heaven when our heart is there before us.

John Newton

World without end.

Old Testament: Isaiah 45: 17

The universe, broad and deep and high, is a handful of dust which God enchants. His is the mysterious magic which possesses—not protoplasm, merely but—the world.

Theodore Parker

They who grasp the world,
The Kingdom, and the power, and the glory,
Must pay with deepest misery of spirit,
Atoning unto God for a brief brightness.

Stephen Phillips: *Herod*, Act III

The world is God's epistle to mankind—his thoughts are flashing upon us from every direction.

Plato

Yes, Heaven is thine; but this
  Is a world of sweets and sours;
  Our flowers are merely—flowers,
And the shadow of thy perfect bliss
  Is the sunshine of ours.

Edgar Allan Poe: *Israfel*

Thro' worlds unnumber'd tho' the God be known,
'Tis ours to trace him only in our own.

Alexander Pope: *Essay on Man*, Ep. I, l. 21

The world's a book, writ by the eternal art
Of the great author; printed in man's heart,
'Tis falsly printed, though divinely penned,
And all the *errata* will appear at the end.

Francis Quarles

Be wisely worldly, but not worldly wise.

Francis Quarles: *Emblems*, Bk. II, em. 2

This fine old world of ours is but a child
Yet in the go-cart. Patience! Give it time
To learn its limbs: there is a hand that guides.

Alfred, Lord Tennyson: *The Princess*

My God, I would not live
Save that I think this gross, hard-seeming world
Is our misshaping vision of the Powers
Behind the world, that make our griefs our gains.

Alfred, Lord Tennyson: *The Sisters*, l. 223

Man draws the nearer to God as he withdraws from the consolation of this world.
How swiftly passes the glory of the world!

Thomas a Kempis

One world at a time, brother, one world at a time.

Henry David Thoreau

The world is a mirror of infinite beauty, yet no man sees it. It is a Temple of Majesty, yet no man regards it. It is a region of Light and Peace, did not men disquiet it. It is the Paradise of God.

Thomas Traherne: *Centuries of Meditations*

Everything is for the best in this best of possible worlds.

Voltaire: *Candide,* I

I look upon the world as my parish.

John Wesley

What is this world? A net to snare the soul.

George Whetstone: *The World*

Let your soul stand cool and composed before a million universes.

Walt Whitman: *Song of Myself,* XLVIII

The splendid discontent of God
With Chaos, made the world.

Ella Wheeler Wilcox: *Discontent,* Rand McNally and Company

The world is too much with us; late and soon,
Getting and spending, we lay waste our powers.

William Wordsworth: *Sonnet*

WORRY

Leave tomorrow's trouble to tomorrow's strength; tomorrow's work to tomorrow's time; tomorrow's trial to tomorrow's grace and to tomorrow's God.

Anonymous

Anxiety springs from the desire that things should happen as we wish rather than as God wills.

Anonymous

The devil would have us continually crossing streams that do not exist.

Anonymous

Take plenty of time to count your blessings, but never spend a minute in worry.

Anonymous

Hence jarring sectaries may learn
Their real interest to discern;
That brother should not war with brother,
And worry and devour each other.

William Cowper: *The Nightingale and the Glow-Worm*

The world is wide
In time and tide,
And God is guide,
    Then—do not hurry.
That man is blest
Who does his best
And leaves the rest,
    Then—do not worry.

Charles F. Deems: *Epigram*

Jesus once said, "Don't worry" . . . That's good advice; but . . . notice . . . Jesus is talking about people who are worrying about themselves. He is not talking of those who are anxious about the welfare of others . . . The more you worry about other people's welfare, the less you will worry about your own.

Alvin E. Magary: *Your Life*

Worry affects circulation, the heart, the glands, the whole nervous system. I have never known a man who died from overwork, but many who died from doubt.

Charles H. Mayo: *American Mercury*

Thou art . . . troubled about many things:
But one thing is needful.

New Testament: Luke 10: 41–42

Nothing in the affairs of men is worth worrying about.

Plato: *Republic,* Bk. X, sec. 604

Blessed is the man who is too busy to worry in the daytime, and too sleepy at night.

Earl Riney: *Church Management*

All worry is atheism, because it is a want of trust in God.

Bishop Fulton J. Sheen

Gainst minor evils let him pray,
Who fortune's favour curries,—
For one that big misfortunes slay,
Ten die of little worries.

George Robert Sims: *Occasional Lines*

WORSHIP

The philosopher aspires to explain away all mysteries, to dissolve them into light. Mystery on the other hand is demanded and pursued by the religious instinct; mystery constitutes the essence of worship.

Henri Frédéric Amiel: *Journal*

God is to be worshipped by faith, hope, and love.

St. Augustine: *On Faith, Hope, and Charity*

For the Christian who loves God, worship is the daily bread of patience.

Honoré de Balzac

I have never known a man, who habitually and on principle absented himself from the public worship of God, who did not sooner or later bring sorrow upon himself or his family.

Henry Whitney Bellows

It is for the sake of man, not of God, that worship and prayers are required; that man may be made better—that he may be confirmed in a proper sense of his dependent state, and acquire those pious and virtuous dispositions in which his highest improvement consists.

Hugh Blair

For worship is a thirsty land crying out for rain,
It is a candle in the act of being kindled,
It is a drop in quest of the ocean, . . .
It is a voice in the night calling for help,
It is a soul standing in awe before the mystery of the universe, . . .
It is time flowing into eternity,
. . . a man climbing the altar stairs to God.

Dwight Bradley: *Leaves From a Spiritual Notebook,* Harper & Row, Publishers, Inc.

He who neglects worship neglects that which separates man from the birds, the animals, the insects, the fishes.

Ibid.

A human being must be graded according to his capacity for worship.

Ibid.

Man is a religious being; the heart instinctively seeks for a God. Whether he worships on the banks of the Ganges, prays with his face upturned to the sun, kneels towards Mecca or, regarding all space as a temple, communes with the Heavenly Father according to the Christian creed, man is essentially devout.

William Jennings Bryan

Ah why
Should we, in the world's riper years, neglect
God's ancient sanctuaries, and adore
Only among the crowd and under roofs
That our frail hands have raised?

William Cullen Bryant: *A Forest Hymn,* l. 16

Worship renews the spirit as sleep renews the body.

Richard Clarke Cabot

The man who does not habitually worship is but a pair of spectacles behind which there is no eye.

Thomas Carlyle

Man always worships something; always he sees the Infinite shadowed forth in something finite; and indeed can and must so see it in any finite thing, once tempt him well to fix his eyes thereon.

Thomas Carlyle: *Essays: Goethe's Works*

Worship is transcendent wonder.

Thomas Carlyle: *Heroes and Hero-Worship.* Lecture I

We should worship as though the Deity were present. If my mind is not engaged in my worship, it is as though I worshipped not.

Confucius

It is only when men begin to worship that they begin to grow.

Calvin Coolidge

The happiest man he is who learns from nature the lesson of worship.

Ralph Waldo Emerson

And what greater calamity can fall upon a nation than the loss of worship.

Ralph Waldo Emerson: *An Address*

They that worship God merely from fear,
Would worship the devil too, if he appear.

Thomas Fuller: *Gnomologia*, no. 6419

Aye, call it holy ground—
The soil where first they trod!
They have left unstained what there they found—
Freedom to worship God!

Felicia D. Hemans: *The Landing of the Pilgrim Fathers*

Man worships because God lays His hand to the dust of our experience, and man miraculously becomes a living soul—and knows it and wants to worship.

Douglas Horton

The dullest observer must be sensible of the order and serenity prevalent in those households where the occasional exercise of a beautiful form of worship in the morning gives, as it were, the keynote to every temper for the day, and attunes every spirit to harmony.

Washington Irving

Worship is the act of rising to a personal, experimental consciousness of the real presence of God which floods the soul with joy and bathes the whole inward spirit with refreshing streams of life.

Rufus Matthew Jones: *The World Within*

Worship is pictured at its best in Isaiah when the young prophet became aware of the Father; aware of his own limitations; aware of the Father's directives; and aware of the task at hand.

David Julius

Worship liberates the personality by giving a new perspective to life, by integrating life with the multitude of life-forms, by bringing into the life the virtues of humility, loyalty, devotion and rightness of attitude, thus refreshing and reviving the spirit.

Roswell C. Long

And learn there may be worship without words!

James Russell Lowell: *My Cathedral*

Ev'n them who kept thy truth so pure of old,
When all our fathers worshipp'd stocks and stones.

John Milton: *On the Late Massacre in Piedmont*

Every one's true worship was that which he found in use in the place where he chanced to be.

Michel Eyquem de Montaigne: *Apology for Raimond Sebond*

If Socrates would enter the room we should rise and do him honor. But if Jesus Christ came into the room we should fall down on our knees and worship Him.

Napoleon Bonaparte

It is written, Thou shalt worship the Lord thy God, and him only shalt thou serve.

New Testament: Matthew 4: 10

For where two or three are gathered together in my name, there am I in the midst of them.

New Testament: Matthew 18: 20

God is a Spirit: and they that worship him must worship him in spirit and in truth.

New Testament: John 4: 24

Worship the Lord in the beauty of holiness.

Old Testament: I Chronicles 16: 29

O come, let us worship and bow down: let us kneel before the Lord our maker. For he is our God; and we are the people of his pasture, and the sheep of his hand.

Old Testament: Psalms 95: 6, 7

They that worship merely from fear,
Would worship the devil too, if he appear.

Proverb

First worship God.
  He that forgets to pray
Bids not himself good-morrow
  Or good-day.

Thomas Randolph

Do not forget that even as "to work is to worship" so to be cheery is to worship also, and to be happy is the first step to being pious.

Robert Louis Stevenson

The instinct to worship is hardly less strong than the instinct to eat.

Dorothy Thompson

It is an axiom of the Christian faith that the mode of worship must correspond to the essence of God, which is spiritual; and the feeling of the worshipper must correspond to the character of God, which is paternal.

Joseph Parrish Thompson

Worship requires only a man and God.

Unity

Here is the naturalness of Christian worship. First, we listen to God speak, then we give ourselves to Him and He Himself to us, in prayer and fellowship. It is the order of family worship; it is the order when you visit the sick; it is the order when you preach to win men for Christ—first, you carry the glad news to them; then, you lead them in confession and commitment of life.

H. W. Vaughan: *The Living Church*

The worship of God is not a rule of safety —it is an adventure of the spirit, a flight after the unattainable.

Alfred North Whitehead: *Science and the Modern World,* Cambridge University Press

WRATH

The wrath of the lion is the wisdom of God.

William Blake: *The Marriage of Heaven and Hell: Proverbs of Hell*

Day of wrath that day of burning
Seer and Sibyl speak concerning,
All the world to ashes turning.

Attributed to Thomas di Celano

He who curbs his wrath merits forgiveness for his sins.

Hebrew Proverb

So fond are mortal men
Fall'n into wrath divine,
As their own ruin on themselves to invite.

John Milton: *Samson Agonistes,* l. 1682

Let not the sun go down upon your wrath.

New Testament: Ephesians 4: 26

And this I know: whether the one True Light
Kindle to Love, or Wrath consume me quite,

One flash of It within the Tavern caught
Better than in the Temple lost outright.
>> Omar Khayyám: *Rubáiyát,* st. 77

Wrath killeth the foolish man.
>> *Old Testament: Job 5: 2*

A soft answer turneth away wrath.
>> *Old Testament: Proverbs 15: 1*

Pardon, not wrath, is God's best attribute.
>> Bayard Taylor: *Poems of the Orient.*
>> *Temptation of Hassan Ben Khaled,*
>> st. 11, l. 31

The divine wrath is slow indeed in vengeance, but it makes up for its tardiness by the severity of the punishment.
>> Valerius Maximus: I, l. 3

Y

YOUTH

I felt so young, so strong, so sure of God.
> Elizabeth Barrett Browning: *Aurora Leigh*, Bk. II, l. 13

Olympian bards who sung
    Divine ideas below,
Which always find us young,
    And always keep us so.
> Ralph Waldo Emerson: *Essays: The Poet*

Young saint, old devil.
> English Proverb

An angelic boyhood becomes a Satanic old age.
> Erasmus: *Fam. Coll.*

Youth is a curse to mortals, when with youth a man hath not implanted righteousness.
> Euripides: *Andromache*, l. 184

There is a feeling of Eternity in youth which makes us amends for everything. To be young is to be as one of the Immortals.
> William Hazlitt: *Table Talk: The Feeling of Immortality in Youth*

The bulwark of religious training is vital if the line is to be held against the forces of corruption, crime and disloyalty. I believe that men imbued with spiritual values do not betray their country. I believe that children reared in homes in which morality is taught and lived rarely become delinquents.
> J. Edgar Hoover

Then, gods, to reverent youth grant purity,
Grant, gods, to quiet age a peaceful end.
> Horace: *Saecular Hymn*, l. 45

The sins of youth are paid for in old age.
> Latin Proverb

Let no man despise thy youth.
> New Testament: *I Timothy 4: 12*

For the imagination of man's heart is evil from his youth.
> Old Testament: *Genesis 8: 21*

Thy youth is renewed like the eagle's.
> Old Testament: *Psalms 103: 5*

Rejoice, O young man, in thy youth; and let thy heart cheer thee in the days of thy youth, and walk in the ways of thine heart, and in the sight of thine eyes: but know thou, that for all these things God will bring thee into judgment.
> Old Testament: *Ecclesiastes 11: 9*

Remember now thy Creator in the days of thy youth, while the evil days come not, nor the years draw nigh, when thou shalt say, I have no pleasure in them.
> Old Testament: *Ecclesiastes 12: 1*

A youth to whom was given
So much of earth, so much of heaven.
> William Wordsworth: *Ruth*

Bliss was it in that dawn to be alive,
But to be young was very Heaven.
> William Wordsworth: *The Prelude*, XI

Z

ZEAL

An Indian, having heard from a white man some strictures on zeal, replied: "I don't know about having too much zeal; but I think it is better the pot should boil over than not boil at all."

Anonymous

For Zeal's a dreadful termagant,
That teaches saints to tear and yant.

Samuel Butler: Hudibras, Pt. III,
Canto II, l. 677

When too much zeal doth fire devotion,
Love is not love, but superstition.

Richard Corbet: R.C.

All zeal for a reform, that gives offence
To peace and charity, is mere pretence.

William Cowper: Charity, l. 533

Awake, my soul! stretch every nerve,
And press with vigour on;
A heavenly race demands thy zeal,
And an immortal crown.

Philip Doddridge: Hymns: Zeal and
Vigour in the Christian Race, st. 1

The weakness of human nature has always appeared in times of great revivals of religion, by a disposition to run into extremes, especially in these three things: enthusiasm, superstition, and intemperate zeal.

Jonathan Edwards

Nothing can be fairer or more noble than the holy fervor of true zeal.

Jean Baptiste Molière

A zeal of God, but not according to knowledge.

New Testament: Romans 10: 2

It is good to be zealously affected always in a good thing.

New Testament: Galatians 4: 18

Zeal then, not charity, became the guide,
And Hell was built on spite, and Heav'n on pride.

Alexander Pope: Essay on Man, Epis III,
l. 261

I think while zealots fast and frown,
And fight for two or seven,
That there are fifty roads to town,
And rather more to Heaven.

Winthrop Mackworth Praed: The Chant
of the Brazen Head, st. 8

Be not too zealous; moderation is best in all things.

Theognis: Sententiae, no. 335

We are often moved with passion, and we think it to be zeal.

Thomas à Kempis: Imitation of Christ,
Pt. II, ch. 5

All true zeal for God is a zeal for love, mercy and goodness.

Robert Ellis Thompson

Persecuting zeal . . . Hell's fiercest fiend!

James Thomson: Liberty, Pt. IV, l. 66

Nothing spoils human nature more than false zeal. The good nature of an heathen is more God-like than the furious zeal of a Christian.

Benjamin Whichcote: Moral and
Religious Aphorisms

INDEX OF AUTHORS

INDEX OF AUTHORS

INDEX OF AUTHORS

INDEX OF AUTHORS

INDEX OF AUTHORS

INDEX OF AUTHORS

INDEX OF AUTHORS

INDEX OF AUTHORS

INDEX OF AUTHORS

INDEX OF AUTHORS

INDEX OF AUTHORS

INDEX OF AUTHORS

INDEX OF AUTHORS

INDEX OF AUTHORS

INDEX OF AUTHORS

INDEX OF TOPICS

INDEX OF TOPICS

BIBLE, I could use the, 452
  if you have, creed, 90
  not in the, alone, 199
  not just a, word, 37
  plainly says he exists, 110
  taste for, study, 269
  truth of the, 61
BISHOP(S), 35
  devil is a busy, 110
  most diligent, 111
BLESSING(S), 35-41
  among God's, 88
  are, in disguise, 341
  are plentiful and rife, 388
  bargain for its, drive, 215
  Bible is one of the greatest, 30
  contented mind is the greatest, 87
  count your, 440
  dismiss us with thy, 233
  enumerate the, 387
  faith is the root of all, 137
  finding a greater, 320
  for curses, 47
  great corner-stone, 440
  greatest of all, 62
  health is the second, 212
  humble man his, 240
  I know no, so small, 347
  nor poverty a, 383
  of the house, 229
  open to receive God's, 213
  poverty is a, 333
  prayer purchases, 439
  prayers should be for, 347
  private and personal, 441
  prosperity is the, 1
  six, bestowed, 265
  source of every, 170
  temporal, a taste of heaven, 204
  there is no one small, 88
  'tis expectation makes a, dear, 219
  to be made a, to all, 355
  upon our daily rod, 1
  we call it a, 208
  what a, Christmas is, 72
  what a, is Sunday, 390
BROTHERHOOD, 36-41
  neighbourhood without, 368
  trying to build the, 171
BROTHER(S)
  a, 's love, 277
  a, 's sufferings, 433
  closer than a, 157
  desires for his, 193
  fold to thy heart thy, 287
  friend equal to a, 156
  mote that is in thy, 260
  than a, far off, 319
BURDEN(S), 41-42
  bearing each other's, 71
  Christians and camels receive their, 61
  cross of Christ is the sweetest, 94
  ease the, of another, 36
  of care in getting rich, 383
  of the day, 444
  of the week lies there, 388
  of the world's divine regret, 58
  to himself the greatest, 287
  selfishness makes Christmas a, 68
  take his, from him, 433
  you make it a, 95

C

CHARITY, 43-48
  and beating begin, 230
  believeth all things, 21
  best creed we can have is, 90
  but, is wanting, 353
  Christian, 48
  enough to see, 270
  faith hope, 234
  flame of, in the heart, 71
  hate and want of, 37
  man's mind move in, 214
  noblest, is to prevent, 4
  O chime of sweet saint, 120
  religion of, 23
  solitary act of, 3
  spoken without, 453
  there is no, 160
  to all men, 159
  truth without, 455
  universal, 375
  we have less, for those, 91
  zeal then not, 483
CHRIST, 48-60
  adopt the principles of, 326
  after the pattern of Jesus, 250
  all that I am I owe to Jesus, 30
  arise and follow, 394
  believe and rejoice in, 407
  believing in Jesus, 307
  between, and war, 467
  brother of mine in, 38
  calls not the righteous, 390
  can make nations, 38
  cannot please, 18
  cautious statistical, 47
  coming to know, 454
  conscience is the palace of, 84
  conscience is the true vicar of, 85
  deny themselves for, 397
  did not simply speak, 454
  died like a God, 105
  dims my vision of, 269
  disarmed every soldier, 468
  faith in, 394
  find the similar to Jesus, 200
  has made death, 99
  help thy kin, biddeth, 45
  history . . . began with, 200
  holiness that is, 227
  humanity of, 256
  humility makes way for, 239
  if antichrist is like, 9
  in you, 234
  is come in the flesh, 9
  is his friend, 154
  is our hope today, 234
  is risen today, 94
  is the centre, 452
  is the master, 30
  is the spirit of missions, 308
  justified by faith in, 197
  last kind word to, 264
  life and character of, 256
  life with, 231
  livery of, 281
  love is the livery of, 286
  may Lord, enter in, 213
  measure of the gift of, 202
  message of, 308
  ministers of, 305
  my blessed savior, 431

506

INDEX OF TOPICS

INDEX OF TOPICS

INDEX OF TOPICS

INDEX OF TOPICS

INDEX OF TOPICS

INDEX OF TOPICS

INDEX OF TOPICS

NEIGHBOR(S), if your, has made one pilgrimage, 329
  is everyone that needs help, 38
  love thy, 283
  make, of us all, 78
  our, for God, 43
  providence was his next door, 362
  regard your, 's gain, 193
  reputation to your, 84
  spiritual needs of his, 61
  that his, does not cheat, 191
  thou shalt not covet thy, 's house, 90
  thy love to thy, 284
  truth with his, 453
  we have Christ in our, 72
  with respect to his, 193

O

OBEDIENCE, 320–322
  Christianity is, 463
  commences with, 334
  insures greatness, 385
  in, to reason, 435
  motions for, 150
  principal act of, 139
  promises to, 256
  resistance to tyrants is, 176
  to God, 367
  to laws, 394
  to the will of God, 463
  true test of, 427

P

PAIN(S), 323
  all, are nothing, 414
  every single, that we feel, 190
  fear is, 143
  is the deepest thing, 431
  marriage has many, 297
  midst of bitterest, 326
  never feels a, 413
  nothing is dead but . . . 107
  of love be sweeter, 278
  pleasure's but, 185
  prayer and, 306
  sweeter for past, 431
  that endless, 220
  thinks, the greatest evil, 435
  would cause you, 192

PATRIOTISM, 324–325

PEACE, 325–328
  add to the, and good will, 8
  and love shall reign, 247
  and the soldier, 350
  at, whose conscience is pure, 86
  be at, henceforth, 39
  brotherhood, 192
  cry out in anguish for, 13
  God is, 183
  God's will is our, 164
  good war or a bad, 467
  good-bye to, 350
  graft of, 281
  health, and competence, 436
  health strength and, 435
  I make, and create evil, 127
  if possible, 453
  ineffable, 366
  is its companion, 263
  marriage with, 298
  may not live in, 319

none with, of soul, 409
obedience and, 321
on earth, good-will to men, 71
prayer is the, of our spirit, 348
preserve the, of the church, 78
Prince of, 49
promise of world, 78
righteousness and, 385
righteousness and, embraced, 14
such, flowing in, 51
thank God for, 439
they are in, 415
try all the ways to, 49
war and, 280
with justice and honor, 332
without brotherhood, is not possible, 37
you will find, 88

PERFECTION, 328–329
  Bible urges us on to, 358
  truth is so great a, 454

PIETY, 329–330
  abode of, 471
  and holiness, 226
  and morality, 311
  and pity, 330
  divorcement of morals and, 311
  little, in big churches, 78
  sentiment of, 316
  temperance is corporal, 436
  that is real, 269
  to carry, as far, 433
  to, more prone, 469
  with the silk of, 385

PITY, 330–331
  claim a brother's, 433
  he that hath, 334, 414
  I learn to, them, 335
  we may learn to, 431

POSSESSIONS, 331–332

POVERTY, 332–334
  its, by how little, 415

POWER, 334–336
  acknowledgment of a divine, 12
  adding, to the strength, 347
  ambitious with, 108
  authority of the, of the spirit, 31
  belief is, 20
  but his attribute, 173
  but of, 304
  by their civilizing, 367
  can n'er be equal, 138
  cannot command, 274
  Christianity is the, of God, 65
  devil hath, 112
  foil the tempter's, 202
  get from it a great, 61
  goodness armed with, 198
  grant that he may have, 108
  great as the, behind us, 137
  greater, to possess, 453
  greatest constraining, 280
  greatest, in the world, 339
  if Christ is the . . ., of God, 50
  in the, of God, 183
  loss of vital, 410
  man of his own, 45
  moulding, uplifting, 64
  no, can the impenitent, 376
  of choosing good, 196
  of gratitude, 439

INDEX OF TOPICS

INDEX OF TOPICS

INDEX OF TOPICS

INDEX OF TOPICS